Biographical
Dictionary Of The Left

D1253342

Biographical Dictionary
Of The Left

Consolidated Volume I

(Combining Volumes I, II, III, and IV of the Preview Series)

by

Francis X. Gannon

WESTERN ISLANDS

PUBLISHERS

BOSTON · LOS ANGELES

TABLE OF CONTENTS

A FOREWORD BY THE PUBLISHER

It is our present expectation that this *Biographical Dictionary Of The Left* will consist of eight consolidated volumes in this Western Islands edition, containing in all about three thousand names. This first volume is a combination of volumes one through four of the Preview Edition of the *Dictionary*. As an aid to the reader and as an important preface to the biographies, we have begun this edition with the fourth volume in the Preview Series, "Organizations Of The Left."

Because of the urgent need for this reference dictionary, we shall continue to follow the basic procedure used in producing this work. As each compilation of some one hundred sketches becomes available, it will be published in the saddle-wire, over-sized-pamphlet format of the Preview Series. When another four volumes of the Series are completed, we shall pull the material together into a second consolidated volume of this same book format, thus giving this vital material greater permanence and effectiveness. But in both editions, all of the names in any one volume will be separately alphabetized into one sequence between its covers. This will require extra work of the reader, in searching for a particular listing. But it is far more practicable, and will make these early volumes far more useful, than if we followed the alternative procedure – as did the French *Encyclopédists,* for instance – of having each new volume simply move that much further down the total alphabet.

Each volume is being prepared by, or under the careful supervision of, Dr. Francis X. Gannon, Head of The Research Department of The John Birch Society. Dr. Gannon, who received his Ph.D. in History at Georgetown University, has long been a worthy disciple of his great teacher – and eminent historian – Charles Callan Tansill. Sound scholarship in his

vii

chosen field, and unimpeachable accuracy in every line he writes, have long been imperative considerations for Dr. Gannon, as they were for Dr. Tansill before him.

Believing that it is better to err a hundred times on the side of restraint and understatement, than to err even once, no matter how slightly, on the side of abuse or exaggeration, Dr. Gannon will give you in these forthcoming volumes as much dependable information concerning contemporary leaders of the liberal-left persuasion as space and time and other practical limitations will permit. And we send this first consolidated volume forth in continuance of the tremendous project we hope will result in a whole series of reference books which will prove very useful to all patriotic students of the planned and subversive confusion which now engulfs us all.

Editorial Staff, Western Islands

Organizations Of The Left

AMERICAN CIVIL LIBERTIES UNION
THE ROGER BALDWIN FOUNDATION

On December 18, 1914, the American League to Limit Armaments was organized "to combat militarism and the spread of the militaristic spirit in the United States." Its members resolved "that the true policy of this country is not to increase its land and sea forces but to retain for productive and humanizing outlay the vast sums demanded for armaments."

The American League to Limit Armaments was an offshoot of the Emergency Peace Federation, a pacifist group directed by Louis Lochner who was — in that era — one of the most notorious Reds in America. The organizers of the American League included Jane Addams, John Haynes Holmes, George Foster Peabody, Stephen Wise, L. Hollingsworth Wood, and Morris Hillquit — all of whom were prominent in radical-pacifist activities.

Early in 1915, the executive committee of the American League to Limit Armaments decided to expand the scope of the organization's activities and change its name to the American Union Against Militarism. Until the United States entered World War I, the AUAM worked to prevent legislation which would increase the United States military establishment.

Once the United States entered World War I, the AUAM set out on a massive anti-draft campaign. In its elaborate plans, the AUAM — through its branch offices in Washington, D. C. and New York City, operating as the Civil Liberties Bureau — would urge its members to cooperate with the Socialist Party; the Intercollegiate Socialist Society; labor unions; women's, farmers', and church organizations; collegiate and social workers' clubs; radical and pacifist groups; and, racial groups — especially Jewish and colored. The plans of the AUAM and its Civil Liberties Bureau had to be scrapped when conscription became the law of the land, six weeks after the United States declared war upon Germany.

In October, 1917, Roger Baldwin who was director of the Civil Liberties Bureau was prompted by his friends in the Fellowship of Reconciliation to reorganize the CLB as the National Civil Liberties

1

Bureau and to separate from the parent organization, the American Union Against Militarism.

The reorganization was accomplished and Baldwin, an anarchist, concentrated most of the energies of the National Civil Liberties Bureau on the issue of conscientious objection. Baldwin's NCLB went to the aid of a small number of avowed conscientious objectors but tried to encourage a much larger number of potential conscriptees to register as "conshies." When he was not proselyting "conshies," Baldwin was aiding other radical groups such as the Wobblies to obstruct the war effort and, in general, to do everything possible to promote Red radicalism.

Baldwin's efforts came to grief, however, when he was imprisoned for his own draft evasion. Upon his release from prison in July, 1919, a party was given in his honor at which time the party-goers decided to organize a movement allegedly to champion civil rights. In attendance were Norman Thomas — the host — who would become the patriarch of the Socialist Party; Elizabeth Gurley Flynn who would become national chairman of the Communist Party; and, Agnes Smedley who would become a Soviet espionage agent in China.

After a few more meetings, Baldwin's associates reorganized the National Civil Liberties Bureau as the American Civil Liberties Union. In 1920, Harry Ward was chairman of the ACLU; Baldwin, the director; and, Louis Budenz (later to become an important official of the Communist Party), the publicity director. The national committee of the ACLU in 1920 was a collection of the era's most active pacifists, Socialists, and Communists. It included Jane Addams, Elizabeth Gurley Flynn, William Z. Foster who became one of the Communist Party's most durable leaders, Felix Frankfurter and his British friend Harold J. Laski (then teaching at Harvard), Morris Hillquit, Robert Morss Lovett, Abraham J. Muste, Jeanette Rankin, Scott Nearing, Vida Scudder, Norman Thomas, Oswald Garrison Villard, and L. Hollingsworth Wood.

In its first decade, the ACLU's board of directors or national committee or general membership was joined by Clarence Darrow, Eugene V. Debs, John Dewey, Morris Ernst, George W. Kirchwey, Alexander Meiklejohn, and Monsignor John A. Ryan; in the 1930's, by Vito Marcantonio, Virginius Dabney, Mary Van Kleeck, William H. Kilpatrick, Heywood Broun, Pearl Buck, Frank P. Graham, Mary Simkhovitch, Quincy Howe, Corliss Lamont, Thurgood Marshall, Bishop G. Bromley Oxnam, Elmer Rice, Sherwood Eddy, Whitney North Seymour, and Robert E. Sherwood; in the 1940's, by Francis Biddle,

George S. Counts, Norman Cousins, Elmer Davis, Melvyn Douglas, Walter Gellhorn, William H. Hastie, Robert M. Hutchins, Freda Kirchwey, Max Lerner, Archibald MacLeish, John P. Marquand, A. Philip Randolph, Elmo Roper, Arthur M. Schlesinger Jr., Lillian Smith, and Roy Wilkins; in the 1950's, by Sarah G. Blanding, Catherine D. Bowen, John Mason Brown, Stuart Chase, Grenville Clark, Henry S. Commager, J. Frank Dobie, Louis Hacker, August Heckscher, John Hersey, Palmer Hoyt, Gerald W. Johnson, Walter Millis, Saul K. Padover, Telford Taylor, James A. Wechsler, Edward Bennett Williams, Alan Barth, Benjamin Kizer, Robert S. Lynd, and James G. Patton.

The ACLU's membership lists are not made public but it is known that among those who have joined the state and city affiliates (which, in 1968, numbered forty-six with more than 130,000 members) have been: J. Robert Oppenheimer, Harold Ickes, Frances Perkins, Harry Ashmore, Emil Mazey, Adolf A. Berle Jr., Thornton Wilder, Alan Westin, Gerard Piel, Michael Harrington, Algernon Black, Thomas I. Emerson, James Farmer, Ralph Bunche, Clifford Case, Herbert Lehman, Walter Lippman, Jerome B. Wiesner, Dore Schary, Frederick L. Schuman, Harlow Shapley, Archibald Cox, Howard Mumford Jones, Robert F. Drinan S. J., Endicott Peabody, John P. Roche, Kirtley Mather, and James Baldwin.

If the ACLU officials and members have not been the most eminent in their primary fields of interest, they at least have been among the most publicized: educators, diplomats, cabinet members, scientists, United States Senators and Representatives, governors, novelists, poets, biographers, playwrights, actors, newspaper and magazine publishers and editors, journalists, columnists and broadcasting news commentators, historians, labor leaders, social workers, businessmen, industrialists, lawyers, jurists, foundation officials, and clergymen. They have held high positions in the Communist, Socialist, Democrat, and Republican parties. They have been officials and members of Americans for Democratic Action, the NAACP, the Council on Foreign Relations, the League for Industrial Democracy, the National Lawyers Guild, the National Committee for an Effective Congress, the Congress of Racial Equality, the Center for the Study of Democratic Institutions, the Anti-Defamation League, and, certainly without exception, every Communist front that has existed in the United States during the past fifty years.

Four consecutive presidents of the United States have showered unequivocal praises upon the ACLU: "The integrity of the American Civil Liberties Union and of its workers in the field has never been, and I feel, never will be questioned. Officers, directors and members of the Union have performed outstanding service to the cause of true freedom." (Harry S. Truman) "During the span of years covered by your organization the American people have given increased attention to progress in the field of civil rights . . . . It is good to be reminded that the members of the American Civil Liberties Union and the overwhelming majority of my fellow citizens are working together in this field with steadfast vigor and understanding." (Dwight D. Eisenhower) "During the 43 years of its existence the American Civil Liberties Union has played a significant role in defending our basic democratic freedoms. Your voice has always been raised clearly and sharply when our liberties have been threatened. America is a stronger nation for your uncompromising efforts." (John F. Kennedy) "The American Civil Liberties Union has an essential role at this critical time. It defends the rights of even the most despised to speak, to assemble, and to petition for redress of grievances. It protects the individual's constitutional guarantees of the right to counsel, to confrontation, and to due process of law. It has come to symbolize racial justice and religious freedom." (Lyndon B. Johnson)

Throughout the entire history of the ACLU, Roger Baldwin has been an official and certainly the most dominating influence in the organization. (On his eightieth birthday, Baldwin received from President Lyndon Johnson a very warm message of congratulations, which read, in part: " . . . I wish to salute you for your long career. Your unremitting fight against injustice and intolerance in this country and across the world has earned you the warm gratitude of countless individuals. In your life, you have shown a devotion to principle and force of personal character which will long be remembered by your countrymen.")

As the ACLU's work, directed by Baldwin, concluded its first decade of existence, it came under the scrutiny of the Special House [of Representatives] Committee to Investigate Communist Activities in the United States. In that Committee's *Report,* dated January 17, 1931, it was stated: "The American Civil Liberties Union is closely affiliated with the communist movement in the United States, and fully 90 per cent of its efforts are on behalf of communists who have come into conflict with the law. It claims to stand for free speech, free press, and free assembly; but it is quite apparent that the main function of the

A.C.L.U. is to attempt to protect the communists in their advocacy of force and violence to overthrow the Government, replacing the American flag by a red flag and erecting a Soviet Government in place of the republican form of government guaranteed to each State by the Federal Constitution.

"Roger N. Baldwin, its guiding spirit, makes no attempt to hide his friendship for the communists and their principles. He was formerly a member of the I. W. W. [Wobblies] and served a term in prison as a draft dodger during the war. This is the same Roger N. Baldwin that has recently issued a statement 'that in the next session of Congress our job is to organize the opposition to the recommendations of the congressional committee investigating communism.' "

The Committee, in its report, quoted some of Baldwin's testimony which he gave as the ACLU's director:

"The Chairman. Does your organization uphold the right of a citizen or alien — it does not make any difference which — to advocate murder?

"Mr. Baldwin. Yes.

"The Chairman. Or assassination?

"Mr. Baldwin. Yes.

"The Chairman. Does your organization uphold the right of an American citizen to advocate force and violence for the overthrow of the Government?

"Mr. Baldwin. Certainly; in so far as mere advocacy is concerned.

"The Chairman. Does it uphold the right of an alien in this country to urge the overthrow and advocate the overthrow of the Government by force and violence?

"Mr. Baldwin. Precisely on the same basis as any citizen.

"The Chairman. You do uphold the right of an alien to advocate the overthrow of the Government by force and violence?

"Mr. Baldwin. Sure; certainly. It is the healthiest kind of thing for a country, of course, to have free speech — unlimited."

The Committee then recalled a previous investigation of the ACLU: "A committee of the New York State Legislature, back in 1928, reached the following conclusion about the American Civil Liberties Union: 'The American Civil Liberties Union, in the last analysis, is a supporter of all subversive movements; its propaganda is detrimental to the interests of the State. It attempts not only to protect crime but to encourage attacks upon our institutions in every form.' Your committee concurs with the above findings."

In 1935, Baldwin, who directed the ACLU for thirty years, described himself and his activities in his college year book: "I have continued directing the unpopular fight for the rights of agitation, as director of the American Civil Liberties Union. . . . I have been to Europe several times, mostly in connection with international radical activities, chiefly against war, fascism and imperialism; and have traveled constantly in the United States to areas of conflict over workers' rights to strike and organize. My chief aversion is the system of greed, private profit, privilege and violence which makes up the control of the world today, and which has brought it to the tragic crisis of unprecedented hunger and unemployment . . . . Therefore, I am for Socialism, disarmament and, ultimately, for abolishing the State itself as an instrument of violence and compulsion. I seek the social ownership of property, the abolition of the propertied class and sole control of those who produce wealth. Communism is the goal."

In 1943, the Legislative Committee investigating un-American activities in California reported: "The American Civil Liberties Union may be definitely classed as a Communist front or 'transmission belt' organization. At least 90 per cent of its efforts are expended on behalf of Communists who come into conflict with the law. While it professes to stand for free speech, a free press and free assembly, it is quite obvious that its main function is to protect Communists in their activities of force and violence in their program to overthrow the government."

In 1948, California's Senate Fact-Finding Committee on Un-American Activities reported that it "reiterates the findings of former legislative committees concerning the Communist character of the American Civil Liberties Union. The International Labor Defense, called 'the legal arm of the Communist Party' by former Attorney General Francis Biddle, has not established a better Communist record than this thinly disguised organization that devotes its energies to the defense of enemies of the United States."

In September, 1939, when the Hitler-Stalin Pact was signed, confusion reigned among Communists, pro-Communists, and liberals throughout the world. Within the ACLU, there arose a great deal of dissension as to what tack should be taken. In 1940, the ACLU adopted the position that individuals who support totalitarian dictatorship in any country could offer no more than token support for civil liberties in the United States. Consequently, the ACLU announced that Communists, Nazis, Fascists, Ku Klux Klansmen, Silver Shirts, and Christian

Fronters would be barred from holding office or employment in the organization. (If any members of these groups, with the exception of Communists, were ever officials of the ACLU, they have yet to be discovered.) With the announcement, the ACLU perpetrated a strategic purge by demanding the resignation of Communist Elizabeth Gurley Flynn. When she refused to resign, she was dismissed. And Harry Ward, a co-founder of the ACLU with Flynn, resigned in protest.

The strategic purge conducted by the ACLU was evidently not understood completely in Communist and pro-Communist circles. In their *Daily Worker* of March 19, 1940, the Communists carried a letter, signed by seventeen pro-Communist "liberal leaders," and addressed to the ACLU: "The phrasing of the resolution is dangerous. Its context is worse. The Civil Liberties [Union] was founded in 1920. The Soviet Union was established in 1917 [*sic*], and with it the 'dictatorship of the proletariat.' We are told that Communists are to be barred from office or employment in the Civil Liberties Union because, while fighting for civil liberties in America, they accept their suppression in Soviet Russia. Why then, did the Civil Liberties Union wait until 1940 before seeking to bar them? . . . Civil liberties within the Soviet Union were no different before the [Hitler-Stalin] Pact than after."

After the disruption of the Hitler-Stalin Pact in 1941, the ACLU continued to abide by its resolution against Communists holding office in the organization. In an advertisement in 1953, in *Nation* magazine, the ACLU stated: "The Union fights for the civil liberties even of those whose anti-democratic opinions it abhors. In order to do so it bars from its governing body all totalitarians of the left and right." And, in its recruiting literature, it was stated: "The A. C. L. U. needs and welcomes the support of all whose devotion to civil liberties is unqualified by Communist, Fascist, KKK, or other totalitarian leanings."

In February, 1954, the national board of the ACLU supplemented its "anti-Communist" resolution of 1940: "Mindful of its responsibilities as a voluntary association of free citizens and in furtherance of its declared principles and purposes to defend the civil liberties of any person in the United States, we today reaffirm the policy of the American Civil Liberties Union not to have as an officer, board member, committee member, or staff member, national or local, any person who does not believe in civil liberties, or who accepts the discipline of any political party or organization which does not believe in civil liberties or which is under the control or direction of any totalitarian government, whether Communist or Fascist, which itself does not believe in civil liberties or in practice crushes civil liberties."

The ostensible exclusion of Communists from ACLU officialdom, if it did nothing else, contributed to the fact that the organization was never investigated or found to be a Communist front by any congressional committee. The entire farce was ended, however, in May, 1968 when the ACLU repealed its "anti-Communist" resolution of 1940, which simply meant that Communists could serve as officials or employees in the organization. Actually, in the period 1940-1968, officials and members of the ACLU remained active in Communist fronts, old and new, working as effectively, if not more so, than if they were dues-paying, card-carrying members of the Communist Party. (It is extremely doubtful if any Communist front in this country has ever been without ACLU members.)

In its entire history, the ACLU has had only three directors: Baldwin from 1920 until 1950, Patrick M. Malin from 1950 until 1962, and John de J. Pemberton Jr. since 1962. Both Malin and Pemberton entered the office with no history of Communist-front or subversive affiliations to live down. But the nature of the ACLU's work, as directed by the undeniably radical Baldwin, underwent no substantive change when first Malin and then Pemberton took over.

While Malin was the director, a pamphlet ("What Is the American Civil Liberties Union?") linked the various areas of activities of the organization under three headings: One, *Freedom of Inquiry and Expression:* "The ACLU opposes all prior censorship of what people may see, read, or hear. The ACLU battles against laws and legislative committees that, under the guise of national security, punish 'advocacy' and 'teaching' of revolutionary philosophy rather than overt acts of violence. The ACLU protects the right of individuals to associate and assemble. The ACLU seeks to broaden public access to government information, convinced an alert and articulate public opinion depends upon information. The ACLU defends the right of religious belief, any, or none at all — no matter what community pressures attack that belief. The ACLU (on the other side of the religious-freedom coin) guards against government intrusion into religion by opposing financial aid to private religious schools and religious exercises in public schools. The ACLU resists invasions of teachers' and students' academic freedom, realizing that a flow of unfettered ideas in the classroom speeds the nation's intellectual growth."

Two, *Equality before the Law:* "The ACLU defends the rights of labor unions, and of members within labor unions, and the rights of employers, too. The ACLU supports non-discrimination in public schools, housing, public accommodations, and employment — South, North, East, or West. The ACLU seeks to win fully protected voting rights for Negroes. The ACLU backs fairer apportionment of voting districts. The ACLU opposes discriminatory quota systems in our immigration laws."

Three, *Due Process of Law:* "The ACLU fights against unfair discharges of government workers under various government security programs. The ACLU seeks to end police abuse of citizens. The ACLU opposes legislation that seeks to block freedom of travel. The ACLU defends aliens from summary deportation. The ACLU opposes 'electronic eavesdropping.' The ACLU strives to obtain legal counsel for Negroes in the South, where fear of reprisal has intimidated many lawyers."

There can be no denying the success that the ACLU has had in promoting its program over the years. A great deal of its work has been conducted in courts at all governmental levels up to and including the Supreme Court of the United States. And, in these courts, ACLU lawyers defend individuals, groups, or institutions or, on occasion, submit an *amicus curiae* brief. But, beyond its work in the courts, the ACLU works as a pressure group upon public officials, has its personnel testify before state legislative and congressional committees, conducts publicity campaigns through its own publications and throughout the entire press media, and reaches church, civic, service, and educational groups through ACLU speakers' bureaus.

There can be no denying that many of the items that the ACLU is "for" or "against," at first glance, would seem to be consonant with a stance that conservatives might take on the same items. But where the conservative has labored for true liberty, for law and order, and for social responsibility, the ACLU has worked for licentiousness, for chaos (approaching anarchy), and for a regimented, totalitarian society. The conservative has been concerned with the victim of a crime, while the ACLU has been solicitous of the criminal's welfare. The conservative has been anti-Communist, while the ACLU has been pro-Communist and anti-anti-Communist. The conservative has recognized the religious basis of government, while the ACLU has fought to separate all moral values from the laws and administrative procedures of the State.

9

As the ACLU has grown older, especially in the past decade or two, it has received impressive support from the press. Glittering encomiums have been showered on its activities by the *New York Times* ("thoroughly patriotic organization"), the *Pittsburgh Post-Gazette* ("the essence of Americanism"), *Atlanta Constitution* ("fights for the rights of men everywhere"), *Denver Post* ("few informed persons or organizations have ever questioned the purity of its motives, the quality of its patriotism, or the depth of its courage"), *Washington Evening Star* ("steadfast devotion to a defense of the civil liberties which are guaranteed to all of us"), *New York Herald Tribune* ("watchdog of the citizen's liberties"), *Washington Post* ("knows and understands what true Americanism means"), *St. Louis Post-Dispatch* ("has established its fearlessly independent reputation, and particularly its freedom from Communist control"), *Toledo Blade* ("earned the hatred of Communists"), *San Francisco Examiner* ("worthy of the support of all freedom loving citizens"), and similar tributes by the *Capital Times* of Madison, Wisconsin, the *Christian Science Monitor,* the *Durham Herald,* the *Des Moines Register,* the *Chicago Daily News* and the *Minneapolis Tribune.*

Many of the ACLU's defenders and apologists in the press have gone to great lengths to disassociate the ACLU from sympathies for Communism or Communists. A notable exception to this type of support in the press occurred in 1935 when the *New York American,* in an editorial entitled "Unmasked," said: "Whenever a patriotic bill is introduced in Congress or in a State Legislature, the American Civil Liberties Union almost always pops up in opposition. Whenever a movement is under way to repeal such a measure, the American Civil Liberties Union will usually be found vociferously demanding repeal. Whenever a deportable alien falls into Federal custody, and is likely to be shipped back where he belongs, the American Civil Liberties Union is generally discovered to be the 'organization' that sends lawyers to his aid . . . . Now, the purpose of all this legislation which the American Civil Liberties Union opposed was to safeguard the States and the nation against the subversive 'isms' of Europe and our alien-minded Americans — against Fascism and Nazism and Communism alike. Communism — due mainly to the aid and comfort given by such disguised Communistic organizations as the American Civil Liberties Union and the American League against War and Fascism — is a real public menace."

Long before the *New York American* characterized the ACLU as a disguised Communistic organization, it was apparent that the ACLU's ties with Communists were something more than ephemeral.

In 1922, Communists William Z. Foster, Scott Nearing, Robert W. Dunn, Benjamin Gitlow, and Clarina Michaelson joined with ACLUers Roger Baldwin, Norman Thomas, Morris Ernst, Freda Kirchwey, James W. Johnson, Robert Morss Lovett, Mary E. McDowell, Judah L. Magnes, and Walter Nelles to establish and staff the American Fund for Public Service (Garland Fund). The Garland Fund, throughout the 1920's was a major source of finances for Communist enterprises. The ACLU was given and lent money for its legal defense of Communists and other radicals.

One of the ACLU's first major projects was the defense of Communists caught in a federal government raid on a Communist underground convention at Bridgeman, Michigan in 1922.

In 1929, in the aftermath of a Communist-led strike in Gastonia, North Carolina, the ACLU defended Communists who were arrested during the strike.

In and out of courts, the ACLU has gone to the defense of individual Communists and/or Soviet espionage agents such as Earl Browder, Gerhard Eisler, Harry Bridges, Paul Robeson, Tom Rabbit, Fred Beal, Claude Lightfoot, Steve Nelson, George Charney, Oleta Yates, Elizabeth Gurley Flynn, Frank Wilkinson, Carl Winter, and Morton Sobell. In the late 1940's, the ACLU opposed the trials of the "Hollywood Ten" and the eleven national Communist leaders.

In 1935, the ACLU issued a manifesto whereby the organization resolved to oppose any and all bills introduced in the Congress or State Legislatures which (1) would make criminal the advocacy of the overthrow of the Government by force or violence; (2) would punish those who encourage disobedience to orders by the military or naval forces; (3) would outlaw from the ballot any political party which advocates the overthrow of the Government; and (4) would require loyalty oaths from school teachers. And it has remained the policy of the ACLU to oppose any and all legislation designed to expose, hamper, or prosecute Communists.

In its solicitude for Communists and fellow travelers, the ACLU has opposed the anti-Communist provisions of the McCarran-Walter Immigration Act, the Smith Act, the Mundt-Nixon Bill, the Communist Control Act, and other internal security legislation.

Anti-Communist investigating committees on both a federal and state level have always been targets of the ACLU. The group has fought to abolish such committees including the Dies Committee, the House Committee on Un-American Activities, and the Senate Internal Security Subcommittee. Similar opposition has been leveled against the Subversive Activities Control Board.

When the occasion has demanded it, the ACLU has gone to the defense of the entire Communist Party. In 1964, when Attorney General Robert Kennedy was going through the motions of trying to have the Communist Party's officials register with the Justice Department, the ACLU requested Kennedy to halt all such action since it was "nothing but harassment."

The ACLU defends the Communist Party of the United States as if it were a legitimate political party whose members are entitled to all the rights, liberties, and privileges enjoyed by loyal American citizens. Yet, in the Communist Control Act of 1954, the Congress of the United States — under the heading: "Findings of Fact" — found and declared "that the Communist Party of the United States, although purportedly a political party, is in fact an instrumentality of a conspiracy to overthrow the Government of the United States . . . [and] the policies and programs of the Communist Party are secretly prescribed for it by the foreign leaders of the world Communist movement. Its members have no part in determining its goals, and are not permitted to voice dissent to party objectives. Unlike members of political parties, members of the Communist Party are recruited for indoctrination with respect to its objectives and methods, and are organized, instructed, and disciplined to carry into action slavishly the assignments given them by their hierarchial chieftains . . . . The peril inherent in its [the Communist Party's] operation arises not from its numbers, but from its failure to acknowledge any limitation as to the nature of its activities, and its dedication to the proposition that the present constitutional Government of the United States ultimately must be brought to ruin by any available means, including resort to force and violence. Holding that doctrine, its role as the agency of a hostile foreign power renders its existence a clear present and continuing danger to the security of the United States." These "Findings of Fact" remain the law of the land and their constitutionality has not been overruled by the courts.

Despite the findings that the Communist Party and its members are under the discipline of hostile foreigners who propose to destroy the United States government by any available means, the ACLU has defended Communists and their associates at every turn. The ACLU has opposed any and all efforts by the federal government to bar or to impede the flow of Communist propaganda into this country. The ACLU has upheld the "right" of Communists to maintain jobs in the motion-picture, radio, television, and theatrical industries; in schools at all levels; in defense plants; in labor unions; in government positions (even positions involving national security); and, in the armed forces.

The ACLU has defended the "right" of Communists to speak on campuses and the "right" of student groups to hear Communist speakers. On the other hand, the ACLU has opposed the use of public schools for anti-Communist seminars.

The ACLU has defended the "rights" of Communists to be issued passports and to travel abroad freely notwithstanding State Department restrictions.

The ACLU has opposed loyalty oaths (designed to find out if an individual is or has been a member of the Communist Party or other subversive organization) for school administrators, faculty members, students, ROTC members, recipients of Medicare, civil service employees, and individuals who receive federal grants and subsidies for teaching, research, or other work. And, in general, the ACLU opposes the entire loyalty-security program of the federal government.

In the area of religion, the ACLU opposed religious exercises — including Bible reading and prayers — in public schools, federal grants and loans to church-related institutions, the use of public funds for parochial school text books or bus transportation for parochial school students, released time for public school pupils to receive religious instruction, the wearing of religious garb by nuns who teach in public schools, the retention of the words "under God" in the Pledge of Allegiance, the rental of publicly owned textbooks to church schools, the enrollment of sectarian school pupils as part-time students in public schools to satisfy compulsory state education requirements, and the involvement of religious groups in Project Headstart which was designed to operate guidance centers for pre-school children. In 1968, the ACLU complained that references made to God and religious philosophy in character guidance courses given to soldiers were, in effect, religious indoctrination.

The ACLU's stand on religion is based on guarantees of church-state separation allegedly found in the First Amendment to the Constitution of the United States. However, on the other end of the moral spectrum, the ACLU has defended the publication, distribution, and sale of obscene and pornographic writings, pictorial materials, and films. Such a defensive campaign has led to the ACLU's opposition to censorship by governmental agencies at all levels (executive, judicial, and legislative) and by private agencies of books, periodicals, films, and advertisements. The ACLU is a foe of the Legion of Decency, the Motion Picture Code, and private groups interested in combatting the propagation of obscene and pornographic materials. For its part, the ACLU claims that obscenity and pornography are undefinable and therefore protected by the First Amendment's provisions for free speech. But other private groups which oppose the propagation of obscene and pornographic materials are branded by the ACLU as vigilante groups.

Using its strained interpretation of the Bill of Rights as a shield, the ACLU has shown disregard for an orderly society by its overbearing concern for homosexuals, prostitutes, sex offenders, drug pushers, rioters, juvenile delinquents, anarchists, draft dodgers, murderers, and others who have broken the law. But through its various facilities, the ACLU is unremitting in its efforts to find alleged loopholes and/or alleged technicalities by which the criminal will escape punishment.

One of the ACLU's favorite targets has been the policeman in the performance of his duties especially when he is making an arrest or interrogating a suspect. Largely through the efforts of the ACLU, with its influence upon the Congress and the federal courts, the police have been severely hampered from making arrests. Police efforts to search for and seize evidence have been virtually nullified by court decisions. The police have been greatly intimidated from making physical arrests for fear that they will be charged with "police brutality" – a slogan used by the ACLU long before it became popular with racist revolutionaries. (As part of its campaign against alleged "police brutality," the ACLU has successfully pioneered in establishing civilian-dominated police review boards.) The police have been virtually hamstrung by ACLU-inspired court decisions on the methods of obtaining confessions. Vagrants, loiterers, and disorderly individuals are now practically immune from arrest and prosecution due to the efforts of the ACLU. The use of wiretaps or other electronic eavesdropping devices are opposed by the ACLU no matter the objective; to trace the source of obscene phone calls, to apprehend national security risks or kidnappers or any other criminals. So blatant is the ACLU's hostility toward the police that the United Press International (December 26, 1966) reported that the ACLU held that a string of four-letter oaths hurled at a policeman may be socially necessary. And, in a twenty-eight-page brief filed with the U. S. Court of Appeals, the ACLU declared that any citizen has the right to make his remarks to a policeman as colorful as he may please: "Free spontaneous expression is as basic and perhaps as vital to the ultimate health of society as laughter and crying."

In its broad range of activities, no issue is too small or too large for ACLU's agitation. The organization works just as frantically in its protests against hair-style and dress codes in high schools as it does in its propagandizing for more liberalized abortion laws. Its opposition to the national motto, "In God We Trust," is matched by its persistent efforts to repeal the Connally Reservation which was designed to preserve the constitutional integrity of the United States from interference by the United Nations' International Court of Justice.

The ACLU has attacked Congress for investigating tax-exempt foundations with the same fervor that it has attacked the Peace Corps for asking applicants if they have a record of arrests. The ACLU is as eager to encourage student strikes and boycotts (for alleged violations of students' civil liberties) as it is to promote governmental dissemination of birth control information.

When teachers or students refuse to salute or pledge allegiance to the flag of the United States, the ACLU defends their "right" to do so as vigorously as it defends the "right" of a Communist to practice law or a Fifth Amendment pleader to hold a sensitive position in government.

In recent years, the ACLU has been extremely active in the promotion of the racial agitation that has been waged under the banner of civil rights. Wherever there have been racial demonstrations, sit-ins, and "freedom" rides, the ACLU's lawyers have been present to defend the "rights" of individuals to disrupt the peace. Whenever the cry of "racial discrimination" has been raised over the franchise, public school enrollment, public housing, or employment procedures, the ACLU has been present with its legal pyrotechnics, twisting and turning some constitutional amendment so as to impose an extreme and regimented egalitarianism on an American society that has been traditionally pluralistic.

Ed Wallace, writing a feature story in the *New York Sunday News* (January 21, 1968), compared the ACLU to "a fusty, crusty, cranky old party, who goes through life demanding to see the manager, finding all rooms too hot or too cold, sending dishes back to the kitchen for whimsical reasons, asking people to exchange seats on buses and trains,

15

and tormenting laundrymen that shirts have too much starch (or too little), the crotchety old American Civil Liberties Union, the curmudgeon's curmudgeon, goes its muling, puling way."

Unfortunately, for the peace of American society, the ACLU's "whimsical reasons" become translated into laws on issues which are vital to the peace and security and moral fiber of society. When a small high school in New Jersey planned its traditional Christmas programs, the ACLU responded: "A program in celebration of a Christmas religious holiday constitutes establishment of religion by the government." When Congress debated a bill, making it a crime to cross state lines to incite a riot, the ACLU said that such a bill violated the free speech and due process of law provisions of the Constitution. The ACLU insists that the Communist Party is no threat to the United States yet, when kindergarten children recited "God is great, God is good, and we thank Him for our food," the ACLU considered such an act of grace a threat to the Constitution of the United States.

In *Barron's* weekly (September 30, 1968), Shirley Scheibla reported that the ACLU has decided to enter upon an activist, offensive phase of its work while still maintaining its defensive nature on behalf of "civil liberties." The activism is being made possible by an Internal Revenue Service ruling that ACLU-sponsored foundations could accept tax-exempt donations.

The ACLU has established the Roger Baldwin Foundation which, within its first year of existence, received grants from the Marshall Field, the New York, the Norman, the Wieboldt, the New World, and other foundations. In turn, the Baldwin Foundation has given financial support to Cesar Chavez and his California grape strike, which is a Communist-sponsored attempt to force compulsory unionism on migrant farm workers. And, the Baldwin Foundation plans to support similar attempts in New York, New Jersey, and Minnesota.

With the flow of tax-exempt funds into the Baldwin Foundation, the ACLU has established "legal centers" and "ghetto offices" around the country. Through these facilities, the ACLU hopes to promote black separatism on a large scale, with emphasis placed on community control over police (e. g. civilian review boards) and schools (e. g. bypass school boards and allow parents, students, and teachers to run the schools). An intensified campaign against alleged police brutality is planned coterminous with agitation for all-civilian review boards. And ACLU's new-found wealth will enable it to continue and to expand its old projects:

the protection of flag-burners, draft dodgers, and Communist fronts; the fights against capital punishment, national security measures, and public school systems which have not yet obliterated religious customs, such as Bible reading, and Christmas and Hanukkah observances.

AMERICANS FOR DEMOCRATIC ACTION
UNION FOR DEMOCRATIC ACTION

Eight months before the Japanese attack upon Pearl Harbor, the Union for Democratic Action was established. According to James Loeb Jr. who became UDA's national director, the organization was formed to "unite for common counsel and action all progressive forces in the nation who are agreed that totalitarian tyranny must be defeated by the vigorous and concerted efforts of all free peoples, and that the preservation and extension of essential democracy in both our political and economic life is not only the prerequisite for victory over our foreign foes, but is equally important for a solution of those problems and a healing of those ills which our civilization faced even before tyranny threatened it and which contributed to the rise and early successes of fascism against the democratic world."

During the course of World War II, the UDA's activities were nowhere near as involved as Loeb's pretentious explanation of its basic purposes. The UDA was plainly a political action force. In the field of foreign affairs, the UDA was primarily concerned with the survival of the Soviet Union. In pursuit of this objective, the UDA promoted the involvement of the United States in the European war. Once the United States became involved, the UDA worked for all-out American aid to the Soviet Union which was portrayed as a gallant ally in wartime and deserving of American support and cooperation in the subsequent peacetime.

While patriotic Americans were naturally preoccupied with achieving victory in World War II, the UDA's main thrust in domestic affairs was directed at the destruction of the Congress of the United States. In this endeavor UDA received the cooperation of *Time* magazine, Marshall Field's leftwing *PM,* the *New Republic* magazine under the editorship of Malcolm Cowley, and from the Communist Party's own publications, the *Daily Worker* and *New Masses.*

The guiding genius behind the UDA was Louis Fraina who was temporary chairman of the first Communist convention ever held in the Western Hemisphere, at Chicago in September, 1919. Among the planks for that Communist convention platform was one written by Fraina: "Participation in parliamentary campaigns, which in the general struggle of the proletariat is of secondary importance, is for the purpose of revolutionary propaganda." In later years, Fraina was on the executive committee of the Communist International, which in its "Theses and Statutes" (the basis of the Communist Party's program in the United States) held that: "Communism repudiates parliamentarism as the form of the future; its aim is to destroy parliamentarism." In 1934, Fraina published (under one of his many aliases, Lewis Corey) *The Decline of American Capitalism* wherein he concluded: "American civilization depends upon Communist revolution, and, given the dominant economic position of the United States, the victory of the American working class will make a mighty contribution to the building of world socialism and a new world civilization."

As "research director" of the UDA, Fraina obviously sensed that he had an ideal vehicle to carry him on his Communist mission. Within the UDA, he had a hard core of Communists to help him. And, while Fraina and his comrades remained somewhat in the background, the UDA operated with such front men as James Loeb Jr., the national director; Reinhold Niebuhr, chairman; and, board members Joseph P. Lash, Eleanor Roosevelt's protégé, and Robert Bendiner, managing editor of *Nation* magazine. Other well-known figures who were original officers or members included: Freda Kirchwey, editor of *Nation* magazine; George S. Counts, professor at Columbia University's Teachers College and president of the American Federation of Teachers; Frank Graham, president of the University of North Carolina; A. Philip Randolph, president of the Brotherhood of Sleeping Car Porters; and, Alfred Baker Lewis, veteran official of the Socialist Party. The general membership, as James Burnham once described it, was "a kind of grab-bag, pro-war, 'anti-fascist' united front of intellectuals, writers and publicists of the Left, combining Liberals, Socialists and Communist fellow travelers."

During its first five years, the UDA was so brazenly pro-Communist that it outlived its usefulness as a front. It had performed efficiently on behalf of the Soviet Union during the war years. But it had suffered a crushing blow in the 1946 congressional elections. For the first time since the 1928 elections, the House of Representatives had a Republican majority, and, for the first time since the 1930 elections, the Senate had a Republican majority. Fraina's scheme to destroy the Congress had gone awry. And one of the main campaign issues contributing to the Republicans' victories was their sharp criticism of recent and heavy Communist infiltration of national life, especially in government, labor, and education circles.

On January 4, 1947, Reinhold Niebuhr convened more than one hundred members of the UDA. Out of that meeting and another two months later came the formation of Americans for Democratic Action. The founders of ADA desired to give the impression that the UDA was defunct. The truth was, however, that the UDA had simply shed a discredited old name and adopted a new one. And, when Niebuhr shifted from the UDA to ADA he was accompanied by James Loeb Jr., Joseph P. Lash, Robert Bendiner, William Bohn, Alison Carter, Nelson Cruikshank, Margaret Edwards, Ethel Epstein, Mortimer Hays, Edward Hollander, Alfred Baker Lewis, Leo Lerner, Eduard Lindeman, Nathalie Panek, Cornelia Pinchot, Marvin Rosenberg, Will Rosenblatt, Mrs. Clyde Johnson, Alex Saltzman, Louis Fischer, Boris Shishkin, Anthony Smith, J. C. Turner, George L. P. Weaver, Hortense Young, and others.

Founders of ADA included union leaders (Jack Altman, Douglas Anderson, George Baldanzi, Harvey Brown, James B. Carey, David Dubinsky, Hugo Ernst, John Green, Sal Hoffmann, Arthur McDowell, Walter Reuther, Willard Townsend, and Barney Taylor); representatives of the press (Joseph Alsop, Steward Alsop, Robert Bendiner, Barry Bingham, Marquis Childs, Kenneth Crawford, Elmer Davis, Edgar Ansel Mowrer, Saul Padover, Nelson Poynter, James Wechsler, and Thomas Stokes); clergymen (Reinhold Niebuhr, G. Bromley Oxnam, William Scarlett, George Higgins, and A. Powell Davis); members or former members of Congress (Andrew Biemiller, John A. Carroll, Frank Hook, Herman Koppelmann, and Jerry Voorhis); prominent New Dealers (Wilson Wyatt, Paul Porter, Edward Prichard Jr., Joseph Rauh Jr., James H. Rowe Jr., Melvin Hildreth, Robert Hudgens, Gardner Jackson, Charles Douds, Richard Gilbert, and David Ginsburg); other political figures (Eugenie Anderson, Genevieve Blatt, Chester Bowles, Dan Hoan, Leon Kowal, Frank McCulloch, Arthur Naftalin, Eleanor Roosevelt, and Franklin D. Roosevelt Jr.); and academicians (John K. Galbraith and Arthur M. Schlesinger Jr.). Also among the founders were officials of various organizations: Walter White of the National Association for the Advancement of Colored People; Gilbert Harrison of the American Veterans Committee; Morris Ernst of the American Civil Liberties Union; and, Evelyn Brandt of Friends of Democracy.

From its beginnings, ADA represented itself as an independent, non-partisan political organization and as an anti-Communist force on the left. In 1950, ADA's Chairman Francis Biddle (Attorney General in the Roosevelt Administration) testified that "the ADA was largely founded to split from the liberal movement in America those elements of communism and fellow travelers which, in my opinion, certainly up until 1945 did great harm to the liberal movement by permitting, with some justice, the accusation of fellow travelers to be pinned on persons before the sheep and goats had been counted." In 1962, ADA's National Director Violet Gunther insisted: "The facts are that ADA was founded . . . to provide a political organization for liberals who were anti-communist." In 1965, ADA's Director of Information Curtis B. Gans explained: "In 1947 when ADA was formed, the Progressive Party was in the process of being overtaken by the non-democratic left. ADA was formed as a non-Communist answer to the Progressive Party. We opposed Henry Wallace and supported the Democratic Party — Harry S. Truman quite reluctantly because we did not think he could win."

If ADA has ever been truly anti-Communist, such has not been readily apparent to some. In 1950, President Sal Hoffmann of the Upholsterers Union resigned from the national board of ADA. Mr. Hoffmann explained: "The most charitable and kindly interpretation I can place on the position of the ADA board is that their opposition to Communists and Communism so strongly proclaimed when I joined in founding the ADA in January, 1947, does not extend to the more remote areas of the world."

In 1954, when ADA was waging relentless attacks on the late Senator Joseph R. McCarthy, Republican Senator Everett M. Dirksen of Illinois described his own reaction to the situation in very strong language: "Here is the Communist Party . . . the *Daily Worker*, and their affiliate organization, the ADA, a great multitude . . . marching with one persecution complex against an humble Senator . . . from Wisconsin."

In 1958, Republican Representative Steven B. Derounian of New York said: "The ADAers are morbidly fascinated by the U. S. S. R. and anything accomplished by the Communists is acclaimed by the ADA as superior to anything accomplished by the United States of America."

James Burnham, in two perceptive articles in *National Review* ("Does ADA Run the New Frontier?," May 7, 1963; "A Coming ADA Government?," November 3, 1964), demolished the myth of ADA's anti-Communism. Some of Mr. Burnham's observations: ADA "is the perfect example of 'anti-anti-Communism.' " — "The ADA ideology is based on thoroughgoing internationalism . . . general and complete disarmament . . . peaceful coexistence with the Soviet Union . . . [withdrawal of] recognition of the Chiang Kai-shek government as the government of China . . . diplomatic recognition of the Peiping regime and its accreditation to the UN as the government of China." — "The ADA ideology calls for the total Welfare State . . . on every *specific* issue in every field, ADA supports government control, planning, financing or takeover." — "The ADA position serves to block, blunt or smother action against domestic subversion or espionage; that time and again in international affairs, the practical consequences of the ADA position serve to advance Communist interests."

Any claims made by ADA that it is anti-Communist in either domestic or foreign affairs are offset by ADA's advocacies throughout its history. On the domestic scene, ADA's programs parallel Marxist and Socialist measures which can only result in a totally leftist system of government and society for the United States. Specifically, the ADA has called for compulsory health insurance; federal controls of prices, wages, and rents; adoption of the Brannan Plan, a Marxist farm program; massive federal subsidies and federal controls of elementary, secondary, and higher education; massive federal expenditures for housing programs; massive federal expenditures for urban commercial, industrial, and cultural development; repeal of the Taft-Hartley Act's provisions which safeguard states' right-to-work laws; and, power for the President of the United States "to modify rates of taxes and expenditures to meet changing conditions."

In the area of internal security, ADA has called for the abolition of the House Committee on Un-American Activities and the Senate Internal Security Subcommittee. ADA has called for the repeal of anti-subversive statutes such as the Smith Act and the Internal Security Act. ADA has opposed the use of wire-taps even in anti-subversive efforts undertaken by federal agencies. ADA has defended the Communist Party as a legitimate political party in the United States. ADA has defended the presence of Communists on the nation's campuses: "We support the rights of teachers and students to full freedom of research, discussion, expression, organization, and publication . . . . Former membership in a Fascist or Communist Party, or refusal to testify under the fifth amendment, should not be automatic grounds to disqualify a teacher." — "We endorse the student bill of rights advocated by Students for Democratic Action. Recent banning of Communist student organizations on college campuses forces us to affirm most strongly the right of Communist student organizations to organize on an equal basis with other student organizations to organize and hear any speaker of their choice."

In 1954, Republican Representative Kit Clardy of Michigan expressed some observations on ADA which retain their accuracy in 1969. Said Mr. Clardy: "While I can cite many instances where ADA members have defended Communists exposed by others, I have never found them on the firing line where Communists were being uncovered. I have never found them exposing Communist fronts or denouncing Communist propaganda. They have reserved their attacks for those of us really engaged in the thankless job they would have you believe they are engaged in. Almost every utterance they make fairly bristles with thunderous denunciations of all of us engaged in carrying the fight to the enemy.

"ADA talks about having made a great and heroic fight against communism in the United States. Well, they have made the battle a bloodless one. ADA had never wounded, let alone decapitated, a single Communist. It has never even wounded the feelings of a Communist — or those of a fellow traveler. Its self-proclaimed great and heroic fight with communism has apparently been carried on in the belief that the really effective way to fight the Communist cause is to kill it with kindness."

In recent years, ADA has expended huge efforts in support of racial agitators in the latter's pursuit of so-called civil rights. ADA was not content with the provisions of the 1964 Civil Rights Act and the 1965 Voting Rights Act. Before these Acts had been tried and found wanting, ADA called for totalitarian, arbitrary, and racist measures to complete the "vast unfinished business in the enforcement of these Acts." ADA proposed legislation which "should make a federal crime every case of murder or assault upon a Negro or civil rights worker where state courts apply one standard of justice to whites and a different standard to Negroes; assure that Southern juries accurately reflect the population composition of the court district; authorize the Attorney General to seek injunctions to prevent violations of Constitutional rights; make possible federal removal of state officials whose denial of constitutional rights results in death or serious bodily injury."

Just as ADA's domestic program could not in any way offend Communists' sensibilities, so too, its foreign program has not only been anti-anti-Communist but, in many instances, unmistakably pro-Communist. On the matter of Red China, ADA has advocated diplomatic recognition by the United States, American support for Red China's admission to United Nations membership, American relief aid to Red China, and the removal of all trade barriers between the United States and Red China.

On foreign "aid" programs, ADA has been critical of the amounts spent by the United States. It has called for not less than a trebling of expenditures. Specifically, ADA has supported handouts to Communist Yugoslavia and Communist Poland but has called for economic sanctions against the anti-Communist regime of South Africa and has opposed any aid to Franco's regime in Spain. (ADA went so far as to urge United States action calling for the exclusion of Spain from the United Nations.)

Toward the United Nations, ADA has displayed an especial fondness. It has called for complete support of the Red-dominated UNESCO and the UN's International Labor Office. It has called for United States ratification of the Red-inspired and Red-supported UN Covenants on Human Rights and Genocide. It has called for repeal of the Connally Reservation which protects, to some degree, domestic matters of the United States from the jurisdiction of the UN's World Court. It has called for a United Nations peace-keeping army.

Peaceful coexistence is the general theme of ADA's attitude toward the Soviet Union. ADA called for United States diplomatic recognition of Outer Mongolia, a Soviet satellite. Toward another Soviet satellite, the ADA has called for a United States hands-off-Cuba policy.

As a major part of its peaceful coexistence stance, the ADA has supported disarmament negotiations and treaties with the Soviet Union by constantly raising the spectre of nuclear warfare. To further its mania for disarmament, ADA has called for total disarmament under United Nations control and a "world government with powers adequate to prevent war."

ADA's claim to non-partisanship and independence in the political arena is just as spurious as its claims to anti-Communism. One of the organization's earliest and staunchest supporters, Dorothy Schiff, publisher of the *New York Post,* said, in 1955: "I question the exactness of the 'non-partisan' label ADA has pinned on itself. It is true that this liberal organization occasionally supports — or rather doesn't campaign against — a few liberal Republicans. But ADA could better be called the conscience of the Democratic Party." In *Commentary* magazine, it was said of ADA that "it abandoned its non-partisan character to become an apologist for the Democratic party, along with the rest of the liberal-left community, on the matter of Communist infiltration of government."

To be precise, ADA has recruited its officers and leaders from the Democratic Party, the Socialist Party, and New York's Liberal Party. But, as a practical matter, ADA has promoted its causes through the candidacies of Democrats. And, from the beginning, ADA has been a highly successful political organization.

Much of ADA's success has undoubtedly been due to the political experience of its officers — experience gained in the Roosevelt, Truman, Kennedy, and Johnson Administrations either as elected or appointed officials or as campaign workers. Then, too, ADA has enjoyed very close ties with leaders of organized labor who have not only served as officials of ADA but have seen to it that the major share of ADA's financial support has come from the nation's unions. (Very early in its history, ADA received a great boost when Walter Reuther urged all trade unionists to work with ADA.)

Among those who have served as ADA officials have been such veteran political figures as Hubert Humphrey, Leon Henderson, Wilson Wyatt, James Loeb Jr., Louis Harris, Joseph L. Rauh Jr., Paul Porter, Eleanor Roosevelt as well as her sons James and Franklin Jr. and her daughter Anna, David Ginsburg, Chester Bowles, William Hastie, Francis Biddle, Frank McCulloch, Wayne Morse, Don Edwards, Daniel Moynihan, Joseph S. Clark, Henry B. Gonzalez, Michael Harrington, Robert W. Kastenmeier, Allard Lowenstein, Charles F. Brannan, Eugene McCarthy, Telford Taylor, Robert Weaver, Herbert Lehman, William Fitts Ryan, Maurine Neuberger, and Leon Keyserling. The academic world has been represented by Arthur M. Schlesinger Jr., James MacGregor Burns, Hans Morgenthau, Samuel Beer, Harold Taylor, and Peter Odegard. From organized labor have come Walter and Victor Reuther, David Dubinsky, James B. Carey, Marx Lewis, Harold Gibbons, Iorwith W. Abel, Joseph Beirne, and James G. Patton. And, from various other facets of the left wing, have come Murray Lincoln, Leo Lerner, Reinhold Niebuhr, Dore Schary, Bayard Rustin, Mrs. Benjamin Spock, and Max Lerner.

In the Congress, ADA has had such members as Paul Douglas, Frank

Graham, Herbert Lehman, Will Rogers Jr., Abraham Ribicoff, William Proxmire, Pat McNamara, Estes Kefauver, Don Edwards, Joseph S. Clark, Francis Myers, Matthew Neely, James Murray, Hubert Humphrey, Maurine Neuberger, Harrison Williams, Jeffery Cohelan, Charles Howell, Richard Bolling, Foster Furcolo, Franklin D. Roosevelt Jr., James Roosevelt, Jonathan Bingham, and Chester Bowles. In the Executive branch, ADA has had G. Mennen Williams, Wilbur J. Cohen, Archibald Cox, Thomas K. Finletter, Carl Rowan, Henry Fowler, Orville Freeman, Theodore Sorensen, Robert Weaver, Arthur Goldberg, and Esther Peterson. Other political figures who have been warm in their praise of ADA have included Lyndon B. Johnson, Dean Acheson, Richardson Dilworth, Averell Harriman, Claude Pepper, Richard L. Neuberger, Martin L. King Jr., Adlai Stevenson, James Farmer, Roy Wilkins, and Bayard Rustin.

Presidential elections have played a major role in ADA's history. In 1948, ADA supported Harry S. Truman. However, this was a second-hand gesture. In April, 1948, ADA's national board had called for the Democratic Party's nomination of Dwight Eisenhower and Associate Justice of the Supreme Court William O. Douglas, for president and vice president, respectively. In 1952 and 1956, ADA supported the candidacy of Adlai Stevenson. In 1960, ADA's affections were divided for awhile between Adlai Stevenson and John F. Kennedy. Some ADA leaders could not forget that Mr. Kennedy had once remarked: "I never joined the Americans for Democratic Action ... I'm not comfortable with those people." Eventually, ADA did endorse Mr. Kennedy who rewarded the organization by saturating his administration with ADA members on his White House staff, in ambassadorships, in his cabinet, and in the upper echelons of all government departments, bureaus, and agencies. In 1964, ADA – with only the slightest and briefest misgivings – campaigned for Lyndon Johnson, who continued the Kennedy policy of keeping ADA leaders and favorites in influential positions throughout the Administration. In 1968, ADA leaders were once again divided in their affections. For a time, they were undecided as to whether to support Robert Kennedy or Eugene McCarthy. After Mr. Kennedy's death, there was some indecision between those who wished to support McCarthy vis-à-vis Hubert Humphrey. Eventually, most ADAers settled on Mr. Humphrey.

ADA, as of 1968, claimed a membership of 55,000. Its major publication is the monthly *ADA World* but influential press support on a continuing basis may be found in such publications as *Nation, New Republic, The Progressive, Atlantic, Harper's, Newsweek,* the *New York Times,* the *New York Post,* the *Boston Globe,* the *Washington Post,* the *Denver Post,* the *Milwaukee Journal,* the *San Francisco Chronicle,* the *St. Petersburg Times,* the *Atlanta Constitution,* the *Louisville Courier-Journal,* the *Providence Journal,* and the *St. Louis Post-Dispatch.* ADA has a campus division. The present national director of ADA is Leon Shull and John Kenneth Galbraith is national chairman.

CARNEGIE CORPORATION
CARNEGIE ENDOWMENT FOR INTERNATIONAL PEACE
CARNEGIE FOUNDATION FOR THE ADVANCEMENT OF TEACHING

Andrew Carnegie, the steel magnate, who amassed one of the all-time great fortunes in American industry, made public gifts and bequests in the amount of $333 million. Three of the many institutions established and endowed by Carnegie were the Carnegie Corporation, the Carnegie Endowment for International Peace, and the Carnegie Foundation for the Advancement of Teaching.

The Carnegie Foundation for the Advancement of Teaching (CFAT) was established in 1905 and endowed with $15 million. (As of June 30, 1966, it had assets of $23 million.) The announced purposes of the CFAT have been varied: retirement allowances for college professors and pensions for their widows (the list of eligible professors was closed in 1931); educational enquiry; publication; consultative services; co-operation with other similar agencies in projects, studies and research, and in other activities which tend to encourage, uphold and dignify the profession of the teacher and the cause of higher education.

The Carnegie Endowment for International Peace (CEIP) was established in 1910 and endowed with $10 million. (As of June 30, 1965, it had assets of $42 million.) The announced purposes of the CEIP have been "to advance the cause of peace among nations; to hasten the renunciation of war as an instrument of national policy; to encourage and promote methods for the peaceful settlement of international differences and for the increase of international understanding and accord; to aid in the development of international law and the acceptance by all nations of the principles underlying such law." The CEIP has described the methodology of promoting its purposes as including the publication of books and pamphlets; the subsidization of study clubs in colleges and universities for the study of international relations; the encouragement (by subsidization) of discussion on international subjects through institutes and international exchange programs of professors and students; the promotion (by subsidization) of better understanding between nations by international visits of representative individuals and groups; the improvement of teaching and the increase of study of international law through fellowships and other financial grants; and, the maintenance of what may be termed a laboratory of observation of the contemporary phenomenon of war and the results of war.

The Carnegie Corporation (CC) was established in 1911 and endowed with $135 million. (As of September 30, 1966, it had assets of $289 million.) It describes its purposes and activities as: "The advancement and diffusion of knowledge and understanding among the peoples of the United States and of the British Commonwealth, excluding India, Pakistan, and the United Kingdom. In the United States, grants are made to colleges, universities, professional associations, and other educational organizations for studies of critical problems facing American education, the improvement of teaching, and research and training programs in public and international affairs."

In 1953, the Carnegie group (CFAT, CEIP, and CC) — along with other foundations and organizations — came under the scrutiny of the Congress which created a Special Committee to Investigate Tax-exempt Foundations and Comparable Organizations (the Reece Committee). The Reece Committee was "authorized and directed to conduct a full and complete investigation and study of educational and philanthropic foundations and other comparable organizations which are exempt from Federal income taxation to determine if any foundations and organizations are using their resources for purposes other than the purposes for which they were established, and especially to determine which such foundations and organizations are using their resources for un-American and subversive activities; for political purposes; propaganda, or attempts to influence legislation."

The Reece Committee was never able "to conduct a full and complete investigation and study." From the beginning, it was hampered by the lack of adequate appropriations and a lack of complete cooperation from the Executive branch and foundation officials. Within the Committee itself, there was marked dissension, exemplified by the obstructionist and disruptive tactics of the ranking minority member, Wayne L. Hays (D. -Ohio). Nevertheless, the Committee did hold sixteen public hearings before the Chairman and the two majority (Republican) members finally voted to discontinue the hearings because they believed that Hays' harassment made it impossible to conduct orderly hearings. Chairman Reece charged that Hays intended all along to frustrate the investigation and to whitewash the foundations. Indeed, Reece went so far as to say that Hays worked hand-in-hand with some of the foundations to prevent the Committee from making the full and complete investigation as authorized and directed by the House.

Chairman Carroll Reece later wrote: "The most difficult assignment of my thirty years in the Congress of the United States was the chairmanship of the Special Committee . . . . This investigation required embarrassingly close scrutiny of the intellectual activities supported by the great and highly respected names of Carnegie, Rockefeller, and Ford . . . [and] I had sensed the power that would spring up in opposition to a complete investigation.

"The obstacles were obvious from the first. We knew that the influential 'liberal' press, characterized by the *New York Times,* the *New York Herald Tribune,* and the *Washington Post-Times Herald,* would throw its editorial power against the Committee. We knew that even the bulk of the conservative press could not be unmindful of the enormous power of these foundations. We knew that many prominent educators, regardless of what they felt, could not be unmindful of the dependency of their institutions upon continued largess from the foundations involved. We knew that the group of prominent men whose decisions would have to be judged extended even to intimates of the White House." (Preface to Reneʹ A. Wormser's *Foundations: Their Power and Influence,* Devin-Adair, 1958.)

Columnist John O'Donnell, writing in the *New York Daily News* (December 21, 1954), described the Reece Committee as having an "almost impossible task" of telling "the taxpayers that the incredible was, in fact, the truth. The incredible fact was that the huge fortunes piled up by such industrial giants as John D. Rockefeller, Andrew Carnegie, and Henry Ford were today being used to destroy or discredit the free-enterprise system which gave them birth."

When the Reece Committee completed its work and was making its findings known, it admitted that, because of the hindrances which had been encountered, its Report "to some extent . . . must be regarded as a pilot study." Enough work had been completed, however, so that the Committee did establish certain findings: (1.) "Foundations are clearly desirable when operating in the natural sciences and when making direct donations to religious, educational, scientific, and other institutional donees. However, when their activities spread into the field of the so-called 'social sciences' or into other areas in which our basic moral, social, economic, and governmental principles can be vitally affected, the public should be alerted to these activities and be made aware of the impact of foundation influence on our accepted way of life."

(2.)"The power of the individual large foundation is enormous. It can exercise various forms of patronage which carry with them elements of thought control. It can exert immense influence on educational institutions, upon the educational process, and upon educators. It is capable of invisible coercion through the power of its purse. It can materially predetermine the development of social and political concepts and courses of action through the process of granting and withholding foundation awards upon a selective basis, and by designing and promulgating projects which propel researchers in selected directions. It can play a powerful part in the determination of academic opinion, and, through this thought leadership, materially influence public opinion."

(3.) "The power to influence national policy is amplified tremendously when foundations act in concert. There is such a concentration of foundation power in the United States, operating in the social sciences and education. It consists basically of a group of major foundations, representing a gigantic aggregate of capital and income. There is no conclusive evidence that this interlock, this concentration of power, having some of the characteristics of an intellectual cartel, came into being as the result of an over-all, conscious plan. Nevertheless, it exists. It operates in part through certain intermediary organizations supported by the foundations. It has ramifications in almost every phase of research and education, in communications and even in government. Such a concentration of power is highly undesirable, whether the net result of its operations is benign or not."

(4.) "A professional class of administrators of foundation funds has emerged, intent upon creating and maintaining personal prestige and independence of action, and upon preserving its position and emoluments. This informed 'guild' has already fallen into many of the vices of a bureaucratic system, involving vast opportunities for selective patronage, preference and privilege. It has already come to exercise a very extensive, practical control over most research in the social sciences, much of our educational process, and a good part of government administration in these and related fields. The aggregate thought-control power of this foundation and foundation-supported bureaucracy can hardly be exaggerated. A system has thus arisen (without its significance being realized by foundation trustees) which gives enormous power to a relatively small group of individuals, having at their virtual command, huge sums in public trust funds. It is a system which is antithetical to American principles."

(5.) "Research in the social sciences plays a key part in the evolution of our society. Such research is now almost wholly in the control of the professional employees of the large foundations and their obedient satellites. Even the great sums allotted by the Federal Government for social science research have come into the virtual control of this professional group."

(6.) "The impact of foundation money upon education has been very heavy, largely tending to promote uniformity in approach and method, tending to induce the educator to become an agent for social change and a protagonist for the development of our society in the direction of some form of collectivism. Foundations have supported text books (and books intended for inclusion in collateral reading lists) which are destructive of our basic governmental and social principles and highly critical of our cherished institutions."

(7.) "In the international field, foundations, and an interlock among some of them and certain intermediary organizations, have exercised a strong effect upon our foreign policy and upon public education in things international. This has been accomplished by vast propaganda, by supplying executives and advisers to government and by controlling much research in this area through the power of the purse. The net result of these combined efforts has been to promote 'internationalism' in a particular sense – a form directed toward 'world government' and a derogation of American 'nationalism.' Foundations have supported a conscious distortion of history, propagandized blindly for the United Nations as the hope of the world, supported that organization's agencies to an extent beyond general public acceptance, and leaned toward a generally 'leftist' approach to international problems."

The Carnegie group was culpable of each charge contained in the findings of the Reece Committee. (The same was true of the Rockefeller and Ford foundations but the effectiveness of these groups was neither as long-lived nor as consistent as the Carnegie group.)

When Andrew Carnegie founded the Endowment for International Peace, he gave to the Trustees (in his eccentric method of spelling) "the widest discretion as to the measures and policy they shall from time to time adopt, only premising that the one end they shall keep unceasingly in view until it is attained is the speedy abolition of international war between so-called civilized nations." The most prominent and, by far, the most active Trustee of the CEIP was Nicholas Murray Butler, one of the leading figures in the Republican Party and president of Columbia University. Butler was not only a rabid internationalist but his Anglophilia was virtually as strong as that of Carnegie whose fervent wish was to see a reunion of the United States and the British Empire.

During World War I, Butler — worried about the fate of Britain — forsook "international peace" in favor of propagandizing for the entrance of the United States into the European war, with the result that the first major project of the Carnegie Endowment for International Peace was an expenditure of funds for intervention. Once the war was over and Britain was safe, Butler led his fellow Trustees toward support of the League of Nations along with a widespread campaign directed toward making Americans international-minded. (Incidentally, one of Butler's books was entitled *The International Mind*.)

From 1910 until 1925, Elihu Root was president of the CEIP. Root, an internationalist, went along with Butler's ideas. From 1925 until 1945, Butler was president and it was during his tenure that the CEIP became the nation's prime propagandist for internationalism. In its 1925 *Yearbook,* the CEIP said: "Underneath and behind all these undertakings there remains the task to instruct and to enlighten public opinion so that it may not only guide but compel the action of governments and public officers in the direction of constructive progress." Constructive progress in the lexicon of the CEIP meant success in the promotion of internationalism.

The Reece Committee summarized the CEIP's program: "An extremely powerful propaganda machine was created. It spent many millions of dollars in: The production of masses of material for distribution; the creation and support of large numbers of international polity clubs, and other local organizations at colleges and elsewhere; the underwriting and dissemination of many books on various subjects,

31

through the 'International Mind Alcoves' and the 'International Relations Clubs and Centers' which it organized all over the country; the collaboration with agents of publicity, such as newspaper editors, the preparation of material to be used in school text books, and cooperation with publishers of text books to incorporate this material; the establishing of professorships at the colleges and the training and indoctrination of teachers; the financing of lecturers and the importation of foreign lecturers and exchange professors; the support of outside agencies touching the international field, such as the Institution of International Education, the Foreign Policy Association, the American Association for the Advancement of Science, the American Council on Education, the American Council of Learned Societies, the American Historical Association, the American Association of International Conciliation, the Institute of Pacific Relations, the International Parliamentary Union and others, and acting as mid-wife at the birth of some of them."

Through the "International Mind Alcoves," the CEIP distributed books written by Communists, Socialists, pro-Communists, and left-wing internationalists. To the "International Relations Clubs and Centers," the CEIP sent a wide assortment of leftwing literature published by the Foreign Policy Association, the Institute of Pacific Relations, and the American-Russian Institute with the result that university and college students in International Relations Clubs were exposed to a barrage of Communist or pro-Communist literature represented as objective scholarship.

While the CEIP was contaminating campuses with leftwing propaganda, it was also exerting powerful influence upon the State Department. As early as 1934 in its *Yearbook,* the CEIP boasted that it was "becoming an unofficial instrument of international policy, taking up here and there the ends and threads of international problems and questions which the governments find it difficult to handle, and through private initiative reaching conclusions which are not of a formal nature but which officially find their way into the policies of governments." It was no idle boast. Personnel from the CEIP and the Council on Foreign Relations, which was subsidized by the CEIP, took consultative and administrative positions in the State Department during the 1930's and 1940's.

The successor to Butler as president of the CEIP was Alger Hiss who took office in 1947. Hiss, whose subversive reputation was already an open secret in governmental circles, had played a key role in the establishment of the United Nations as director of the Office of Special Political Affairs in the State Department. He moved directly from the State Department to the presidency of CEIP and immediately began to promote the United Nations as a top priority project for the CEIP.

In the 1947 *Yearbook* of the CEIP, Hiss told the Trustees that the presence of the UN in New York meant that "the opportunity for an endowed American institution having the objectives, tradition and prestige of the Endowment, to support and serve the United Nations is very great." He recommended that the CEIP focus its work on aiding the UN in every way possible. He mentioned a "widely educational" program directed at the general public and he encouraged the Trustees to "aid in the adaption of wise policies, both by our own government in its capacity as a member of the United Nations, and by the United Nations Organization as a whole."

Hiss wanted the CEIP to use not only its own resources to promote the UN but also those of its subsidiaries and other leftwing organizations. He explained to the Trustees: "The number and importance of decisions in the field of foreign relations with which the United States will be faced during the next few years are of such magnitude that the widest possible stimulation of public education in this field is of major and pressing importance. In furthering its educational objectives the Endowment should utilize its existing resources, such as The International Relations Clubs in the colleges, and *International Conciliation,* and should strengthen its relationships with existing agencies interested in the field of foreign affairs. These relationships should include close collaboration with other organizations principally engaged in the study of foreign affairs, such as The Council on Foreign Relations, The Foreign Policy Association, The Institute of Pacific Relations, the developing university centers of international studies, and local community groups interested in foreign affairs of which the Cleveland Council on World Affairs and the projected World Affairs Council in San Francisco are examples.

"Of particular importance is the unusual opportunity of reaching large segments of the population by establishing relations of a rather novel sort with the large national organizations which today are desirous of supplying their members with objective information on public affairs, including international issues. These organizations — designed to serve, respectively, the broad interests of business, church, women's,

33

farm, labor, veterans', educational, and other large groups of our citizens — are not equipped to set up foreign policy research staffs of their own. The Endowment should supply these organizations with basic information about the United Nations and should assist them both in selecting topics of interest to their members and in presenting those topics so as to be most readily understood by their members. We should urge The Foreign Policy Association and The Institute of Pacific Relations to supply similar service on other topics of international significance.

"Exploration should also be made by the Endowment as to the possibilities of increasing the effectiveness of the radio and motion pictures in public education on world affairs."

Hiss' successor as president of the CEIP was James T. Shotwell, emeritus professor of international relations from Columbia University and a trustee of CEIP since 1924. His internationalism dated back to his experience on Edward Mandell House's "Inquiry," at the Paris Peace Conference. Shotwell's tenure lasted but a year and, in 1950, he was succeeded by Joseph E. Johnson who had been Hiss' chief assistant in the State Department. Johnson was also an official of the leftwing-pacifist World Peace Foundation, the leftwing-internationalist Council on Foreign Relations, and the soft-on-Communism Foreign Policy Association.

Since Johnson became president, the CEIP has continued and increased its work on behalf of the United Nations. In 1953, the Carnegie International Center was built opposite the United Nations headquarters in New York City. In 1957, the CEIP and the Foreign Policy Association founded the Foreign Policy Association-World Affairs Center where corporation executives, educators, civic leaders, and journalists could be briefed (or brainwashed) on the virtues of the United Nations.

One of the CEIP's major projects during the 1950's was a massive propaganda effort on behalf of a United Nations "Peace" Force. But Johnson's most important work as president of the CEIP has been his overseership of *Apartheid and United Nations,* a blueprint for a United Nations military invasion and conquest of the Republic of South Africa, a member-nation of the UN. According to CEIP's analysts, the conquest of South Africa could be accomplished within four months because the United States and the Soviet Union would be supporting the "massive direct military intervention." (As of January, 1967,

Apartheid and United Nations had gone through three printings.) Other officials of the CEIP in the period, who must have shared Johnson's penchant for wanton aggression against South Africa, included: Andrew Cordier, Ernest Gross, Gabriel Hauge, William L. Langer, Ralph McGill, Whitney North Seymour, George N. Shuster, and Arthur K. Watson.

While the CEIP has labored to subvert America's nationalist interests in favor of a collectivist one-world, the Carnegie Corporation and the Carnegie Foundation for the Advancement of Teaching have been corrupting educational processes.

Alone or in combination, the CC and the CFAT have heavily subsidized the American Council on Education, the National Education Association, the Progressive Education Association, the National Council on Parent Education, and the American Youth Commission which serve as clearing-houses for progressive-modernist-permissive educationist techniques and materials in higher, secondary, primary, and adult education.

One of the Carnegie group's major strokes in education came about when the Carnegie Corporation granted $340,000 to the American Historical Association for the production of a study by the AHA's Commission on Social Studies. The Commission published its study in sixteen sections, the last of which appeared in 1934 under the title *Conclusions and Recommendations.*

Without regret, *Conclusions and Recommendations* stated that "a new age of collectivism is emerging" in the United States, replacing "the age of individualism and laissez faire in economy and government." The study continued:

"10. As to the specific form which this 'collectivism,' this integration and interdependence, is taking and will take in the future, the evidence at hand is by no means clear or unequivocal. It may involve the limiting or supplanting of private property by public property or it may entail the preservation of private property, extended and distributed among the masses. Most likely, it will issue from a process of experimentation and will represent a composit of historic doctrines and social conceptions yet to appear. Almost certainly it will involve a larger measure of compulsory as well as voluntary cooperation of citizens in the conduct of the complex national economy, a corresponding enlargement of the functions of government, and an increasing state intervention in fundamental branches of economy previously left to the individual discretion and initiative – a state intervention that in some instances may be direct and mandatory and in others indirect and facilitative. In any event the Commission is convinced by its interpretation of available empirical data that the actually integrating economy of the present day is the forerunner of a consciously integrated society in which individual economic actions and individual property rights will be altered and abridged.

"11. The emerging age is particularly an age of transition. It is marked by numerous and severe tensions arising out of the conflict between the actual trend toward integrated economy and society, on the one side, and the traditional practices, dispositions, ideas, and institutional arrangements inherited from the passing age of individualism, on the other. In all the recommendations that follow the transitional character of the present epoch is recognized.

"12. Underlying and illustrative of these tensions are privation in the midst of plenty, violations of fiduciary trust, gross inequalities in income and wealth, widespread racketeering and banditry, wasteful use of natural resources, unbalanced distribution and organization of labor and leisure, the harnessing of science to individualism in business enterprise, the artificiality of political boundaries and divisions, the subjection of public welfare to the egoism of private interests, the maladjustment of production and consumption, persistent tendencies toward economic instability, disproportionate growth of debt and property claims in relations to production, deliberate destruction of goods and withdrawal of efficiency from production, accelerating tempo of panics, crises, and depressions attended by ever wider destruction of capital and demoralization of labor, struggles among nations for markets and raw materials leading to international conflicts and wars.

"13. If historical knowledge is any guide, these tensions, accompanied by oscillations in popular opinion, public policy, and the fortunes of the struggle for power, will continue until some approximate adjustment is made between social thought, social practice, and economic realities, or until society, exhausted by the conflict and at the end of its spiritual and inventive resources, sinks back into a more primitive order of economy and life. Such is the long-run view of social development in general, and of American life in particular, which must form the background for any educational program designed to prepare either children or adults for their coming trials, opportunities, and responsibilities."

The study then continued with a discussion of "distribution" and "redistribution" that was indisputably Marxian. Under the heading, "Choices Deemed Possible and Desirable," it was stated: "Within the limits of the broad trend toward social integration the possible forms of economic and political life are many and varied, involving wide differences in modes of *distributing* wealth, income, and cultural opportunity, embracing various conceptions of the State and of the rights, duties, and privileges of the ordinary citizen, and representing the most diverse ideals concerning the relations of sexes, classes, religions, nations, and races. . . ."

Then, under the heading, " The Redistribution of Power," the nation's educators were told how they might prepare to conduct themselves in a collectivist society: "1. If the teacher is to achieve these conditions of improved status and thus free the school from the domination of special interests and convert it into a truly enlightening force in society, there must be a redistribution of power in the general conduct of education — the board of education will have to be made more representative, the administration of the school will have to be conceived more broadly and the teaching profession as a whole will have to organize, develop a theory of its social function and create certain instrumentalities indispensable to the realization of its aims.

"2. The ordinary board of education in the United States, with the exception of the rural district board, is composed for the most part of business and professional men; the ordinary rural district board is composed almost altogether of landholders. In the former case the board is not fully representative of the supporting population and thus tends to impose upon the school the social ideas of a special class; in both instances its membership is apt to be peculiarly rooted in the economic individualism of the 19th century.

"3. If the board of education is to support a school program conceived in terms of the general welfare and adjusted to the needs of an epoch marked by transition to some form of socialized economy, it should include in its membership adequate representation of points of view other than those of private business.

"4. With the expansion of education and the growth of large school systems, involving the coordination of the efforts of tens, hundreds and even thousands of professional workers and the expenditure of vast sums of money on grounds, buildings and equipment, the function of administration has become increasingly important and indispensable."

The AHA's Commission on Social Studies seemed to leave nothing

37

to chance in its recommendations for the collectivization of education. There was to be a consolidation of traditional subjects (history, civics, political science, sociology, geography, and economics) into the single and amorphous category of "social sciences." The American Historical Association was to take over *The Historical Outlook,* a journal for social science teachers, and rename it *The Social Sciences.* Textbook authors were "expected to revamp and rewrite their old works in accordance with this frame of reference and new writers in the field of the social sciences will undoubtedly attack the central problem here conceived" — the problem being: how to educate a collectivist society. "Makers of programs in the social sciences in cities, towns and states" would "recast existing syllibi and schemes of instruction." Colleges and teachers' schools would revise their programs and *conform* to the "frame of reference" so that there would be a guarantee of "a supply of teachers more competent to carry out the philosophy [collectivism] and purpose here presented."

When Harold Laski read the AHA's *Conclusions and Recommendations,* he said: "At bottom, and stripped of its carefully neutral phrases, the report is an educational program for a socialist America." The Carnegie Corporation hailed the "educational program for a socialist America" in its 1933-1934 *Annual Report*: "That its [the Commission's] findings were not unanimously supported within the *Commission* itself, and that they are already the subject of vigorous debate outside it, does not detract from their importance, and both the educational world and the public at large owe a debt of gratitude both to the [American Historical] Association for having sponsored this important and timely study in a field of peculiar difficulty, and to the distinguished men and women who served upon the *Commission*."

The Carnegie group was not content to promote socialist education merely through the AHA's *Conclusions and Recommendations.* Along with the Rockefeller and Russell Sage Foundations, the Carnegie Corporation subsidized the *Encyclopedia of the Social Sciences,* the most widely used reference for the "social sciences." The major portion of the editorial work was done on the *Encyclopedia* by Alvin Johnson whose flair for Socialism had been made evident when he was editor of *New Republic* and through his directorship of the ultra-radical New School for Social Research. (Two of Johnson's assistant editors were known to him as Socialists.) For the major articles in the *Encyclopedia,* Johnson chose as authors Socialists, Marxists, pro-Communists, Communist fronters, and other radicals. This group included British Socialists Harold Laski and G. D. H. Cole; a Hungarian Socialist, Oscar Jassi; a German Socialist, Werner Sombart; a German Marxist, Max Beer; Communist-fronters Robert Morss Lovett, J. B. S. Hardman, Horace M. Kallen, Max Lerner, Roger Baldwin, Philip Klein, George Soule, John Fitch, Bernhard Stern; and such radicals as Gardiner Means, Adolf A. Berle Jr., George Counts, and Myron Watkins. The net effect was a massive collection of articles praising Socialism, Communism, and other collectivisms. As the Reece Committee indicated: "What is amazingly characteristic of the Encyclopedia is the extent to which articles on 'left' subjects have been assigned to leftists; in the case of subjects to the 'right,' leftists again have been selected to describe and expound them."

The Carnegie Corporation and the Carnegie Foundation for the Advancement of Teaching have contributed heavily to the financial support of the Social Science Research Council which has served as a central agency to promote conformity of so-called research in the so-called social sciences. The SSRC's thirty-member board of directors has twenty-one designated by the American Anthropological Association, the American Economic Association, the American Historical Association, the American Political Science Association, the American Psychological Association, the American Sociological Association, and the American Statistical Association. The SSRC also cooperates with the National Research Council, the American Council of Learned Societies, and the American Council on Education, and there exists between these four clearing houses an interlock of members which helps to constitute a virtual monopoly in the matter of research in the various disciplines included under the heading of social sciences.

The Carnegie Corporation, the Carnegie Foundation for the Advancement of Teaching, and the Carnegie Endowment for International Peace have all heavily subsidized the American Council on Education. The ACE is the council of national and regional education associations and colleges and universities. It is a clearing house for the exchange of information and opinion; it establishes policy and acts as a distributing agent for foundations who make grants in the field of education; it is a liaison agent between educational institutions and federal departments and agencies; it distributes literature produced by a selected group of individuals on social and educational problems; and, it strives for a conformist educational policy on a national level and holds virtually totalitarian control over accreditation standards for universities and colleges.

One of the Carnegie Corporation's most notorious and consequential projects was the financing ($250,000) of Gunnar Myrdal's *An American Dilemma: The Negro Problem in Modern Democracy*. Myrdal, a Swedish Socialist of the Marxian variety, called upon the services of a host of Communists and fellow travelers to write on race problems in the South. What Myrdal produced was a vicious diatribe against the American people, the United States and its Constitution, and, especially, against the people of the Southern states. In 1954, in the case of *Brown v. Board of Education*, Chief Justice Earl Warren cited Myrdal's *An American Dilemma* in its entirety as an authority for his rabble-rousing decision on the matter of segregation in local schools.

In recent years and currently, the Carnegie group has expanded its influence into every facet of education: educational television, international exchanges of students, remedial studies, aptitude tests, college newspapers, surveys of parochial schools, rehabilitation of drop-outs, Negroes' schools, and teachers' education. At the same time, the group has not neglected its promotion of pacifism and internationalism.

COMMITTEE ON POLITICAL EDUCATION
POLITICAL ACTION COMMITTEE (CIO)
LEAGUE OF POLITICAL EDUCATION (AFL)

In 1943, Sidney Hillman established the National Citizens Political Action Committee of the Congress of Industrial Organizations. (Hillman, one of the founders of the CIO, was – in 1943 – president of the Amalgamated Clothing Workers of America. He had also been, since 1936, the leader of the American Labor Party of New York. The ALP was a political front organization of the Communist Party. Through the ALP, the Communists were able to present their candidates for elective office under other than a straight Communist label.)

When Hillman formed the PAC, his immediate purpose was to ensure a fourth term victory for Franklin Roosevelt while the long-range goal was to be a complete takeover of the Democrat Party.

Hillman assumed the chairmanship of the PAC. Other officers included James G. Patton, a veteran fellow traveler and president of the National Farmers Union; Freda Kirchwey, publisher and editor of the fellow-traveling *The Nation*; Clark Foreman, president of the Southern Conference for Human Welfare, a Communist front; Robert C. Weaver, who, in 1966, became the first Negro cabinet member as Lyndon Johnson's Secretary of Housing and Urban Development; and, James Loeb, who, in 1945, became national director of the Union for Democratic Action and, in 1947, was a founder and national director of Americans for Democratic Action. Members of the PAC included such well-known fellow travelers as Max Lerner, Frederick L. Schuman, Carey McWilliams, Lillian Smith, Mary McLeod Bethune, and Aubrey Williams; Communists Paul Robeson, Louis Adamic, and James Dombrowski; Nelson Poynter, the Florida publisher, who, in 1944, founded the Congressional Quarterly publications; Alfred Baker Lewis, Socialist Party activist; John Kenneth Galbraith, who became a founder and eventually national chairman of Americans for Democratic Action; Reinhold Niebuhr, an influential leader of the Union for Democratic Action, who became a founder and vice chairman of Americans for Democratic Action; and labor leaders Philip Murray, David McDonald, and James Carey. It was only natural that Hillman and his PAC with its glittering array of leftists received the total support of the Communist Party.

In 1947, the American Federation of Labor formed its own political wing, the League of Political Education. The LPE took an active role in campaigns for federal, state, and local offices. It distributed campaign material and solicited and distributed campaign funds.

In 1955, the year of the AFL-CIO merger, the political arms (LPE and PAC) were consolidated into the Committee on Political Education, which, from the beginning, has always been dominated by Walter Reuther. From 1955 until 1957, Jack Kroll (Hillman's successor as head of the PAC) and James McDevitt, the head of the AFL's League of Political Education, were co-chairman of COPE. From 1957 until 1963, McDevitt was the sole chairman and, since 1963, the post has been held by Al Barkan. Kroll, McDevitt, and Barkan were never more than front-men for Reuther and they were totally committed to the promotion of ultra-liberal Democratic candidates.

COPE's political interests have been all-inclusive on the American scene. It has actively supported candidates for mayoralties, governorships, state legislatures, the Congress, and the presidency. With very few exceptions, COPE has campaigned for far-left Democrats. It has supported with great reluctance a few Republicans since the term "Republican" is virtually anathema to Reuther who fears that support for a Republican — even one who is ideologically a captive of labor — might result in other Republicans riding in on the coattails of a COPE-sponsored one. (For example, in 1966, COPE endorsed only fifteen Republicans in the 435 Congressional races.)

In recent years, COPE's especial favorites have included the Kennedys (John, Robert, and Edward); Lyndon Johnson; Hubert Humphrey; Adlai Stevenson; Estes Kefauver; Pierre Salinger; G. Mennen Williams; Edmund G. (Pat) Brown; Thomas Kuchel; Mayors James Tate (Philadelphia), Carl Stokes (Cleveland), and Richard Hatcher (Gary, Indiana); Senators Birch Bayh and George McGovern; and, Representatives William Hathaway, James Hanley, and Joseph Vigorito. No political race in any state is too obscure for COPE's interest.

There is no denying COPE's efficiency as it follows its four-point program of (1) voter registration; (2) political propaganda distribution; (3) get-out-the-vote campaigns; and, (4) financing of political candidates. And COPE cooperates with other organizations with the same ideological leftism: Americans for Democratic Action, the National Committee for an Effective Congress, the National Farmers Union, the Institute for American Democracy (and its predecessor the National Council for Civic Responsibility), rural electric co-operatives, civil rights groups, the Democratic Study Group, and the National Council of Senior Citizens. It uses the materials of Group Research.

Pro-labor legislation takes priority in COPE's efforts through its political captives. But COPE has also worked for federal subsidies to education, urban renewal, public power, medicare, federal housing, and other socialistic projects. And, in COPE's publications, there has always been a vigorous anti-anti-Communist campaign.

CONGRESS OF RACIAL EQUALITY

In 1942, Jack Spratt's Coffee Shop in Chicago was the scene of a sit-in demonstration. George Houser led a group of white and Negro agitators in the sit-in which was ordered by James Farmer. (Farmer, at the time, was race relations secretary of the Fellowship of Reconciliation, one of the oldest and certainly the largest leftwing-pacifist group in the country. FOR was headed by Abraham J. Muste, a notorious, longtime collaborator of the Communist Party.)

The sit-in at the coffee shop was successful from the viewpoint of the agitators; business was disrupted and the owner was coerced into serving the integrated group.

Farmer and Houser chose as their next target a roller skating rink.

Before their second sit-in, however, they organized their demonstrators as the Congress of Racial Equality which would allegedly apply Gandhian techniques of nonviolence to combat racial discrimination and segregation. (Houser was CORE's national director from its beginnings in 1943 until 1955. He left CORE to become executive director of the leftwing American Committee on Africa. In CORE's early history, Houser was aided by Bayard Rustin, the group's first and only field secretary. Rustin, like James Farmer, worked for Muste's Fellowship of Reconciliation and it was Muste who assigned Rustin to CORE. But Rustin, during World War II, was a conscientious objector and by violating the selective service law he spent twenty-eight months in prison.)

During CORE's first decade, the organization's activities were sporadic but sit-ins to desegregate lunch counters in St. Louis and Baltimore and swimming pools in New York and Los Angeles were successful. It was not until 1960, however, that CORE made any strenuous efforts in the South. In February, 1960, the organization began a yearlong campaign to desegregate lunch counters. And the sit-ins were successful in more than 130 Southern communities. By this time, it became evident that CORE's demonstrators were especially anxious to be arrested during their sit-in spectacles so that they might attract widespread publicity and sympathy.

In 1961, James Farmer, who had founded CORE along with George Houser, became CORE's national director — a post he held until 1966. (Farmer ended his employment with the Fellowship of Reconciliation in 1945. From 1946 until 1950 and from 1954 until 1959, he worked for organized labor. From 1950 until 1954, he was field secretary for the socialist League for Industrial Democracy. For the two years prior to his return to CORE, he was program director for the National Association for the Advancement of Colored People.)

Under Farmer's direction, CORE became a major force in racist agitation as he instituted the so-called freedom rides throughout the South to protest segregation on interstate carriers and at terminal facilities. Demonstrators — whites and Negroes — came from all parts of the country to join the freedom rides. (Two of the freedom riders had previously gained notoriety in a widely publicized "pacifist" stunt. Albert Bigelow, in 1958, had sailed his ketch *Golden Rule* into the United States nuclear test zone in the Pacific. When Bigelow was arrested, James Peck took his place and, in turn, he was arrested. They, along with twenty others, became the original freedom riders in 1961.)

The freedom rides generally ended in mass arrests and imprisonments. But such results were welcomed by Farmer and his cohorts who attracted wide sympathy with their cries of "police brutality." (Farmer set the tone for the rides when he announced, in March, 1961: "Should nonviolence fail, then violence is a better course than complete acquiescence." He was as careful as Martin L. King Jr. in never advocating violence but simply mentioned it as a possibility. But, by remarkable coincidence, violence followed the nonviolent Farmer with the same frequency it followed King.) Television and radio facilities and newspaper reporters from all over the country served as Farmer's sycophantic publicity agents. And the Communist press was ecstatic over the freedom rides. This was understandable since the entire freedom ride movement was replete with fellow travelers and Communists. (CORE's advisory committee included an imposing representation of individuals who had activist connections with subversive organizations. As of 1963, they were Martin L. King Jr., Fred L. Shuttlesworth, Roger Baldwin, Algernon Black, Allan Knight Chalmers, Earl Dickerson, Rabbi Roland Gittelsohn, Abraham J. Muste, E. Stanley Jones, A. Philip Randolph, Ira DeA. Reid, Lillian Smith, Goodwin Watson, and Charles S. Zimmerman. Other advisors to CORE along the way included: labor leader Walter Reuther, Harold Gibbins of the Teamsters Union, John Cogley of the ultra-liberal *Commonweal* magazine, athletes Jackie Robinson and Bill Russell, novelist James Baldwin, actor Sidney Poitier, and Southern Christian Leadership Conference leader Ralph Abernathy.)

As CORE grew stronger (82,000 members in 1964), its program broadened. It demonstrated at the New York World's Fair, the United Nations, banks, supermarkets, theaters, amusement parks, apartment houses, chain stores of various sorts, and the national conventions of the Republican and Democrat parties. Aside from integration, CORE instigated rent strikes and agitated for civilian review boards to harass local police forces. CORE worked for urban renewal projects and cooperatives in "ghettoes," and it engaged in local political activities. By its own description, CORE was: "Persons of various races committed to the use of nonviolent direct action in specific attacks on segregation and discrimination, who are accepted through local groups after screening. [Membership or former membership in the Communist Party or any other subversive organization was not a bar to membership in

CORE.] To promote better race relations through action projects aimed at change of discriminatory policies: in the South concentrating on voter registration and establishment of full Negro rights; in the North concentrating on community problems of minority groups such as slum improvement, adequate urban renewal, [and] police brutality."

Despite CORE's leaders' constant prattling about nonviolence, CORE demonstrations were fraught with violence. This was not an unusual development because the same situation held true for the Student Nonviolent Coordinating Committee and Martin L. King's Southern Christian Leadership Conference, the two organizations which were the main collaborators in CORE's demonstrations. The net result was that CORE, as it became more and more riotous, lost its financial support and by January, 1965 its leaders admitted that the organization was in debt.

When CORE fell on such troublous financial times, its leadership opted for new tactics. And, in 1965, CORE formed an alliance with the ultra-racist Black Muslims. It became evident that CORE as "persons of various races" was undergoing a drastic change. In the spring of 1966, the change was confirmed when Floyd McKissick succeeded James Farmer as CORE's national director. McKissick, who had served the organization as general counsel and national chairman, made no secret of his racism. For the white man, he advised: "If you want to help, keep your mouth shut and get out of my way." He talked of a Negro revolution and downgraded civil rights and nonviolence: "Forget about civil rights. I'm talking about black power." — "Negroes are not geared to nonviolence."

As McKissick made "black power" the rallying cry for CORE, he worked alongside Lincoln Lynch, CORE's associate director. Lynch was equal to McKissick as a rabble rouser: "If America doesn't come around, we're gonna burn it down." — "We have gone from the nonviolent to the self-protection to the most important step of them all, the open revolution." (In 1966, Lynch spoke at the Communist weekly *National Guardian's* anniversary dinner. In 1967, he spoke at the Communists' *The Worker's* anniversary celebration. He was to succeed McKissick as national director but instead resigned from CORE in December, 1967.)

In December, 1968, Roy Innis was named as associate director of CORE. He was a dedicated black nationalist and the executive director of the Harlem Commonwealth Council which was concerned with rebuilding and creating black economic institutions. (The Council was financed by the federal government.)

In July, 1968, at CORE's annual convention, Innis became CORE's acting director, replacing McKissick who was retiring because of ill health. Innis announced at the convention that CORE was now "clearly a black nationalist organization," with plans for Negroes to take control of the economic, political, and social institutions in their communities. In effect, Innis said, CORE was going to create "a new political subdivision" for Negroes.

In September, 1968, CORE reconvened its annual convention. Innis was elected as national director. A new constitution was adopted wherein CORE formally advocated black nationalism. To Innis, black nationalism includes a new constitution for the United States whereby blacks will be guaranteed representation in the Congress (at present, by Innis' computations, ten black Senators and forty-three Representatives); the creation of black corporations with loans from private industry — the loans being guaranteed by the federal government; and, the "transfer of institutional control of management of those agencies that serve the black community." Whites are now excluded from CORE membership, but Innis says that they may continue to play a role in the civil rights movement by contributing their skills and experience.

COUNCIL FOR A LIVABLE WORLD

The late Leo Szilard, a Hungarian-born scientist, came to the United States in 1939. For five years, he had been developing a theory of chain-reaction to devise a system for releasing atomic energy. By 1939, he was quite convinced that uranium could sustain a chain reaction that might be used in "the construction of bombs which would be extremely dangerous in general and particularly in the hands of certain governments." He was further convinced that the United States must construct such an atomic bomb before the German regime of Adolf Hitler did. So intent was Szilard on preventing the Germans from developing an atomic weapon, he tried to persuade nuclear physicists outside of Germany to censor their findings in order to keep knowledge of progress in the study of atomic energy away from German scientists.

In 1939, Szilard prevailed upon the well-known scientist Albert Einstein to send a memorandum, prepared by Szilard, to President Franklin Roosevelt urging the latter to support the development of an atomic bomb ("some recent work by E. Fermi and L. Szilard, which has been communicated to me in manuscript, leads me to expect that the element uranium may be turned into a new and important source of energy."). Einstein's importunities convinced Roosevelt, and the resources of the U. S. government were placed behind the development of the A-bomb. Then, in 1942, Szilard and Enrico Fermi invented a chain-reaction system for releasing atomic energy and – in less than three years – an A-bomb became a reality.

As was the case with so many scientists, Szilard was obsessed with the idea of using the A-bomb against Germany but, when German resistance collapsed in 1945, Szilard worked feverishly to prevent usage by the United States against Japan. He argued that the United States, too, would become vulnerable to A-bomb attacks, that the Soviet Union would make its own A-bomb within a few years, and that the United States should work to bring the A-bomb under international control.

On October 2, 1964, U. S. Senator Milward L. Simpson (R. -Wyo.), from the Senate floor, summarized Szilard's post-1945 activities: "President Truman's refusal to accept the Szilard proposal apparently pushed the scientist all the way over to the left. He devoted the next few years first, to opposing further nuclear armament, then to opposing development of the hydrogen bomb and to supporting Dr. J. Robert Oppenheimer in his clearance case before the Atomic Energy Commission.

"It was also during this period that Szilard began his long correspondence with leaders of the Soviet Union. First he wrote, over State Department protests, to Stalin and Molotov, later to Khrushchev. This latter correspondence culminated in a tête-à-tête with Krushchev in New York. Khrushchev was in New York for the U. N. meeting. It was at this time that he made a mockery of international procedure with his shoddy, shoe-pounding appearance before the world body. The performance didn't appear to bother Szilard, however.

"His appointment with the Kremlin dictator started out as a 15-minute interview, ended up as a 2-hour conference. Neither party ever revealed fully the extent of their talk.

"Meanwhile, Szilard had teamed with Lord Bertrand Russell of England and Cyrus Eaton – American bankroller of leftist causes – in an extragovernmental series of talks with Communist scientists. Szilard, along with Russell and Eaton, helped create the first international conference of scientists which became known as the Pugwash Conferences, named for Eaton's plush hideaway at Pugwash, Nova Scotia. Szilard was a regular at succeeding conferences.

"With the change of administrations in 1961 Szilard suddenly found he had comparatively free access to the White House, to the Disarmament Agency and to high-level Government circles."

In September, 1961, at a Pugwash Conference in Stowe, Vermont, Szilard presented a disarmament plan to his scientific colleagues. Columnist Holmes Alexander summarized Szilard's contribution: "1. An informer system among Americans: The President would post a $1 million tax-free award to any American who reported nuclear treaty violations to a U. N. Control Commission. To enable the squealer to become happily adjusted, Szilard adds that 'the recipient of such an award who wishes to enjoy . . . a life of leisure and luxury abroad . . . would not be hampered by currency restrictions . . . .

"2. A head-hunt system: A U. N. Peace Court, following a barbaric precedent of the Middle Ages, would pass the death sentence upon any American citizen or Government official deemed guilty of violating 'peace.' In almost incredible savagery Szilard told this international group, which included some vicious enemies of America, that: 'The Court could deputize any and all Americans to try and execute the sentence. An American citizen killing an 'outlaw' could not be legally tried for murder in an American court, inasmuch as the treaty . . . would be the law of the land.'"

The startling proposals made by Szilard to his Pugwash comrades were not merely the dabblings of a "peace" theoretician. He was determined to be an activist. And, for one of his goals, he set out to establish "the most powerful lobby that ever hit Washington." He was greatly encouraged in his activism as a result of an article in *Life* magazine in September, 1961. The article mentioned that Szilard was in Washington "trying to find out if there was a market for wisdom." According to Szilard, he was immediately besieged with requests from colleges and universities inviting him to give lectures. He declined them all until Brandeis University invited him to attend a special convocation and receive an honorary doctorate. He accepted the offer from Brandeis and spoke informally to the trustees and fellows of the university about his "peace" proposals.

After his experience at Brandeis, Szilard developed a formal speech ("Are We on the Road to War?") which he delivered to the Law School Forum at Harvard University on November 14, 1961. Within a few months, Szilard delivered the same speech at nine American colleges and universities. (The entire speech was printed in the April, 1962 issue of the *Bulletin of the Atomic Scientists*, which is the propaganda outlet for the Pugwashers.)

To his audiences, Szilard recounted how he had met with Khrushchev in October, 1960: "At that time, it was not known whether Kennedy or Nixon would get elected, and I started off the conversation by saying that no matter who is elected, the government would try to reach an understanding with Russia on the issue of stopping the arms race. Khrushchev answered — and he spoke in all seriousness — that he believed this also."

A month after Szilard had assured the Soviet dictator as to the future policy of the U. S. government, he traveled to Moscow where he attended the sixth Pugwash Conference. When the Conference concluded, Szilard remained another month: "I stayed on in Moscow in order to engage in private conversations with our Russian colleagues, because I knew from experience that only in private conversations is it possible to get anything across to them or to discover what they really believe to be true.

"None of our Russian colleagues brought up the issue of bomb tests in any of these conversations in Moscow .... I found, however, an undiminished interest in far-reaching disarmament which would result in substantial savings ....

"I tried to impress upon our Russian colleagues that the Kennedy administration would make a serious effort to reach an understanding with Russia on the issue of arms control, but that the new administration would need time — six months and more than six months perhaps — to find its bearings on this issue and to get organized to deal with it."

In February, 1961, Szilard returned to Washington from Moscow. He liked what he found there: "With President Kennedy, new men moved into the administration. Many of them understand the implications of what is going on and are deeply concerned. But, they are so busy trying to keep the worst things from happening, on a day-to-day basis, that they have no time to develop a consensus on what the right approach would be, from the long-term point of view. There are also a number of men in Congress, particularly in the Senate, who have insight into what is going on and who are concerned, but mostly they lack the courage of their convictions."

It was at this point that Szilard decided to set up "the most powerful lobby that ever hit Washington." He planned that the lobby would bring to Washington "scholars and scientists who see current events in their historical perspective. These men would speak with the sweet voice of reason, and our lobby could see to it that they be heard by people inside the administration, and also by the key people in Congress."

Szilard was concerned that "the sweet voice of reason" might go unheeded unless the "distinguished scholars and scientists" were able to deliver votes. But, to his mind, this was not an insurmountable problem: "The minority for which they speak might represent a few per cent of the votes, and a few per cent of the votes alone would not mean very much. Still, the combination of a few per cent of the votes and the sweet voice of reason might turn out to be an effective combination. And, if the minority for which these men speak were sufficiently dedicated to stand ready not only to deliver votes, but also to make very substantial campaign contributions, then this minority would be in a position to set up the most powerful lobby that ever hit Washington."

Szilard deplored the fact that a Russian was not the director of the International Atomic Energy Agency. He urged the lifting of all travel restrictions for Russian "scientists" who visit the United States. He called for the United States government to resolve and proclaim: (1) "that she would not resort to any strategic bombing of cities or bases of Russia (either by means of atomic bombs or conventional explosives), except if American cities or bases are attacked with bombs, or if there is an unprovoked attack with bombs against one of America's allies"; (2) "that America could and should adopt the policy that, in case of war, if she were to use atomic bombs against troops in combat, she would do so only on her own side of the prewar boundary."

Aside from Szilard's penchant for American appeasement gestures toward the Soviet Union, his major objective was disarmament and, of course, in his opinion the American policy-makers were chiefly responsible for not making disarmament a reality: "On the issue of how to secure the peace in a disarmed world, progress could probably be made reasonably fast, through nongovernmental discussions among Americans and Russians. *I believe that such discussions ought to be arranged through private initiative, but with the blessing of the administration.*

"The Russians know very well that America is *not* ready seriously to contemplate general disarmament and this, to my mind, explains why, in spite of being strongly motivated for disarmament, the Russian government displays in its negotiations on this issue much the same attitude as does the American government. As far as negotiations on disarmament are concerned, hitherto both governments have been mainly guided by the public relations aspect rather than by the substantive aspect of the issue.

"The Soviet Union's attitude might change overnight, however, if it became apparent that America was becoming seriously interested in disarmament.

"The Russians are very much aware of the economic benefits they would derive from disarmament, and I believe that the Soviet Union would be willing to pay a commensurate price for obtaining it."

To promote appeasement and to achieve disarmament, Szilard proposed a movement which would be composed of a research organization and a political organization. And, in June, 1962, his proposals resulted in the establishment of the Council for a Livable World. In its recruiting literature, the CLW said: "Through its members who pledge annually 2% of their incomes, the Council conducts a broad operational program. It makes substantial contributions to the campaigns of Congressional candidates who are concerned about the present course of events, who have insight into what needs to be done and who can be counted upon not only to support the Administration's constructive foreign and defense policies, but also to press for improvements in these policies.

"The Council intends to initiate research projects related to arms reduction and disarmament. It has proposed a joint Russian-American non-governmental study on the problem of securing the peace in a disarmed world.

"A third major undertaking is the Washington lobby. The Council brings to Washington scientists, scholars and others who, speaking to members of the Administration and Congress with the 'sweet voice of reason,' press for specific changes in policy and legislation based on the objectives set forth in this Action Program."

Szilard died in 1964 but the Council for a Livable World was firmly entrenched as a political force. In 1967, as the CLW was making its preparations for the congressional elections of 1968, it recapitulated its achievements: "The Council and its supporters have participated in three Congressional election campaigns – 1962, 1964, and 1966 – with striking results. In 1962, six Senatorial candidates backed by the Council won their contests: incumbents Joseph Clark, Pennsylvania;

Frank Church, Idaho; J. W. Fulbright, Arkansas; Jacob Javits, New York; Wayne Morse, Oregon; and challenger, George McGovern of South Dakota. [The 1962 candidates were Democrats with the sole exception of Javits, a Republican.] In 1964, nine victorious Senatorial candidates were supported: incumbents Albert Gore, Tennessee; Philip Hart, Michigan; Eugene McCarthy, Minnesota; Gale McGee, Wyoming; Frank Moss, Utah; Edmund Muskie, Maine; Ralph Yarborough, Texas; and two challengers: Joseph Montoya, New Mexico; and Joseph Tydings, Maryland. [The 1964 candidates were all Democrats.] In 1966, the following Council supported Senators were either elected or re-elected: E. L. Bartlett, Alaska; Edward Brooke, Massachusetts; Clifford Case, New Jersey; Mark Hatfield, Oregon; Lee Metcalf, Montana; Walter Mondale, Minnesota; and John Sparkman, Alabama." The 1966 candidates included Republicans Brooke, Case, and Hatfield. The other four were Democrats.

The CLW has also endorsed and supported the Senatorial candidacies of Thomas Kuchel, California; Hiram Fong, Hawaii; and Winston Prouty, Vermont – all Republicans; and Democrats Genevieve Blatt, Pennsylvania; and John Carroll, Colorado. Candidates for the House of Representatives supported by the CLW have included Republicans John Lindsay and Seymour Halpern, New York; Jerry Pettis, California; Abner Sibal, Connecticut; Stanley Tupper, Maine; and Democrats Ralph Harding, Idaho; Charles Officer, New Hampshire; Weston Vivian, Michigan; and Donald Fraser, Minnesota.

In the 1968 Senatorial campaigns, the CLW focused its support very heavily upon the re-election of Democrats George McGovern of South Dakota and Gaylord Nelson of Wisconsin.

On the Washington scene, the CLW "conducts a continuing series of seminars for Senators and their staffs to which key members of the executive branch and outstanding non-governmental figures are also invited . . . . Each year the Council sponsors a number of larger conferences on the most pressing issues . . . . These conferences are attended by Senators and their aides, by members of the Departments of Defense and State, the Arms Control and Disarmament Agency, by staff members of key Congressional Committees, and by members of the permanent Washington press corps."

Currently, on the CLW's board of directors, are four veterans of the Pugwash Conferences: Ruth Adams, Bernard T. Feld, Jerome Frank, and Matthew Meselson. Also on the board are the ultra-leftists James G.

Patton, past president of the National Farmers Union, and Charles C. Price, past president of the United World Federalists.

The CLW and those congressmen it supports are definitely committed to a program of arms limitations and controls leading toward general and comprehensive disarmament. But, in keeping with the spirit of Pugwash, the implementation of the CLW's program is fraught with anti-American, pro-Soviet measures. The CLW's officials are not so rash as to call for unilateral disarmament by the United States, but they go to great lengths to make certain that concessions in any and all negotiations between the United States and the Soviet Union on disarmament are made by the United States. And, basic to the CLW's objective of establishing "a livable world free from war," are vital gestures of appeasement to be made by the United States — with no provision for reciprocation by the Soviet Union.

In what the CLW describes as its action program, it says: "Unilateral initiations in arms control and in partial disarmament measures can help to create a more favorable atmosphere for fruitful disarmament negotiations — as, for example, if the United States were to adopt a strategic policy of using its nuclear weapons only for retaliation in kind, or if we were to dismantle vulnerable missile bases in Europe." There is never a hint by the CLW that the Soviet Union should ever take a first step toward appeasement; the burden rests solely upon the United States.

COUNCIL ON FOREIGN RELATIONS
FOREIGN AFFAIRS

In 1954, a special committee (the Reece Committee) of the House of Representatives investigated tax-exempt foundations. In its report, the Committee said of the Council on Foreign Relations that "its productions are not objective but are directed overwhelmingly at promoting the globalism concept. There are, after all, many Americans who think that our foreign policy should follow the principle consistently adopted by the British and the French, among others, that the national interest comes first and must not be subordinated to any theoretical internationalistic concept; that international cooperation is essential but only as directed in favor of the national interest. That point of view goes begging in the organizations [the CFR, for example] supported by the Carnegie, Rockefeller and Ford organizations. If private fortunes were being used to the exclusive support of the globalist point of view, that would be beyond criticism. But it is important to keep constantly in mind that we are dealing with the public's money, public trust funds.

"We would like to make it clear that this Committee does not speak from an 'isolationist' standpoint. It is obvious enough that the world has grown smaller and that international cooperation is highly desirable. But the essence of intelligent international cooperation can be measured by its direct usefulness to our national interest. Globalists may be correct in believing we should ignore the national interest in the wider interest of creating a world collectivism; but we feel confident we are right in our conclusion that a public foundation has no right to promote globalism to the exclusion of support for a fair presentation of the opposite theory of foreign policy."

The globalism of the CFR had its genesis in the fertile mind of Edward M. House, who favored himself with the title of "Colonel," which had been conferred on him by a governor of Texas as a political payoff. From political machinations in Texas, House moved onto the national political scene to discover and to sponsor Woodrow Wilson as a candidate for the Presidency of the United States. Wilson, in the White House, was never more than a stooge for House who, for reasons that may have been maniacal or sinister, planned a socialist United States in a socialist one world. And, whatever the real nature of House's reasons, the corruption of the American Republic and major strides in the direction of one world were the significant features of Wilson's domestic and foreign policies.

The House-Wilson relationship was the subject and title of the book *The Strangest Friendship in History* by George Sylvester Viereck. But, in truth, the relationship was no stranger than that which existed between any puppeteer and his puppet. While Wilson campaigned for re-election to the presidency in 1916 on a platform of non-involvement for the U. S. in the European war, House was behind the scenes planning how Wilson would save the world for "democracy" by plunging American troops into the carnage. And, beyond military involvement, House planned that Wilson would take advantage of America's first participation in a European war to promote a world government.

In September, 1917 — five months after the United States declared war upon Germany — House convinced Wilson to commission a group of "intellectuals" to devise peace terms and to draft a program for a world government. The group, called The Inquiry and led by House, incorporated peace proposals and the League of Nations covenant into

54

a single document which the United States Senate refused to approve.

When House realized that his grandiose scheme was not acceptable to the Senate, he made immediate plans to promote globalism through more subtle means than the abortive confrontation with the Senate. The CFR has furnished an account of how House regrouped his internationalist forces: "In the spring of 1919, a group of men at the Peace Conference in Paris concluded that facilities were badly needed in their respective countries for the continuous study of international relations. The Conference had revealed many points of disagreement, not only between national delegations, but within the delegations themselves.

"Sometimes these divergencies represented differing judgments on accepted facts. Sometimes they represented a conflict between the short-term and the long-term view of national interest. Sometimes they were merely opposing positions occupied in the weakness of ignorance. Under the pressure of a public opinion which was impatient to be done with war-making and peace-making, decisions had to be made in haste, and the minds of diplomats, generals, admirals, financiers, lawyers and technical experts were not sufficiently well furnished to enable them to function satisfactorily on critical issues at top speed. Realizing their own shortcomings, some of these men began to talk about a way of providing against such a state of things in the future.

"Conversations between General Tasker H. Bliss, Colonel E. M. House, Prof. Archibald Cary Coolidge, Whitney H. Shepardson, Dr. James T. Shotwell, and others of the American delegation, and such British officials as Lord Robert Cecil, Lionel Curtis, Sir Valentine Chirol, Lord Eustace Percy and Harold Temperly led to a dinner meeting at the Majestic Hotel, on May 30, 1919.

"There it was formally agreed that an organization be created for the study of international affairs."

The British globalists, who attended the Majestic Hotel meeting, formed what is now known as the Royal Institute of International Affairs. The Americans, under House's direction, formed the Council on Foreign Relations, which was incorporated in 1921.

In its early years, the CFR's directors included Isaiah Bowman, Archibald Gary Coolidge, Paul Cravath, John W. Davis, Norman Davis, Stephen Duggan, John Finley, Edwin Gay, David Houston, Otto Kahn, Frank Polk, Whitney Shepardson, William Shepherd, Paul Warburg, and

George Wickersham. In later years, some of the better known directors were Frank Altschul, Hamilton Fish Armstrong, Arthur Dean, Allen Dulles, Thomas K. Finletter, William C. Foster, Averell Harriman, Philip Jessup, Joseph E. Johnson, Grayson Kirk, Walter Lippmann, John J. McCloy, David Rockefeller, Adlai Stevenson, Owen Young, and Henry Wriston. Who were these men? They were bankers, industrialists, diplomats, and academicians. They were, for the most part, Wilsonian cultists whose flair for internationalism was so strong that in the interests of world government and world law they were willing to sacrifice American independence, integrity, and sovereignty for the sake of an experiment in globalism not unlike the globalism sought by socialists and Communists.

The CFR directors, with rare exceptions, have never been elected to political office but their ties have been very strong with foundations, foundation-supported research centers, internationalist and pacifist groups, and such international organizations as the League of Nations, the United Nations, and the North Atlantic Treaty Organization.

The lack of elective political positions has not deterred the CFR's directors and members from exerting a dominant influence in foreign and domestic policy-making for the United States government. In the most critical periods of U. S. diplomacy, CFR members have held the most important ambassadorships (Edwin Reischauer, John Kenneth Galbraith, George F. Kennan, Livingston Merchant, Philip Jessup, James Gavin, Thomas Finletter, Adolf A. Berle, Charles Bohlen, Chester Bowles, Adlai Stevenson, Averell Harriman, Winthrop Aldrich, Arthur Dean, Jonathan Bingham, Lewis Douglas, Foy Kohler, Angier Biddle Duke, Harlan Cleveland, David Bruce, Robert Murphy, Frederick Reinhardt, Claude Bowers, William C. Bullitt, Joseph C. Grew, Carlton Hayes, and John Hay Whitney).

Since World War II, the CFR has been represented in presidential cabinets by such important foreign and domestic policy-makers as John F. Dulles, Arthur Goldberg, Dean Acheson, Robert S. McNamara, Christian Herter, Luther Hodges, Dean Rusk, Douglas Dillon, John Gardner, Charles W. Yost, Alexander B. Trowbridge, Henry Morgenthau, Marion Folsom, Robert B. Anderson, and George C. Marshall. Of equal importance in the promotion of statism at home and internationalism abroad have been such CFR members in high echelon governmental positions as Ernest Gross, Allen Dulles, Herbert Lehman, David Lilienthal, Arthur F. Burns, Daniel Bell, Andrew Cordier, Hans

Morgenthau, Roswell Gilpatric, Edward R. Murrow, Doak Barnett, Joseph F. Barnes, Philip Mosely, Paul Nitze, George Ball, Sumner Welles, Leo Pasvolsky, Arthur M. Schlesinger Jr., General Lyman Lemnitzer, Isidor I. Rabi, Eugene Black, McGeorge and William Bundy, Benjamin V. Cohen, John K. Fairbank, William C. Foster, General Alfred Gruenther, Paul Hoffman, Henry Kissinger, Eugene and Walt Rostow, Harold Stassen, Jerome B. Wiesner, and John Stewart Service. Some of the more notorious CFR members who held government positions included Alger Hiss, Harry Dexter White, J. Robert Oppenheimer, and Lauchlin Currie. Just outside the pale of government but very influential in policy-making were CFR members Owen Lattimore and Frederick V. Field.

When the CFR was incorporated in 1921, its ostensible trappings were no more than that of an elaborate study group. Its stated objectives were "to afford a continuous conference on international questions affecting the United States, by bringing together experts on statecraft, finance, industry, education and science . . . to create and stimulate international thought among the people of the United States, and to this end . . . to cooperate with the Government of the United States and with international agencies, co-ordinating international activities by eliminating, insofar as possible, duplication of effort, to create new bodies, and to employ such other and further means, as from time to time may seem wise and proper."

During its first six years, the CFR — despite its membership of dignitaries — was relatively quiet. Then, in 1927, the Rockefellers, through their various foundations, began to finance the CFR. Later, Carnegie foundations joined in the subsidization.

With the outbreak of World War II in 1939, the CFR entered into an official alliance with the U. S. Department of State. Once the official relationship was established, the Rockefeller Foundation, through the CFR's Committee on Studies, initiated and financed a project, "War and Peace Studies," on: Security and Armaments Problems; Economic and Financial Problems; Political Problems; and Territorial Problems. The "War and Peace Studies" project was later taken over by the State Department which used the same personnel who had been working on the CFR's Committee on Studies. In 1942, the "War and Peace Studies" were expanded to include a "Peace Aims" project.

In 1954, the Reece Committee reported that the CFR — in the same fashion as other private organizations — had "undertaken vital research projects for the [State] Department; virtually created minor departments or groups within the Department; supplied advisors and executives from their ranks [and] fed a constant stream of personnel into the State Department, trained by themselves or under programs which they have financed, and have had much to do with the formulation of foreign policy both in principle and detail. They have, to a marked degree, acted as direct agents of the State Department. And they have engaged actively, and with the expenditure of enormous sums, in propagandizing in support of the policies which they have helped to formulate."

Former Ambassador John Kenneth Galbraith, a member of the CFR, has said of the CFR that it is "as much a part of the ruling establishment" as the State Department. For all practical purposes, Mr. Galbraith could have described the CFR as The Ruling Establishment, superceding the State Department and all other departments of the federal government. The CFR's membership has produced Presidents Hoover, Eisenhower, Kennedy, and Nixon and presidential candidates Thomas Dewey, Henry A. Wallace, Wendell Willkie, and Hubert Humphrey. In the Senate, the voice of the CFR has been heard through Jacob Javits, Stuart Symington, Clifford Case and Gale McGee, among others. In the press media, the CFR viewpoint has been promoted by A. H. Sulzberger, Henry Luce, Gardner Cowles, Norman Cousins, Max Ascoli, David Lawrence, C. D. Jackson, Whitelaw Reid, Eugene Meyer, Palmer Hoyt, Philip Graham, Mark Ethridge, Elmo Roper, George Gallup, William L. Shirer, Roscoe Drummond, Joseph Kraft, Walter Lippmann, and Marquis Childs.

Collectively, the CFR's members began as die-hard League of Nations devotees anxious to make political, economic, and diplomatic intervention throughout the world the basic foreign policy of the United States. All of this in contrast to what had been the traditional aloofness of the United States toward entangling alliances, involvement in the domestic affairs of other nations, and a belligerent status in wars between other nations. The CFR crowd refused to acknowledge that U. S. entrance into World War I — an exceptional departure from traditional U. S. behavior — was detrimental in any way toward the integrity and independence of the United States. They were titillated by the spectacle of the United States becoming inextricably implicated in the military, diplomatic, and economic quarrels of the world.

Franklin Roosevelt's precipitate plunge into globalism was completely agreeable to CFR leaders. They were solidly behind U. S.

involvement in World War II, long before Pearl Harbor. They favored Roosevelt's fawning overtures to the Soviet Union and its barbaric leader Stalin. They were overwhelmingly in evidence at the creation of the United Nations.

Upon the cessation of World War II, it became evident that the CFR was determined in its role as The Ruling Establishment to brook no interference in its campaign to stamp the United States with its brand of modern liberalism and its facets of statism and internationalism. The CFR's drive to shape U. S. policy to the globalistic ambitions of Wilsonian and Rooseveltian cultists began in 1946 when the Rockefeller Foundation and the CFR launched what they hoped would be a massive brainwashing of the American people.

In the 1946 Report of the Rockefeller Foundation, it was stated: "The Committee on Studies of the Council on Foreign Relations is concerned that the debunking journalistic campaign following World War I should not be repeated and believes that the American public deserves a clear and competent statement of our basic aims and activities during the second World War." This all meant that the big brotherhood of the CFR realized that the aberrations of the Rooseveltian war policy and plans for the post-war period must be hidden lest the American people by discovering the truth decided to reject the path to globalism so ardently desired by The Ruling Establishment. And, as a barrier to the truth, the Rockefeller-CFR conspirators decided to sponsor a three-volume history, to be prepared under the direction of William Langer of Harvard University, in which the official propaganda of World War II would be perpetuated. The Rockefeller Foundation went so far as to grant $139,000 for the CFR's court history.

The distinguished historian and political scientist Charles A. Beard, who was making a belated but only partial flight away from liberalism, recognized the implications of the Rockefeller-CFR project: "In short, they hope that, among other things, the policies and measures of Franklin D. Roosevelt will escape in the coming years the critical analysis, evaluation and exposition that befell the policies and measures of Woodrow Wilson and the Entente after World War I."

The Langer project was never realized but the CFR and its cohorts in the foundations continued their conspiracy against historical truth. As the Reece Committee noted: "Parties to this conspiracy are a good many of the professors of history with notable names; the State Department of former years; publishers who, under some misapprehension of their duty to the public, refuse to publish critical books; and newspapers which attempt to suppress such books by ignoring them or giving them for review to rabidly antagonistic 'hatchet-men.'"

There can be no denial that the CFR leaders and their ideological supporters in the foundations were quite successful in establishing the Rooseveltian policies as worthy of imitation and elaboration. Of particular import was the love affair that had blossomed between the White House and the Kremlin. What Roosevelt had begun would be consummated by the CFR and its parasites in government, in the academy, and in the press media.

The pattern of CFR promotions in the post-World War II period has been consistently jelly-soft on Communism and steel-hard against anti-Communism. The CFR through its leaders, its members, and its publications has promoted a globalism that is compatible with the most extreme ambitions of international Communism. CFRers were in the vanguard of those who desired that the secrets of the A-bomb be shared with the world's scientific community. They opposed development of the H-bomb. They have propagandized for the post-war orgy of spending in the name of foreign aid; for so-called cultural relations with the anti-cultural Communist bloc; for diplomatic and trade relations with Communist enemies; for the entangling alliances of NATO, SEATO, and CENTO; for the supra-government of the United Nations; and, for the disarmament proposals of the Communist, pro-Communist, and soft-on-Communist conferees of Pugwash. They have been the leaders of the Red China lobby and the foes of anti-Communist regimes in Free China, Spain, Portugal, South Africa, and Rhodesia. They have joined their voices in the anti-colonialism cries of the Communists.

At well-publicized meetings, the CFR has had for its honored guests and speakers Fidel Castro; the pro-Communist UN Secretary General Dag Hammarskjöld; the Soviet Union's First Deputy Premier Anastas Mikoyan; Ghana's Communist Prime Minister Kwame Nkrumah; the pro-Communist Socialist Mayor of Berlin Willy Brandt; Oscar Lange, high-ranking Communist Party official from Poland; and, a host of other Communist and Socialist officials from all over the world.

But it is in its prestigious quarterly, *Foreign Affairs*, where the CFR shows its consistent and unmistakable left-wing bias. According to its own advertising literature, *Foreign Affairs* "has one aim only — to provide the most expert opinion procurable on the problems of American foreign policy, and on the political, social and economic currents which are affecting men's thoughts and action all over the world. It stands alone in its special field, without rival either in the United States or abroad. Its reputation is such that it secures as contributors the leaders of opinion everywhere, eminent statesmen and scholars and men of affairs who rarely find occasion to write for periodicals.

"*Foreign Affairs* is read by heads of governments, Foreign Ministers and party leaders ... businessmen and bankers ... professional men and women ... officials in Washington and in posts abroad, and in the professor's study; it is used in libraries and in the classrooms of great universities; it is quoted in the newspapers, and referred to in scholarly journals and in debates in Congress.

"*Foreign Affairs* commands this following and awakens this interest because of its unvarying standard of reliability and authority, and because its editorial direction gives it sound historical perspective in combination with the most timely interest."

Since its inception in 1922, by objective standards, *Foreign Affairs* has been a forum for Communists, Socialists, pacifists, internationalists, and other leftwingers from America and abroad. Exceptions have existed but in the greater majority of instances the articles in *Foreign Affairs* have been preachments for some facet of leftwing internationalism, and in many instances the authors have been CFR members parroting the CFR line. Contributors have included Nikita Khrushchev, Leon Trotsky, Marshal Tito, Jawaharlal Nehru, Gamal Abdel Nasser, Paul-Henri Spaak, Lester B. Pearson, Nikolai Bukharin, Kwame Nkrumah, Hugh Gaitskell, Harold Laski, and H. G. Wells — all of whom belonged in the world's hierarchy of Communists or Socialists. From the ranks of American internationalists, *Foreign Affairs* presented "Colonel" Edward M. House, Frank Kellogg, Franklin Roosevelt, Wendell Willkie, Dean Acheson, Dean Rusk, John Foster Dulles, Adlai Stevenson, George Lodge, Nelson Rockefeller, Arthur Dean, Paul Hoffman, John Kenneth Galbraith, George F. Kennan, Henry Kissinger, John F. Kennedy, Eugene Black, John J. McCloy, Henry Wriston, Grayson Kirk, and Security Risk J. Robert Oppenheimer.

It would be idle and foolish to assume that every member of the CFR or — for that matter — that every contributor to *Foreign Affairs* is committed by intellectual conviction to the sacrifice of American independence on the altar of world Socialism. To make such an assumption would be to deny the presence of professional and political ambitions and the elements of flattery and persuasion which can drive an individual into such an elite gathering as The Ruling Establishment. These observations are even more emphatically true with regard to the number of American businessmen who have contributed their money and prestige to the support of the CFR. But businessmen — the technological, industrial, and economic geniuses of America — whose success is the most outstanding material refutation of Socialism have gathered in the company of the CFR's "intellectuals" who are hell-bent on destroying the very system wherein these same businessmen have flourished.

For the affluent businessman, ignorance of public affairs will not debar him from the inner sanctum of The Ruling Establishment. He is welcomed among the elitists as long as he has the proper credentials — money and position: "Subscribers to the Council's Corporation Service (who pay a minimum fee of $1,000) are entitled to several privileges. Among them are (a) free consultation with members of the Council's staff on problems of foreign policy, (b) access to the Council's specialized library on international affairs . . . , (c) copies of all Council publications . . . , (d) an off-the-record dinner, held annually for chairmen and presidents of subscribing companies at which a prominent speaker discusses some outstanding issue of United States foreign policy, and (e) two annual series of Seminars for business executives appointed by their companies. These Seminars are led by widely experienced Americans who discuss various problems of American political or economic policy." What it all means is that businessmen are sold on the merits of government policies by CFR "intellectuals" who formulate and administrate the policies. Of course, the decisive factor in the spiel during the brainwashing sessions for the businessmen is the aura of secrecy under which they receive the off-the-record, inside information.

No matter the CFR project (the sellout of Southeast Asia; the socialization of Latin America; the support of civil rights revolutionists; rapprochement with Communist regimes), it is financed and extolled through the vast network of interlocking influences exerted by CFR members in tax-exempt foundations, in political and quasi-political organizations, in pacifist groups, in television and radio networks, in metropolitan newspapers, in mass magazines and scholarly journals, in major universities, in publishing houses, in church organizations, and — of course — those government departments and agencies which have propaganda outlets to reach the public. This massive aggregate of control virtually precludes any effective opposition to CFR policies since no counter-inner circle exists even as a loyal opposition to The Ruling Establishment.

FEDERAL UNION
INTER-DEMOCRACY FEDERAL UNIONISTS
FREEDOM AND UNION
ATLANTIC UNION COMMITTEE
INTERNATIONAL MOVEMENT FOR ATLANTIC UNION
ATLANTIC COUNCIL OF THE UNITED STATES
ATLANTIC INSTITUTE
ATLANTIC TREATY ORGANIZATION
COMMITTEE ON ATLANTIC STUDIES

Clarence Streit was a correspondent for the *Philadelphia Public Ledger* (1920-1924) and for the *New York Times* (1925-1939). From 1929 until 1939, he covered the League of Nations in Geneva for the *Times*.

In 1938, Streit published a three hundred-page book, *Union Now*. The first edition was published privately in France but, within a year, *Union Now* was published in the United States and England and was translated into Swedish.

Union Now was a proposal for a federal union of fifteen "democracies" as a preliminary step toward a great federal union of the world. The "democracies" were the United States, Great Britain (England, Scotland, Wales, and India), Canada, Australia, New Zealand, South Africa, Ireland, France, Belgium, The Netherlands, Switzerland, Sweden, Denmark, Norway, and Finland. In Streit's Union, there would be a bicameral congress and a five-man supreme executive. There would be a single postal system and a single currency system – the latter would require that each nation would contribute its gold holdings to a central treasury. All colonies would come under the governance of the Union's congress and executive. And there would be a standing invitation to all other nations to enter the Union once they had become experienced in "democracy." To promote Streit's program, the Inter-Democracy Federal Unionists was established but, in 1940, Streit, Percival Brundage (a partner in the accounting firm of Price, Waterhouse), and Melvin Ryder (editor and publisher of *Army Times*) formed Federal Union (to replace the Inter-Democracy Federal Unionists) which has endured down to the present although it has undergone two name changes.

In 1941, Streit, a former Rhodes scholar and an Anglophile, published *Union Now with Britain* in which he suggested that the "democracies" be incorporated into the British Empire as a basis for an eventual world government. The British-dominated union was not to be exclusively or initially reserved for the "democracies" mentioned in *Union Now.* It was especially *not* reserved for capitalistic regimes; there would be room for Socialist, even Communist, regimes in Streit's "democratic Union." (Unsurprisingly, *Union Now with Britain* was a selection of the leftist-dominated Book-of-the-Month Club in 1941.)

In 1942, Streit conducted an advertising campaign in major American newspapers urging the President and the Congress of the United States to take immediate steps to form "a powerful union of free peoples to win the war, the peace, the future." Streit was joined in the campaign by John Foster Dulles, Secretary of the Interior Harold Ickes, and Associate Justice of the Supreme Court Owen J. Roberts. (Roberts, in 1945, resigned from the Court to devote his full-time energies working for Streit's Federal Union proposals.) They were hopeful that the Congress would adopt a joint resolution committing the United States to a federal union with Britain, Ireland, Canada, Australia, New Zealand, South Africa, "together with such other free peoples, both in the Old World and the New as may be found ready and able to unite on this federal basis." They argued that the Soviet republics were united in one government and "surely, we and they must agree that union now of the democracies wherever possible is equally to the general advantage."

For their rallying cry, Streit and his cohorts used: "Let us begin now a world United States." For a starter, they did not envision an ephemeral union but rather one whose government would be empowered to impose a common citizenship upon the peoples of the federated nations; to impose direct taxation upon the federation's new citizens; to make and enforce laws; to coin and to borrow money; to control the armed forces of the federated nations; and, to admit new membernations to the union.

In 1942, the Congress was not yet willing to sacrifice the sovereignty, independence, and integrity of the United States to Streit's dream of world government but Streit continued his propaganda through Federal Union. In 1945, he was greatly encouraged when the United States joined other "peace-loving states" in the United Nations

Organization and, in 1946, Streit began publication of *Freedom and Union,* a monthly magazine which he has edited ever since.

In 1949, the United States joined the North Atlantic Treaty Organization along with Canada, Belgium, The Netherlands, Denmark, Iceland, Luxembourg, France, Italy, Norway, Portugal, and Britain. NATO was represented to the American people as primarily a defensive military alliance against Communism. However, there was enough latitude in the text of NATO's treaty so that it could be interpreted as authorizing an international political union. Streit and his unionist colleagues naturally favored such an interpretation.

In 1949, Streit, taking advantage of the popular reception accorded to the new NATO, formed the Atlantic Union Committee to replace his ten-year-old Federal Union. From its beginnings, the AUC would work to have the Congress of the United States resolve to have the President invite delegates from other NATO nations to a convention where they could consider the feasibility of a "free federal union."

A resolution to that effect was introduced in the Congress on July 26, 1949 by Senator Estes Kefauver (D. -Tenn.). An impressive bipartisan group co-sponsored Kefauver's resolution including: Republicans Raymond Baldwin (Conn.), Harry Cain (Wash.), Zales Ecton (Mont.), Robert Hendrickson (N.J.), Joseph McCarthy (Wis.), Edward Thye (Minn.), and Milton Young (N.D.), and Democrats Virgil Chapman (Ky.), J. William Fulbright (Ark.), Walter George (Ga.), Guy Gillette (Iowa), Frank Graham (N.C.), Lister Hill (Ala.), Harley Kilgore (W. Va.), Burnet Maybank (S.C.), Bert Miller (Ida.), John Sparkman (Ala.), and Garrett Withers (Ky.). In the House, the resolution was sponsored by Republicans James W. Wadsworth (N.Y.) and Walter Judd (Minn.), and Democrats Hale Boggs (La.), Clifford Davis (Tenn.), and George Smathers (Fla.). The resolution, however, never reached a vote in 1949-1950.

On January 15, 1951, Senator Kefauver again introduced the Atlantic Union Resolution. Twenty-seven Senators, including Richard M. Nixon (R. -Cal.) and nine Representatives, including Christian Herter (R. -Mass.) were co-sponsors but the resolution never reached a committee hearing.

On February 9, 1955, Senator Kefauver introduced the resolution under a new title: "Resolution for an Atlantic Exploratory Convention." This time he had for co-sponsors Republican Senators Ralph

Flanders (Vt.) and Frederick Payne (Me.), and Democrats Hubert Humphrey (Minn.), Henry Jackson (Wash.), Herbert Lehman (N.Y.), Russell Long (La.), Pat McNamara (Mich.), James Murray (Mont.), Matthew Neely (W. Va.), Richard Neuberger (Ore.), Kerr Scott (N.C.), and John Sparkman (Ala.). In the House, the co-sponsors were Democrats Hale Boggs (La.), Clifford Davis and Percy Priest (Tenn.), Chet Holifield (Calif.), Lee Metcalf (Mont.), Barratt O'Hara (Ill.), Francis Walter (Pa.), and Clement Zablocki (Wis.), and Republicans Sterling Cole (N.Y.), Robert Hale (Me.), and Walter Judd (Minn.). The resolution was heard before the Senate Committee on Foreign Relations but never came to a vote either in the Senate or in the House.

In 1958, Streit, in an attempt to bolster his cause, founded the International Movement for Atlantic Union. He mustered an impressive roster from several NATO nations of individuals to serve on IMAU's board of directors. (Streit became president of IMAU. Other Atlantic Union Committee members on the board were Mrs. Chase Osborn, Percival Brundage, Melvin Ryder, A.W. Schmidt, and Robert Strausz-Hupé.)

IMAU's immediate goal was to urge the NATO governments to call a conference of eminent, private citizens to "examine exhaustively and recommend how greater unity . . . within the Atlantic Community may best be developed." IMAU also favored exploring all possibilities for revising the NATO treaty "to improve political, economic, social and cultural relations, and meanwhile doing everything possible under the present treaty to harmonize the foreign policies of member nations, exchange technical information and advance common measures against the recession and economic warfare and for economic expansion."

In 1958, the year in which IMAU was founded, Streit and his unionists were very optimistic. Senator Theodore Green (D. -R.I.) had introduced S.C.R. 62, a resolution by which Congress would endorse the citizens' convention on NATO which IMAU and the Atlantic Union Committee considered the most desirable immediate goal. Green's resolution was approved unanimously in the Senate Foreign Relations Committee but when Green tried to railroad the bill through the Senate by the procedure of asking unanimous consent, Senator William F. Knowland, the minority leader, barred the procedure on grounds that the measure should be debated. Streit took solace in that fact that Knowland was retiring from the Senate and Streit was hopeful that in the congressional elections of 1958 the Democrats would greatly increase their control of both the Senate and the House.

When the returns were completed for the 1958 elections, Streit could scarcely retain his joy. Opponents of the Atlantic Union Resolution had been defeated: Senators Frank Barrett (R. -Wyo.), Charles Potter (R. -Mich.), Chapman Revercomb and John Hoblitzell (R. -W. Va.), John Bricker (R. -Ohio), Arthur Watkins (R. -Utah), and George Malone (R. -Nev.). Republican Senators Edward Martin (Pa.) and William Jenner (Ind.) had retired. Liberal Republicans Hugh Scott (Pa.) and Kenneth Keating (N.Y.) had been elected. Streit was also happy that Nelson Rockefeller, a devotee of Atlantic Union, was elected governor of New York. The election of Democrats, who were Atlantic Unionists, to the Senate was especially pleasing to Streit. They included Eugene McCarthy (Minn.), Clair Engle (Calif.), Thomas Dodd (Conn.), and, Harrison Williams (N.J.). Streit did bemoan the loss of retiring Senator Ralph Flanders (R. -Vt.) and the defeats suffered for re-election to the House of Representatives by Democrat Brooks Hays of Arkansas and Republican Robert Hale of Maine. But Streit was somewhat comforted by the election of Chester Bowles (D. -Conn.) to the House and by the elevation to the chairmanship of the House Foreign Affairs Committee of Thomas Morgan (D. -Pa.). Clement Zablocki (D. -Wis.), an ardent Atlantic Unionist, became the third ranking Democrat on Morgan's committee.

By 1959, Streit's policy had become familiar to readers of *Freedom and Union*. In almost every issue, either all or a large part of the policy was printed. In its entirety, it read: "To think, write and act always in terms of all the democratic world, and not of any one country in it.

"To mean by 'we' (except editorially) the citizens of the coming Atlantic Union or Federation of All the Free, not merely those of any existing democracy.

"To speed its coming by helping its people understand better the principles of individual freedom and federal union, and their importance to peace, production, higher living standards and greater spiritual growth and happiness.

"To advance it also by helping the people of this Free Atlantic Community to see that they do form a community which they need to govern democratically.

"To provide a forum for all views in the vast field of freedom and federation.

"To bring out the facts in this field by objective, imaginative research.

"To favor calling now a federal constitutional convention, representing the experienced civil liberty democracies, to work out and submit to their people a plan for uniting them in a Federal Union of the Free, or United States of the Atlantic, under a Constitution that would: 1) guarantee their Bill of Rights; 2) give them a free government in those fields where they agreed this would best advance individual freedom; 3) provide that this government shall be elected by, be responsible to, and operate on, the citizens and be federally balanced in its representation of them; 4) secure the right of each nation in the Union to continue to govern all its national affairs in complete independence.

"To seek to extend the Union's free federal relationship to other nations peacefully and as rapidly as this will advance liberty and peace until eventually it grows into a free federal world republic.

"To assure that, pending universality, this union shall be a loyal member of the United Nations."

On March 19, 1959, Senator Humphrey introduced S. C. R. 17 with the strongest bi-partisan support the resolution had yet had. It was a revision of the resolutions which had been previously offered by Senators Kefauver and Green. But it was, in its essence, merely another call for a citizens convention to explore how NATO nations might become more unified — economically and politically. Senator Kefauver co-sponsored the resolution as did Republican Senators Clifford Case (N.J.) and John Sherman Cooper (Ky.). In the House, the co-sponsors were Democrats A. S. J. Carnahan (Mo.), Clement Zablocki (Wis.), and Thomas Morgan (Pa.), and Republican Walter Judd (Minn.).

In August, 1959, Secretary of State Christian Herter endorsed the resolution on behalf of the Eisenhower Administration.

Meanwhile, the NATO Parliamentarians' Conference had sponsored a five-day Atlantic Congress in London in June. Although American delegates attended the Atlantic Congress in the role of private citizens, they were for the most part individuals who had served or were serving in either elective or appointive government positions and, in almost all cases, had expressed support for an Atlantic Union. They included Eugenie Anderson, William Benton, Robert Bowie, Percival Brundage, Cass Canfield, Lewis Douglas, Thomas K. Finletter, William C. Foster, James M. Gavin, Ernest Gross, Wayne Hays, Hubert Humphrey, Jacob Javits, Estes Kefauver, Clark Kerr, Henry A. Kissinger, Robert McKinney, Maurine Neuberger, Paul Nitze, Frank Pace, James Patton, Charles S. Rhyne, and Thomas J. Watson Jr. When the Atlantic

Congress concluded its session, a "Declaration" was agreed upon by the various delegations and they endorsed the "citizens convention" on NATO — the same as the Humphrey-Kefauver resolution then pending in the Congress.

In 1960, the Humphry-Kefauver resolution (re-numbered as S. J. R. 170 and entitled: "U. S. Citizens Commission on NATO") had smooth sailing through the Senate Foreign Relations and House Foreign Affairs Committees. From outside the government, support came from Erwin Canham of the *Christian Science Monitor,* Adlai Stevenson, Henry Ford II, and other prominent liberals. The Senate Majority Leader Lyndon Johnson and Vice President Richard Nixon were most helpful. In the Senate, the resolution's floor manager was Frank Church (D. -Ida.) and the left wing of both parties voted for it (51 to 44): Democrats included John F. Kennedy (Mass.), Stuart Symington (Mo.), John Sparkman (Ala.), Gale McGee (Wyo.), Paul Douglas (Ill.), Albert Gore (Tenn.), Ernest Gruening (Alaska), William Proxmire (Wis.), John Pastore (R. I.), Warren Magnuson (Wash.), Wayne Morse (Ore.), Eugene McCarthy (Minn.), and Vance Hartke (Ind.). Republicans included Jacob Javits (N.Y.) and Thomas Kuchel (Calif.).

In the House, leading the fight for S. J. R. 170, where the vote was 288-103 in favor, were Republicans John Lindsay and Robert Barry (N.Y.), James Fulton and Robert Corbett (Pa.), and Walter Judd (Minn.), and Democrats Thomas Morgan (Pa.), Clement Zablocki (Wis.), Wayne Hays (Ohio), Porter Hardy (Va.), Barratt O'Hara (Ill.), and Ray Madden (Ind.).

The breakthrough, so long awaited by the one-worlders, came on September 7, 1960 with the passage of Public Law 86-719 by which the U. S. Citizens Commission on NATO was created.

Streit was jubilant. He revised his *Union Now* and, in 1961, published a new edition entitled *Freedom's Frontier — Atlantic Union Now.* He viewed Public Law 86-719 which had been signed by President Eisenhower, as "so significant as to give in itself reason enough for new faith in freedom's future," because the U. S. Citizens Commission would meet with "Citizens of North Atlantic Democracies with a view to exploring fully and recommending concretely how to unite their peoples better."

No longer was Streit's policy statement in *Freedom and Union* calling for "a federal constitutional convention" of "the experienced civil liberty democracies." After the passage of P. L. 86-719, he called for "action by an Atlantic Convention of Citizens from NATO."

The sponsors of Public Law 86-719 went to great lengths to explain that the U. S. Citizens Commission on NATO was merely an exploratory body and that its members would not speak for or represent the U.S. government. This defensive gesture, however, was merely a smokescreen. Appointments to the U. S. Citizens Commission were made by two old political cronies House Speaker Sam Rayburn and Vice President Lyndon Johnson who named as the dominant commissioners former Secretary of State Christian Herter, David Rockefeller, Elmo Roper (President of the Atlantic Union Committee), and William L. Clayton (Vice president of the Atlantic Union Committee).

Shortly after the U. S. Citizens Commission on NATO was formed, Streit and his one-world colleagues began a hectic period of reorganization. The Atlantic Union Committee was superseded by the Atlantic Council of the United States, formed by a merger of the American Council on NATO, the United States Committee for the Atlantic Institute, and the Atlantic Council. (The proliferation of titles involved in the "Atlantic" network also included: The Atlantic Institute, the international parent of the Atlantic Council of the United States, founded in 1961 as an "international, non-governmental organization which seeks to assist and promote the unified action of countries of North America and Western Europe." The new Atlantic Council of the United States represented, in the United States, the Atlantic Treaty Organization which was founded in 1953 as a federation of fifteen associations in the NATO countries "to educate and inform the public concerning aims and goals of NATO and Atlantic cooperation." The Committee on Atlantic Studies is sponsored by the Atlantic Council of the United States and its international parent, the Atlantic Institute, "to foster the study of economic, political, and cultural developments affecting Western civilization," and to propagandize among college faculties for "the teaching of European and American history as a cohesive topic.")

In January, 1962, the U. S. Citizens Commission on NATO attended the twelve-day Atlantic Convention of the NATO countries in Paris. Christian Herter, in an opening day address to the Convention, talked about the "necessary compression of our [United States] sovereignty" and he deplored the "excessive insistence on complete and uncoordinated national freedom." As co-chairman of the U. S. Citizens Commission, Herter said: "Our gathering here to prospect an international breakthrough evidences growing confidence in the effectiveness of private efforts to improve the governance of men."

At the conclusion of the convention, the Americans joined the other national groups in adopting the Delcaration of Paris which proposed to the governments of the NATO countries: (1) A special governmental commission should be appointed to study the organization of the Atlantic community; (2) A permanent high council should be established "to prepare and concert policies on political, economic, cultural, and military matters"; (3) A high court of justice should be created; and, (4) There should be a transference of "a measure of delegated sovereignty in the Atlantic area" to an Atlantic community.

Streit's reaction to the Atlantic Convention appeared in the combined February-March, 1962 issue of *Freedom and Union* where he wrote: "We would agree both that the Convention fell far short of what it should, or even could, have done, and that it nonetheless gave important impetus toward Atlantic Union. This would have been true, and cause for rejoicing, had it done no more than inspire the impressive series of three editorials in the *New York Times* . . . which welcome the Declaration as 'the first internationally agreed proposal for converting the vision of an Atlantic Union into practical reality.' To this powerful newspaper the Convention proved that 'the idea of Atlantic Union is on the march.' This was ironic justice for the Convention had sought to conceal this fact; its Declaration did not venture to mention 'Atlantic Union.'"

On the pessimistic side, Streit wrote: "We regret that the bird in hand – the Convention itself, which took 12 years to bag – was dropped needlessly to reach for a most elusive fowl so quickly – before the Convention had assured better its capture by tackling itself the job of working out an Atlantic government, as its imitators intended."

Streit's disappointment over the Convention's failure to take a major step toward one-world government was alleviated somewhat by Nelson Rockefeller's widely publicized Godkin Lectures at Harvard in February, 1962, when the New York Governor urged the United States to take the initiative in leading free nations into a federal union. So enthusiastic was Streit over Rockefeller's lectures, that he serialized them in *Freedom and Union* and advertised the hardbound version of the lectures (*The Future of Federalism*, published by Harvard University Press) as "required reading in the course of human events."

On June 18, 1962, the U. S. Citizens Commission on NATO made its first and only report to the Congress of the United States. The Commission urged that steps must be taken to make the Atlantic community a reality and they must be taken soon — even if this involved some yielding of sovereignty. The Commission further urged that all the recommendations, contained in the Declaration of Paris, be implemented by the United States government.

On November 12, 1962, a "Declaration of Atlantic Unity," was presented to the NATO Parliamentarian Conference. The "Declaration" included the measures recommended by the Atlantic Congress of January, 1962 and two additional ones: "Promote measures to ensure more effective defense including further development of a unified Atlantic Command; a common strategy both inside and outside the Atlantic area; greater standardization and a more rational production of arms and equipment; and defense contributions fairly shared among our respective countries. Support and expand the Atlantic Institute as an intellectual and spiritual centre for the Atlantic Community."

The 242 signers of the "Declaration," who represented only themselves, came from every NATO nation except Portugal. Sixty-seven Americans signed the Declaration, including Senators Hubert Humphrey, Estes Kefauver and Jacob Javits; California's Governor Edmund (Pat) Brown; Henry A. Kissinger; Walter Reuther; Ellsworth Bunker; Ernest Gross; Christian Herter; Eugene Rostow; and, Clarence Streit and a host of his Atlantic Union associates. Presentation of the "Declaration" to the NATO Parliamentarians was made by Estes Kefauver and the Parliamentarians unanimously endorsed the "Declaration" in all its parts.

In 1963, there were no Atlantic Union resolutions in the Congress, nor were there any tangible advances made to implement the "Declaration." Streit, however, made strenuous and successful efforts to collect hundreds of names for the Advisory Council of the International Movement for Atlantic Union. Business executives, clergy, artists, theatrical personalities, educators, heads of farm and labor organizations, jurists, lawyers, scientists, and government officials (active and retired) lent their prestige to Atlantic Union.

Atlantic Union's twenty-fifth anniversary year was 1964. Streit was far from discouraged as he wrote that his organization had only begun a far-reaching fight. He admitted to his one-world ambitions: "The Atlantic Union it means to see constituted now will be but a nucleus, designed to grow in peace through generations to come, until the Federation of the Free embraces the whole race of mortal man."

Writing in the January, 1965 issue of *Freedom and Union,* Streit reviewed 1964: "The past year did more to improve the prospects for Atlantic unification in general and Atlantic federation in particular than any year I recall in the past decade or so." Streit was especially encouraged by the support accorded the cause of Atlantic unification by Republicans Nelson Rockefeller, Barry Goldwater, Dwight Eisenhower, and the House Republicans' Project Committee on NATO which urged President Johnson to "form a blue-ribbon delegation of U. S. Citizens to meet with similar delegations from other NATO nations" in order to "formulate and propose for ratification improvements in the structure of NATO."

By 1965, however, the most ardent Republican disciple of Streit was Representative Paul Findley of Illinois. On February 22, 1965, in a letter to President Johnson, Findley respectfully recommended that Johnson "call a constitutional convention of North Atlantic Treaty Organization nations. The object of the convention would be to propose for ratification a plan to unify the military, monetary, trade, and foreign policies of the nations which make up NATO." Findley hewed to Streit's habit of equating the proposed Atlantic Union to the American Republic: "A government for the whole of NATO is just as indispensable today as it was for the 13 original U. S. states in 1787, when a constitutional convention was called."

On October 18, 1965, a concurrent resolution, calling for a "constitutional convention" of NATO citizens, was introduced by Democrats Eugene McCarthy (Minn.) and Lee Metcalf (Mont.) and Republican Frank Carlson (Kans.). In the House, a similar resolution was introduced by co-sponsors Republicans Paul Findley (Ill.), Albert Quie (Minn.) and Robert Ellsworth (Kans.), and Democrats Clement Zablocki (Wis.) and Donald Fraser (Minn.).

By January, 1966, the original three co-sponsors in the Senate were joined by fourteen of their colleagues: Republicans Paul Fannin (Ariz.), Hiram Fong (Hawaii), Jacob Javits (N.Y.), and Winston Prouty (Vt.), and Democrats E. L. Bartlett and Ernest Gruening (Alaska), Ross Bass (Tenn.), Thomas Dodd (Conn.), Vance Hartke (Ind.), Daniel Inouye (Hawaii), Frank Lausche (Ohio), Frank Moss (Utah), Claiborne Pell (R. I.), and Harrison Williams (N. J.).

In March, 1966, Findley announced that he had received endorsements for his bill from Barry Goldwater and Richard Nixon and four

Republican Governors: Rockefeller of New York, George Romney of Michigan, William Scranton of Pennsylvania, and Mark Hatfield of Oregon.

By April, 1966, there were ninety co-sponsors of Findley's bill in the House (fifty-five Democrats and thirty-five Republicans). And, in May, 1966, Findley announced that his bill had been endorsed by former President Eisenhower. By that time eighteen Senators and ninety-seven Representatives (divided between seventy-five Democrats and forty Republicans) were on record as co-sponsors or known supporters of the Atlantic Union bill. Once again, however, the Atlantic Unionists were disappointed as their bill never reached a vote either in the Senate or the House.

In 1967, the Atlantic Union bill was re-introduced in the Senate and the House. By April, 1967, sixteen Senators and ninety-four Representatives were either co-sponsors or known supporters. Finally, on July 2, 1968, the House Committee on Foreign Affairs approved H. C. R. 48, introduced by Zablocki and Findley and calling for a "constitutional convention" on NATO. But that is the most extensive progress made by an Atlantic Union bill to the present time. In the meantime, Clarence Streit remains optimistic that President Nixon will lead the way to a surrender of United States sovereignty and independence by promoting Atlantic Union.

FELLOWSHIP OF RECONCILIATION
NATIONAL RELIGION AND LABOR FOUNDATION
WORKERS DEFENSE LEAGUE
CHURCH PEACE MISSION
NATIONAL COUNCIL AGAINST CONSCRIPTION
TURN TOWARD PEACE

In 1955, California's Senate Investigating Committee on Education investigated the Fellowship of Reconciliation. The Committee's Chairman received a letter from John M. Swomley Jr., FOR's Secretary, in which Mr. Swomley said: "This letter is to point out that our fellowship has had a long and consistent record of not collaborating with Communist or Communist front groups. We are a non-partisan religious pacifist organization." (When the Committee found evidence contrary to Swomley's assertion, the Fellowship distributed Alfred Hassler's *The Anatomy of a Smear,* an alleged exposé, according to FOR, of "A California legislative committee's attempt to link pacifism with subversion.")

74

The Fellowship was established in England, shortly after the outbreak of World War I, "as a movement of Christian protest against war and of faith in a better way than violence for the solution of all conflict." Original members of the Fellowship were drawn from more than twenty countries. They subscribed to a Statement of Purpose, which read in part: "They refuse to participate in any war, or to sanction military preparation; they work to abolish war and to foster good will among nations, races and classes; they strive to build a social order which will suffer no individual or group to be exploited for the profit or pleasure of another."

In 1915, Henry T. Hodgkin, an English Quaker and chairman of the British Fellowship of Reconciliation, came to the United States. In response to his visit, 130 persons were invited to meet with Hodgkin at a conference where he hoped that an American Fellowship might be instituted. Those invited to the conference were YMCA leaders, Quakers, and non-Quaker social workers, reformers, and philanthropists.

On November 24, 1915 at Garden City, Long Island sixty-eight persons established an American Fellowship of Reconciliation. Fifty years later, in *Fellowship* magazine, it was recalled that "among those sixty-eight were Rufus Jones the Quaker, later to become one of America's great mystics; John R. Mott, patriarch of the International YMCA; George Foster Peabody, the humanitarian [and banker] in whose name broadcasting's most distinguished [sic] award is given; Jessie Wallace Hughan, then suffragette, later poet, teacher and officeseeker [on the Socialist Party ticket]; Mary Simkovich [Simkhovitch], who came to be known as dean of American social work [and a zealous joiner of Communist fronts]; Isaac Sharpless, who was then president of Haverford College. Later on one founder, L. Hollingsworth Wood, was first chairman of the National Civil Liberties Bureau, predecessor of the ACLU, and Miss Hughan founded the War Resister's League."

Early Fellowship members included Harry F. Ward, Norman Thomas, Abraham J. Muste, Jane Addams, and Emily Greene Balch. Ward, if he never joined the Communist Party, at least became one of the Party's most active and influential fellow travelers. Thomas, who became the six-time presidential candidate on the Socialist Party ticket, spent a lifetime collaborating with the Communists. Muste spent more than thirty years supporting Communist fronts and causes and, at one time, he was national chairman of the now-defunct Workers Party, a

Communist party. Jane Addams and Emily Balch participated in Communist fronts and projects and both were awarded the Nobel Peace Prize, the only two American women recipients of the award. From 1915 until her death in 1935, Addams was chairman and first international president of the leftist International Committee of Women for Permanent Peace. In 1939, the group changed its name to Women's International League for Peace and Freedom and Balch became its general secretary. She was also WILPF's honorary international president from 1937 until her death in 1961.

Although the Fellowship has represented itself as non-partisan, it and its affiliates had a peculiarly strong attraction for Socialists including Norman Thomas, Murray Baron, George Clifton Edwards, Mary Fox, Murray Gross, Louis Hacker, Powers Hapgood, Harry Laidler, Robert Morss Lovett, A. Philip Randolph, Carl Raushenbush, Morris Shapiro, Joseph Schlossberg, Tucker Smith, and Harold Fey.

When the Fellowship was founded in 1915, its initial activity was directed toward opposing the entry of the United States into World War I. Once the United States entered the war, the Fellowship concentrated on the support of conscientious objectors. (According to literature of the Fellowship, all of its "members of military age, unless deferred or exempt for other reasons, have been conscientious objectors" during both World Wars, and under the continuing draft law since World War II.) Out of the Fellowship's "conshie" program, there developed, in 1916, the National Civil Liberties Bureau (the chairman and vice chairman were L. Hollingsworth Wood and Norman Thomas, respectively) which was reorganized in 1920 as the American Civil Liberties Union. (At one time or another, nearly every leading radical in America was an official of the ACLU including: Harry Ward, Roger Baldwin, Louis Budenz, Eugene V. Debs, Felix Frankfurter, Alexander Meiklejohn, Elmer Davis, Roy Wilkins, Norman Cousins, Freda Kirchwey, Archibald MacLeish, Henry S. Commager, Corliss Lamont, Francis Biddle, John Dewey, Max Lerner, Elizabeth Gurley Flynn, and William Z. Foster.)

In 1918, the Fellowship established its second enterprise: Brookwood Labor College of Katonah, New York. Brookwood was Communistic and was heavily subsidized by the Garland Fund which was a major source for the financing of Communist Party enterprises. (Another FOR enterprise, the Committee on Militarism in Education, was also subsidized by the Garland Fund.)

In 1923, the Fellowship was the main force behind the establishment of the National Conference of Christians and Jews which originated as a project of the leftist Federal Council of Churches. The FCC had been created by a group from the Fellowship.

In 1928, the Fellowship founded the National Religion and Labor Foundation. The House Special Committee on Un-American Activities (Seventy-fifth Congress) reported that the NRLF "was organized to propagandize the New Social Order (socialism and communism) within the Catholic, non-Catholic, and Hebrew Churches. Its atheistic bulletin is styled 'Economic Justice,' and its vileness is only equaled by publications of Soviet Russia." (The members of the National Committee and Executive Committee of the National Religion and Labor Foundation were also members of the National Council and Executive Secretaries of the Fellowship of Reconciliation. In addition, the NRLF had three honorary presidents: J. E. Hagerty, president of the Catholic Conference on Industrial Problems; Sidney Hillman, the notorious leftwing labor leader; and, Methodist Bishop Francis J. McConnell, a fellow-traveler and the president of the Federal Council of Churches.)

In 1932 and 1933, the National Religion and Labor Foundation was one of the most active organizations working for U.S. diplomatic recognition of the Soviet Union. The pro-Soviet stance of the NRLF was explained by the group's "economic adviser," Francis A. Henson: "We believe that the primary job today is one of achieving economic justice. We believe that this will require revolutionary changes in our social and economic order. Therefore, instead of attacking [sic] Soviet Russia, we are anxious to appreciate the contributions which it has made and, at the same time, build here in this section of the world an order that has all of the values of the one that is being created in the Soviet Union, without the sacrifice of other important values."

In its literature, the Fellowship of Reconciliation also takes credit for the creation of the Workers Defense League. The House Special Committee on Un-American Activities (Seventy-fifth Congress) reported: "Just as the Communist Party has its defense movement, the International Labor Defense, so also has the Socialist Party, the Workers Defense League. The latter organization was formed in May, 1936, by leading members of the Socialist Party. . . . The national committee of the Workers Defense League is composed of . . . Socialists and extreme left-wingers. . . . The executive committee of the league is likewise composed of Socialists and extreme left-wingers. . . . Norman Thomas, Socialist Party candidate for the President of the United

States, is the real head of the league. . . ." (As recently as 1964, the late Norman Thomas was still honorary president of the Workers Defense League. Officers included labor leaders Joseph A. Beirne, A. Philip Randolph, and James B. Carey. On the WDL's national board were Babette Deutsch, Theodore Draper, George Counts, John Henry Faulk, Donald Harrington, Murray Kempton, Norman Mailer, Emil Mazey, Joseph L. Rauh Jr., Victor Reuther, Bayard Rustin, and Roy Wilkins. In earlier years, individuals working with the WDL included Harry Gideonse, Arthur M. Schlesinger Jr., and Arthur Goldberg.) The Workers Defense League describes itself as an "anti-Communist and pro-democratic" legal aid society, concerned with political cases and the protection of minority rights. It is true that periodically the WDL has gone through futile motions by protesting against well-publicized and undeniable acts of barbarism perpetrated by Communist regimes. But the real energies of the WDL have been expended on the protection of labor agitators working among sharecroppers, migratory agricultural workers, and merchant seamen. The defense of political undesirables, subject to deportation proceedings, and individuals charged with security/loyalty violations have been a major concern of the WDL.

In its area of primary interest, conscientious objection, the Fellowship established the Church Peace Mission and the National Council against Conscription.

The Church Peace Mission, according to its own literature, was an effort "to secure a wider hearing in colleges and seminaries, and in youth groups in the various churches, for the pacifist interpretation of the Gospel." And, "help in planning for youth, lay, and camp programs for those who wish to consider the Christians' responsibility for peacemaking, with a special view to being helpful to young men who face the draft and to their ministers and parents who counsel them." Literature of the Fellowship has described the Church Peace Mission as an "effort to bring the pacifist position to the attention of the Christian Church in the United States. It has initiated and published several pamphlets on the theology of the pacifist position, and has been largely responsible for such discussion and debate as have taken place on that subject within the World Council of Churches."

In 1948, the California Senate's Un-American Activities Committee devoted its entire annual report to an analysis and enumeration of Communist front organizations. Of the National Council against Conscription, the report said: "Pamphlets of this Communist front are being distributed by the American Civil Liberties Union in Los Angeles.

"The current Communist Party line is presently directed against military preparedness, and the Communist Party of the United States is doing everything within its power to keep the United States militarily weak, while it demands that American armed forces abroad be returned to the United States. . . .

"The latest Communist front in this field is the new National Council against Conscription launched in Washington, D. C., November 9, 1946. . . .

"The committee points out that this type of Communist front is organized for the purpose of attracting many good American citizens, who, because of religious convictions, are against war at any time. There are many pacifists and members of religious groups who are not disloyal in any sense of the word. This same statement applies with equal validity to many good citizens who were attracted to the American Peace Mobilization and other Communist fronts organized for the purpose of assisting Hitler during his partnership with Stalin for the conquest of Europe. Undoubtedly many of these good people will be innocently attracted to a Communist front such as the National Council against Conscription.

"The distinction the committee wishes to make is that the record of a substantial number of the members of the National Council against Conscription have indicated in the past their close affiliation with Communist-front organizations operating for Communist purposes and causes.

"There are no humane or religious purposes being served by Communist organizations in this field. Soviet Russia and its imperialist expansionist policies alone are served while the United States is kept weak and impotent, and, of course, that is the purpose behind the National Council against Conscription."

Among the better known members of the Fellowship's National Council against Conscription were Frank Graham, Robert Kenny, Vito Marcantonio, Mary McLeod Bethune, Jerome Davis, Francis J. McConnell, and Reinhold Niebuhr.

In 1942, James Farmer who was, at the time, race relations secretary of the Fellowship, instigated inter-racial sit-ins which were led by George Houser. In 1943, Farmer and Houser organized their demonstrators in the Fellowship-sponsored Congress of Racial Equality, allegedly to apply Gandhian techniques of nonviolence to combat racial discrimination and segregation. (Houser was CORE's national director from its beginnings in 1943 until 1955. He left CORE to become executive director of another Fellowship enterprise, the American Committee on Africa. In CORE's early history, Houser was aided by Bayard Rustin, a Fellowship staff member, who was CORE's first and only field secretary. Farmer, from 1961 until 1966, was CORE's national director.)

In 1947, the Fellowship began its stormy history of so-called freedom rides in the southern states with the "Journey of Reconciliation" and, a few years later, sent interracial teams into the South to teach "nonviolent" techniques for racial demonstrations. In 1961, the freedom rides program was resumed on a large scale under the direction of James Farmer. These activities, conducted by CORE, eventually expanded into the North where CORE instigated rent strikes, agitated for civilian review boards to harass local police forces, engaged in local political activities, and propagandized and demonstrated for "urban renewal" programs. In 1965, CORE formed an alliance with the ultra-racist Black Muslims.

During World War II, the Fellowship started an anti-bombing campaign that has lasted down to the present time. The campaign began in 1944 when the Fellowship began propagandizing against saturation bombing tactics of the allied forces. The A-bombing of Hiroshima in 1945 found the Fellowship extending apologies on behalf of the United States to Japan. In 1961, the Fellowship struck out against bomb shelters. Then, in 1962, the Fellowship established Turn toward Peace, an "umbrella organization of national peace, labor, public affairs and religious groups." Through TTP scores of leftist organizations were coordinated on a national level.

In 1963, Turn toward Peace listed fifty "initial steps to provide for establishment of a world government controlled by the United Nations." Among the "initial steps" suggested by TTP were: Recognition of Red China and repeal of the McCarran Immigration Act to allow up to one million people from Red China to move to America each year; a United Nations-controlled transfer of North Africa to Nasser and Ben Bella; placement of all U. S. long-range missiles under UN control by 1964; amend the United States Constitution to allow the UN to levy a direct tax on the American people; establish a national security police force under UN control to harass all anti-UN American citizens; and, repeal of the Connally Amendment to permit the World

Court to try such Fascists [*sic*] as Barry Goldwater, Billy Graham, General Walker, and others if they engage in anti-UN activities.

When Turn toward Peace held a conference at New York City in December of 1963, participant organizations included the American Baptist Convention, Americans for Democratic Action, B'na B'rith, the National Association for the Advancement of Colored People, the Catholic Daughters of America, and the Foreign Policy Association. Among the conferees were Martin Luther King Jr., Senator Joseph Clark, J. Robert Oppenheimer (the security risk), Dean Erwin Griswold of Harvard Law School, Eugene Carson Blake, Arthur Larson, and James G. Patton. Officials of TTP included Norman Thomas and Bayard Rustin and the roster of TTP included Eleanor Roosevelt, Walter Reuther, and Martin Luther King Jr.

The Vietnam War has been a special target for the Fellowship in recent years. In 1965, the Fellowship formed the Clergymen's Emergency Committee for Vietnam. In 1965, this committee, through an advertisement in the *New York Times,* demanded that the United States should halt all bombing in Vietnam, declare a cease-fire, show willingness to enter unconditional discussions to end the war, and agree to conduct negotiations with the Vietcong. (At the same time, the Catholic Peace Fellowship — another enterprise of the Fellowship of Reconciliation — was offering a similar anti-Vietnam War program. Its leaders included Dorothy Day of the *Catholic Worker,* Publisher Edward M. Keating of *Ramparts* magazine, and the two radical and revolutionary brothers and priests Daniel Berrigan S.J. and Philip Berrigan S.S.J. A Jewish Peace Fellowship under the leadership of Rabbi Isidor Hoffman was later absorbed by the Fellowship.) In 1966, in the *New York Times,* a Fellowship advertisement read: "To the people and government of the United States: The horrors that your planes and massive fire power are inflicting on the people of Viet Nam are beyond moral or political justification." At that time, funds for the Fellowship were being solicited by Martin Luther King Jr., President Jacob Weinstein of the Central Conference of American Rabbis, President Dana McLean Greeley of the Unitarian-Universalist Association, and Methodist Bishop Raymond Grant — all of whom were fellow-travelers.

In 1966, in connection with the Vietnam War, the Fellowship began a project called "They are our Brothers." The stated purposes of the Brothers Project were "to raise funds for the purchase and shipping of medical and other humanitarian aid to the civilian victims of the war, in all sections of Vietnam; to express the profound sorrow and penitence many Americans feel for the extent to which their government has contributed to this suffering; to underline the nature of this war, in which there are far more civilian casualties than combatant; and, to speak across the battlelines a word of reconciliation and brotherhood to those who are our brothers, who kill and are being killed, attempting to increase the insistence on peace and to erode the concept of enmity."

Sponsors of "They are our Brothers" included the Berrigan brothers; Chaplain William Sloane Coffin Jr. of Yale University; Sister Mary Corita of Los Angeles (now an ex-nun); former President Edwin T. Dahlberg of the National Council of Churches; President Dana McLean Greeley of the Universalist-Unitarian Association, Rev. Robert Moon, national chairman of the Fellowship, President Jacob Weinstein of the Central Conference of American Rabbis; Episcopal Bishop William Crittenden, vice president of the National Council of Churches; and Catholic monsignors Paul H. Furfey of Catholic University and Thomas J. Reese, director of the Catholic Social Service of Wilmington, Delaware.

On the Vietnam War issue, the Fellowship has demanded the withdrawal of all U. S. military aid from South Vietnam and that the Vietnam problem should be placed before the United Nations and that a peace conference should include Red China.

Earlier, the Fellowship's pro-Communist position on foreign policy had been very much in evidence, about a year after Fidel Castro had seized Cuba and placed it under his tyrannical, Communist regime. The Fellowship urged that the United States display a generous and sympathetic attitude toward Communist Cuba by (1) immediately rescinding all economic sanctions against Cuba; (2) offering long-term, low-interest loans to Cuba which could be used in compensating owners of expropriated American properties; (3) withdrawing from the United States naval base at Guantanamo; and, (4) acknowledging that the United States has no right to impose its will on Cuba in the matter of political, economic or military ties with the Soviet bloc even though such adherence might pose a "serious threat to world peace." The Fellowship went so far as to organize a "reconciliation team" but the U. S. government refused to use or sanction it.

In 1967, the Fellowship began a massive Draft/War Project to give "hundreds of thousands of draft age men a chance to register their convictions on the Vietnam War." Always careful to avoid violations of the selective service laws, the Fellowship does not counsel draft evasion but it goes to great lengths to encourage those eligible for the draft to become conscientious objectors or to avoid military service in some other way. Among the pamphlets and brochures distributed by the Fellowship and directed toward The Conscientious Objector are *Questions and Answers on the Classification and Assignment of Conscientious Objectors* ("invaluable for persons taking the CO stand"); *Handbook for Conscientious Objectors* ("standard reference for counselor and counselee"); *The Conscientious Objector and the Armed Forces* ("avenues open to a soldier who reaches the CO position after induction"); *The Non-Cooperator and the Draft* ("reasons for non-cooperation and the consequences of civil disobedience"); and, *Guide to Conscientious Objection,* published by the Communistic Students for a Democratic Society.

The Fellowship's own publications include the monthly *Fellowship Magazine,* in which have appeared such contributors as Martin L. King Jr., Benjamin Spock, Milton Mayer, Alan Paton, Henry Hitt Crane, George F. Kennan, and assorted other leftists; *Current Issues,* published irregularly and containing the leftist-pacifist analyses of world problems by the *Fellowship's* foreign affairs consultant John M. Swomley Jr.; and, *Hi-Issues,* a leftist-pacifist newsletter written expressly for high school students.

The Fellowship also distributes publications of the American Friends Service Committee, the World Council of Churches, and the Center for the Study of Democratic Institutions. Under such headings as The Bomb — Civil Defense — Disarmament — and, War and Militarism, the classified catalog of the Fellowship recommends the extremely leftward slanted writings of Benjamin Spock, Thomas Merton, Claude Eatherly (the phony "Hiroshima A-bomb pilot"), Sidney Lens, Arthur Larson, Walter Millis, James Real, Victor Gollancz, Jerome Davis, Harold Taylor, Lenore Marshall, Tristram Coffin, Victor Perlo, Brock Chisholm, Fred J. Cook, and Arthur Waskow. On the question of Civil Rights, the Fellowship's catalog leans heavily on racial agitators and their apologists: James Baldwin, James Peck, James Farmer, Bayard Rustin, Martin L. King Jr., William Stringfellow, Nat Hentoff, and Howard Zinn. On Communism, the catalog's selection could not be more ludicrous: Sidney Lens, George F. Kennan, Felix Greene (the prolific apologist for Mao Tse-tung), Oliver Edmund Clubb (a long-time member of the Red China Lobby), and David Dellinger, whose *Libera-*

tion magazine has been, since its founding in 1956, an outlet for Communist and pro-Communist propaganda and left-wing pacifism.

Under such headings as Man in the Modern World — Foreign Policy Problems — Peace and Nonviolence — Poverty — The Social Revolution — and, Vietnam, the Fellowship's catalog recommends the writings of Socialists, anti-anti-Communists, pro-Communist apologists, and anti-Americans: Jerome D. Frank, Erich Fromm, William O. Douglas, Barbara Ward, Bertrand Russell, Milton Mayer, Felix Greene, C. Wright Mills, Paul Goodman, Robert Moon, Charles E. Osgood, Abraham J. Muste, Arnold Toynbee, Michael Harrington, Robert Theobald, Hannah Arendt, Gerard Piel, W. H. "Ping" Ferry, Denna F. Flemming, and Robert Scheer.

As is common with left-wing pacifists, the Fellowship pays homage to Thoreau and Gandhi and also to the American Emily Greene Balch, Kagawa of Japan, and Alcock of Canada. But these old-time pacifists are being replaced in the affections of the hero-worshipping Fellowship by the recently deceased Abraham J. Muste and Martin L. King Jr.

As of 1968, the Fellowship claimed that it had 13,000 members. According to the Fellowship's Statement of Purpose: "Although members do not bind themselves to any exact form of words, 1. They refuse to participate in any war or to sanction military preparations; they work to abolish war and to foster good will among nations, races, and classes; 2. They strive to build a social order which will suffer no individual or group to be exploited for the profit or pleasure of another, and which will assure to all the means for realizing the best possibilities of life; 3. They advocate such ways of dealing with offenders against society as shall transform the wrongdoer rather than inflict retributive punishment; 4. They endeavor to show reverence for personality — in the home, in the education of children, in association with persons of other classes, nationalities, and races; 5. They seek to avoid bitterness and contention, and to maintain the spirit of self-giving love while engaged in the struggle to achieve these purposes."

It must be remarked that despite the Fellowship's flowery protestations of idealism and assumed mantle of religiosity, its entire history since 1915 has demonstrated a remarkable consistency in its repeated sympathizing with tyrannical and anti-religious regimes (the Soviet Union, North Vietnam, Red China, Communist Cuba). The Fellowship has worked for the identical goals of international Socialism: a radical reorganization of society and the replacement — wherever it exists — of individual capitalism by collective ownership.

The shibboleth of "nonviolence" flaunted so ubiquitously by the Fellowship is belied by the violence engendered by Fellowship-sponsored demonstrations against war and defense preparations and in labor and "civil rights" disputes. And the Fellowship makes a mockery of "nonviolence" by its persistent advocacy of disarmament programs for the United States which is precisely what the ever-arming, violence-ridden Communist regimes have been promoting through diplomatic channels and especially through private pacifist groups such as the Fellowship.

FORD FOUNDATION
FUND FOR THE REPUBLIC
CENTER FOR THE STUDY OF DEMOCRATIC INSTITUTIONS

In 1936, the Ford Foundation was incorporated in Michigan. Its donors were Henry Ford and his son Edsel.

The Foundation was one of many studied by the House Special Committee to Investigate Tax-Exempt Foundations in 1954. The Special Committee, known as the Reece Committee, in its report, said of the Foundation: "The Ford Foundation affords a good example of the use of a foundation to solve the death tax problem and, at the same time, the problem of how to retain control of a great enterprise in the hands of the family. Ninety per cent [eighty-eight per cent, according to other sources] of the ownership of the Ford Motor Company was transferred to the Ford Foundation, created for the purpose. Had it not been, it is almost certain that the family would have lost control. The only practical alternative might have been to sell a large part of the stock to the public or to bankers, or to sell the entire Company.

"The huge taxes payable by the Ford estates could not have been paid without liquidating a considerable part — possibly a controlling part — of the family business. The solution selected was to give away ninety [or eighty-eight] per cent of the Company to 'charity,' so that the greater part of the estates would be free of death taxation.

"The 'charitable' transfers could have been made, of course, direct to universities, churches, hospitals and other institutions. But this would have put the donated stock of the Ford Company into the hands of strangers. For this reason, we assume, a foundation was created, and to make doubly certain that there would be no interference with the Company's management, the donated stock was in the form of non-voting shares. Not only did the family thus retain one hundred per cent voting control, but the Ford Company lost no working capital whatsoever. Moreover, even non-voting stock can be something of a nuisance in the hands of strangers but, held by an amiable creature, operated by friendly nominees of the family, it would not be likely to bring any pressure to bear on the management of the Company of the kind which might be expected of an alert general stockholder."

The Reece Committee called attention to the April, 1954 issue of *The Corporate Director* where a study of the Ford Foundation appeared and in which it was pointed out "that members of the Ford family, as officers of the Ford Company, are able to draw salaries and are thus in a position, being assured of their own income, to allow the Company to operate on a cost basis, without having to pay dividends.

In its early years, the Ford Foundation directed most of its grants to charities in Michigan. But, after the deaths of Henry and Edsel Ford, the Foundation became a national and international operation. And, after 1949, the Ford family and other trustees surrendered to the Foundation's employees almost all of their responsibility for the detailed supervision of the Foundation's programs. This situation came about as a result of the Ford Foundation's "Report of the Study for the Ford Foundation on Policy and Program," dated November 19, 1949. The Report, which was accepted by the trustees, said: "Individual members of the Board of Trustees should not seek to decide the technical questions involved in particular applications and projects. Nothing would more certainly destroy the effectiveness of a foundation. On the contrary, the Trustees will be most surely able to control the main lines of policy of the Foundation, and the contribution it will make to human welfare, if they give the President and the officers considerable freedom in developing the program, while they avoid influencing (even by indirection) the conduct of projects to which the Foundation has granted funds.

"As individuals, the Trustees should learn as much as they can by all means possible, formal and informal, about the program of the Foundation in relation to the affairs of the world. But the Board of Trustees, as a responsible body, should act only according to its regular formal procedures, and usually on the agenda, the dockets, and the recommendations presented by the President.

"The meeting of the Board should be arranged so that the discussion will not be directed mainly at the individual grants recommended by the officers and institutions to receive them. Nothing could destroy the effectiveness of the Board more certainly than to have the agenda for its meetings consist exclusively of small appropriation items, each of which has to be judged on the basis of scientific considerations, the academic reputation of research workers, or the standing of institutions. If the agenda calls solely for such discussions the Board will necessarily fail to discuss the main issues of policy and will inevitably interfere in matters in which it has no special competence."

Until the Ford Foundation became a national and international operation, there was no definite policy to govern the Foundation's grants. But, in 1948, the Trustees appointed a study committee, headed by H. Rowan Gaither Jr., to propose how the Foundation might spend the vast sums of money which were coming from the estates of Henry and Edsel Ford. The Gaither Committee spent two years interviewing more than one thousand "experts" with the result that the Trustees were told that the Ford Foundation should try to solve the problems of mankind in five areas: The Establishment of peace; the strengthening of democracy; the strengthening of the economy; education in a democratic society; and individual behavior and human relations. Columnist Raymond Moley (*Newsweek,* January 9, 1956) said of the Committee that it was "composed of a lawyer, H. Rowan Gaither, Jr., now president of the foundation; a doctor; a school administrator; and five professors. None of these was experienced in foundation work. It could hardly be a coincidence that the five 'areas' which they recommended for the foundation correspond, to a degree, to the academic departments in which the professors had been teaching. The plan substantially ruled out medical research, public health and natural science on the vague ground that 'progress toward democratic goals are today social rather than physical.' 'Democratic goals' are nowhere defined."

Once the Ford Foundation was reorganized to solve the problems of mankind, it became a sprawling conglomeration of projects: *Adult Education* (Continuation of liberal education beyond formal schooling. Areas of effort: international, political and economic understanding); *Advancement of Education* (1. Institutional content. 2. Institutional execution. Clarification of educational philosophy and of functions and improvement; teacher improvement; education of armed forces; financial support of educational institutions.); *East European Fund* [first called the *Free Russia Fund*] (1. Orientation of Russian refugees; 2. Assistance to scholars and scientists in their chosen fields; 3. Aid in social integration.); *Intercultural Publications* (Improved understanding of differing cultures and backgrounds via publications and their circulation.); *Resources for the Future* (Availability and conservation of national resources required for the Nation's growth, welfare, and security.); *Fund for the Republic* (Pressing problems; legislative hearings; Government loyalty procedure; private censorship; loyalty oaths; due process of law; academic freedom; free speech and free assembly; democracy in labor unions.); *Center for Advanced Study* (Training of behavioral scientists at post-doctoral levels: 1. Greater number of qualified scholars. 2. Increase competency of faculty members. 3. Development of better content and methods. 4. New designs and materials for research training.); *TV-Radio Workshop* (Omnibus programs: literary, musical, artistic, historical, and scientific.); *Foundation External Grant* (Foreign activities; domestic educational institutions; public administration; social and scientific research; and, fellowships and grants-in-aid); and, the *Behavioral Sciences Division.*

The Behavioral Sciences Division had three facets: one, *Research and Training Abroad* (1. Aid to scholars in western European institutions. 2. Comparative training and research.); two, *Institutional Exchange Program* (1. Interchange of scholars at doctoral levels. 2. Applies to graduate students and faculty members.); three, *Grants-in-Aid* (1. Individual grants to outstanding scholars. 2. Applies to scholars at home and abroad. 3. Spending under the discretion of the individual.)

One of the Ford Foundation's first ventures into international affairs consisted of grants in 1951 and 1952 to the American Friends Service Committee. The officers of the Ford Foundation "felt that the American Friends Service Committee had demonstrated over a long period its capacity to deal effectively with many of the economic, social and educational conditions that lead to international tensions."

For at least twenty years prior to receiving the Ford Foundation's largesse, the AFSC, under the leadership of fellow traveler Clarence Pickett, had been a notorious outlet for Communist propaganda. Behind its facade of religion-oriented pacifism, the AFSC had become a collection of apologists for the belligerent and barbaric international Communist conspiracy. In January, 1950, the AFSC was one of the first large organizations to urge President Truman to recognize Red

China on grounds that "by treating Communist China as an enemy and by refusing to recognize her, we are isolating ourselves."

In explanation of their grants to the AFSC, the Foundation's officers said: "Our policy in Asia has failed to lead us to the real objectives of the American people because its preoccupation with strategy and ideology has prevented our giving sufficient weight to the economic, social and political realities of Asia. There, as elsewhere, we have tended to label as Communist any movement that sought a radical change in the established order, without consideration of the roots of such a movement. Quaker workers [the AFSC is a Quaker organization], during years of service in the troubled Orient, have witnessed the great changes taking place and the increasing hostility with which the United States has regarded them. They are convinced that an effective policy must take into account the actual conditions that have produced these changes, as well as the new situation that revolution has created in Asia. Our fundamental ignorance of the East is costing us dear, but the situation has been further complicated by the fact that United States policy towards Asia has recently been exposed in an unusual degree to the hazards of domestic criticism arising from political partisanship.

"It is surprising that we have not been able to understand the situation in Asia because Americans should be peculiarly able to comprehend the meaning of revolution. Our own independence was achieved through a revolution, and we have traditionally sympathized with the determined attempts of other peoples to win national independence and higher standards of living. The current revolution in Asia is a similar movement, whatever its present association with Soviet Communism."

At the time this extraordinary tribute to Communist "revolution" in Asia was offered, the United States was in the midst of the Korean War fighting against Communist China's armies. The two most prominent officers of the Ford Foundation, at the same time, were Paul Hoffman and Robert Maynard Hutchins both of whom held unimpeachable credentials as leftwingers, which goes a long way toward explaining why the AFSC received grants of $1,134,000 in 1951 and 1952.

Hoffman was the first president of the national/international Ford Foundation. His successors have been H. Rowan Gaither Jr., Henry T. Heald, and McGeorge Bundy. As of December, 1968, the Ford Foundation had dispensed $3.1 billion in every state and in more than eighty countries. (The assets of the Ford Foundation — more than $3 billion —

are nearly four times those of the next wealthiest trust, the Rockefeller Foundation.) And the Hoffman precedent of subsidizing the left has been scrupulously followed by his successors no matter what the project.

Within twenty-two months in 1952 and 1953, the Ford Foundation granted $759,950 to one of its creations, Intercultural Publications. This outfit was formed "in an attempt to increase understanding among the peoples of the world and to advance mutual appreciation of differing cultural and intellectual backgrounds through the exchange of ideas and literary productions . . . [and] to help maintain world peace and to promote better understanding between peoples of different nations, races and relations; to increase without the United States knowledge of the culture, art, intellectual works, customs, and interests of the United States and its peoples."

Mrs. Alice Widener, a competent and scholarly journalist, analyzed *Perspectives USA,* one of the Intercultural Publications. She found that the contents were "largely culled from the small literary *avant-garde* magazines which pride themselves on a lack of appreciation of contemporary American life as it is enjoyed by the vast majority of American citizens."

Mrs. Widener studied the second issue of *Perspectives USA* for which Lionel Trilling, a leftwinger, was the guest editor. She noted that Trilling stated that he chose for that particular issue the writings of American authors belonging to a group who "are especially aware of the social and political context in which the intellectual and creative life is lived." According to Trilling, a typical member of the group would say: "We are not trying to represent the American Spirit or the American Quality . . . . We don't know what the American Spirit or the American Quality is, and we have no intention of trying to find out."

Trilling's selection for the lead article in the second issue of *Perspectives USA* was "America the Beautiful" by Mary McCarthy, which contained such un-beautiful sentiments as: "1. The inalienable right to life, liberty and the pursuit of happiness appears, in practice, to become the inalienable right to a bathtub, a flush toilet, and a can of Spam. 2. There is a great similarity between the nation with its new bomb and the consumer with his new Buick. 3. Only among certain groups where franchise, socially speaking, has not been achieved, do pleasure and material splendor constitute a life-object and an occupation. Among the social outcasts — Jews, Negroes, racketeers and homosexuals — . . . the

90

love of fabrics, gaudy show, and rich possessions still anachronistically flaunts itself."

The totally leftist character of *Perspectives USA* was an accurate reflection of the publication's advisory board which included such well-known leftwingers as Mortimer Adler, Aaron Copland, Malcolm Cowley, James T. Farrell, Kenneth Rexroth, Arthur M. Schlesinger Jr., and Gilbert Seldes.

Since 1950, the greater share of the Ford Foundation's expenditures has been in the general area of "education." The Foundation's Fund for Adult Education has granted substantial subsidies to the American Council on Education (a leftwing clearing-house and liaison agency between educational institutions and the federal government, especially the State Department, the Army, and the Navy); the American Labor Educational Service (staffed by fellow travelers and specializing in the circulation of pro-Communist propaganda); and, the Inter-University Labor Education Committee (another outlet for pro-Communist propaganda).

The Fund for Adult Education has also subsidized the Great Books program which is sponsored by the Great Books Foundation using the Great Books of the Western World, published in fifty-four volumes by the Encyclopedia Britannica. The whole project was devised by Mortimer Adler and Robert Maynard Hutchins, two political leftists who had been closely associated at the University of Chicago and the Encyclopedia Britannica, and who both received generous finances from the Ford Foundation's cornucopia. The Great Books Program simply promoted the leftwing globalism so dear to the ideological hearts of Adler and Hutchins.

The Foreign Policy Association, which is and always has been leftwing from roof to cellar, has also been subsidized by the Fund for Adult Education.

Another vehicle for the Ford Foundation's spending spree on "education" has been the Fund for the Advancement of Education. Dr. Thomas H. Briggs, professor emeritus of Columbia University, served on the advisory committee of this Fund but resigned when he realized that he was wasting his time. Dr. Briggs found that the trustees had turned over their responsibilities to the Fund's administrative officers. Dr. Briggs testified about these men before the Reece Committee: "These administrative officers doubtless present to the board, as they do to the public, a program so general as to get approval and yet so indefinite as to permit activities which in the judgment of most competent critics are either wasteful or harmful to the education program that has been approved by the public.

"Not a single member of the staff, from the president down to the lowliest employee, has had any experience, certainly none in recent years, that would give understanding of the problems that are met daily by the teachers and administrators of our schools. It is true that they have from time to time called in for counsel experienced educators of their own choosing, but there is little evidence that they have been materially influenced by the advice that was proffered. As one prominent educator who was invited to give advice reported, 'any suggestions for changes in the project (proposed by the fund) were glossed over without discussion.' As a former member of a so-called advisory committee I testify that at no time did the administration of the fund seek from it any advice on principles of operation nor did it hospitably receive or act in accordance with such advice as was volunteered."

Based on his experiences as an advisor whose advice was not sought, Dr. Briggs indicted the Fund: "In summary, I charge: (1) That The Fund for the Advancement of Education is improperly manned with a staff inexperienced in public elementary and secondary schools, ignorant at firsthand of the problems that daily confront teachers and school administrators, and out of sympathy with the democratic ideal of giving an appropriate education to all the children of all of the people; (2) That the Fund is using its great resources, mostly contributed by the public by the remission of taxes, to deprecate a program of professional education of teachers and school administrators that has been approved by the public with legislation and appropriations; (3) That the Fund has ignored the professional organizations of teachers and school administrators, neither seeking their advice and cooperation nor making appropriations to support projects proposed by them; (4) That the Fund has made grants to favored localities and individuals for projects that are not likely to have any wide or important influence; (5) That the Fund has given no evidence of its realization of its obligation as a public trust to promote the general good of the entire Nation; (6) That the Fund has in some cases been wastefully prodigal in making grants beyond the importance of the projects; and (7) That the Fund either has no balanced program of correlated constructive policies, or else it has failed to make them public."

At least several of the items in Dr. Briggs' indictment were applicable to the Fund's grant of $565,000 to the Institute for Philosophical Research which, according to Robert Hutchins' globalistic soul-mate Mortimer Adler, director of the Institute, was "undertaking a dialectical examination of Western humanistic thought with a view to providing assistance in the clarification of basic philosophical and educational issues in the modern world."

It was more than ironical that the Fund for the Advancement of Education was showering American taxpayers' dollars on Adler whose predilection for world government and Socialism were unmistakable. Adler had described the thesis of his 1945 book, *How to Think about War and Peace*: "world peace depends on world federal government; that world federal government requires the *total* relinquishment and abolishment of the external sovereignty of the United States as well as that of all other presently existing sovereign nations; that this may seem a high price to pay for peace, but that it is nevertheless the *absolutely minimum* condition, without which we shall have another world war in less than fifteen years. Since I think that the atomic warfare which impends will be absolutely destructive of the civilization of the United States, whether we win or lose that war, I feel that I am justified in strongly recommending action by the American people to prevent that war — even if it means *the loss of our national sovereignty.*" (Emphases added.)

Writing in January, 1949, in an article, "The Quiet Revolution," Adler scarcely concealed his joy that the United States had gone beyond the point-of-no-return in the direction of Socialism: "The basic trend toward socialism, which began with Wilson's New Freedom, and which was greatly accelerated by Roosevelt's New Deal, has been confirmed by Truman's return to the presidency on a platform which does not yield an inch to the right and in many respects goes further to the left. That fact suggests the possibility that some form of socialism is quite compatible with democracy — as in England and the United States — may prove to be the middle ground between the free enterprise capitalism and the oligarchical politics of the 'economic royalists' on the one hand, and the dictatorship of the proletariat and the despotism of the party on the other . . . . It all adds up to a clear picture. It looks like a quiet but none the less effective revolution. If we still wish to be cautious we need say no more than that we have reached a turning point in American politics at which it has become evident that the general social process of the last twenty years is irreversible — except by force. By choice the American people are never going to fall back to the right again. That deserves to be called a revolution accomplished. But it is also a revolution which will continue. Either the Democratic Party will move further to the left or a new political party will form to the left of the Democrats."

The case of the globalist-socialist Adler was by no means an isolated one. The Ford Foundation, once it became national and international, financed the most extreme leftwingers in educational circles all over the world. At the same time, expenditures made on seemingly worthwhile projects helped to obscure the basic leftwingism of the Foundation's program.

Attention was called to some of these projects by Philip M. Stern in *Harper's* magazine of January, 1966 ("An Open Letter to the Ford Foundation"). Stern was not only a friendly critic of foundations but president of two of them. He wrote: "To me, Ford in its largest grants has been guilty of pouring too many barrels in the ocean. The clearest examples are the $200 million grant distributed among 3,254 private nonprofit hospitals, adding only infinitesimally to their aggregate operating budgets; and the $210 million for an endowment to raise faculty salaries at 615 private colleges by an average of only $4 per week per teacher. Another example, slightly less clear perhaps, is the $275 million devoted to the general development of some 70 private colleges and universities (which has attracted an additional $725 million in matching funds required by Ford). I am not saying these grants were harmful. I am well aware that each filled a need and resulted in measurable benefits. Yet in appraising the dispensing of two-thirds of a *billion* dollars (a third of everything Ford has given away), I insist on asking, what is there to show for this prodigious sum, in new ideas sparked, new directions charted?"

If Mr. Stern really wanted to be perceptive, he would have discovered that the prodigious sum of two-thirds of a billion dollars purchased for the Ford Foundation the reputation of a benevolent philanthropy. The most nefarious of the Foundation's many enterprises, the Fund for the Republic, was launched with $15 million — a paltry sum when compared with the multi-hundreds of millions spent on teachers, hospitals, and colleges and universities.

The Fund for the Republic was established in 1953. Allegedly, it was to promote one of the programs of the Ford Foundation: "The Foundation will support activities directed toward the elimination of restrictions on freedom of thought, inquiry, and expression in the United States and the development of policies and procedures best adapted to protect these rights in the face of persistent international tension. . . . The maintenance of democratic control over concentrations of public and private power, while at the same time preserving freedom for scientific and technological endeavor, economic initiative, and cultural development. The strengthening of the political processes through which public officers are chosen and policies determined, and the improvement of the organizations and administrative procedures by which governmental affairs are conducted. The strengthening of the organization and procedures involved in the adjudication of private rights and the interpretation and enforcement of law. Basic to human welfare is general acceptance of the dignity of man. This rests on the conviction that man is endowed with certain unalienable rights and must be regarded as an end in himself, not as a cog in the mechanics of society or a mere means to some social end. At its heart, this is a belief in the inherent worth of the individual and the intrinsic value of human life. Implicit in this concept is the conviction that society must accord all men equal rights and equal opportunity. Human welfare requires tolerance and respect for individual, social, religious, and cultural differences, and for the varying needs and aspirations to which these differences give rise. It requires freedom of speech, freedom of the press, freedom of worship, and freedom of association. Within wide limits, every person has a right to go his own way and to be free from interference or harassment because of nonconformity."

Robert M. Hutchins said that the Fund was established "to defend and advance" the Declaration of Independence and the Constitution and to keep under scrutiny "those areas in which these principles seemed to be in danger."

Paul Hoffman, the Fund's chairman of the board, told the Ford Foundation that the Fund would operate in five areas of action: (1) Restriction and assaults upon academic freedom; (2) Due process and equal protection of the laws; (3) Protection of the rights of minorities; (4) Censorship, boycotting, and blacklisting activities of private groups; and, (5) Principle and application of guilt by association.

Almost as soon as the Fund for the Republic was established, it became evident that it had a dual purpose: an all-out attack upon congressional investigating committees and a massive anti-anti-Communist drive.

The Ford Foundation's choice for president of the Fund was Clifford Case of New Jersey. Case, a Republican, was in his fifth term in the House of Representatives when he resigned to become the Fund's first president, a position that "challenged my imagination." In his congressional career, Case was so far to the left that he became one of the first Republicans ever endorsed by Americans for Democratic Action. He was especially noted for his hostility toward the House Committee on Un-American Activities and his attacks upon Senator Joseph R. McCarthy, who was successfully uncovering Communist influences within government circles. (McCarthy was particularly abhorrent to Robert Hutchins who, while reflecting on the establishment of the Fund and its early critics, said: "Particularly in an era in which Senator McCarthy was at the height of his power, the Fund could not expect the applause of those who in the opinion of the Board of Directors were threatening the principles it was called on to defend and advance.")

Clifford Case, despite the imaginative challenge of defending and advancing the Declaration of Independence and the Constitution, resigned the Fund's presidency after a mere eight months. His successor was Robert Hutchins whose antagonism toward congressional investigating committees was not only as strong but even pre-dated Case's.

Within five years after he took over as president of the Fund, Hutchins managed to spend $10 million. Among the fellow travelers on the Fund's payroll were Julien Bryan and Helen Lynd. Earl Browder, former head of the Communist Party in the United States – but still a Communist – went to work as a consultant to the Fund. Amos Landsman was hired by Hutchins as a press agent just three weeks after he pleaded protection under the fifth amendment when asked about his relationship with the Communist Party. Walter Gellhorn was given a fellowship by the Fund. Gellhorn's fellow traveling included his affiliations with the National Lawyers Guild ("the foremost legal bulwark of the Communist Party"); the International Juridical Association (an organization "which actively defended Communists and consistently followed the Communist Party line"); the National Emergency Conference for Democratic Rights ("Communist front"); and, the Non-Partisan Committee for the Re-election of Congressman Vito Marcantonio ("Communist front").

Adam Yarmolinsky, a member of the Fund's staff, wrote *Case Studies in Personnel Security* an attack upon the federal government's loyalty-security program. The Yarmolinsky project cost the Fund $192,170.

John Cogley was assigned to compile a two-volume report on alleged blacklisting of fellow travelers in the radio and television industries. When the report was completed, it became obvious that the Fund had set out to discredit anti-Communist investigating committees. With Cogley on the project was Michael Harrington, a Socialist; Elizabeth Poe, who had previously been active in a Communist Party cell at *Time* magazine; and Marie Jahoda, a Socialist who came to this country from Austria in 1945. She had a history of attacking the federal government's loyalty programs.

Mary Knowles was employed by the William Jeanes Memorial Library in Plymouth Meeting, Pennsylvania. She had been identified as a member of the Communist Party and had pleaded the fifth amendment when questioned about this association. When her employers would not fire her after she pleaded the fifth amendment, the Fund gave the library $5,000 for "courageous and effective defense of democratic principles."

When J. Robert Oppenheimer became the nation's most celebrated security risk, the Fund selected Edward R. Murrow of the Columbia Broadcasting System to whitewash Oppenheimer's reputation. Murrow's format was an hour-long "interview" with Oppenheimer on Murrow's "See It Now" television program. For its part, the Fund distributed 110 reprints of the program free to colleges and civic groups. Also in the same vein: *The Bulletin of Atomic Scientists* printed a special issue praising Oppenheimer and denouncing the federal government's loyalty-security program — the program which had brought about Oppenheimer's downfall. The Fund made a free distribution of 25,000 copies of the special issue.

On American Broadcasting Company's television network, the Fund sponsored a series called "Survival and Freedom." For the second program of the series, Mike Wallace interviewed Cyrus Eaton, the multimillionaire industrialist whose apologetics on behalf of Communism and Communists have earned him the Lenin Peace Prize, an award reserved only for those who have made a significant contribution to the Soviet Union. On the Mike Wallace program, Eaton attacked and smeared the Federal Bureau of Investigation and its personnel.

At one time, the Fund planned to spend $200,000 for a television news commentary series, featuring Herbert Block (Herblock), whose anti-anti-Communist cartoons have long been the most extreme tributes to the Left found in the pages of the venomously anti-anti-Communist *Washington Post.* Advance publicity of the proposed Herblock series attracted unanswerable queries as to Herblock's qualifications for news analysis and the project was abandoned.

When Erwin N. Griswold, a director of the Fund, wrote an article, "The Fifth Amendment," (with the theme that when a witness pleads the Fifth Amendment privilege no inference should be drawn as to the possibility of the witness hiding his guilt) the Fund distributed 35,000 copies. When Richard Rovere, a notorious anti-anti-Communist, wrote "The Kept Witnesses" for *Harper's* magazine, the Fund distributed 25,000 reprints. Rovere castigated the use of former Communists as witnesses in loyalty-security proceedings.

The Fund approached several universities with a project whereby an analysis would be made of testimony of witnesses in proceedings relative to Communism. Since the underlying purpose of the Fund was to discredit former Communists who testified about their experiences and associations in the Communist Party, the universities turned the proposal down. Finally, however, Stanford University's Law School accepted $25,000 for the "study."

The Association of the Bar of the City of New York was granted $100,000 by the Fund "for a study and report on the federal loyalty-security program. Walter Millis, a member of the Fund's staff, supervised the work even though he was flatly opposed to the very existence of a federal loyalty-security program.

When Paul Hoffman of the Fund wrote his viciously anti-anti-Communist "To Insure the End of Our Hysteria" for the *New York Times Magazine,* the Fund distributed 10,000 reprints to the Emergency Civil Liberties Committee, a Communist front with the avowed purpose to abolish the House Committee on Un-American Activities and to discredit the Federal Bureau of Investigation.

One of the Fund's most ludicrous productions was a *Bibliography on the Communist Problem in the United States,* a 474-page compilation prepared under the direction of Clinton Rossiter. It was a travesty on scholarship that cost the Fund $67,000 before the volume was allowed to go out-of-print. But in its short life, Rossiter's sorry work found its way onto library shelves throughout the country as a "reference" work. In another venture of book distribution, federal judges and college presidents received from the Fund free copies of leftwing books by Samuel Stouffer, Alan Barth, and Telford Taylor.

The most important and durable action taken by the Fund was the establishment, in 1959, of the Center for the Study of Democratic Institutions. The Center was allegedly organized to foster "the discussion of a Free Society, with the motto "Feel Free." In its formal literature, the Center described itself as "a non-profit educational enterprise established by the Fund [for the Republic] to promote the principles of individual liberty expressed in the Declaration of Independence and the Constitution." Harry Ashmore, chairman of the Center's executive committee, was a bit more specific when he said that the Center's purpose was "to do what governments ought to be doing and ultimately will have to do." On another occasion, Ashmore said: "We are in the rather absurd position of running what amounts to a privately financed, understaffed, and wholly unaccredited foreign service."

Four years after the Center began its work, Mrs. Alice Widener, in her excellent bi-weekly *U.S.A.*, accurately appraised the Center when she wrote: "The Fund's subsidized intellectuals allege that we need a new civilization run by a New American State. It should be unilaterally disarmed, advised by a National Planning Agency, and empowered to control all U. S. corporations by coercion under 'law' — but not law as we now know it." Mrs. Widener, who obviously studied the Center's literature, said that "seen in focus through its publication, it seems the Center . . . is for: Destruction of the first strike nuclear capability of the United States; unilateral U. S. disarmament; and a better Red-than-dead U. S. foreign policy.

"Abolition of the FBI's counterintelligence activities and removal of J. Edgar Hoover from office as director of the F.B.I.

"Abolition of Congressional power to investigate Communist activities and of all existing U. S. anti-Communist legislation.

"Conversion of all industries to peacetime production only and their total subjection to control by the Federal Government.

"Federal control over what is broadcast internationally by Telstar.

"Creation of a Corporate Republic of the United States of America to be achieved by: (a) Curtailing all powers of Congress except that of debate permitted by the President of the Corporate Republic; (b) Concentrating all power in the hands of the President; (c) Enabling him to use the Supreme Court as his instrument for legalizing his exercise of absolute power; (d) Incorporation of the Corporate Republic of the United States into a World Government ruling disarmed peoples by a World Police armed with nuclear weapons."

When the Ford Foundation created the Fund for the Republic, the Foundation disavowed any further responsibility for the Fund's actions. In similar fashion, the Center for the Study of Democratic Institutions disavows responsibility for what is written by contributors in the Center's publications: "Contributors to publications issued under the auspices of the Center are responsible for their statements of fact and expressions of opinions. The Center is responsible only for determining that the material should be presented to the public as a contribution to the discussion of a Free Society."

Such disclaimers are meaningless. There could never be any doubt that with Paul Hoffman and Robert Hutchins directing the Fund for the Republic, the Ford Foundation had merely moved two of its favorite ultra-liberals into a position where their mischief making could have the trappings of autonomy. And when Hutchins as head of the Fund became head of the Center, the farce was merely carried one step further. It would be idle to suppose that Hutchins' choice of staff members and consultants for the Center was ignorant as to the leftist ideological slant of these individuals who, within three years, produced 105 publications uniformly leftist. And Hutchins' enthusiasm for this leftist output was demonstrable as he sold or gave away 3,500,000 copies of the 105 publications.

What Hoffman and Hutchins had done with the Fund for the Republic was to create an ultra-liberal fief exclusively endorsed and staffed by ultra-liberals, all of whom had distinguished themselves as anti-anti-Communists, pro-Communists, Socialists, globalists, statists, or in some other specialized collectivism. The press was represented by Harry Ashmore, Alicia Patterson, William C. Baggs, Barry Bingham, James A. Linen, Max Lerner, Chet Huntley, and Harry Golden; the theater and arts by Dore Schary, Paddy Chayefsky, Melvyn Douglas, Ben Shahn, Eli Wallach, and Aaron Copland; government circles by William Benton, Chester Bowles, William J. Brennan Jr., Ralph Flanders, Henry Cabot Lodge, Luis Muñoz-Marín, Abraham Ribicoff, Eugene V. Rostow, and Robert Meyner (as well as his mother-in-law Eleanor Stevenson); labor by Walter Reuther, James B. Carey, James G. Patton, and Joseph A. Beirne; religion by Henry Van Dusen, Francis J. Lally. Others included J. Robert Oppenheimer, Stanley Marcus, Lillian Smith, Elmo Roper, Lyle Spencer, Edward Lamb, and Jerome Wiesner.

When the Center was established, the Hutchins-Hoffman fief merely underwent an expansion and the roll call of ultra-liberal sycophants simply became longer. Founding members of the Center (expected to contribute $1000 a year) included Robert Strange McNamara, Herbert Lehman, and Bart Lytton. On the board of directors with Hoffman and Hutchins were Elmo Roper, Justice William O. Douglas, Bruce Catton, and Monsignor Francis J. Lally. Consultants included Adolf A. Berle, Harrison Brown, Scott Buchanan, Eric Goldman, Clark Kerr, Henry Luce, Reinhold Niebuhr, and Isidor I. Rabi. The staff included Frank Kelly, Walter Millis, Harvey Wheeler, Eugene Burdick, Paul Jacobs, John Cogley, Richard Lichtman, Milton Mayer, Linus Pauling, Rexford Tugwell, William V. Shannon, Arthur Waskow, and Fred Warner Neal.

Individually and collectively those connected with the Fund and the Center represented and still represent the highest echelons of opinion-molding and policy-making influences. Beyond this situation, the Fund for the Republic had a complete tie-in with the leftwing Pacifica Foundation, operators of radio stations WBAI-New York, KPFA-San Francisco, and KPFK-Los Angeles. The Center, within a year after it was established, was called upon by Encyclopedia Brittanica for guidance and cooperation.

The Center has boasted that its publications are used in hundreds of universities, colleges, and high schools as reference material or classroom texts and also used in the Senior Officer's Course of the State Department's Foreign Service Institute.

In 1961, the Center was host to five Soviet "scientists" at a meeting arranged by Harrison Brown of the Center's staff and Amrom Katz of the RAND Corporation, the U. S. Air Force's main "think factory." At the meeting, there was a discussion of disarmament problems and scientific cooperation. The bases of the discussion were papers prepared by Brown and Millis, two devotees of disarmament and coexistence.

Excursions into the realm of international relations, which properly belong in the province of the nation's Executive, have not been unusual for the Center's personnel. One of the most celebrated instances was a trip taken to Hanoi by the Center's board chairman Harry Ashmore and William C. Baggs, Florida newspaper publisher and a Fund director. Baggs and Ashmore visited with Ho chi Minh and invited the Communist leader of North Vietnam to visit the Center's second *Pacem in Terris* convocation, being held at Geneva, Switzerland. (Ashmore returned from Hanoi describing Ho chi Minh as "a man of great charm, great sophistication, great intelligence . . . quite outgoing, quite frank.) The Center's first *Pacem in Terris* convocation was held at New York City. Both convocations were nothing short of a viciously anti-American seminar whose main theme was to extort peace at any price from the United States.

Ostensibly, both convocations were to be inspired by the principles enunciated in Pope John XXIII's encyclical *Pacem in Terris.* But, in reality, the encyclical was sacrilegiously distorted or ignored by the speakers.

At the first convocation, held in 1965, American peaceniks were very much in evidence: Steve Allen, Eugene Burdick, Grenville Clark, John Cogley, Norman Cousins, James Farmer, Jerome Frank, Paul Hoffman, H. Stuart Hughes, Robert M. Hutchins, Philip Jessup, George F. Kennan, Edward Lamb, Henry Luce, Marya Mannes, Walter Millis, Hans Morgenthau, Fred Warner Neal, James G. Patton, Linus Pauling, Gerard Piel, Elmo Roper, Stanley K. Sheinbaum, Abram Chayes, George N. Shuster, Bayard Rustin, Harold Stassen, Paul Tillich, and Dagmar Wilson. Foreign leftists included Abba Eban of Israel, N. N. Inozemtsev and M. D. Millionshchikov of the Soviet Union, Yevgenyi Zhukov of Communist Hungary, Arnold Toynbee and Barbara Ward of Britain, Paul-Henri Spaak of Belgium, Adam Schaff of Communist Poland, and Vida Tomsic of Communist Yugoslavia. Although they appeared as private citizens, American governmental leaders lent their prestige to the gathering. From the U. S. Supreme Court came Chief Justice Earl Warren and Associate Justice William O. Douglas. The Executive Department was represented by Vice President Hubert Humphrey and Ambassador Adlai Stevenson. The Congress was represented by Senators J. William Fulbright, George McGovern, Claiborne Pell, and Eugene McCarthy, and Representative William Fitts Ryan.

The chairman of the convocation was the Center's President Hutchins who, at the outset, reminded those in attendance that it was "a political meeting." The strange bedfellows in the political meeting then listened to a series of speeches extolling the United Nations, pleading for disarmament, and urging "coexistence." Time and time again, the bogey of nuclear warfare punctuated peacenik platitudes. Brickbats were reserved for the United States but the Communist world emerged unscathed.

In the spring of 1966, Robert M. Hutchins presided over a planning session for a second *Pacem in Terris* convocation. Among the planners were Justice William O. Douglas; N. N. Inozemtsev, a director of the Soviet Union's Academy of Sciences and a consultant to the Center for the Study of Democratic Institutions; and, Professor Lachs of Communist Poland. The planning group agreed unanimously "that this should be a convocation aimed at bridging gaps, especially between the United States and the [Communist] People's Republic of China."

The second Center-sponsored *Pacem in Terris* meeting was held in May, 1967 at Geneva, Switzerland. For reasons which were never revealed, most Communist regimes boycotted this second convocation. Notable exceptions were East Germany and Communist Poland.

Americans who went to Geneva included William O. Douglas, J. William Fulbright, Bishop James Pike, Marya Mannes, Martin Luther King Jr., James Roosevelt, Linus Pauling, John Kenneth Galbraith, Robert Hutchins, and Harry Ashmore.

Miss Mannes, then a columnist for *McCall's* magazine, blasted the United States for its "brutal" policy in Vietnam. She *demanded* "the end of bombing" as the "one act of trust which could open the only avenue to reason and peace." (Miss Mannes, who had been a writer for *Vogue, Glamour,* and *The Reporter* magazines, became a monthly columnist for the *New York Times* in 1967.)

Harry Ashmore, the Center's board chairman, paid tribute to Ho chi Minh: "There is nobody else in the world today in any country who seems to provide a similar blend of spiritual and political power."

Justice Douglas went out of his way to criticize Chaing Kai-shek and Free China but heaped praises on Nikita Khrushchev and Ho chi Minh. And for his pro-Communist pièce de résistance he compared America's Revolution of 1776 to the Bolshevik Revolution of 1917.

Senator Fulbright contributed his ritualistic and dovish criticism of U. S. involvement in the Vietnam War and urged that the UN's Security Council call for a cessation of U. S. bombings of North Vietnam. He was especially regretful that the Soviet Union had not sent delegates to the convocation. He wanted to tell them that the Soviet Union should take the initiative in raising the Vietnam issue in the Security Council. Martin Luther King joined delegates from Cambodia and Communist

Poland in a three-pronged attack upon the United States participation in the Vietnam War. He called upon the convocation's delegates to ask the United States to end the bombing of North Vietnam and to declare a cease-fire.

Linus Pauling demanded an end of the U. S. bombings of North Vietnam and condemned the United States for "the murder of tens of thousands, hundreds of thousands of men, women and children in the war in Vietnam." According to Pauling, the United States was guilty of "carrying on a cruel and vicious attack on a poor, small, weak people on the other side of the world."

At the end of the four-day convocation, Robert Hutchins announced that the delegation of more than three hundred had adopted an eleven-point manifesto: (1) The United Nations should be strengthened and made more independent; (2) Membership of the United Nations must be made more universal; (3) The Vietnam War, at best, is a mistake; (4) All southeast Asia must be neutralized; (5) The Cold War must be ended and the myths of Communist conspiracy and capitalistic imperialism must be seriously modified if not abandoned; (6) Racial discrimination is intolerable; (7) Aid must be given to developing countries; (8) Present terms of trade are intolerable for developing countries; (9) No military solutions are adequate for present day problems; (10) No national solutions are adequate for present day problems; (11) Coexistence is a necessary but not sufficient condition for human life.

Aside from the work of Hutchins and Ashmore, the Center has been well-publicized through the efforts of its vice-president W. H. "Ping" Ferry. Ferry is one of the Center's leading advocates of compulsory controls over all American corporations by national planning "accomplished by statute, not by executive order," and with provisions for enforcement. He has hopes that the presidential cabinet will one day include a national planning agent.

In 1962, Ferry attracted a great deal of notoriety when he spoke at a Democratic Party Conference and used the occasion to slander and blast the FBI and its director J. Edgar Hoover. In the same speech he downgraded any threats from the Communist conspiracy or from Communist espionage. The remarks were so incredibly bad that Attorney General Robert Kennedy, on behalf of the Democrats, apologized for Ferry's display of rudeness and stupidity.

Another of the Center's luminaries, Richard Lichtman, complemented Vice President Ferry's antagonism toward business. In "Toward

Community: A Criticism of Contemporary Capitalism," Lichtman issued a routine Marxian attack upon capitalism coupled with a call for a Marxian dictatorship in the United States.

To promote the Center's creed of unilateral disarmament and peace at any price, the Center has relied upon the writings of Eugene Burdick, Harvey Wheeler, Walter Millis, Fred Warner Neal, James Real, and Arthur Waskow.

By 1966, the Fund for the Republic declared that its only activity was to support the Center. Coincidentally, in that same year, the Center's headquarters at Santa Barbara, California became the birthplace for the National Conference for New Politics. The NCNP was soon revealed as a classical, united front, third party movement largely controlled by the Communist Party. Also, in 1966, Robert Scheer and Stanley Sheinbaum — both associated with the Center — ran for Congress in California: Sheinbaum on the New Left ticket and Scheer as a "peace" Democrat.

Meanwhile, the Ford Foundation — from which were spawned the Fund and the Center — was changing its leadership. Henry T. Heald after ten years as president gave way to McGeorge Bundy, who had served as a special assistant for national affairs to Presidents John Kennedy and Lyndon Johnson. By this time, the Foundation's trustees, headed by Julius Stratton, included Eugene Black, publisher John Cowles, Benson and Henry Ford, Edwin Land of Polaroid, Roy Larsen of Time, Inc., J. Irwin Miller, and Federal District Court Judge Charles E. Wyzanski Jr.

Under Bundy, the Foundation became obsessed with the Negro "civil rights" problem. In Cleveland, the Congress of Racial Equality was granted $175,000 by the Foundation for a voter registration program that would insure the mayoralty election of Negro Carl Stokes. Other grants were lavished on such agitational groups as the NAACP, the National Urban League, the Anti-Defamation League, the Southern Educational Conference, and various collegiate and religious institutions.

Along with "civil rights," Bundy went all out on poverty and urban "problems." When Walter Reuther began his phony Citizens Crusade against Poverty, the Foundation granted $508,500 to the CCP. Other generous grants went to the American Friends Service Committee, the National Council of Churches, the National Council of Negro Women, the National Committee against Discrimination in Housing, and other organizations which traditionally took a leftwing approach toward society and its real and alleged problems.

In his first two years with the Foundation, Bundy gave $45 million in grants to New York City for its urban "problems." And, under his direction, noncommercial-educational television became a virtual monopoly for Ford Foundation influences. As of September 30, 1967, the Foundation had granted more than $22 million to such television enterprises.

No matter the field, Bundy has seen to it that leftwing institutions and individuals are not neglected: the National Student Association, the London School of Economics, Leroi Jones, Milton Galamison, the Sex Information and Educational Council of the U. S., the Planned Parenthood Federation, the Population Council, the United Nations Association of the U. S., the Institute of International Education, the Council on Foreign Relations, the World Affairs Council, the Carnegie Endowment for International Peace, the Committee for Economic Development, American Assembly, the Social Science Research Council, the National Planning Association, the Atlantic Institute, the League of Women Voters, the African-American Institute, and hundreds of other organizations in the U. S. and more than eighty other nations.

In early 1969, Bundy appeared before the House Ways and Means Committee which was investigating tax-exempt foundations. Some of the committee's members questioned Bundy as to the Foundation's involvement in politics. Mr. Bundy, for at least four hours, denied that the Foundation was political or involved in politics.

FOREIGN POLICY ASSOCIATION
"HEADLINE SERIES"
FOREIGN POLICY BULLETIN
WORLD AFFAIRS COUNCILS
INTERNATIONAL RELATIONS CLUBS
WORLD AFFAIRS CENTER
GREAT DECISIONS PROGRAMS

In 1918, the League of Free Nations was founded. It was just one of the many organizations established in that era by the radicals, Socialists, internationalists, and pacifists who were caught up in the excitement of World War II, the Bolshevik Revolution, and Woodrow Wilson's international messianism.

In 1921, the League of Free Nations became the Foreign Policy

Association and, in 1928, the FPA was incorporated in New York as an educational and nonpartisan organization concerned with world affairs.

Once the FPA was incorporated, it embarked upon its first major project: propagandizing for United States diplomatic recognition of the Soviet Union. The propaganda appeared in pamphlets prepared by Vera Micheles Dean who spent more than thirty years making the FPA and its publications highly effective pro-Communist vehicles. Matthew Woll, vice president of the American Federation of Labor, who opposed recognition of the Soviet Union, wrote of Dean's efforts: "These pamphlets are not merely partisan in adopting the Soviet view on this question but by wholly repressing important sections of the U. S. documents quoted, and by giving other sections out of their context, have misrepresented our State Dept. policy to the point of presenting it as being the very reverse of what it actually is."

The chairman of the FPA, from 1919 until 1933, was James G. McDonald who, in 1949, became the first United States Ambassador to Israel. In his tenure as FPA's chairman, McDonald professed ignorance of Red activities in America but, at the same time, insisted that the Soviet Union was searching for peace. To those who opposed recognition of the Soviet Union, McDonald explained that the Soviet government's peaceful "intentions are hampered frequently by the activities of the Russian Communist Party and the Third International neither of which the government has power to control" — all of which was nothing less than the line handed out by the Kremlin to persuade dupes all over the world that the Party, the International, and the Soviet government were separate entities, instead of a united force run by Stalin.

The FPA's pro-Communist line, even in the first few years, had many outlets: radio programs, lectures, study and discussion groups, and luncheon meetings. But the most durable outlets were the pamphlets, prepared under the editorial direction of Vera Dean, and which — under the name Headline Series — became staple reference works in public libraries and school libraries. Early contributors to the pamphlet series included John Dewey, Morris Hillquit, George Soule, Paul Douglas, Maurice Hindus, William E. Borah, Monsignor John A. Ryan, Max Eastman, Harry Gideonse, and George H. Blakeslee — all of whom were notorious radicals. (The officers of the FPA in that era were equally radical. They included Jane Addams, Bishop Francis J. McConnell, Stephen P. Duggan, Lillian Wald, Francis Biddle, Paul Kellogg, and Bruce Bliven.)

Other publications of the FPA have been the periodical "Reports," *Intercom,* and the *Foreign Policy Association Bulletin.* Readers of these publications were treated to the pro-Communist and/or anti-anti-Communist writings of such conspicuously leftist "experts" as: Max Lerner, Senators Jacob Javits and Joseph Clark, Walter Lippmann, Emil Lengyel, Herbert Matthews, James Warburg, Henry Steele Commager, Edwin O. Reischauer, Joseph Harsch, Oliver Edmund Clubb, C. L. Sulzberger, William Clayton, Nathaniel Peffer, Thomas A. Bisson, Maxwell Stewart, John K. Fairbank, Chester Bowles, Arthur M. Schlesinger Jr., Brooks Emeny, Ernest Gross, Eustace Seligman, and Peggy Durdin. Other leftists whose writings were promoted by the FPA's publications included Harry and Bonaro Overstreet, Edgar Faure, Doak Barnett, Richard Butwell, Amry Vandenbosch, Richard Wright, E. Franklin Frazier, Isaac Deutscher, Louis Fischer, and Telford Taylor.

The overwhelming presence of leftists in the pages of FPA literature was not accidental. It was attributable in almost totality to the determined efforts of Vera Micheles Dean.

Two competent observers — a decade apart — analyzed Dean's work. Shepard Marley in "Mrs. Dean's Foreign Policy Lobby," *Plain Talk,* November, 1946, described Dean as supervising "a factory for propaganda to appease the Soviet Union and to apologize for its expansion in all directions." Marley found a persistent scheme in Dean's personal writings or in those of her contributing authors: "(1) Point out that the Soviet Union is being criticized for some action. (2) Admit that the action is (slightly) 'deplorable.' (3) Show that Russia is after all not much to blame for what it has done, in view of the lack of 'understanding' between it and the West. (4) Show that the 'Western Allies' have committed mistakes too. (5) Philosophize about such chicanery being quite common in international affairs. (6) Point out that all such misconduct must be eliminated by strengthening the Big Three and the United Nations. (Occasionally step No. 2 is omitted.)" [In the 1930's, the FPA-Dean slavish affection for the Soviet Union had been complemented by devotion to the League of Nations.]

William Henry Chamberlin, in "Anti-anti-Communism: A Ford Investment," *National Review,* April 11, 1956, wrote: "The genus anti-anti-Communist has these eight distinctive traits: (1) A strong American guilt complex; (2) A conviction that, while Communism is undesirable, the real enemy is militant anti-Communism; (3) Extreme deference to the views of Nehru and other 'uncommitted' and unfriendly neutrals;

(4) A desire to lean heavily, in difficult situations, on that weak reed, the UN; (5) As regards Soviet Communism, an attitude of minimizing its threat to U. S. security; (6) A pathological fear of losing alleged friends in Europe and Asia by any strong, clear-cut action against Communist expansion; (7) A belief that the American taxpayer owes a living to the 'underprivileged' nations of the world; (8) A conviction that only old-fashioned prejudice accounts for our objections to admitting Red China to the United Nations.

"A careful study of FPA literature and of the writings of Mrs. Dean shows a pattern compounded of the foregoing ideas, repeating itself again and again, whether the subject under discussion is resistance to Communist aggression in Korea, support of the Chinese Nationalist Government in Formosa, rearming of West Germany, or setting up American air and naval bases in Spain."

The FPA did not enjoy a monopoly on the services of the pro-Communist, anti-anti-Communist "experts" who were under the editorial direction of Vera Dean. The same individuals were involved with the Communist-controlled Institute of Pacific Relations or were writing pamphlets for Maxwell Stewart's Public Affairs Institute or were active in one way or another with any number of Communist fronts and leftwing-pacifist groups.

The FPA's principal sources of finances were the Carnegie Endowment for International Peace, the Rockefeller Foundation, and – in later years – the Ford Foundation's Fund for the Republic. And with such support the FPA was not content to be a mere publishing house. Parallel to its pamphleteering efforts, the FPA has conducted its World Affairs Councils, scattered in cities across the nation.

The World Affairs Council, which describes itself as "a non-partisan, non-profit organization which promotes international understanding through education," has boasted of its affiliation with sixteen different governmental agencies. Over the years, the WAC has worked in cooperation with the State Department, the American Assembly, the American Friends Service Committee, the United World Federalists, the American Veterans Committee, the Women's International League for Peace and Freedom, and other one-world, leftwing, and pacifist groups.

The most impressive effort of the WAC is its "diplomats-off-the-record" series, wherein WAC members and their guests listen to ambassadors and other prominent leaders of foreign nations speak on world affairs. There are also luncheon meetings and regional conferences where the WAC members may hear such distinguished leftwingers as Dean Rusk, Doak Barnett, Grayson Kirk, Philip Mosely, Paul Hoffman, Gerard Piel, Henry A. Kissinger, Adrain Fisher, and Robert Scalapino. And, in some cities, the WAC has an annual meeting addressed by noted foreign correspondents who report on the state of world affairs.

A major work of the WAC is propagandizing for the United Nations. The WAC sponsors tours for students and adults to the United Nations headquarters in New York. Model United Nations assemblies and United Nations essay contests in various school programs are under the aegis of the WAC. Also, on behalf of the UN, the WAC conducts seminars for teachers, conferences for college and high school students, and lecture series for junior high school students. The local offices of the WAC also distribute State Department and United Nations publications and, of course, the output of the Foreign Policy Association.

In 1954, the Foreign Policy Association extended its influence over the nation's students by absorbing the International Relations Clubs on over six hundred college campuses. The Clubs had been founded and subsidized by the Carnegie Endowment for International Peace. Members of the Clubs received free literature from the Carnegie Endowment including various publications of the Institute of Pacific Relations, the American-Russian Institute, and the Foreign Policy Association. Through this massive pro-Communist brainwashing effort, the International Relations Club members were given the writings of such notorious leftists as Owen Lattimore, Thomas A. Bisson, Corliss Lamont, Evans Clark, Ruth Benedict, Nathaniel Peffer, and Alexander Werth. (Needless to say, no foundation or any other institution has ever given members of the International Relations Clubs literature to offset the pro-Communist materials from the leftist network of the FPA, the Institute of Pacific Relations, and the other leftwing groups — including the State Department and the United Nations — which cooperate with the tax-exempt foundations that are determined to push anti-Americanism and pro-Communism on every college campus in the country.)

In 1957, the Foreign Policy Association — in cooperation with the Carnegie Endowment — established the World Affairs Center in New York City. This project was financed by the Carnegie Endowment, the Ford Foundation, the Rockefeller Brothers Fund, the A. W. Mellon Educational and Charitable Trust, and the Lilly Endowment. The announced purpose of the Center was "to serve as a central point to which anyone can turn for accurate information on international matters ... [and] to serve as a central point to which anyone can turn for information about what citizens are doing in world affairs. And, most important, to help bring about better communication among organizations and individuals concerned with world affairs, to encourage constructive activity, and to contribute to raising the level of effective and responsible non-government engagement in this field." The real purpose of the Center, however, was indicated by its address: United Nations Plaza. And, at the World Affairs Center, day-long briefings were given on the United Nations and world affairs to brainwashing victims, including corporation executives, educators, civic leaders, and journalists. In 1960, the World Affairs Center was merged with the Foreign Policy Association and the "briefings" are now held at the FPA-WAC headquarters in New York City.

In 1955, the FPA began its most ambitious and probably its most successful project: Great Decisions — an annual eight-week study and discussion program in which "eight critical foreign policy problems facing the American people" are reviewed. Thousands of small informal groups in communities throughout the nation participate in the study-dicussion programs. The participants are furnished "fact sheet kits" by the Foreign Policy Association-World Affairs Center-World Affairs Councils complex. The "fact sheet kits" reflect the FPA's traditional obeisance to pro-Communism, pacifism, internationalism, anti-anti-Communism, and anti-Americanism.

The Great Decisions have received tremendous support from hundreds of newspapers which provide free promotional support as well as editorial endorsement. The Mutual Broadcasting System has offered a series of eight radio programs, prepared at Wayne State University, to its more than five hundred affiliated states. Hundreds of commercial and educational television channels have provided free time for the study-discussion series. United Press International, in over one hundred newspapers, has provided an eight-part series on Great Decisions each year. The program has even reached into secondary schools and, in 1967, more than a quarter of a million high school children participated in Great Decisions.

In effect, the Great Decisions is the most widely publicized and fastest growing study-discussion group in existence. It all means that, through the facilities of newspapers, radio, television, and classrooms, millions of Americans are being propagandized to discredit anti-

Communism and to minimize the threat of Communism. They are swamped with pro-United Nations, pro-internationalist, pro-State Department literature from the same breed of "experts" in the Foreign Policy Association who, over the years, have made heroes of Stalin, Khrushchev, Krishna Menon, Sukarno, Ben Bella, Castro, Tito, Mao Tse-tung, and Ho chi Minh. It is little wonder that Great Decisions has been boosted by the Communists in *The Worker* and *People's World*.

The influence of the Foreign Policy Association complex is immeasurable. Its officials have tangible ties with the largest foundations, the largest corporations (especially those active in international trade), and the largest universities and colleges. They have been in the highest echelons of the State Department. They have been prominent in foreign "aid" programs, in disarmament movements, in diplomatic posts, in state and municipal governments, in medicine, law, and science, in political and semi-political groups, in the clergy, and in service organizations.

Such well known members of the Liberal Establishment as Henry Cabot Lodge, Arthur Goldberg, Christian Herter Sr. and Jr., Samuel P. Hayes, Victor Reuther, Joseph E. Johnson, James B. Conant, Anna Lord Strauss, Walter H. Wheeler Jr., Andrew Cordier, Morris Abram, Robert Bowie, Ellsworth Bunker, Dexter Perkins, John Richardson Jr., Francis O. Wilcox, and Arthur K. Watson have lent their prestige to the FPA complex in one way or another. The presence of these national figures has undoubtedly attracted many individuals on a community level to the support of the FPA's World Affairs Councils. It defies credibility that even a large minority of those individuals who sponsor local World Affairs Councils are ideologically sympathetic to the half-century anti-Americanism program of the Foreign Policy Association. Many of the local individuals undoubtedly believe that they are contributing to a worthwhile, educational dialogue on foreign affairs and they would be shocked out of their dupery and do-goodism if they realized that the FPA, in all its facets, has always loaded the deck against the best interests of the United States and the free world.

FREEDOM HOUSE

In the *New York Times* of August 24, 1966, Barnard L. Collier began his news item as follows: "Just 37 days before the Japanese bombed Pearl Harbor and plunged the United States into World War II, Freedom House was established in New York.

"It was George Field's idea. Under one roof would go most of the major organizations that had concluded that the United States participation in the war was right, good and inevitable.

"The retirement of Mr. Field after nearly 25 years as executive director of Freedom House was announced yesterday . . . .

"Freedom House, of course, is no longer concerned with being an answer to Hitler's Braunhaus in Munich. But it is still dedicated to the ideas in its original articles of incorporation: ' . . . resisting the totalitarian movement now threatening civilization . . . in terms of the aspirations of all peoples for a world of freedom, peace and security; to promote the concrete application of the principles of freedom and democracy in the everyday affairs of the U. S. A., governmental and otherwise, so that by sacrifice, intelligence and justice this country can be an example to both the present and post-war world of democracy at its best . . . .'

"It was easy to operate Freedom House during the war, Mr. Field says, 'because we were practically the civilian spokesman against totalitarianism.'

"Since then, with nothing so black and white anymore, Freedom House has steered a course that is described by Mr. Field as 'centerist' — always well reasoned, now and then in advance of the times, seldom at odds with the Government but constantly constructively critical.

"That is what Mr. Field is like, too.

"'He always remained behind the scenes,' said Roscoe Drummond, the columnist, who is also the chairman of the board of trustees. 'He is the one who made things work. If we wanted money or an important "name" to back up our policy statements, we'd call on George and he'd do it. He was the group's careful guiding force.'"

There is no doubt that George Field enjoyed a successful and interesting twenty-five year tenure as the executive director of the prestigious Freedom House. His previous career, however, was equally interesting. He was born in New York City. He attended evening classes for a few semesters at New York University. From 1929 until 1932, he was in the advertising business. From 1932 until 1936, he worked in radio publicity. In 1936, at the age of thirty-two, he was chairman of the board of the Rand School of Social Science in New York City. (The Rand School was established in 1906. It was originally owned by the American Socialist Society and was heavily financed for many years by the Garland Fund, which was a major source for financing Communist

Party enterprises. In 1933, when the Rand School was in financial distress, the Socialist Party and fellow travelers came to its rescue. By the time George Field became Rand's chairman of the board, the Socialist Party had saved the school which catered not only to Socialists but also to assorted radicals of the left.)

In 1937, Field wrote the *American Labor Party Political Handbook* for Fiorello La Guardia's mayoralty campaign. (In that same year, the entire membership of the Communist Party had been instructed to join the American Labor Party.) Also, in 1937, Field began a three-year stint as radio program director for Station WEVD in New York City. (WEVD, named in honor of Victor E. Debs, one of America's earliest Bolsheviks, was founded in 1927 by the Socialist Party. The Station was nothing less than a propaganda outlet for Communists, Socialists, and other radicals of the left, including the grande dame of the Left, Eleanor Roosevelt.)

From 1938 until 1963, Field was the director of WEVD's University of the Air, a program that presented a forum for the most extreme leftists from political, labor, and educational circles. And WEVD's audience was barraged by Communist and Socialist propaganda in the guise of lectures, panel discussions, and dramas. The Station lived up to its original purpose "to champion the cause of liberty and social justice in the broad and liberal spirit of Eugene V. Debs," who, in an address to a Socialist Party gathering, has said: "I am going to speak to you as a Socialist, as a Revolutionist, and as a Bolshevist, if you please."

In 1940 and 1941, aside from his duties with WEVD, George Field was secretary of the Committee to Defend America by Aiding Allies, one of the many interventionist, warmongering groups that arose in that era. And, it was in this period when he helped to found Freedom House and began his long career as its executive director.

According to its promotional literature: "The positive position of Freedom House, conveyed by its name, is necessarily coupled with a strong anti-Communist posture. Since it is *for* freedom, it is *against* tyranny. Since it is *for* representative democracy, it is *against* all kinds of dictatorship. And it regards aggressive dictatorships as the greatest threat to peace." To make the "strong anti-Communist posture" viable, Freedom House has had on its board of trustees what some overly charitable critics would describe as the anti-Communist left. In reality, George Field and his successor Leonard Sussman have been surrounded by Socialists, Communist fronters, pacifists, ban-the-bomb advocates, architects of appeasement, vigorous enemies of anti-Communist investigations, internationalists and inveterate anti-anti-Communists. The trustees have been generally drawn from the ranks of liberal Democrats, holding strong ties with such leftwing groups as Americans for Democratic Action, the Council on Foreign Relations, the National Committee for an Effective Congress, the Anti-Defamation League and the League for Industrial Democracy. The few Republicans who have been on the Freedom House board have been of the "modern Republican" group which coalesced during the Eisenhower Administration. There may have been, in a few instances, an occasional political innocent but, for the most part, the individuals in Freedom House have been interlocking stalwarts of the Leftist Establishment: Whitney North Seymour, Harry Gideonse, Leo Cherne, Roscoe Drummond, Rex Stout, Irving Brown, Christopher Emmet, Arthur J. Goldsmith, Paul Hoffman, Jacob Javits, J. M. Kaplan, Maxwell Kriendler, John Lindsay, Edgar Ansel Mowrer, Bonaro Overstreet, Whitelaw Reid, Mrs. Kermit Roosevelt, Elmo Roper, Eric Sevareid, Roy Wilkins, James A. Pike, Spyros Skouras, Ralph Bunche, Herbert Agar, Zbigniew Brzezinski, Daniel Moynihan, Richard N. Gardner and Wendell Willkie.

One of Freedom House's practices is to present an annual Freedom Award. In not a single instance has the award been given to any individual who could be judged in any other light than as an anti-anti-Communist. The recipients of the award have included Harry S. Truman, Dwight Eisenhower, Lyndon B. Johnson, Dean Acheson, George C. Marshall, Lucius Clay, Winston Churchill, Jean Monnet, Pablo Casals, James B. Conant, Arthur H. Vandenberg, David E. Lilienthal, Paul Hoffman, Willy Brandt, Walter Lippmann, Paul H. Douglas, Roy Wilkins, Paul-Henry Spaak, Luis Muñoz-Marín, Edward R. Murrow, George Kennan, Franklin D. Roosevelt, and Sumner Welles.

In 1959, a Freedom House Bookshelf program was instituted. Books selected by a committee ("America's foremost men of letters, scholars, composers, artists, historians and social scientists") are sent "to leaders and scholars in Africa, Asia and Latin America selected with the help of responsible American agencies operating in those areas."

The treasurer of the Bookshelf has been Rex Stout whose leftism does not seem to have mellowed since the days when he was one of the original publishing team of *New Masses,* a Communist weekly. The Bookshelf Committee has been comprised of the most brazen-faced leftists in the literary and academic worlds: Archibald MacLeish,

Gordon Allport, Max Lerner, Cass Canfield, Bennett Cerf, Henry Steele Commager, James B. Conant, Norman Cousins, Foster Rhea Dulles, Clifton Fadiman, Buell Gallagher, Oscar Handlin, Granville Hicks, Howard Mumford Jones, Grayson Kirk, the Arthur Schlesingers, Junior and Senior, Upton Sinclair, Elmer Rice, Saul Padover, Allan Nevins, Samuel Eliot Morison, Ashley Montagu, Erich Fromm and William L. Langer. Also, aiding in selection of "the good books that make men's hearts catch fire," have been such other leftists as Ben Shahn, Edward R. Murrow, William Benton, Chester Bowles, Erwin Canham, Leo Cherne, Aaron Copland, William O. Douglas, and Roscoe Drummond.

By the standards of the Bookshelf Committee, "the writings of the foremost spokesmen of freedom" include works by committee members Max Lerner, Arthur M. Schlesinger Jr., Ashley Montagu, Bonaro Overstreet (in collaboration with her fellow-traveling husband), and Saul Padover. Other recommended leftwing authors include Carl Sandburg, J. Kenneth Galbraith, Ruth Benedict, Theodore Draper, and the Yugoslav Communist Milovan Djilas. *Profiles in Courage* by John F. Kennedy is distributed by the Bookshelf Committee, but none of Herbert Hoover's or Douglas MacArthur's works are so favored. And the Freedom House's self-proclaimed "strong anti-Communist posture" evidently does not provide for its Bookshelf Committee to distribute a single volume of any sort that deals with the exposures of Communist espionage and subversion in the United States or recent Communist aggression in any part of the world.

At the close of every year, Freedom House issues a report on the gains and losses of freedom throughout the world. The report receives generous publicity in the press. As might be expected, the evaluation does not approach the full truth about Communist advances. And, in recent years, "freedom" in the United States is studied only from the perspective of so-called civil rights and, by Freedom House's standards, freedom gains only if racist agitators have been successful. Also, in recent years, Freedom House has devoted a great deal of attention to the Vietnam War and, in the annual progress reports, freedom has made gains as long as the Johnson Administration has clung to a no-win policy. (A military victory by the United States and its allies in Vietnam would be a blow to freedom, according to Freedom House.)

[AMERICAN] INSTITUTE OF PACIFIC RELATIONS

In 1925 the Institute of Pacific Relations was established as an association of national councils which were to cooperate in a program of research, publications, and conferences. The program came to be directed by a Pacific Council in which each national council was represented. The administration of the program was conducted by an international secretariat in New York City.

As of 1950, the IPR included national councils from the United States (AIPR), Australia, Canada, France, India, Britain, Japan, New Zealand, Pakistan, and The Philippines. (Between 1934 and 1939, the Soviet Union had a member-council. Also, at other times in its history, the IPR has included councils from China, The Netherlands, and Indonesia.)

From 1925 until 1950, the IPR received 77 per cent of its finances from American foundations and the American Institute of Pacific Relations (AIPR). In turn, the AIPR received 50 per cent of its financial support from the Rockefeller Foundation, the Carnegie Corporation, and the Carnegie Endowment.

As of 1950, the major institutional contributors — aside from the Rockefeller and Carnegie foundations — to the AIPR included: Standard-Vacuum Oil; International General Electric; National City Bank; Chase National Bank; Bankers Trust Company; International Business Machines; International Telephone and Telegraph; Electric Bond and Share Company; Rockefeller Brothers Fund; Time, Incorporated; J. P. Morgan Company; Studebaker Corporation; Reader's Digest; American President Lines; Alexander & Baldwin; American Trust Company; Matson Steamship Lines; Bank of Hawaii; Pan American Airways; Bank of America; Firestone Tire and Rubber; Shell Oil; Wilbur Ellis Company; American Foreign Power Company; and, National Cash Register. Individual major contributors included Juan Trippe, Henry Luce, Mrs. Thomas W. Lamont, Frances Bolton, Arthur Dean, Gerard Swope, and Joseph E. Davies. (In earlier years, individual major contributors included Frederick Vanderbilt Field and Thomas W. Lamont.)

Ostensibly, the AIPR, whose membership fluctuated between 1200 and 1800, was devoted to research and discussion of those economic, social, and political problems of the Pacific and the southern and eastern parts of Asia pertinent to the interests of the United States. In reality, the AIPR waged a far-reaching campaign to promote the interests of international Communism in the Pacific and in Asia. The main features of the campaign included attacks upon the Chiang Kai-shek regime in China, the independent Republic of South Korea, and the imperial family of Japan.

Through its members, staff, publications, and close collaborators, the AIPR promoted its pro-Communist campaign in the White House, the State Department, and other departments and agencies of the federal government. So close were the ties between the AIPR and the federal government that AIPR officials were asked to make personnel recommendations for positions in the State Department and other departments and agencies.

In the 1930's and 1940's, the AIPR enjoyed a virtual monopoly in popular magazine articles, published books (including textbooks), and pamphlets devoted to the Far East. (During World War II, the orientation programs of the armed forces were literally saturated with AIPR pamphlets.)

In 1952, the Senate Internal Security Subcommittee reported that, from 1945 until 1950, "the IPR stalwarts constituted for the American reading public during those years a virtual screening and censorship board with respect to books on the Far East and the Pacific . . . [and] a major preoccupation of the reviewers was the launching of each other's books." The Subcommittee's judgment was based on a survey of book reviews made by the Legislative Reference Service of the Library of Congress. The survey was made of *New Republic,* the *New York Times, Saturday Review, Nation,* the *New York Herald Tribune,* and other major book review media. The surveyors uncovered 286 reviews written by AIPRers. Almost every book under review had been written by well-known AIPRers and, with one or two exceptions, every book dealt with the Pacific or the Far East. This all meant that the pro-Communist AIPR line was lauded and recommended through the most influential book review sections in America.

The AIPR was not content to promote its line only through its organizational facilities. It maintained a vast interlock with Communist-controlled organizations and publications, including: Allied Labor News Service, *Amerasia,* the American Committee in Aid of Chinese Industrial Cooperatives (Indusco), American Friends of the Chinese People, *China Today,* the American-Russian Institute, the China Aid Council, the Committee for a Democratic Far Eastern Policy, *Far East Spotlight,* Federated Press, Friends of Chinese Democracy, the Japanese-American Committee for Democracy, Russian War Relief, and

Soviet Russia Today. (*Amerasia,* which had been organized under Communist auspices, became the center of a cause célèbre in 1945 when hundreds of classified U. S. government documents were discovered in *Amerasia's* offices. According to the Senate Internal Security Subcommittee, the "IPR family ordinarily treated it [*Amerasia*] as simply another of their own publications ... [and] articles and writers were readily shunted back and forth among [IPR's] *Pacific Affairs,* [IPR's] *Far Eastern Survey* and *Amerasia*.")

In 1951, after five months of preliminary investigation, the Senate Internal Security Subcommittee held hearings on the AIPR. Between July 25, 1951 and June 20, 1952, the SISS heard sixty-six witnesses in one of the most extensive congressional hearings ever held. The SISS sought to determine: "(a) Whether or to what extent the Institute of Pacific Relations was infiltrated and influenced or controlled by agents of the communist world conspiracy; (b) Whether or to what extent these agents and their dupes worked through the Institute into the United States Government to the point where they exerted an influence on United States far eastern policy; and if so, whether and to what extent they still exert such influence; (c) Whether or to what extent these agents and their dupes led or misled American public opinion, particularly with respect to far eastern policy."

During the course of the hearings, the SISS heard sworn testimony in which many IPRers were identified as Communists. They included: Solomon Adler; James S. Allen (Sol Auerbach); Asiaticus (Heinz Moeller, Hans Mueller, or M. G. Shippe); Hilda Austern; Joseph F. and Kathleen Barnes; T. A. Bisson; Evans Carlson; Abraham Chapman (John Arnold); Chen Han-seng (Geoffrey or Raymond D. Brooke); Chi Ch'ao-ting (Hansu Chan or T. B. Lowe); Harriet Levine Chi; Frank V. Coe; Len De Caux; Israel Epstein; John K. Fairbank; Frederick Vanderbilt Field; Julian Friedman; Talitha Gerlach; Kumar Goshal; Alger Hiss; Philip Jaffe (James W. Phillips); Anthony Jenkinson; Benjamin H. Kizer; Corliss Lamont; Olga Lang; Owen Lattimore; William M. Mandel; Kate Mitchell; Harriet L. Moore; E. Herbert Norman; Hotsumi Ozaki; Mildred Price; Lee Pressman; Lawrence K. Rosinger; Helen Schneider; Agnes Smedley; Nym Wales (Mrs. Edgar Snow); Andrew Steiger; Maxwell Stewart; Anna Louise Strong; Ilona Ralf Sues; Daniel Thorner; Mary Van Kleeck; John Carter Vincent; and, Ella Winter. (John K. Fairbank, Julian Friedman, Benjamin Kizer, Corliss Lamont, Owen Lattimore, Kate Mitchell, Maxwell Stewart, and John Carter Vincent have denied, under oath, their alleged membership in the Communist Party.)

Many of the IPRers were identified as collaborators of the Soviet Union's intelligence apparatus (including Solomon Adler, Frank V. Coe, Lauchlin Currie, Laurence Duggan, Israel Epstein, Frederick V. Field, Michael Greenberg, Alger Hiss, Owen Lattimore, Hotsumi Ozaki, Fred Poland, Lee Pressman, Kimikazu Saionji, Agnes Smedley, Guenther Stein, Anna Louise Strong, Victor Vakhontoff, and Harry Dexter White. Only Owen Lattimore, under oath, denied the alleged collaboration.) Many IPRers were identified as writers for Communist Party publications, while others were the subjects of action by an agency of the U. S. government or a foreign non-Communist government on grounds involving loyalty or national security.

The State Department was of special interest to the AIPR where such AIPRers as Dean Rusk, Ralph Bunche, George Catlett Marshall, Esther Brunauer, Oliver Edmund Clubb, Arthur Dean, John Paton Davies, Harlan Cleveland, Robert Barnett, Philip Jessup, Charles Yost, William T. Stone, Edwin O. Reischauer, Sumner Welles, Joseph E. Johnson, Bernard Noble and Haldore Hanson thrived on controversy as they made the IPR line the official foreign policy of the United States.

One of the most prolific publicists for the AIPR was Edgar Snow who, for thirty-five years, has been an ardent apologist and propagandist for Mao Tse-tung. Aside from his articles in IPR publications and his many books, Snow was with the *Saturday Evening Post* from 1942 until 1951 during which time sixty-one of his pro-Communist articles appeared in that magazine.

Other prominent Americans who lent their prestige to the activities of the AIPR included educators Derk Bodde, George S. Counts, Raymond Dennett, James T. Shotwell, William H. Kilpatrick, Isaiah Bowman, Quincy Wright, and Nathaniel Peffer; fellow travelers Marguerite Stewart, Vera Micheles Dean, and Vilhjalmur Stefansson; novelists John Hersey and Pearl Buck; Admiral Harry Yarnell; and, journalists Ernest K. Lindley, Joseph C. Harsch, Walter Lippmann, Edgar Ansel Mowrer, Frank Noyes, and Raymond Gram Swing.

The investigation of the IPR and the AIPR by the Senate Internal Security Subcommittee in 1951-1952 was really inspired by a disgruntled member and official of the AIPR, Alfred Kohlberg. Mr. Kohlberg, a scholarly businessman, became aware in 1940 that AIPR was loaded with Communists on its staff. Then, in 1944, after making a trip to China, Mr. Kohlberg studied every article on the Chinese military and/or political situation published in IPR publications, beginning in 1937. After preparing an eighty-eight-page study of his findings that the publications were presenting thinly veiled Communist propaganda, Mr. Kohlberg urged Edward C. Carter, the Secretary General of the IPR, and all of the AIPR's trustees to clean house. The executive committee of the AIPR summarily rejected Mr. Kohlberg's suggestion. (Arthur Dean, vice chairman of the IPR, assured Mr. Kohlberg that the IPR was "lily-white.") Despite Mr. Kohlberg's strenuous efforts, the situation remained static until 1951. By that time, Mr. Kohlberg's campaign against the Communists in the IPR was so well publicized that the Senate Internal Security Subcommittee naturally gravitated to a thorough investigation.

Seven years after Mr. Kohlberg had made his own thorough study of the IPR, the SISS completed its hearings and offered its conclusions (which bore out Mr. Kohlberg's findings in every particular): "The Institute of Pacific Relations has not maintained the character of an objective, scholarly, and research organization. The IPR has been considered by the American Communist Party and by Soviet officials as an instrument of Communist policy, propaganda and military intelligence. The IPR disseminated and sought to popularize false information including information originating from Soviet and Communist sources.

"A small core of officials and staff members carried the main burden of IPR activities and directed its administration and policies. Members of the small core of officials and staff members who controlled IPR were either Communist or pro-Communist.

"There is no evidence that the large majority of its members supported the IPR for any reason except to advance the professed research and scholarly purposes of the organization. Most members of the IPR, and most members of its Board of Trustees, were inactive and obviously without any influence over the policies of the organization and the conduct of its affairs.

"IPR activities were made possible largely through the financial support of American industrialists, corporations, and foundations, the majority of whom were not familiar with the inner workings of the organization. The effective leadership of the IPR often sought to deceive IPR contributors and supporters as to the true character and activities of the organization. Neither the IPR nor any substantial body of those associated with it as executive officers, trustees or major financial contributors, has ever made any serious and objective investigation of the charges that the IPR was infiltrated by Communists and was used for pro-Communist and pro-Soviet purposes. The names of eminent individuals were by design used as a respectable and impressive screen for the activities of the IPR inner core, and as a defense when such activities came under scrutiny.

"Owen Lattimore was, from some time beginning in the 1930's, a conscious articulate instrument of the Soviet conspiracy. Effective leadership of the IPR had by the end of 1934 established and implemented an official connection with G. N. Voitinski, Chief of the Far Eastern Division of the Communist International. After the establishment of the Soviet Council of IPR, leaders of the American IPR sought and maintained working relationships with Soviet diplomats and officials. The American staff of IPR, though fully apprised that the Soviet Council of IPR was in fact an arm of the Soviet Foreign Office, was simultaneously and secretly instructed to preserve the 'fiction' that the Soviet council was independent. IPR officials testified falsely before the Senate Internal Security Subcommittee concerning the relationships between IPR and the Soviet Union. Owen Lattimore testified falsely before the subcommittee with reference to at least five separate matters that were relevant to the inquiry and substantial in import.

"John Paton Davies, Jr., testified falsely before the subcommittee in denying that he recommended the Central Intelligence Agency employ, utilize and rely upon certain individuals having Communist associations and connections. This matter was relevant to the inquiry and substantial in import.

"The effective leadership of IPR worked consistently to set up actively cooperative and confidential relationships with persons in Government involved in the determination of foreign policy. Over a period of years, John Carter Vincent was the principal fulcrum of IPR pressures and influence in the State Department. It was the continued practice of IPR to seek to place in Government posts both persons associated with IPR and other persons selected by the effective leadership of IPR. The IPR possessed close organic relations with the State Department through interchange of personnel, attendance of State Department officials at IPR conferences, constant exchange of information and social contacts.

"The effective leadership of the IPR used IPR prestige to promote the interests of the Soviet Union in the United States. A group of persons operating within and about the institute of Pacific Relations exerted a substantial influence on United States far eastern policy. The IPR was a vehicle used by the Communists to orientate American far eastern policies toward Communist objectives.

"A group of persons associated with the IPR attempted, between 1941 and 1945, to change United States policy so as to accommodate Communist ends and to set the stage for a major United States policy change, favorable to Soviet interests, in 1945. Owen Lattimore and John Carter Vincent were influential in bringing about a change in United States policy in 1945 favorable to the Chinese Communists. During the period 1945-49, persons associated with the Institute of Pacific Relations were instrumental in keeping United States policy on a course favorable to Communist objectives in China. Persons associated with the IPR were influential in 1949 in giving United States far eastern policy a direction that furthered Communist purposes.

"A chief function of the IPR has been to influence United States public opinion. Many of the persons active in and around the IPR, and in particular though not exclusively Owen Lattimore, Edward C. Carter, Frederick V. Field, T. A. Bisson, Lawrence K. Rosinger, and Maxwell Stewart, knowingly and deliberately used the language of books and articles which they wrote or edited in an attempt to influence the American public by means of pro-Communist or pro-Soviet content of such writings. The net effect of IPR activities on United States public opinion has been such as to serve international Communist interests and to affect adversely the interests of the United States."

The IPR did not collapse once the SISS had made its findings known. As late as 1960, the IPR was advertising itself as "a non-partisan, unofficial organization devoted to the study of contemporary Asian problems. It has no axe to grind, and takes no stand on issues of public policy." But, after the SISS hearings, the IPR — as a viable institution — was an embarrassment to those who had been caught red-handed in the midst of international Communist conspirators. Finally, in 1961, the death of the IPR in the United States occurred when it was announced that, as of March, 1961, IPR publications would be distributed from the University of British Columbia in Vancouver, Canada. Of course, the pro-Communist line has lived on in federal policy-making positions as IPR alumni are as much in evidence in the Nixon Administration as they have been in every administration during the past four decades.

LEAGUE FOR INDUSTRIAL DEMOCRACY
INTERCOLLEGIATE SOCIALIST SOCIETY
STUDENT LEAGUE FOR INDUSTRIAL DEMOCRACY
STUDENTS FOR A DEMOCRATIC SOCIETY

On September 12, 1905, about one hundred men and women met at Peck's Restaurant in New York City. They had answered a call "by ten prominent persons for the purpose of promoting an intelligent interest in socialism among college men and women, graduate and undergraduate, through the formation of study clubs in the colleges and universities, and the encouraging of all legitimate endeavors to awaken an interest in socialism among the educated men and women of the country. The signers of this call were: Oscar Lovell Triggs, Thomas Wentworth Higginson, Charlotte Perkins Gilman, Clarence S. Darrow, William English Walling, J. G. Phelps Stokes, B. O. Flower, Leonard O. Abbott, Jack London and Upton Sinclair." (Mina Weisenberg, *The LID: 50 Years of Democratic Education – 1905-1955.*)

At the meeting there was established the Intercollegiate Socialist Society. The first president of the ISS was Jack London, the novelist, who traveled to campuses in 1906 in order to establish collegiate chapters of the new organization.

The first campus chapters of the ISS were formed in 1905 at Columbia University and Wesleyan University by William M. Feigenbaum and Harry Laidler, respectively. (Laidler, who had been raised by his uncle, Theodore Atworth, a Socialist, had attended the American Socialist College in 1904 and 1905. At the organizational meeting of the ISS, Laidler was elected as the only student member of the executive committee. He was an executive director of the ISS from 1914 until 1956. His co-executive director during most of that period was Norman Thomas, the Socialist Party leader.) In 1906, ISS chapters were formed at Yale and Harvard. (Charter members of the Harvard chapter, which was called the Harvard Socialist Club, included Arthur N. Holcombe, Kenneth Macgowan, Heywood Broun, and Walter Lippmann. Lippmann later explained what motivated the young Socialists: "The only evil we really fear is blind ignorance. In a general way our object was to make reactionaries, standpatters; standpatters, conservative liberals; conservative liberals and liberals, radicals; and radicals, Socialists. In other words, we tried to move everyone up a peg.") Other early chapters were organized at Princeton University, Amherst College, the University of Pittsburgh, Barnard College, the University of Michigan, and Cornell University. And, by 1917, largely through the work of Laidler, there were sixty chapters with a total membership of twelve hundred on campuses and one thousand in alumni chapters.

In 1908, the publishing efforts of the ISS began on a modest scale with a quarterly Bulletin, devoted mostly to news of chapters' activities. Then, in 1913, the Bulletin became the *Intercollegiate Socialist*. Contributors to the *Intercollegiate Socialist* included such renowned Fabian Socialists as Norman Angell, Keir Hardie, Ramsay MacDonald, George Bernard Shaw and Beatrice and Sidney Webb from Great Britain, and American radicals such as Paul Douglas, Morris Hillquit, Alexander Trachtenberg and Eugene V. Debs. In 1919, the ISS became a little more ambitious by replacing the *Intercollegiate Socialist* with a monthly, the *Socialist Review*. The new publication lasted only eighteen months but, even in that brief span, it served as a showcase for some of the leading radicals of the era: Harry Elmer Barnes, Lewis Gannett, Norman Thomas, Harold Laski, Charles Steinmetz, Harry Overstreet, Stuart Chase, Abraham J. Muste, Evans Clark, and Clark's wife, Freda Kirchwey.

During World War I, the ISS experienced somewhat of a decline, especially on the campuses, as membership and activities were reduced. Socialists, at home and abroad, had quarreled among themselves over the question of American participation in the war. Further internecine differences arose when American Socialists could not decide how much support they should give to the Bolshevik Revolution in Russia. Some of the American Socialists were dismayed that the Russians were using the terms "Communist" and "Socialist" interchangeably. And there was little doubt that the term "Socialist" had fallen into disfavor since so many observers of the political scene were equating Socialism with the most extreme types of radicalism.

The flagging fortunes of the ISS called for drastic measures in the post-war period. In 1921, the ISS changed its name to the League for Industrial Democracy. ("Industrial Democracy" was no more than a transparent euphemism for Socialism.) The campus chapters were placed under the umbrella of the Intercollegiate Liberal League, which was organized in 1921 at Harvard University. In 1928, the student division of the LID was given the name: Student League for Industrial Democracy.

When the name League for Industrial Democracy was adopted, the slogan of the ISS ("Light, more light") was discarded in favor of

"Education for a new social order based on production for use and not for profit." (Karl Marx could not have expressed his objectives in more precise terms.)

Over the years since the LID adopted the simple slogan, "Education for a new social order based on production for use and not for profit," its objectives have gone through an interesting evolution of terminology. For a time during the 1920's, it was boldly stated that: "The League for Industrial Democracy is a militant educational movement which challenges those who would think and act for a new social order based on production for use and not for profit." Evidently, someone in the higher echelons of the LID felt that the phrase "militant educational movement" smacked too much of extremism and a change was made: "The League for Industrial Democracy is a membership society engaged in education for a new social order based on production for use and not for profit." Then, the obviously Marxian phrase, "production for use and not for profit," was dropped as the description became: "The League for Industrial Democracy is a non-profit educational organization committed to a program of education in behalf of increasing democracy in our economic, political and cultural life." Today, the LID's letterhead carries the simple phrase: "Education for increasing democracy in our economic, political and cultural life."

From its beginnings in 1905, the ISS-LID-SLID, through its literature and by statements of its leaders, attempted to portray itself as independent from the Socialist Party and denied that it was a vehicle for the promotion of Socialism. The same sort of disclaimers were also attempted with relation to Communists and Communism. But in the face of overwhelming evidence, it cannot be denied that the ISS-LID-SLID has always been inextricably involved with Socialism and Socialists and that its ties with Communism and Communists have been more than tenuous.

Early in the history of the ISS-LID-SLID, when the organization was being criticized as an incubator for Socialists, one of the founders, Thomas Wentworth Higginson, writing in *Collier's* magazine, insisted: "The primary aim of the society was to create students of socialism, not to produce Socialists." And Mina Weisenberg wrote in her *The LID: 50 Years of Democratic Education:* "The ISS constantly reiterated that 'to study socialism commits the students to nothing whatever. They may reject it in theory and combat it in practice.' Dr. Laidler explained to them that 'the society has never in its history committed its mem-

126

bers to any creed or line of tactics." However, throughout the entire history of the ISS-LID-SLID, active Socialist Party leaders (Elizabeth Gilman, Arthur McDowell, Alfred Baker Lewis, Michael Harrington, Paul Blanshard, and Norman Thomas, among others) have been simultaneously active leaders of the organization. In 1922, Thomas became Laidler's co-executive director of the LID and Blanshard became the group's field director. Said Laidler of Thomas and Blanshard and their work for the LID: "From then through part of the thirties, these two magnetic speakers carried the message of industrial democracy to student and civic groups in all parts of the country, and proved towers of strength to the progressive movement."

The first regular headquarters for the ISS was in the Rand School of Social Science. In 1906 — just one year after the ISS was organized — the American Socialist Society established the Rand School. For many years, the Garland Fund contributed considerable financial support to the Rand School and the ISS-LID. (At the same time, the Garland Fund was a major source for financing Communist Party enterprises.) The intimate relationship of the ISS—LID with the Rand School and the Garland Fund was not merely financial. The personnel of the three organizations were familiar to each other.

Associated with the Rand School as officials, lecturers, pamphleteers, or fundraisers were Alexander Trachtenberg, Norman Thomas, Algernon Lee, John Dewey, John Haynes Holmes, Morris Hillquit, Upton Sinclair, Paul Douglas, William Kilpatrick, Stuart Chase, Broadus Mitchell, Heywood Broun, Clarence Senior, Charles A. Beard, Oswald Garrison Villard — all of whom were connected with ISS-LID officers, members, lecturers, pamphleteers, or cooperators (a term used by ISS-LID to describe those who were receptive to ISS-LID awards or who, in other respects, demonstrated their sympathy and support for ISS-LID objectives). Officials of the Garland Fund included Roger Baldwin, William Z. Foster, Lewis Gannett, Robert Morss Lovett, Morris Ernst, Norman Thomas, Freda Kirchwey, and Elizabeth Gurley Flynn — all of whom had close ties with the ISS-LID. (In 1933, when the Rand School was in financial distress, the Socialist Party and fellow travelers came to its rescue. The head of the Socialist Party was, of course, Norman Thomas who was also a director of the Garland Fund and a co-executive director of the LID.)

The relationship of the ISS-LID-SLID to Socialism and Socialists is further demonstrable. In 1912, Governor Chase Osborn of Michigan, in praise of the ISS chapter on the campus of the University of Michigan, said: "The right way of the future is to be discovered by those who are making earnest search for the truth, and I believe that you are doing that above all other considerations, and before you take any thought of political profit. The truth is what we should all desire, and, if it can come through the work of educated socialism, it will be none the less welcomed." Mina Weisenberg, who went to such pains to divorce ISS-LID-SLID from activist Socialism in her *The LID: 50 Years of Democratic Education,* inexplicably included in her booklet Governor Osborn's recognition of the ISS as a training ground for Socialists. And, in 1932, Felix Cohen, writing in the LID's magazine *Revolt* as a spokesman for the organization, said: "A socialist attack on the problem of Government cannot be restricted to presidential and congressional elections or even to general programs of legislation. We have to widen our battle front to include all institutions of government, corporations, trade unions, professional bodies, and even religious bodies, as well as legislatures and courts. We have to frame the issues of socialism and democracy and fight the battles of socialism and democracy in the stockholders meetings of industrial corporations, in our medical associations and our bar associations and our teacher associations, in labor unions, in student councils, in consumers and producers' cooperatives — in every social institution in which we can find a foot hold."

It is true that all LID officers, members, and cooperators did not always toil under the banner of the Socialist Party. Some did, of course. (Norman Thomas, Michael Harrington, Maurice Calman, Paul Blanshard, Morris Hillquit, Alfred Baker Lewis, Samuel Friedman, Clarence Senior, Eugene V. Debs, James Maurer, and Darlington Hoopes.) Others, however, fought for the Socialist revolution in academic circles: John Dewey, the father of progressive and permissive education; William Kilpatrick and George Counts, Dewey's foremost disciples, who wielded their influence at the mecca of the educationists, Columbia University's Teachers College; Arthur Holcombe, professor of government at Harvard University and president of the American Political Science Association; Julius Bixler, president of Colby College; Laurence Seelye, president of St. Lawrence University; Charles A. Beard, the dean of America's liberal political scientists; Harold U. Faulkner, whose socialistic economic textbooks saturated the classrooms of America's colleges and universities; Jerome Davis, a widely traveled college professor and president of the American Federation of

Teachers; Bryn Hovde, president of the New School for Social Research; Alexander Meiklejohn, president of Amherst College; Harold Taylor, president of Sarah Lawrence College; Broadus Mitchell, professor of economics at many major universities and colleges for almost half a century; Eliot Pratt, chairman of Goodard College's board of trustees; and, a host of university and college professors of sociology, political science, economics, history, English, philosophy, mathematics, psychology, and law.

Many officials, members, and alumni of ISS-LID-SLID became prominent in the publishing business and the press, including: Daniel Bell, labor editor of *Fortune*; Carroll Binder, editorial editor of the *Minneapolis Tribune*; Bruce Bliven, editorial director of *New Republic*; James Henle, president of Vanguard Press; Freda Kirchwey, editor and publisher of *Nation*; Joseph P. Lash, correspondent for the *New York Post*; William E. Bohn, editor of *New Leader*; Lewis Gannett, literary editor of the *New York Herald Tribune*; Robert Morss Lovett, editor of *New Republic*; Oswald Garrison Villard, editor and publisher of *Nation*; Morris Rubin, editor of *Progressive*; Daniel Mebane, publisher of *New Republic*; James Wechsler, editor of the *New York Post*; and columnists or correspondents including: Walter Lippmann, Max Lerner, William L. Shirer, Quincy Howe, Heywood Broun, Murray Kempton, and John Temple Graves.

The ISS-LID-SLID brand of Socialism has been promoted in the trade union movement by David Dubinsky, Iorwith W. Abel, Jacob Potofsky, Walter and Victor Reuther, James B. Carey, Jay Lovestone, Marx Lewis, and Arthur McDowell.

Some ISS-LID-SLID alumni and cooperators went to the Congress of the United States including Senators Paul Douglas, Wayne Morse, Hubert Humphrey, Frank Graham, and Herbert Lehman, and Representatives Andrew Biemiller, Jerry Voorhis, and Will Rogers Jr. Others were leaders in the Liberal Party: Donald Harrington, John L. Childs, Murray Baron, and George S. Counts. In the literary world were the muckrakers Upton Sinclair, Lincoln Steffens, and Charles E. Russell, along with such widely-read individuals as James T. Farrell, Irving Stone, Edna St. Vincent Millay, Babette Deutsch, Jack London, and Louis Fischer. The clergy has been represented by Reinhold Niebuhr, Sherwood Eddy, and John C. Bennett. In high positions in the federal government were Leland Olds, chairman of the Federal Power Commission; Paul R. Porter, who held many diplomatic posts in the Truman

Administration; John Roche, a special assistant to President Lyndon Johnson; Oscar L. Chapman, Secretary of the Interior; Gordon Clapp, chairman of the Tennessee Valley Authority; and, Ralph Bunche, who served in the State Department during the Roosevelt and Truman Administrations. Other notorious radicals who were affiliated with ISS-LID-SLID included: Stuart Chase, Eleanor Roosevelt, Clarence Darrow, Thorstein Veblen, Morris Ernst, Algernon Lee, David Saposs, Abraham J. Muste, Selig Perlman, Harry Overstreet, George Soule, Bayard Rustin, Charles Steinmetz, Lewis Mumford, Emily Balch, Roger Baldwin, A. Philip Randolph, Elmer Davis, Stephen Raushenbush, Alvin Hansen, and Bjarne Braatoy.

The ISS-LID-SLID alumni have had such a wide variety of vocations and avocations that they have held high offices in institutions and organizations of all sorts, including: the American Civil Liberties Union, Americans for Democratic Action (and, its predecessor, Union for Democratic Action), the National Council of Churches (and, its predecessor, the Federal Council of Churches), the National Labor Relations Board, the Research Institute of America, Union Theological Seminary, the American Jewish Congress, the Tennessee Valley Authority, UNICEF, the Congress of Racial Equality, the American Newspaper Guild, the Public Affairs Institute, the YWCA, the American Economic Association, the New School for Social Research, the Bell Telephone Laboratories, Lever Brothers, the Twentieth Century Fund, Chrysler Corporation, Statler Corporation, the National Association for the Advancement of Colored People, the Office of War Information, and the Communist Party.

In December, 1935, at a convention in Columbus, Ohio, the Student League for Industrial Democracy merged with the National Student League to form the American Student Union. The National Student League had been organized in 1932 and remained completely controlled by the Communist Party. The merger of SLID with the NSL was due mainly to the efforts of the SLID's secretary Joseph P. Lash, who — in later years — would gain considerable notoriety as Eleanor Roosevelt's protégé and close friend. Once the merger was effected, the SLID lost its identity with the American Student Union which was nothing less than a Communist Party enterprise, and Joseph P. Lash was the ASU's national secretary.

Between 1935 and 1941, the American Student Union with its ex-SLIDers rallied to the defense of teachers and students who were charged with engaging in Communist activities; cooperated with and supported numerous Communist fronts; participated in May Day parades organized by the Communist Party; and, supported every twist and turn of the Soviet Union's foreign policy.

Mina Weisenberg, in her *The LID: 50 Years of Democratic Education,* explained the 1935 action of the SLID: "Work for peace, for aiding underground activities in Fascist countries, for preserving civil rights, for strike aid – all these were of interest to the young collegians. But the young people could not resist the increased pressure and clamor for unity resulting from the Communist Party's popular front line. With great reluctance and against the advice of the general organization, the autonomous student LID gave up its identity and its connection with the LID, and merged with other youth groups to form in 1935 the American Student Union."

The Weisenberg account could not be more misleading. When the SLID merged with the NSL to form the American Student Union, adult leaders of the LID formed a majority of the ASU's Advisory Board: Roger Baldwin, George S. Counts, Quincy Howe, Freda Kirchwey, Robert Morss Lovett, Alexander Meiklejohn, Reinhold Niebuhr, Norman Thomas, Bertha Weyl, Ethel Clyde, and Mary Fox. And, in 1937, when the American Student Union held a dinner "for alumni of the student movement," the ASU's sponsoring committee of fifty contained at least thirty-one officials or members of the LID. It all meant – contrary to the impression given by Weisenberg – that not only did the SLID throw its support to the Communists but many of the most influential leaders of the LID did the same.

A close relationship between Communists and the ISS-LID-SLID was not unusual. In attendance at the founding meeting of the ISS in 1905 were William Z. Foster, Ella Reeve Bloor, and Elizabeth Gurley Flynn – all of whom would become high-ranking officials of the Communist Party. Louis Fraina, who had served on the executive committee of the Communist International, lectured under the auspices of the LID, using his alias of Lewis Corey. Other Communists affiliated with the ISS-LID-SLID included Jay Lovestone, Nathaniel Weyl, Frederick V. Field, and Alexander Trachtenberg.

Harry Laidler went to great lengths to present the League for Industrial Democracy as non-Marxian: "We never promoted the Marxian cult. We conceived of the socialist society as one with a mixed economy, an economy with public, cooperative and private ownership, the ultimate objective of which was real equality of opportunity for every man and woman so he or she could achieve the fulfillment of his or her potentialities."

Mina Weisenberg wrote: "The history of the LID might be written by listing the thousands of names of leaders in every field of American life — economic, political, legal, scientific, educational, social and literary — who received their initial introduction to the problems confronting a democratic society in college chapters of the organization. Or it may be written by listing the books and the pamphlets published under LID auspices — works on housing, transportation, social security, public utilities, labor, international affairs, monopolies, etc. — or by mentioning the numerous lectures, meetings, conferences, addressed by outstanding speakers, greatly influencing public opinion during the past half century."

The fact remains, however, that the substance of the ISS-LID-SLID program has conformed in all respects to the substance of Marx's precepts as delineated in the Communist Manifesto and elsewhere. Furthermore, it would be impossible to discover any Communist front, project, or enterprise during the past fifty years that has not been supported by members, officers, or cooperators of the ISS-LID-SLID. Even a casual study of the roster of those who have received the annual awards of the LID indicates that only extreme leftists and determined anti-anti-Communists find the organization's favor: Walter Reuther, George Meany, David Dubinsky, Jacob Potofsky, Leland Olds, Paul Porter, Clarence Senior, Hubert Humphrey, Wayne Morse, Herbert Lehman, Ralph Bunche, William Green, Harry Laidler, Upton Sinclair, Trygve Lie, Eleanor Roosevelt, and John L. Childs.

There can be little doubt that the LID suffered setbacks in growth and public acceptance when the SLID and even LID leaders were caught so flagrantly in the midst of the Communist conspiracy during the days of the American Student Union. After the SLID merged into the ASU, ten years passed before there were any signs of revival. But, by the fall of 1946, there was enough interest to warrant a convention of a new breed of SLIDers. And, in 1947, at the second post-World War II convention, a new constitution was adopted which specifically barred "advocates of dictatorship and totalitarianism" from membership in SLID. No particular type of totalitarianism, such as Communism, was mentioned. And, of course, the fiction that Socialism is not totalitarian was maintained and the emphasis in SLID literature was upon the term "democracy."

The program and activities of the LID-SLID during the post-World War II period were essentially the same brand of Socialism that prevailed in the organization's earlier history. In 1956, the SLID became a member of the International Organization of Socialist Youth and, in the same year, Bjarne Braatoy, who had been president of LID, became chairman of the Socialist International. Such affiliations indicated that the LID-SLID was confident enough of its strength to affiliate with extreme radicals all over the world.

In June, 1962, at Port Huron, Michigan, SLID leaders decided to change their organization's name to Student for a Democratic Society. With the change of name, they also became bolder in their radical pronouncements, beginning with their Port Huron Statement of 1962. The Statement was a dull, rambling, high-flown discourse which, in its essentials, was a call for a Marxian-Socialist state to be achieved through "participatory democracy," a euphemism for Communism. The childish authors found virtually nothing of any worth in the United States. Their dismal heritage, according to their manifesto at Port Huron, was the "cold" war, The Bomb, McCarthyism, racial bigotry, the military-industrial complex, automation, poverty, colonialism, paranoiac anti-Communism, and just about any other alleged ill that could be found in the history of socialist/Communist protests. They were discontented with the status of political parties, the national economy, organized labor, universities, foreign "aid" programs, and mental health programs.

In their broad program, the SDS were to work for civil rights, especially by supporting the Student Nonviolent Coordinating Committee. They would participate in activity for peace and disarmament. They would dramatize economic injustices. They would "inject controversy into a stagnant educational system. SDS works on campus against paternalistic deans; lobbies at the National Student Congress for student freedom; stimulates the creation of new or improved courses on peace-related and economic problems." They would "support political insurgents in the fight for a government that would promote social justice. SDS produces studies of the political and electoral situation; SDS members unofficially have participated in New York reform movements and in 'peace candidacies' such as that of H. Stuart Hughes."

The parent LID continued to give its financial support and approval

133

to SDS. The adult radicals did not forsake the so-called New Left. As the SDS became more and more overtly communistic, they continued to receive the plaudits of Walter Reuther, Bayard Rustin, Harold Taylor, William Fitts Ryan, James Farmer, Erich Fromm, Norman Thomas, W. H. "Ping" Ferry, Arthur Waskow, Dagmar Wilson, Abraham J. Muste, and Staughton Lynd.

As late as 1965, LID literature carried the notice that: "Students for a Democratic Society is the student department of the L.I.D. It seeks to bring together all those − liberals and radicals, activists and scholars − who share its vision of a truly democratic society. Among the most active groups on the campus scene, the SDS strives to implement its vision and analysis by engaging students in study-action projects, both through its campus structure and through the community organizing projects administered by SDS's Economic Research and Action project."

In testimony in February, 1966, before the House Committee on Appropriations, FBI Director J. Edgar Hoover appraised the status of the SDS in 1965: "One of the most militant organizations now engaged in activities protesting U. S. foreign policy is a student youth group called Students for a Democratic Society. Communists are actively promoting and participating in the activities of this organization, which is self-described as a group of liberals and radicals. This organization currently claims a membership in excess of 3,000 in over 100 chapters throughout the United States, and its members are most vocal in condemning the American way of life and our established form of government.

"This organization sponsored a march on Washington to protest U.S. action in Vietnam which took place on April 17, 1965. Communists from throughout the Nation participated in this march and over 70 past or present Communist Party members from New York City alone, including several national leaders, were observed among the participants.

"A national convention of this organization was held at a camp near Kewadin, Mich., in June 1965. Practically every subversive organization in the United States was represented by delegates to this convention. There were delegates from the Young Socialist Alliance, the youth and training section of the Trotskyite Socialist Workers Party, which has been designated as subversive pursuant to Executive Order 10450.

"Also represented were the Communist Party, U.S.A. and the Spartacist group, a Trotskyite splinter organization. Other delegates represented the Progressive Labor Party, a Marxist-Leninist organization following the line of Communist China, and the May 2 Movement, a front group of the Progressive Labor Party.

"At this convention, a number of proposals were made to further oppose the U. S. action in Vietnam. One Students for a Democratic Society leader called for deliberate violation of the sedition statutes by Students for a Democratic Society members which it was hoped would result in mass arrests and a 'political trial' of the organization. Members were urged to attempt to enter military bases to persuade soldiers that they should refuse to fight in Vietnam.

"At a meeting of the national council, the governing body of the Students for a Democratic Society which was held over the 1965 Labor Day weekend, 20 of the approximately 100 participants had past or present affiliations with the Communist Party or other subversive groups. A vigorous antidraft program was proposed at this meeting, which included plans to counsel draft-age youth on how to avoid the draft. This proposal was later submitted to the Students for a Democratic Society membership by referendum for approval but was defeated by a narrow majority.

"In spite of this, Students for a Democratic Society leaders recently announced that each local chapter would make its own decisions as to whether an antidraft program would be undertaken by that particular chapter.

"During the last week of December 1965, the antidraft program and the Vietnam protest movement again were subjects which dominated discussions at a national membership conference of this group held at Urbana, Ill. Heated exchanges took place between various factions, some of which wanted to continue with a 'hard line' and others wanting to retreat entirely from all protest activity in connection with the Vietnam issue. Although no foreign policy decisions resulted from this conference, the Students for a Democratic Society has continued to sponsor and participate in demonstrations throughout the United States protesting U. S. action in Vietnam."

Among other SDS activities in 1965 were trips to Hanoi, North Vietnam by SDS president Carl Oglesby, who said that the United States was fighting the Vietnam war "under the banner of cold war colonialism," and Tom Hayden, founder of SDS and major author of the Port Huron Statement, who was accompanied by Staughton Lynd and Communist Herbert Aptheker.

In October, 1965, Paul Booth, national secretary of SDS, revealed that the SDS was beginning a drive to enlist high school students who, as soon as they were eligible for the draft, would file as conscientious objectors. This was to be tied to the major SDS anti-draft campaign wherein selective service offices would be picketed, pacifist tracts would be distributed, and local draft boards would be reviled as "undemocratic" and recruiters and officer trainees as "war criminals."

By October, 1965, the flagrantly revolutionary activities of SDS were jeopardizing the tax-exempt status of the LID, the parent organization. In a joint statement, leaders of the LID and SDS announced that a friendly separation had been arranged "for tax reasons." (The LID's adult leaders showed no concern, earlier in the year, when the SDS at their national convention, announced that they were not only not opposed to Communism but that their membership was open to Communists.)

Even without overt and formal ties to the LID, SDS continued to grow. In 1966, it claimed six thousand members at 150 colleges and universities, including the Universities of Michigan, Illinois, Wisconsin, Chicago, Ohio, Texas, Maryland, Indiana, Rhode Island, Kansas, Kentucky, California, and Oklahoma; Johns Hopkins University; Brandeis University; Cornell University; Harvard University; Yale University; and, colleges: Northeastern, Vassar, Oberlin, Detroit, Swarthmore, Reed, and Haverford.

In January, 1967, SDS participated in a riotous anti-Vietnam War demonstration at the University of Oklahoma; in February, Central Intelligence Agency recruiting was the excuse for an SDS demonstration at Columbia University; in February, also, at Harvard Law School, the SDS protested against a speaking engagement of Arthur Goldberg who was portrayed as a hawkish advocate of the Vietnam War; and, in April, Marine Corps recruiting served to launch SDS on a riotous and destructive rampage at Columbia University.

In the *New York Times* issue of May 7, 1967, Greg Calvert, national secretary of SDS, was quoted: "We are actively organizing sedition." The SDS leaders were especially interested in helping draft dodgers by "insubordination, legal and illegal emigration to Canada, going underground in America — everything." The New Left, personified in SDS, was not content any longer with "protests" — *resistance* was the theme.

In October, 1967, at the University of Michigan, SDS demonstrated against the university's research relationship with the Defense Department. In March, 1968, SDS caused a gift to be withdrawn from the Boston University School of Nursing when the would-be donor was castigated as a slum landlord. In April, 1968, SDS conducted their most notorious disruption of a university's activities when Mark Rudd, the campus president of SDS, using admittedly phony pretexts literally seized physical control of the university. In a letter to Columbia's President Grayson Kirk, Rudd said: "If we win, we will take control of your world, your corporations, your university, and attempt to mold a world in which we and other people can live as human beings. Your power is directly threatened since we will have to destroy that power before we take over." Only when university officials belatedly called for police assistance was any semblance of order restored to the campus.

In November, 1968, SDS combined with the National Mobilization Committee to End the War in Vietnam and Clergy and Laymen Concerned about Vietnam to lead an "election offensive" across the country with demonstrations on behalf of "peace" in Vietnam. In the same month, SDS combined with the Black Students Union in demonstrations against "racism" by authorities at San Fernando State College and San Francisco State College.

At hearings of the House Subcommittee on Appropriations in February, 1968, FBI Director J. Edgar Hoover, in his summary of SDS activities, said: "The new left student movement in this country has so captured the attention of the Nation in the past several years as to merit hundreds of articles in the news media and to initiate a broad range of speculation about its future role in our country.

"It is many-sided. It is a political theory, sociology, and bitter protest. It is linked with civil rights, the fight against poverty, the American war in Vietnam. It involves students, faculty members, writers, intellectuals, beatniks, most of them being quite young. The mood of this movement, which is best typified by its primary spokesman, the Students for a Democratic Society, is a mood of disillusionment, pessimism, and alienation. At the center of the movement is an almost passionate desire to destroy, to annihilate, to tear down. If anything definite can be said about the Students for a Democratic Society, it is that it can be called anarchistic.

"A national leader of the Students for a Democratic Society during the summer of 1967 claimed a membership of 30,000 for the organization. 'New Left Notes,' a weekly publication of Students for a

Democratic Society, in its issue dated June 26, 1967, stated there was a recorded membership of 6,371 with a total of nearly 250 chapters, mostly on college campuses. Of the 6,371 members, only 875 had paid dues since January 1, 1967. The organization is infiltrated by Communist Party members and Party Leader Gus Hall has described the organization as part of the 'responsible left' which the party has 'going for us.'

"In late June, 1967, the Students for a Democratic Society held its national convention on the campus of the University of Michigan, Ann Arbor, Mich. In continuance of past programs, the organization called for acts of civil disobedience when necessary. It called for continued demonstrations against U. S. policy in Vietnam, radicalizing the student power movement by connecting it with radical off-campus issues, and the taking over of the colleges and universities by the students.

"The Students for a Democratic Society is opposed to conscription in any form and if it has any one program at this time, it is draft resistance. It called for the formation of antidraft unions and the utilization of such tactics as disrupting the Selective Service System apparatus by demonstrations and civil disobedience. It advocated agitation by those men in uniform and urged members of the armed services to desert and go 'underground.'

"In keeping with its past course of action and to put into practice its programs that were outlined at the 1967 national convention, the Students for a Democratic Society has seized upon every opportunity to foment discord among the youth of this country.

"Student dissent and behavior are not what really concern perceptive citizens today. Student unrest and dissatisfaction have been erupting through the centuries and dissent is an integral part of our American way of life. What is of concern in the new left movement is its alienation from our democratic thought, processes, and ideals; the open hostility of these students to law and order, to civilized behavior and the concept of liberty under law.

"The new left identifies itself with the problems of American society, such as civil rights, poverty, disease, and slums. With its anarchistic bent, however, it refuses to cooperate sincerely with other groups interested in eradicating these same problems, and despite the new leftist's protestations of sincerity, he is not legitimately interested in bringing about a better nation. On the contrary, he is dedicated – in his bizarre and unpredictable ways – to cut the taproots of American society.

"The new left should not be arbitrarily equated with the traditional old-line left. Although they become prey to the superior organizational ability and talents of the old-line subversive organizations, such as the Communist Party-U.S.A., the Socialist Workers Party, and the like, to simply identify them as Moscow or Peking Communists would be missing the point. To put it bluntly, they are a new type of subversive and their danger is great. In a population which is becoming increasingly youthful, the new left can be expected to find wider fields of endeavor and to try to do all that it can to infect the rising generation with its anti-American prattle."

That Mr. Hoover had not exaggerated the extremism of SDS was perhaps best demonstrated by the SDS's interorganizational secretary Bernardine Dohrn who, when asked if she considered herself a socialist, replied: "I consider myself a revolutionary communist." Or by Mark Rudd, who said of himself and his SDS associates: "We are all Marxists . . . we are all socialists."

There can be no doubt of SDS's ties with the Communists. In January, 1965, Clark Kissinger, then national secretary of SDS, was a speaker, along with Gus Hall, at the Fortieth Anniversary of International Publishers, the Communists' major printing establishment. The SDS has regularly advertised in *National Guardian,* the Communist weekly. In 1967, SDS accepted invitations to the Communists' Tri-Continental Congress in Havana and the Fiftieth Anniversary celebration of the Bolshevik Revolution in Moscow.

Meanwhile, the LID has continued without its collegiate branch, just as it had to do when the SLID broke away in the 1930's. As of 1968, the head of the Socialist Party, Michael Harrington, was chairman of the LID's board of directors. The ties with trade unionism remain as strong as ever with the presence of Nathaniel Minkoff as LID's president. And, the list of LID's vice presidents, directors, and national council is markedly similar to the calibre of radicals that have guided the organization since 1905.

Since 1962, the leaders of SDS have achieved a notoriety that rivals the radical leaders of the LID. Such names as Paul Booth, Rennie Davis, Tom Hayden, Clark Kissinger, Carl Oglesby, and Paul Potter have become nationally and internationally famous as flaming red revolutionaries.

NATIONAL ASSOCIATION FOR THE ADVANCEMENT OF COLORED PEOPLE

"The wisest among my race understand that the agitation of questions of social equality is the extremest folly, and that progress in the enjoyment of all the privileges that will come to us must be the result of severe and constant struggle rather than of artificial forcing. No race that has anything to contribute to the markets of the world is long in any degree ostracized. It is important and right that all privileges of the law be ours, but it is vastly more important that we be prepared for the exercises of these privileges. The opportunity to earn a dollar in a factory just now is worth infinitely more than the opportunity to spend a dollar in an opera-house." These were the words of Booker T. Washington — Negro educator, a native Virginian born in slavery, and founder of Tuskegee Institute.

Throughout his adult life, Washington labored to impress upon Negroes that they would have a rewarding role in America's progress if only they developed industrial and agricultural skills through vocational training in a massive "self-help" program among Negroes. From the whites Washington asked for cooperation and understanding which would result in "interlacing our industrial, commercial, civil, and religious life with yours in a way that shall make the interests of both races one. In all things that are purely social we can be as separate as the fingers, yet one as the hand in all things essential to mutual progress." There were Negro intellectuals who disagreed sharply with Washington. They alleged that Washington was leading his fellow Negroes into a surrender of political rights and a permanent system of social segregation.

The most prominent among the anti-Washington Negroes was W. E. Burghardt DuBois — a native of Massachusetts with a doctorate and two lesser degrees from Harvard. (DuBois, before the turn of the century, was a Statist. Later, he formally joined the Socialist Party, resigned and became an active fellow traveler of the Reds, and eventually became a member of the Communist Party. And, today his name is memorialized in the Communists' DuBois Clubs.)

In a total misrepresentation of Washington's views, DuBois said: "Mr. Washington apologizes for injustice, North and South, does not rightly value the privilege and duty of voting, belittles the emasculating effects of caste distinctions, and opposes the higher training and ambition of our brighter minds ... [therefore] we must unceasingly and firmly oppose him."

To offset Washington's "self-help" program, DuBois — in 1905 — and a group of collectivists founded the Niagara Movement. DuBois planned, as an immediate goal, to train a Negro elite — "the Talented Tenth" — which could lead the Negro masses in a militant program to agitate for unconditional political and social equality.

Out of the Niagara Movement, there emerged — in 1909 — the National Association for the Advancement of Colored People with its announced purposes: "To promote equality of rights and eradicate caste or race prejudice among the citizens of the United States; to advance the interest of colored citizens; to secure for them impartial suffrage; and to increase their opportunities for securing justice in the courts, education for their children, employment according to their ability, and complete equality before the law."

The formation of the NAACP was urged by the leading radicals of the era including Jane Addams, John Dewey, William Lloyd Garrison, John Haynes Holmes, Lincoln Steffens, Brand Whitlock, Lillian Wald, Rabbi Stephen Wise, and Ray Stannard Baker. Among the first officials of the NAACP were more radicals including: Mary White Ovington, Oswald Garrison Villard, Walter E. Sachs, John Milholland, Frances Blascoer, and William English Walling. Other radicals were among the first NAACP members: Florence Kelly, William Pickens, James W. Johnson, Charles E. Russell, and E. R. A. Seligman. (Many of these individuals were already or would soon become enrolled in the newly formed Intercollegiate Socialist Society [which later became the League for Industrial Democracy] and, within a few years, they were prominent in various pacifist groups, including the Fellowship of Reconciliation, and the American Civil Liberties Union. The NAACP gave them one more vantage point — agitation for Negroes' equality — from which they could promote Socialism and other facets of radicalism.)

Moorfield Storey, a white attorney from Boston, was the first president of the NAACP. DuBois became the organization's first director of publicity and research and the editor of the organization's monthly magazine, *The Crisis.* For twenty-four years, *The Crisis* served as DuBois' regular outlet for unbridled racism. In one of his editorials, he set the tone for the magazine when he wrote that "the most ordinary Negro is a distinct gentleman, but it takes extraordinary training and opportunity to make the average white man anything but a hog."

From 1909 until 1934, DuBois — in this country and abroad — was the most prominent spokesman for the NAACP. In that same period,

Mary White Ovington, a white social worker and an official of the organization, was second only to DuBois in propaganda efforts for the organization. The NAACP has also been fortunate in having three very able men serve as executive secretary: James Weldon Johnson (1920-1928), Walter White (1929-1955), and Roy Wilkins since 1955. Wilkins also was editor of *The Crisis* from 1934 until 1949. Long tenure in office has also been characteristic of the NAACP's presidents — all white men: Moorfield Story (1910-1915), Joel Spingarn (1915-1940), Arthur Spingarn (1940-1966), and, since 1966, Kivie Kaplan.

During its first year, the NAACP recruited 329 members. At the end of twenty years, there were 88,000 members. The peak of membership was reached in 1963 with 510,000 and, at the end of 1968, there were 449,000 members.

In its early history, the NAACP proved to be a natural attraction for Communists. DuBois, the real leader of the organization, "hailed the Russian Revolution of 1917," and he traveled to the Soviet Union in 1926 and 1936. He especially liked "the racial attitudes of the Communists."

In 1920, the question of the Negro in America had been discussed at the second world congress of the Communist International. At that time, the Negro in America was described as a "national" minority rather than a "racial" minority.

By 1922, the Communists in America had received their orders from the Communist International to exploit Negroes in the Communist program against the peace and security of the United States. In 1923, the NAACP began to receive grants from the Garland Fund which was a major source for the financing of Communist Party enterprises. (Officials of the Fund included Communists William Z. Foster, Benjamin Gitlow, Elizabeth Gurley Flynn, Scott Nearing, and Robert W. Dunn, along with prominent leftwingers Roger Baldwin, Sidney Hillman, Ernest Gruening, Morris Ernst, Mary E. McDowell, Harry F. Ward, Judah L. Magnes, Freda Kirchwey, Emanuel Celler, Paul H. Douglas, Moorfield Storey, and Oswald Garrison Villard.) The grants continued until, at least, 1934.

There could be no doubt that the NAACP was of particular interest to the Communist Party. At the fourth national convention of the Workers (Communist) Party in 1925, the comrades were told that it was "permissible and necessary for selected Communists (not the party membership as a whole) to enter its [NAACP's] conventions and to make proposals calculated to enlighten the Negro masses under its influence as to the nature and necessity of the class struggle, the identity of their exploiters . . . ."

In 1928, the Communist International instructed American Negro Communists to work for a Negro-controlled State composed of all contiguous Southern countries having majority black populations — the so-called Black Belt. In 1930, the Communist International instructed the entire Communist Party, USA to organize the Negroes of the South for the purpose of setting up a separate state and government in the South.

The noted Negro journalist George Schuyler, who was familiar with the personnel and operations of the NAACP, has written of this era: "This was the time the veteran Socialist, Dr. W. E. B. Dubois (then the acknowledged intellectual leader of Aframerica, and editor of *The Crisis* since 1910), wrote an editorial in January 1934 to plug *for* segregation. He declared that 'the thinking colored people of the United States must stop being stampeded by the word *segregation*.' With considerable exaggeration, he held that segregation was 'more insistent, more prevalent and more unassailable by appeal and argument' than ever before; that Negroes must 'fight segregation with segregation,' and he told them to 'voluntarily and insistently organize our economic and social power no matter how much segregation is involved.' This shocked the NAACP directors. But, DuBois continued to urge that Negroes 'cut intercourse with white Americans to the minimum demanded by decent living.'" (Mr. Schuyler's observations appeared in *The Review of the News,* December 18, 1968.)

DuBois' views, so overtly compatible with the Communists' plans for a segregated Negro America, were an embarrassment to the NAACP which, of necessity, had to depend upon financial and other support from white America. And, in 1934, DuBois separated from the NAACP. (He returned ten years later but within four years he left the NAACP permanently and devoted his energies full-time working for Communist projects.)

The departure of DuBois from the NAACP did not mean that the organization was averse to Communists. George Schuyler has narrated: "Meanwhile, the Association [NAACP] was playing patsy with the forces of the Left . . . and were thereby floating on financial beds of ease. Evil associations corrupt good manners, and also good sense. As the Communists, crypto-Communists and fellow travelers moved in on the New Deal and took charge, the NAACP was more and more affected. The indefatigable Walter F. White, NAACP executive secretary, was weekly in Washington cultivating white power which was often Red. Then the New York Communist organizers, Manning Johnson and Leonard Patterson, traveled to Washington, contacted the Red faculty members at Howard University, and 'sold' them on organizing an activist National Negro Congress (NNC). Among the first suckered into it was the NAACP's executive secretary. This committed the Association to supporting an outfit tailored originally by the Communist Party of the U.S.A. to destroy it." (The NAACP's affiliation with the National Negro Congress was not an isolated tie-in with the Communists. In 1938, the NAACP was represented in the World Youth Congress, a Communist enterprise. And, in the 1940's the NAACP was affiliated with American Youth for a Free World, the American affiliate of the World Federation of Democratic Youth, a Communist clearing house.)

As was the case with so many Communist fronts, the National Negro Congress foundered amidst the confusion of the Hitler-Stalin Pact.

The National Negro Congress, however, had a short-lived revival. George Schuyler recounted: "With War's end and the return of the Communist Party to its pre-War line (crying for 'Self-Determination for the Black Belt' and trying to invade the province of the NAACP with the hastily-organized Civil Rights Congress), there was no difficulty in getting high Association officials to join. Soon the National Negro Congress, in one of its last gasps, presented a petition to the United Nations charging the United States with genocide on its Negro population — which, curiously, had increased since 1790 to 1940 from 750,000 to 15 million. Not to be outdone, Dr. DuBois, who had again been given executive office by the NAACP, the following year presented a *similar* petition charging American genocide against the Negroes. It followed the general line of the Communist plea, and Walter White and DeBois traipsed out to Lake Success to present it."

One of the NAACP's most literate apologists was the late Langston Hughes. (From 1925 until his death in 1967, Hughes was openly associated with Communist Party projects and enterprises. In 1956, the Senate Internal Security Subcommittee included Hughes in its list of eighty-two names of the most active and typical sponsors of Communist front organizations. In sworn testimony, former Communist Party functionary Manning Johnson identified Hughes as a member of the Communist Party as of December, 1935.)

In 1962, Hughes wrote *Fight for Freedom: The Story of the NAACP*. In his book, Hughes said: "Attempts to label the NAACP subversive, Communist-influenced, or out-and-out Communist have continued for a long time. The late Negro professional witness, ex-Communist Manning Johnson, since discredited, testified before two southern legislative committees to the effect that the NAACP was 'a vehicle of the Communist Party designed to overthrow the government of the United States.'" [Johnson was not a professional witness but a genuinely repentant American who, from his years as a top Negro Communist, testified accurately before, and cooperated fully with, federal and state investigating committees and agencies. He was discredited only by the Communist Party, its fellow travelers, and its dupes. He did identify Hughes as a Communist. He did testify as to the Communist character of the NAACP since he had been assigned the job of bringing Negro organizations into the Communist orbit.)

Hughes, however, in his whitewash of the NAACP (which, by the way, had conferred its highest award — the Spingarn Medal — upon him in 1960), wrote: "Utterly disregarding the truth, these malicious and irresponsible accusations ignore evidence, so clearly on the record, that the NAACP is not and was not Communist and has never even remotely been under Communist influence. Since its earliest years, its top officials from Joel Spingarn and James Weldon Johnson to Walter White and Roy Wilkins have attacked communism in no uncertain terms in both speaking and writing . . . [and] until recently, the official Communist program for Negroes called for the establishment of a separate Negro nation, an idea that was directly opposite to the NAACP's philosophy of integration." (Spingarn and Johnson were officials when the NAACP was receiving grants from the Garland Fund, the outfit which was created to finance Communist enterprises. White, as George Schuyler noted, worked hand-in-hand with the Communists. Wilkins, on the NAACP's staff since 1931, went out of his way to praise the Communist Party for the help it gave to the Negroes. And, from 1937 until 1949, Wilkins was affiliated with a number of Communist fronts and enterprises. He did become somewhat discreet after 1949 [in 1949 and 1950, he was acting executive secretary and, since 1955, he has been the executive secretary of the NAACP] but in 1965 he joined with notorious Communist leaders to memorialize the deceased Communist W. E. B. DuBois. And, Hughes conveniently forgot that the Communists and the NAACP set aside temporarily the idea of a separate Negro nation only because American Negro masses simply showed no interest in such a segregation.)

It is true that from time to time the NAACP went through the motions of denouncing Communism and Communists but, at the same time, the NAACP harbored in its roster of officials and in its membership a legion of Communist-fronters, individuals whose prestige and influence made their presence in the fronts of far more importance to the Communist Party than if they were dues-paying members of obscure and secretive party cells. Among these individuals who represented every Communist front, project, and enterprise ever to appear in this country have been: Roger N. Baldwin, George S. Counts, J. Frank Dobie, Dorothy Canfield Fisher, Arthur Garfield Hays, Freda Kirchwey, Alfred Baker Lewis, Archibald MacLeish, Reinhold Niebuhr, A. Philip Randolph, Guy Emery Shipler, Lillian Smith, Norman Thomas, Leonard Bernstein, Eugene Carson Blake, Sarah Gibson Blanding, Ralph Bunche, Morris Ernst, Buell Gallagher, Rabbi Roland Gittelsohn, Frank Graham, Bishop James A. Pike, Carl Rowan, Eleanor Roosevelt, Walter Reuther, Channing Tobias, Algernon D. Black, Bishop G. Bromley Oxnam, Van Wyck Brooks, Henry Hitt Crane, Benjamin E. Mays, S. Ralph Harlow, and Oscar Hammerstein II. Hughes even boasted that the NAACP membership included Jawaharlal Nehru of India, Averell Harriman, Herbert Lehman, Harry Golden, Harry Belafonte, G. Mennen Williams, Chester Bowles, Nelson Rockefeller, Alan Paton, and Adam Clayton Powell — none of whom could be considered as anything less than extremely soft on Communism. Even after the publication of Hughes' book, there appeared on NAACP letterheads such names as Walter Gellhorn, Telford Taylor, William Sloane Coffin Jr., Dick Gregory, Ossie Davis, Steve Allen, Ruby Dee, Aaron Copland, Helen Buttenwieser, Erwin N. Griswold, Senator Edward M. Kennedy, John A. Volpe, Kirtley Mather, Elliot L. Richardson, and Henry Cabot Lodge.

Among those honored by the NAACP with its annual Spingarn Medal have been: W. E. B. DuBois, Mary McLeod Bethune, A. Philip Randolph, William Hastie, Paul Robeson, Thurgood Marshall, Richard Wright, Martin L. King Jr., Ralph Bunche, Walter White, and Langston Hughes.

From its inception to the present, no matter the protestations of Langston Hughes or any other NAACP apologist, the organization's officials and its known members, collectively and individually, have represented the influential left, the leadership of Communist fronts and leftwing political and pacifist groups, and the most effective of the anti-anti-Communist establishment.

In 1946, the NAACP cooperated with the Communist Party as the latter, in one of its most ambitious political projects of all time, established the Progressive Citizens of America — the basis for Henry Wallace's Communist-dominated Progressive Party in the presidential election of 1948. In 1951, when the Massachusetts legislature was considering a bill to outlaw the Communist Party, the Boston branch of the NAACP, through its legislation committee, opposed the bill. The Committee's chairman, Edward W. Brooke (now U.S. Senator), argued that the bill was "against democratic principles and endangers American civil liberties."

The Communists in the United States have certainly recognized the value of the NAACP as an ally. In 1950, Communist leader Robert Thompson boasted: "The emergence of a powerful left, anti-imperialist, anti-fascist current among the Negro people is unmistakable and is clearly discernible in the NAACP. This Left, anti-imperialist trend in the Association insists upon much greater attention by the organization to the pressing economic and political problems facing the Negro masses." (*Political Affairs,* February, 1950.)

In 1953, an unusual and total endorsement was given to the NAACP by the Communists in their *Daily Worker* (September 30): "It should be clear that we Communists are the first to insist that the labor movement, all sections of it, should give every possible support to any and all campaigns conducted by the NAACP."

Four years later, a similar endorsement appeared in the *Daily Worker* (February 19, 1957): "Communists in labor unions are thus pledged to get their unions to support the NAACP, to better express the alliance of labor with the Negro people. Communists in communities are pledged to aid in increasing the membership and financial strength of the NAACP, whether as members or not."

The relationship between the NAACP and the Communist Party has been demonstrable through the activities of those attorneys who have held office in the NAACP, its branches, or the "Committee of 100" which supports the NAACP's Legal Defense and Educational Fund.

Among the more prominent attorneys associated with the NAACP have been Morris Ernst, Robert W. Kenny, Earl B. Dickerson, Clarence Darrow, Bartley Crum, Osmond Fraenkel, Hubert Delany, and Loren Miller — all of whom had an unusual affinity for Communist fronts and projects. For ten years prior to his appointment in 1939 to the Supreme Court of the United States, Felix Frankfurter, an unreconstructed Bolshevik, served as a legal adviser to the NAACP. That intimate association never deterred Frankfurter from sitting and writing decisions on cases where the NAACP was directly involved. But, in its entire history, the NAACP owes its most dramatic successes to the work of Thurgood Marshall. From 1936 until 1961, he was with the NAACP as assistant special counsel (1936-1938), special counsel (1938-1940), and director and counsel for the Legal Defense and Educational Fund (1940-1961). [In 1962, Marshall was appointed by President Kennedy to be U.S. Circuit Court Justice for the Second Judicial Circuit; in 1965, President Johnson appointed him to be Solicitor General of the United States; and, in 1967, President Johnson appointed him to the Supreme Court of the United States.]

From 1938 to 1961, Marshall represented the NAACP thirty-two times before the Supreme Court. He won twenty-nine of the cases. His most notable achievement before the Supreme Court came in 1954, when he successfully argued the *Brown v. Board of Education* case with the resultant revolutionary decision by the Court that segregation in public schools was unconstitutional. There were circumstances, however, which dulled Marshall's victory and the Court's decision.

Seven years after *Brown v. Board of Education*, Dr. Alfred H. Kelly, an historian who served as an aide to Marshall in the preparation of a brief for the case, revealed that Marshall set out to deceive the Court with dishonest historical arguments. In an address to the American Historical Association, Dr. Kelly told how he was asked by Marshall "to prepare a research paper on the intent of the framers of the Fourteenth Amendment with respect to the constitutionality of racially segregated schools."

Dr. Kelly then described his research efforts: "As a constitutional historian, I knew, of course, that the Fourteenth Amendment had evolved, in some considerable part, out of the Civil Rights Act of 1866. Accordingly, I went to work on the 1866 volumes of the 'Congressional Globe,' reading anew the story of the debates that winter and spring for clues concerning the intent which [Lyman] Trumbell, [John A.]

Bingham, [Thaddeus] Stevens and the other congressional Radicals might have had with respect to legalized segregation in particular.

"I did not really expect to find very much of anything . . . .

"As any reasonably competent historian could have told the Court and the lawyers on both sides, the historical questions they had framed [in 1953] did not necessarily have very much relevance at all to the issues that seemed consequential then to the embattled Radicals who had hammered out the Civil Rights Act and the Fourteenth Amendment that spring of 1866 . . . .

"To my surprise, the debates reprinted in the 1866 volumes of the 'Globe' had a good deal to say about school segregation. Unhappily, from the NAACP's point of view, most of what appeared there at first blush looked rather decidedly bad . . . .

"The conclusion for any reasonably objective historian was painfully clear. The Civil Rights Act as it passed Congress was specifically rewritten to avoid the embarrassing question of a congressional attack upon State racial-segregation laws, including school segregation . . . .

"The paper I prepared for the September conference [with Mr. Marshall in 1953] was not adequate by any standard. I was trying to be both historian and advocate within the same paper, and the combination, as I found out, was not a very good one . . . .

"I was facing, for the first time in my own career, the deadly opposition between my professional integrity as a historian and my wishes and hopes with respect to a contemporary question of values, of ideals, of policy, of partisanship and of political objectives. I suppose if a man is without scruple, this matter will not bother him, but I am frank to say that it bothered me terribly . . . ."

Dr. Kelly's work, however, was not completed. He was recalled for help by Marshall, and, along with Robert Ming Jr., a former law professor at Howard University and the University of Chicago, Kelly drafted a brief for Marshall to present to the Supreme Court. And thus began an extraordinary marriage of phony history and highly questionable legal ethics: "I am very much afraid that for the next few days I ceased to function as a historian, and, instead, took up the practice of law without a license. The problem we faced was not the historian's discovery of the truth, the whole truth and nothing but the truth; the problem instead was the formulation of an adequate gloss on the fateful events of 1866 sufficient to convince the Court that we had something of a historical case . . . .

"It is not that we were engaged in formulating lies; there was nothing as crude and naïve as that. But we were using facts, quietly ignoring facts and, above all, interpreting facts in a way to do what Marshall said we had to do — 'get by those boys down there.'

"There was one optimistic element in all this, as Marshall pointed out: it was obvious that the Court was looking for a plausible historical answer . . . .

"In other words, Marshall said, we didn't need to win a historical argument hands down — all we needed was a face-saving draw. 'A nothing-to-nothing score,' Marshall put it, 'means we win the ball game.' I believe, by the way, that this was a correct interpretation of the Court's mood . . . .

"I am convinced now that this interpretation, which we hammered out with anything but historical truth as our objective, nonetheless contains an essential measure of historical truth.

"History is art as well as fact; everyone in this room knows that the facts do not automatically arrange themselves without the historian's creative leap, which occurs in our craft as well as in the exact sciences . . . .

"But the historians had produced at least the 'draw' that Marshall and his colleagues had asked for. It was all they needed in order to win.

"So we historians can assure ourselves, I think, that we had something to do with the victory. Thurgood Marshall, at all odds, presently wrote some of us letters of thanks, assuring us that enlisting the history profession on his side had been the NAACP's smartest move in the whole complicated case."

Twelve years later, Marshall admitted that the favorable ruling he and the NAACP received in the 1954 segregation case "initiated and required social change." As the NAACP's top attorney, Marshall viewed the Supreme Court as no more than a social reform group before which deceit was proper as long as it advanced the interests of the NAACP. Marshall's contempt for representative government was his excuse for legal trickery. It is not surprising, therefore, to find that while Marshall was the NAACP's top lawyer, he was on the national committee of the International Juridical Association, which actively defended Communists and consistently followed the Communist Party line. He was also on the executive board of the National Lawyers Guild and associate editor of *Lawyer's Guild Review,* at the time when the NLG was unquestionably the foremost legal bulwark of the Communist Party, its front organizations, and its controlled unions and which "never failed to rally to the legal defense of the Communist Party and individual members thereof, including known espionage agents."

Shortly after the NAACP's victory in the segregation case, the Communist Party decided to intensify agitation in the South by taking advantage of the unrest attendant upon forcible integration of the public schools. The unrest was aggravated when the bus boycott began in Montgomery, Alabama in 1955. It was that boycott that brought the opportunistic Martin L. King Jr. into national prominence. The boycott lasted a year and although King had not initiated it, he was given credit for its success. And, in 1957, he established the Southern Christian Leadership Conference.

It was not long before King became the racial agitation hero in the liberal and Communist press. Despite its four decades of seniority, the NAACP, which had no hero-figure such as King, began to lose its popularity, especially among young agitators, to King's Southern Christian Leadership Conference. This became even more apparent when King organized the Student Nonviolent Coordinating Committee to manage sit-in demonstrations.

In the realization that physical agitation was the order of the day, James Farmer, who had been the NAACP's program director in 1959 and 1960, became national director of the Congress of Racial Equality in 1961. CORE had been relatively quiet for many years although in 1960 it had begun a wide-spread campaign in the South to desegregate lunch counters. However, under Farmer's direction, CORE instituted the so-called freedom rides throughout the South to protest segregation on interstate carriers and at terminal facilities.

Once the "freedom rides" went into full swing, the NAACP decided to recoup its popularity by giving its full support to Farmer and his CORE freedom riders. Soon the NAACP was cooperating with King's SCLC and Snick and with A. Philip Randolph and Bayard Rustin in their political agitation projects.

The public position of the NAACP changed considerably in the early 1960's. Whereas before it had concentrated on its "legal" and "educational" programs, it now became involved with sit-ins at theaters, beaches, and swimming pools; picket lines at chain stores; "peace" marches; and boycotts. It supported the drive to impose civilian review boards upon police departments and it gave its financial and moral support to those who shouted "police brutality" and "black power."

While the NAACP has expended much of its finances and energies upon the support of the demonstrative groups, it has not forsaken its other projects. It continues to agitate for government housing and government "created" jobs for Negroes; for socialized medicine; for forcible integration of public schools; for federal interference with state voting laws, and, for federal interference with intrastate travel laws. In other projects, the NAACP has campaigned against the House Committee on Un-American Activities, against Barry Goldwater, against South Africa, for the peace corps, and for the United Nations.

In July, 1968, in an advertisement in *Esquire* magazine, the NAACP seemed to revert to the racism that had been characteristic of W. E. B. DuBois. In the ad, the NAACP charged that "white America denies black America its constitutional rights. White America creates the ghetto and slams the door on efforts to escape. White America traps the Negro in a cycle of prejudice and poverty that denies his humanity and destroys his dignity." Meanwhile, the NAACP was holding its fifty-ninth annual convention.

At the six-day convention in June, 1968, the delegates worked on the theme: "the building of economic and political power within the nation's ghettoes." A group of NAACP officials and leaders, organized as the National Committee to Revitalize the NAACP Movement, were obviously disturbed at the organization's loss of influence in the black community because of the rising popularity of black militant groups. These Leaders said: "We must rid ourselves of a solely middle-class image and organize our black stakeless and hopeless; the down and out, the inferiority complex-ridden." They also expressed their shock at "the thundering silence of the association's top leadership on issues of concern to black people."

The remedies suggested by the leaders to restore confidence in the NAACP included the formation of a black-oriented political bloc, similar to labor and farmer blocs; lobbying for more federal handouts for blacks, especially through a guaranteed annual wage plan; and, the introduction into more schools of a "black history" program in an effort "to restore a lost sense of pride and self-worth."

The trouble in the ranks of the NAACP continued after the annual convention. In October, 1968, a lawyer on the NAACP staff wrote an article for the *New York Times* magazine. He was bitterly critical of the Supreme Court for not doing more for Negroes. The utter ridiculousness of the article caused the lawyer to be fired. To protest his firing, the entire legal staff resigned. It all meant that black separatists were embarrassing the NAACP with their enthusiasm for black power.

In the November, 1968 issue of *The Crisis,* by means of an editorial, the NAACP tried to repair the damage done to its public image by renouncing the black separatists and their cries for violence and preferential treatment. In January, 1969, Alfred Baker Lewis — a white, a long-time Socialist, and a leader and treasurer of the NAACP — went on a tour of the South, carrying a message: "The NAACP is in favor of integrating Negro citizens on all levels — jobs, housing, education, politics and others. We are, however, as opposed to black separatism as to white-imposed segregation or racism."

Lewis was obviously concerned that, if black separatists were heeded, Negroes would be politically isolated — a precarious position since the 1969 NAACP program was largely concentrated on lobbying for federal expenditures to gain for Negroes low-rent housing, jobs in public works projects, and larger relief payments.

NATIONAL COMMITTEE FOR A SANE NUCLEAR POLICY

In 1957, Clarence Pickett and Norman Cousins organized the National Committee for a Sane Nuclear Policy. Pickett, who died in 1965, was at the time of SANE's founding, secretary emeritus of the American Friends Service Committee. He had a long history of associations with pro-Communist causes. Cousins, editor of *Saturday Review,* was a founder of the United World Federalists which had for its objective the creation of "a world federal government with authority to enact, interpret, and enforce world law adequate to maintain peace."

On November 15, 1957, in the *New York Times,* SANE published its first full-page advertisement and inaugurated its persistent "ban-the-bomb" campaign. Cousins and Pickett had no trouble recruiting names to grace their advertisements, letterheads, brochures, and other promotional literature. They called upon Socialists, fellow travelers, pro-Communist apologists, leftwing pacifists, and racist agitators. To add an international touch to SANE, honorary sponsors included such prominent leftwingers as Gunnar Myrdal of Sweden, Bertrand Russell and Philip Noel-Baker of Britain, Brock Chisholm of Canada, Pablo Casals — the Spanish expatriate — of Puerto Rico, and Albert Schweitzer — the French expatriate — of Gabon.

The theatrical world has been heavily represented among SANE's officials, sponsors, and entertainers: Steve Allen, Robert Ryan, Dore

Schary, Harry Belafonte, Tony Randall, Leonard Bernstein, Gene Kelly, Joan Baez, Pete Seeger, Mike Nichols, Elaine May, Ruby Dee, Ossie Davis, Helen Gahagan Douglas, Hildy Parks and Tom Poston.

The veteran fellow travelers in SANE were led by Eleanor Roosevelt. She was accompanied by Stringfellow Barr, Stuart Chase, Jerome Frank, Lewis Mumford, Louis Untermeyer, Mark Van Doren, Roger Baldwin, Clark Eichelberger, Hugh Hester, Kirtley Mather, Isidor F. Stone, Robert Havighurst.

The leftwing stalwarts of organized labor have been headed by Walter and Victor Reuther, A. Philip Randolph, and James G. Patton. From high positions in the federal government have come G. Mennen Williams, Benjamin V. Cohen, Edward U. Condon, Oliver Edmund Clubb, Rexford Tugwell.

The Protestant clergy have been represented by John C. Bennett, Edwin T. Dahlberg, and Dana McLean Greeley; the Catholic clergy by Daniel Berrigan S.J.; and, of the many rabbis involved with SANE are Rabbis Roland B. Gittelsohn, Maurice Eisendrath, and Edward Klein. Donald Harrington of New York City's Community Church had also been a SANEer but he had been, perhaps, better known as the state chairman of New York's Liberal Party.

From the academic ranks, SANE has received the support of Linus Pauling, Albert Szent-Györgyi, Erich Fromm, Seymour Melman, Quincy Wright, Denna F. Flemming, Hans Morgenthau, Harold Taylor, John P. Roche, David Riesman.

The racial agitators have included Martin Luther King Jr. and his wife, Julian Bond, John Lewis, James Farmer, and James Baldwin. From the Fund for the Republic came W. H. "Ping" Ferry and Fred Warner Neal; from the Socialist Party, Norman Thomas; from the press, cartoonists Walt Kelly and Jules Feiffer; from the literary world, John Hersey, Lillian Smith, and Laura Z. Hobson.

Prominent in the activist ranks of SANE have been such officers as Benjamin Spock, the baby doctor, whose gloomy visage has been featured in SANE advertisements; H. Stuart Hughes, who, in 1948, somehow discovered that the State Department's position was hardening against the Soviet Union; Homer Jack, a Gandhian, who had been vice chairman of the Illinois section of the American Civil Liberties Union from 1947 until 1959; and, Sanford Gottlieb, who was a labor editor and organizer for five years before he became SANE's political director.

SANE's announced basic program has always been opposition "to the testing, use, or threatened use of nuclear weapons." Such a program promoted by Americans was, of course, very agreeable to both home grown and foreign Communists. And SANE as the most prestigious ban-the-bomb group proved to be a boon for Communist infiltrators.

Inevitably, even though belatedly, the question of Communist infiltration of the SANE group became the subject of hearings held by the Senate Internal Security Subcommittee. Senator Thomas Dodd (D.-Conn.), a member of the subcommittee, delivered a speech in the Senate on May 25, 1960. Dodd said of these hearings: "Evidence that has come into the hands of the Subcommittee on Internal Security indicates that the Communist Party has made the nuclear test ban movement the chief target of its infiltration operations . . . on a foreign policy issue of overriding importance like the test ban, if a legitimate organization adheres to a policy which coincides with Communist policy, then it must be prepared to expect a concerted effort at infiltration by the Communist termites."

Dodd went on to discuss a major rally sponsored by SANE at Madison Square Garden, and held on May 19, 1960. He pointed out that "the unpublicized chief organizer [Henry Abrams] of the Madison Square Garden rally was a veteran member of the Communist Party; that there was also evidence of serious Communist infiltration at chapter level throughout the Committee for a Sane Nuclear Policy; that the Communist Party and its front organizations had done their utmost to promote the meeting; [and] that the Communists provided much of the organizing machinery for the meeting because they planned to use it as a pressure instrument in support of Soviet nuclear policy." On March 8, 1961, when the situation within SANE had shown no dramatic improvement, Dodd again warned his colleagues that there remained "a serious Communist infiltration in the local chapters of the Committee for a Sane Nuclear Policy."

The SANE leaders did dismiss Abrams, whose long record of service in the Communist Party could not be successfully denied. But, if any attempts were made to rid SANE of other Communists, such efforts were carefully concealed from public notice. And the Communists, if we may judge by their press, did not turn against SANE because of its token expulsion of Abrams. In the March, 1963 issue of *Political Affairs,* the Communists said that "the objective fact is that in the American scene, Dr. [Homer] Jack [then the executive director of

SANE] and a number of similar personalities are regarded as peace advocates, and are leaders in the struggle for peace, and through the work of SANE they do make an important contribution to peace." In *The Worker* (November 21, 1965), the Communists described SANE as "one of the many peace organizations which carry on positive work." ("Positive work" in the Communists' lexicon could only mean work that furthers the cause of international Communism.)

SANE, in an obvious ploy to lure political innocents to its membership, did indicate that it was not wholly on the side of the Communists: "While we disagree with the Communist nations in many ways, we also have common interests: in avoiding nuclear war; in ending radioactive fallout; in reducing money spent on arms which is needed to combat poverty, illiteracy, disease and deprivation both at home and abroad; in slowing and then ending the suicidal arms race." However, whatever points of disagreement might exist between SANE and the Communist nations have been studiously unmentioned. As a matter of fact, in its approach to Red China, SANE has made a strong overture for Communist approbation the world over. SANE has urged the seating of Red China in the United Nations, the lifting of travel bans between the United States and Red China, the resumption of U.S.-Red China trade relations, and the extension of American "humanitarian aid" to Red China — all projects which meet with the approval of international Communists.

SANE's leaders have not been so stupid as to advocate complete and total submission of U.S. foreign policy to the will of the Kremlin. They have, however, contrived a sugar-coated, idealistic plan of gradual surrender down the road of appeasement. They claim that their ultimate goal for the world is general and complete disarmament: "general" to include all types of weapons; "complete" to mean down to police levels. Such a goal would be reached in phases of arms control with inspections that would be fair to every nation in the world.

Of course, SANE's leaders realize only too well that the Communists are not going to make any genuine and credible moves toward peace. Therefore, SANE places the burden on the United States: "A series of initiative actions by the U.S., publicized in advance, independent of continued negotiations and carried out over a period of years as a definite and continuing strategy, offers hope of impressing all nations with the seriousness of the U.S. in its pursuit of its proclaimed goal of general and complete disarmament in a peaceful world." Of course, SANE never suggests that the Communists make a first move toward peace nor does it anticipate the disastrous consequences to American security after "a period of years" of U.S. initiatives without reciprocation by the Communists.

In the theoretical give-and-take between the U.S. and the Communist powers, the give must always be an American gesture in SANE's program. For example, SANE has stressed the need for economic justice throughout the world. But, to achieve this need, SANE suggests: "The U.S. and the West should challenge the Communist bloc to join them in providing aid through U.N. channels on a scale far greater than that of existing programs. If the Communist states do not adequately respond to this challenge, the Western countries should nevertheless continue to direct much of their aid into U.N. programs, which are more acceptable than the bilateral ones. In the case of non-cooperation by the Communist nations, however, the U.S. and other Western countries should reserve the right to provide bilateral aid geared to promoting peaceful social change."

The insistence upon American initiative to placate the Communists has also been the basis for SANE's attitude toward Communist Cuba: "The U.S. should initiate steps that will lead toward a normalization of diplomatic, trade, and cultural relations with Cuba, as well as freedom of travel between the two nations." SANE reasons that "the Castro regime in Cuba has become a severe test for the maturity of the U.S. and for its ability to adapt to a changing world," and "since the existing U.S. policies have not prevented the spread of Soviet influence to the Western hemisphere, the U.S. must reexamine those policies." In other words, the U.S. must accept a Communist stronghold in the Caribbean as a *fait accompli* and, in the future, should adopt a foreign policy of accommodation so that future spreads of Soviet influence in the Western hemisphere will not provoke hard feelings in the United States.

On the question of the Vietnam War, SANE's penchant for accommodation with the Communists has again been evident: "While the guerrilla campaign is executed through the use of terror, it has its roots in peasant aspirations for a better life." (Note: SANE will not admit that North Vietnam has waged a war of aggression to usurp more territory, resources, and subject peoples.) "Once again the U.S. is supporting the *status quo* in Asia in the face of a revolutionary tide." (Note:

By SANE standards, an independent Vietnam — that is, the *status quo* — should be forsaken in the face of Communist aggression, which, evidently by SANE standards, is progress.)

SANE has advised: "The U.S. Government should treat the situation in South Vietnam for what it is: A Communist 'war of liberation,' or a political-military-economic struggle to bring about a Communist regime in a colonial or formerly-colonial country. This situation cannot be resolved unilaterally: it requires both international assistance for political and economic change and a new international arrangement to stop the entry of arms and men. The burden should be shared among the U.N., the U.S., and other individual nations." The only possible interpretation of this SANE position is that the United States should recognize the futility of trying to prevent by military measures a Communist takeover, and should make the best of a bad situation by giving political and economic aid so that a new Communist regime might be stabilized. By December, 1968, SANE confirmed such an interpretation when it called for "the immediate withdrawal of substantial numbers" of American troops and weapons from Vietnam as a unilateral move by the United States. There was, of course, no call by SANE for the Communists to make any reciprocal gesture.

No matter what the area or source of trouble — Cuba, Berlin, Vietnam, Red China, the Soviet Union — SANE inevitably places its reliance for a peaceful world upon the United Nations. SANE advocates that the United Nations should have a permanent peace force to discourage aggression, that massive world-wide economic development be conducted through UN auspices, and — most important — that "the U.N. must be given authority to enact, interpret, and enforce world law to assure world security." Along with the so-called peace force, the United Nations would have "a World Court whose jurisdiction is accepted without reservation by all nations to settle disputes."

To achieve its one-world, disarmed and under United Nations control, SANE lobbies in the U.S. Congress and the United Nations, circulates its propaganda through more than one hundred other national leftwing, pacifist organizations, and supports political candidates.

In 1966, SANE's political activism was expressed through the Voters' Pledge Campaign, led by Norman Thomas, William Sloane Coffin Jr., and Sanford Gottlieb. (Thomas and Coffin, in 1967, were convicted of conspiracy to violate the federal draft laws.) Through the VPC, SANE supported congressional candidates who were committed

to a U.S. policy of scaling down the fighting in Vietnam and of supporting U.S. initiatives to encourage negotiations which would include the
Vietcong at the bargaining table. In 1968, SANE was the first national
non-partisan organization to support the presidential candidacy of
Senator Eugene McCarthy.

NATIONAL COMMITTEE FOR AN EFFECTIVE CONGRESS

In 1944, the League for Franchise Education was established. Its
announced purpose was to encourage maximum electoral participation
through the distribution of information about voting rights and voting
procedures. Its leaders included Henry Luce, Henry Kaiser, Winthrop
Aldrich, and John Cowles. The LFE was somewhat active during the
1944 presidential campaign but then became more or less defunct.

In 1948, some of the LFE's leaders and others decided to create the
National Committee for an Effective Congress in order to take a more
direct and active part in politics by supporting candidates for the
Congress of the United States. From its beginnings, the NCEC also —
according to its own promotional literature — provided "a nonpartisan,
practical service of arranging face-to-face get-togethers between community leaders and Members of Congress for exchange of information
and viewpoints on important issues . . . [and rendered] technical
research assistance to Members of Congress upon request."

The NCEC has always advertised itself as "the only independent
nonpartisan organization in American politics devoted solely to
Congress," and has attributed its success to "the fact that . . . [it] does
not represent any section of the country, any interest or any special
group." The history of NCEC, however, reflects an entirely different
situation because, unexceptionally, it has supported the most notorious
leftists in Congress, and with a very heavy emphasis upon Democrats.
The first chairman of NCEC was James Roosevelt, then a national
committeeman for the Democratic Party and who would later make his
mark in the Congress by leading a futile but vituperative fight to abolish
the House Committee on Un-American Activities.

Over the years, officials of the NCEC have included a few starry-
eyed liberals but the greater majority have taken an active role in
Communist fronts or one-world groups or various leftwing political
organizations, characterized mainly by their anti-anti-Communism.
Behind the scenes of the NCEC's formation were Arthur Goldsmith,
Maurice Rosenblatt, and Sidney Scheuer, all of whom were prominent

in the leadership of the defamatory Anti-Defamation League. Goldsmith and Rosenblatt have worked together in the Coordinating Committee for Democratic Action, a smear outfit which had for its targets members of Congress who refused to be rubber stamps for President Franklin Roosevelt and his interventionist foreign policy. (The Coordinating Committee for Democratic Action eventually merged with Friends of Democracy which was led by Communist-fronters Rex Stout and Leon Birkhead who wielded their dirty hatchets against anti-Communists.) Scheuer had been an executive director in the Foreign Economic Administration during the Roosevelt Administration. Two of his superiors at FEA were Frank Coe and Lauchlin Currie, both of whom had been members of Nathan Silvermaster's Communist cell which, in the 1930's, was an important part of the Soviet espionage network within the United States government.

The roster of NCEC officials has included Robert E. Sherwood, who had been a ghost writer for Franklin Roosevelt; Frederick L. Allen, an historian of liberal persuasion; Paul Appleby, the Dean of Syracuse University's Maxwell School of Citizenship and a former New Dealer in the Department of Agriculture where he had been Under Secretary for four years after serving seven years as executive assistant to Henry A. Wallace; Thurman Arnold, who had been a favorite in Roosevelt's New Deal, but who, in 1948, was a law partner of Abe Fortas and Paul Porter; Stringfellow Barr, a leftwing pacifist and Communist-fronter who was, in 1948, just beginning a ten-year tenure as president of the Foundation for World Government; Henry Seidel Canby, chairman of the board of the liberal *Saturday Review* and chairman of the board of judges of the Book-of-the-Month Club, which has been a financial and ideological boon for liberal-leftist authors; Evans Clark, husband of Freda Kirchwey who was the editor and publisher of the radical *Nation* magazine while Clark, in his own right, was formerly executive director of the Twentieth Century Fund which specialized in supporting pro-Communist projects; William L. Clayton, who had been a prominent official in the Roosevelt and Truman Administrations before assuming the vice presidency of the internationalist Atlantic Union; Mark Ethridge, the bleeding-heart publisher of the *Louisville Courier Journal;* Oscar Hammerstein II, the celebrated librettist, who was a familiar figure in Communist fronts; Palmer Hoyt, formerly a director in Elmer Davis' Red-lined Office of War Information, and who, in 1948, was propagating his ultra-liberalism as editor and publisher of the *Denver*

Post; Gardner Jackson, a veteran Communist fronter; Paul Hoffman, an ubiquitous socialist; Archibald MacLeish, a veteran Communist fronter, a former assistant director of Elmer Davis' Red-lined Office of War Information, and the individual given the most credit for establishing UNESCO which became a nesting place for international Reds and radicals who wanted to subvert traditional educational norms and principles under the aegis of the United Nations; Michael Straight, editor of the leftist *New Republic* magazine; Telford Taylor, a lawyer noted for defending leftists in the courtroom and attacking anti-Communists everywhere; George Hamilton Combs, a former congressman, who brought his ultra-liberal views to his profession as radio news analyst; Sumner Welles who, while Under Secretary of State in the Roosevelt Administration, scandalized diplomatic circles with his perverted behavior; and Arthur Schlesinger Sr., an historian from Harvard University, who lent his name to many Communist fronts and causes.

In later years, the NCEC added such officials as Harry Ashmore, formerly the executive editor of the *Arkansas Gazette* who, in 1948, supported Henry Wallace, the Communists' choice for the American presidency, and later campaigned for Adlai Stevenson, became a director of the ultra-leftist Fund for the Republic, editor-in-chief of the Encyclopedia Britannica, and, in 1967, an apologist for Ho chi Minh of Communist North Vietnam; Henry Steele Commager, an ultra-liberal historian, who ranks as one of the most hysterical bleeding-hearts in the entire academic world in his denunciations of McCarthyism, loyalty oaths, security statutes, and committees investigating subversion; Hans Morgenthau, a political scientist, whose leftwing pacifism became nationally known during the wave of anti-Vietnam "teach-in" demonstrations; James A. Pike, the former Bishop of the Episcopal Church in California whose eccentric religious views attracted the criticism of his co-religionists while his leftist political views gained him a haven at the ultra-leftist Center for the Study of Democratic Institutions; and Barbara Tuchman, whose career in leftwing journalism did not prevent her winning the Pulitzer prize in general non-fiction for her *The Guns of August.* Arthur M. Schlesinger Jr., whose affectations as an historian brought him to a key role in the Kennedy administration and made him a much heralded spokesman in radical politics and John K. Galbraith, one of the nation's most influential Keynesian economists, who became national chairman of Americans for Democratic Action in 1968, worked in 1967 for NCEC candidates by speaking at fund-raising events.

After its formation in 1948, the NCEC wasted no time in starting its political activity. In that year, its support went to the Senatorial campaigns of Paul Douglas of Illinois, Guy Gillette of Iowa, Hubert Humphrey of Minnesota, James Murray of Montana, Estes Kefauver of Tennessee, and Matthew Neely of West Virginia – all Democrats. In 1949, in a special Senatorial election, the NCEC supported Democrat Herbert Lehman of New York.

In 1950, Claude Pepper of Florida and Frank Graham of North Carolina were supported by the NCEC in Senatorial primaries. In that same year, in Senatorial elections, support was given to Democrats Helen Gahagan Douglas of California, John Carroll of Colorado, William Benton and Brien McMahon of Connecticut, Thomas Hennings of Missouri, Herbert Lehman of New York, and Warren Magnuson of Washington, along with Wayne Morse of Oregon, then an Independent, and Republican Charles Tobey of New Hampshire.

In 1952, the NCEC supported the Senatorial candidacies of Democrats Mike Mansfield of Montana, Harley Kilgore of West Virginia, Dennis Chavez of New Mexico, Henry Jackson of Washington, Stuart Symington of Missouri, and Joseph O'Mahoney of Wyoming, and Republicans Alexander Wiley of Wisconsin, Ralph Flanders of Vermont, Frederick Payne of Maine, Irving Ives of New York, Dwight Griswold of Nebraska, and John Sherman Cooper of Kentucky. Members of the House of Representatives Gracie Pfost of Idaho and Lester Johnson of Wisconsin received NCEC support in 1952 and 1953, respectively.

In 1954, the NCEC entered upon its most celebrated escapade. Its leaders, particularly Paul Hoffman – President Dwight Eisenhower's confidante – decided that the time was opportune to destroy Senator Joseph R. McCarthy whose anti-Communist investigations were proving embarrassing to the left-wingers, such as those found in NCEC, who felt that they had a sanctuary in government service from which they could continue their un-American, anti-American activities.

The NCEC set up its base of operations in the Carroll Arms Hotel, across the street from the Senate Office Building. Republican Senator Ralph Flanders of Vermont, whose campaign had been supported by the NCEC in 1952, was chosen as stooge for the NCEC. On July 30, 1954, Flanders introduced in the Senate an NCEC-drafted resolution to condemn McCarthy for "conduct unbecoming a member." On August 2, Flanders' resolution became Senate Resolution 301. Amendments to

SR301, proposed by Flanders and two other NCEC favorites — J. W. Fulbright of Arkansas and Wayne Morse of Oregon — added up to forty-six counts of allegedly improper conduct on the part of McCarthy.

The forces of the left rallied behind Flanders: the Communist Party, Americans for Democratic Action, the Congress of Industrial Organizations, and such individuals as William Clayton, John Cowles, Lewis W. Douglas, Samuel Goldwyn, Erwin Griswold, Palmer Hoyt, Ralph McGill, Reinhold Neibuhr, Henry Wriston, James D. Zellerbach, Spyros Skouras, Walter Reuther, John P. Marquand, Paul Helms, Fred Lazarus Jr., and Cass Canfield.

After two months of hearings and deliberations, a Special Committee, headed by Republican Senator Arthur Watkins of Utah, dismissed all but two of Flanders' forty-six counts against McCarthy. On December 2, 1954, by a vote of 67 to 22, the Senate condemned McCarthy on two counts, based on opinions McCarthy expressed outside the Senate. Neither of the two counts were contained in Flanders' original charges, but only twenty-two Republicans (out of forty-five) voted contrary to the NCEC's vendetta. The entire representation of Democrats in the Senate followed meekly in the footsteps of Flanders. (On July 19, 1956, Flanders apologized to McCarthy from the Senate floor for having introduced the censure resolution two years earlier. But, four years after McCarthy's death, Flanders — in his autobiographical *Senator from Vermont* — recanted his apology and once again attacked McCarthy.)

The campaign against McCarthy cost the NCEC at least $73,372. And, from the viewpoint of the left, it was money well spent. As McCarthy admitted, the NCEC "masterminded the censure movement" — a quotation still used by NCEC in its promotional literature.

In 1954, the year of the NCEC's victory over McCarthy, the organization was extremely busy supporting the Senatorial candidacies of Democrats Hubert Humphrey of Minnesota, John Sparkman of Alabama, Richard Neuberger of Oregon, James Murray of Montana, Paul Douglas of Illinois, Joseph O'Mahoney of Wyoming, John Carroll of Colorado, Claude Wickard of Indiana, and Earle Clements of Kentucky.

In 1956, the NCEC supported the Senatorial candidacies of Wayne Morse of Oregon and Millard Tydings of Maryland. In that campaign year, the NCEC claimed to have spent $157,989 — allotting two-thirds of the sum to Democrats and one-third to Republicans. (By 1957, the NCEC claimed that it had seventeen Democrats and eight Republicans in the Congress.)

During the Senatorial campaign of 1956, the NCEC established a front which it called: A Clean Politics Appeal. The front was headed by Elmer Davis and Archibald MacLeish, two old comrades who had served as director and assistant director, respectively, during World War II in the Red-lined Office of War Information. The targets for the dirty politics of Davis and MacLeish were Senators Herman Welker of Idaho and Everett Dirksen of Illinois, who — in the eyes of the left — had committed the unpardonable sin of defending Joe McCarthy against the NCEC's 1954 campaign of destruction. Against Welker and Dirksen, the NCEC-Davis-MacLeish front supported the candidacies of Democrats Frank Church in Idaho and Richard Stengel in Illinois. Church defeated Welker but Dirksen retained his Senate seat.

Another front was established in 1956 by the NCEC. It was called Citizens' Fund for Cooper and was headed by Mayor Charles P. Taft of Cincinnati. The committee not only raised $50,000 for Republican John Sherman Cooper of Kentucky but helped to provide personnel for his campaign staff and bought advertising and television time for him. Cooper had served in the Senate on two occasions (1946-1949 and 1952-1955) but on each occasion he had been defeated for re-election. After his defeat in 1954, President Dwight Eisenhower made him Ambassador to India where he served from March, 1955 until August, 1956. Cooper, however, since he had the resources of the NCEC behind him, did not have to wage a lengthy campaign for the Senate and, in the fall election, he gained a Senate seat for the third time. (Cooper has not been ungrateful. He has endorsed his generous benefactors: "The NCEC . . . works with members to discover what things need to be done in the national interest, what things can be done, and how to do them." Of course, Cooper — during his second stint in the Senate — had voted to condemn Joe McCarthy as did all the Republican recipients of NCEC's largesse but no other Senator enjoyed a $50,000 campaign gift as did Cooper.)

In 1958, a major solicitation for funds to support NCEC Senatorial candidates was made by Eleanor Roosevelt on behalf of Democrats Fred M. Anderson of Nevada, Clair Engle of California, Eugene McCarthy of Minnesota, and Gale McGee of Wyoming. In 1960, the chief beneficiaries of the NCEC's financial support in the Senatorial races were the Democrats Hubert Humphrey of Minnesota, Robert L.

Knous of Colorado, George McGovern of South Dakota, Pat McNamara of Michigan, Lee Metcalf of Montana, Maurine Neuberger of Oregon, Quentin Burdick of South Dakota, and Frank Theis of Kansas.

In 1961, Democratic Senators Eugene McCarthy, Lee Metcalf, and Estes Kefauver along with Republican Senators John Sherman Cooper and Clifford Case expressed their appreciation to NCEC by soliciting funds on its behalf through a mass mailing to "Dear Friend." They began their letter with a rather curious sentence: "If the National Committee for an Effective Congress were to try to dictate what we should do (like so many organizations), it would (like them) achieve little that would not have been achieved anyhow." The disclaimer was curious since Chairman Sidney Scheuer of NCEC had admitted that those candidates supported by the NCEC (for example, Case, Cooper, Kefauver, McCarthy, and Metcalf) received such support "contingent on the candidates' promise to help develop a creative American foreign policy; work with other Congressional liberals as an affirmative team; and call on the committee whenever he needed it, after being elected." Whether the Senators liked it or not, they responded to the NCEC's whip or else they lost the organization's support.

In 1962, Democrats Frank Church of Idaho, John Carroll of Colorado, George McGovern of South Dakota, and David King of Utah received the NCEC's financial support in their Senatorial campaigns.

Seventy candidates for House and Senate seats were supported in 1964 by the NCEC. It was a most productive year since sixty-two of the seventy were elected. More than $500,000 was spent in that year by the NCEC.

Senator Eugene McCarthy and Henry Steele Commager, the ultra-liberal historian, solicited NCEC campaign funds by mail and through advertisements in *New Republic, Saturday Review,* and other liberal journals. They sought support for liberal Senatorial candidates "and some 50 men in the House who represent clear-cut choices against right-wing opponents." The McCarthy-Commager efforts brought in $40,000 and, even though 1966 was an off-year, the NCEC contributed a total in excess of $200,000 to elect Democratic Senators Clinton Anderson of New Mexico, E. L. Bartlett of Alaska, Fred Harris of Oklahoma, Thomas J. McIntyre of New Hampshire, Walter Mondale of Minnesota, Claiborne Pell of Rhode Island, John Sparkman of Alabama, and William Spong of Virginia, and Republicans J. Caleb Boggs of Delaware, Edward Brooke of Massachusetts, Howard Baker of

Tennessee, Clifford Case of New Jersey, John Sherman Cooper of Kentucky, and Margaret Chase Smith of Maine. In the House races, the NCEC had fifty-five of its endorsees elected — thirty-eight Democrats and seventeen Republicans. Such victories offset the defeats suffered by four NCEC Senatorial candidates — all Democrats: Ralph Harding of Idaho, G. Mennen Williams of Michigan, Frank Morrison of Nebraska, and Teno Roncalio of Wyoming.

Intrigue was the keynote for the NCEC in 1967. At an NCEC-sponsored meeting in the home of Laughlin Phillips, publisher of the ultra-liberal *Washingtonian* magazine and an NCEC member, a group of Republicans were urged by Republican Senator Hugh Scott of Pennsylvania to emulate Republican Senators Jacob Javits of New York and Clifford Case of New Jersey by batting from the party line on key issues. According to *Human Events* (July 1, 1967): "Many in the gathering were reportedly opposed to the GOP's 'budget cutting' proposals and its general stand against LBJ's 'soft on Soviet' policies, particularly expanded East-West trade." Republicans who attended the NCEC conclave included: Senator J. Caleb Boggs of Delaware, Representatives James G. Fulton and Joseph McDade of Pennsylvania, Florence Dwyer of New Jersey, Charles Whalen of Ohio, Charles Mathias of Maryland, Seymour Halpern of New York, Robert Stafford of Vermont, and Bradford Morse of Massachusetts. Morse's presence was of special significance since he was and remains the leader of the so-called Wednesday Club, a group of very liberal House Republicans.

Chairman Sidney Scheuer of the NCEC, when questioned about the meeting in the Phillips home, said: "Just as the Democratic Study Group [an organization of very liberal House Democrats] exerts pressure on the Democratic leadership, these Republicans should exert pressure on GOP leadership." With Senator Scott leading such an intra-party revolution, aided and abetted by Representative Bradford Morse and his Wednesday Club, Scheuer could not help but be pleased since Scott — at the meeting — had been lavish in his praise of NCEC. It all meant that the NCEC was cementing its control of liberals of both parties in both the Senate and the House. Back in 1959, when the Democratic Study Group was organizing, it received the encouragement of the NCEC and finances in order that the DSG could meet its operating budget and personnel assistance to coordinate the DSG's research and campaign activities. In their turn, the DSG leaders such as Senators Eugene McCarthy and Mike Monroney and Representative

James O'Hara of Michigan helped the NCEC by raising funds and coordinating DSG's political moves with those of the NCEC.

In the summer of 1967, the NCEC launched its fund-raising campaign for the 1968 congressional elections. Henry Steele Commager and Barbara Tuchman sent an appeal through the mails: "The National Committee for an Effective Congress believes that Congress itself can be the source of fresh ideas and of leadership. It is the independent Congressmen of both parties who have, so far, stood up to the military extremists and it is to them that we must look." Of course, the NCEC was not really looking for "independent Congressmen of both parties." It was looking for liberal stooges who would receive support from NCEC under the contingency that they promise to work for NCEC's goals in the Congress and to look for advice, while in the Congress, from the NCEC's leaders.

By the summer of 1968, Commager and Tuchman were becoming hysterical in their NCEC fund-raising appeals: "We can no longer afford a Congress crippled by narrow interests, parochial fears and dominated by a coalition of Southern Democrats and Northern conservatives . . . . The liberal heart of the Senate is at stake."

For the Senate in 1968, the NCEC endorsed Democrats Frank Church of Idaho, Joseph Clark of Pennsylvania, J. William Fulbright of Arkansas, Ernest Gruening of Alaska, John Gilligan of Ohio, George McGovern of South Dakota, Mike Monroney of Oklahoma, Wayne Morse of Oregon, and Gaylord Nelson of Wisconsin, and Republicans George Aiken of Vermont, Thomas Kuchel of California, Charles Mathias of Maryland, and Thruston Morton of Kentucky. Kuchel was defeated in the primaries. Morton decided to retire. Clark, Gruening, Gilligan, Monroney, and Morse were defeated. In the House races, the NCEC concentrated on the election of Democrats Charles Vanik of Ohio, Morris Udall of Arizona, Charles Weltner of Georgia, and John Brademas of Indiana. All but Weltner were victorious.

NATIONAL COMMITTEE TO ABOLISH THE
HOUSE UN-AMERICAN ACTIVITIES COMMITTEE

In 1946, the Committee on Un-American Activities became the only investigative standing committee in the House of Representatives. Ever since, the Communist Party and its fellow travelers have waged a campaign to abolish the Committee. The campaign has fluctuated in its intensity but in 1959, for reasons best known to themselves, the Communists made "abolition" a high-priority project. Throughout that year, in the Party's newspapers, *The Worker* and *People's World,* there appeared increasing agitation for "abolition." In the *Washington Post and Times Herald* of January 7, 1959, there appeared, in an advertisement, a petition to "eliminate the HCUA as a Standing Committee." The signatories were well-known fellow travelers and included: Eleanor Roosevelt, Aubrey Williams, Clarence Pickett, Alexander Meiklejohn, Abraham J. Muste, Stewart Meacham, Dorothy Marshall, Stringfellow Barr, Eugene Carson Blake, and Robert Kenny.

In December, 1959, at the Communist Party's Seventeenth National Convention in New York City, there was a call directed at all Communists to "abolish the witch-hunting House Un-American Activities Committee." Less than a month later, it was announced in *People's World* that Eleanor Roosevelt and Frank Wilkinson had agreed on a joint effort to push the "abolition" campaign. Shortly thereafter, Eleanor's dutiful son James, then serving in the House of Representatives from California, introduced a bill to abolish the HCUA. (He carried on his futile "abolition" campaign until he left the Congress five years later.)

In the spring of 1960, the HCUA announced that it would hold hearings in San Francisco for the purpose of investigating Communist Party activities in California. In April, 1960, the San Francisco chapter of the Citizens Committee to Preserve American Freedoms held its first meeting. The CCPAF had been chosen by the Communist Party's leaders to guide the attack against the HCUA when it held its hearings in San Francisco. (The CCPAF, which had been organized in 1952, was a Communist front that specialized in propaganda aimed at abolishing the HCUA and discrediting the Federal Bureau of Investigation.) Frank Wilkinson, the head of the CCPAF, was the Communist Party's principal field agent to organize demonstrations against the HCUA. (Wilkinson was formerly the head of the security unit of the Communist Party in Los Angeles. He had also worked for the Emergency Civil Liberties Committee, a Communist front organized in 1951, which had as its main purpose the abolition of HCUA.)

On or about May 6, 1960 — a week before the HCUA hearings were scheduled to begin — Wilkinson arrived in San Francisco. The Communist Party's plan of attack against the HCUA was distributed to Communists in the San Francisco area. Wilkinson rallied Communist fronters and dupes to follow the Communists. And, on May 12, 13, and

14, 1960, the HCUA held its hearings in San Francisco's City Hall. Behind Communist leadership, collegians and others rioted in the rotunda outside the hearing room, disrupted committee proceedings within the hearing room, and established massive picket lines outside the City Hall.

Unfortunately for Wilkinson's cause, the demonstrations were recorded on film and shown to millions of Americans through the auspices of the HCUA and a number of anti-Communist organizations. The film, "Operation Abolition," was definitely an embarrassment to the Communists. They had been caught in the act of creating riots against a duly constituted committee of the Congress. The exposé called for a change of tactics in the "abolition" campaign and Frank Wilkinson was ready.

On August 15, 1960, Wilkinson organized the National Committee to Abolish the House Un-American Activities Committee. There has probably never been a Communist front which attracted so many notables to its support. Listed as founders of the NCAHUAC were three long-time fellow travelers Alexander Meiklejohn, Clarence Pickett, and Aubrey Williams — all of whom are now deceased. Original officers of the front included Communists Harvey O'Connor, Florence Luscomb, Russ Nixon, Richard Criley, William Howard Melish, and Otto Nathan, and fellow travelers James Imbrie, Robert Kenny and Dorothy Marshall. Wilkinson's position has always been that of executive director. The top-heavy representation of Communists in official positions indicated that the Communist Party's leaders were taking no chances that the NCAHUAC would deviate in the slightest degree from the Party's line.

Wilkinson's strategy as the leader of the NCAHUAC soon became obvious. Newspaper advertisements, calling for the abolition of the HCUA, and containing hundreds of names, were placed in the *New York Times* (February 9, 1961 and February 22, 1962) and the *Washington Post* (January 2, 1961). The names of the NCAHUAC did not appear in the advertisements but, instead, the device of Ad Hoc Committees was used in two of the advertisements along with the names of Clarence Pickett and James Imbrie, both of whom were original officials of the NCAHUAC. (The third advertisement merely carried names of signatories to a petition to abolish the HCUA.) There was no question about the true sponsorship of the advertisements. They stemmed from Wilkinson and his NCAHUAC.

Along with the large advertisements which were reprinted and widely distributed by Wilkinson, regional branches of the NCAHUAC were organized. In Massachusetts, the branch was headed by Vern Countryman of Harvard University's Law School. He was joined by his faculty colleagues Mark De Wolfe Howe, Clark Byse, David Cavers, Louis Jaffe, John Dawson, and Albert Sacks. The Rev. Robert F. Drinan S.J., dean of Boston College's Law School, wrote an article (*Boston Globe,* August 28, 1966), condemning the HCUA and praising the efforts of Countryman and his branch of the NCAHUAC. Also from the Boston College Law School, Rev. William J. Kenealy became a sponsor of the Massachusetts branch. Other clergymen from Massachusetts who joined the "abolition" campaign included Protestant Bishops Malcolm Peabody and William Appleton Lawrence, Rabbi Roland Gittelsohn, and Rev. Joseph H. Fichter S.J. and Joseph Fletcher of the Harvard Divinity School's faculty. They were in company with Paul Dudley White, the heart specialist, and such well-known fellow travelers as Henry Steele Commager, Howard Mumford Jones, Kirtley Mather, Albert Szent-Györgyi, and Dirk Struik.

Vice chairmen for the Southern region's NCAHUAC activities were racial agitators Rev. C. T. Vivian, Rev. Wyatt Tee Walker, and John Lewis, and Communist Carl Braden.

In the House of Representatives, abolition leaders, besides James Roosevelt, included George Brown, Don Edwards, Edward Roybal, Jeffery Cohelan of California; Leonard Farbstein, Abraham Multer, Benjamin Rosenthal, William Fitts Ryan, John Lindsay, Adam Clayton Powell, Theodore Kupferman, Jonathan Bingham, and James Scheuer of New York; John Conyers, Charles Diggs, John Dingell, Neil Staebler, and Lucien Nedzi of Michigan; Thomas Ashley of Ohio; Robert Duncan and Edith Green of Oregon; Donald Fraser of Minnesota; Thomas Gill of Hawaii; Henry Gonzalez of Texas; Barratt O'Hara of Illinois; and Robert Kastenmeier of Wisconsin.

From the theatrical world, would-be abolitionists of HCUA included Alan Alda, Melvyn Douglas and his wife Helen Gahagan, Ossie Davis, Ruby Dee, Pete Seeger, Howard Da Silva, James Whitmore, Sterling Hayden, and Robert Ryan; literary figures included James Baldwin, James Jones, John Ciardi, Louis Untermeyer, Elmer Rice, Catherine Drinker Bowen, and Mark Harris.

In 1966, at a private fund-raising party for the NCAHUAC Representative Theodore Kupferman, who was succeeding to John Lindsay's seat in the Congress, made a speech to the gathering of about seventy. The speech was, of course, an anti-HCUA diatribe. In attendance at the meeting were two who had pleaded the Fifth Amendment before the HCUA, Frank Donner and Russ Nixon; John Henry Faulk who had won a very lucrative libel suit on grounds that he had been falsely accused of pro-Communist activities; and, Alger Hiss (!) whose appearances before the HCUA resulted in a federal prison term. (Hiss' publisher Alfred A. Knopf has signed an anti-HCUA petition.)

Many of those individuals who have joined Wilkinson's "abolition" campaign have unhappy memories of their own experiences before the HCUA or its counterparts in the U.S. Senate and various States. Others have a long history of supporting organizations which the HCUA had investigated and found to be Communist fronts. And some of the largest and most influential Communist fronts have contributed hugely to the roster of signatories found on the anti-HCUA petitions gathered by Wilkinson and his colleagues. These fronts include: the American Committee for Protection of Foreign Born [Americans]; the Chicago Committee to Defend the Bill of Rights; the Emergency Civil Liberties Committee; the Methodist Federation for Social Action; the National Lawyers Guild; the Southern Conference Educational Fund; the National Assembly for Democratic Rights; the Citizens Committee for Constitutional Liberties; the Committee to Secure Justice for Morton Sobell; and, the National Council of American-Soviet Friendship.

The Senate Internal Security Subcommittee's 1956 list of the "most typical sponsors of front organizations" has been well represented in the anti-HCUA campaign. The "typicals" include Elmer Benson, Jerome Davis, Robert Dunn, Thomas I. Emerson (NCAHUAC's "advisor on constitutional law"), Robert J. Havighurst, James Imbrie, Robert Kenny, Freda Kirchwey, Corliss Lamont, Carey McWilliams, Clyde Miller, Harlow Shapley, Isidor F. Stone, Dirk Struik, and Willard Uphaus. Other perennial front-joiners include such leftwing elder statesmen as Norman Thomas, Stringfellow Barr, Reinhold Niebuhr, Robert Lynd, Lewis Mumford, W. E. B. DuBois, Paul Tillich, Jerome Davis, Matthew Josephson, Derk Bodde, Harry Bridges, Edward U. Condon, Clyde Miller, Broadus Mitchell, Quincy Wright, Hugh Hester, Oscar Handlin, Robert MacIver, Thurman Arnold, Robert M. Hutchins, W. H. "Ping" Ferry, John C. Bennett, Vincent Hallinan, William A. Williams, Sidney Lens, Matthew Josephson, Walter Millis, Clark Foreman, Erich Fromm, Ben Shahn, and Harold Taylor. The ban-the-bomb crowd has been represented by Benjamin Spock, Linus Pauling, Donna Allen, Dagmar Wilson, and H. Stuart Hughes. The Warren Commission has been represented by Norman Redlich, counsel to the commission, and Mark Lane, whose writings on the commission's work have been anti-Commission, pro-Lee Harvey Oswald. The eccentric Bishop James A. Pike is anti-HCUA as is the racist agitator Monsignor Charles Owen Rice of the *Pittsburgh Catholic* and as was the deceased agitator Martin Luther King Jr.

The preponderance of Communists and Communist fronters in the Wilkinson-led "abolition" campaign virtually precludes the idea that any of the hundreds of educators, businessmen, clergymen, jurists, politicoes, authors, artists, or others who have signed the NCAHUAC-sponsored petitions can plead ignorance of the fact that they are co-operating in a major project of the Communist Party.

NATIONAL COUNCIL FOR CIVIC RESPONSIBILITY
PUBLIC AFFAIRS INSTITUTE
GROUP RESEARCH, INC.
INSTITUTE FOR AMERICAN DEMOCRACY

In 1947, there was organized the Public Affairs Institute, described in its own literature as "a liberal-oriented, action-research center." In reality it was a socialist propaganda mill, financed by the left wing of organized labor. Among its original sponsors were Chester Bowles, Thurman Arnold, Stuart Chase, Morris Ernst, James G. Patton, Fiorello La Guardia, Hubert Humphrey, and Arthur M. Schlesinger Jr. Among its leftist boosters have been Edmund G. (Pat) Brown, Joseph S. Clark, Paul Douglas, Abe Fortas, Pat McNamara, Frank Moss, James Roosevelt, Jacob Javits, Estes Kefauver, Eugene McCarthy, Gale McGee, Wayne Morse, William Proxmire, and Stuart Symington. ("Since its inception, the PAI has been under the executive direction of Dr. Dewey Anderson, an economist with varied experience in public welfare in California and on the national level. A liberal Democrat, he was prominent in official Washington during the FDR-New Deal. The Senate Internal Security Subcommittee in hearings, April 16, 1953, on Interlocking Subversion in Government Departments introduced into the record a federal government application Form 57 for Nathan Gregory Silvermaster which showed Dewey Anderson to have been a reference, in 1944, for Mr. Silvermaster. At that time, Dr. Anderson was chief of field operations for UNRRA. Silvermaster was named by Elizabeth

Bentley as the leader of a Communist underground group in Washington during 1941-44 from whom she secured secret information and Communist Party dues. Mr. Silvermaster invoked the 5th Amendment rather than answer questions based on Miss Bentley's charges.") (The Church League of America, *News & Views,* March, 1965.)

"Shortly after the 1960 election, a group of left wing publicists and activists decided that never again should conservatives be allowed to threaten the liberal-left-labor coalition as it had in the presidential photo-finish which won John F. Kennedy the presidency.

"This group had no formal designation or membership lists. But it included official and unofficial representatives of the tax-exempted AFL-CIO, the Jewish Labor Committee, Americans for Democratic Action, and a number of other organizations. As a result of informal meetings and consultations, a systematic and sustained campaign against conservatives and other right wingers was launched." (Ralph de Toledano, *Manchester Union-Leader,* October 8, 1964.)

Meanwhile: "In October-November of 1960 the Soviets convened a 'Meeting of Representatives of the Communist and Worker's Parties' in Moscow which was attended by delegates from 81 Communist Parties throughout the world representing 36 million voluntary and involuntary Communists. At the close of the meeting the Communist leaders issued a Manifesto which was a scorching attack on the 'reactionaries' of America as the principal enemies of what the Communists call progressive change. At that meeting a world 'party-line' was laid down to start a drive on those 'reactionaries' who stand in the way of the new social order.

"The Communists in America almost immediately began the crusade against what they termed the 'ultra-Right.' This party line was announced to the comrades at large and the hitch-hiking liberals in a Party magazine called *Political Affairs* which is regularly used for that purpose. In its issue of August, 1961, Communist leader Gus Hall did the announcing with an article titled 'The Ultra-Right: Kennedy and the Role of Progressives.' All through the article he pounded hard on the terms 'Ultra-Right' and 'extreme right.' This was the same Gus Hall who, in the Communist *Daily Worker,* April 5, 1950, was the first on record to introduce the term 'McCarthyism.' Our American liberal-coterie quickly grabbed that shibboleth and wore it threadbare flagellating the individuals and groups they did not like. Almost everyone not left of center suddenly became a 'McCarthyite.' When time dulled the edge of that ugly word, the crusading-left eagerly grasped the new slogan-weapons of 'Ultra-Right' — 'Extremists' — and 'Radical-Right' so conveniently provided for them." (The Church League of America, *News & Views,* January, 1965.)

"On December 19, 1961, a memorandum was completed and transmitted to the then Attorney General of the United States, Robert Kennedy. Sent by long-time leftist labor leaders Walter and Victor Reuther, the memo called for a sharp cut-back in FBI action against Communists, and a strong Federal effort to curb the effectiveness of so-called 'rightists.' The Reuther memo was nothing less than a comprehensive plan for the muzzling of conservatives and anti-Communists.

"The memo itself was an out-growth of a general understanding reached by various leaders of the AFL-CIO, Americans for Democratic Action and other left wing groups. Something had to be done, they agreed, to silence conservative leaders and isolate their followers. In 1962, [six weeks] after the Reuther memo, a new front group set up offices in Washington, D.C. calling itself Group Research, Inc. Its purpose was for a time shrouded in secrecy." (Robert E. Bauman, "NCCR and Smear Tactics of the Left," *New Guard,* January, 1965.)

"This outfit [Group Research], conceived by Emanuel Muravchik, an active Socialist whose nominal job is with the Jewish Labor Committee and Labor's powerful Committee on Political Education [COPE], set itself up in business as an open blacklister of conservatives. To 'subscribers' it sent out a stream of material purporting to give the backgrounds of all those who opposed the liberal-left-labor coalition. It urged these 'subscribers' to protest — and if possible prevent — the appearance of conservatives on lecture platforms, TV programs, or on radio. It aimed its fire primarily on the scattering of conservatives in the mass communications media." (Ralph de Toledano, *Manchester Union Leader,* October 8, 1964.)

"Group Research, Inc., was incorporated as non-profit and educational . . . by three men: Wesley McCune, Dan Singer, and James Heller. [The papers of incorporation were notarized by Mary C. Asay, office secretary of Joseph Rauh Jr., an executive of Americans for Democratic Action.] McCune was assistant to Charles F. Brannan when he was Secretary of Agriculture, [then McCune was a staff member of the Democratic National Committee], and later was associated with James Patton in the National Farmers Union [described by Patton as a 'militant, progressive, left-wing farm organization'] in which McCune was public information officer. The latter two men are Washington attorneys, and Heller is secretary of the Washington chapter of the American Civil Liberties Union. [Singer was secretary-treasurer of Leo Szilard's leftwing, pacifist Council for a Livable World, wherein James Patton was on the board of directors.]

"Group Research, Inc. is a creature and subsidiary of the AFL-CIO's Industrial Union Department (I.U.D.). The I.U.D. enjoys complete autonomy inside the merged labor federation. It was set up by Walter Reuther at the time of the merger to ensure a power center under his absolute control inside the 'family of labor.'" (The Church League of America, *News & Views,* September, 1963.)

Under the leadership of Wesley McCune and with the complete co-operation of Reuther's IUD and the AFL-CIO's COPE, Group Research set out to destroy the so-called right wing. Emanuel Muravchik, as field director of the Jewish Labor Committee, wrote to labor union officials across the nation, requesting their assistance in collecting information about the "activities of the ultra-rightists and their relation to the right-to-workers and anti-labor employers" in their communities. Muravchik, of course, was seeking ammunition for Group Research's campaign.

Walter Reuther's IUD urged recipients of its Group Research mailings to send "clippings, publications or other evidence of (right-wing) activity in your area." The purpose, of course, was to find material for Group Research. In March, 1963, COPE distributed a memorandum ("Combatting Right-wing Activity in Your Community") to state and local union officials. Group Research received its greatest boost from this memorandum which said, in part: "In the past year or two countless right-wing groups have sprouted, both national and local. They distribute a staggering variety of misleading smear literature, attack democratic institutions, disrupt school systems, harass civic groups, provide speakers, distribute films, censor textbooks and generally make their influence felt.

"Although the right-wingers talk most about the menace of communism, impeaching Chief Justice Warren, repealing the income tax, 'getting the U.S. out of the U.N. and the U.N. out of the U.S.,' and the alleged 'no-win' foreign policy, at the root of their efforts is determined anti-labor activity and an all-out drive against social welfare legislation.

"Combatting them at the national and community level is essential for organized labor, and the fight must be waged in cooperation with other groups under attack. By working with teachers, clergymen, foreign policy groups, liberal farm organizations, PTA's, youth movements, minority groups, civil liberties groups and many others, unions can find a common ground which will help counteract right-wing activities and build future support on labor questions.

"Intelligent opposition to right-wing extremists is based on two things: research and action.

"1. *How to use research.* We have made arrangements to get special material on right-wing organizations and other pressure groups from Group Research, Inc., in Washington D.C.... Your city central body and state federation office have received this material .... (A) Let key people in your community know you have this kind of information. Share it with them. (B) When you hear that a right-wing speaker is coming to town, check him immediately in the [Group Research] Directory and alert friendly groups. Inform your local newspaper by personal visit if possible of the character, background and connections of the speaker. A list of some right-wing speakers who get around the country is attached for your convenience, including some who are not in the Directory ....

"2. *Community action.* Armed with facts about extremist groups, labor union members can take some leadership in combatting them, either by heading them off before they really get started or by limiting the damage they do and helping to dry them up.

"(a) *Preventive* action is best, of course, but is not easy. The idea is to alert democratic [sic] groups to the possibility of trouble and meet with their representatives. Ordinarily it is best not to pass resolutions or take a vote. But there is sometimes an advantage in arranging a meeting at which community leaders actually sign a warning statement, for release to the press, in advance of a right-wing meeting, exposing its nature and intent.

"(b) Action *after* a right-winger has disrupted the Community is more difficult, but it hinges on getting at least a few community leaders to stand up and be counted. Labor can provide real leadership in such a maneuver. Editors and broadcasters should be visited with facts about right-wingers which they presumably do not have at hand. They should be urged to publish such material ....

"(c) ... If a right-wing spokesman appears on local radio or television in an interview program, request equal time to rebut him. If you have access to a labor-sponsored or liberal farm organization-sponsored radio or TV program, request equal time to rebut them."

In Group Research's promotional literature, it was stated: "The right-wing is dedicated to: Destruction of the United Nations as an effective instrument of peace; discrimination against minority groups; barring all immigration; abolition of trade unions as effective instruments of protection for working people; vigilante action against all other groups with whom they disagree; domination of our schools and intimidation of the clergy; nullification of virtually all social legislation passed in the last 30 years; questioning the loyalty of those with whom they disagree." It is worth nothing that Group Research has never found any single right-wing organization or combination of such organizations "dedicated" to any one or any combination of these items. However, truth proved to be no barrier to Group Research's published materials. From the very beginning, McCune's anti-right wing campaign was buoyed on a sea of smears, lies, half truths, innuendoes, clumsily contrived guilt-by-association, exaggeration, anonymous charges, and character assassination.

Group Research materials were disseminated widely under the auspices of organized labor. Also serving as outlets for McCune's propaganda were the American Jewish Committee and the National Council of Churches. But, one of the biggest boosts ever received by Group Research was delivered by Chairman John M. Bailey of the Democratic National Committee. On August 3, 1965, Bailey wrote to fellow Democrats that his office had been besieged with requests for help to counteract the "Radical Right," and "so far as possible we have tried to provide this help. But to do so we have had to depend heavily on the only national research organization that has systematically kept track of the activities of the Radical Right and has readily available the information on individuals and organizations that is so essential to combatting their activities.

"This organization is Group Research, Inc., which was established four years ago as a private, non-profit organization. Since then it has rendered invaluable assistance to organizations with Right Wing problems — among them the League of Women Voters, the National Education Association, the Parent-Teachers Association of America, the National Council of Churches, and the A.F.L.-C.I.O.

"Enclosed is a brochure describing this organization, and a sample copy of the newsletter that is its principal publication. If the Radical Right is active in your area you may want to give serious consideration to subscribing to the newsletter, and perhaps the other services that are available. It is our experience, and that of others, that you will find them extremely valuable in countering Right Wing activities."

In the Congress, stooges for Group Research included Senator Gale McGee (D.-Wyo.) and Representatives Ronald Cameron (D.-Calif.) and John Brademas (D.-Ind.).

In 1964, still in keeping with the letter and spirit of the 1961 Reuther memorandum, the left wing created another group. On September 22, 1964, Arthur Larson announced the formation of the National Council for Civic Responsibility. He insisted that it was only coincidental that the NCCR was being formed simultaneously with the beginning of the Johnson vs. Goldwater presidential campaign. (Larson, though nominally a Republican, endorsed Johnson.) Despite Larson's denials, it soon became obvious that the left wing, through the NCCR, viewed the Goldwater campaign as opportune for continuing its attacks upon anti-Communists and conservatives, for linking Goldwater to "extremism," and for insuring Lyndon Johnson's re-election.

Larson, who had held high federal government positions in the Roosevelt and Eisenhower Administrations, was, in 1964 when the NCCR was organized, a consultant to the State Department — a position he had also held in the Kennedy Administration. He was most famous, however, as the author of *A Republican Looks at His Party* (1956), which was a disavowal of the traditional Republican Party's principles and a call for "modern Republicanism," an improvement upon and expansion of the socialist New Deal of Franklin Roosevelt. In 1958, Larson became director of the World Rule of Law Center at Duke University where he has labored tirelessly to sell out American sovereignty to the interests of the one-worlders. In August, 1964, just a few weeks before the birth of the NCCR, Larson was co-chairman with Norman Cousins of an American "peace" delegation to the Soviet Union which met for six days with Soviet leaders in Leningrad.

Larson, as chairman and the only officer of the NCCR, surrounded himself with an array of councilors, recruited from Americans for Democratic Action, the Council on Foreign Relations, the United World Federalists, the National Council of Churches, organized labor, the anti-HCUA crowd, veteran anti-anti-Communists and fellow travelers representing just about every Communist front that ever existed in the United States, and the left wing of both major political parties.

The academic world was represented to an unusual degree including such educational institution presidents as: Hurst Anderson of American University; Gordon Blackwell of Florida State University; Samuel Belkin of Yeshiva University; James Nabrit of Howard University; Stuart Anderson of the Pacific School of Religion; John C. Bennett of Union Theological Seminary; Detlev Bronk of Rockefeller Institute; John Fischer of Columbia University's Teachers College; Robert Goheen of Princeton University; Thomas Hamilton of the University of Hawaii; Robert MacIver of the New School for Social Research; John Meng of Hunter College; Thomas Mendenhall of Smith College; Everett Clinchy of the Institute on Man and Science; James Coles of Bowdoin College; James P. Dixon of Antioch College; Douglas Knight of Duke University; Nathan Pusey of Harvard University; Calvin Plimpton of Amherst College; Charles Cogen of the American Federation of Teachers; Frederick Burkhardt of the American Council of Learned Societies; Hudson Hoagland of the American Academy of Arts and Sciences; Norris Darrell of the American Law Institute; Laurence Gould of the American Association for the Advancement of Science; Samuel P. Hayes of the Foreign Policy Association; and, Alvin Rogness of the Lutheran Theological Seminary.

Larson's Council included law school deans: Jefferson Fordham of the University of Pennsylvania; Paul R. Dean of Georgetown University; Vernon Miller of Catholic University; Lehan Tunks of the University of Washington; Erwin Griswold of Harvard University; Frank Newman of the University of California (Berkeley); Eugene Rostow of Yale University; Benjamin Small of Indiana University; Allan Smith of the University of Michigan; divinity and theological school deans: Gray Blandy of the Episcopal Theological Seminary of the Southwest; Jerald Brauer of the University of Chicago's Divinity School; William Finch of Vanderbilt University's Divinity School; Roger Hazelton of Oberlin College's Graduate School of Theology; and Samuel Miller of Harvard University's Divinity School. Other Councillors holding deanships included William Carmichael at Cornell University; William Haber at the University of Michigan; Carl Kaysen and Don Price at Harvard University; and, J. Carlyle Sitterson at the University of North Carolina.

There were also many religious leaders including Episcopal Bishops James A. Pike, John Craine, Everett Jones, C. R. Haden Jr., M. George Henry, George L. Cadigan, Arthur Lichtenberger, and F. W. Lickfield;

Methodist Bishops A. Raymond Grant, Lloyd Wicke, and Donald Tippett; President Uri Miller of the Synagogue Council of America; President Reuben H. Mueller of the National Council of Churches; President Dana McLean Greeley of the Unitarian Universalist Association; and President Louise Wallace of the United Church Women.

Other institutional high-ranking officials included: Frank Altschul, vice president of the Council on Foreign Relations; Hamilton Fish Armstrong, editor of *Foreign Affairs;* Harry Ashmore, executive chairman of the Center for the Study of Democratic Institutions; Jacques Barzun, provost of Columbia University; Barry Bingham, publisher of the *Louisville Courier Journal;* Cass Canfield, board chairman of Harper & Row; Norris Darrell, president of the American Law Institute; Jennie Haldenstein, president of the Child Study Association of America; Lewis W. Jones, president of the National Conference of Christians and Jews; Ralph McGill, publisher of the *Atlanta Constitution;* Jennelle Moorhead, president of the National Congress of Parents and Teachers; Joachim Prinz, president of the American Jewish Congress; Gilbert White, chairman of the American Friends Service Committee; Alan Waterman, board chairman of the American Association for the Advancement of Science; Roy Wilkins, executive director of the National Association for the Advancement of Colored People; Morris Abram, president of the American Jewish Committee; Bernard Feld, president of the Council for a Livable World; Label Katz, president of B'nai B'rith; A. William Loos, president of the Council on Religion and International Affairs; Robert Stein, editor of *Redbook* magazine; Herman Steinkraus, president of the United Nations Association of the United States; and, Dore Schary, national chairman of the Anti-Defamation League. (Just three days before Larson announced the formation of the NCCR, Schary announced at a press conference that the ADL was publishing *Danger on the Right* by two of the ADL's most accomplished defamers, Arnold Forster and Benjamin Epstein. In his foreword to the Foster-Epstein diatribe, Schary wrote: "The authors of *Danger on the Right* have attempted to write a definitive book on the attitudes, personnel and influence of the Radical Right and the Extreme Conservatives on the American scene. I believe they have succeeded." What they succeeded in doing was to ridicule, excoriate, and defame anti-Communists and conservatives. The entire book blended perfectly into Walter Reuther's campaign against anti-

Communists as engaged in by the National Council for Civic Responsibility.

In a press conference on October 17, 1964, Larson insisted that the NCCR had nothing to do with the presidential campaign or the right-wing views of the Republican candidate, Barry Goldwater. Such a disclaimer, however, fell flat in light of the politicoes who appeared on the NCCR's council: Charles F. Brannan, Truman's Secretary of Agriculture; Jerome Wiesner, Kennedy's science advisor; Thurman Arnold, Leon Keyserling, Stuart Chase, and Benjamin Cohen, from Franklin Roosevelt's New Deal; General Lawton Collins, Truman's Army Chief of Staff; Oscar Ewing, Truman's Federal Security Administrator; David Lilienthal, Truman's Atomic Energy Commission chairman; Mortimer Caplin, Kennedy's Internal Revenue commissioner; James Mitchell and Marion Folsom from Eisenhower's cabinet; Ernest Gross from the Roosevelt and Truman Administrations; and, the arch-eccentric Harold Stassen, Eisenhower's "peace" secretary — truly a representative group of anti-Goldwaterites. The same leftwing flavor was present in all groups, no matter what their area of interest, which followed Larson: the labor leaders James Patton, Jacob Potofsky, Joseph A. Beirne, and A. J. Hayes; the literary figures Archibald MacLeish, John Mason Brown, Marcia Davenport, Elmer Rice, Irving Stone; theatrical personalities Fredric March and his wife Florence Eldridge; Robert Kennedy's sycophant David Ginsburg; and, leftwing academicians Saul Padover, James B. Conant, Hans Morgenthau, David Riesman, and Lewis Mumford.

The Communists greeted the formation of the NCCR with editorial praise in *The Worker* (September 27, 1964). For an allegedly nonpartisan, apolitical group in a presidential election year, the NCCR received an extraordinary amount of publicity in the press: the *New York Times,* the *Washington Post,* the *Washington Star,* the *New York Herald Tribune,* the Associated Press, the United Press International, and organized labor's journals. And, the Democratic National Committee contributed $60,000 to NCCR by funneling the contribution through the "tax-exempt, nonprofit Public Affairs Institute." (Larson was serving as vice chairman of Senior Citizens for Johnson and Humphrey.)

The announced purpose of the NCCR was "the collection and dissemination of facts on the activities of irresponsible extremists as

181

expressed in the beliefs, actions and activities of the recognized Left and Right now operating in the United States."

"To defend the democratic process and institutions from both the extreme Right and Left," the NCCR's grandiose battle plans included a series of radio broadcasts and documentaries; a "living library" which would make available to the public reliably checked information on the extremist groups of the Right and Left; a research and publications program where the live issues of the day would be analyzed and discussed by leading experts; and, the organizing and strengthening of regional and community Councils which would meet the problems right where they occur.

In the six weeks preceding the 1964 presidential election, the NCCR did produce a radio program ("Spotlight") and regional Councils were established. But almost immediately after the election, the radio programs began to go off the air. (This was no surprise to NCCR employees in New York City. They had been told that their jobs would expire with the November election. Radio stations, which carried "Spotlight," were told at first that the program would be of long duration. But, a week before the presidential election, the NCCR informed the stations that programs would be reduced from five to two times a week. Then, four days before the election, the program was cancelled on various stations in such cities as Houston, San Francisco, Chicago, and Washington, D.C.) (See, Robert Bauman, "NCCR and Smear Tactics of the Left," *New Guard,* January, 1965.)

"Spotlight" — during its very brief history — was nothing else than one more outlet for Group Research's venomous anti-Communist, anti-conservative diatribes geared to make Barry Goldwater appear to be a far-out kook. The Communists and, for that matter, the entire Left escaped completely unscathed from the wrath of the NCCR-Group Research fire.

On February 4, 1965, Larson announced that he had resigned as chairman of the NCCR. The man, who — only five months earlier — was going "to defend the democratic process and institutions from both the extreme Right and Left," remembered that he had to make an April 26 deadline for the revision of his *Law of Workmen's Compensation,* first published in 1952. As he fled from the battlefront, he said: "I hope the work of the council will continue, if not under the same name, possibly under another name. But that will be under the supervision of the Public Affairs Institute, the parent organization in Washington."

On February 17, 1965, Dewey Anderson, executive secretary of the Public Affairs Institute, announced the demise of NCCR, claiming that the organization — despite its galaxy of dignitaries — could not raise enough money to continue its activities.

On November 18, 1966, at a press conference in Sheraton-Carlton Hotel in Washington, D.C., President Franklin H. Littell of Iowa Wesleyan College announced the formation of a new organization, the Institute for American Democracy. The IAD was pledged to combat extremists of both the right and the left. Its chairman would be Littell, whose anti-anti-Communist credentials were impeccable. And, just as Arthur Larson had done with the NCCR in 1964, Littell surrounded himself with an imposing group of dignitaries. Originally, Littell's "sponsoring committee" consisted of forty-seven but grew to sixty-five by 1968. Of the sixty-five, twenty-three had been on Larson's NCCR (Dore Schary, Morris Abram, Roy Wilkins, Bishop A. Raymond Grant, Marion Folsom, Leon Keyserling, Oscar Ewing, Thurmond Arnold, Jacob Blaustein, Oscar de Lima, James Patton, Jacob Potofsky, John C. Bennett, William Haber, George C. Lodge, Harry Ashmore, Ralph McGill, Dana McLean Greeley, A. William Loos, Bishop Reuben Mueller, Stanley Marcus, Roger Sonnabend, and *Arthur Larson*).

Also on Littell's IAD were U. S. Senators Clifford Case, Gale McGee, and Frank Moss; labor leader Walter Reuther, whose 1961 memorandum to Robert Kennedy was still viable; Whitney Young, executive director of the National Urban League; Samuel Dalsimer, chairman of the program division of the Anti-Defamation League; Steve Allen, a tireless fund-raiser for the leftwing, pacifist National Committee for a Sane Nuclear Policy; former U.S. Attorney General Francis Biddle; and, Roger Baldwin, patriarch of the American Civil Liberties Union.

"*Broadcasting,* the official journal of the broadcasting industry for March 13, 1967 carried an interview on page 48, with Charles R. Baker, Executive Director of the 'newly formed' IAD in which the following was stated: Mr. Baker said IAD grew out of discussions involving members of the National Council of Churches and of the Anti-Defamation League of B'nai B'rith who felt 'let down' after the Larson group folded and who were concerned about 'extremists of both left and right.' These concerned individuals, Mr. Baker said, saw similarities between the two extremes in that 'they were at war' with those occupying the middle ground. *Broadcasting* stated that IAD is a kind of spiritual successor to the National Council for Civic Responsibility . . . ." (*News & Views,* November, 1968.)

For two years, Littell and his organization went on their nefarious way, attacking anti-Communists and conservatives as had Group Research and the NCCR in keeping with the spirit and letter of the Reuther brothers' memorandum of 1961. And, in the IAD's newsletter *Homefront,* Baker, the executive director of IAD, stated that the basic information which the organization disseminated came from the files of Group Research and the Anti-Defamation League.

Then, in November, 1968, the Church League of America's staff, in their publication *News & Views,* accused Littell and Baker "of perpetuating a gigantic deception and hoax on the press and on the people of the United States." After an extensive investigation, they discovered that IAD was not founded in 1966, but in 1943 when it was incorporated in New York. On June 27, 1944, the IAD received a tax-exempt status as a non-profit organization. But, on October 15, 1952, the IAD was disolved by proclamation of New York's Governor because the organization had failed to file a mandatory annual report with the Department of Social Welfare. The IAD filed a certificate of annulment of this dissolution on November 18, 1952 and was then reinstated.

On March 6, 1956, the Attorney General of New York — Jacob Javits, now U.S. Senator — wrote an opinion to the Commissioner of the Department of Social Welfare and stated that it was no longer necessary for the IAD to file an annual report because the IAD was a department of the Anti-Defamation League.

This all means that when Littell held his press conference in November, 1966, he was merely reviving a branch of the Anti-Defamation League, whose national chairman Dore Schary was on Larson's "Council" and Littell's "sponsoring committee." After being dormant for ten years, IAD came out of the woodwork to help the Anti-Defamation League defame legitimate and patriotic anti-Communists and conservatives.

Since 1966, the IAD — was not only involved with the Anti-Defamation League and Group Research — but has been allied in its anti-anti-Communist program with the National Congress of Parents and Teachers; the American Civil Liberties Union; the National Education Association; the American Jewish Committee; the National Council of

Churches; the National Association for Mental Health; the Department of Communications of the United Church of Christ; the AFL-CIO's Committee on Political Education (COPE); the United Nations Association of the United States; and, National Education Television.

Although Littell and his IAD are persistent in claims that they are fighting both the Right and the Left, the Left is downgraded as to its influence and numbers. For the Right, however, there have been no bounds to the hysterical, fear-mongering charges leveled against it by IAD, its informants, and a host of anonymous collaborators. As for Littell, he would be merciless against the Right. Speaking to a convention of the National Education Association in 1967, he said: "Right-wingers are not a loyal opposition. Their style and their stench is disloyalty .... Extremists [of the Right] should be thrown out of whatever groups they are in — churches, synagogues, political parties, school boards, professional organizations. The question is not how their opinions can be changed. The question is how soon they can be muted and rendered ineffective." The Left has not been threatened by Littell with such an extermination.

STUDENT NONVIOLENT COORDINATING COMMITTEE

On February 1, 1960, the history of Negro sit-in demonstrations began in Greensboro, North Carolina. Within the next few weeks, college towns in the southern States were swept by the sit-ins. They were billed as spontaneous demonstrations but they bore a marked similarity from one scene to another. They were successful — of that there can be no doubt. They attracted nation-wide attention as metropolitan newspapers and the major television networks gave the sit-ins high-priority publicity.

If the sit-ins had ever been "spontaneous," they did not remain so very long. Martin L. King Jr., the head of the Southern Christian Leadership Conference, brought into being the Student Nonviolent Coordinating Committee (Snick) to manage the sit-ins. Once Snick became the major front for King's sit-ins, demonstrations became commonplace at lunch counters, restaurants, theaters, hospitals, service stations, and parks throughout the South.

A great deal of Snick's early activities were centered around the Nashville Student Movement at Fisk University and the Atlanta Student Movement at Atlanta University. With the notorious Martin L. King Jr. as the guiding hand behind Snick, the organization attracted the support of the U.S. National Student Association (subsidized by the Central Intelligence Agency); and the New World Foundation (founded by Anita McCormick Blaine. One of New World's directors was Whitney North Seymour, then president of the American Bar Association, and formerly board chairman of Freedom House, board chairman of the trustees of the Carnegie Endowment for International Peace, and national board member of the American Civil Liberties Union); Attorney General Robert F. Kennedy's Department of Justice; the National Association for the Advancement of Colored People; the Congress of Racial Equality; Martin L. King's Southern Christian Leadership Conference; and, the civil rights agitators of the Medical Committee for Human Rights.

The sit-ins have only been a part of Snick's activities. The organization has conducted so-called freedom rides, voter registration drives, and so-called freedom schools. In the beginning, Snick's leaders – in imitation of Martin L. King Jr. – paid lip service to Gandhian nonviolence to achieve racial integration in public, semi-private, and private facilities of various sorts. Gradually, however, the goal of integration gave way to segregation under the banners of black power and black nationalism.

In September, 1963, Snick's leaders were confident enough to announce a massive program of intimidation against the people and the government of the State of Alabama. The program was drafted by Diane Bevel. (She is the wife of James Bevel, who, in 1963, was one of Martin L. King's most militant lieutenants. Diane achieved national and international notoriety in 1966 when she made an unauthorized trip to Hanoi, North Vietnam and returned to the United States extolling the virtues of the Communist tyrant Ho chi Minh.)

Diane Bevel's program, endorsed by Snick's chairman John Lewis, threatened to raise a "uniformed nonviolent army of 25,000 in the South. The army would have its own flag as it practiced enough militant civil disobedience to paralize the state capital at Montgomery. There were also plans to call a "general work strike" and to refuse to pay state and local taxes. As part of the "nonviolent" tactics, Snick would conduct lie-ins on airport runways, highways, and train tracks.

The Snick-Bevel program never made much headway and its militant tone began to make some of Snick's white liberal supporters a bit squeamish. And, somewhere in the higher echelons of Snick, a decision was made to concentrate – at least for a little while – upon political activity. In Lowndes County, Alabama Snick organized an independent political party with an appeal for nation-wide support. The new political party had as its symbol a black panther. Then, in 1964, Snick was instrumental in founding the Mississippi Freedom Democratic Party, a group which caused a great deal of commotion in the Democratic National Convention of that year.

In 1965, Snick reached its high point of achievement when it was the major force in Martin L. King Jr.'s violence-ridden voter registration drive in Selma, Alabama. Earlier in the same year, the red complexion of Snick had become so obvious that liberal columnists Rowland Evans and Robert Novak commented: " . . . There is no doubt that SNCC is substantially infiltrated by beatnicks, left wing revolutionaries and — worst of all — by Communists." (As early as 1964, Snick was using the mailing plates of the Communist weekly *National Guardian.* And, at least on one occasion in 1965, an advertisement for a Snick celebration was placed in the same journal.)

As befitted an organization with such strong ties to the Communists, Snick could find no charges too extravagant to make against the United States government. A Snick memo of March, 1965 said, in part: "The whole racist structure of the enormously complex U.S. government provides those who govern too many 'outs' — the constitutionalism and legalism which always has been used to explain why the U.S. government must condone lynching, mass murder, [and] systematic terrorism." Six months after issuing this thoroughly dishonest and inflammatory statement, Snick raised $50,000 at a Hollywood party. The donors included Marlon Brando, Richard Burton, Harry Belafonte, Sidney Poitier, James Garner, Paul Newman, Burt Lancaster, Elizabeth Taylor, Joanne Woodward, and Mike Nichols.

In 1966, Snick dropped all pretenses of working for integration through nonviolent methods. Shunted aside were such Snick leaders as Robert Moses (Parris), Julian Bond, John Lewis, Tom Hayden, and James Forman. In their stead was Stokely Carmichael who, as Snick's chairman, would harangue his audiences with calls for "Black Power." (With the advent of Carmichael into Snick's leadership, one of the organization's most dedicated apologists, the ultra-liberal Ralph McGill, was forced to admit that: "Snick today seeks conflict between races — not peace and an equality of opportunity and political power." And McGill was one of the few liberal columnists to admit that Snick had gone overboard with the Reds: "In early 1966 talk of 'Havana money' became current. SNCC, unable to meet payrolls, suddenly could form a front and purchase a $65,000 building. That a once honorable idealistic student action group should now be taken over by what amounts to a secret klan-type group which openly states its racial hatreds and its objectives to foment disorder and chaos in order to destroy Western civilization is one of the more melancholy stories of our time."

As chairman of Snick, Carmichael traveled with his gospel of hatred for whites and cries for black power to Britain, France, Spain, Czecho-Slovakia, Cuba, North Vietnam, Guinea, Tanzania, Egypt, Algeria, Syria and Sweden, and to college campuses throughout the United States. He threatened Mississippi, Washington, D.C., Cleveland, and other places with destruction. He ranted and raved against the United States government and its officials but lauded Cuba's Castro and Guevara. He made threats against the lives of President Johnson and his cabinet, but somehow Snick's chairman remained above and beyond legal punishment.

In May, 1967, Hubert Geroid (Rap) Brown succeeded Carmichael as Snick's chairman. (Within a month of his election, Brown was openly advocating wholesale murder of whites by Negroes: "How can you be nonviolent in America, the most violent country in the world . . . . You better shoot that [white] man to death; that's what he's been doing to you.")

With Brown's ascendancy, the policies and programs of Snick were outlined at a press conference: "SNCC is a Human Rights organization interested not only in Human Rights in the United States, but throughout the world; that, in the field of International Relations, we assert that we encourage and support the liberation struggles of all people against racism, exploitation, and oppression. We see our struggle here in America as an integral part of the world-wide movement of all oppressed people, such as in Vietnam, Angola, Mozambique, South Africa, Zimbabwe, and Latin America. Furthermore, we support the efforts of our brothers in Puerto Rico who are presently engaged in a fight for independence and liberation there.

"We shall seek to build a strong nation-wide Black Anti-Draft Program and movement to include the high school students, along with college students and other black men of draft age. We see no reason for black men who are daily murdered physically and mentally in this country to go and kill yellow people abroad, who have done nothing to us, and are, in fact, victims of the same oppression that our brothers in Vietnam suffer.

"Our major thrust will be in the building of National Freedom Organizations which will deal with all aspects of the problems facing black people in America. The political objective will manifest itself in creation of a viable, independent political force. The economic objective will be (1) to expel the exploiters who presently control our community, (2) to gain economic control of our communities, and (3) to create an economic system which will be responsible to and benefit the black community, rather than a few individuals. Our cultural objective will be (1) to destroy the myths and lies propagated by white America concerning our history in Africa and in this country and (2) to develop an awareness and appreciation of the beauty of our thick lips, broad noses, kinky hair and soul. In obtaining these objectives, we will work with all other black groups who are fighting for the same goals."

Brown, as chairman of the self-defined Human Rights organization, advised Negroes in Washington, D.C.: "Get you some guns . . . burn this town down. You have to tell the [white] man if you come into my community you are going to come in with the intent of dying or you don't come in at all. I say there should be more shooting than looting, so if you loot, loot a gun store. You've got to decide for yourself if you kill your enemy because that is an individual decision. But the white man is your enemy. You got to destroy your enemy. If you give me a gun and tell me to shoot my enemy, I might shoot Lady Bird [Johnson]."

In July, 1967, Brown was arrested by FBI agents and charged with inciting a riot in Cambridge, Maryland. But the arrest did not deter Brown's defiance, as he stated: "We stand on the eve of a Black revolution. Masses of our people are on the move, fighting the enemy, tick for tack, responding to counter-revolutionary violence with revolutionary violence, an eye for an eye, a tooth for a tooth and a life for a life. These rebellions are but a dress rehearsal for the real revolution." Out on bail, Brown continued to travel the country, screaming "Black Power" and urging his black audiences to "stop looting and start shooting." He addressed Black Panther meetings and spoke at a dinner sponsored by the Communist weekly *National Guardian.*

Meanwhile, Stokely Carmichael — Brown's predecessor as Snick's chairman — had continued working for Snick. He effected a complete alliance between Snick and the Black Panthers who are dedicated to warfare against whites throughout the United States. He negotiated a protocol of cooperation with the Pro-Independence Movement of

Puerto Rico, a Communist group willing to join Snick in their "common struggle against U.S. imperialism." He established a direct relationship with the Revolutionary Action Movement, which is "dedicated to the overthrow of the capitalist system in the United States by violence if necessary."

In its issue of October 5, 1968, *Human Events* reported: "FBI Director J. Edgar Hoover disclosed last week that the Student Nonviolent Coordinating Committee held a top-secret conference earlier this year at which plans were discussed for the 'elimination by Mau Mau tactics' of mayors, chiefs of police and other local officials. Hoover said the closed-door conference was held in mid-April. A majority of participants were armed.

"Among the tactics discussed was the preparation of maps showing the homes of local officials who could be wiped out Mau Mau style, Hoover said. The deployment of snipers along travel routes of National Guard units and police forces was also discussed.

"Participants were urged to recruit Viet Nam war veterans to train militant blacks in demolition and guerrilla warfare. Black college students were to instruct ghetto residents in the care and use of firearms, the preparation of Molotov cocktails, and the reloading of spent cartridges."

The formal merger of Snick and the Black Panthers took place in February, 1968. Officials of Snick — Forman, Carmichael, and Brown — assumed official positions in the Black Panthers. The merger, however, lasted only until August when, after a power struggle, Snick expelled Carmichael from its membership and broke off relations with the Black Panthers.

On November 27, 1968, the Associated Press reported: "An alliance between the Student Nonviolent Coordinating Committee and the National Black Liberators has been formed to ward off what the two groups call 'mounting repressions facing black communities.'"

UNITED NATIONS ASSOCIATION OF THE UNITED STATES
COLLEGIATE COUNCIL FOR THE UNITED NATIONS
COMMISSION TO STUDY THE ORGANIZATION OF PEACE
UN WE BELIEVE
AMERICAN ASSOCIATION FOR THE UNITED NATIONS
UNITED STATES COMMITTEE FOR THE UNITED NATIONS
NATIONAL CITIZENS COMMITTEE FOR UN DAY

CONFERENCE GROUP OF U. S. NATIONAL
ORGANIZATIONS ON THE UNITED NATIONS
VISTA

In 1965, the United Nations Association of the United States was founded through means of a merger between the American Association for the United Nations (AAUN) and the United States Committee for the United Nations (USCUN).

From 1948 until 1952, the USCUN was known as the National Citizens Committee for UN Day. The AAUN was the successor organization to the League of Nations Association which was founded in 1923 and dissolved in 1945.

Along with the 1965 merger, the United Nations Association of the United States (UNAUS) absorbed the Conference Group of U.S. National Organizations on the United Nations which was founded in 1949.

Affiliates of the UNAUS are the Commission to Study the Organization of Peace, a research arm, and the Collegiate Council for the United Nations. (The Collegiate Council, with chapters on more than four hundred university and college campuses, sponsors model United Nations, General Assemblies, and Security Councils, and conferences and seminars dealing with various aspects of the United Nations.)

Before the merger of the AAUN and the USCUN, the two groups created UN We Believe to work for "a more effective United Nations." This has been a brainwashing operation aimed at business, industry, and labor leaders who, in turn, are expected to brainwash employees, stockholders, customers, and union members. All are expected to commit themselves to the "principles" of the United Nations and "to accept the fact that they are participants in world events, not spectators." UN We Believe conducts luncheon meetings at which chief executives of major corporations and labor unions confer with ambassadors and UN employees as to how their organizations can propagandize on behalf of the United Nations. The most publicized result of this operation has been the display by these executives of the UN emblem and the slogan, *UN We Believe,* on commercial vehicles, stationery, business forms, postage meters, and elsewhere.

Despite the confusion of organizational titles, there is an individual, Clark Eichelberger, whose career provides the cement binding the organizations for four decades.

Eichelberger, from 1929 until 1934, was the director of the midwest office of the League of Nations Association (LNA). From 1934 until 1945, he was national director of the LNA and, from 1945 until 1964, he was national director of the successor organization, the American Association for the United Nations. Meanwhile, Eichelberger was director (1939-1948) and, since 1948, chairman of the Commission to Study the Organization of Peace, the research arm of the League of Nations Association, the American Association for the United Nations, and the United Nations Association of the United States.

When the United Nations Association of the United States came into being in 1964, Eichelberger was shunted aside in favor of Porter McKeever. McKeever had ideal liberal credentials as he assumed leadership of the UNAUS. He had worked for the Red-lined Office of War Information, the State Department, the United States Mission to the UN, the Council on Foreign Relations, the Ford Foundation, and the Committee for Economic Development.

The UNAUS (and its predecessor AAUN) has served as a propaganda organization for the United Nations, for one worldism, for disarmament, and for admission of Red China to UN membership. Its officers, advisors, members, and sponsors have represented the far leftwing of the democrat Party; the most extreme of "modern" Republicans; the Red China lobby; the leftwing of organized labor; the leadership of leftwing political groups and pacifist organizations; leftwing clergy; soft-on-Communism State Department functionaries; executives of foundations that have made substantial contributions to the socialization of the United States; disarmament fanatics; inveterate Communist fronters; and, vociferous anti-anti-Communists.

The New Deal - Fair Deal - Modern Republican - New Frontier - Great Society Establishment has given to the UNAUS (AAUN) Alger Hiss, Eleanor and Anna Roosevelt, Arthur Goldberg, Hubert Humphrey, Adlai Stevenson, Sumner Welles; Joseph E. Davies, Benjamin V. Cohen, Ralph Bunche, Ernest Gross, Arthur H. Dean, Joseph E. Johnson, Eugenie Anderson, Charles W. Yost, Arthut Larson, Andrew Cordier, Luther Evans, Paul Hoffman, Sol Linowitz, James J. Wadsworth, John Foster Dulles, Philip Jessup, Thomas K. Finletter, Grayson Kirk, Frank P. Graham, Arthur J. Goldsmith, G. Bernard Noble, Helen Gahagan Douglas, Detlev Bronk, Herbert Lehman, Charles P. Taft, and Elmo Roper.

From organized labor have come the ubiquitous Walter Reuther, James B. Carey, Jacob Potofsky, and James G. Patton. From the Red

China lobby have come Owen Lattimore, Edwin O. Reischauer, Nathaniel Peffer, Doak Barnett, and John K. Fairbank. They have been joined by individuals whose names have repeatedly appeared on letterheads of various leftist organizations: James T. Shotwell, Douglas Fairbanks Jr., Thomas J. Watson, Robert W. Kenny, G. Bromley Oxnam, Roger Baldwin, Bruce Bliven, Cass Canfield, Dorothy Canfield Fisher, Thomas S. Mann, Albert Einstein, Telford Taylor, Bartley Crum, Channing Tobias, J. Raymond Walsh, Rex Stout, Guy Emery Shipler, Virginius Dabney, Palmer Hoyt, Benjamin Kizer, Anna Lord Strauss, and Arthur Upham Pope.

Many of the individuals connected with the UNAUS (AAUN) have had a very personal and vested interest in the United Nations. Some were present at the founding conference of the UN; many have been employed by the UN or the U.S. Mission to the UN; and still others have served on various UN commissions.

As is the custom of globalist organizations, the UNAUS dwells on the alleged indispensability of the United Nations for the survival of the universe. In promotional literature for *Vista* the UNAUS monthly magazine, the scaremongering clichés of the globalists are very much in evidence: "The UN has survived two decades of international tensions, strife, Cold War and hot combat; it has grown to be a force to reckon with in world affairs, and it is today man's one hope of peace — yet its future hangs trembling on the slender thread of international opinion. If people *believe* in the UN and support it, their governments will make it survive." Mrs. Arthur Goldberg, soliciting members for UNAUS and subscribers to *Vista,* presented a slight variance on this theme by remarking that when an individual becomes a member he is "able to answer the charges of those who do not share our enthusiasm and hopes for peace . . . [and] save you from that sense of helplessness in the face of the bigness of all these world problems. But more than all that, instead of just being an observer, you too will be participating in our country's support of the United Nations. Then, if we have grandchildren or hope to have them, we will be able to look them in the eye when they ask: 'What did you do besides just wish and talk about peace in the world?'"

Vista has never been anything but a mawkish series of articles and editorials extolling the virtues of the United Nations, members of its secretariat, and the various UN agencies. What critical viewpoints do appear are generally directed against the United States for not completely surrendering its national interests to the last "one hope of peace."

In 1966, the UNAUS reaped a full harvest of publicity when it issued a report on U.S.-Red China relations. It was all a part of a project financed by the Ford Foundation and done in cooperation with the State Department and individuals in the Johnson Administration who were most anxious to sell the American public on the wisdom of admitting Red China to membership in the United Nations.

The UNAUS chose a panel that can only be described as a travesty. The chairman was Robert V. Roosa, a banker and partner of Averell Harriman. Roosa was completely lacking in diplomatic experience. (If he sought and followed Harriman's advice, he would do all he could to placate Mao Tse-tung.) The vice-chairman was Frederick Beebe, chairman of the board of the ultra-leftist *Newsweek-Washington Post* Company. Members included Detlev Bronk (a scientist and a veteran of the Pugwash Conferences which were attended by Americans bent on appeasing the Soviet Union); Robert Benjamin (a motion picture tycoon, lacking in diplomatic experience); Everett Case (a foundation executive with no diplomatic experience); Doak Barnett (one of the better known of the Red China lobbyists); Arthur Dean (a veteran of the State Department who had favored Red China's admission to the UN for many years); Leland Goodrich (a well-known apologist for the UN); Ernest Gross (a former UN employee, who had been pushing for Red China's admission to the UN for at least eight years); Joseph E. Johnson (president of the leftist-pacifist Carnegie Endowment with a personal reputation for being soft-on-Communism); Harry Knight (a management consultant with no diplomatic experience but a board member of the Foreign Policy Association, a leading group in the Red China lobby); Arthur Larson (the ubiquitous anti-anti-Communist who was pushing for Red China's admission to the UN before he became a panel member); Jacob Potofsky (an extreme leftist labor leader who also had urged Red China's admission to the UN before joining the panel); Lucian Pye (a political scientist and consultant to the State Department); Anna Lord Strauss (a well-known peacenik and apologist for the UN); George E. Taylor (a college professor whose writings on China indicated he would urge appeasement of Red China); Eleanor Worley (a magazine publisher with no diplomatic experience but with a reputation as a globalist); Stephen Wright (president of the United Negro College Fund, an educator with no diplomatic experience); and,

Charles Yost (a veteran of the State Department and, in 1966, a senior fellow at the Council on Foreign Relations — another major force in the Red China lobby).

With the committee so obviously stacked with individuals either holding preconceived notions or else having no experience upon which to base their judgment, the panel's report — a tortuous exercise in circumlocution — favored admission of Red China to the UN, retention of Free China in the UN, further debate on the question of Red China's admission to the UN's Security Council, and "further study to the possible terms" under which the United States would enter into full diplomatic relations with Red China.

The panel, with exemplary hypocrisy, expressed the fear that, unless the United States government made such appeasing overtures to Red China, other member-nations of the UN might expel Free China and seat Red China. (The *New York Times* hailed the panel's report as "clear-headed, stripped of wishful thinking, and is concentrated on the fundamentals, on the bleak alternatives and on the escalating urgency of the problem." It was, of course merely coincidental that the panel's report was identical with the *Times'* long-standing editorial policy on the matter of Red China. It was, of course, merely coincidental, also, that Harding Bancroft, vice president of the *Times*, participated in the work of the Roosa panel until this task was interrupted by his appointment to the U.S. delegation to the 1966 UN General Assembly.)

The entire project with the phony panel-report and equally phony concern for Free China was a typical ploy of the UNAUS whereby the interests of the United States and the free world are set aside in favor of a universal United Nations (a long-time goal of the UNAUS leaders) as a further step toward world government (another long-time goal of the UNAUS leaders).

UNITED WORLD FEDERALISTS
WORLD ASSOCIATION OF WORLD FEDERALISTS

The utterly tasteless full-page advertisement read: "O'er the ramparts we watched . . . as a V.C. killed a U.S. and vice versa. It was beautiful — a stranger shot a stranger and *no one knows why*. We are now on the razor's edge of decision and reason. We can decide on a simple one-bomb suicide, or a one-world law; the sort of law that will create one world of peace and national sovereignty. This is what we are working for. You can join the group: It's cheap life insurance."

The advertisement appeared in the November, 1966 issue of *Ramparts,* an iconoclastic and leftwing magazine. The advertisement was sponsored by United World Federalists which described itself as an "American association for world peace through enforceable world law by strengthening the United Nations."

The UWF was created on February 22, 1947 from a merger of six groups: Americans United for World Government, World Federalists, World Republic, Student Federalists, World Citizens of Georgia, and the Massachusetts Committee for World Federation.

Instrumental in the founding of the UWF were Stringfellow Barr, Raymond Gram Swing, Norman Cousins, Albert Einstein, Thomas S. Mann, Rex Tugwell, Clifton Fadiman, Carl and Mark Van Doren, Robert Sherwood, Lewis Mumford, Rex Stout, Elmer Rice, Vito Marcantonio, Glen H. Taylor, Harlow Shapley, Emanuel Celler, Waldo Frank, James P. Warburg, Upton Sinclair, James B. Carey, and Thomas K. Finletter.

The extreme leftwing founders were ideologically matched by the early members of the UWF who included Boris Artzybasheff, Louis Bromfield, Cass Canfield, Jerome Frank, Frank Graham, Albert Guerard Sr., Oscar Hammerstein II, Donald Harrington, John Hersey, John Haynes Holmes, Alfred Baker Lewis, Robert M. MacIver, Frederic March, James G. Patton, Quentin Reynolds, Rosika Schwimmer, Alan Cranston, and Ralph Sockman.

The early UWFers were recruited from such one-world groups as Federal Union, the Atlantic Union Committee, Students for Federal World Government, the Foundation for World Government, Citizens Committee for a World Constitution, Action for World Federation, the Committee to Frame a World Constitution, World Citizen Movement, World Movement for World Federal Government, World Constitutional Convention, Student Federalists, the Campaign for World Government, and Writers' Board for World Government. Represented among the early membership, also, were the Socialist and Communist Parties, virtually every Communist front in America, pacifist organizations, and a host of political pressure groups.

When local branches of UWF were formed, they were urged to cooperate with Quaker, Methodist, Baptist, Episcopalian, Presbyterian, Congregational, and Unitarian church groups, and, also, the Grange, Jaycees, Kiwanis, the Brotherhood of Railroad Trainmen, certain AFL-CIO unions, the League of Women Voters, the Foreign Policy Association, the World Affairs Council, Americans for Democratic Action, the American Veterans Committee, the American Association for the United Nations, the Atlantic Union Committee, and the Women's International League for Peace and Freedom. And the UWF, itself, is a member of the World Association of World Federalists which includes affiliated and associated organizations from Australia, New Zealand, Canada, Britain, Austria, Belgium, Denmark, France, West Germany, Greece, Italy, Lebanon, Iran, The Netherlands, Norway, Switzerland, Sweden, Turkey, Cameroon, Ghana, Madagascar, Nigeria, Sierra Leone, The Philippines, South Vietnam, South Korea, Japan, India, Pakistan, Puerto Rico, Colombia, Argentina, Brazil, Chile, Costa Rica, Ecuador, Guyana, Haiti, Mexico, and Peru. Officials of the World Association have included such renowned leftists as Pablo Casals, Brock Chisholm, Indira Gandhi, Earl Atlee, and Lord Boyd Orr.

American presidents and presidential candidates have lauded the work of the UWF: "I sincerely hope that your organization will continue to grow in influence, particularly in regard to the strengthening of the United Nations." (Harry Truman) — "You are on the right track. The greatest seers of our generation have proclaimed again and again that mankind's only hope of survival lies in rising above nationalist parochialism and building the minimum institutions of world order. I share these beliefs." (Adlai Stevenson) — "The United World Federalists, adhering to common standards of justice and international conduct, requires the continued support of all those dedicated to freedom." (Dwight Eisenhower) — "Your consistent support of the United Nations and your unflagging advocacy of the means whereby it might be strengthened represent a genuine contribution to public education." (John F. Kennedy) — "Every one of us is committed to brotherhood among all nations, but no one pursues these goals with more dignity and dedication than the United World Federalists." (Hubert Humphrey) — "Your organization can perform an important service by continuing to emphasize that world peace can only come through world law." (Richard Nixon).

In 1968, the UWF had approximately twenty thousand members in two hundred local groups. Its presidents have included Cord Meyer Jr., Alan Cranston, Norman Cousins, Donald Harrington, Charles C. Price, James G. Patton, and for 1969, former U.S. Senator from Pennsylvania Joseph S. Clark.

The UWF lobbies at the Congress of the United States; it maintains a permanent observer at the United Nations; it conducts letter-writing campaigns; its staff members testify before congressional committees; it maintains a speaker's bureau; its officers host breakfast meetings for members of Congress; it organizes United Nations Day celebrations; it has sponsored intercollegiate and high school debates on the merits of world government; it has worked in various States to have legislatures adopt resolutions favoring United States participation in a world government; it sponsors discussion and study groups; and, it propagandizes for world government through pamphlets, press releases, and advertisements in newspapers and magazines.

The literature of the UWF is saturated with scare phrases, hyperbole, and clichés: "The world is incredibly small today." — "The cold war is thawing." — "One bulwark against disaster [the United Nations]." — "One World or none." — "A strengthened United Nations is humanity's only hope." — "Extremists of the right and left, here and abroad, are doing all they can to weaken the United Nations, to starve it, to undermine its authority, and to discredit it — even at the risk of war." — "We have in the United Nations the beginning of that essential moral and political perfectibility in our universal institutions." — "A military-industrial complex and negative approach to the challenge of militant communism seems to dominate American foreign policy." — "If the UN fails, and Thermonuclear War I comes, it could lead to the annihilation of every man, women, and child on earth — including you and yours."

Paramount in the UWF's program has been agitation to have the United Nations charter revised by a series of amendments which would: "(1) Grant the United Nations power to make laws . . . which prohibit any nation from using force or threats of force in international disputes and which also prohibit the manufacture, possession, or use of armaments beyond those required for internal policing. These laws must be binding on individuals as well as on nations. At the same time a schedule for universal and complete disarmament must be adopted. (2) Grant the United Nations power to govern the high seas and outer space, as well as other carefully defined international jurisdictions. (3) Grant the United Nations authority to raise adequate and dependable revenue under carefully defined and limited taxing power. (4) Establish a system for enforcing world law through inspectors, civilian police, courts and an adequate armed peace force. (5) Establish a civilian executive branch of the UN, without the veto, responsible to the General

Assembly for controlling the UN forces which will maintain law and order. (6) Provide a voting system on legislative matters more just and realistic than the present one-nation-one vote formula in the General Assembly. (7) Provide for universal membership without right of secession. (8) Confer on an expanded UN judiciary the final authority to interpret world laws, including existing international law; to settle disputes between nations by peaceful means; to try all individuals accused of violating world laws governing disarmament and prohibiting aggression. (9) Provide a Bill of Rights protecting individuals against arbitrary or unjust action by the United Nations, and prohibiting UN interference with any rights or liberties guaranteed to citizens by their own national or state institutions. (10) Reserve to individual nations and their people all powers not expressly delegated to the United Nations, thus guaranteeing each nation complete freedom to manage its domestic affairs and to choose its own political, economic and social institutions."

The World Association of World Federalists, to which the UWF is affiliated, in its program for amending the UN charter advocates: "A strict United Nations control should be exercised over all nuclear material which could be used for war purposes. Outer Space must be placed under the control of the United Nations." — "A court of international delinquency shall be established for adjudicating cases of persons considered to be guilty of acts that lead to war." — "In matters of a non-legal character, that is political matters not directly connected with world law, an appropriate conciliation body shall propose a settlement. If this is not accepted by one of the parties concerned, a World Equity Tribunal, should make a binding decision in the case."

The UWF had advocated membership in the United Nations for Red China. It has worked for authorization for the U.S. Treasury Department to make United Nations "peace bonds" available to American citizens. It has urged *compulsory* arbitration through the United Nations for a settlement of difficulties in the Middle East. It has promoted a large expansion of United States foreign "aid" programs. It has proposed that the Panama Canal and U.S. bases in the Pacific be made "World Federal Districts" under control of "World Government." It has actively supported every test-ban treaty to go before the Senate. It has lobbied to achieve permanent status for the U.S. Arms Control and Disarmament Agency. It has called for a ceasefire in Vietnam and for peace negotiations wherein the Vietcong would participate.

Of special interest to the UWF throughout its entire history has been its campaign to repeal the Connally Reservation whereby the United States has reserved to itself the power to decide what matters are essentially within the domestic jurisdiction of the World Court. The UWF wants repeal of the Connally Reservation so that the United States will accept "as binding the rulings of the International Court of Justice [World Court] on disarmament, on interpretation of the UN Charter and laws, and on international treaties." (The World Association of World Federalists proposes: "Governments should accept the compulsory jurisdiction of the International Court of Justice . . . and without crippling reservations [such as the Connally Reservation] ." And, going a step further, WAWF advocates: "Future treaties should contain provision for their binding interpretation by the International Court of Justice should any dispute with respect to them arise between the parties.")

The most influential individual in UWF has been Norman Cousins who more than anyone else was responsible for the group's founding in 1947. Cousins is not only America's leading "ban-the-bomb" leader but is one of the most vocal pleaders for co-existence with the Soviet Union's Communist regime. He has held high office in the World Association of World Federalists and he has been a top official of the left-wing-pacifist National Committee for a Sane Nuclear Policy. (For a time in 1964, there was a serious effort made to merge UWF and SANE but, at the last moment, negotiations broke down.)

Next in influence to Cousins was the late Grenville Clark who, along with Louis B. Sohn, wrote *World Peace through World Law* which serves more or less as a textbook for the UWF. Clark's interest in world government dated back at least to 1939 when he drafted a blueprint for world government – *A Federation of Free Peoples.* (Clark also had a long history of being soft on Communists and Communism.)

U.S. Senators who lent their names and prestige to the cause of UWF included Ralph Flanders, Claude Pepper, Jacob Javits, and Frank Church. In the House of Representatives, Donald Fraser of Minnesota and James Fulton of Pennsylvania have been UWF favorites. Other government figures in UWF have been James J. Wadsworth, G. Mennen Williams, Justice William O. Douglas, Will L. Clayton, George V. Allen, and Chester Bowles. From the academic world have come Harold Urey, Frederick L. Schuman, Hans Morgenthau, Harrison Brown, and Harry Overstreet. Organized labor leaders Walter Reuther, Arnold Zander, and

A. Philip Randolph; newspapermen Mark Ethridge, Paul Smith, and Harry Ashmore; pacifist Benjamin Spock; UN apologist Clark Eichelberger; theatrical personalities Dore Schary and Douglas Fairbanks Jr.; clergymen Dr. Howard Thurman, Edward A. Conway S. J., Rabbis Maurice Eisendrath, Solomon Freehof, and Daniel J. Silver, Bishop Henry K. Sherrill, Bishop Bernard J. Sheil, and Philip S. Moore C.S.C.; and many high-ranking executives from business and industry have served as officers and active members of the UWF.

"Membership in UWF is open to any American except persons Communist or Fascist oriented," according to the group's own literature. (Such a stricture, however, has not prevented individuals, with long records of Communist front activity, from becoming officers and/or members of the UWF.) The ostensible district of domestic Communists is in sharp contrast to the UWF's faith in foreign Communists.

The UWF is anxious for the United States to support free elections in Vietnam "on the sole condition that the sovereign independence and neutrality of an all-Vietnamese government . . . be guaranteed by the major powers, including [Red] China and the Soviet Union." Needless to say, nowhere in UWF's literature is there a single instance cited whereby either Red China or the Soviet Union has ever guaranteed "the sovereign independence and neutrality" of any government.

When the UWF is confronted with skepticism concerning the willingness of Communist regimes to cooperate in the altruistic plans of the UWF for world peace, the organization answers: "What about the Communist nations? We must seek honorable alternatives to war for moral and for political reasons. So must the Communist nations." When any Communist nation has ever acted for "moral" reasons goes unmentioned by UWF. And, though the UWF's leaders have cultivated close relationships with Communist leaders throughout the world, there is no organization comparable to the UWF in Red China, in North Vietnam, in North Korea, in Cuba, in the Soviet Union, or in the Communist-bloc countries of Eastern Europe and Africa.

Biographical Dictionary Of The Left

IORWITH WILBUR ABEL was born on August 11, 1908 in Magnolia, Ohio, son of Mary Jones and John Abel. He married Bernice Joseph. He is a graduate of Canton (Ohio) Actual Business College.

From 1925 to 1937 Abel worked for the American Sheet & Tin Plate Company, the Canton Malleable Iron Co., and Timken Roller Bearing Co. In 1937, he joined the staff of the United Steelworkers of America. In 1942, he became director of the Canton-Massillon United Steelworkers. In 1953, he became the national Secretary-Treasurer and, in 1965, the national President of the United Steelworkers of America.

As a labor organizer and labor leader, Abel has been an active Socialist. He has been a vice president and national board member of the Americans for Democratic Action, the center of the radical left in American politics. And, in the 1964 presidential campaign, he traveled with and campaigned for his old friend Hubert Humphrey. One of Abel's most notable achievements as President of the Steelworkers has been the absorption by his union of the Mine, Mill and Smelter Union which, in 1950, was so strongly controlled by the Communists that it was expelled from the leftist CIO. In 1962 and 1964, the Subversive Activities Control Board and the Senate Internal Security Subcommittee, independently, decided that the Communist domination and control of Mine-Mill was still present. But, despite these decisions which were not amended in the meantime, Abel's Steelworkers absorbed Mine-Mill in 1967.

Abel has a demagogic approach to politics as was clearly evident in the fall elections of 1966, when he wrote a letter to all members of the Steelworkers Union, saying: "Reports reaching us show that many of our good union members have deserted labor's proven friends and embraced the candidacies of sworn enemies of the union. It happened in Maryland, Louisiana and Georgia. It could happen in California and Illinois and elsewhere.

"What has prompted good, reliable union men and women to do this? Apparently they have permitted their justifiable concern over recent racial rioting to affect their better judgment in choosing candidates . . . .

"We should be short-sighted indeed if we did not recognize that many of the traditional enemies of labor — from the far left and the far right — are today actively agitating and exploiting the unrest that exists among Negroes and other minority groups.

"These forces are not trying to solve our racial problems; they are trying to magnify them. They oppose men like Governor Brown in California and Senator Douglas of Illinois because they don't want solutions. They want turmoil and hope to create it by arousing Negro against white, and white against Negro.

"If our members fall for this engineered confusion and allow the extremists to trick them into voting like the Birchers or Communists would like them to vote, they will only help defeat your friends and allies in Congress on November 8."

All this could only mean that by Abel's standards, unless an individual voted for a candidate endorsed by the

Steelworkers, he was a racist, a Bircher, or a Communist.

RALPH D. ABERNATHY was born on March 11, 1926 in Linden, Alabama, son of Louivery Bell and W.L. Abernathy. He married Juanita Jones. He is an alumnus of Alabama State College (B.S., 1950) and Atlanta University (M.A. 1951).

At the age of 22 while still an undergraduate at Alabama State, Abernathy was ordained to the Baptist ministry. While studying for his master's degree from Atlanta University, he was a social science instructor at Alabama State and held a pastorate in Demopolis, Alabama.

In 1951, Abernathy became pastor of the First Baptist Church in Montgomery, Alabama. In 1955, he was a leading organizer of the Montgomery Improvement Association, the leading force behind the 381-day bus boycott of 1955 and 1956 in Montgomery. Abernathy's MIA used Rosa Parks to initiate the trouble. (Mrs. Parks had attended the Highlander Folk School at Monteagle, Tennessee. Highlander was ostensibly an independent labor school but in reality was a training school for agitators, guided by fellow travelers who worked in close cooperation with the Communist Party.) Mrs. Parks deliberately violated Montgomery ordinances, was arrested and fined, and then became a heroine for the Communist Party. She became an especial favorite of the Emergency Civil Liberties Committee, a Communist front.

Once the Montgomery bus boycott began, Martin Luther King moved into the situation, assumed leadership, gained nation-wide notoriety as a racial agitator, and began his close association with Abernathy. After the boycott, King returned to his home base in Atlanta where he organized the Southern Christian Leadership Conference. He brought Abernathy along as an organizer for SCLC. King served as president of SCLC until his death in 1968. Abernathy was treasurer and vice president and, in 1968, succeeded King in the presidency. (King had described Abernathy as "my closest associate and most trusted friend.")

Although Abernathy's energies were mainly expended in his role as aide to King, he did find time to be a pastor at the W. Hunter St. Baptist Church in Atlanta. He has held membership in the NAACP, has served on the advisory committee of the Congress of Racial Equality, and has been on the board of directors of Chicago's Industrial Areas Foundation, Saul Alinsky's base for revolutionary activities.

While Martin L. King lived, Abernathy could be found invariably at his side, whether in a jail cell, a lecture platform, or in street demonstrations. Abernathy's utterances were merely echoes of King's monotonous tributes to Gandhi and the hollow prattlings about non-violence. Like King, Abernathy criticized the Vietnam War as a peacenik and as a racist agitator: "It is not too much to say that the war in Vietnam is being waged not only against Hanoi, but also against the Negro revolution. The grossly undemocratic operation of the military draft has thrown the heaviest burden on the Negro. The number of Negro combat troops is far out of proportion to our percentage of the total population. Thus, the war is extending in a grisly form the traditional pattern of imposing upon Negroes the hardest and dirtiest tasks .... The war in Vietnam cannot be justified on moral or security grounds."

Abernathy has displayed the same willingness to cooperate with Communists as did King. When the National Conference for New Politics was threatened in 1967 with an investigation by the Senate Internal Security Subcommittee, Abernathy petitioned against any SISS hearings. The concern of Abernathy and his fellow petitioners was based on public reports that SISS had found substantial evidence that the NCNP was not only heavily infiltrated by Communists but that the decisions made at the NCNP's 1967 convention were dictated by the Communist Party.

Abernathy has evidently steered clear of direct involvement with Communist fronts but he did petition for Carl Braden's freedom when that Communist was in federal prison and when the Communists were making Braden's release a major party project. On international matters, aside from the Vietnam War, Abernathy has been relatively quiet although he has come out strongly for the admission of Red China to the United Nations.

Before Martin L. King was killed, plans had been made for a massive demonstration in Washington, D.C. with the announced purpose of bringing the functions of the federal government to a halt until demands by Negro agitators for federal handouts were met. When King died, Abernathy decided to fulfill King's plans with the so-called Poor People's March.

Abernathy proved to be as demagogic as King whose death he blamed on "white racism." He assured his followers that in the wake of a conference with the Lord (in some versions, he had a vision), he had been chosen "by God and Martin Luther King" to lead Negroes to the promised land. For the benefit of the federal officials, he declared that "we're bringing all our rats, our lice, and our roaches, and we're going to dump all of them in Congress' front yard and wait until Congress decides to do something about them."

While he repeatedly adjured violence, Abernathy was not above some veiled threats as he organized the Washington, D.C. demonstration: "Things that you've never heard of, never dreamed of, will happen in this campaign if Congress does not act with all deliberate speed." He predicted that Negro militants would "burn the country down," if his Poor People's March failed, because it was probably the "last attempt anybody is going to make to deal with these problems peacefully."

From the federal government, Abernathy demanded jobs, education, and a guaranteed annual income for the "poor" – and in the context of his remarks, his "poor" were almost exclusively Negroes.

As his "poor people" headed for Washington from all parts of the nation, by a symbolic mule train and by more comfortable private cars and air-conditioned buses, Abernathy described himself as "a leader that's a rough boy" and "believe me, as Ralph Abernathy, this nation is going to have hell on its hands." While pre-fabricated shelters were being constructed for Abernathy's "poor" people on federal lands in the nation's capital, he was recruiting behind the screen of non-violence ("We're not going to bring violence to Washington. That's not our way. But anything else may happen in Washington when we get there."). But he was asking for no promises from his followers to remain nonviolent, as he vowed "to plague the Pharaohs of this nation with plague after plague until they agree to give us meaningful jobs and a guaranteed annual income." Unless the demands were met, Abernathy would not guarantee that there would be no violence. Not even Martin Luther King has ever produced such extortionate demands against the Congress and the people of the United States.

DEAN ACHESON was born on April 11, 1893 in Middletown, Connecticut, son of Eleanor Gooderham and Edward Acheson. He married Alice Stanley. He is an alumnus of Yale University (A.B., 1915) and Harvard University (LL.B., 1918).

From 1919 until 1921, Acheson was private secretary to Associate Justice Louis Brandeis of the U.S. Supreme Court. In 1921, Acheson began his private law practice which has continued until the present time with interruptions only while he was in federal government service.

In 1933, Acheson served as Under Secretary of the Treasury for six months but President Roosevelt dismissed him as a "lightweight." Until that time, Acheson's chief claim to fame was that as an attorney he had represented the Soviet Union's dictator Joe Stalin's interests prior to United States diplomatic recognition of the U.S.S.R. When Acheson's appointment to the Treasury Department was being considered by the Senate Finance Committee, he admitted that he had practically no finance experience and had never made a study of public finances.

In 1941, although he had no previous diplomatic experience, Acheson entered the State Department as Assistant Secretary. From 1945 until 1947, he was Under Secretary of State. Then, after a brief return to his law practice, he became Secretary of State – a position he held throughout the rest of the Truman years.

For the approximately nine years that Acheson was in the State Department, he was unquestionably the leader of a clique which at best can only be described as very soft on Communism and, at its worst,, pro-Communist. It is certainly no coincidence that while Acheson surrounded himself with the likes of Alger Hiss, Owen Lattimore, John Stewart Service, Oliver Edmund Clubb, John Carter Vincent, and Lauchlin Currie, the Soviet Union with the connivance of American diplomats made its greatest gains at the expense of free nations.

Acheson, more than any other individual, was responsible for the promotion of Alger Hiss into a position of such influence that Hiss would become the power behind the formation of the United Nations Organization which Hiss would staff with Red agents. Even after Hiss was convicted of perjury in denying that he had given American secrets to Soviet agents, Acheson was his foremost character witness as he said: "I will not turn my back on Alger Hiss." To this day he hasn't turned his back.

Acheson, along with the pro-Red China clique he sheltered in the Department, bears a major share of the blame for the American betrayal of China into the hands of Mao Tse-tung. In 1949, Acheson released a "White Paper" on U.S. relations with China. That document is probably the most dishonest ever foisted upon the American people by the State Department. Indeed, it was so patently fraudulent that even the *New York Times* criticized it editorially. It was Acheson whose machinations with UNRRA allowed that UN agency to be used by the Soviet Union to enslave Central Europe by the Communists' control of distribution of American food. It was Acheson who extended diplomatic recognition to the Communist regime of Tito in Yugoslavia just two months after President Truman had promised there would be no recognition of any regime that was not elected by the people. It was Acheson who sold the American people a bill of goods about the post-war peaceful intentions of the Soviet Union. It was Acheson who fought valiantly at every turn to protect security risks in their State Department positions. Acheson capped his career in the State Department with his betrayal of South Korea by combining an attack upon General MacArthur's military position with assurances to the Red Chinese that their territory would not be jeopardized if they joined forces with the North Korean aggressors against American troops.

No American Secretary of State has ever received or deserved more favorable treatment in the Communist press than Acheson, and it is well to remember that his influence within the State Department remains down to the present time.

In recent years, Acheson has been uttering sentiments which have caused some, who should be more perceptive, to think that he has turned over his red leaf and is now a fighting anti-Communist. He should remind observers of an alcoholic in the midst of his most recent hangover lecturing on the evils of John Barleycorn.

GARDNER ACKLEY was born on June 30, 1915 in Indianapolis, son of Margaret McKenzie and Hugh Ackley. He married Bonnie Lowry. He is an alumnus of Western Michigan University (A.B., 1936) and the University of Michigan (A.M., 1937, Ph.D., 1940).

Ackley was an instructor in economics at Ohio State University (1939-1940) and the University of Michigan (1940-1941). During the next six years,

he was with the Office of Price Administration (1941-1943 and 1944-1946) and the Office of Strategic Services (1943-1944). He was back in the Office of Price Administration in 1951 and 1952. In 1946, Ackley rejoined the economics faculty at the University of Michigan as an assistant professor (1946-1948), becoming an associate professor in 1949, a professor in 1952, and serving as department chairman from 1955 until 1962. In 1950, he served as a consultant to the Economic Stabilization Agency and was a visiting professor at the University of California. He has held a Fulbright scholarship and a Ford Foundation research fellowship.

In 1962, Ackley became a member of President Johnson's Council of Economic Advisers and, in 1964, he became chairman of the Council. From the time he joined the Johnson administration, Ackley proved himself to be a vigorous foe of free enterprise and especially hostile toward big industry. If Ackley had his way, the federal government would fix all prices and wages and regulate all consumer spending through the application of frenetic Keynesian economics.

On New Year's Day in 1968, Ackley was named U.S. Ambassador to Italy by President Johnson who described him as "one of my most trusted and closest friends and advisers."

SAUL ALINSKY was born on January 30, 1909 in Chicago, Illinois, son of Sarah Tannenbaum and Benjamin Alinsky. He was married to the late Helene Simon, and is married to Jean Graham. He is an alumnus of the University of Chicago (Ph.B.) where he also did some graduate work for about two years. Alinsky is the author of *John L. Lewis: A Biography* and of *Reveille for Radicals.*

Throughout most of the period 1931-1939, Alinsky was employed as a sociologist with the Institute for Juvenile Research in Chicago. During that same era, Alinsky was also a member of the Illinois State penitentiary system's classification board, did some organizing for John L. Lewis' Congress of Industrial Organizations (CIO), and raised money for the Communists' International Brigade in the Spanish Civil War.

In 1939, with the financial backing of leftist millionaire Marshall Field Jr., Alinsky established the Industrial Areas Foundation as a base for his personal revolutionary activities which have continued down to the present time. In the guise of a sociologist and as a self-described professional radical, Alinsky has preached and waged class warfare — the haves vs. the have-nots — by organizing poor people, especially Negroes, against "the white Establishment" and the city hall "power structure" in such places as Buffalo, Rochester, Chicago, Los Angeles, Detroit, and Syracuse. His utterances and writings cannot be identified with a single ideology. They contain elements of Marxism, Fascism, anarchism, Socialism, and racism, along with contempt for religion, the business world, and traditional American political processes.

In his efforts to bring about social revolution, Alinsky creates training schools for agitators whose mission is to create chaos in urban areas through boycotts, sit-ins, rent strikes, and street demonstrations. Alinsky's agitators work with Negro leaders, Protestant and Catholic clergymen, and so-called civil rights organizers (Alinsky admires Stokely Carmichael and his black power militancy). Wherever Alinsky and his revolutionaries have worked, they have left in their wake social chaos and racial bitterness.

Incredible as it may seem, Alinsky found employment during World War II with the federal government in various agencies, including the Labor and Treasury Departments. More recently he has been involved with the "War on Poverty" program and the Peace Corps.

DONNA ALLEN was born on August 19, 1920 in Petoskey, Michigan, daughter of Louise Densmore and Casper Rehkopf. She married Russell Allen. She is an alumna of Duke University (B.A., 1943) and the University of Chicago (M.A., 1952).

In 1944 and 1945, Mrs. Allen was an assistant to the research director in the metal trades department of the American Federation of Labor. In 1948 and 1949, she was a research writer for the National Labor Bureau in Chicago. From 1953 until 1955, she was a member of the faculty at Cornell University's School of Industrial and Labor Relations. In 1960, she was an assistant to Representative William H. Meyer (D.-Vt.).

For several years, Mrs. Allen has been the Washington, D.C. representative for the National Committee to Abolish the House Un-American Activities Committee, established and directed by the Communist Party. The Executive Secretary of NCAHUAC is Frank Wilkinson, who has been identified under oath as a Communist. (Wilkinson, an associate of Alger Hiss, has also worked for such Communist fronts as the Citizens Committee to Preserve American Freedoms and the Emergency Civil Liberties Committee.)

Mrs. Allen has been an active member of the Women's International League for Peace and Freedom, a left-wing group with a varied program of agitation. The WILPF lobbies and demonstrates for expanded foreign "aid" programs, disarmament, abolition of nuclear tests, forcible desegregation, and civil "rights" legislation. (The California Senate Fact-Finding Subcommittee on Un-American Activities, in its 1961 Report, found that WILPF had been substantially infiltrated by Communists in its local branches throughout the United States.)

Mrs. Allen has been an active and one of the better known members of Women's Strike for Peace, the largest feminine leftwing pacifist group in the United States. (Arnold Johnson, a top official of the Communist Party, USA, has described WSP as the "most vital mass force in the peace movement of our country today." WSP lobbies and demonstrates against nuclear tests, for disarmament, and for U.S. diplomatic recognition of Red China.)

As a member of WSP and WILPF in 1963, Mrs. Allen accompanied Russ Nixon, the general manager of the Communist weekly *National Guardian,* on two visits to the State Department's visa division in an effort to gain entry into the United States for Kaoru Yasui, a prominent Japanese Communist and a recipient of the Lenin "Peace" Prize. Nixon and Mrs. Allen were successful in their efforts on behalf of Yasui, who visited the United States on a ten-day speaking tour which began in Honolulu in November 1963, when the notorious red labor leader Harry Bridges held a "stop-work-meeting" to hear Yasui, the head of the pro-Communist Japan Council against A-and H-Bombs.

In 1964, the House Committee on Un-American Activities, which – at that time – was charged with the responsibility of surveillance over the McCarran-Walter Immigration Act of 1952, investigated the visit of Communist Yasui as part of a study to determine whether U.S. government agencies were improperly granting special waivers to foreigners who should not be allowed to enter the United States. From March 12 to September 9, 1964, the HCUA held nine executive sessions in its study of the waiver practices. On December 7, 1964, Nixon, Mrs. Allen, and Dagmar Wilson (leader of WSP) appeared under subpoena at HCUA's tenth executive session. It was explained that they had been summoned because of their role in arranging Yasui's visit and because testimony heard in previous executive sessions indicated that they might have information as to possible abuses of the immigration laws by U.S. government agencies.

Nixon protested that the HCUA was in executive session and refused to be sworn to testify unless the hearing were made public. Mrs. Wilson was sworn but refused to answer questions and also protested the executive nature of the hearing. Donna Allen took an affirmation, rather than an oath. She refused to give her name and address or to answer any questions of the HCUA in protest to the executive session. On December 10, 1964, the HCUA voted unanimously to report the conduct of the three witnesses to the Speaker of the House. On December 11, the Speaker certified to the U.S. Attorney for the District of Columbia that Allen, Nixon, and Wilson were in contempt of the Congress. On December 30, the three witnesses were indicted by a federal grand jury on charges of contempt. On February 26, 1965, defense motions to dismiss the indictments were denied and the three were tried and found guilty of the charges on April 8. On June 4, each of the defendants was sentenced to pay a fine of $100 and to serve jail terms of four to twelve months. The execution of the sentences was suspended. The three defendants then appealed their convictions to the U.S. Court of Appeals. A national committee, Defenders of 3 against HUAC, was organized and it was publicized in the Communist press to raise funds for Allen, Nixon, and Wilson.

On August 2, 1966, a three-man U.S. Court of Appeals, by a vote of two to one, reversed the contempt convictions on the technicality that the Speaker had certified the acts of contempt to the U.S. Attorney while the Congress was not in session. Neither Mrs. Allen nor her two co-defendants have been recalled by HCUA to give testimony. And Mrs. Allen continues to be active with NCAHUAC, WILPF, and WSP.

GEORGE V. ALLEN was born on November 3, 1903 in Durham, North Carolina, son of Harriet Moore and Thomas Allen. He married Katharine Martin. He is an alumnus of Duke University (A.B., 1924).

From 1924 until 1929, Allen was a public school teacher and principal and newspaper reporter in North Carolina.

In 1930, Allen joined the U.S. foreign service, and held minor diplomatic positions in Jamaica, China, Greece, and Egypt until 1938 when he was assigned to the State Department's Middle Eastern division in Washington. From 1946 until 1948, he was U.S. Ambassador to Yugoslavia during which time he did a great deal to impress the American people by propagating the fraud that Tito's brand of Communism was different from Stalin's.

From 1953 until 1955, Allen was U.S. Ambassador to Nepal and India. In 1955 and 1956, he was Assistant Secretary of State for Near Eastern, South Asian, and African affairs in Washington. In 1956 and 1957, he was U.S. Ambassador to Greece.

From 1957 until 1960, Allen was director of the U.S. Information Agency which, in effect, made him a front man for the Central Intelligence Agency.

While in the State Department, Allen was a conferee at some of the most important American sellouts to the Soviet bloc — the Cairo, Moscow, Potsdam, and the San Francisco (organizing the United Nations) conferences.

In 1960, Allen retired from government service and became president of the Tobacco Institute, but President Johnson brought Allen back into government as director of the Foreign Service Institute where government employees and families receive orientation and language training before going on overseas assignments. If Allen's principles apply to such orientation, then the trainees from the Institute can only emerge as full-blown internationalists. Allen belongs to Clarence Streit's Atlantic Union, which is working towards a political merger of Western Europe and the United States, as a major step towards world government, and has been an official of the United World Federalists, an anti-American sovereignty group.

JOSEPH ALSOP was born on October 11, 1910 in Avon, Connecticut, son of Corinne Robinson and Joseph Alsop. He married Susan Patten. He is an alumnus of Harvard University (A.B., 1932).

From 1932 until 1937, Alsop was on the staff of the *New York Herald Tribune,* first in New York, then in Washington. From 1937 until 1940, along with Robert E. Kintner, Alsop wrote a syndicated column on politics for the North American Newspaper Alliance.

During the war years (1940-1945), Alsop served in the U.S. Navy, the

American Volunteer Air Force (Chennault's Flying Tigers), and the U.S. Air Force. For a brief time in 1942 and 1943, he was chief of the Lend-Lease mission to China.

From 1945 until 1958, Alsop teamed with his brother Stewart in writing a column for the *New York Herald Tribune Syndicate*. Since 1958, Alsop has continued writing the column alone and it is now syndicated by the *Washington Post*. Alsop has written two books with his brother Stewart (*We Accuse, The Reporter's Trade*), two with Robert E. Kintner (*Men Around the President, American White Paper*), one with Turner Catledge (*The 168 Days*), and one by himself (*From the Silent Earth*).

There are some occasions when Alsop, writing on foreign affairs, makes some sensible observations. But as a founder of the ultra-liberal Americans for Democratic Action, Alsop with rare exceptions follows the ADA's socialist line when writing about domestic affairs. He is a persistent apologist for the foreign policy mistakes made in every administration, from Roosevelt's through Lyndon Johnson's. Alsop's ADA venom is particularly noticeable when he has cause to write about anti-Communist activists in general (the late Senator Joseph R. McCarthy, in particular), or Republicans of the Goldwater or Reagan stamp, or anyone to the political right of Hubert Humphrey.

STEWART ALSOP was born on May 17, 1914 in Avon, Connecticut, son of Corinne Robinson and Joseph Alsop. He married Patricia Hankey. He is an alumnus of Yale University (A.B., 1936).

Before World War II, Alsop was an editor with Doubleday Doran. During the war years, he served with the British Army and the U.S. Army.

From 1945 until 1958, Alsop collaborated with his brother Joseph in writing a column for the *New York Herald Tribune Syndicate*. Since 1958, he has been with the *Saturday Evening Post*, first as a national affairs contributing editor, and later as the Washington editor.

Alsop was a founder of the ultra-liberal Americans for Democratic Action and his presentation of the ADA's socialist line in his regular column has blended perfectly with the *Saturday Evening Post's* frantic move toward the far left in jouralism during recent years. Alsop is impartial toward liberals: he doesn't seem to care whether they belong to the Democrat or Republican Party. And his estimates range from Khrushchev as "rational" to Hubert Humphrey as an ideal President of the United States. At the other extreme, Alsop's hysteria reaches its heights when he recalls the late Senator Joseph McCarthy or anyone who has been an active anti-Communist.

FRANK ALTSCHUL was born on April 21, 1887 in San Francisco, son of Camilla Mandlebaum and Charles Altschul. He married Helen Goodhart. He is an alumnus of Yale University (B.A., 1908).

Altschul has retired from the activity of the business world where he was a great success as head of his General American Investors Corporation. But Altschul is a prototype of that curious breed of businessmen who, despite their debt owed to the opportunities presented by this nation's free enterprise system, attack that very system's future by their support of organizations which are unquestionably socialistic and a threat to the independence which made this nation's free enterprise system's existence possible.

Altschul has been an active official of the Council on Foreign Relations, the informal supra-State Department of the United States; an active official of the National Planning Association, which has the most ambitious program extant for the absolute centralization of all government in Washington, D. C.; a trustee of the Committee for Economic Development, the major propaganda arm of the Council on Foreign Relations, in the important work of socializing the American economy; a member of Arthur Larson's National Council for Civic Responsibility, an election year's drive by the Democratic Party against anti-Communists; and, an active official of the Atlantic Council, an internationalist organization which stresses the need for closer cooperation, especially economic, between the United States and the socialist nations of Western Europe – a program similarly endorsed by another of Altschul's internationalist affiliates, the National Planning Association.

CLINTON P. ANDERSON was born on October 23, 1895 in Centerville, South Dakota, son of Hattie Presba and Andrew Anderson. He married Henrietta McCartney. He attended Dakota Wesleyan University and the University of Michigan for a total of three years, but ill health prevented him from completing his collegiate studies.

In 1916 and 1917, Anderson was a reporter for the *Mitchell* (S.D.) *Republic.* For reasons of health, Anderson moved to New Mexico where, from 1918 until 1922, he worked as a reporter and editor for the *Albuquerque Journal.* In 1922, he entered upon a forty-one-year career in the insurance business and, during this same period, acquired a large working ranch near Albuquerque.

Aside from his private business in the

1930's, Anderson served as Treasurer of New Mexico (1933-1934), administrator of the New Mexico Relief Administration (1935), field representative for the Federal Emergency Relief Administration (1935-1936), and chairman and executive director of New Mexico's Unemployment Compensation Commission (1936-38). In 1939 and 1940, he was managing director of the U.S. Coronado Exposition Commission.

In 1940, Anderson was elected for the first of three consecutive terms to the U.S. House of Representatives as Congressman-at-Large from New Mexico. In June 1945, Anderson's poker-playing crony, President Harry S. Truman, appointed him to be Secretary of Agriculture – a position he held for three years. In 1948, Anderson was elected to the U.S. Senate from New Mexico and has been re-elected for second, third, and fourth terms.

During his years in the Senate, Anderson has been relatively quiet on foreign affairs, seemingly content generally to cast his vote along liberal lines. On domestic matters, however, he has been an ardent Populist and a sturdy workhorse during the Truman, Kennedy, and Johnson Administrations. He has successfully labored for socialized agriculture, socialized medicine, minimum wages, so-called civil rights legislation, and federal power projects vis-à-vis privately owned power companies.

Anderson's most important Senatorial committee work has been with the Joint Committee on Atomic Energy where he can usually be found to be right half of the time – but only half. The second half, however, is so wrong that he can assume much of the blame from his senior position for the disastrous atomic energy policy which has brought the United States so close to total disarmament.

JACK ANDERSON was born on October 19, 1922 in Long Beach, California. He married Olivia Farley.

In connection with a pending libel suit, Anderson was interrogated during pre-trial hearings. He testified that "his family had moved from Long Beach to Salt Lake City, Utah, when he was about two and that he had lived in Salt Lake City until World War II, attending Granite High School and the University of Utah in 1940-41, finishing one year of college. He said that he took courses at 'either George Washington or Georgetown' in Washington after World War II while working but never acquired a degree." (Frank Kluckhohn and Jay Franklin, *The Drew Pearson Story,* 1967, page 99.)

Anderson testified that he worked two years on the city desk of the *Deseret News* while he was a high school senior and a college freshman. Then, according to Anderson, he accepted a call as a missionary for the Mormon Church, after having been ordained a Mormon minister. Mormon authorities said that Anderson could not have been ordained, that he was an unsalaried volunteer missionary, and worked in various southern States from December 20, 1941 until February 22, 1944.

Anderson testified that in 1944 he voluntarily joined the U.S. Navy and was sent to and attended the Merchant Marine Academy at San Mateo, California. Anderson said he was at "the Merchant Marine Officer Training School" for about three months as a "midshipman." The Merchant Marine Academy authorities have no record of having had a Jack Anderson in attendance, and they note that its student officers are referred to as "cadets" – not midshipmen. Furthermore, the Merchant Marine Academy is not an adjunct of the Navy which Anderson says he joined.

Anderson testified that he went to sea in the Merchant Marine, aboard the *Cape Elizabeth* for seven or eight months, but the Maritime Bureau's records do not indicate that Jack Anderson was ever on a ship's crew. According to Anderson, his Merchant Marine career ended in early 1945 when he became a reporter for the *Deseret News* and he went to China as an accredited correspondent of that journal. He claimed that he filed stories from China about guerrilla campaigns and "air raids" but couldn't recall what newspapers, if any, printed his stories. Then, sometime after the war (Anderson does not remember when precisely), he was inducted into the U.S. Army. ("I think there was a brief period that I was in the Quartermaster Corps . . . . I cannot recall my own serial number.") And, according to Anderson, he was eventually assigned to the Army newspaper *Stars and Stripes,* while he saw service in the Pacific. But in his testimony Anderson provided no details as to his experience with *Stars and Stripes.*

In 1948, Anderson went to work for columnist Drew Pearson, and presently the Pearson column is often written by Anderson or as a collaborative effort of Pearson and Anderson. If Anderson and Pearson have had any disagreement on subject matters for their columns, it has never been made public.

They are indistinguishable in their persistent anti-anti-Communist stance, their carelessness with historical facts, their use of half-truths and innuendos and their obsession with "rightists." Anderson would make an ideal successor and heir to the Pearson column.

GLENN L. ARCHER was born on March 29, 1906 in Densmore, Kansas, son of Adah Burnap and Garfield Archer. He married Ruth Ford. He is an alumnus of Greenville College of Illinois (B.A., 1927), the University of Colorado (M.S., 1938), and Washburn University (L.L.B., 1946). He has also studied at Central Academy and College of Kansas and at Northwestern University.

From 1927 until 1939, Archer was a school superintendent in Kansas. From 1939 until 1942, he was an administrative assistant to the Governor of Kansas. In 1942 and 1943, he was director of professional relations for the Kansas State Teachers Association. In 1943 and 1944, he was an associate director of the National Education Association and, in 1946, was a special counsel to the NEA.

In 1946, Archer was admitted to the Kansas bar and, in 1947 and 1948, was dean and professor of law at Washburn University's School of Law.

In 1948, Archer became executive director of Protestants and Other Americans United for Separation of Church and State (POAU). According to Edgar Bundy's *News & Views* (March 1962): "Of the eighty-three original members of the POAU's 1948 National Advisory Council, at least thirty had Communist front records of varying degrees from minor and unimportant to extremely long and significant." Archer's only known affiliation of the sort was his sponsorship of the founding conference of the Emergency Civil Liberties Committee ("Communist front" – "subversive"). But in his 20 years as the guiding light of the POAU, Archer's stock in trade has been a virulent anti-Catholicism in which Archer portrays Catholicism as a greater enemy of the American people than Communism. Archer combines his anti-Catholicism with anti-anti-Communism in POAU's monthly magazine *Church and State*.

HAMILTON FISH ARMSTRONG was born on April 7, 1893 in New York City, son of Helen Neilson and D. Maitland Armstrong. He was married to Helen Byrne and to Carman Barnes. He is married to Christa von Tippelskirch. He is an alumnus of Princeton University (A.B., 1916).

In 1917, Armstrong was a military attaché to the Serbian War Mission in the United States. In 1918, he was a military attaché to the U.S. Legation in Belgrade, Serbia. From 1919 until 1921, he was on the editorial staff of the *New York Evening Post* and, in 1921 and 1922, was a special correspondent in eastern Europe for that same journal.

In 1922, Armstrong became co-editor with Archibald Cary Coolidge of *Foreign Affairs*, the quarterly journal of the Council on Foreign Relations, and since Coolidge's death, in 1928, Armstrong has been the editor of *Foreign Affairs*. Also, since 1928, he has been a resident member of the CFR and has served as a director of that organization, which is the informal supra-State Department of the United States.

From 1942 to 1944, Armstrong was with the Department of State as a member of its advisory committee on post-World War II problems, as a special assistant – with ministerial rank – to the U.S. Ambassador in London, as a special adviser to the Secretary of State, and as an adviser to the U.S. delegation at the San Francisco organizing conference of the United Nations.

Among Armstrong's better known books are *Can We Be Neutral?* and *Can America Stay Neutral?* (two pleas for American intervention in Europe, written in collaboration with Allen W.

Dulles), and *Tito and Goliath*, outstanding as a propaganda piece for the Yugoslav Communist tyrant.

As editor of *Foreign Affairs*, Armstrong has offered a most hospitable forum to the ultra-liberal internationalists, American and foreign, as they drive toward their one-world goal, at the expense of American sovereignty and security and for the advantage of Communist and Socialist regimes everywhere.

THURMAN ARNOLD was born on June 2, 1891 in Laramie, Wyoming, son of Annie Brockway and Constantine Arnold. He married Frances Longan. He is an alumnus of Princeton University (A.B., 1911), Harvard University LL.B., 1914), and Yale University (M.A., 1931).

Arnold began the practice of law in Chicago in 1914; then practiced in Laramie from 1919 until 1927. He lectured in law at the University of Wyoming from 1919 until 1927. From 1927 until 1930, he was dean of the College of Law at West Virginia University, and, in 1930, he joined the faculty of Yale University's law school, serving successively as a visiting professor and professor of law until 1938.

In 1938, Arnold began a five-year period as an Assistant Attorney General of the United States, in charge of the anti-trust division of the Department of Justice. From 1943 until 1945, he was an associate justice in the U.S. Court of Appeals for the District of Columbia. He then joined the firm of Arnold, Fortas & Porter. Along the way, in 1933 and 1934, Arnold did some legal work for the Department of Agriculture. He is the author of *The Symbols of Government; Cases on Trials; Judgments and Appeals; The Folklore of Capitalism; The Bottlenecks of Business; Democracy and Free Enterprise;* and *Fair Fights and Foul — A Dissenting Lawyer's Life.*

Arnold has been affiliated with Arthur Larson's National Council for Civic Responsibility, an election year's drive by the Democrat Party against anti-Communists; Franklin Littell's Institute for American Democracy, hysterical successor to Larson's abortive NCCR; the leftwing American Committee on Africa; the National Committee for an Effective Congress, a group which, since 1952 has campaigned for and financed ultra-leftist candidates for the House and Senate; the International Movement for Atlantic Union, working towards a political merger of Western Europe and the United States, as a major step towards world government; the American Civil Liberties Union, that motleyed collection of defenders of subversion, crime, and licentiousness; and, the Institute for Policy Studies, which is nothing less than a leftwing propaganda agency for disarmament.

Arnold's world is one of extreme likes and dislikes. Among his heroes are Earl Warren, the late Franklin D. Roosevelt, Lyndon Johnson, J. William Fulbright, Wayne Morse, and Owen Lattimore. His favorite villain was and remains the late Senator Joseph R. McCarthy, who, according to Arnold's fantasy, "frightened both the Truman and Eisenhower administrations into establishing procedures by which citizens were tried and condemned as subversive on secret evidence without the American constitutional right of confrontation and cross-examination."

Arnold is a cheer leader for the Warren Court, for the no-win policy in Vietnam, for the admission of Red China into the United Nations, for an American foreign policy of coexistence with the Communist nations, and for the lessening of anti-subversive activities by the federal government.

MANACHEM S. ARNONI was born in 1918 in Lodz, Poland. He claims to have been imprisoned in German concentration camps for five years. As a citizen of Israel, he entered the United States in October 1952 as a visiting journalist. He claims that he adjusted his status to permanent residence in the United States in December 1954. He has not filed application for American citizenship.

In 1959, Arnoni began publishing *Minority of One,* a monthly magazine, in Richmond, Virginia. In 1961, he moved his publishing operation to Passaic, New Jersey.

From the beginning, *Minority of One* has featured on its masthead and as authors of its articles notorious leftwing pacifists and Communist fronters. Articles from *Minority of One* have been reprinted in Moscow's *New Times.* The Fair Play for Cuba Committee, subsidized by Castro, has used sample copies of *Minority of One* to solicit funds. The Communist dictator of North Vietnam, Ho chi Minh, has used *Minority of One* as a propaganda forum.

Arnoni and *Minority of One* have received very favorable notices in the Communist press. Arnoni has advertised his publication in the Communist weekly *National Guardian* and he sent greetings to *The Worker's* annual banquet in 1965.

In 1967, Arnoni predicted that the United States would launch a nuclear attack upon Red China before the 1968 national elections.

MAX ASCOLI was born on June 25, 1898 in Ferrara, Italy, son of Adriana Finzi and Enrico Ascoli. He married Marion Rosewald. He is an alumnus of the University of Ferrara (LL.D., 1920)

and the University of Rome (Ph.D., 1928). From 1926 until 1931, he was a professor of jurisprudence in Italian universities.

In 1931, Ascoli applied for and received a Rockefeller Foundation fellowship to study in the United States. Upon completion of his studies, he decided not to return to Italy. The Foundation's officials helped him to obtain a professorship in political science on the graduate faculty of the ultra-left New School for Social Research. And, during his first year at the New School, the Foundation paid half of Ascoli's salary.

Ascoli was at the New School until 1941 and during his last two years there he was dean of the graduate faculty. Meanwhile, he was naturalized in 1939 and, from 1940 until 1942, he was in the State Department as assistant director for cultural relations and coordinator of inter-American affairs.

From 1944 until 1954, Ascoli was president of Handicraft Development, Inc., but in 1949 he became editor and publisher of his own magazine *The Reporter.* He is the author of *Intelligence in Politics* and *The Power of Freedom,* and co-author with Arthur Feiler of *Fascism for Whom.*

Ascoli is a member of the Council on Foreign Relations, the informal supra-State Department of the United States. And Ascoli and his wife were among the earliest financial supporters of Americans for Democratic Action, the center of the radical left in American politics.

In its publishing history, Ascoli's *The Reporter* has been a mirror for the most extreme leftwing views of the Council on Foreign Relations and the Americans for Democratic Action. It combines preachments for Fabian socialism with anti-anti-Communism. Ascoli, himself, enjoys a reputation as an anti-Fascist but this posture is not a denial of his soft-on-Communism attitude.

In 1950, Ascoli called for United States diplomatic recognition of Red China. In 1952, Ascoli was a pioneer, discovering the legendary and almost totally imaginary Nationalist China lobby. In the McCarthy years, he joined the liberal chorus, yapping at the heels of the Wisconsin Senator. In 1954, Ascoli did his best to destroy the political career of New Hampshire's Styles Bridges, the most durable anti-Communist in the United States Senate at the time. And, over the years, heroes of *The Reporter* would include luminaries of the Fair Deal, Modern Republicanism, the New Frontier, and the Great Society, and their foreign counterparts — the socialist revolutionaries on every continent.

HARRY ASHMORE was born on July 28, 1916 in Greenville, South Carolina, son of Nancy Scott and William Ashmore. He married Barbara Laier. He is an alumnus of Clemson College (B.A., 1937) and he was a Nieman Fellow at Harvard University in 1941-1942.

From 1937 until 1939, Ashmore was a reporter-columnist for the *Greenville* (N.C.) *Piedmont.* From 1939 until 1941, he was a political writer for the *Greenville News* and *Charlotte* (N.C.) *News.* From 1945 until 1947, he was, successively, an associate editor and editor of the *Charlotte News.* In 1947, he was editor of the editorial page of the *Arkansas Gazette* and, from 1948 until 1959, was executive editor of that journal.

In 1948, Ashmore supported the candidacy of Henry Wallace, the Communists' choice for the presidency. In 1955 and 1956, Ashmore took a leave of absence from the *Gazette* while he worked on the campaign staff of presidential candidate Adlai Steveson.

In 1959, Ashmore became a consultant to the ultra-leftist Fund for the Republic's Center for the Study of Democratic Institutions. Later he became a director of the Fund.

From 1960 to 1963, Ashmore was editor-in-chief of the Encyclopedia Brittanica and, since 1963, has been director of research and development for editorial projects of the Brittanica. He is the author of *The Negro and the Schools; An Epitaph for Dixie;* and *The Other Side of Jordan.*

Ashmore received his greatest notoriety as a modern day scalawag. His writings defending the Supreme Court's decisions and executive actions which brought forced integration to the southern States gained for Ashmore the Sidney Hillman and Freedom House Awards, which are invariably reserved for outstanding leftwingers.

Ashmore has been affiliated with Arthur Larson's National Council for Civic Responsibility, an election year's drive by the Democrat Party against anti-Communists; Franklin Littell's Institute for American Democracy, hysterical successor to Larson's abortive NCCR; the National Committee for an Effective Congress, a group which, since 1952, has campaigned for and financed ultra-leftist candidates for the House and Senate; the Atlantic Union, which is working towards a political merger of Western Europe and the United States as a major step towards world government; and the United World Federalists, an anti-American sovereignty group.

In January 1967, Ashmore visited Hanoi, North Vietnam to invite Ho chi Minh, the Communist leader of the war against the United States and its allies, to attend a "Pacem in Terris Convocation," sponsored by the Center for the Study of Democratic Institutions. Ashmore found Ho to be "a man of great charm, great sophistication, great intelligence . . . . quite outgoing, quite frank . . . . I believe historically he will rank with Gandhi and it occurs to me there is nobody else around in the world today in any country who seems to provide a similar blend of spiritual and political power."

JOHN M. BAILEY was born on November 23, 1904 in Hartford, Connecticut, son of Louise Moran and Michael Bailey. He married Barbara Leary. He is an alumnus of Catholic University (A.B., 1926) and Harvard University (LL.B., 1929).

Bailey was admitted to the Connecticut and Massachusetts bars in 1929 (his present law practice is as a senior partner in Bailey & Wechsler).

From 1931 until 1933, Bailey was executive secretary to the Mayor of Hartford. From 1933 until 1935 and from 1939 until 1941, he was a judge in Hartford's Municipal Court. In 1937, he was a law clerk with the U.S. Senate Judiciary Committee. From 1941 until 1946, he was commissioner for statute revision, working for the Connecticut Legislature. In 1946, he was executive secretary to the Governor of Connecticut.

In 1932, Bailey became a member of Connecticut's Central Committee of the Democrat Party and, in 1946, he became Chairman of the Central Committee. He was the first State Chairman to endorse the presidential candidacy of John F. Kennedy in 1960.

In 1961, Bailey became National Chairman of the Democratic Party. In his role as Chairman, Bailey has combined the characteristics of a hatchet-man and a demagogue. He has constantly represented the Republican Party, as the party of wealthy people – a cliché that should have been discarded decades ago but the use of which fits in very well with Bailey's predilection for appeals to class distinctions.

It is true that in his public utterances Bailey usually offers little else but equivocation and double-talk, but when he does say anything substantive on either domestic or foreign policy, he follows the left-of-center line laid down in the New Deal era and perpetuated throughout the Administrations of the New Frontier and Great Society.

In 1965, Bailey insisted that he was merely a party organizer. "My deal with the White House has been simple," he said. "They'll take care of foreign policy and I'll take care of the precincts." Then he posed the question: "What should be done in Vietnam?" And gave his answer: "I don't know anything about the issues. But, by 1967, Bailey's education had evidently broadened his understanding of Vietnam as he launched a vicious, slanderous attack upon Republicans: "President Johnson seeks to prevent World War III [in Vietnam], while most Republicans are busy trying to win the 1968 election any way they can. We [Democrats] must point this out to American voters. We must drum away, day after day, at the theme that preventing the world from blowing up must take precedent [sic] over partisan politics."

In the congressional election year of 1966, Bailey described the Republican Party as the party of ultra-conservative extremists who include "political witch doctors, retired martinets, and neurotic victims of the neo-Fascist lecture circuit." Bailey never offets his bogey of ultra-conservatives with any alarms about the real threat of ultra-leftists who have saturated the Democrat Party. And in the same vein, his cries against the alleged evils of big business are not matched by warnings against the socialistic Democrats who labor so tirelessly to destroy free enterprise and revolutionize the economic system of the United States.

Bailey, in the past few years, has also added to his bag of demagoguery bleeding-heart references to the "poor people." How far he will go to prove a point was best demonstrated when he offered this inane and corrupt version of constitutional law: "The general welfare clause of the Constitution does not include bankers, investors or bondholders, but is for the poor people of this country." It is ironic that periodically Bailey joins his Republican counterpart to sign a code of fair campaign practices which is supposedly a promise that campaigns will be in the "best American tradition free from distortion and misrepresentation." Perhaps Bailey feels that all is fair in the war he wages — class warfare.

JAMES BALDWIN was born on August 2, 1924 in New York City, son of Berdis Jones and David Baldwin.

Baldwin has written for periodicals including: *Harper's, Atlantic, Mademoiselle, Nation, New York Times* magazine, the *New York Times Book Review, Reporter, Commentary, Partisan Review, New Leader,* and *Esquire.* His books include the novels *Go Tell It on the Mountain; Giovanni's Room;* and *Another Country;* and collections of essays *Notes of a Native Son; Nobody Knows My Name;* and *The Fire Next Time.* He has written the plays *Blues for Mr. Charlie* and *Amen Corner.* And he has also contributed to a book, *Harlem, U.S.A.,* which was distributed by the Communists' Jefferson Bookshop.

Columnist Morrie Ryskind said of Baldwin's *Another Country*: "Frankly, I'm damned if I can see how this story of the sex life of a bunch of abysmal slobs and sluts, told in a dialogue that never uses a five-letter word when a foul four-letter synonym can do the trick, can be classified as literature." Ryskind was understandably disturbed when he discovered that Baldwin's *Another Country* was being promoted as required reading for school children.

Throughout his career, Baldwin has been unusually capable of attracting help for the promotion of his work. He has been the recipient of a Rosenwald fellowship, a *Partisan Review* fellowship, a Guggenheim fellowship, a Eugene F. Saxton Memorial Trust Award, and a grant from the Ford Foundation. When his play, *Blues for Mr. Charlie,* was closing because of box-office slump, two daughters of Nelson Rockefeller contributed $5,000 each to keep the play going at least another week. And, in 1965, Baldwin's play *Amen Corner* was sponsored for a tour in Austria, The Netherlands, Switzerland, France, and West Germany.

Baldwin has been the subject of a nine-page spread in *Life* magazine and a cover story in *Time* magazine. He has had widespread exposure on television and radio programs. He has lectured before many high school and college audiences.

In his writings, Baldwin is preoccupied with themes revolving around sexual perversion and his pet hatreds: Christianity, America, American customs, and white people. William F. Buckley Jr. has called Baldwin an "eloquent menace" and his attitude "morose nihilism." The descriptions are certainly appropriate as far as they go.

In recent years, Baldwin has been one

of America's most inflammatory racial agitators. He denies being a spokesman for Negroes but is easily recognized as such despite protestations. He has raised money for the Student Nonviolent Coordinating Committee and he has been an official of and speaker for the Congress of Racial Equality – two of the more militant Negro groups in the current era of demonstrations and riots.

Baldwin also insists that he is neither a Marxist nor a socialist, but he is portrayed in heroic posture throughout the Communist press. Such praise has not been idly given. Baldwin was a sponsor of the Castro-financed Fair Play for Cuba Committee. He worked for Junius Scales' amnesty after that Red terrorist had been convicted under the Smith Act. He worked for Carl Braden's freedom when that Communist was in federal prison.

The House Committe on Un-American Activities has been a special target of Baldwin's activities. He has sponsored the National Committee to Abolish the House Un-American Activities Committee, a Communist Party enterprise. He has written a postscript for *A Quarter Century of Un-Americana,* a rambling diatribe against the HCUA, which was published by Marzani & Munsell. (Carl Marzani served a federal prison term for perjury when he denied his activities as a member of the Communist Party. Alexander Munsell refused under oath to answer questions about his Communist Party activities.)

In 1962, Baldwin helped to raise funds for the Committee to Aid Southern Lawyers, a creation of the National Lawyers Guild which had been described by the HCUA as "the foremost legal bulwark of the Communist Party," and by the Senate Internal Security Subcommittee as "a bulwark of protection" for the Communist Party.

Baldwin takes the same tack on the Vietnam War as do many other racists: white America is using black Americans to kill colored people in Asia; and, as do many other leftists, Baldwin joins with the ban-the-bomb crowd in sponsoring the leftwing, pacifist National Committee for a Sane Nuclear Policy.

ROGER BALDWIN was born on January 21, 1884 in Wellesley, Massachusetts, son of Lucy Nash and Frank Baldwin. He married and was divorced from Madeleine Doty, and was married to the late Evelyn Preston. He is an alumnus of Harvard University (A.B., 1904; M.A., 1905).

In the academic field, Baldwin was an instructor in sociology at Washington University of St. Louis and was a member of the faculty at the New School for Social Research. In government, Baldwin has been a counsel to the United Nations, and a counsel on civil liberties to the United States occupation authorities in Japan (1947), Korea (1947), Germany (1948), and Austria (1950). He also served as counsel in 1956 to the United States governing authorities in Puerto Rico and the Virgin Islands. Baldwin is the author of *Liberty under the Soviets; Civil Liberties and Industrial Conflict* (Harvard's Godkin lectures); and *A New Slavery: Forced Labor.*

Baldwin's continuous radical career of association and cooperation with Communists, anarchists, and Socialists is of more than fifty years' duration. He was a member of the subversive, un-American Industrial Workers of the World (Wobblies) and a convicted draft dodger during World War I. He has been affiliated with Russian Reconstruction Farms ("Communist enterprise"); Consumers' National Federation ("Communist front"); the All-America Anti-Imperialist

League ("Communist enterprise"); American Youth Congress ("subversive and Communist"); American Committee for Struggle against War ("Communist front"); Book Union ("distributors of Communist literature"); the American Fund for Public Service, the Garland Fund ("a major source for the financing of Communist Party enterprises"); the International Labor Defense ("legal arm of the Communist Party); the National Committee to Abolish the Poll Tax ("Communist front"); the National Committee to Aid Victims of German Fascism ("Communist front"); the National Congress for Unemployment and Social Insurance ("Communist front"); American Friends of Spanish Democracy ("subversive"); the American League for Peace and Democracy ("subversive and Communist"); Friends of the Soviet Union ("to propagandize for and to defend Russia and its system of government" – "directed from Moscow"); the American Student Union ("Communist front"); the New York Tom Mooney Committee ("Communist front"); the National People's Committee against Hearst ("subsidiary" to the American League for Peace and Democracy – "subversive and Communist); the American League against War and Fascism ("subversive and Communist"); the American Committee for Protection of Foreign Born [Americans] ("subversive and Communist" – "one of the oldest auxiliaries of the Communist Party in the United States" – under the "complete domination" of the Communist Party); National Committee to Defeat the Mundt Bill ("a Communist lobby"); Citizens' Committee to Free Earl Browder ("Communist"); National Student League ("Communist front"); Consumers' National Federation ("Communist front"); the United States Con-

gress against War ("completely under the control of the Communist Party"); American Congress for Peace and Democracy ("Communist front"); Frontier Films ("Communist front"); *New Masses* ("Communist periodical"); Federated Press ("Communist-controlled" news syndicate); the Japanese-American Committee for Democracy ("Communist-controlled"), the American Friends of the Chinese People ("Communist front"); Chicago Sobell Committee ("active in the Communist propaganda campaign exploiting atomic spies"); Greater New York Emergency Conference on Inalienable Rights ("Communist front"); the International Workers' Order ("subversive and Communist"); and *Liberator* ("Communist magazine"). Baldwin has also been associated with the leftwing pacifist National Committee for a Sane Nuclear Policy; the radical, pacifist *War/Peace* magazine; the League for Industrial Democracy (socialist); the leftwing American Committee on Africa; and, the leftwing International League for the Rights of Man. In 1966, Baldwin was a sponsor of the National Voters' Pledge Campaign, which was led by Socialist Norman Thomas, veteran Communist-fronter Reverend William Sloane Coffin, and Sanford Gottlieb, the political director of the National Committee for a Sane Nuclear Policy. The Voters' Pledge Campaign was designed to support "peace" candidates, who would work for a cease-fire in Vietnam and encourage negotiations in which the Vietcong would be participants.

But Baldwin's major contribution to un-Americanism has been his 47-year career with the American Civil Liberties Union, of which he was a founder and original officer, along with such notables of Communist Party history as Elizabeth

Gurley Flynn, Louis Budenz, and William Z. Foster.

On his 80th birthday, Baldwin received from President Lyndon Johnson a very warm message of congratulations, which read, in part: "In your life, you have shown a devotion to principle and force of personal character which will long be remembered by your countrymen."

GEORGE W. BALL was born on December 21, 1909 in Des Moines, Iowa, son of Edna Wildman and Amos Ball. He married Ruth Murdoch. He is an alumnus of Northwestern University (B.A., 1930; J.D., 1933).

From 1933 until 1935, Ball was in the general counsel's office of the U.S. Treasury Department. From 1935 until 1942, he practiced law in Chicago. In 1942, at the suggestion of Adlai Stevenson, a legal associate of Ball's, Ball was brought back into the federal government. From 1942 until 1944, he was an associate general counsel of the Lend-Lease Administration, which had changed its name to the Foreign Economic Administration. In 1944 and 1945, he was director of the U.S. Strategic Bombing Survey in London and, in 1945 and 1946, he was general counsel of the French Supply Council in Washington, D.C.

From 1946 until 1961, Ball was a member of a law firm (Cleary, Gottlieb, Steen & Ball) which he helped to found in 1946. The firm represented the European Common Market, the European Coal and Steel Community, the European Atomic Energy Community, and the French government. During this period, Ball was a registered lobbyist for these foreign interests.

Although Ball was a veteran political supporter of Adlai Stevenson, President Kennedy appointed him to the number three post in the State Department — Under Secretary for Economic Affairs. Within a year, Ball became Under Secretary of State, second only to Rusk in the Department but generally described as Rusk's alter ego and troubleshooter. Ball left the Department in 1966 to become chairman of Lehman Brother International.

During his years with the Kennedy and Johnson Administrations, Ball was one of Washington's most vociferous internationalists — his favorite theme being the necessity for United States economic and military interdependence with other nations.

From his lofty position in the State Department, Ball was consistently soft on Communism and Communists. He advocated lifting of restrictions on the sale of military goods to Communist nations by countries which were recipients of U.S. foreign aid. He worried that name-calling might be resented by the Communists. Therefore, he advocated Communism not be described as "the enemy," or that Communist tactics be called "brutal," or that "slavery" be used to characterize the Communists' hold on the captive nations.

Within days after Kenya's President Jomo Kenyatta, the former leader of the savage Mau Mau, had dedicated a Communist training institute, Ball described Kenyatta as "a pretty mature individual trying to follow something of a middle path."

Ball was a leader in the muzzling-the-military scandals when anti-Communist references in speeches made by military men were vigorously censored by the State Department. Ball took a leading role in the State Department's betrayal of the anti-Communist regime of Katanga Province in the Congo. Ball, as much as anyone in the Department, soft-pedalled the truth about Communist influence in Africa and the Soviet Union's influence in Cuba.

Ball is a non-resident member of the Council on Foreign Relations, the informal supra-State Department of the United States; a trustee of The American Assembly, a Columbia University brain-washing project wherein American business executives are fed an up-to-date version of the State Department's soft-on-Communism, internationalist line; and, a member of Clarence Streit's Atlantic Union, which is working towards a political merger of Western Europe and the United States, as a major step towards world government.

FREDERICK BARGHOORN was born on July 4, 1911 in New York City, son of Elizabeth Brust and Elso Barghoorn. He is an alumnus of Amherst College (A.B., 1934) and Harvard University (A.M., 1935; Ph.D., 1941).

From 1942 until 1947, Barghoorn was on the staff of the United States Embassy in Moscow. In 1947, he joined the political science faculty of Yale University, becoming a professor in 1957. He has also lectured at the University of Chicago and Columbia University. He has been on the staff of the Ford Foundation, which has been a horn of plenty for leftwingers and leftwing projects on every continent, and is a non-resident member of the Council on Foreign Relations, the informal supra-State Department of the United States. From 1949 until 1951, on leave from Yale, Barghoorn was employed by the State Department in West Germany. He is the author of *The Soviet Image of the United States; Soviet Russian Nationalism; The Soviet Cultural Offensive;* and *Soviet Foreign Propaganda.*

Barghoorn is widely heralded as an expert on the Soviet Union. Yet, writing in the *New York Times Magazine* (January 19, 1964), Barghoorn attributed Lenin's seizure of power in 1917 and 1918 to his "promises of bread, peace, land and self-determination" as "overwhelmingly persuasive propaganda." Not even Lenin's most ardent adherents in the Kremlin would make such a ridiculous claim.

Barghoorn became an international celebrity in October and November, 1963 when he was arrested and imprisoned for sixteen days in Moscow. Barghoorn said that he was approached outside his Moscow hotel by a young stranger who thrust a roll of papers toward him. "Unwittingly, perhaps foolishly," said Barghoorn, the expert on the Soviet Union, "I took it and put it in my coat pocket." Within a matter of seconds, Soviet police leaped from a car and arrested Barghoorn. President Kennedy told Kremlin authorities that Barghoorn was not a spy and, in an outburst of "good fellowship," Barghoorn was released from Lubyanka Prison. The odor of the entire affair lingers on for those who still don't believe in peaceful coexistence.

Fifteen months later, Barghoorn was a guest at a reception for a Soviet "cultural" group at Yale and he endorsed a long-range exchange program with the Soviet Union. Perhaps, he thinks more American "tourists" should have a taste of Lubyanka Prison.

JOSEPH BARNES was born on July 21, 1907 in Montclair, New Jersey, son of Anna Kohler and Earl Barnes. He married Elizabeth Brown.

From 1928 to 1931, Barnes was employed by the Equitable Trust Company in New York City. From 1931 to

1934, he was on the staff of the Institute of Pacific Relations ("a vehicle used by the Communists to orientate American far eastern policies toward Communist objectives") in the Soviet Union, Manchuria, China, and Japan. In 1935, he joined the staff of the *New York Herald Tribune* and he remained with that journal until 1948, except for the war years. From 1941 to 1944, Barnes was a deputy director in Elmer Davis' Red-lined Office of War Information.

In 1942, Barnes accompanied Wendell Willkie on a trip to the Soviet Union and China – a trip memorialized in Willkie's book *One World* (with collaboration by Barnes), in which the ultra-liberal Willkie made a fervent plea for a post-war one world of accommodation between the United States and the Soviet Union. A few years later, Barnes would be a ghost writer for Dwight Eisenhower's *Crusade in Europe.*

Barnes is the author of only one book, *Willkie,* published in 1952. But in earlier years, Barnes contributed articles to the IPR's *Pacific Affairs;* the *Annals* of the American Academy of Political and Social Science; the *Bulletin* of the American-Russian Institute; *Foreign Affairs;* the IPR's *Far Eastern Survey;* and the *American Scholar.* The pro-Communist views, evident in Barnes' writings, come as no surprise when it is recalled that, in sworn testimony, Whittaker Chambers, Louis Budenz, Alexander Barmine, Karl Wittfogel, and Hede Massing, swore of their own personal knowledge that they had known Barnes as a Communist agent.

Since 1948, when he left the *New York Herald Tribune,* Barnes was editor of the leftwing *New York Star* for about two years. He is presently a senior editor with the publishing firm of Simon and Schuster. He is a resident member of the Council on Foreign Relations (the informal supra-State Department of the United States) and a member of the National Committee to Abolish the House Un-American Activities Committee ("to lead and direct the Communist Party's 'Operation Abolition' campaign").

DOAK BARNETT was born on October 8, 1921 in Shanghai, China, son of United States citizens Bertha Smith and Eugene Barnett. He married Jeanne Badeau. He is an alumnus of Yale University (B.A., 1942; M.A., 1947).

From 1947 until 1950 and in 1952 and 1953, he was a fellow of the Institute of Current World Affairs in China and South Asia. In those same years he was a correspondent for the *Chicago Daily News.* In 1950 and 1951, he was a consultant to the Economic Cooperation Administration and, in 1951 and 1952, he served as a consultant and public affairs officer to the United States Consul-General in Hong Kong. From 1953 until 1955, he was an associate on the American University's field staff.

In 1956 and 1957, Barnett was department head for foreign area studies in the State Department's Foreign Service Institute. In 1958 and 1959, he was a research fellow with the Council on Foreign Relations, the informal supra-State Department of the United States. From 1959 until 1961, he was a program associate with the Ford Foundation, which has been a horn of plenty for leftwingers and leftwing projects on every continent.

In 1961, he joined the faculty at Columbia University as a professor of political science and chairman of the contemporary China studies committee. He is the author of *Communist Eco-*

nomic Strategy: The Rise of Mainland China; Communist China and Asia: Challenge to American Policy; Communist China in Perspective; China on the Eve of Communist Takeover; and *Communist China: The Early Years.*

Barnett has long been in the van of this nation's Red China lobbyists. As long ago as November of 1956, before an American Assembly seminar at Arden House, Barnett urged United States diplomatic recognition of Red China. In his *Communist China and Asia,* he not only advocated *de facto* diplomatic recognition of Mao Tse-tung's regime but also withdrawal of *de jure* recognition from Chiang Kai-shek's regime. He also suggested that the United States exert pressure on Nationalist China to surrender its offshore islands Quemoy and Matsu to Red China. Barnett argued that retention of the offshore islands was contrary to the wishes of Britain, India, and Red China.

In 1958, at a preparatory meeting of the Fifth Annual World Study Conference, conducted by the National Council of Churches, Barnett's high regard for Red China was demonstrated when he said: "We must realistically face . . . not only the question of what we can or cannot do in respect to Communist China itself, but also the question of whether or not we are capable of competing effectively with Communist China [in pursuit of industrial and political goals], and with the ideas, the values, and institutions which it represents, in the whole non-Western, Asian-African world."

In 1962, in his *Communist China in Perspective,* Barnett was uncritically receptive to anything and everything the Chinese Communists claimed as to their industrial accomplishments, political objectives, and their ideas, values, and institutions.

In 1966, Barnett joined with such prominent Red China lobbyists as John K. Fairbank, Oliver Edmund Clubb, Bayard Rustin, Anna Lord Strauss, Roger Hilsman, Clark Kerr, and Robert A. Scalapino to form the National Committee on United States-[Red] China Relations. This group, according to its organizers, was to sponsor public debate – as if it were needed – on United States policy toward Red China, which simply meant to lobby and propagandize for a sellout of Nationalist China, United States diplomatic recognition, and United Nations membership for Red China.

In 1966, Barnett unequivocally endorsed Red China's admission to the United Nations and membership for Red China on the UN's Security Council after a probationary period. Also, in 1966, when Senator William J. Fulbright, chairman of the Senate Foreign Relations Committee, held his infamous scaremongering hearings – war with Red China was just around the corner – his first witness was Doak Barnett. Barnett did not disappoint Fulbright as he presented testimony that must have warmed the red cockles of Mao Tse-tung's heart.

ROBERT BARNETT was born on November 6, 1911 in Shanghai, China, son of United States citizens Bertha Smith and Eugene Barnett. He married Patricia Glover. He is an alumnus of the University of North Carolina (A.B., 1933; M.A., 1934) and Oxford University of England (B.A., 1936; B. Litt., 1937), where he was a Rhodes scholar. At Yale University (1937-1939), he was a General Education Board fellow. In 1940 and 1941, he was a Rockefeller Foundation fellow and, in 1959 and 1960, he was a fellow at Harvard University's Center for International Affairs.

He also was a graduate student at the Universita per Stranieri of Perugia, Italy, in 1935, and at the University of Michigan in 1938.

In 1941 and 1942, Barnett was on the staff of the Institute of Pacific Relations ("a vehicle used by the Communists to orientate American far eastern policies toward Communist objectives") and affiliated with the Communist-controlled magazine *Amerasia*. The Senate Internal Security Subcommittee classified Barnett as pro-Communist.

In 1945, Barnett began a career in the State Department and continued that career despite the disclosures of his pro-Communist background by the Senate Internal Security Subcommittee in 1952. In the Department, he has been a member of the economics and reparations committees for the Far Eastern Commission in Japan, the officer-in-charge of China economic affairs, the officer-in-charge of western European economic affairs, the officer-in-charge of European economic organizations, economic counselor to the U.S. Embassy in The Hague, counselor to the U.S. mission to European communities, deputy director of the foreign economic advisory staff, and, in his present position, deputy assistant secretary of state for Far Eastern Affairs.

Barnett is a non-resident member of the Council on Foreign Relations, the informal supra-State Department of the United States.

There is no reason to believe that Barnett's views are any different today than they were when he was a staff member of the Institute of Pacific Relations. And in the Far Eastern section of the State Department, he is in an ideal position to promote the pro-Red China views of his brother Doak and the similar views of IPR veterans within the government such as Secretary of State Rusk and those with influence upon government officials such as former Ambassador Edwin O. Reischauer, John K. Emmerson, and John K. Fairbanks.

STRINGFELLOW BARR was born on January 15, 1897 in Suffolk, Virginia, son of Ida Stringfellow and William Barr. He married Gladys Baldwin. He is an alumnus of the University of Virginia (B.A., 1916; M.A., 1917) and Oxford University (B.A., 1919; M.A., 1921), where he was a Rhodes scholar. He also studied at the University of Paris (diplôme, 1922) and the University of Ghent, Belgium (1922-1923).

From 1924 until 1937 and from 1951 until 1953, Barr was on the University of Virginia's faculty, serving successively as assistant professor, associate professor, professor, and visiting professor. In 1936 and 1937, he was a visiting professor at the University of Chicago. From 1937 until 1946, he was President of St. John's College in Maryland. At St. John's, Barr – along with Scott Buchanan, who served as Dean – became famous in the academic world when he completely reorganized the curriculum of the college. He introduced a non-elective, four-year system wherein candidates for the A.B. degree were required to read "the Great Books of the Western World" and discuss them in seminars. In the meantime, from 1944 until 1946, Barr was an advisory editor to the Encyclopedia Brittanica's publication of Great Books.

In 1948, Barr began a ten-year term as president of the Foundation for World Government. The FWG was established with a $1,000,000 contribution from the octogenarian Mrs. Emmons McCormick Blaine of Chicago. (Mrs. Blaine, who was vice-chairman of Henry Wallace's Progressive Party in Illinois, was a well-known angel for leftwing causes. She contributed $2,000,000 to *The Compass,* the pro-Communist successor to Marshall Field's defunct *PM* of New York.) With Barr in the FWG was his colleague from St. John's College, Scott Buchanan, and Harris Wofford Jr. (Buchanan was a founder of World Federalists and Wofford was a founder of Student Federalists.) At the same time, Barr was also on the Committee to Frame a World Constitution, headed by Robert M. Hutchins and Mortimer Adler, both of whom were associated with Brittanica's Great Books project. Also on the CFWC were Rexford Tugwell, Albert Guerard, Charles McIlwain, Wilbur Katz, and Guissepe Borgese — all of whom were Communist-fronters and associated with various "world government" groups. For his part, Barr — aside from his affiliations with the Foundation for World Government and the Committee to Frame a Constitution — belonged to United World Federalists, Students for Federal World Government, Federal Union, Action for World Federation, and Citizens Committee for a World Constitution — all of which were a part of the Fabian Socialist movement in the United States, Britain, and elsewhere. Most of the "world government" leaders, as well as their membership in a number of "world government" groups, usually had affiliations with various Communist fronts, projects, and enterprises. Barr was no exception. He was affiliated with the National Federation for Constitutional Liberties ("under [Communist] Party domination and headed by responsible Party functionaries"); the National Committee to Defeat the Mundt Bill ("a Communist lobby"); and, the Emergency Civil Liberties Committee ("Communist front" — "subversive"). He had signed petitions and statements on behalf of Communists and Communist causes. He was a vigorous opponent of the House Committee on Un-American Activities and a sponsor of the leftwing, pacifist National Committee for a Sane Nuclear Policy.

While president of the Foundation for World Government, Barr joined the faculty of Rutgers University's Newark College in 1955. He retired as emeritus professor in 1964. In the past few years, Barr has been on the staff of the Center for the Study of Democratic Institutions where he rejoined his fellow leftwing one-worlders, Robert M. Hutchins, Scott Buchanan, and Rexford Tugwell.

ALAN BARTH was born on October 21, 1906 in New York City, son of Flora Barth and Jacob Lauchheimer. He married Adrienne Mayer. He is an alumnus of Yale University (Ph.B., 1929) and was a Nieman fellow at Harvard University in 1948 and 1949.

In 1936, Barth was a reporter for the *Beaumont* (Tex.) *Enterprise.* In 1937 and 1938, he was an editorial writer for the *Beaumont Journal.* From 1938 until 1941, he was a Washington correspondent for the McClure Newspaper Syndicate.

In 1941 and 1942, Barth was an editorial assistant to U.S. Secretary of the Treasury Henry Morgenthau. In 1942 and 1943, he edited reports for Elmer Davis' Red-lined Office of War Information. In 1943, he began a career as an editorial writer for the leftwing *Washington Post.*

Barth is the author of *The Loyalty of Free Men; Government by Investigation; The Price of Liberty;* and *Heritage of Liberty.* He is a member of the American Civil Liberties Union.

In his books and editorial work, Barth

has proven to be one of the most persistent critics of any and all law enforcement agencies and congressional committees which investigate subversive activities. His writings have earned for Barth such leftwing tributes as the American Newspaper Guild, the Sidney Hillman Foundation, and the Oliver Wendell Holmes Bill of Rights awards. He has been praised for his *Post* editorials and books in the unmistakably pro-Communist *National Guardian* as "one of our most effective American writers in support of civil liberties." And when a Communist talks of liberties, he only means revolutionary license.

LUCIUS BATTLE was born on June 1, 1918 in Dawson, Georgia, son of Jewel Durham and Warren Battle. He is an alumnus of the University of Florida (A.B., 1939; LL.B., 1946).

In 1942 and 1943, Battle was a personnel administrative officer in the War Department. After World War II, he began a career in the State Department. From 1946 until 1953, he held minor positions in Washington, D.C. From 1953 until 1956, he served in Europe at the U.S. Embassy in Copenhagen and at NATO headquarters in Paris. From 1956 until 1961, he was vice president of the historical restoration project at Williamsburg, Virginia.

In 1961, Battle returned to the State Department as a special assistant to Secretary of State Dean Rusk and as executive secretary for the Department. He also served as Assistant Secretary of State for educational and cultural affairs before his appointment, in 1964, as U.S. Ambassador to the United Arab Republic. He served as Ambassador until April 1967, when he returned to Washington as Assistant Secretary of State for Near Eastern and South Asian Affairs.

As Ambassador to the United Arab Republic, Battle must assume a large share of the responsibility for the disastrous U.S. policy carried on by the Johnson Administration whereby the United States was sending millions of dollars of food to the Kremlin's puppet Nasser and in return would be insulted as no self-respecting sovereign nation ever should. Battle's role was to send the usual meaningless notes of protest to Nasser. Battle's mission to the U.A.R. must be reckoned as one of the greatest failures in American diplomatic history.

BIRCH BAYH was born on January 22, 1928 in Terre Haute, Indiana, son of Leah Hollingsworth and Birch Bayh. He married Marvella Hern. He is an alumnus of Purdue University (B.S., 1951) and Indiana University (J.D., 1960). He was admitted to the Indiana bar in 1961.

In 1952, Bayh settled down to farming in Vigo County, Indiana. However, in 1954, he was elected to the Indiana House of Representatives. He served four terms as a legislator, two as minority leader and one as speaker of the House.

In 1962, Bayh ran for the U.S. Senate in opposition to the conservative Republican incumbent Homer Capehart. As a three-term Senator, Capehart apparently considered himself unbeatable. He conducted a totally lackadaisical campaign. Bayh, on the other hand, campaigned vigorously for more than a year and a half. He had the complete support of Indiana's Democrat Party and organized labor, particularly the AFL-CIO. And, in one of the most startling political upsets of 1962, Bayh defeated Capehart by a margin of 10,944 votes, slightly more than one-half of one per cent of the total votes cast.

During his first term in the Senate, Bayh has placed himself in the ranks of leftwing Democrats. He has been a reliable rubber stamp voter for Kennedy and Johnson Administration measures. On domestic matters he is a spendthrift in the custom of New Frontier-Great Society socialism. He is a bleeding heart on so-called civil rights and welfare state legislation. In foreign affairs, he is totally committed to the appeasement policy toward our nation's Communist enemies — the policy that has been so markedly a characteristic of the Kennedy-Johnson years.

JACOB BEAM was born on March 24, 1908 in Princeton, New Jersey, son of Mary Prince and Jacob Beam. He married Margaret Glassford. He is an alumnus of Princeton University (B.A., 1929). He also studied at Cambridge University of England in 1929 and 1930.

He is a non-resident member of the Council on Foreign Relations, the informal supra-State Department of the United States.

In 1931, Beam began his career in the State Department. For more than twenty years, he held minor posts in Geneva, Germany, Washington, England, and Indonesia. In 1952 and 1953, he was acting head of the U.S. Embassy in Moscow. In 1953 and 1954, he was deputy director of the policy planning staff of the State Department in Washington. From 1955 until 1957, he served on the East European desk and then as a deputy assistant for European affairs.

In 1957, he was appointed U.S. Ambassador to Communist Poland, a position he held for four and a half years. During this time, Beam also served as the United States representative in the periodic talks with Red Chinese representatives. The talks began in 1955 and have been continued ever since, numbering more than 130 at the end of 1967.

The meetings between Beam and his Communist counterpart served to dignify the Communist regime of Mao Tse-tung as the diplomatic equal of our government. If anything productive for United States interests ever came out of Beam's talks with the Communists, it is one of the State Department's most closely guarded secrets. All that the American taxpayer gets out of these meetings is a bland communiqué that the meeting was held. Ambassador Averell Harriman has said that "the only thing they [the Red Chinese] ever want to talk about [at Warsaw] is our handing Taiwan over to them."

Beam's reward for taking part in these ritualistic meetings has been a four-year stint with our surrender bureau, the U.S. Arms Control and Disarmament Agency, and his present position as U.S. Ambassador to Communist Czecho-Slovakia.

SAMUEL BEER was born on July 28, 1911 in Bucyrus, Ohio, son of Jesse Hutchinson and William Beer. He married Roberta Reed. He is an alumnus of the University of Michigan (A.B., 1932), Oxford University of England, where he was a Rhodes scholar (B.A., 1935), and Harvard University (Ph.D., 1943).

Fresh from his Rhodes scholarship, Beer joined Roosevelt's New Dealers as a writer for the Resettlement Administration and the Democratic National Committee in 1935 and 1936.

From 1936 until 1938, Beer was a reporter for the *New York Post* and a writer and researcher for *Fortune* magazine.

In 1938, Beer joined the government faculty at Harvard University, where he was, successively, an instructor, associate professor, professor, and departmental chairman of government. Along the way, he was the recipient of Fulbright and Guggenheim fellowships. He is the author of *The City of Reason* and *Treasury Control: The Coordination of Financial and Economic Policy in Great Britain.*

Beer is one of this country's leading Fabian socialists. From 1955 until 1957, he was chairman of the Massachusetts Chapter of Americans for Democratic Action, and, from 1959 until 1962, he was national chairman of Americans for Democratic Action. In this latter position Beer recommended to his good friend President-elect John F. Kennedy that the New Frontier-ADA program would be advanced if Kennedy appointed such liberal stalwarts as Chester Bowles, Orville Freeman, Adlai Stevenson, and G. Mennen Williams to high office. Mr. Kennedy did as Beer suggested. And Mr. Kennedy, who once said of ADAers, "I don't feel comfortable with those people," smothered his Administration with Beer's kind of people.

JOSEPH BEIRNE was born on February 16, 1911 in Jersey City, son of Annie Gilbin and Michael Beirne. He married Anne Abahaze. He was an evening student at Hudson College of St. Peter in New Jersey and at New York University, from 1933 until 1939.

Beirne worked as an instrument repairman for Western Electric from 1928 until 1939. In 1937 and 1938, he was president of Western Electric Employees. In 1937, he organized the National Association of Telephone Equipment Workers and was president of the Association from 1938 until 1945. He was vice president (1940-1943) and president (1943-1947) of the National Federation of Telephone Workers and has been president of its successor union, Communication Workers of America, since 1947.

Beirne was a vice president of the Congress of Industrial Organizations (CIO) from 1949 until 1955, and, since 1955, has been a vice president of the AFL-CIO. Since 1958, he has been a vice president of the Workers Defense League, a group that defends political undesirables who are subject to deportation. He is a director of the Americans for Democratic Action, the center of the radical left in American politics.

Beirne and his union have been just as much a part of Democrat Party politics as Walter Reuther and the United Automobile Workers, and the Communication Workers Union gives one hundred per cent support to Reuther's socialist program. In the Truman Administration, Beirne was on the Wages Stabilization Board. In the Kennedy Administration, Beirne was an advisor to the Peace Corps, the Alliance for Progress, and the Committee on Youth Development. In the Johnson Administration, he is on the Automation Commission.

CEDRIC BELFRAGE was born on November 8, 1904 in London, England, son of Grace Powley and Sydney Henning Belfrage. He married Mary Bernick. He was educated at Cambridge University (England) and Grenoble University (France).

Belfrage began his lifetime career as a writer and journalist in 1926 while still in his native England. The details of his career, however, are somewhat obscure. In 1953, when he appeared before the House Committee on Un-American Activities, Belfrage was asked about his employment. At first, he pleaded protection under the Fifth Amendment. Then, after a brief talk with his counsel, he admitted to writing in England and the United States for motion picture fan magazines and motion picture trade publications in the late 1920's and early 1930's. He also admitted to having worked as a publicity agent in England for two years on behalf of Samuel Goldwyn, the famous Hollywood producer.

Belfrage has never been an American citizen. He did take out his first U.S. citizenship papers but when asked by the HCUA staff why he went no further to seek citizenship, he pleaded the Fifth Amendment. He made a similar plea when asked about his relationship with the Communist Party and its fronts and projects. The HCUA had information that he had been affiliated with the League of American Writers ("subversive and Communist"); the National Council of American-Soviet Friendship ("subversive and Communist" – "specializing in pro-Communist propaganda"); and, the United American Spanish Aid Committee ("Communist"). There was also information that he had been a contributing author to *New Masses* ("Communist periodical"); that he had been a board member of the National Committee for People's Rights (entirely under the control of the Communist Party"); that he had been on the executive committee of Commonwealth College in Mena, Arkansas ("Communist"); that he had been a board member of the People's Institute of Applied Religion ("subversive and Communist"); and, that for the People's Institute, he had written – using the pseudonym, John Goley – a biography of Rev. Claude Williams, a Communist Party member. Belfrage was also asked if his Communist Party name was George Oakden and if he had used that name when writing for *New Masses* and other leftwing magazines in the 1930's and 1940's. But, to all questions related directly or indirectly to his alleged Communist activities and affilia-

tions, Belfrage pleaded the Fifth Amendment.

The HCUA's interest in Belfrage was traceable in part to his longtime residence in the U.S. where he had been employed, yet never had acquired citizenship. Over the years, the HCUA knew Belfrage had worked (1941-1943) for British Intelligence during World War II, then was employed (1944-1945) in the Psychological Warfare Division at SHAEF. Furthermore, HCUA had knowledge that, while with the British Intelligence, Belfrage took information from British Intelligence files and turned it over to Soviet espionage agents. Also, while at General Eisenhower's headquarters (SHAEF), Belfrage was a press control officer. In this position, he was given an assignment to see that postwar German newspapers were "democratic." Belfrage's method of "democratizing" those newspapers was to hire Communists to work on them.

In 1948, Belfrage helped to establish and became an editor of *National Guardian,* published in New York. From the beginning, *National Guardian* was obviously nothing less than a pro-Communist outlet for propaganda, despite its self-styled label of "progressive."

The interest shown by HCUA in Belfrage's activities led to his deportation in 1955 under the provisions of the McCarran-Walter Immigration and Naturalization Act of 1952. But Belfrage continued to write – as "editor-in-exile" – for *National Guardian,* filing dispatches from Cuba, Hong Kong, New Zealand, and British Guiana. Finally, in 1967, Belfrage, after nineteen years service, resigned from *National Guardian* during a dispute described by that journal's staff as "non-ideological" and strictly related to disagreements over "news" coverage and format.

During his "exile," Belfrage wrote at least two books which were published under Communist auspices in the United States: *Seeds of Destruction,* published by Cameron and Kahn; *The Man at the Door with the Gun,* published by Monthly Review. And, while Belfrage continues to remain in "exile," his daughter Sally continues the family tradition by fellow-traveling in this country.

DAVID BELL was born on January 20, 1919 in Jamestown, North Dakota, son of Florence Boise and Reginald Bell. He married Mary Barry. He is an alumnus of Pomona College (B.A., 1939) and Harvard University (M.A., 1941).

From 1942 until 1951, with time out for Marine Corps service, Bell was either on the staff of the Budget Bureau or a special assistant at the White House. From 1951 until 1953, he was an administrative assistant to President Truman. From 1954 until 1957, he was a project field supervisor for a Harvard University Advisory Group on general economics to the Government of Pakistan's Planning Board.

Bell joined the faculty at Harvard University in 1957 and lectured on economics for four years and was secretary of Harvard's Graduate School of Public Administration from 1959 until 1961.

In 1961 and 1962, Bell was director of the Budget Bureau and, from 1962 until 1967, he was administrator of the foreign aid program, the Agency for International Development.

Throughout his academic and governmental career Bell has been a proponent of fiscal insanity. When President Kennedy appointed him to be head of the foreign aid program, the distinguished columnist Henry J. Taylor commented, "Bell is a White House clans-man. This Robin Hood of the red ink is also a professor-turned-politician, straight out of the Fabian socialist mold, who hit the Budget Bureau (which he formerly headed) like a breath of fresh ether. The rest is the record of a man so impervious to fiscal arithmetic and the taxpayers' groups that his contempt for thrift and solvency is internationally notorious."

JOHN C. BENNETT was born on July 22, 1902 in Kingston, Ontario, son of United States citizens Charlotte Coleman and William Bennett. He is an alumnus of Williams College (A.B., 1924), Oxford University (B.A., 1926; M.A., 1930), and Union Theological Seminary (B.D., 1927; S.T.M., 1929). He married Anne McGrew.

In 1930 and 1931, Bennett was an instructor in theology at Union Theological Seminary. From 1931 to 1938, he was on the faculty of Auburn Theological Seminary, teaching Christian Theology. In 1939, he was ordained to the ministry of the Congregational Church. From 1938 to 1943, he was a professor of Christian Theology and philosophy of religion at the Pacific School of Religion. In 1943, he re-joined the faculty of Union Theological Seminary, serving that institution successively as the Reinhold Niebuhr professor of social ethics, dean of the faculty, and, since 1964, as president. He has been a visiting lecturer at Queens Theological College, Chicago Theological Seminary, Yale University, Grinnell College, Lancaster Theological Seminary, Bangor Theological Seminary, the University of Virginia, Hartford Theological Seminary, Eden Theological Seminary, Colgate-Rochester Divinity School, Berea College, and Garrett Bible Institute. He is the author of *Social Salvation; Chris-*

tian Ethics and Social Policy; Christianity and Communism; The Christian as a Citizen; and *Christian and the State.*

In 1960, the former FBI counterspy Herbert A. Philbrick, in a telegram to the Religious News Editor of the *New York Herald Tribune,* questioned the treatment accorded Dr. Bennett by that journal. Said Philbrick: "Cannot understand your apparent neglect to check the voluminous John Bennett files in the New York Herald Tribune morgue which contains one of the longest and most notorious Communist and Communist Front records of anyone in the country."

At that time, Mr. Philbrick was concerned with "Bennett's attempt to stampede Protestant churches in America behind the Communist drive to admit Red China into the United Nations. It seems to me that fair and impartial reporting would call for the truth concerning Bennett's extreme pro-Soviet bias."

As long ago as 1941 and 1943, Bennett had signed statements opposing renewal of the House Committee on Un-American Activities. These statements were issued under the auspices of the National Federation for Constitutional Liberties, which was cited as "subversive and Communist" by U.S. Attorney General Tom Clark. Twenty years later, Dr. Bennett had not changed his views. He signed "An Appeal to the House of Representatives – Abolish HUAC" (*New York Times,* February 22, 1962). FBI Director J. Edgar Hoover has described abolition of HCUA as a "long-standing [Communist] party aim." Along the way, Bennett became a member of the National Committee to Abolish the House Un-American Activities Committee ("to lead and direct the Communist Party's 'Operation Abolition' campaign").

In 1955, Dr. Bennett was an initiator of a petition seeking amnesty for Communist Party leaders who were convicted under the Smith Act. (*New York Times,* December 21, 1955.) In July 1959, Dr. Bennett signed an appeal on behalf of Morton Sobell, a co-defendant with the atom bomb spies, Julius and Ethel Rosenberg. This appeal was made under the auspices of the National Committe to Secure Justice for Morton Sobell – a "Communist front." On August 25, 1961, Dr. Bennett signed a petition for the pardon of Junius Scales, a convicted Communist. One of Scales' specialties in the Communist Party was teaching his comrades how to murder a person with a pencil point. On November 8, 1961, Dr. Bennett was an initiator of an appeal on behalf of two well-known Communists, Carl Braden and Frank Wilkinson, who were sentenced to a year in jail for contempt of Congress.

Appearing on the David Susskind television program, *Open End,* on December 10, 1961, Dr. Bennett said that "the Church should not fight Communism." His reason for such a statement may be found in a speech Bennett delivered in Chattanooga, Tennessee on May 15, 1961, when he said: "Communism is not wholly evil. It is the wrong solution to a real problem."

This was an old refrain for Bennett who wrote in *Christian Century* (June 11, 1952): "Communism wins power because it has much truth in its teachings, because it appeals to the loyalties and not primarily to the cynical self interests of man ... as he [the Christian] studies communism he finds many things to approve in it. I refer to such things as the Communist criticism of many features of capitalism and imperialism, the Communist practice in regard to racial discrimination, the Communist goal of a classless society, the generous motives that inspire many people to give themselves to communism with selfless commitments."

Then there was this illuminating passage from Bennett in *Theology Today* (October 1950): "Why must they conclude that there is a conflict between Christianity and communism? . . . Certainly we cannot find the difficulty in the Communist economic system or in Communist social goals. There is much overlapping between Communist goals and Christian goals. Also, I think it is a mistake to put the emphasis upon the materialism of communism or upon the moral relativism of communism or even upon the atheism of communism. Each of these elements in communism is a crude way of protesting against something that is false in the dominant religious and moral ideas which the Communist prophets, Marx and Engels, especially, found it necessary to reject. Dialectical materialism was a partly justified protest against a one-sided idealism . . . . I do not believe that American Christians could condemn Communism because of its belief that revolution, even violent revolution, is sometimes necessary."

Bennett has been affiliated with the National Committee for a Sane Nuclear Policy (leftwing, pacifist), the League for Industrial Democracy (Socialist), and is a resident member of the Council on Foreign Relations (the informal supra-State Department of the United States). From 1955 to 1965, Bennett was vice chairman of New York's ultra-leftist Liberal Party.

In 1964, Bennett was a member of Arthur Larson's National Council for Civic Responsibility, an election year's drive by the Democratic Party against anti-Communists, and in 1966, he joined Franklin Littell's Institute for American Democracy, hysterical successor to Larson's abortive NCCR. In 1965, Bennett was affiliated with the Inter-University Committee for a Public Hearing on Vietnam, sponsors of the anti-Vietnam "teach-in" movement, which the Communist propaganda apparatus exploited for purely Communist purposes, and in 1967, was on the guiding committee of Negotiation Now!, an ad hoc committee led by leftwing luminaries for appeasement in Vietnam, including Martin Luther King Jr., Joseph L. Rauh Jr., Victor Reuther, Arthur Schlesinger Jr., Reinhold Niebuhr, and John Kenneth Galbraith.

WILLIAM BENTON was born on April 1, 1900 in Minneapolis, son of Elma Hixson and Charles Benton. He married Helen Hemingway. He is an alumnus of Yale University (A.B., 1921).

After his collegiate work, Benton was employed by the Lord & Thomas advertising agency. In 1929, he became founder and president of the Benton & Bowles advertising agency. He resigned as president in 1935 but remained with the agency as chairman of the board in 1935 and 1936.

In 1937, Benton's classmate from Yale, Robert M. Hutchins, who was then president of the University of Chicago, persuaded him to become vice president of the University. For the next eight years, Benton served at Chicago on a part-time basis. In 1945, he became assistant to Chancellor Hutchins.

While at the University of Chicago, Benton bought the common stock of *Encyclopedia Britannica* on behalf of the University. Since 1943, he has been chairman of the board of the *Britannica's* American, Canadian, and British publishing companies.

In 1940, Benton saw his first service in the federal government. From 1940 until 1945, he was a member of the advisory committee to the State Department's Coordinator of Inter-American Affairs. From 1942 until 1945, he was vice chairman of the U.S. Commission to the Inter-American Development Commission. (In 1942, Benton also became a founding vice president of the Committee for Economic Development. He served as vice president from 1942 until 1945 and as trustee from 1947 until 1960. The CED was and is the major propaganda arm of the Council on Foreign Relations in the important work of socializing the American economy. Although neither the CED nor the CFR are government agencies, the influence their members in and out of government have upon federal domestic and foreign policies is indisputable.)

In 1945, Benton was appointed to be an Assistant Secretary of State. President Truman was hopeful that Benton could apply the expertise of his advertising experience to organize the State Department's propaganda facilities. But within two years' time Benton had so antagonized congressional committees through his arrogant demands for appropriations that he was eased out of his job — not too graciously — by Mr. Truman.

While in his position as Assistant Secretary, Benton had become involved with UNESCO affairs. In 1945, he was the U.S. delegate to UNESCO's constitutional convention in London. In 1946 and 1947, respectively, he was chairman of the U.S. delegation to the UNESCO general conferences in Paris and Mexico City. Benton appeared to thrive in the Communist-ridden atmosphere of UNESCO. In an address to his "educational, scientific, and cultural" colleagues from free and Communist na-

tions, he exulted: "We are at the beginning of a long process of breaking down the walls of our national sovereignty. In this UNESCO can be, and indeed must be, the pioneer."

In 1948, Benton kept his contact with Washington by serving as chairman of the U.S. delegation to a United Nations conference on freedom of information at Geneva.

In 1949, Benton reaped dividends from an old friendship. Chester Bowles, who had become wealthy under the tutelage of Benton in the advertising business, was, in 1949, Governor of Connecticut. U.S. Senator Raymond Baldwin, a Republican, accepted an appointment from Bowles to Connecticut's Supreme Court and thereby vacated the Senate seat. Bowles then appointed his old benefactor Benton to take Baldwin's seat. After serving one year by appointment, Benton won an election for a two-year term which completed Baldwin's original term in the Senate.

In the Senate, Benton gained notoriety as the original State Department-inspired hatchetman against the late Senator Joseph R. McCarthy. In August 1951, Benton introduced a resolution demanding McCarthy's expulsion from the Senate on charges of "bearing false witness and practicing deceit and falsehood." McCarthy, in turn, charged that Benton, while in the State Department, surrounded himself with "a motley, red-tinted crowd," and that he had protected seven employees (McCarthy furnished the names) who were Communists, fellow travelers, or complete dupes.

In his own defense, Benton denied McCarthy's particulars and said: "I know there were Communists in the State Department because I helped to drive them out." But when pressed for details as to what Communists he tried to drive out, Benton replied: "I cannot give you the names of Communists in the State Department because I do not know any. I did not know any then, I do not know any now."

McCarthy was not content to let Benton's hostility get the best of him. And, in 1952, when Benton sought re-election for a full six-year term to the Senate, McCarthy entered Connecticut and campaigned for William Purtell, Benton's Republican opponent. Despite campaign efforts by Adlai Stevenson and Harry Truman on behalf of Benton, he was defeated by Purtell. McCarthy, on the other hand in that same election year, was re-elected for a six-year term by the voters of Wisconsin. (In 1958, Benton made one more attempt for elective office when he and his old partner Chester Bowles were both seeking the Democratic nomination for U.S. Senator from Connecticut but Thomas E. Dodd won the nomination and election.)

After 1958, Benton remained busy with his activities on the aforementioned Committee for Economic Development and in his chairmanship of *Britannica*. Then, in 1963, he returned to UNESCO as U.S. Ambassador where he has labored diligently to break down the walls of U.S. national sovereignty while simultaneously serving as an apologetic lackey for Soviet Communists whose claims to educational, scientific, and cultural achievements Benton accepts as the omega of truth.

ADOLF A. BERLE JR. was born on January 29, 1895 in Boston, Massachusetts, son of Augusta Wright and Adolf Berle. He married Beatrice Bishop. He is an alumnus of Harvard University (A.B., 1913; M.A., 1914; LL.B., 1916).

He has been in the practice of law since 1916.

Berle served the Woodrow Wilson administration on the Commission to Negotiate Peace with Germany. As a very influential New Dealer, he was a special counsel for the Reconstruction Finance Corporation and Assistant Secretary of State in the Franklin Roosevelt administration. In the Truman administration, Berle was United States Ambassador to Brazil. In the Kennedy administration, he was chairman of a presidential task force in Latin America and a consultant to Secretary of State Dean Rusk. He is an emeritus professor of law at Columbia University and the author of several books on law, as well as *Natural Selection of Political Forces; The 20th Century Capitalist Revolution; Tides of Crisis;* and *The American Economic Republic.*

Berle played a major role in the Whittaker Chambers-Alger Hiss story. It was Berle to whom Chambers told of Hiss' and other government officials' activities in Soviet espionage. Berle was asked by Chambers to inform Roosevelt of the traitors within his administration. But more than eight years passed before Hiss was finally convicted − not for treason or espionage − but for the lesser crime of perjury.

In the liberal press, Berle enjoys a reputation as an expert on Latin America, which simply means that Berle has disparaged the threat of Communism in Latin America and portrayed the pro-Communist demagogues of Latin America (Betancourt, Figueres, Bosch) as defenders of social justice.

Berle is a resident member of the Council on Foreign Relations, the informal supra-State Department of the United States; a consultant to the ultra-leftist Center for the Study of Democratic Institutions; and, a member of the Committee for Economic Development, the major propaganda arm of the Council on Foreign Relations, in the important work of socializing the American economy. He has been chairman, and is presently honorary chairman, of the ultra-leftist Liberal Party of New York. If Berle's history of professional and political associations and his utterances, writings, and activities are given an accurate appraisal, he must be recognized as one of America's leading Socialists.

ALVAH BESSIE was born on June 4, 1904 in New York City, son of Adeline Schlesinger and David Bessie. His second wife is Sylviane Molla. He is an alumnus of Columbia University (A.B., 1924).

For about four years after his college days, Bessie tried to make a career out of acting on the legitimate stage but failed. In the meantime, he turned to writing short stories and, between 1926 and 1934, translated six books from French to English. In 1935, he wrote his first novel and, in that same year, received a Guggenheim fellowship in creative writing.

In 1936 and 1937, Bessie was editor of the *Brooklyn Eagle's* Sunday magazine. He resigned from that journal to go to Spain where he fought for a year with the Abraham Lincoln Brigade on the side of the Reds. In December 1938, the Communists' *Daily Worker* described Bessie as the commissar of 150 veterans of the Abraham Lincoln Brigade who had returned from Spain. (For his service with the Reds, Bessie received the Dombrowski Medal, awarded by Polish Veterans of the International Brigade.) He has commemorated his Spanish Civil War experiences in several of his books, including *Men in Battle; The Heart of Spain;* and his autobiographical *Inquisition in Eden.*

From 1939 until 1942, Bessie was a film, drama, and book critic for *New Masses,* a Communist publication. In the 1930's and 1940's, he would write or do editorial work for such other Communist publications as *People's World; Fight; Soviet Russia Today; New Currents; Mainstream;* and *Independent.* In that same period, he was affiliated with the Independent Citizens Committee of the Arts, Sciences and Professions ("Communist front"); the International Workers Order ("subversive and Communist"); the Artists' Front to Win the War ("Communist front"); the League of American Writers ("subversive and Communist"); the American Committee for Spanish Freedom ("Communist"); the Veterans of the Abraham Lincoln Brigade ("subversive and Communist"); the Joint Anti-Fascist Refugee Committee ("subversive and Communist"); the Workers School of New York City ("Communist Party school"); the International Labor Defense ("legal arm of the Communist Party"); the American-Russian Institute of Southern California ("Communist"); the American Council on Soviet Relations ("established by the Communist Party"); the National Council of American-Soviet Friendship ("subversive and Communist" – "specializing in pro-Soviet propaganda"); and American Youth for Democracy ("subversive and Communist").

From 1943 until 1945, Bessie was a contract screenwriter for Warner Brothers. After 1946, he was a free-lance screenwriter. Among his films have been "The Very Thought of You," "Northern Pursuit," "Objective Burma," "Hotel Berlin," and "Smart Woman." His film work has been exemplary of Bessie's versatility. He has written stories, articles, and criticisms in magazines and newspapers in England, France, Spain, Germany, Austria, the United States, and the Soviet Union. His writings have appeared in *Scribner's, Collier's, Esquire, Yankee, Screenwriter, Theatre Arts,* and the *New York Herald Tribune's* "Books." He has written radio and/or television plays for Radio Berlin, the British Broadcasting Company, and for Czecho-Slovak outlets.

In October 1947, when the House Committee on Un-American Activities was investigating Communist infiltration of the motion picture industry, Bessie was subpoenaed as a witness. He proved to be somewhat obstinate to the extent that he was charged with contempt of the Congress. Instead of seeking the legitimate protection of the Fifth Amendment, Bessie refused to answer two questions: "Are you a member of the Screen Writers Guild?" and "Are you now, or have you ever been, a member of the Communist Party?" He was found guilty of the contempt charges and served a year in federal prison.

Since his release from prison, Bessie has continued his writing career. He has written for the Communists' West Coast daily, *People's World,* under the pseudonym of David Ordway. For a brief time, he worked for *The Dispatcher,* the publication of Harry Bridges' International Longshoremen's and Warehousemen's Union.

In 1965, Macmillan published Bessie's *Inquisition in Eden.* He frankly admitted that his "real reason for writing this book was to attack the House Committee and the drive to conformity." (Bessie had done a similar job in his 1957 book, *The Un-Americans.)* And *Inquisition* was given very sympathetic reviews in *People's World* (Communist), *The Worker* (Communist); the *Prov-*

idence (R.I.) *Journal,* the *San Francisco Chronicle, Newsweek,* and a host of other unsurprising sources of that ilk.

HANS A. BETHE was born on July 2, 1906 in Strassburg, Alsace-Lorraine, son of Anna Kuhn and Albrecht Bethe. He married Rose Ewald. He is an alumnus of the University of Frankfurt and the University of Munich (Ph.D., 1928). He came to the United States as a refugee from Germany in 1935. He became an American citizen during World War II.

From 1928 until 1933, Bethe was a physics instructor at the German Universities of Frankfurt, Stuttgart, Munich, and Tübingen. From 1933 until 1935, he lectured at the British Universities of Manchester and Bristol. In 1935, he became an assistant professor and, in 1937, a professor at Cornell University. He is presently at Cornell's Laboratory of Nuclear Studies.

During World War II, Bethe did some work at the radiation laboratory of the Massachusetts Institute of Technology. Then, from 1943 until 1946, he was director of the theoretical division of the A-Bomb project in Los Alamos, New Mexico. From 1956 until 1964, he was a member of the President's Science Advisory Committee. In 1958, he headed a Presidential Study of Disarmament. In 1961, he received the Atomic Energy Commission's Enrico Fermi award and, in 1967, he received the Nobel Prize in Physics.

A writer friendly to Bethe, Lee Edson, has called Bethe "America's most outstanding and influential advocate of nuclear disarmament." ("Scientific Man for All Seasons," *New York Times* magazine, March 10, 1968.) Bethe represents himself as having undergone struggles with his conscience when he accepted a directorship in the A-bomb project. His acceptance was not based upon motives of patriotism in the framework of his newly acquired American citizenship but rather was based on his experiences as a Jewish refugee from Nazi Germany and he feared that the Germans might develop an A-bomb before the Americans did.

In the post-World War II period, Bethe joined J. Robert Oppenheimer in strong opposition to development of the H-bomb. But after the outbreak of the Korean War, Bethe changed his mind when he became reconciled to the idea that his aversion to nationalist self-defense and obsession with internationalist harmony was not overwhelmingly popular. And, in a mood of "if-you-can't-lick-'em, join-'em," Bethe went to work on the H-bomb project — "If I were around Los Alamos, I might still be a force for disarmament." Neither patriotic motives nor dedication to science prompted Bethe to work on the H-bomb; he was more concerned with infiltrating the scientific community to propagandize for his political stance on disarmament.

In 1950, Bethe and eleven other physicists held a press conference during which they called upon the United States government to promise that Americans would not be the first to use the H-bomb. In the context of their behavior, the physicists assumed that the Soviet Union's leaders would never initiate H-bomb warfare. (Years later, Bethe again displayed his unbounded trust in the humaneness of Communists when he exulted that the Chinese Communists propagandized that they wouldn't be the first to launch an H-bomb attack.) Bethe argued that, instead of following the course we did, "It would have been perfectly possible for us to have made an agreement with the Russians to go ahead with hydrogen

fusion experimentation, but not to test the bomb." Bethe was quite willing to trust the Russians to keep their part in such an agreement. This implicit faith in the Communists has become a notable characteristic of Bethe's non-scientific meddling in foreign policy. As a close advisor to President Kennedy, he pleaded for executive action to halt atmospheric nuclear testing by the United States. In 1962, President Kennedy announced that the U.S. was going to resume atmospheric testing for the first time since President Eisenhower had announced a unilateral moratorium in 1958. Mr. Kennedy explained that the resumption was being made to maintain national security. Testing by the Soviet Union had become public knowledge. Bethe, however, rushed to the defense of the Russians: " . . . We should not accuse the Russians of breaking an agreement by their resumption of tests. No agreement has been concluded; in fact, the U.S. insisted repeatedly that the moratorium was temporary and could be terminated any day . . . . There has not been any evidence that the Russians cheated by testing during the moratorium." Bethe's was nothing less than a straw-man argument: cheating was not the issue. What was of importance to the United States was the fact that its almost four-year moratorium was simultaneous to the manifest truth that the Communists ignored the Americans' exemplar, made no announcement of a moratorium, and conducted forty or fifty tests which – if they were productive – could jeopardize the security of the United States. Bethe seemed to realize that his defense of "cheating" was not too convincing and so he embellished his plea by downgrading the tests: " . . . The value of tests has been grossly exaggerated. We already know so much about atomic weapons that there is very little more to be learned. We have weapons of all sizes, for all reasonable military purposes. Only relatively minor improvements can be made on the yield of weapons for a given weight." Mr. Kennedy's preoccupation with national security was of brief duration and, in 1963, a treaty was concluded with the Soviet Union banning atmospheric nuclear tests. Bethe was an active participant in the negotiations for that treaty.

During the Johnson Administration, when proposals were being made that the United States construct an antiballistic missile system, Bethe was again in the forefront of the disarmament pleaders. He argued against the ABM on grounds that it was too expensive and of doubtful technical efficiency. But the crux of his opposition was pure scaremongering. The ABM "will create instability in the arms race. We exist in peace today only because each side knows it cannot win a nuclear war. Once this balance of terror is broken – as it will be with the ABM since that will let one side think it has an advantage – then we will have a continuing spiral of increasing arms and further instability." To Bethe – as is the case with so many ban-the-bomb-niks – there is "peace" as long as there is no nuclear warfare. It is a retreat from reality as Bethe and his ilk ignore the sacrifices and deaths of soldiers and civilians, the destruction of economies, and the losses of freedom in any other kind of war. Bethe, who could appreciate the belligerence of Nazis, refuses to recognize the unremitting hostility of the entire Communist apparatus even while the Vietnam War is going on: nuclear weapons are not being used, therefore "we exist in peace."

There is no question as to Bethe's competence in physics, nor can there be

any quarrel with his right to plead for disarmament. But his closeness to three successive White House Administrations has provided him with unique opportunities to use his prestige as a scientist as a means of propounding his soft-on-Communism views in the political-diplomatic area. The Communist press has paid him homage for his peacenik efforts and he has accented his internationalist political activities by petitioning for the abolition of the House Committee on Un-American Activities and by urging the repeal of the McCarran Act (Internal Security Act of 1950) – both of which are Communist Party projects within the United States.

JAMES BEVEL was born about 1937. He is a native of Itta Bena, Mississippi and he is a Baptist minister. He married Diane Nash, an energetic civil rights agitator, who achieved national and international notoriety in 1966 when she made an unauthorized trip to Hanoi, North Vietnam and returned to the United States extolling the virtues of the Communist tyrant Ho chi Minh.

Bevel first became notorious in his own right in 1960 when he took a prominent part in so-called civil rights sit-in demonstrations in Nashville, Tennessee. In 1963, Bevel became recognizable as one of Martin L. King's most militant lieutenants during the latter's widely publicized racist demonstrations in Birmingham, Alabama. And, by 1965, Bevel was such an important figure on the staff of King's Southern Christian Leadership Conference that he was assigned the task of directing King's voter registration drive in Selma, Alabama – a racial demonstration which featured the infamous "march" to Montgomery, the highlight of King's career as an agitator.

In 1965, one of the most radical and militant of all Negro agitators, Albert Raby, was making futile attempts to plague Chicago by leading protest marches. Raby had raised the phoney issue of de facto segregation in Chicago schools but his efforts attracted few followers. Martin L. King Jr. decided to heed the call for help from his old comrade Raby, and Bevel was chosen to represent King in the latter's first major effort to disrupt law and order in a northern city.

In Chicago, Bevel discarded Raby's strategy of protesting against alleged de facto segregation. Instead, Bevel made a strong but vain attempt to seize political power for Negroes. Aside from some success in organizing Negroes who were welfare cases or who were living in public housing projects, Bevel's mission on the whole was a failure. Eventually King followed Bevel to Chicago but even King's efforts were fruitless when he attempted to recruit Chicago's Negroes into his revolutionary demonstrations.

After the Chicago fiasco, Bevel's career as a would-be demagogue went into a partial eclipse. He remained on the staff of King's Southern Christian Leadership Conference until King decided to grant him a leave of absence so that Bevel could serve as national director of the Spring Mobilization Committee to End the War in Vietnam. That outfit was formed on November 26, 1966 at a meeting in Cleveland, Ohio. No overt Communists were elected as officers of the Mobilization Committee which Bevel headed, but the entire project was publicly supported and sponsored by the Communist Party, speaking through its official publications and some of its better known comrades, including Arnold Johnson, Ben Dobbs, Bettina Aptheker, James R. Lindsay, Albert J. Lima, and Al Richmond.

In April 1967, Bevel's "Mobilization Committee" held massive demonstrations in New York City and San Francisco. In the words of the House Committee on Un-American Activities, the purpose was "to reverse the U.S. policy of resisting Communism in Vietnam . . . . The organization and planning of the Vietnam Week demonstrations provide an excellent example of successful implementation by the Communists of their 'united front' strategy. Dr. Martin Luther King's agreement to play a leading role in the April 15 demonstrations in New York City, and his freeing Rev. James Bevel from his key position in the Southern Christian Leadership Conference to head up the Spring Mobilization Committee, are evidence that the Communists have succeeded, at least partially, in implementing their strategy of fusing the Vietnam and civil rights issues in order to strengthen their chances of bringing about a reversal of U.S. policy in Vietnam." (See, HCUA's Report, "Communist Origin and Manipulation of Vietnam Week," 1967.)

Bevel's assignment by King to lead a Communist-dominated project was not a trick upon some poor dupe. Bevel had previously given his personal support, on at least two occasions, to the Communists' DuBois Clubs. He had the Communist line on the Vietnam War down pat ("White Americans are not going to deal in the problems of colored people when they're exterminating a whole nation of colored people." – "The purpose of the American Army [in Vietnam] is not to keep invaders out but to keep you enslaved, not to fight for freedom but to suppress people everywhere, particularly colored people." – "A peace movement that is serious must take the position of the folks [in Vietnam] whose kids were burned up this morning." — "Each passing day makes more and more plain to millions of Americans the hollowness and wickedness of this war of oppression against a foreign colored people, which parallels in military terms what has been done to the American Indians and the colored people of America for centuries.")

During the course of Ralph Abernathy's 1968 "poor people" spectacle in Washington, D.C., Bevel was on the job as the chief disciplinarian of the demonstrators. U.S. Senator Charles Percy (R.-Ill.), in an extraordinary gesture of stupidity, provided Bevel with a forum where he could regale an audience of congressional staff assistants who were urged by Percy to listen to Bevel. Bevel's theme was pure Marxism: Every American official in authority is a fascist; the capitalist system is defunct and "economic class warfare" has arrived in this country. "I feel no responsibility to a nation-state," said Bevel. "I represent conscious energy which is a universal phenomenon. As a result, I don't get too excited when I see a rag on a stick which is called a flag."

No Communist Party spokesman could have improved upon Bevel's demagoguery as he ranted: "You people got to understand what we mean by nonviolence is not just some people marching peaceably in a parade. We mean the whole restructuring of our inter-relationships.

"Some of the scenes will be violent. If there's violence, we won't worry about it. We will come back and re-educate.

"Our goals are to eliminate all disciplinary relationships. We do not believe in a parent making a kid conform to a certain norm. That is a violent relationship. We want to eliminate it.

"The wealth must be re-distributed and the means of production turned over to the people. Money is a product of militarization. Armaments must be eliminated. The police must be re-oriented. The God versus devil philosophy of Judeo-Christian tradition must be eliminated.

"Personally, capitalism is intellectually incompatible with me. Why should I compete for things that are mine?"

JONATHAN BINGHAM was born on April 14, 1914 in New Haven, Connecticut, son of Alfreda Mitchell and Hiram Bingham. He married June Rossbach. He is an alumnus of Yale University (B.A., 1936; LL.B., 1939).

Bingham has practiced law intermittently since 1939 in New York City. In 1941 and 1942, he was in the Office of Price Administration. After military service in World War II, Bingham went to work for the State Department. He was chief of the Alien Enemy Control Section, assistant director of the Office of International Security Affairs, and deputy administrator of Truman's Point Four program. From 1955 until 1958, he was secretary to Governor Averell Harriman of New York.

From 1961 until 1964, Bingham was at the United Nations. He was U.S. representative on the UN's Trusteeship Council, an alternate U.S. representative to the 15th, 16th, 17th, and 18th General Assemblies, U.S. representative (holding ambassadorial rank) to UNESCO, and principal advisor on economic social matters to Ambassador Adlai E. Stevenson.

Bingham is the author of *Shirt-Sleeve Diplomacy: Point 4 in Action,* which is nothing less than a blueprint for the expansion of international socialism at the expense of American taxpayers.

Since 1965, Bingham has represented

the 23rd New York district in the House of Representatives. In the Congress he has distinguished himself as a foremost defender of the United Nations and an arch foe of Rhodesia's anti-Communist regime.

Bingham is a member of the Council on Foreign Relations, the informal supra-State Department of the United States, and Americans for Democratic Action, the center of the radical left in American politics. His voting record is consistent with the CFR-ADA line.

THOMAS A. BISSON was born on November 8, 1900 in New York City, son of Marie Felesina and Noel Bisson. He married Faith Williams. He is an alumnus of Rutgers University (B.S., 1923) and Columbia University (M.A., 1924).

From 1924 until 1928, Bisson was in China as a missionary teacher, affiliated with the Presbyterian Church. From 1929 until 1941, he was on the research staff of the Foreign Policy Association, which was one of the most effective pro-Communist vehicles of that era. In 1942 and 1943, he was the principal economist of the Board of Economic Warfare. While he was with the BEW, Bisson's loyalty to the United States was the subject of investigations by the Dies Committee (Un-American Activities) and a House Appropriations Subcommittee, but nothing of consequence resulted from these investigations. From 1943 until 1945, he was on the staff of the Institute of Pacific Relations as an associate editor of IPR's publication *Pacific Affairs*. (The IPR was a vehicle used by the Communists to orientate American far eastern policies toward Communist objectives.) In 1945 and 1947, he was an economist with the U.S. Strategic Bombing Survey in Japan. In 1947, he was a

special assistant to the chief of the government section at General Headquarters of the Supreme Command of the Allied Powers in Tokyo. In 1948, he joined the political science faculty of the University of California. In recent years, he has been on the faculty of the Western College for Women in Ohio.

Students of far eastern affairs cannot help but encounter Bisson's name in footnotes and bibliographical references. Few individuals have ever written in such a wide variety of publications on the Far East, particularly China, than has Bisson. His writings have appeared in the *New York Times;* the *New York Herald Tribune; Soviet Russia Today* (a "Communist-controlled" publication); the *Nation* magazine; *New Republic* magazine; *Political Science Quarterly; China Today* (the "official organ" of the Communist-controlled American Friends of the Chinese People); *Annals* of the American Academy of Political and Social Science; the *Saturday Review of Literature;* the *Foreign Policy Bulletin; Foreign Policy Reports;* and, *Pacific Affairs, Amerasia,* and *Far Eastern Survey* – all three of which were outlets for the Institute of Pacific Relations and its outpourings of Communist policy and propaganda. (In *China Today,* for which he wrote at least nineteen items, Bisson used the pseudonym "Frederick Spencer." By a remarkable coincidence, Frederick Spencer was the name used by Bisson's friend Frederick Vanderbilt Field in his activities as a member of the Communist Party.)

Bisson wrote two major books: *Japan in China* and *America's Far Eastern Policy.* (The latter was written as an assignment from the Institute of Pacific Relations.) He also wrote at least three pamphlets for the Foreign Policy Association. One of his pamphlets, "Shadow

Over Asia," was written under the general title of Headline Books. The War Department purchased 30,000 copies of "Shadow Over Asia" for distribution to army camps.

In his writings, Bisson made little or no attempt to disguise his pro-Soviet and pro-Chinese Communist sympathies or his antipathy for Nationalist China. (It was his strategy to present Nationalist China as feudal and reactionary and Communist China as democratic and progressive.) His pro-Communist sympathies were also demonstrated through his activities in American Friends of the Chinese People ("Communist front"); Friends of Chinese Democracy ("Communist controlled" organization); the Committee for a Democratic Far Eastern Policy ("Communist") where he was a member of the board of directors and a consultant; the American Committee for Non-participation in Japanese Aggression ("Communist front"); and, the International Release Committee (a very important world-wide Communist project).

Bisson's professional and social intimates included such notorious pro-Communist propagandists as Owen Lattimore, Edgar Snow, Frederick Vanderbilt Field, Philip Jaffe, Corliss Lamont, and the rest of the IPR crowd which contributed so mightily to the takeover of the Chinese mainland by Mao Tse-tung. And, along the way, Bisson's friendship with the pro-Communist powers-that-be enabled him to pursue his academic-propaganda career with the help of a Carnegie Foundation grant and at least two Rockefeller Foundation grants.

Bisson has spent most of his recent years on college and university campuses but he has not forsaken all opportunities to reaffirm his old pro-Communist sympathies. In 1965, when the "teach-in" craze was at its height, he sponsored the Inter-University Committee for Public Hearings on Vietnam, which the Communist propaganda apparatus exploited for purely Communist purposes.

Although Bisson has been identified at least once in sworn testimony as a Communist, he has sworn under oath that he has never been a Communist or subject to Communist Party discipline.

ALGERNON BLACK was born in 1900 in New York City, son of Sonya and Adolph Ballachowsky. He married Elinor Goldmark. He is an alumnus of Harvard University.

After graduating from Harvard, Black went to work for the New York Society for Ethical Culture, becoming leader of the Society in 1934. For more than forty years, Black has lectured at various Ethical Culture schools. He has been a director and vice president of the National Association for the Advancement of Colored People. He has been a board member of the American Civil Liberties Union. Black has been an active socialist and one of this country's most notorious and persistent supporters of Communist fronts, Communist causes, and Communist projects. He is an apologist for Red China, an advocate for unilateral disarmament, and a bitter critic of anti-Communists.

Black has been affiliated with the American Committee for Protection of Foreign Born [Americans] ("subversive and Communist" -- "one of the oldest auxiliaries of the Communist Party in the United States" -- under the complete domination" of the Communist Party); the American Committee to Save Refugees ("Communist enterprise"); the American Committee for Spanish Freedom ("Communist"); American Friends of Spanish Democracy ("subversive"); the American-Russian Institute ("subver-

244

sive" – "Communist" – "specializing in pro-Soviet propaganda"); the American Student Union ("Communist front"); the American Youth Congress ("subversive and Communist"); Associated Film Audiences ("Communist front"); Citizens' Victory Committee for Harry Bridges ("Communist front"); the Committee for a Democratic Far Eastern Policy ("Communist"); the Committee of One Thousand ("Communist created and controlled front organization"); the Conference on Pan-American Democracy ("Communist front"); Continuations Committee of the Conference on Peaceful .Alternatives to the Atlantic Pact ("Communist front"); the Coordinating Committee to Lift the [Spanish] Embargo ("Communist front"); The Council on African Affairs ("subversive and Communist"); Exiled Writers Committee of the League of American Writers ("Communist enterprise"); Film Audiences for Democracy ("Communist front"); the Greater New York Emergency Conference on Inalienable Rights ("Communist front"); the International Workers Order ("subversive and Communist"); the League of American Writers ("subversive and Communist"); the Mid-Century Conference for Peace ("aimed at assembling as many gullible persons as possible under Communist direction and turning them into a vast sounding board for Communist propaganda" – "Communist front"); the National Committee to Defeat the Mundt Bill ("a Communist lobby"); the National Council of American-Soviet Friendship ("subversive and Communist" – "specializing in pro-Soviet propaganda"); the National Council of the Arts, Sciences and Professions ("a Communist front used to appeal to special occupational groups"); the National Emergency Conference ("Communist front"); the National Federation for Constitutional Liberties ("under [Communist] Party domination and headed by responsible Party functionaries" the Non-Partisan Committee for the Re-election of Congressman Vito Marcantonio ("Communist front"); the Reichstag Fire Trial Anniversary Committee ("Communist front"); the United American Spanish Aid Committee ("Communist"); the Veterans of the Abraham Lincoln Brigade ("subversive and Communist"); the Veterans against Discrimination of Civil Rights Congress ("subversive and Communist"); and, the National Committee to Abolish the House Un-American Activities Committee ("to lead and direct the Communist Party's 'Operation Abolition' campaign"). Black has a sense of humor. He said that he resigned from the American Committee for Protection of Foreign Born [Americans] in 1953 because he was told it was controlled from the left!

In 1966, Republican Mayor John Lindsay of New York City appointed Black as chairman of Lindsay's short-lived police review board.

EUGENE BLACK was born on May 1, 1898 in Atlanta, Georgia, son of Gussie Grady and Eugene Black. He graduated from the University of Georgia in 1917. He married Susette Heath.

In his private banking career, Black was associated with the Chase National Bank of New York City.

From 1947 until 1962, Black was, successively, executive director, president, and chairman of the executive directors of the International Bank of Reconstruction and Development – the same bank which has propped up socialist regimes all over the world. Later, Black would become financial consultant to the Secretary General of the United Nations; a member of the advisory board to the UN's Special Fund which is headed by the socialistic Paul Hoffman; and, a member of the permanent advisory commission to evaluate U.S. foreign aid programs.

Black has been a director of the American Express Company, the New York Times, Chase Manhattan Bank, Royal Dutch Shell Corporation, International Telephone and Telegraph, Olin Mathieson Chemical, among others. He is a trustee and chairman of the finance committee of the Ford Foundation, which has been a horn of plenty for leftwingers and leftwing projects on every continent. He is a trustee of the Atlantic Council, an organization which stresses the need for closer cooperation, especially economic, between the United States and the socialist nations of Western Europe; and, the leftwing Institute of International Education. He is on the board of directors of the Atlantic Council. He is chairman of the board of the Brookings Institution, a unique "think factory" which has influenced internationalist trends in the federal government for the past fifty years. He is a non-resident member of the Council on Foreign Relations, the informal supra-State Department of the United States.

HUGO L. BLACK was born on February 27, 1886 in Harlan, Alabama, son of Martha Toland and William Black. He married the late Josephine Foster. He is married to Elizabeth DeMeritte. He is an alumnus of the University of Alabama (LL.B., 1906).

Black began practicing law in Birmingham, Alabama in 1906. In 1910 and 1911, he served eighteen months as a police court judge. From 1915 until 1917, he was prosecuting attorney for Jefferson County, Alabama. Along the way, Black was, for a brief time, a member of the Klu Klux Klan. From 1927 until 1937, Black was U.S. Senator from Alabama. Then, in 1937, President Franklin D. Roosevelt appointed him as Associate Justice of the Supreme Court of the United States. For thirty years Black has been the best friend that Communists have ever had on the bench. Black's leftwing views have always been years ahead of the Congress, the executives, and his judicial associates from the days of the New Deal down to the Great Society.

EUGENE BLAKE was born on November 7, 1906 in St. Louis, Missouri, son of Lulu Carson and Orville Blake. He married Valina Gillespie. He is an alumnus of Princeton University (A.B., 1928) and Princeton Theological Seminary (Th.B., 1932). He also studied at New College in Edinburgh, Scotland in 1929 and 1930.

From 1932 until 1951, Blake served in various Presbyterian pastorates. In 1951, he was elected Stated Clerk of the General Assembly of the Presbyterian Church, U.S.A., and, in 1958, was elected Stated Clerk of the General Assembly of the United Presbyterian Church, U.S.A.

From 1954 until 1957, Blake was president of the National Council of Churches of Christ, U.S.A. In 1966, he became the general secretary of the World Council of Churches.

As a churchman, Blake has been a well-publicized commentator on public affairs. He has long been an outspoken critic of any and all congressional committees investigating subversion and has recommended the abolition of all such committees. He talks a good game against Communism but after periodic visits to the Soviet Union, he has spouted utter nonsense about the position of churches under the Communists.

In his high positions with the National and World Councils of Churches, Blake has cooperated in a program of "religious peaceful coexistence" with Communist agents who have infiltrated national churches. Blake has represented the war in Vietnam as a racial one; he has urged that the Vietcong be represented at any peace conferences; and, he follows the Martin Luther King line that the war in Vietnam is waged at the expense of Lyndon Johnson's phony "war on poverty."

When Blake's pious preachments are stripped down to their essentials, he emerges as an ultra-liberal, soft-on-Communism, socialistic propagandist.

PAUL BLANSHARD was born on August 27, 1892 in Fredericksburg, Ohio, son of Emily Coulter and Francis Blanshard. He was married to the late Julia Anderson. He is married to Mary Hillyer. He is an alumnus of the University of Michigan (A.B., 1914) and Brooklyn Law School (LL.B., 1937). He did graduate work at Harvard University, Columbia University, and Union Theological Seminary.

In 1917, Blanshard was ordained as a Congregational minister but, after holding only one pastorate, he retired from active ministerial work. From 1920 until 1924, he was educational director for the Amalgamated Clothing Workers of America in Rochester, New York. From 1925 until 1933, he was field secretary for the socialist League for Industrial Democracy. Meanwhile, he was an associate editor of the leftwing *Nation* magazine (1928-1929) and director of the city affairs committee in New York City.

In 1933, Blanshard was the research director in the New York City mayoralty campaign of Fiorello La Guardia, a political and ideological eccentric. By that time, Blanshard was one of the best known Socialists in the nation. In 1932, he had written: "The church's survival, it seems to me, depends largely on whether the ministry has the courage to rise to the moral level of Socialism." And Blanshard spelled out in detail the Socialist goals of himself and his colleagues: "If we [Socialists] gained control of the American government, we probably would begin with a complete revision of the national governmental system. We would do one of two things. We would write an amendment to the Constitution giving the federal government the right to regulate all private business, and to enter into any business which it deemed proper, or we would abolish the Constitution altogether and give the national congress the power to interpret the people's will, subject only to certain general principles of free speech and assemblage." But La Guardia, who was elected mayor, overlooked Blanshard's notoriety as a Socialist and appointed him to be the city's Commissioner of Accounts, a post he held until 1938. It was during this period that the *New York Times* (October 27, 1937) reported that Blanshard had allowed Communist funds to be collected in his office and permitted literature to be circulated in the office urging the election of Earl Browder, head of the Communist Party, to the presidency of the United States. The *Times* quoted Blanshard as saying: "Having once captured the government and shelved the Supreme Court, we Socialists would nationalize as many large industries as we could chew and as speedily as such masticulation could be accomplished."

In 1938, at the age of 46, Blanshard

was admitted to the bar in New York and practiced law from 1939 until 1941. In 1942, Blanshard became an employee of the very government he wished to revise completely. With absolutely no credentials for the job, he became an economic analyst and consultant to the Caribbean Commission of the State Department, and he remained in this position until 1946. Since 1946, he has been almost exclusively a writer.

In earlier years, Blanshard wrote two books. The first was *An Outline of the British Labor Movement,* written in collaboration with Norman Thomas, the six-time Socialist candidate for the presidency of the United States. The second was *What's the Matter with New York* (it wasn't Socialist enough for Blanshard).

In 1947, Blanshard wrote *Democracy and Empire in the Caribbean* which merely demonstrated that the Socialism he took to the Caribbean Commission of the State Department had not been forsaken. Then in 1949, Blanshard began a career as a professional anti-Catholic. He began a series of books with *American Freedom and Catholic Power,* published in 1949. The main theme of this work was that alleged Catholic power was the most serious threat to American freedom. The book thrust Blanshard into the national limelight and he became an especial hero of Protestants and Other Americans United for Separation of Church and State (POAU). The POAU had been recently organized and was under the executive directorship of Glenn L. Archer, a virulent anti-Catholic who portrayed Catholicism as a greater enemy of the American people than Communism. Blanshard became an official of POAU, joining a number of individuals who had long records of Socialist or pro-Communist affiliations and activities.

Blanshard followed his initial anti-Catholic diatribe with *Communism, Democracy and Catholic Power* (1951); *The Irish and Catholic Power* (1953); *God and Man in Washington* (1960); *Freedom and Catholic Power in Spain and Portugal* (1962); and *Religion and the Schools* (1963).

Blanshard's quarrel with the Catholic Church is not merely his disagreement on doctrinal matters. He charges that Catholicism is a political threat to any nation where it is allowed to thrive. He equates Catholicism with Fascism and shows a reckless disregard for truth in his efforts to prove his contention that individual Catholics are political captives of a Rome-based totalitarian conspiracy against "democracy." Although Blanshard levels his heaviest cannonades at Catholicism, a close study of his works indicates that he is opposed to all organized religion and, though he professes to be a Unitarian, his materialistic Socialism remains his forte. It has not been diluted over the past four decades.

HERBERT BLOCK was born on October 13, 1909 in Chicago, son of Tessie Lupe and David Block. He studied at Lake Forest College in Illinois and the Art Institute of Chicago.

Herblock (his professional signature) has been an editorial cartoonist since 1933. He was four years with the *Chicago Daily News,* ten years with the Newspaper Enterprise Association Service, and, since 1946, has been with the *Washington Post.*

One of Herblock's journalistic admirers (Max Freedman) has written of Herblock that he "is not only a genius at his craft but is also a man of generous loyalties and wide sympathies. He can draw a cartoon that can scorch and sting as if with scorpions. This gift of ridicule is a terrible gift, for it can be so easily abused." Communist Joe North, writing in *The Worker* (October 4, 1964), said: "Herblock . . . has the God given gift of satire. He is, to my taste, the best man in the current field."

Herblock has been showered with the type of prizes that are the usual milestones in a successful leftwing career: the American Newspaper Guild Award; two Pulitzer prizes; the Heywood Broun Award; the Grenville Clark Editorial Award; the Lauterbach Award; and, the Sidney Hillman Award. But perhaps the most fitting tribute paid to Herblock was that by the Moscow *New Times* when it had a full-page reproduction of a Herblock cartoon on the inside cover of its July 6, 1966 issue.

It is inarguable that, throughout his career, Herblock's "generous loyalties and wide sympathies" have been directed solely to the left. While his scorpion-like "scorch and sting" have been heaviest against anti-Communists, political conservatives, efficient and honest law enforcement officials, and military men who are dedicated to the preservation of our nation's security.

DERK BODDE was born on March 9, 1909 in Brant Rock, Massachusetts, son of Margaret Peddle and Theodore Bodde. He married Galia Speshneff. He is an alumnus of Harvard University (B.A., 1930) and the University of Leiden of The Netherlands (Ph.D., 1938). He did graduate study at Harvard in 1930 and 1931, and was a fellow at the Harvard-Yenching Institute in Peiping, from 1931 until 1935. During World War II, he was with the Office of Strategic Services and Elmer Davis' Red-lined Office of War Information.

Bodde has been on the faculty at the University of Pennsylvania since 1938,

specializing in Chinese studies. Among his books are *China's Gift to the West; Chinese Ideas in the West;* and *Peking Diary.*

Bodde has been affiliated with the American Committee for Protection of Foreign Born [Americans] ("subversive and Communist" − "one of the oldest auxiliaries of the Communist Party in the United States" − under the "complete domination" of the Communist Party); the American Forum for Socialist Education ("subversive"); the Emergency Civil Liberties Committee ("Communist front" − "subversive"); the International Workers' Order ("subversive and Communist"), the Institute of Pacific Relations ("a vehicle used by the Communists to orientate American far eastern policies toward Communist objectives"); the Committee for a Democratic Far Eastern Policy ("Communist"); and, the National Committee to Abolish the House Un-American Activities Committee ("to lead and direct the Communist Party's 'Operation Abolition' campaign"). He has also been affiliated with the National Committee for a Sane Nuclear Policy (leftwing, pacifist); and the American Civil Liberties Union, that motleyed collection of defenders of subversion, crime, and licentiousness.

He has petitioned on behalf of Communists and against state and federal anti-subversive laws and activities.

In 1965, he was affiliated with the Inter-University Committee for a Public Hearing on Vietnam, sponsors of the anti-Vietnam "teach-in" movement which the Communist propaganda apparatus exploited for purely Communist purposes.

CHARLES BOHLEN was born on August 30, 1904 in Clayton, New York. He married Avis Thayer. He is an alumnus of Harvard University (A.B., 1927).

Bohlen began his State Department career in 1929. During his first fourteen years in the Department, Bohlen held minor posts in Prague, Moscow, Tokyo, and Washington. In 1943, he was assistant chief in the Division of European Affairs. From 1943 until 1945, he was first secretary in Moscow, then chief of the Division of Eastern European Affairs, and an assistant to the Secretary of State for White House liaison. In 1946, he was a special assistant to the Secretary of State. In 1947 and 1948, he was a counselor at the Department. From 1949 until 1951, he was U.S. Minister in Paris. In 1951 and 1952, he was back in Washington as a counselor.

In 1953, Bohlen began a four-year tenure as U.S. Ambassador to the Soviet Union. From 1957 until 1959, he was U.S. Ambassador to T Philippines. From 1959 until 1961, he was a special assistant on Soviet affairs to the Secretary of State. From 1962 until 1967, he was U.S. Ambassador to France. In December 1967, he was named to succeed Foy Kohler as Deputy Under Secretary of State for Political Affairs.

In the entire history of the State Department, it is extremely doubtful if any one diplomat ever attended more top level diplomatic meetings than Bohlen.

In the Roosevelt years, Bohlen was at the Moscow, Teheran, Dumbarton Oaks, and Yalta conferences. In the Truman years, he was at the Potsdam Conference, the London Council of Ministers the two Moscow Conferences of Foreign Ministers, the San Francisco Conference to Organize the United Nations, the Paris Conference of Foreign Ministers, and two United Nations General Assemblies. The late U.S. Senator Styles Bridges said

of Bohlen: "In most every diplomatic horsetrade at which Bohlen was present, the Russians got the fat mare and the U.S. ended up with the spavined nag. Bohlen is an experienced failure." Senator Bridges may well have erred on the charitable side. Bohlen certainly made no secret of his appeasable attitude toward the Soviet Union.

Bryton Barron writes in *The Untouchable State Department* that when Bohlen was ending his ambassadorial term in Moscow in 1957, Khrushchev said: "We hate to see you go." Khrushchev need not have been so sad. Wherever Chip Bohlen went, he would continue to be one of the most outrageous apologists for Communist perfidy.

CHESTER BOWLES was born on April 5, 1901 in Springfield, Massachusetts, son of Nellie Harris and Charles Bowles. He married Julia Mayo Fisk and was divorced. He married Dorothy Stebbins. He is an alumnus of Yale University.

In 1924 and 1925, Bowles was a reporter for the *Springfield* (Mass.) *Republican*. From 1925 until 1941, he was in the advertising business.

By 1940, Bowles had become very active in Democratic politics and, in that year, he was a Connecticut delegate to the Democratic national convention. (He was also a delegate in 1948 and 1956.)

During World War II, Bowles served, successively, as rationing administrator for Connecticut, director in Connecticut for the Office of Price Administration, national general manager for the Office of Price Administration, and national price administrator. In that same period, he was a member of the War Production Board and of the Petroleum Council for War.

In the first Truman Administration,

Bowles was director and chairman of the Economic Stabilization Board. In 1947 and 1948, he was a special assistant to United Nations Secretary General Trygve Lie.

From 1949 until 1951, Bowles was Democrat Governor of Connecticut. In 1951, President Truman appointed Bowles to be Ambassador to India and Nepal, where he remained until the end of the Truman years. During the two Eisenhower Administrations, Bowles busied himself lecturing at Bryn Mawr College, the University of California, Harvard University, and Yale University. Then Bowles returned to active politics. He was elected a Representative from Connecticut to the 86th Congress (1959-1961) and, in 1960, he climbed on the Kennedy bandwagon and became platform chairman of the Democratic national convention.

President Kennedy made Bowles Under Secretary of State but Bowles lasted less than a year in that lofty position and he was put out to pasture in the do-nothing position of presidential special representative for Asian, African and Latin American Affairs. Finally, President Kennedy sent Bowles back to India as Ambassador — a position he still holds. In his two missions to India, there has been justifiable confusion on the part of observers as to whether Bowles is the U.S. Ambassador or the Indian Ambassador-in-Residence.

Bowles is a charter member of the be-nice-to-Castro-club. He is a bitter foe of Chiang Kai-shek and has recommended that U.S. foreign policy should be geared to supporting the "less arrogant and less dangerous, less expansionist" of the Chinese Communists and settle on a two-China policy of diplomatic recognition. He is a fanatic proponent of U.S. foreign aid programs and of world-wide agrarian "reforms."

Bowles was a founder of Americans for Democratic Action, the center of the radical left in American politics. He has been an official of the leftwing Institute of International Education. He has also been affiliated with Clarence Streit's Atlantic Union, which is working towards a political merger of Western Europe and the United States, as a major step towards world government, and with the Council on Foreign Relations, the informal supra-State Department of the United States.

In January 1968, Bowles was sent by President Johnson to Cambodia for talks with Cambodia's double-talking Chief of State Prince Sihanouk. Bowles was to discuss the years-old problem of North Vietnamese and Vietcong troops using Cambodia as a sanctuary. True to form, Bowles' mission was an abject failure as Sihanouk found Bowles apparently eager to prove himself to be zealous of retaining his standing as America's most inadequate diplomat.

HARRY BRIDGES was born on July 28, 1901 in Melbourne, Australia, son of Julia Dorgan and Alfred Bridges. He was married to Agnes Brown and to Nancy Berdico. He is married to Noriko Sawada.

Bridges came to the United States as a seaman in 1920. In 1921, he joined the Marine Transport Workers Union, which was affiliated with the Industrial Workers of the World (Wobblies). In 1924, he belonged for a brief time to the International Longshoremen's Association (ILA). In 1933, he rejoined the ILA. In various indictments, federal government officials have charged that Bridges also joined the Communist Party, U.S.A. in 1933.

In 1934, Bridges was chairman of the

ILA's Strike Committee and the Joint Marine Strike Committee. A strike called by Bridges in that year brought him to the forefront of the Pacific Coast labor movement. Within two years, he was elected Pacific Coast President of the ILA and became a member of the American Federation of Labor's executive committee. In 1937, Bridges and his union were expelled from the AFL, and the ILA then changed its name to the International Long-shoremen's and Warehousemen's Union (ILWU).

In 1938, the U.S. Immigration and Naturalization Service began proceedings to deport Bridges for his Communist activities. Attempts to deport him were also made in 1941, 1949, and 1954. All attempts failed. In the meantime Bridges applied for and received U.S. citizenship.

Despite the fact that many ex-Communists testified under oath, as did Bridges' first wife, that he was a member of the Communist Party, Bridges was saved from deportation at various times by former Harvard Law School Dean James M. Landis, Mrs. Eleanor Roosevelt, Labor Secretary Frances Perkins, and the Supreme Court of the United States.

In 1950, the ILWU was expelled from the CIO on grounds that Bridges' union was controlled by the Communists. But no amount of adverse publicity has ever been a deterrent to the growth of Harry Bridges' power. He controls the shipping of Alaska, Hawaii and the west coast of the United States. He is the most powerful single influence in all of Hawaii's political life. And through cooperation with other Communist-controlled union, Bridges is in a position to control shipping throughout the world. And Bridges has made just such plans.

DAVID BRINKLEY was born on July 10, 1920 in Wilmington, North Carolina, son of Mary West and William Brinkley. He married Ann Fischer.

Brinkley began his journalism career as a reporter with the *Wilmington Star-News* in 1938. From 1941 until 1943, he was a reporter and bureau manager for the United Press in southern States. In 1943, he joined the staff of the National Broadcasting Company and has worked as a news writer, news reader, and commentator on radio and television, generally from Washington. In recent years, Brinkley has teamed with Chet Huntley on a five-night-a-week news program. Brinkley and Huntley became prominent through their coverage of national political conventions, beginning in 1956.

Brinkley brought to television and radio coverage of the news the wry commentary and wisecrack. Unfortunately for the sake of objectivity in journalism, Brinkley's wryness of humor is used almost exclusively to promote extreme liberalism.

DETLEV BRONK was born on August 13, 1897 in New York City, son of Marie Wulf and Mitchell Bronk. He married Helen Ramsey. He is an alumnus of Swarthmore College (A.B., 1920) and the University of Michigan (M.S., 1922; Ph.D., 1926).

In 1921, Bronk was an instructor of physics at the University of Pennsylvania. From 1921 until 1924, he was an instructor of physics and, from 1924 until 1926, he was an instructor in physiology at the University of Michigan. From 1926 until 1929, he served, successively, as assistant professor, associate professor, and professor of physiology and biophysics at Swarthmore College. From 1929 until 1949, he was at the University of Pennsylvania as a professor of biophysics and a director of research in medical physics. In this same period, he held a professorship in physiology at Cornell University's Medical College. And, in this period, he lectured at the Philadelphia College for Physicians, McGill University, Pennsylvania State College, Princeton University, New York University, and Brown University.

From 1942 until 1946, Bronk was a special consultant to the Secretary of War and he coordinated research for the U.S. Army Air Corps' Air Surgeon. From 1944 until 1946, he was chief of the aviation medicine division in the Office of Scientific Research and Development. In 1946, he became a member and, in 1948, vice-chairman of the United States Commission for the United Nations Educational, Scientific, and Cultural Organization (UNESCO). In 1946, he became a member of the Naval Research Advisory Board. From 1948 until 1950, he was a member of the National Advisory Committee for Aeronautics.

From 1946 until 1950, Bronk was chairman of the National Research Council, in which position he supervised the choice and distribution of research fellowships for the Atomic Energy Commission. In 1949, the Joint Congressional Committee on Atomic Energy discovered that one of the AEC's fellowships had been granted to an individual who had publicly acknowledged his membership in the Communist Party. The committee questioned Bronk about the circumstances and he proved to be quite evasive. At first, he admitted that the grant to a Communist was an embarrassment. But, he argued that it was necessary to take a calculated risk of having an occasional Communist in the research program if the government wanted to build up its pool of scientific researchers. When the Communist in question was quoted as saying that his loyalty to the United States was not compromised by his Communist Party membership, Bronk said: "It sounds to me as if he doesn't think very clearly and that he is not likely to make a good scientist." How the Communist's defense of his ideological views affected his scientific talents, Bronk never explained; nor did Bronk suggest that grantees should undergo a rigid security investigation before being considered for a grant. Bronk was content to let the grantee's school officials submit an estimate of his general character and activities. In Bronk's opinion, an occasional Communist would not do any harm in the AEC program "except to sound off a lot of nonsense."

From 1949 until 1953, Bronk was president of The Johns Hopkins University. In 1953, when Rockefeller University, a research center, was reorganized into a graduate university, Bronk became its president. In 1968, Bronk retired as president but has retained an office and biophysics laboratory at the University.

During his tenure as Rockefeller's president, Bronk was also president of the National Science Foundation Board (1956-1964) and president of the National Academy of Sciences (1950-1962). He was a member of President Eisenhower's and President Kennedy's Science Advisory Committee and a consultant to President Johnson's Science Advisory Committee.

Bronk has long been a close associate of the Pugwash scientists, an international group dominated by Russians and Americans who meet periodically to discuss disarmament proposals which inevitably lead to concessions by the United States government and to the advantage of the Soviet Union's program of conquest. In 1958, Bronk was elected to the Soviet Academy of Sciences. In 1959, he was given a special medal by the Society for Promoting International Scientific Relationships. For many years, he has been a sponsor of the *Bulletin of the Atomic Scientists*. The major advocacies of the *Bulletin* have included the elimination of all secrecy and security surrounding the development of U.S. atomic bombs and other devices. The *Bulletin* has called for international control of atomic energy without inspections. It has called for disarmament based upon mutual trust of the various national scientific communities, whose members are expected to take an active political role in their respective governments. The *Bulletin* provides a forum for Soviet Union propagandists to reach American scientists. And, the *Bulletin* has given its pages over to the world's most famous pleaders for appeasement, surrender, and coexistence as the desirable relationship between the Communist bloc and free nations.

In 1964, Bronk became a charter member of Arthur Larson's National Council for Civil Responsibility, an election year front inspired by Walter Reuther to combat anti-Communists and conservatives. Bronk's colleagues on the NCCR represented just about every Communist front, Communist project, and Communist enterprise of the past thirty or thirty-five years.

In 1966, Bronk was on a panel of twenty-seven prominent persons, convened by the leftwing United Nations Association, who urged that the United States adopt a policy that would permit both Communist China and Free China to be members of the United Nations. The policy, according to the panel, would strengthen the U.S. position in world affairs and provide timely encouragement to moderate (?) elements in Red China.

Bronk has been very close to the Rockefeller establishment, aside from his presidency of Rockefeller University: He has been a trustee of the Rockefeller Brothers Fund and a member of the Council on Foreign Relations which has been heavily subsidized by the Rockefeller Foundation.

In 1964, Bronk (along with such notorious leftwingers as A. Philip Randolph, Edward R. Murrow, Walter Lippmann, Carl Sandburg, Lewis Mumford, Ralph McGill, and Reinhold Niebuhr) received from Lyndon Johnson the Presidential Medal of Freedom for having "made freedom stronger for all of us."

EDWARD W. BROOKE was born on October 16, 1919 in Washington, D.C., son of Helen Seldon and Edward Brooke. He married Remigia Ferrari-Sacco. He is an alumnus of Howard University (B.S., 1941) and Boston University (LL.B., 1948; LL.M., 1949). He wrote *The Challenge of Change*, published in 1966.

In 1948, Brooke was admitted to the Massachusetts bar. In 1950, he began his private practice of law in Boston, Massachusetts. During the 1950's, he was an unsuccessful candidate for the state legislature on two occasions. In 1960, he was the Republican nominee for Secretary of State of Massachusetts but was defeated in the election. In 1961 and 1962, he served as chairman of the Boston Finance Commission. In 1962, he was elected Attorney General of Massachusetts and he was re-elected in 1964. In 1966, he was elected to the United States Senate (the Communists, through the pages of *New World Review,* rejoiced over his election as did liberals throughout the press media).

During the Republican National Convention of 1964, Brooke gained national prominence as a leader of the anti-Goldwater wing of the Republican Party. Brooke's hostility toward Barry Goldwater's candidacy was so intense that he refused even to appear on the same platform with Goldwater after the latter had been nominated. Brooke favored the ultra-left Republicans such as John Lindsay, George Romney, Nelson Rockefeller, Mark Hatfield, and Charles Percy. But, when Brooke was campaigning for the U.S. Senate in 1966, he accepted contributions from Barry Goldwater and Goldwaterite Clare Booth Luce. On two electoral occasions, Brooke has accepted endorsements from Americans for Democratic Action, the center of the radical left in American politics. And, in 1966, Brooke was supported by the National Committee for an Effective Congress which has supported only ultra-leftist candidates since it was organized in 1952.

Although Brooke has often disclaimed ideological labels, he has been represented in the press and political circles as a moderate, a conservative, a progressive, and — infrequently — as a leftist. However, his position on national and international issues — despite his disclaimer of labels — places him unmistakably to the left of center. As a matter of fact, it would be difficult — if not impossible — to find a single issue where Brooke has made his views known which would be offensive to American leftists.

On economic matters, Brooke is a complete Keynesian in his belief that government spending is the panacea for all ills. He goes so far as to pronounce that government spending increases the gross national product — a total absurdity. He advocates increased unemployment insurance, an increased minimum wage, a guaranteed annual wage, a postponement of debts owed by "developing" nations paired with large increases of foreign aid to those same nations, increased government spending in all areas of education, and — as might be expected — increased taxes coupled with deficit spending.

Once Brooke was elected to the Senate, he set out to become an instant expert on foreign affairs. This ambition caused him to make widely publicized trips to Asia and Africa during his first year as a freshman Senator. From Asia, he returned with the liberal line on the Vietnam War. He called for a halt to the bombing of North Vietnam, for negotiations with the Viet Cong, and even for a political settlement which is not wholly satisfactory to the United Sates rather than have an increase of military involvement in Vietnam.

Brooke has advocated United States recognition of Red China. He insists that Red China's threat to the rest of Asia has been vastly overrated and that Mao Tse-tung has been concerned predominantly with the internal affairs of Red China.

From his African experiences, Brooke adopted a strong pro-Israeli stance vis-à-vis the Arab nations. He called for strong United States economic and political sanctions against Rhodesia and the Republic of South Africa. He also called for United States pressure upon Portugal to grant independence to the latter's overseas provinces of Angola and Mozambique. It is significant that the three targets of Brooke's aggressiveness — Rhodesia, South Africa, Portugal — are the three most important anti-Communist forces in Africa.

Brooke is also an ardent devotee of the United Nations. He preaches that it has been a positive good for peace and order in the past but could become even more efficient in the future if only a UN military force was created to police the world.

As a Negro, Brooke has been politically astute by avoiding a direct activist role with any one Negro group or an alliance with any individual racial agitators. He did not hesitate, however, to shower praises on the late Martin L. King Jr. and the veteran Harlem agitator Adam Clayton Powell Jr. He has insisted that he has no intention of becoming a national leader of the Negro people but nevertheless from his prestigious position as a Senator he has adopted the bleeding-heart approach to riots which he blames upon poverty, illiteracy, and hunger – a thesis which squares with the foolishness uttered by leaders of the NAACP, the ADA, and President Johnson's Commission for Civil Rights – of which Brooke is a member.

Brooke has advocated civilian review boards over the police. He has opposed all literacy tests as requirements for voting in federal, state, and local elections. He has voted right down the line for all so-called civil rights legislation. He has joined a Memorial Committee to honor the late W. E. B. DuBois, the most famous of all American Negro Communists. In other words, despite his insistence that he is not a national leader for the Negroes, Brooke is fast becoming their Senatorial voice. His activities have not gone unrewarded. In 1968, the NAACP presented him the Spingarn Medal – which is an annual recognition given to those who have contributed to racial agitation (earlier recipients included Ralph Bunche, Roy Wilkins, Robert Weaver and Thurgood Marshall).

There is no denying Brooke's political cleverness. In January 1965, when interviewed by the staff of *U.S. News &*
World Report, he described the United States as the greatest country in the world for the Negro – a statement which was obviously made for creating a national image of Brooke as an objective-minded Negro politician, because two months later at the Community Church of Boston under the auspices of Reverend Donald Lothrop, Brooke decried the "fact" that in this country the Negro did not have the right to walk down a road. It is reasonable to suspect that before the latter audience, Brooke wished to reassure the left that he had not deserted the ranks of racial agitators. (As recently as 1958, a Massachusetts legislative Special Commission to Study and Investigate Communism concluded that the Community Church is "the most active center of Communist Party activity now in Boston" and that the Church and Lothrop "have been a great source of aid and comfort through the years to the Communist Party.")

It was also in 1965 that Brooke made another obeisance to the left in his home state. At that time, Brooke was president of the Boston Opera Group. Luigi Nono, a notorious and active member of the Italian Communist Party and a composer, applied for a visa to visit the United States. Nono's opera *Intolleraza 1960* was to have its premiere performance by Brooke's Boston Opera Group. But when Nono applied for a visa, it was automatically and legally denied him because he admitted his Italian Communist Party membership. Brooke, at the time, was Attorney General of Massachusetts. Through his efforts and those of U.S. Senator Edward F. Kennedy, the State Department reversed its legal decision and Nono received his visa. Two months after the premiere of *Intolleraza 1960,* Nono displayed his gratitude by writing a vicious anti-Boston, anti-American diatribe in *Rinacita,* the Italian Communist weekly.

Shortly after Brooke took his seat in the Senate, he announced: "I intend to do my job as a Senator from Massachusetts." But, in his first year and a half, he has been a notable absentee from Washington, D.C. as he has spent so much time in his Asian and African travels, followed by his 1968 efforts campaigning on behalf of Nelson Rockefeller's candidacy for the Republican presidential nomination. It is doubtful if any State has ever been so neglected by a freshman Senator as has been Massachusetts in 1967 and 1968.

EDMUND G. (PAT) BROWN was born on April 21, 1905 in San Francisco, son of Ida Schuckman and Edmund Brown. He married Bernice Layne. He is an alumnus of the San Francisco Law School (LL.B., 1927).

Brown was admitted to the California bar in 1927 and, from 1927 until 1943, he practiced law in San Francisco. From 1943 until 1950, he was District Attorney for the city and county of San Francisco.

In 1950, Brown, running as a Democrat, was elected Attorney General of California. His election was attributable in great part to his close friend Earl Warren, then the Republican Governor of California.

Brown served as Attorney General until 1958 when he was elected Governor of California. He was re-elected in 1962. In 1958 and 1962, respectively, Brown defeated former U.S. Senator William Knowland and former Vice President Richard M. Nixon in two campaigns which were especially marked by deep and serious divisions within the Republican Party.

Of great help to Brown throughout his political career has been the campaign support he has received from the International Longshoremen's and Warehousemen's Union, led by the notorious Red labor leader Harry Bridges. When Brown was District Attorney of San Francisco, the U.S. government was making rather strong efforts to deport Bridges. But District Attorney Brown rallied to Bridges' defense and denounced the U.S. immigration authorities who were trying to send Bridges back to his native Australia. Brown also threw his active support behind a move to grant U.S. citizenship to Bridges. Such patronizing efforts toward Bridges produced an unbroken history of political support by the ILWU for Brown.

Brown's tie-up with the ILWU was not his only association with the left. In his numerous political campaigns, he has been supported at various times by the ultra-leftist California Democratic Council, by the Hollywood Independent Citizens Committee of the Arts, Sciences and Professions (a Communist front), and, when the latter merged with the C.I.O. Political Action Committee to become the Progressive Citizens of America, by the new political Communist front.

Throughout his public life, Brown has enjoyed and earned very favorable treatment in the Communist press. As a top law enforcement official in California, he denounced anti-Communist legislative investigations as witch hunts. He opposed loyalty oaths for public officials and employees. He favored the appearance of Communist speakers on state-financed campuses. He opposed anti-subversive legislation and he raised the phony spectre of McCarthyism in order to stifle anti-Communism in a state where there has been a long history of concentration and activities by Communists and their fellow travelers.

Brown apparently has steered clear of direct involvement with Communist fronts with one major exception. He has been an off-and-on member and official over the past twenty years of the National Lawyers Guild which the House Committee on Un-American Activities has cited as a Communist front: It "is the foremost legal bulwark of the Communist Party, its front organizations, and controlled unions" and "since its inception has never failed to rally to the legal defense of the Communist Party and individual members thereof, including known espionage agents."

The years when Brown was California's Attorney General were particularly notable for the unprecedented increase in the State's crime rate. As Governor he followed the demagogue's course of tax and spend, tax and spend. In eight years, he managed to almost double the cost of state government.

In 1964, Brown became quite active in the presidential campaign of that year with his vigorous denunciation of the Republican candidate Barry Goldwater. Brown charged that Goldwater had "ruthlessly encouraged the racist, the bigot, the Ku Klux Klan, and even the Communist to assault the constitutional rights of those who oppose him." Brown's hysterical extremism in the campaign of 1964 undoubtedly contributed to his defeat two years later when he sought re-election as Governor in a campaign against Ronald Reagan — Brown's first political setback in twenty-four years. The defeat was remarkable since few state governors had been so strongly endorsed by the Kennedy dynasty and the Johnson Administration. And no Californian enjoyed closer ties with the politically influential Chief Justice Earl Warren and the politically powerful Red labor leader Harry Bridges.

Since 1966, Brown has been in somewhat of a political eclipse. He did emerge from the shadows briefly, early in 1968, when President Lyndon Johnson commissioned him to go to Greece during its monarchial crisis. The mission was not subject to much publicity nor has there been any word on what Brown might have accomplished. Except for spouting the ultra-liberal line on foreign policy (resume trade with Red China; support the United Nations; spend more on foreign aid), Brown has made few forays into foreign affairs. He has, however, on several occasions ingratiated himself with Communist leaders from the Soviet Union and Yugoslavia. But for all practical purposes, his mission to Greece was his novitiate in diplomacy.

DAVID BRUCE was born on February 12, 1898 in Baltimore, son of Louise Fisher and William Bruce. He was married to Ailsa Mellon and is married to Evangeline Bell. Bruce studied at Princeton University and the Law Schools of the University of Virginia and the University of Maryland.

From 1921 until 1940, Bruce divided his time between law practice, business, and farming in Maryland with the exception of the period 1926-1928 when he was a vice consul in Rome. In 1940 and 1941, he was the chief representative of the American Red Cross in Britain. During the war years, 1941-1945, Bruce was with the Office of Strategic Services, eventually becoming the OSS director in the European Theater of Operations.

In 1947 and 1948, Bruce was Assistant Secretary of Commerce. In

1948 and 1949, he was head of the U.S. foreign aid program (Economic Cooperation Administration) in France. From 1949 until 1952, he held the first of his three ambassadorial posts in France. Later (1957-1959), he was in Germany and, since 1961, has been in Britain. In 1952 and 1953, he was Under Secretary of State and, in 1953 and 1954, the U.S. representative to the European High Authority for Coal and Steel. Bruce is a non-resident member of the Council on Foreign Relations, the informal supra-State Department of the United States.

Journalist Charles Bartlett, who was a very close friend of the late John F. Kennedy, wrote that President Kennedy's final choice for Secretary of State lay between Dean Rusk and David Bruce. There is no reason to believe that, had his choice been Bruce, the soft-on-Communism foreign policy of the Kennedy-Johnson Administrations would have been any different than it has been under Rusk.

ZBIGNIEW BRZEZINSKI was born on March 28, 1928 in Warsaw, Poland, son of Leonia Roman and Tadvsz Brzezinski. He came to the United States in 1938 and was naturalized in 1958. He married Emilie Benes. He is an alumnus of McGill University of Canada (B.A., 1949) and Harvard University (M.A., 1950; Ph.D., 1953).

From 1953 until 1960, Brzezinski was at Harvard University in the Russian Research Center and the Center for International Affairs. He served as an instructor and assistant professor of government, a research fellow, a research associate, and a consultant. From 1960 until 1966, he was on the faculty of Columbia University as an associate professor and professor of public law and government. While at Columbia, he was also the director of the University's Research Institute on Communist Affairs and a faculty member of the University's Russian Institute.

In 1962, Brzezinski became a consultant to the Rand Corporation, a "think factory" which, since 1946, has held research contracts financed mainly by the U.S. Air Force, but also by the Atomic Energy Commission, the National Aeronautics and Space Administration, and the Defense Department.

It was also in 1962 that Brzezinski became a consultant to the State Department and, in 1966, he relinquished his faculty position at Columbia to become a member of the State Department's Policy Planning Council. He is the author of *The Permanent Purge: Politics in Soviet Totalitarianism; The Soviet Bloc: Unity and Conflict;* and *Ideology and Power in Soviet Politics.* He is co-author of *Totalitarian Dictatorship and Autocracy* and *Political Power: USA-USSR.*

Brzezinski has long since proved himself as a master of accommodation and appeasement with Communists. Basic to his alleged expertise is a United States policy of recognizing the status quo for Europe — meaning that Soviet aggression and Soviet captivity of nations receive an American seal of approval and acquiescence. Brzezinski advocates that the United States promote a massive all-Europe Marshall Plan, under which countries on both sides of the Iron Curtain would join in an economic development — which, of course, would solidify the Soviet Union's hold on its satellites. Brzezinski further proposes that the United States "consider ways of minimizing Soviet fears of "Germany" — meaning that American pressure be applied to force Germany into appeasement.

In March 1965, FBI Director J. Edgar Hoover warned that "few things would give the Communist Party, U.S.A. more comfort than a widespread underestimation of the menace which it presents to the internal security of the Nation." Three months later, Brzezinski provided such comfort when he said: "The Communist Party in the United States is a weak, faction-riddled group of political and social outcasts."

In 1967, while the United States was at war against Communists of North Vietnam, whose military efforts were made possible by Communists of Red China and the Soviet Union and its satellites, Brzezinski proclaimed that "Communism, the principal and until recently the most militant revolutionary ideology of our day, is dead."

Brzezinski is a non-resident member of the Council on Foreign Relations ("the informal supra-State Department of the United States") and the NAACP, the fountainhead of Negro agitation for the past fifty-eight years. In 1964, Brzezinski was a member of the honorary steering committee of Young Citizens for Johnson — credentials which probably were as good as any to make Brzezinski — as *Newsweek* put it — "one of the fastest-rising stars in the Johnson Administration" and "one of the architects of U.S. foreign policy."

After eighteen months in the State Department, Brzezinski resigned his post in December, 1967 and was reported to be resuming his professorship of government and directorship of the Research Institute on Communist Affairs at Columbia University. Simultaneously with his resignation, an article by Brzezinski was published in *Foreign Affairs*, the quarterly publication of the Council on Foreign Relations. In what had all the earmarks of a State Depart-

ment trial baloon, Brzezinski called for a diplomatic accommodation between NATO (which supposedly has been the military defensive posture against Communist military threats in Europe) and the Warsaw Pact nations (the Communist bloc's reaction to the establishment of NATO). Brzezinski's proposal makes as much sense as a veterinarian urging cats and dogs to be friends.

RALPH BUNCHE was born on August 7, 1904 in Detroit, Michigan, son of Olive Johnson and Fred Bunche. He married Ruth Harris. Bunche is an alumnus of the University of California (A.B., 1927) and Harvard University (A.M., 1928; Ph.D. 1934). He also did postdoctoral work in anthropology and colonial policy at Northeastern University, the London School of Economics, and the University of Capetown in South Africa.

In 1928, Bunche joined the faculty of Howard University as an instructor of political science. During the next twenty-four years, he rose through the academic ranks to become a professor and head of the department of political science. He also served as assistant to the university's president and as a professor of government.

While on the Howard faculty, Bunche received a Rosenwald Fellowship (1931-1932) for study in Europe, England, and North and West Africa; and, a Social Science Research Council postdoctoral fellowship (1936-1938) for study in Europe, South Africa, East Africa, Malaya, and the Dutch East Indies.

During the war years (1941-1944), Bunche was the senior social science analyst in charge of research on African and other colonial areas for the British Empire section of the Office of Strategic

Services, deputy chief of the Near East-Africa section, and chief of the African section.

From 1944 until 1947, Bunche was with the Department of State and began his work with the United Nations. In his UN activities, Bunche has worked in the Department of Trusteeship and has traveled on special assignment to Palestine, the Congo, and Yemen. From 1955 to 1958, he was Under Secretary for Special Political Affairs. In 1954, the Theodore Roosevelt Memorial Association presented Bunche with a medal for distinguished service in international affairs during 1954. The late President's son, Archibald, was so horrified at the news of the presentation that he issued a protest to the president of the Association in the form of a 49-page history of Bunche's close affiliation with Communists and the Marxism evident in Bunche's writings and utterances.

As uncovered by Mr. Roosevelt, the most damaging affiliations of Bunche included his part in originating and serving with prominent Communists on the national governing body of the National Negro Congress ("subversive and Communist"), his activities as an official of the Institute of Pacific Relations ("a vehicle used by the Communists to orientate American far eastern policies toward Communist objectives"), and his editorial position, from 1935 until 1940 with *Science and Society* ("a Communist publication").

In 1954, at the time when Bunche was made Under Secretary for the United Nations, a United States Civil Service special loyalty board for international organizations passed judgment on Bunche's qualifications. In the background, aside from Bunche's long-time proclivity for leftwing organizations, were his close connections with Alger Hiss. Bunche had rushed to Hiss' defense almost as soon as Hiss had been identified as a Communist by Whittaker Chambers. And when Bunche had first applied for a position in the UN, he had listed Hiss as a reference. Bunche had been Hiss' assistant secretary at the Dumbarton Oaks Conference of 1944, when the framework of the United Nations was established. And, in 1945, Bunche went to San Francisco with Hiss, who was secretary general of the UN's organizing conference.

At the loyalty board hearing, two former high-ranking Communists, Manning Johnson and Leonard Patterson — both Negroes, swore under oath that they had known Bunche within the Communist Party. In an editorial on May 31, 1954, the Communists' *Daily Worker,* while rushing to the defense of Bunche, excoriated Johnson and Patterson as "two stool pigeons."

Chesly Manly, the *Chicago Tribune's* UN correspondent for eight years, wrote in his book *The UN Record* of a report that Max Rabb, Dwight Eisenhower's trouble-shooter with minority groups, "was insistent that Bunche should be whitewashed to avoid any risk of offending Negro voters in the 1954 elections." Whatever the underlying reasons, Bunche was whitewashed and neither the loyalty board nor UN officials ever made a public report of the damaging evidence presented by Johnson and Patterson.

In pursuit of his UN duties, Bunche, as a truce negotiator in the Palestine crisis, alienated the Arab bloc from the United States and other Western nations; in the Congo, Bunche had a major share of responsibility in the ruthless suppression of the anti-Communist regime in Katanga Province. And from his lofty position in the UN, Bunche has added his prestige to the "civil rights" agitation in the United States and has been an outspoken critic of the United States policy of opposition toward Red China's admission to the United Nations.

Perhaps the most fitting tribute paid to Bunche was that of the Communists' *Worker* of June 16, 1964 when Communist Party spokesman Mike Davidow urged Bunche's nomination as the Democratic candidate to the United States Senate from New York.

McGEORGE BUNDY was born on March 30, 1919 in Boston, Massachusetts, son of Katharine Putnam and Harvey Bundy. He married Mary Lothrop. He is an alumnus of Yale University (A.B., 1940).

During World War II, Bundy was an aide to Admiral Alan Kirk. After the war, he collaborated with former Secretary of War Henry L. Stimson in writing the latter's memoirs *On Active Service*. For a brief time, Bundy worked in the Marshall Plan foreign aid program and, in 1948, he was a foreign affairs adviser to the Republican presidential candidate Thomas E. Dewey.

In 1948 and 1949, Bundy was a political analyst for the Council on Foreign Relations. Then in 1949, Bundy joined the faculty at Harvard University. From 1949 until 1951, he was a visiting lecturer; from 1951 until 1954, an associate professor of government; from 1954 until 1961, a professor of government; and, dean of the faculty of arts and sciences from 1953 until 1961. In 1959, when Fidel Castro visited the Harvard campus to extol the virtues of his "non-Communist" regime, Bundy was the University's smiling and genial host to the Communist tyrant.

In 1960, Bundy, who had been a Republican, campaigned for John F. Kennedy, helping to organize a scientific and professional committee in support of Mr. Kennedy's presidential candidacy.

From 1961 until 1966, Bundy served President Kennedy and President Johnson as a special assistant for national security affairs. In 1966, Bundy became president of the Ford Foundation.

While Bundy was in the White House, it was commonly remarked in the press that he ran his own State Department. Milton MacKaye, an old friend of Bundy's writing in the *Saturday Evening Post* of March 10, 1962, described the influential nature of Bundy's work in national security affairs: "Bundy's job is highly important. He is, of course, the President's chief staff adviser on foreign affairs. But his basement office in the west wing of the White House also serves as a vital communications center. Dispatches and cables which may warrant the President's attention go first to Bundy's office; departmental memoranda concerning security and foreign relations – a daily torrent of paper – go there, too. It is Bundy's task to filter the inflow and see to it that the President is properly informed . . . . In a real sense, Bundy is a custodian of the President's time, which must be strictly rationed. Security issues which can be settled later stay on Bundy's desk."

Newsweek (March 4, 1963) elaborated on MacKaye's estimate: "Along with his role as the President's adviser on crunching global problems, Bundy is director of the National Security Council and boss of its high-powered staff. From the White House, he coordinates the many arms of government involved in 'national security' – State, Defense, Treasury, Atomic Energy, Disarmament, Central Intelligence, Foreign Aid, even Agriculture – slashing across bureaucratic lines to deal with Cabinet members and agency heads."

Time magazine (June 25, 1965) appraised Bundy's role as "the President's foremost personal analyzer, arranger and adviser on all matters touching the fields of foreign policy, defense and intelligence. Half a dozen times each day, a red light on Bundy's telephone console flashes, and 'Mac' picks up the receiver to hear L.B.J. ask: 'What do you think about . . . ?' And dozens of times each day Bundy, in talking to others, utters the most galvanizing words in U.S. Government: 'The President wants . . . .' "

Nothing could be more ironical than to associate Bundy with sensitive security matters. When he was Dean of the Faculty at Harvard, Bundy placed himself squarely in opposition to federal security. He alleged that the government's security program "creates needless confusion and fear, spreads confusion far beyond the range of reason, and tends to discourage that confidence and eager sense of participation which has so often distinguished the relationship between American scholars and their Government since the day of Benjamin Franklin."

WILLIAM BUNDY was born on September 24, 1917 in Washington, D.C., son of Katharine Putnam and Harvey Bundy. He married Mary Acheson. He is an alumnus of Yale University (A.B., 1939) and Harvard University M.A., 1940; LL.B., 1947).

Bundy practiced law from 1947 until 1951. In 1951, he began a ten-year career with the Central Intelligence Agency and, in 1960, while still with the CIA, he was staff director of the Presidential Commission on National Goals.

From 1961 until 1964, Bundy was with the Defense Department, first as deputy assistant secretary, then as assistant secretary of defense for international security affairs. Since 1964, he has been Assistant Secretary of State for Far Eastern affairs. He is a non-resident member of the Council on Foreign Relations, the informal supra-State Department of the United States, and a trustee of the American Assembly, a Columbia University brainwashing project wherein American business executives are fed an up-to-date version of the State Department's soft-on-Communism, internationalist line.

In 1953, Bundy was a prime target of the late Senator Joseph R. McCarthy, who was laboring in vain to focus attention upon security risks and subversives within the malodorous Central Intelligence Agency. In his *The Twenty-Year Revolution,* Chesly Manly describes the Bundy-McCarthy encounter: "In July, 1952, Allen Dulles, head of the Central Intelligence Agency, who is a brother of Secretary [John Foster] Dulles, obstructed Senator McCarthy's efforts to question William P. Bundy, a CIA official. McCarthy told the Senate that Bundy, a son-in-law [and law firm associate] of former State [Department] Secretary Acheson, contributed $400 to the defense fund of Alger Hiss, who was an Acheson favorite. McCarthy said Bundy had submitted, in writing, the following explanation for his contribution to the Hiss defense fund: (1) it would help out Bundy's father-in-law; (2) it was 'imperative' to exonerate Hiss; and (3) the trial was important to the Democratic Party.

"McCarthy heard that Bundy was to be appointed to a new job as liaison officer between the Atomic Energy Commission and the National Security Council, the nation's top strategic planning agency. Whe he summoned Bundy to appear for questioning about his fitness for this job, he was advised by Walter Pforzheimer, legislative liaison officer of the CIA, that Bundy had gone away on a vacation and that, anyway, Dulles had prohibited CIA personnel from testifying before Congressional committees.

"McCarthy accused Dulles of 'blatantly defying the authority of the Senate' and of 'covering up' information concerning the activities of Bundy."

In the Johnson Administration, Bundy must take a large share of the blame for the disastrous no-win policy in the Vietnam War. While in the Defense Department, he was so closely associated with Defense Secretary McNamara that he might rightly be considred as McNamara's legacy to the State Department.

ELLSWORTH BUNKER was born on May 11, 1894 in Yonkers, New York, son of Jean Cobb and George Bunker. He was married to the late Harriet Butler. He is married to Carol Laise (U.S. Ambassador to Nepal). He is an alumnus of Yale University (A.B., 1916).

Until 1951, Bunker was an executive of the National Sugar Refining Company which his father had helped to found.

In 1951, Bunker assumed the first of what would be a long series of ambassadorial posts: Argentina, 1951; Italy, 1952-1953; India, 1956-1961; Nepal, 1956-1959; the Organization of American States, 1964-1966; South Vietnam, 1967-1968. And he has also served on special ambassadorial missions in the Kennedy and Johnson Administrations.

In 1962, Bunker became involved in the sell-out of West New Guinea to Achmed Sukarno's Communist regime of Indonesia. There are few chapters in American diplomatic history more sordid. It all began on March 12, 1956

when Secretary of State John Foster Dulles was paying a state visit to Indonesia. At that time Dulles "made it clear to President Sukarno that the United States was giving no support to the Dutch on the [West New Guinea] issue . . . 'the general trend is in your favor' [Dulles told Sukarno]." (*New York Times,* March 18, 1956.)

In 1962, Robert F. Kennedy, then Attorney General, went to Indonesia and culminated the hatchet-job begun by Dulles. When Kennedy was through fawning over Sukarno and arm-twisting the Dutch, Bunker went through the rituals of negotiations. And Bunker's diplomatic pirouette concluded Kennedy's dance of death over West New Guinea's independence.

Dutch Premier Jan de Quay and four members of his cabinet excoriated Bunker's work as they presented a memorandum to the Second Chamber of the States-General, the lower house of the Dutch Parliament, on September 4, 1962. De Quay and his colleagues were convinced that the United States had double-crossed the Dutch Government and the Papuans of West New Guinea.

Bunker's handiwork in the sell-out of West New Guinea to Sukarno's Communist regime was no surprise to those who have followed Bunker's diplomatic career from the days when Dean Acheson first brought him into the State Department in 1951 and down to Bunker's 1967 appointment as Ambassador to South Vietnam. Conceivably it could be coincidental that wherever Bunker has served as Ambassador there has been a distinct rise of anti-United States sentiment and/or a noticeable increase of Communist strength – Argentina, India, Italy, the Dominican Republic, Nepal, and the Organization of American States. He must also be given

264

credit for saving the Communist regime of Yemen from the wrath of Saudi Arabia's King (then Crown Prince) Faisal.

Bunker has long had an affinity for leftwing internationalist groups. He has been a trustee of the Institute for International Social Research, Education in World Affairs, Experiment in International Living, the Council on World Affairs, the Foreign Policy Association, and the Institute of International Education. He has also been affiliated with Clarence Streit's Atlantic Union, working towards a political merger of Western Europe and the United States, as a major step towards world government; the radical New School for Social Research; and, he is a non-resident member of the Council on Foreign Relations, the informal supra-State Department of the United States.

JAMES MacGREGOR BURNS was born on August 3, 1918 in Melrose, Massachusetts, son of Mildred Bruce and Robert Burns. He married Janet Thompson. He is an alumnus of Williams College (B.A., 1939) and Harvard University (M.A. and Ph.D., 1947). He has also studied at the National Institute for Public Affairs (1939-1940) and at the London School of Economics (1949).

In 1941 and 1942, Burns was an instructor in political science at Williams College. In 1942 and 1943, he was an executive secretary within the National War Labor Board. In 1947, he returned to the political science faculty at Williams as an assistant professor. Later he became an associate professor, professor, and chairman of the political science department. He has held the A. Baston Hepburn chair of political science and the James Phinney Baxter chair of history and public affairs.

Among Burns' better known books are *Roosevelt: The Lion and the Fox; John Kennedy; A Political Profile;* and *The Deadlock of Democracy.*

In the past four national Democratic conventions, Burns has been a delegate from Massachusetts. He was an unsuccessful candidate for Congress in 1958. Burns was a campaigner for, and an ardent devotee of, John F. Kennedy. And, in his writings, he is the complete Fabian socialist, as befits his activity in Americans for Democratic Action. In his promotion of Lyndon Johnson's candidacy in 1964, he was not a bit subtle in his call for a socialist revolution: "Our need is not to win an election or a leader; we must win a government."

In 1963, Burns visited the Soviet Union under the auspices of the Soviet Academy of Sciences and the American Council of Learned Societies. He gave a series of four lectures to Soviet historians on "FDR and World War II" and "FDR and the New Deal." Upon his return to this country, Burns said he had been received very politely and had encountered no incidents or hostility. His experiences should have been no surprise since he was merely extolling the virtues of one of the all-time patsies and heroes of the Soviet Union.

[DONALD] ANGUS CAMERON was born on December 25, 1908 in Indianapolis, son of Minnie Groeschel and Joseph Cameron. He married Sheiler Smith. He is an alumnus of DePauw University (A.B., 1930).

In 1931, Cameron began his lifetime career in the book publishing business. From 1931 until 1938, he was a sales promotion manager for Hurty-Peck Company of Indianapolis (1931-1934) and Bobbs-Merrill Company in Indianapolis (1934-1938). Briefly in 1938, he was

265

an editor for Bobbs-Merrill. Later that year, he joined Little, Brown and Company and, over the next thirteen years, held positions as editor, editor-in-chief, secretary of the corporation, vice president, and director.

Cameron testified under oath before the Senate Internal Security Subcommittee that he resigned from Little, Brown and Co. because his associates in that company wanted to censor his outside activities. Cameron's activities had been publicized in September, 1951 in the pages of *Counterattack,* an anti-Communist newsletter. (On the other side of the coin, Clem Hodges, writing in the Communist Party magazine, *Masses and Mainstream* of November 1, 1951, came to Cameron's defense in an article, "Burning Books, Banning Authors – Crisis in Publishing.") In 1948, Cameron was treasurer of the National Wallace for President Committee, chairman in Massachusetts of the Progressive Party, and a financial contributor to Wallace's campaign – a campaign thoroughly endorsed by the Communist Party whose leaders found Wallace to be an ideal front-man for their program. *Counterattack* also reported accurately that Cameron had been a trustee of the Samuel Adams School ("adjunct of the Communist Party"); a member of the board of directors of the Progressive Citizens of America, which – in California, at least – was found to be a Communist front; and, a member of the Committee of Welcome for Rev. Hewlett ("Red Dean") Johnson, England's most notorious pro-Soviet apologist among the clergy.

Cameron had also been affiliated with the Civil Rights Congress ("subversive and Communist"); the World Peace Congress in Paris in 1949 ("Communist front"); the Waldorf Peace Conference ("Communist front"); the American Continental Congress for Peace ("another phase in the Communist 'peace' campaign, aimed at consolidating anti-American forces throughout the Western Hemisphere"); the Committee for a Democratic Far Eastern Policy ("Communist"); the National Federation for Constitutional Liberties ("subversive and Communist" – "under [Communist] Party domination and headed by responsible Party functionaries"); the National Conference on American Policy in China and the Far East ("Communist"); and the National Youth Assembly against Universal Military Training ("Communist-promoted project"). When Communist Howard Fast was jailed for contempt of Congress, Cameron spoke on Fast's behalf at a rally held by *Masses and Mainstream,* a Communist magazine. When the Congress of Industrial Organizations (CIO) planned to expel Communist Party-directed unions, Cameron signed an open letter in protest of the plan. In 1951, ex-Communist Louis Budenz testified under oath, before the Senate Internal Security Subcommittee, that he had known Cameron to be a member of the Communist Party. On May 7, 1953 and March 9, 1955, Cameron was given the opportunity in SISS hearings to contradict Budenz. But, Cameron pleaded his rights under the protection of the first, fifth, and ninth amendments to the Constitution of the United States.

In 1953, Cameron began a six-year career as an independent publisher. He organized the publishing firm of Cameron and Kahn. (Albert H. Kahn was a Communist at the time.)

In 1954, Cameron organized Cameron Associates and Liberty Book Club. (In both of these enterprises, Carl Marzani was an officer. Marzani had been convicted in a district court in Washington, D.C. on charges of concealing his Communist Party membership when applying for a government job.)

In 1955, the firm of Cameron and Kahn made its greatest impact on the American scene when it published Harvey Matusow's *False Witness.*

In 1950, Harvey Matusow went voluntarily to the Federal Bureau of Investigation, offering to serve as an informant on Communist Party activities and personnel. Over the next two years, Matusow testified at length as a friendly witness before the House Committee on Un-American Activities and the Senate Internal Security Subcommittee. The Department of Justice cross-checked individuals identified by Matusow and found corroborating evidence in ninety per cent of the cases. Of the remaining ten per cent, no information was found to disprove the accuracy of Matusow's identifications. Not a single individual identified by Matusow before HCUA or SISS ever appeared before either committee to dispute Matusow's identification.

After Matusow's testimony was printed by HCUA and SISS as a part of the public record, the Communist Party decided to have Matusow recant his testimony through means of a book – *False Witness.* The book was prepared under the direction of Communist Albert Kahn and Nathan Witt. (Witt, too, was a Communist and had been a member of the Harold Ware cell, along with Alger Hiss.) The SISS, after extensive hearings in 1955, concluded that *False Witness* was "a confection of falsehoods" and part of a campaign that was "a collective product of the Communist conspiracy," and that the campaign had as its immediate goal "to secure new trials in the cases of Communist leaders who had been convicted. Its broader and long-range goals were to discredit Government witnesses, the Department of Justice, the courts, the FBI, and con-

gressional investigative committees, and thus to immobilize the prosecution and investigation of the Communist conspiracy."

After Matusow agreed to cooperate with the Communists in the production of *False Witness,* he was contacted by the firm of Cameron and Kahn. The book was financed by Communists, distributed through Communist-controlled unions, and publicized in the Communist press throughout the United States and Europe. The Communists were not the only ones to hail the book's appearance. Cameron and Kahn solicited and received early boosts for *False Witness* from columnists Joseph and Stewart Alsop, Drew Pearson, and Murray Kempton of the *New York Post.* None of those involved in the Matusow conspiracy were ever punished. Angus Cameron, as a matter of fact, moved ahead in the publishing world. In 1959, he became an editor in the large publishing house of Alfred A. Knopf, Inc. And, in 1967, Cameron was named senior editor of Knopf's, which is now a Random House subsidiary.

ERWIN CANHAM was born on February 13, 1904 in Auburn, Maine, son of Elizabeth Gowell and Vincent Canham. He married Thelma Hart. He is an alumnus of Bates College (B.A., 1925). He also received a B.A. and M.A. from Oxford University where he was a Rhodes scholar.

Since 1925, Canham has been on the staff of the *Christian Science Monitor.* He has worked as a reporter, general news editor, special correspondent, managing editor, and editor. He is presently editor-in-chief of the *Monitor* and president of the Christian Science Church. He has been president of the U.S. Chamber of Commerce and has held minor positions with the United States delegation to the United Nations. He is the author of *New Frontiers for Freedom* and *Commitment to Freedom*.

In his writings and public utterances, Canham gives every indication of being a dedicated statist, socialist, and internationalist. *Human Events* once described him as a super-liberal, which is probably as good a description of him as any. He has been a vigorous critic of congressional committees investigating subversive activities. He has long been an advocate of U.S. diplomatic recognition for Red China. He is a pacifist.

It is ironical that Canham, who has proven to be a foe of capitalism, an apologist for socialism, and an ignoramus on Communism should have been president of the U.S. Chamber of Commerce.

JAMES B. CAREY was born on August 12, 1911 in Philadelphia, son of Margaret Longhery and John Carey. He married Margaret McCormick. He was an evening student at Drexel Institute (1929-1931) and the Wharton Evening School of the University of Pennsylvania (1931-1932).

From 1929 until 1934, Carey was an electrical worker. In 1933, he became active in unions and would hold executive positions in various unions until his ouster in 1965 after fifteen years as president of the International Union of Electrical, Radio and Machine Workers of America, AFL-CIO. Between 1933 and 1950, Carey was president of the Radio and Allied Trades; general organizer for the American Federation of Labor; national secretary and secretary-treasurer of the Congress of Industrial Organizations; and, president of the United Electrical, Radio and Machine Workers of America. He was also a vice president of the AFL-CIO.

Carey was close to every White House Administration from Roosevelt to Johnson. Positions he held included: membership on the production planning board of the Office of Production Management (1941); membership on the Presidential Commission on Civil Rights (1946); membership on the Presidential Nonpartisan Commission (1947); adviser to the Economic Cooperation Administration (1948); labor representative on the Commission on Judicial and Congressional Salaries (1953); membership on the labor advisory committee of the Foreign Operations Administration (1954); and, membership on the Commission on White House Fellows (1964).

In 1958, Carey was a member of the foreign policy and labor policy advisory committees of the Democratic National Committee. He has been a national officer of the Americans for Democratic Action, the center of the radical left in American politics; the Workers Defense League, a group that defended political undesirables who were subject to deportation; and, the League for Industrial Democracy (socialist).

Carey has been affiliated with the American League for Democracy and Intellectual Freedom ("Communist front" – "subversive and unAmerican"); the American Congress for Peace and Democracy ("Communist front"); the American Peace Mobilization ("subversive and Communist"); the American Student Union ("Communist front"); the American Youth Congress ("subversive and Communist"); the Committee for Peace through World Cooperation ("Communist front"); the Greater New York Emergency Conference on Inalienable Rights ("Communist front"); the International Workers Order ("subversive and Communist"); the Jewish People's Committee ("subversive and Communist"); the Joint Committee for Trade Union Rights ("Communist front"); the League of American Writers ("subversive and Communist); the National Citizens Political Action Committee ("Communist front"); the Negro People's Committee to Aid Spanish Democracy ("Communist front"); the New York Tom Mooney Committee ("Communist front"); the Southern Conference for Human Welfare ("Communist front"); the Washington Committee for Democratic Action ("headed by responsible [Communist] Party functionaries"); and, the World Youth Congress ("Communist front").

In 1959, over the Voice of America, Carey suggested the formation of a new world federation of trade unions to include unions in Communist-bloc countries and Communist-controlled labor groups in other countries.

STOKELY CARMICHAEL was born on June 29, 1941 in Port-of-Spain, Trinidad, son of Adolphus and Lynette Carmichael. When Stokely was eleven years of age, he came to the United States to live with his parents who were then permanent residents of this country. By 1953, both of Stokely's parents had become citizens which fact gave him derivative American citizenship at the age of twelve. He attended and graduated from the Bronx High School of Science in New York City. He is an alumnus of Howard University (A.B., 1964). He married Miriam Makeba.

When Carmichael was a high school student, he began to develop his interest in leftism by studying and absorbing the writings of Marx and associating with young Socialists.

In 1960, Carmichael's interest turned toward activism in so-called civil rights demonstrations. He began this career at a sit-in demonstration in Virginia. In 1961, he went on a "freedom ride" in Mississippi which resulted in a jail sentence of forty-nine days for him. By mid-1966, he had been jailed twenty-seven times. And it was in 1966 that Carmichael became a prominent national figure when he was elected to be head of the Student Nonviolent Coordinating Committee (Snick) which had been organized in 1960 at the urging of Martin Luther King Jr.

Snick, as the most militant racist organization among Negroes, was the ideal front for Carmichael. As summer follows spring, riots ensued when Carmichael spoke — Puerto Rico; Selma and Prattville, Alabama; Nashville; Atlanta; and, other southern cities and towns. He helped to organize the first Black Panther party in Mississippi. Later, he would do the same in New York City. He became a familiar sight on campuses (Texas Southern University, Vanderbilt University, Howard University, the University of California, Western Michigan University, and others), at church gatherings, and even at high schools. His press conferences commanded the attention of the most prestigious news media. And wherever he spoke he brought his messages of hate, racism, anti-Americanism, and pro-Communism.

In 1966, Carmichael began to harangue his audiences with his call for "Black Power." That phrase epitomized his virulent hatred of all whites and he reminded his listeners that he never knew a white man he could trust. "Move on over, or we'll move over you," he warned the whites.

To Mississippians, Carmichael said: "We want black power! Every courthouse in Mississippi ought to be burned down to get rid of the dirt." To a Negro audience in Boston, he advised: "I don't ever want to hear you apologizing for a black man. Don't you apologize for anyone who's driven to throw Molotov cocktails. And don't you call them riots, call them rebellions, for that's what they are." His counsel for Washingtonian Negroes was: "I don't think black people ought to wait to get the vote .... You ought to get together and tell the [white] man that if you don't get the vote you're going to burn down this city. Tell him, 'if we don't get the vote you're not going to have a Washington, D.C.' "

In Cleveland, Carmichael urged Negroes to defy Selective Service by not registering for the draft. For Clevelanders who were still reeling from the effects of diastrous Negro riots, Carmichael observed: "They're building stores in Cleveland with no windows. It just means we have to move from Molotov cocktails to dynamite."

Both before and after Carmichael assumed leadership of Snick, he exploded the myth of "non-violence" which had become the favorite disarming cliché of Negro racists and their white supporters. In February 1966, in California during the course of an interview, he said: "This nonviolence bit is just a philanthropic handout. I don't see why people keep thinking about that. The violence is inevitable. I don't try to stop the fight. I try to prepare the people I am organizing so that when the right time comes they will be able to win it. Our country does not run on reason; it is run on violence. That's the reality of how things are done here. It is to my benefit to get the Negro out on the streets to stop the machine which is keeping me from my rights. Whether they do it by marching, singing, dancing or fighting is irrelevant." On another occasion, he threw aside all caution as he ranted: "Any time they give a black man

a gun and tell him to shoot his enemy and he don't shoot Lurleen and George and little junior [the Wallaces], he's a fool. Lurleen Wallace is your enemy. These white helmeted cops are your enemies." As leader of Snick, Carmichael said: "I tried it [non-violence] for five years and now he [a policeman] is no longer going to beat his humanity into my head. If he touches me, I'm going to kill him." And, if that wasn't plain enough, he emphasized that he was "not opposed to violence, nor have I ever been.

In 1967, Carmichael went to work making good his promise that Snick wanted to link itself with leftist forces in other areas of the world. He traveled to Tanzania, Egypt, Algeria, Syria, Sweden, Spain, England, France, North Vietnam, Guinea, Czecho-Slovakia, and Cuba. In France, he cried: "We do not want peace in Vietnam. We want the Vietnamese people to defeat the United States." In Guinea, he said: "We will win our rights or we are going to burn the country [U.S.A.] down to the ground." In London, he boasted: "In Newark we applied tactics of the guerrillas. We are preparing groups of urban guerrillas for our defense in the cities. The price of these rebellions is a high price that one must pay. This fight is not going to be a simple street meeting. It is going to be a fight to the death." From Syria, Carmichael was quoted as saying that American Negroes were not fighting for integration, but "to crush the capitalist system of the United States." And he called on America's enemies abroad to support the Negroes' objective of an "armed struggle within America." But it was in Cuba in 1967 where Carmichael was at his peak of virulence.

Cuba's Communist leader Fidel Castro welcomed Carmichael to Cuba as

270

"the representative of the Negro people of the United States." Carmichael responded by hailing the virtues of Castro, his hatchetman, Ché Guevara, and the Cuban revolution. He especially praised Castro for standing up to the United States. He also took time out to hail Ché Guevara "my fellow comrade wherever you are," and said, "Afro-Americans in the United States have a great deal of admiration for you. We eagerly await your writings in order to digest them and to plan our tactics based on them."

Carmichael's visit to Cuba coincided with the Castro regime's celebration of its revolutionary beginnings (July 26) and with a conference of the Communists' Latin American Solidarity Organization (LASO). Carmichael arrived as an observer to LASO but was soon named an honorary delegate so that he could deliver a fifteen-minute speech to the conference. And Carmichael took advantage of the opportunity to call for a revolution to make the Western hemisphere one country: "Our [American Negroes'] struggle is not confined to the boundaries of the United States. We are for a truly United States of America from Tierra del Fuego to Alaska." As he stressed the need for unity between American Negroes and Latin Americans, Carmichael quoted his hero, Ché Guevara: "The next Vietnam will be on this continent, perhaps in Bolivia, Guatemala, Brazil, or the Dominican Republic." Said Carmichael: "Yankee imperialism has existed too long. We [Negroes] are ready to destroy it from the inside. We hope you [Latin Americans] are ready to destroy it from the outside. We must join those who are for armed struggle throughout the world . . . . As we develop our revolutionary conscience, we must begin to develop urban guerrilla warfare. We are ready to

meet the savagery of the white United States with arms." In an earlier interview, Carmichael had used Guevara's words as a springboard to his own call for warfare in the United States: "We must internationalize our struggle and if we are going to turn into reality the words of Ché to create two, three, and more Viet Nams, we must recognize that Detroit and New York are also Viet Nam."

During a press conference in Cuba, Carmichael made what was probably his most brazen threat when he said that American Negroes "are taking the offensive now. They want to settle the score and will kill first and aim for the head. We must take our vengeance against the leaders of the United States. We don't know if our people are ready yet, but our list is ready: McNamara, Dean Rusk, Johnson, etc."

From his Cuban forum, Carmichael spoke to American Negroes as he remarked that "the United States has taught us how to kill. Our brothers returning from Vietnam are going to use that training well in the cities of the United States." He made no secret of his hopes that guerrilla warfare would devastate America as he advised that Negro guerrillas "must develop a consciousness so that when people who are struggling get killed, the retaliation will be against the leaders of the West. Let us develop a consciousness that when they touch one guerrilla, Lyndon Johnson, Dean Rusk, Robert McNamara and Harold Wilson must pay the price. We are not waiting for them to kill us. We will come to kill them first or rather, we are working towards that goal. We have no alternative but to use aggressive armed force, violence, in order to own the land, houses and stores inside our communities and to control the politics of those communities."

When Carmichael returned to the United States from his world travels, federal officials relieved him of his passport since he had made an unauthorized visit to North Vietnam. But a few months later, the passport was returned to him when he said that he was going on a honeymoon and promised not to visit unauthorized countries.

In August 1968, Carmichael and Snick came to a parting of the ways. Officials of Snick said that the organization and Carmichael were moving in different directions. Carmichael's explanation was that political differences had caused the rift. But whatever the real reason, Lester McKinnie, head of Snick in Washington, denied that Snick had renounced Carmichael's equating black power with black violence.

Carmichael left quite a legacy for his Snick successors: a complete tie-in with the Black Panthers who are dedicated to warfare against whites throughout the United States; a protocol of cooperation with the Pro-Independence Movement of Puerto Rico, a Communist group willing to join Snick in their "common struggle against U.S. imperialism"; and, a direct relationship with the Revolutionary Action Movement, which is "dedicated to the overthrow of the capitalist system in the United States by violence if necessary." And Carmichael gave Snick its rallying cry: "To hell with America . . . [which is] racist from top to bottom, from left to right."

WILLIAM GEORGE CARR was born on June 1, 1901 in Northampton, England, son of Alice Bailey and Alfred Carr. He came to the United States in 1915. He married Elizabeth Vaughan. He studied at the University of California (1920-1923) and is an alumnus of Stanford University (A.B., 1924; A.M., 1926; Ph.D., 1929).

In 1924 and 1925, Carr was a high school teacher in California. In 1926 and 1927, he taught education at Pacific University. In 1928 and 1929, he was research director of the California Teachers Association.

In 1929, Carr went to work for the National Education Association as assistant director of research. Over the years, he became director of research, associate secretary, and, since 1952, executive secretary. He also lectured in summer sessions at Stanford University, the University of Michigan, the University of California (Berkeley), the University of Oregon, the University of California (Los Angeles), and the University of Pennsylvania. He has written or contributed to at least a dozen books on education including *Education for World Citizenship; Education and the People's Peace; Only by Understanding;* and *One World in the Making.* He has held minor positions with the United States delegation to the United Nations.

Under Carr's direction, the National Education Association has been the foremost group in this country promoting socialism and internationalism through educational systems. The NEA is also the most powerful lobbying force behind federal intervention, financially and ideologically, in the educational processes.

HODDING CARTER was born on February 3, 1907 in Hammond, Louisiana, son of Irma Dutarte and William Carter. He married Bette Werlein. He is an alumnus of Bowdoin College (B.A., 1927). He also studied at Columbia University's School of Journalism (1927-1928) and Tulane University (1928-1929). He was a Nieman fellow at Harvard University, in 1939, and he has held a Guggenheim fellowship.

In 1929, Carter was a reporter for the *New Orleans Item-Tribune*. In 1930, he was a night bureau manager for United Press in New Orleans. In 1931 and 1932, he was manager of the Associated Press bureau in Jackson, Mississippi. From 1932 until 1936, he was editor and publisher of the *Hammond Daily Courier* and held the same positions, from 1936 until 1938, with the *Greenville* (Miss.) *Delta Star*. In 1939, he was editor for a brief time of the radically red *PM* in New York.

Since 1939, Carter has been the editor and publisher of the *Greenville* (Miss.) *Delta Democrat-Times*. In the meantime, he has been, since 1962, a writer-in-residence at Tulane University and, from 1951 until 1961, he was a member of the Pulitzer Prize advisory board. He has written more than a dozen books, almost all of which deal with the South.

Early in his journalistic career, Carter decided to become a combination flaming liberal-scalawag, defending the federal government's intrusion, through all of its branches, into the social and economic life of the southern States.

Carter has been affiliated with Clarence Streit's Atlantic Union, working towards a political merger of Western Europe and the United States, as a major step towards world government; Arthur Larson's National Council for Civic Responsibility, an election year's drive by the Democrat Party against anti-Communists; and, Littell's Institute for American Democracy, hysterical successor to Larson's abortive NCCR. Carter was also a founder of Americans for Democratic Action, the center of the radical left in American politics.

CLIFFORD CASE was born on April 16, 1904 in Franklin Park, New York, son of Jeannette Benedict and Clifford Case. He married Ruth M. Smith. He is an alumnus of Rutgers University (A.B., 1925) and Columbia University (LL.B., 1928).

In 1928, Case was admitted to the New York bar and joined the law firm of Simpson, Thatcher & Bartlett in New York City. He was an associate in the firm until 1939 and, from 1939 until 1953, was a member of the firm.

In 1937, Case became actively involved in Republican party politics. He sought and received elections to the Rahway, New Jersey Common Council and served on it for five years. In 1942, he was elected as Representative to New Jersey's State Assembly, where he served two terms. From 1945 until 1953, he served in the U.S. House of Representatives.

In 1953, Case resigned from Congress. He accepted an offer to become the first president of the Ford Foundation's Fund for the Republic. He later explained that the position "challenged my imagination." Case had either little imagination or his imagination was easily satisfied, because he quit that job within eight months.

In 1954, Case decided to return to politics and seek the Republican nomination for the U.S. Senate. New Jersey's Treasurer, Walter Margetts, also sought the Republican nomination but a little arm-twisting by the White House clique convinced Mr. Margetts to realize his political ambitions otherwise. Case was handpicked by Dwight Eisenhower or whoever was practicing White House puppetry. President Eisenhower said that he wanted Case in the Senate. Vice President Nixon went to New Jersey and spoke throughout the State for Case.

During his years in Congress, Case had emerged as a "progressive" Republican, which put him not only leftward of most of his Republican colleagues but even to the left of most Democrats in the Congress. He was one of the original crowd of "draft-Ike" Republicans, many of whom had studiously avoided the Republican label throughout their public lives. In the House, Case became conspicuous by his strong stand against the House Committee on Un-American Activities and also by his suddenly discovered concern for so-called civil rights legislation. He voted a pro-organized labor line and was one of the first Republicans ever endorsed by the ultraliberal Americans for Democratic Action (later he would become a pet endorsee of the equally ultra-liberal National Committee for an Effective Congress). He especially endeared himself to President Dwight Eisenhower and Vice President Richard Nixon when he joined the braying leftwing Republicans who were attacking Senator Joseph R. McCarthy. But Case's flagrant leftism and the mighty political influence of the White House almost proved inadequate during the 1954 campaign. However, an ill-advised third party candidate – a conservative – obtained 35,000 votes and thereby undoubtedly but unwittingly threw the election to Case whose margin of victory was only 3,300 votes out of more than a million cast.

In the U.S. Senate, Case merely added a sheen to the leftist record he had established in the House. But his repetitious labors did not go unrewarded. In 1960, fifty Washington columnists and correspondents voted Case as one of the Senate's ablest men – which is more a reflection upon the press than on Case. And, in 1960, when Case sought re-election, Eisenhower and Nixon went overboard for their old friend.

Before Case could be re-elected, he had to win the Republican nomination from the opposition of Robert Morris, who was avowedly and undeniably a conservative. Morris had gained prominence as Counsel for the Senate Internal Security Subcommittee, a post he resigned in 1958. And for two years, Morris had campaigned vigorously to win support of organizational Republicans throughout New Jersey and he had met with some success. In many instances, when Morris could not get one of these organization men to support him, he was able to get a promise of neutrality in the Republican primary. Such was the case with Eisenhower's Secretary of Labor James P. Mitchell, a very prominent and influential New Jersey Republican.

Before the primary campaign was over, however, Morris found himself being trampled by a herd of G.O.P. elephants. Ranged on Case's side with slanted contributions were *Time* magazine, the Columbia Broadcasting System, the *New York Herald Tribune,* and the *Newark Evening News* – a fair cross-section of modern Republican influence. To Case's campaign chest went generous and well-publicized financial contributions from Secretary of State Christian Herter; Gabriel Hauge, a close friend of Vice President Nixon and a former assistant to Eisenhower on economic affairs; John Hay Whitney, owner of the *New York Herald Tribune;* and, Henry Luce of *Time* magazine. Then Secretary of Labor James Mitchell announced on the eve of the election that he and his wife had cast their absentee ballots for Case (a curious way of maintaining his neutrality pledge made to Morris).

In the course of the campaign, Morris' religion (Catholicism) became an issue for smears. *Time* magazine "reported" that Morris had been a longtime lieutenant and key aide of Senator Joseph R. McCarthy – which Morris never was, but "guilt-by-association," even without foundation in truth, was not beyond Luce's *Time*. And, since no campaign of conservative versus liberal would be complete without Drew Pearson, that merry-go-rounder produced one of his dirtier smears in a piece that was widely published in New Jersey — even in papers that ordinarily did not carry Pearson's column. To round out Case's campaign, the *Newark Evening News* portrayed him as an underdog allegedly on a purge list of the Teamsters' Union boss, Jimmy Hoffa, who was then in the midst of some unsavory publicity. (The fact that Teamsters' Union officials were campaigning for Case in New Jersey simply proved that in 1960 politics were as dirty as ever.)

Robert Morris was swamped in the primary returns by almost a 2-to-1 margin, and Case has since become — apparently — a fixture in the U.S. Senate. He is still the spear-carrier for Americans for Democratic Action, the National Committee for an Effective Congress, and organized labor. His support for so-called civil rights legislation and extreme socialist measures of all sorts almost puts him beyond the pale of major party labels. On the Vietnam War, Case has demonstrated simplicity and callousness. He offers as a solution to the Communist aggression the withdrawal of United States forces. His reason: no nation — in this instance South Vietnam — has a right to an independent existence unless it can defend itself. This alone should brand as a travesty Case's presence on the Senate Foreign Relations Committee.

EMANUEL CELLER was born on May 6, 1888 in Brooklyn, New York, son of Josephine Muller and Henz Celler. He married Stella Baar. He is an alumnus of Columbia University (A.B., 1910; LL.B., 1912).

Celler began the practice of law in New York City in 1912. In 1922, he was elected as a Democrat to the House of Representatives and has served there ever since.

Celler's affiliations have included the American Committee for Protection of Foreign Born [Americans] ("subversive and Communist" — "one of the oldest auxiliaries of the Communist Party in the United States" — under the "complete domination" of the Communist Party); the American Committee to Save Refugees ("Communist enterprise"); the American Committee for Yugoslav Relief ("subversive and Communist"); the American Slav Congress ("subversive and Communist"); the Committee for a Democratic Far Eastern Policy ("Communist"); the Exiled Writers Committee ("Communist enterprise"); the American Fund for Public Service ("a major source for the financing of Communist Party enterprises"); the Greater New York Emergency Conference on Inalienable Rights ("Communist front"); the Joint Anti-fascist Refugee Committee ("subversive and Communist"); the League of American Writers ("subversive and Communist"); the United American Artists ("Communist front"); and, the United American Spanish Aid Committee ("Communist"). He has also been affiliated with the United World Federalists (the organization's program is a very serious threat to American sovereignty of all free nations).

As Chairman of the powerful House Judiciary Committee during the Eisenhower, Kennedy, and Johnson Administrations, Celler has been a consistent collaborator of the extreme left wing of the federal judiciary, blocking any and all legislative attempts to halt judicial usurpation of congressional and state governmental powers. He has been a vigorous and successful foe of anti-subversion legislation and investigations. His voting record marks him as an absolute socialist.

MARQUIS CHILDS was born on March 17, 1903 in Clinton, Iowa, son of Lilian Marquis and William Childs. He married Lué Prentiss. He is an alumnus of the University of Wisconsin (A.B., 1923) and the University of Iowa (A.M., 1925). Childs began his career in journalism with *United Press* in 1923. From 1926 until 1944, he was with the *St. Louis Post-Dispatch.* From 1944 until 1954, he wrotee a column for *United Feature Syndicate.* In 1954, he became a special correspondent for the *St. Louis Post-Dispatch* and the Washington correspondent for the same journal in 1962.

Childs has written or co-authored more than a dozen books. He has lectured at the University of Oregon and Columbia University's School of Journalism. He is a non-resident member of the Council on Foreign Relations, the informal supra-State Department of the United States; and, he was a founder of Americans for Democratic Action, the center of the radical left in American politics.

Whether in books or in newspaper writings, Childs has never hidden his bent for socialist principles, and his column is little more than an exposition of the current ADA line. He was an ardent admirer of Roosevelt's New Deal and of whatever socialist embellishments have been added in subsequent administrations. Apparently Childs was affiliated with only two Communist fronts (the Washington Friends of Spanish Democracy and the Coordinating Committee to Lift the Embargo) but he has been a vigorous critic of anti-Communists and congressional committees investigating Communist activities. The late Senator Joseph R. McCarthy was a particular villain in Childs' eyes which may have been due in some part to McCarthy's publicizing that Childs had supported Communists William Remington and Alger Hiss and had bitterly attacked General Douglas MacArthur's headquarters staff for exposing Communist agent Agnes Smedley.

FRANK CHURCH was born on July 25, 1924 in Boise, Idaho, son of Laura Bilderback and Frank Church. He married Bethine Clark. He is an alumnus of Stanford University (B.A., 1947; LL.B., 1950).

Church was admitted to the Idaho bar in 1950 and he engaged in private law practice in Boise until 1956. From 1952 until 1954, he was state chairman of the Young Democrats of Idaho. In 1956, he was elected to the United States Senate. In 1960, he was temporary chairman and keynote speaker of the Democratic National Convention. He was re-elected to the Senate in 1962.

Church's election to the Senate in 1956 was attributable to the Republican incumbent Herman Welker's complacency and the strong support Church received from Walter Reuther's Committee on Political Education (COPE). Before he had completed his first senatorial term, Church proved to be one of the most reliable rubber stamps for organized labor. Nor did his ultra-liberalism end there.

In general, Church votes right down the line for welfare statism. He favors federal handouts to the States for the aged, the blind, the disabled, dependent children, public health, hospital construction, and control of water pollution. He is a complete devotee of federal handouts for education: school lunch programs, vocational rehabilitation, school construction, subsidies for students.

Church carries his ultra-liberalism into the area of foreign policy which is especially pertinent since he is a member of the Senate Foreign Relations Committee. He readily admits to being a confirmed internationalist, a position certified by his close adherence to the views of Chairman J. William Fulbright of the Foreign Relations Committee.

Church is a strong supporter of the United Nations, foreign aid programs, and the Peace Corps. He has gone out of his way to extol the virtues of NATO as a bulwark against Communism yet he downgrades the threat of Communism as he sees the Communist world falling to pieces. But perhaps his chief contribution to foreign policy has been his anti-anti-Communist stand in such areas as Algeria, Yugoslavia, and the Congo during the Tshombe regime.

Most puzzling of all is Church's attitude toward nuclear warfare. Unsurprisingly he is a scaremonger. He warns of a possible nuclear disaster but at the same time believes that western Europe should arm itself with a genuine nuclear-deterrent capability in a project which should be encouraged and supported by the United States. He believes that such a development would allow the United States to withdraw its forces from Europe. And, under such conditions, the United States would enjoy a stronger Atlantic partnership and the "artifical" division of Europe between East and West might break down.

On the Vietnam War, Church has been on the side of the most dovish in the Senate. He holds to the thesis that it is a civil war where from the beginning the South Vietnamese were fighting only against the Viet Cong. He admits that the Viet Cong — somewhere along the way — began to receive support from North Vietnam and Red China but the nature of the war did not change. In his view, it remained a civil conflict. For the United States, Church advocates a political settlement of the war. He discounts any thought that Red China might wish to invade Southeast Asia and he refuses to believe that Ho chi Minh takes orders from Communist leaders outside North Vietnam. Central to all of Church's dovish views is his insistence that Communism is too "poor" a system to take over the world.

It is understandable that Church, during the election year of 1968, has received the complete endorsement and active support of the National Committee for an Effective Congress. The NCEC, of impeccable ultra-liberal credentials, places Church in the category of Senators Wayne Morse, J. William Fulbright, Ernest Gruening, Clifford Case, John Sherman Cooper, George McGovern, Gaylord Nelson, and George Aiken — wheelhorses of the senatorial left.

JOSEPH S. CLARK was born on October 21, 1901 in Philadelphia, son of Kate Avery and Joseph Clark. He is an alumnus of Harvard University (B.S., 1923) and the University of Pennsylvania (LL.B., 1926).

In 1926, Clark was admitted to the Pennsylvania bar and began his practice of law, which continued until 1951, interrupted only by his four-year wartime service in the U.S. Army Air Force. In 1934 and 1935, he was a deputy attorney general of Pennsylvania. From 1949 until 1951, he was city controller in Philadelphia. In 1952, he was elected mayor of Philadelphia – the first Democrat to hold the office in sixty-eight years. In 1956, he resigned the mayoralty to run for the U.S. Senate seat, held by the one-term incumbent, seventy-three-year old James H. Duff. Clark's victory margin was 18,000 votes – 4,500,000 were cast.

During his two terms in the Senate, Clark's modern liberalism has made most of his colleagues in the Americans for Democratic Action appear to be arch conservatives. By any standards, he must be considered the Senate's all-time champion advocate of big spending on government boondoggles. He believes that anyone who does not believe in deficit federal spending is hopelessly out of date – by at least forty years. He is such a staunch believer in big government that he claims any reduction in the monstrous federal governmental powers and controls would result in anarchy. And, in his topsy-turvy world, the expansion of federal government does not lead to curtailment of individual freedoms. He once defined his type of liberal "as one who believes in using the full force of government for the advancement of social, political and economic justice at the municipal, state, national, and international levels."

During the Kennedy Administration when there was a move under way to get Chester Bowles out as Under Secretary of State, Clark rushed to the defense of his fellow ADAer and added somewhat to his definition of a liberal and, as an aside, gave an estimate as to how many of his Senate colleagues were in his good graces: "It is suggested that one reason why it is necessary to get rid of Mr. Bowles is that he is alleged to be a devotee of the planned economy and welfare state. If Mr. Bowles is to be indicted for such views it will be neces-

sary to indict about three-fourths of the Senators on this side [Democrats], and about one-fourth of the Senators on the other. If we do not get more planning into our economy and go forward with the welfare measures advocated by the President of the United States, the country will be in a far worse condition than it otherwise would be. I should say that the majority of the Senate will heartily support the well-known views of Mr. Bowles on domestic policy. Furthermore, I am confident that one reason why the President of the United States has made the decision to retain Mr. Bowles is that, by and large, the President of the United States himself shares those views. It is said that Mr. Bowles is unpopular with the conservative wing of the Democratic Party. So are 45 other Democrats who serve in this body. I suspect their number is not confined to the Senate and the House of Representatives, but I assert also that the views of Mr. Bowles and other members of this body in that regard are shared also by the President of the United States." It may or may not have been a case of guilt-by-association, but the Clark-type liberal, Chester Bowles, was moved out of his job as Under Secretary and was sent to India as an Ambassador. Mr. Clark's legislative colleagues made no clamorous demand to keep Bowles in Washington.

On another occasion during the Kennedy Administration, Clark set out to purge the late Harry Byrd (D.-Va.) of his chairmanship of the Senate Finance Committee. Byrd had had and intended to keep an archly conservative position on government spending. Byrd's distinguished twenty-eight-year career in the Senate did not dissuade Clark from taking his purge-fight to the Senate floor, where he failed to win the support of a single other Senator. The Bowles and Byrd incidents undoubtedly helped to prompt Clark to say, at a later date, that it is "my deep conviction that the legislatures of America, local, state and national, are presently the greatest menace to the successful operation of the democratic process."

But Clark's contempt for representative government was not merely based on isolated incidents in his own Senatorial career. He long held contempt for local governments and for the entire context of the Constitution of the United States. Everywhere he turned, Clark could see the several branches of government on all levels conspiring to retard the growth of the welfare state. He despised constitutional restraints and, as is the wont with the ultra-liberal, he considered the Constitution of the United States hopelessly passé: "In a day when governmental action, if needed at all, could afford to be slow, when the 'tyrant' George III was fresh in men's minds, this original conception [constitutional restraints], favoring inaction, made good sense. Does it still do so? I think not."

To Clark, conservatives are hallucinatory but he can see hope for the days when all Americans will be his kind of liberal. The hope lies in the field of modern education: "It is significant that what used to be called 'history' is now 'social studies'. Spiritually and economically youth is conditioned to respond to a Liberal program of orderly policing of society by government, subject to the popular will, in the interests of social justice."

But for Clark there is room for improvement in the Amerian educational system. We should look elsewhere for a model. He found one: "They plan well in Russia. There someone decides where little Ivan is going to work. If, at the age of eleven, he seems unresponsive, he goes back to the collective farm. If he shows promise, his education is continued at state expense through technical school and the university. Education and incentives for different occupations are adjusted to meet the personnel needs required by the Five or Seven Year Plan."

Clark's admiration for the way Communists do things is not confined to their "educational" practices. He has a particular liking for Karl Marx's guidline: "From each according to his ability, to each according to his needs." Clark's version reads: "I realize that it is not considered nice to refer in America to anything like a 'class struggle.' That is too Marxian. In America, it is considered nicer to pretend that, 'What's good for General Motors is good for the country.' Yet the tax issue is at heart a class issue." And to resolve the class issue Clark wants the federal government to use its taxing power to "redistribute the wealth downward."

Clark has long fancied himself an expert on foreign policy and for years he practically begged for a position on the Senate Foreign Relations Committee. He finally made it in 1964. As in domestic affairs, Clark thinks Big in foreign affairs. In 1963, he submitted a paper to a seminar conducted by the ultra-leftwing, internationalist Fund for the Republic. His hopes for foreign policy were to see the role of government increase in five major international areas in the next 10 years: (1) General and complete disarmament, verified by an international disarmament organization, enforced by an internationally recruited and commanded peace force. International controversy will be settled by international judicial peace-keeping agencies with adequate budgets and power under world law to enforce their decrees. (2) An international agency, perhaps an outgrowth of the present United Nations, adequately financed with funds saved from the armament race, will direct its activities toward assisting under-developed nations to that economic breakthrough which is necessary to enable them to raise living conditions within their borders to standards acceptable in the modern world. (3) An expansion of the powers and activities of the World Bank and the International Monetary Fund will result in the establishment of a world currency as the medium of exchange for international transactions. (4) An extensive development of interlocking regional agreements for the orderly conduct of world trade, including stabilization of raw commodity prices and reduction of impediments to trade such as tariffs and quotas. (5) An international attack on the population problem . . . . " *Human Events,* November 9, 1963.

In 1964, Clark spelled out a few of these items in more detail. On the matter of disarmament, he proposed an international disarmament commission composed of the United States, the Soviet Union, Red China, and other powers. He further proposed "a permanent, international peace force of individuals rather than nations which would police and maintain disarmament." (Clark is a member of the Senate Subcommittee on Disarmament.) For universal economic boondoggling, Clark suggests an international development authority "to mitigate the vast and excessive economic disparities between the 'have' and 'have-not' nations."

With such an array of ultra-liberal credentials, it is not surprising that Clark, as he seeks re-election to the Senate in 1968, has the support of the ultra-leftist National Committee for an Effective Congress and the equally radical AFL-CIO's Committee on Political Education (COPE).

RAMSEY CLARK was born on December 18, 1927 in Dallas, Texas, son of Mary Ramsey and Tom Clark. He married Georgia Welch. He is an alumnus of the University of Texas (B.A., 1949) and the University of Chicago (A.M. and J.D., 1950).

From 1951 until 1961, Clark practiced law in Dallas, Texas. In 1961, he entered the Department of Justice as Assistant Attorney General. From 1965 until 1967, he was Deputy Attorney General. In March 1967, President Lyndon Johnson appointed Clark as Attorney General.

When Clark was appointed to the cabinet position, *Human Events* (March 11, 1967) made these perceptive comments: "There were some glum faces on Capitol Hill when Ramsey Clark, son of retiring Supreme Court Justice Tom Clark, was picked by LBJ to be U.S. Attorney General. The 39-year-old lawyer has the reputation of being a liberal. He is unalterably opposed to capital punishment, favors vigorous prosecution of the much-abused antitrust laws and has a tendency to be overly zealous is protecting the rights of criminals.

"Clark, moreover, does not seem to be too concerned about Communist activity in this country. Last year he determinedly fought enactment of the Pool bill, which would have made it a federal crime for groups in the United States to send supplies to North Viet Nam or the Viet Cong. He light-heartedly brushed off U.S. Communist activity on behalf of the Viet Cong as 'eccentric behavior.'

"Young Clark is not only vigorously opposed to using eavesdropping devices for the purpose of combatting organized crime, but he was instrumental in persuading LBJ to veto the 1966 D.C. Omnibus Crime Bill. Though this bill, aimed at holding down the soaring crime rate in the District, passed both the Senate and the House by overwhelming margins, Clark thought it dealt too harshly with suspected criminals. In this opinion he voiced arguments similar to those of ADA bigwig Joseph Rauh and the American Civil Liberties Union.

"Hence, the uneasiness among many Washington politicos over Clark's appointment."

As a matter of fact, it would be virtually impossible to find Clark assuming anything but an ultra-liberal stance on any issue. He has called for more federal handouts for education, housing, health programs, and the so-called war on poverty. He has called for the forcible elimination of segregation in housing and school patterns where such segregation has been a perfectly natural development and not enforced by state or local governments. He is in favor of civilian review boards which are a high-priority project for leftwingers so that they might hamper effective police work. He is an ardent apologist for the Supreme Court decisions which have proven to be such a boon for criminals and a hindrance to law enforcement officials. There seems to be little doubt that Clark, if he remains in office long enough, will make serious increases of federal control over state and local police forces.

HARLAN CLEVELAND was born on January 19, 1918 in New York City, son of Marian Van Buren and Stanley Cleveland. He married Lois Burton. He is an alumnus of Princeton University (A.B., 1938). He also attended Oxford University as a Rhodes scholar, in 1938 and 1939, and was an intern at the National Institute of Public Affairs, a hotbed of socialism, in 1939 and 1940. At Princeton, Cleveland was president of the Anti-War Society for three years and in the Princeton yearbook he listed himself as a "Socialist."

From 1940 until 1942, Cleveland was a writer in the information division of the Farm Security Administration, which agency was "considered so important as an incubator for Communist infiltration into other government agencies that Soviet spymaster Nathan Silvermaster had esconced himself there as Director of the Labor Division." (Frank L. Kluckhohn, *Lyndon's Legacy,* 1964, page 195.)

In 1942, Cleveland became an official of the Board of Economic Warfare and its successor, the Foreign Economic Administration. Louis Budenz, former editor of the *Daily Worker,* described the Board of Economic Warfare as a "special nesting-place for large-scale Communist colonization into governmental posts."

From 1944 until 1947, Cleveland spent most of his time in Rome. At first, he was executive director of the economic section of the Allied Control Commission, an early version of the United States foreign aid program. Then, in 1945, Cleveland became associated with UNRRA (the United Nations Relief and Rehabilitation Administration). And, in 1946 and 1947, he was deputy chief of the UNRRA mission in Italy. The head of the mission was Harold Glaser, a Soviet espionage agent. In 1947 and 1948, Cleveland also worked as director of UNRRA's program in China. Throughout Eastern Europe and China in the post-World War II years, UNRRA was financing the establishment of Communist regimes with American money.

From 1948 until 1953, Cleveland worked in the foreign aid program, under its names of Economic Cooperation Administration and the Mutual Security Agency. Cleveland would later advise the Senate Foreign Relations Committee that all U.S. foreign aid should be turned over to the United Nations which would then distribute it as United Nations foreign aid.

In 1953, Cleveland left government service and, over the next three years, he was associated as an executive editor and publisher with Max Ascoli's leftwing *Reporter* magazine.

In 1956, Cleveland became dean of the Maxwell Graduate School of Citizenship and Public Affairs at Syracuse University.

While at the Maxwell School, Cleveland found the time to publish a study, *The Theory and Practice of Foreign Aid,* written for the Special Studies Project of the Rockefeller Brothers Fund. He advocated a vast increase in U.S. foreign aid to underdeveloped countries as a means of preventing these countries from becoming Communist. It mattered not to Cleveland that the history of foreign aid proved just the contrary. Also, during his deanship, Cleveland found time to be an official at the World Brotherhood Conference on "World Tensions" at the University of Chicago. Other conference officials were such leftwing dignitaries as Paul Hoffman, Marquis Childs, Norman Cousins, Adlai Stevenson, and Ralph Bunche. As might be expected, these officials, including Cleveland, decided that the Communists were looking for peaceful coexistence; they were not interested in political subversion; they had no plans for world conquest; and, they wanted to trade with the United States (and the United States should reciprocate). The United States, on the other hand, should increase its foreign aid program and seek closer relations with all the nations in the Communist bloc.

In February 1961, Cleveland was appointed by President Kennedy as Assistant Secretary of State for International Organization Affairs and UN Affairs. The State Department's security officials investigated Cleveland's background and activities and ruled against even a temporary security clearance for him. But Secretary of State Rusk personally waived a clearance for Cleveland. During Cleveland's four years as Assistant Secretary, he showed a remarkable interest in placing old associates of Alger Hiss in responsible positions in the State Department. And, on one occasion, Cleveland had even inquired as to the prospects for the reemployment of Hiss by the government. Cleveland's sympathies for security risks was nothing new. Previously, he had interceded for eleven individuals employed in the foreign aid program when security officials were trying to remove them as security risks.

Since 1965, Cleveland, with the rank of Ambassador, has been the United States representative to NATO. His favorite line is that the Communists are mellowing, the cold war is all but over, and progress toward compromise with the Communists is being made through an East-West dialogue.

OLIVER EDMUND CLUBB was born on February 16, 1901 in South Park, Minnesota. He entered the University of Washington for undergraduate studies in 1922 and, in the following year, transferred to the University of Minnesota from which he graduated in 1927. He received a master's degree from the University of California in 1940.

In 1928, Clubb took and passed examinations for the Foreign Service and began his twenty-four-year career with the State Department. From 1929 until 1941, he held various posts in China at Peiping, Hankow, Tientsin, and Nanking. In 1941, he was assigned as consul to Saigon but was detailed temporarily to Hanoi. He was interned by the Japanese in Indochina and released in an exchange program in 1942. In 1943, he returned to China and served in Lanchow and Tihwa. From 1944 until 1950, he served as consul general at Vladivostok, U.S.S.R. (1944-1946); Mukden, Manchuria (1946-1947); and, Peiping, China (1947-1950). When all the U.S. consulate offices were closed in China in 1950, he was assigned to the State Department in Washington, D.C. and, from 1950 until 1952, he was Director of the Office of Chinese Affairs.

In 1951, Clubb was summoned to testify before the House Committee on Un-American Activities on three occasions. Clubb's experiences before the Committee are described in the *Annual Report* of HCUA for 1951: "His appearances before the committee were an outgrowth of a continuing investigation conducted by the committee staff on the basis of information supplied by Whittaker Chambers, confessed former Soviet espionage agent.

"Mr. Chambers had advised the committee that a member of the State Department's consular service in China had called at the office of the Communist magazine, *New Masses,* in the summer of 1932. Mr. Chambers said the individual had asked to see Walt Carmon, whom Mr. Chambers had just succeeded as editor of the publication. In Mr. Carmon's absence, the individual saw Mr.

Chambers. Mr. Chambers recalled the name of the State Department officer as being 'Clubb.'

"The committee first subpoenaed Oliver Edmund Clubb to appear before an executive session of the committee on March 14, 1951. Mr. Clubb had been a Foreign Service officer for the State Department for 23 years, approximately 18 of which involved assignments in China. He was recalled from China in 1950 and appointed director of the Office of Chinese Affairs, State Department, Washington – a post which he held at the time of his executive testimony.

"In the course of this testimony, Mr. Clubb stated that he had been vice consul at Hankow, China, in 1932 and in the same year had returned to the United States on vacation leave. He could not recall Whittaker Chambers, however, or having any association whatever with the magazine *New Masses.*

"On July 12, 1951, the State Department announced that Oliver Edmund Clubb had been suspended pending a loyalty investigation and hearing.

"Five days later, Mr. Clubb addressed a letter to the committee advising that he had obtained from Peiping, China, his personal diaries for the year 1932 and that an entry of July 9, 1932, recorded a meeting between himself and Whittaker Chambers in the *New Masses* office in New York. The committee subpoenaed Mr. Clubb and his diaries for a public hearing on August 20, 1951.

"The following extract from Mr. Clubb's diaries was read into the record of the hearing: 'The most interesting meeting thus far was that with the *New Masses.* Their so-called revolutionary organ is a horrible rag, but Agnes had given me a letter of introduction to Walt Carmon and so I went to see. It was a ramshackle place to which one went by a rambling, rickety staircase. There were many *Masses* cartoons on the walls. A charming Jewess, typing, who acted as secretary. She introduced me to Michael Gold as "Comrade Clubb," and I talked to him a while waiting. He spoke of revolution but had no "hopes" of it for the United States at the present, bemoaning the lack of organizers when the field is prepared and the crops so ripe for the harvest. He asked of China, and then the successor to Walt Carmon, one Whittaker Chambers, a shifty-eyed, unkempt creature, who nevertheless showed considerable force and direction, asked me about the Red movement in China. In turn I asked him of conditions in the United States, but we didn't talk smoothly. I was, after all, out of my bailiwick, masquerading almost under false pretenses, so that I felt too much like a stranger to show the proper "revolutionary enthusiasm." '

"Despite the aid of the diaries, Mr. Clubb maintained at this second hearing that he still had no independent recollection of the *New Masses* visit. He denied that he deserved the appellation 'Comrade Clubb.' He surmised he had visited *New Masses* out of a desire to learn about conditions in the United States during his infrequent 'home leaves.' Yet, he admitted he had known *New Masses* to be a Communist magazine since his college days.

"The Foreign Service officer named the late Agnes Smedley as the author of his letter of introduction to Walt Carmon of *New Masses*. Agnes Smedley has been identified before the committee as an international Communist agent who, at the very time she furnished Mr. Clubb with letters of introduction, was actively working with the notorious Sorge espionage ring in China.

"Mr. Clubb's diaries noted that he had twice sought out Miss Smedley in Shanghai in May 1932, prior to leaving for the United States, and 'got from her [Smedley] letters of introduction to many interesting people in New York.' Mr. Clubb, under questioning, explained he had received five such letters from Miss Smedley. He admitted also that he had had a number of other contacts with Miss Smedley, which he said were either social in nature or for the purpose of obtaining information on the Chinese Communist revolutionary movement. He also admitted that he knew at the time that Miss Smedley was 'very sympathetic' to the Chinese Communists.

"At the time of his *New Masses* visit, Mr. Clubb delivered other letters of introduction in New York. His diaries, however, labeled his New York trip 'singularly unsuccessful' because 'the chief of those I wanted to see have been out of town — Villard, Lovett, Chappell, Sanger.' Letters to Oswald Garrison Villard and Robert Morss Lovett were among those supplied to Mr. Clubb by Agnes Smedley. A letter to Winifred Chappell had been furnished by a missionary friend of Mr. Clubb's in China, one Joseph Bailey. Committee files reflect that Mr. Villard and Miss Chappell each have a record of approximately 20 Communist-front affiliations, while Robert Morss Lovett's Communist-front associations total more than 70.

"The diaries further disclosed that Mr. Clubb sought out Lawrence Todd of *Tass* News Agency in the city of Washington during his 1932 vacation. Mr. Todd was brother to Oliver J. Todd, hydraulic engineer in China and close friend of Mr. Clubb. Lawrence Todd dined with Mr. Clubb on July 5, 1932, and on the following day took Mr. Clubb to see one Skvirsky, head of the Soviet

Information Bureau in Washington, who questioned him about sovietized sections of China, and discussed recognition of the U.S.S.R. by the United States. Mr. Todd also conducted the State Department officer to the press room of the State Department, where Mr. Clubb met columnist Drew Pearson. Mr. Clubb subsequently dined at the latter's home, in the company of Lawrence Duggan and Frank P. Lockhart, both since deceased. Mr. Clubb again professed to have no recollection of these associations.

"In this connection, it should be noted that Whittaker Chambers identified Mr. Duggan as having been a member of the pro-Soviet bloc in the State Department. Drew Pearson, avowedly an intimate friend of Mr. Duggan, has stated publicly that he knew Mr. Duggan to have attended Communist meetings in Alexandria, Va., in the year 1932, while employed by the State Department. In the late 1930's, however, Mr. Duggan rejected efforts of Soviet agents Hede Massing and Boris Bykov to draw him into an espionage apparatus within the United States Government, according to a report he made 10 years afterward to the FBI.

"The committee hearing on August 20, 1951 brought to light contacts in China between Mr. Clubb and Frank Glass and Harold Isaacs. Communist hearings on the operations of the Sorge espionage ring in China in the early 1930's had disclosed that Frank Glass and Harold Isaacs were associates of the Comintern agent Agnes Smedley during that period. Mr. Glass was identified as a British Communist, and Harold Isaacs as editor of the China Forum, an English-language Communist periodical.

"Mr. Clubb admitted under questioning that he had shared his apartment in Hankow, China, with Mr. Glass and Mr. Isaacs when the two men arrived in that town in 1931 during a period of flood. Mr. Clubb also said that, following their departure, he had continued to correspond with both men until approximately 1934.

"One of Mr. Clubb's colleagues in Chungking, China, according to his testimony, was Solomon Adler, A Treasury Department attaché. Mr. Adler was a member of the 'Silvermaster' espionage group which operated within United States Government agencies during World War II, according to the testimony of Elizabeth T. Bentley, confessed former courier for the spy group. Mr. Clubb also knew Philip Jaffe in China. Mr. Jaffe, as an editor of the pro-Communist magazine *Amerasia* in 1945, was fined $2,500 in a case involving the channeling of classified Government information to the magazine.

"Mr. Clubb admitted associations with millionaire Communist Frederick Vanderbilt Field, but insisted he could not remember the circumstances. At a third hearing before the committee on August 23, 1951, Mr. Clubb was shown photostatic copies of what appeared to be a letter introducing him to Frederick Field, and another letter addressed to Field by Clubb himself. The letter of introduction, dated January 22, 1937, was signed by Karl August Wittfogel, who had admitted membership in the Communist Party of Germany from 1920 to 1933. Mr. Clubb's letter to Mr. Field, dated March 24, 1937, promised that the Foreign Service officer would visit Mr. Field shortly and 'should very much enjoy seeing and talking with you again.' The letters failed to stir any recollection on the part of Mr. Clubb."

Meanwhile, Clubb was being investigated by the State Department's Loyalty Board. On February 11, 1952, the State

Department announced that Clubb was "absolutely cleared" of charges against his loyalty and security, and that he was restored to duty. Senators Homer Ferguson (R.-Mich.) and Joseph R. McCarthy (R.-Wisc.) discovered that Clubb was not "cleared" – absolutely, or otherwise – by the Loyalty Board but rather that its three members voted unanimously against him. The two Senators also found that Assistant Secretary of State Carlisle Humelsine, who was in charge of State Department security, approved of the vote against Clubb.

On March 5, 1952, Secretary of State Dean Acheson – in the course of a press conference – admitted that Senators Ferguson and McCarthy had unearthed the truth: the vote of the Loyalty Board was a 3-0 against Clubb and Humelsine had approved the vote. But Acheson reversed the ruling of the Loyalty Board and Humelsine's concurrence and cleared Clubb. Clubb then resigned from the State Department with a lifetime pension of $5,800 a year.

In recent years, Clubb has been on the political science faculty at Columbia University. In 1965, he was a sponsor and participant in the "teach-in" movement, agitating against American participation in the Vietnam War. It was Clubb's contention that if the United States chose to expand the war in Vietnam, there was the grim prospect that American troops would be fighting against millions of Chinese and Russian soldiers. Clubb's solution was negotiation by the United States to "achieve some neutral status for [South] Viet Nam" – which, of course, was neutral prior to the aggression of Ho chi Minh's North Vietnamese forces.

In 1966, Clubb joined with Red China lobbyists (John K. Fairbank, Roger Hilsman, Bayard Rustin, Doak Barnett, Clark Kerr, Anna Lord Strauss, and Robert A. Scalapino) to form the National Committee on United States-China Relations to promote appeasement of Red China.

Clubb's lectures on collegiate campuses and elsewhere reflect the hoary policy of the Institute of Pacific Relations, to which he belonged for twenty or twenty-five years; extreme hostility toward Chiang Kai-shek's Free China regime and great sympathy for the Communist regime of Mao Tse-tung. Clubb is especially grieved that the United States is a captive of its extreme anti-Communist policy. He wants U.S. diplomatic recognition and UN membership for Red China. After all, he fictionalizes, "the Communists unified the country, redistributed and collectivized the land to increase food supply and made remarkable progress in industry."

As is the case with so many IPR veterans, Clubb is now considered an expert in the liberal community on U.S. policy in Asia. When *Diplomat* magazine (now defunct) published a special China issue in September, 1966, Clubb contributed an article along with other never-right, always-left "experts" such as Doak Barnett, John K. Fairbank, Harold Isaacs, David Schoenbrun, Morton Halperin, and Felix Greene. The intensity of the pro-Red Chinese propaganda offered by this clique matches anything produced by the infamous IPR crowd in their heyday of the 1930's and 1940's. And, as recently as December, 1967, Clubb used the letters-to-the-editor column of the *New York Times* to bemoan "the war we wage upon the poor, misery-ridden Vietnamese" and our hostility toward Red China "and its presumed accomplices."

WILLIAM S. COFFIN JR. was born

on June 1, 1924 in New York City, son of Catherine Butterfield and William Coffin. He married Eva Rubinstein. He is an alumnus of Yale University (B.A., 1949; B.D., 1956).

In 1949 and 1950, Coffin attended Union Theological Seminary in New York City. (For half a century, Union has been a hotbed of Red activities. Its alumni constitute a hierarchy of Communist fronters.) From 1950 until 1953, he was with the Central Intelligence Agency. In 1956, upon completion of his divinity studies at Yale, he was ordained to the ministry of the Presbyterian Church. In 1956 and 1957, he was acting chaplain at Phillips Academy in Massachusetts. In 1957 and 1958 he was a chaplain at Williams College. Since 1958, he has been chaplain of Yale University.

Coffin has been very active in the so-called civil rights movement. In 1961, he was arrested for participating in a Montgomery, Alabama sit-in demonstration. In 1963, he was arrested in Maryland where he was protesting against racial segregation at a privately-owned amusement park. In 1964, he was arrested in St. Augustine, Florida for taking part in an illegal demonstration.

In 1965, Coffin became a leader in opposition to United States participation in the Vietnam War and to the selective service system. In 1966, he joined the veteran Communist fronter and Socialist Party leader Norman Thomas as co-chairman of the National Voters' Pledge Campaign. Coffin and Thomas were joined in the Campaign's leadership by Sanford Gottlieb, the political director of the leftwing-pacifist National Committee for a Sane Nuclear Policy. The NVPC was designed to have voters pledge their support for "peace" candidates for Congress, who would work for a cease-fire in Vietnam and encourage negotiations in which the Vietcong would be participants.

In 1967, Coffin signed the call for the National Conference for New Politics which was nothing less than a classical united third party movement largely controlled by the Communist Party.

Coffin's activities against the selective service system led to his indictment by a federal grand jury, a trial, and a conviction. Specifically, he was charged with joining in an illegal conspiracy to violate the federal draft laws which forbid counselling, aiding, or abetting draft evasion. Co-defendants with Coffin were Benjamin Spock, Mitchell Goodman, Marcus Raskin, and Michael Ferber. (The group quickly became known as The Boston Five, and their defense received extremely sympathetic attention in the nation's Communist press.)

When Coffin was indicted, he said that he and his co-defendants welcomed "the chance to confront the Government in the courts of the United States in the traditional American way. Of course we are prepared to go to jail. When throughout the ages men have suffered death rather than subordinate their allegiance to conscience to the authority of the state, to go to jail is obviously a small thing." Coffin's bravado suffered somewhat once he was convicted. He immediately appealed his prison sentence.

In 1967 and 1968, a great deal of Coffin's energies were spent in helping to organize and finance the activities of Clergy and Laymen Concerned about Vietnam. He was joined by names which have long been familiar in pacifist groups and Communist fronts, including John C. Bennett, Eugene Carson Blake, Dana McLean Greeley, Hans Morgenthau, Reinhold Niebuhr, and Ralph Sockman. In their statement of protest against the

Vietnam War, the Clergy and Laymen incorporated the clichés which featured the leftwing teach-ins which saturated universities and other institutions across the nation: the war is immoral; *widespread* use of napalm is killing and maiming women, children, and the aged; there is *systematic* destruction of Vietnamese crops; the guilt of the United States is far more than we have courage to admit; United States military presence in Vietnam serves to unite Communist *societies;* military expenditures in Vietnam jeopardize domestic programs to help minority groups; initiative for peace negotiations must be unconditional and unilateral on the part of the United States; the National Liberation Front must be, by *right*, a partner in peace talks; and, the United Nations must be given a major role in peace negotiations.

Coffin has spoken often and at length on his own personal views of the Vietnam War. He has said, as recently as 1968: "It's true that we're fighting Communists [in Vietnam], but it is more profound to say that we have been intervening in another country's civil war . . . .

"The war is being waged with unbelievable cruelty and in a fashion so out of character with American instincts of decency that it is seriously undermining them. The strains of the war have cut the funds that might otherwise be applied to antipoverty efforts at home and abroad — which is the intelligent way to fight Communism — and, finally, the war would have a good chance of being negotiated to an end were we to stop the bombing in Vietnam."

When Coffin was asked if withdrawal by the United States might not result in a victory for the Communists, he answered: "Probably, to some extent it will. I'm not in any way happy about Vietnam going to the Communists, but I am against our intervention — unsuccessfully — to prevent it."

Coffin was also asked if a United States withdrawal might not bring a blood bath to South Vietnam. Evasively he replied: "And as for blood baths, how many innocent civilians, men, women and children, are we killing every day with our indiscriminate [*sic*] bombardment?"

There is nothing on record to indicate that Coffin has ever encouraged the burning of draft cards. But he has encouraged young men to return their draft cards to the government. Even while under indictment, Coffin said publicly that clergymen should be "trying to organize 1000, 2000, 5000 students to gather on a specified date in 10 different centers in order to surrender their draft cards at previously designated Federal buildings with a simple, moving statement? [*sic*]" No matter how simple and moving the statement, the fact remains that by surrendering a draft card a young man violates the selective service laws. Coffin, however, rationalizes lawbreaking: No man ever had the right to break a law but every man upon occasion has the duty to do so."

Even after his conviction for conspiring to counsel, aid, and abet draft evasion, Coffin would not be silenced. He contended: "Thousands of youths must either violate their consciences or go to jail." Evidently, Coffin believes that he is flirting with treason. He has compared himself and others who are resisting the draft laws to George Washington and Thomas Jefferson who "were traitors until crowned with success."

Coffin's status as a university chaplain is apparently not in jeopardy because of his extensive off-campus activities. Yale's President Kingman Brewster says that he is constrained to "disagree with the chaplain's position on draft resistance, and in this instance deplore his style," but "thanks in large part to his personal verve and social action, religious life, within and without the church, [he] reaches more people at Yale than on any other campus I know about. More important, the rebellious instinct, which elsewhere expresses itself so often in sour withdrawal, cynical nihilism and disruption, is here more often than not both affirmative and constructive, thanks in considerable measure to the chaplain's influence."

Brewster, however, overlooks the fact that Coffin's opposition to the draft ranges far beyond religion. He encourages draft resistance in connection with his opposition to the Vietnam War, not merely on religious grounds, but — as he has phrased it — the war is "stupid politically, inept militarily and morally unjust."

WILBUR COHEN was born on June 10, 1913 in Milwaukee, son of Bessie Rubenstein and Aaron Cohen. He married Eloise Bittel. He is an alumnus of the University of Wisconsin (Ph.B., 1934).

In 1934 and 1935, Cohen was a research assistant to the Executive Director of Staff of the Committee on Economic Security. In 1936, Cohen moved onto the staff of the Social Security Administration (which later became a part of the Department of Health, Education and Welfare), where he would remain for the next twenty-two years. Successively, Cohen served as a technical adviser, assistant director, and director of the Bureau of Research and Statistics.

When Cohen resigned from his directorship in 1958, he remained on HEW's payroll as a consultant to the Social Security Commissioner until December, 1959. Meanwhile, Cohen went to the University of Michigan as professor of Public Welfare Administration, and remained there until 1961 when he rejoined Health, Education and Welfare as an assistant secretary. In 1965, he was promoted to Under Secretary of HEW.

For more than three decades, Cohen — more than any other individual — has labored successfully to bring nationalized, socialized medicine to this country. In doing so, he has worked hand-in-hand with Socialists and Communists. In 1967, Dr. Marjorie Shearon, a veteran researcher and legislative observer, published a brilliant account of Cohen's socialistic career (*Wilbur J. Cohen: Pursuit of Power*), which is a vivid history of the remarkable progress that Cohen has made in Sovietizing the federal social security racket and HEW's federal "health" monstrosity. In 1961, when President Kennedy was bringing Cohen back into government as an Assistant Secretary of Health, Education and Welfare, Dr. Shearon testified before the Senate Finance Committee in opposition to Cohen's appointment. Said Dr. Shearon of Cohen: "He probably is more conversant with the Social Security Act, its history, its provisions, its costs, its administration than any other person in the country. He has drafted, or aided in the drafting, of every significant Social Security bill that has come to hearings in the Congress since 1935. He has, either by himself or through his subordinates, aided in formulating the language of Committee reports, Advisory Council reports, Messages from Presidents to the Congress, etc. I doubt if there is another person in the United States who has been so intimately connected with Federal Social Security legislation since 1934 as Professor Cohen, especially with respect to aid to Congressional Committees and to individual Members of Congress."

While Cohen worked in the government, he was affiliated with the Washington Committee for Aid to China ("Communist controlled"); the Washington Committee for Democratic Action ("subversive and Communist"); and, the Washington Book Shop Association ("subversive and Communist"). He has also been a member of Americans for 'Democratic Action, the center of the radical left in American politics.

HENRY S. COMMAGER was born on October 25, 1902 in Pittsburgh, Pennsylvania, son of Elisabeth Dan and James Commager. He married Evan Carroll. He is an alumnus of the University of Chicago (Ph.B., 1923; A.M., 1924; Ph.D., 1928). He also studied at the University of Copenhagen in 1924 and 1925.

From 1926 until 1938, Commager was at New York University as an instructor, assistant professor, associate professor, and professor of history. From 1939 until 1956, he was a professor of history at Columbia University and, since 1956, he has been a professor of history and American studies at Amherst College.

Commager has lectured for the Department of State in Germany, Israel, Trinidad, Italy, and Chile. He has also lectured at Cambridge University and Oxford University in England, Boston University, the University of Virginia, Uppsala University in Sweden, the University of Copenhagen, Aix-en-Provence at Nice, the University of Jerusalem, and the University of Mexico.

Commager is the author, co-author, or editor of more than thirty books. His own books include *The American Mind,*

Living Ideas in America, and *Freedom, Loyalty, Dissent.* His best known collaborative work is *The Growth of the American Republic,* written with Samuel E. Morison.

Few American historians are cited more in footnotes and bibliographies than is Commager in liberal textbooks. And he certainly ranks as one of the most hysterical bleeding-hearts in the entire academic world in his denunciations of McCarthyism, loyalty oaths, security statutes, and committees investigating subversion. He has been affiliated with the Chicago Sobell Committee ("active in the Communist propaganda campaign exploiting atomic spies"); the National Federation for Constitutional Liberties ("under [Communist] Party domination and headed by responsible Party functionaries"); and, the American Committee for Democracy and Intellectual Freedom ("Communist front" – "subversive and un-American"). He has been a national officer of the American Civil Liberties Union, that motleyed collection of defenders of subversion, crime, and licentiousness. He is a non-resident member of the Council on Foreign Relations, the informal supra-State Department of the United States; and has been a leader in the Foreign Policy Association, which is a propaganda affiliate of the Council on Foreign Relations and promotes its soft-on-Communism, anti-anti-Communist views through its World Affairs Councils and "Great Decisions" programs. The FPA is a major part of the Red China lobby, working for U.S. diplomatic recognition and admission to United Nations membership for Red China. He has petitioned on behalf of Communists. He was on the Committee of Welcome for the Very Reverend Hewlett Johnson, the "Red" Dean of Canterbury, one of England's all-time notorious apologists for the Soviet Union.

Commager has also been affiliated with the National Committee for a Sane Nuclear Policy (leftwing, pacifist), and, in 1967 and 1968, he has been working for the National Committee for an Effective Congress, which is campaigning for the re-election of such notable doves as Senators Church of Idaho, Clark of Pennsylvania, Fulbright of Arkansas, Gruening of Alaska, McGovern of South Dakota, Aiken of Vermont, Javits of New York, Nelson of Wisconsin, and Morse of Oregon.

EDWARD U. CONDON was born on March 2, 1902 in Alamagordo, New Mexico, son of Caroline Uhler and William Condon. He married Emilie Harzik. He is an alumnus of the University of California (A.B., 1924; Ph.D., 1926).

In 1926 and 1927, Condon was a research fellow at the University of Göttigen and the University of Munich. In 1928, he was a lecturer of physics at Columbia University. In 1928 and 1929, he was an assistant professor of physics at Princeton University. In 1929 and 1930, he was professor of theoretical physics at the University of Minnesota, then, in 1930, he returned to Princeton as an associate professor of physics, remaining there until 1937 when he became assistant director of the Westinghouse Research Laboratory.

In 1945, Condon became the director of the National Bureau of Standards. While in this position, in 1948, the House Committee on Un-American Activities investigated Condon. In its Report of May 18,1948, the HCUA said that the associations of Condon and his wife were a cause of great concern to agencies charged with the security of the United States. Condon had entertained and associated with persons who were alleged to be Soviet espionage agents.

On May 15, 1947, FBI Director J. Edgar Hoover had written to Secretary of Commerce Averell Harriman and said that FBI files indicated that, as late as 1947, Condon had been in contact with an individual alleged, by a self-confessed Soviet espionage agent, to have engaged in espionage activities with Soviet agents in Washington, D.C. fron 1941 to 1944.

Mr. Hoover mentioned that Condon and his wife associated with several individuals from Communist Poland's Embassy in Washington. These associates included the wife of the Polish Ambassador, the secretary of the Embassy, and a former counselor of the Embassy. The latter Ignace Zlotowski, a nuclear scientist, had worked as a Soviet espionage agent in direct contact with the Soviet Embassy in Washington.

Mrs. Condon applied for a passport to travel to the Soviet Union in 1945, but, for reasons not explained by Mr. Hoover, the passport was withdrawn. Condon was issued a passport in 1946, to travel and study in Germany, France, Holland, Italy, Czecho-Slovakia, Britain, Denmark, and Switzerland. Previously in 1946, Condon had applied for and been issued a passport for travel to the Soviet Union, but the passport was cancelled by the Army.

The HCUA found that Condon and his wife had been guests in the homes of persons who were attached to Soviet satellite embassies, and present on these occasions were representatives of official Soviet agencies. The HCUA also found that, for at least five years, Condon had been in personal contact with American citizens who were members of the Communist Party. Although the HCUA had no evidence that Condon was a member of the Communist Party, he was a member of the executive committee of the American-Soviet Society, an affiliate of the subversive National Council of American-Soviet Science Friendship, one of the principal Communist endeavors in the United States.

In the opinion of the HCUA, Condon was one of "the weakest links in our atomic security" – of especial significance since Condon had been a scientific advisor to the Senate's Special Committee on Atomic Energy and, as Director of the Bureau of Standards, Condon was at a focal point of interest for espionage agents. Condon remained with the Bureau of Standards until 1951 when he resigned and became director of research and development at the Corning Glass Works.

In 1954, the U.S. Navy gave Condon a security clearance but when Condon made the fact known two days later, the clearance was withdrawn for further review.

In 1956, Condon joined the faculty of Washington University of St. Louis as a physics professor. In 1963, he became a fellow in the joint institute for laboratory astrophysics and a professor of physics at the University of Colorado. At Colorado, all of Condon's salary has been paid by federal contract funds and the university receives an additional fifty per cent to cover overhead.

In his academic career, Condon has also taught at the University of Michigan, Massachusetts Institute of Technology, Stanford University, and Oberlin College. Condon's off-campus activities have included his sponsorship of the National Committee for Abolition of the House Un-American Activities Committee ("to lead and direct the Communist Party's 'Operation Abolition' campaign"); his sponsorship of the National Committee for a Sane Nuclear Policy ("leftwing, pacifist"); his signing of clemency petitions for the imprisoned Communists Frank Wilkinson and Carl Braden; his signing of clemency petitions for the convicted spies Julius and Ethel Rosenberg; his service on the national council of the Emergency Civil Liberties Committee ("Communist front" – "subversive"); and, his opposition to nuclear weapons tests.

In 1966, Condon was appointed as head of an Air Force-sponsored program at the University of Colorado to check the validity of reports on unidentified flying objects (UFO's). The Air Force signed a fifteen-month, $313,000 contract with the University of Colorado for Condon's program.

JOHN CONYERS JR. was born on May 16, 1922 in Detroit, son of Lucille Simpson and John Conyers. He is an alumnus of Wayne State University (B.A., 1957; LL.B., 1958). In 1959, he was admitted to the Michigan bar and began practicing law in Detroit.

From 1958 until 1961, Conyers was a legislative assistant to Representative John Dingell (D.-Mich.). From 1961 until 1965, he was a referee in Michigan's Workmen's Compensation Department.

Since 1965, Conyers has been in the House of Representatives as a Democrat, representing Michigan's First District. In and out of Congress, Conyers is a black racist militant and a leftwing extremist. He has been a vice-chairman of Americans for Democratic Action, the radical center of American politics. He has been on the national executive board of the National Lawyer's Guild, the foremost legal bulwark of the Communist Party, its front organizations, and controlled unions.

In 1966, Conyers spoke at the founding convention of Trade Unionists for Peace which was established by leftwing labor leaders as a lobby against United States forces remaining in Vietnam. (TUP was run by Charles Walters, a shop steward for the United Automobile Workers. Former Communist Bereniece Baldwin testified under oath, in 1954, before the House Committee on Un-American Activities, that Walters was in the Communist Party. In 1966, Walters was editor of *Labor Today* which FBI Director J. Edgar Hoover described as an organ of Communist propaganda. Conyers has written for *Labor Today*.)

Conyers has adopted the position that the Vietnam War is a racist conflict and he was one of only four members of the House of Representatives to vote against military support for U.S. troops in Vietnam. But consistent with his racism, he proposed that Congress spend an additional thirty billion dollars a year in Negro areas around the United States. (Other than his opposition to the Vietnam War, Conyer's interest in foreign affairs seems to have been confined to his adulatory support of the Communist Kwame Nkrumah, former head of Ghana.)

On the House Judiciary Committee, Conyers was the only member to oppose legislation designed to make desecration of the American flag a crime.

In 1967, Conyers led the fight against, and voted against the "riot bill" which made it a federal crime to cross state lines for the purpose of inciting violence.

In 1968, Conyers told *The Worker* (Communist) that he was organizing a committee of blacks to evaluate candidates for the 1968 election. It was part of his overall program to organize American Negroes into one voting bloc. For his evaluating committee, he had chosen, among others, the revolutionaries Stokely Carmichael, Ralph Abernathy and Floyd McKissick.

FRED COOK was born on March 8, 1911 in Point Pleasant, New Jersey, son of Huldak Compton and Frederick Cook. He married Julia Simpson. He is an alumnus of Rutgers University (Litt.B., 1932).

From 1933 until 1936, Cook was a reporter with the *Asbury Park* (N.J.) *Press*. In 1936 and 1937, he was an editor of the *New Jersey Courier*. From 1938 until 1944, he was a desk man and city editor of the *Asbury Park Press*. From 1944 until 1959, he was a rewrite man and feature writer for the *New York World Telegram and Sun*. Cook was fired from that journal for lying, while appearing on David Susskind's TV show, about having been offered a bribe by New York City officials.

Since 1959, Cook has been a free lance writer, although *National Review,* a few years ago, described him more accurately as a professional mudslinger. Most of Cook's prolific output has been in the pages of the leftwing *Nation* magazine, to which he had contributed articles while he still was with the *World Telegram*.

In 1957, Cook's *Nation* article "Hiss" was the first of several he wrote in defense of the convicted perjurer. According to Cook, Hiss was framed by the Federal Bureau of Investigation. The articles later became the framework for a book, *The Unfinished Story of Alger Hiss.*

In 1958, Cook's *Nation* article "The FBI" was a vitriolic attack, later expanded into a book, *The FBI Nobody Knows.* The article was reviewed enthusiastically in the pro-Soviet *National Guardian.* The Communists' west coast paper *People's*

World described the book as "brilliantly documented." *The Worker* said the book was "well worth reading."

In 1961, Cook's *Nation* article "Jugernaut" appeared. It would later be expanded into the book, *The Warfare State.* Cook's thesis was that American military men were trying to provoke war with peace-loving nations so that the military could impose a fascistic dictatorship upon the United States.

In 1962, in his "The Ultras" which appeared in *Nation,* Cook imagined that anti-Communists were taking over this country, and naturally he was repelled at the thought. The *World Marxist Review* loved this diatribe.

In 1966, when Cook's *The Corrupted Land* appeared, *People's World* described him as "one of the best reporters in the country." The book grew out of his *Nation* article "The Corrupt Society," which Moscow's *New Times* liked since the thesis was that American life was mostly rotten. Another *Nation* article by Cook was "Hate Clubs of the Air," which can only be classified as fantasy since its theme was that anti-Communists were pretty much monopolizing radio broadcast time across the country.

More recently, Cook has written *The Plot against the Patient,* a wholesale attack upon the American Medical Association, the medical profession in general, and American hospitals in particular.

JOHN SHERMAN COOPER was born on August 23, 1901 in Somerset, Kentucky, son of Gertrude Tartar and John Cooper. He married Lorraine Shevlin. He is an alumnus of Yale University (A.B., 1923). He attended Centre College of Kentucky in 1918 and 1919 and Harvard University's Law School from 1923 until 1925. In 1928, he was admitted to the Kentucky bar and began his private practice of law in Somerset.

From 1928 until 1930, Cooper was a member of Kentucky's House of Representatives. From 1930 until 1938, he was an elective judge (an administrative position) in Pulaski County. In 1939, he was an unsuccessful candidate for the governorship of Kentucky. While in the U.S. Army in 1945, he was elected as a circuit judge. In 1946, a few months after he assumed the judgeship, he resigned the office to run for the U.S. Senate seat vacated by Albert Chandler, who resigned. Cooper went to the U.S. Senate, as a Republican, but failed in his attempt to be re-elected in 1948. During his twenty-six months in the Senate, Cooper joined leftwing Republicans (Wayne Morse of Oregon, George Aiken of Vermont, and Charles Tobey of New Hampshire) in opposition to the conservative Republican bloc led by Robert A. Taft of Ohio. The leftwingers, including Cooper, were pressing for a bipartisan internationalist foreign policy with a heavy emphasis on handouts to foreign nations. On domestic matters, Cooper's votes were generally of a conservative nature.

In 1949, for a few months, Cooper resumed the practice of law in Washington, D.C. In September, 1949, President Harry Truman appointed Cooper to the U.S. delegation to the United Nations General Assembly. He replaced John Foster Dulles and served with three outstanding leftwing internationalists: Warren Austin, Philip Jessup, and Eleanor Roosevelt.

In April, 1950, Cooper became an advisor to Secretary of State Dean Acheson. He accompanied Acheson to London and Brussels for meetings of the Council of Ministers of the North Atlantic Treaty Organization. In 1950 and 1951, Cooper was an alternate delegate to the UN General Assembly.

In 1952, Cooper was elected to the U.S. Senate, replacing the incumbent Virgil Chapman who had died. In 1954, Cooper was an unsuccessful candidate for re-election.

From March, 1955, until August, 1956, Cooper was U.S. Ambassador to India. He resigned this position to run for the U.S. Senate seat vacated when Alben Barkley died. Cooper was re-elected in 1960 and 1966. In 1964, Cooper was a member of The President's Commission on the Assassination of President Kennedy (Warren Commission).

Cooper has long since abandoned any pretensions to conservatism. He has become one of the most liberal Republicans in that party's history. He has moved so far to the left, in both foreign and domestic affairs, that he is one of the very few Republicans favored with endorsement and active support from the AFL-CIO, the ultra-leftist National Committee for an Effective Congress, and the leftwing-pacifist National Committee for a Sane Nuclear Policy.

AARON COPLAND was born on November 14, 1900 in Brooklyn, New York, son of Sarah Mittenthal and Harris Copland. He has been a composer of music since 1920. From 1927 until 1934, he lectured on music at the New School for Social Research. From 1935 until 1944, he was music lecturer at Harvard University and at Harvard, in 1951 and 1952, he was the Charles Eliot Norton professor of poetry.

In an interview with Hans Eisler, the Karl Marx of the musical field, the *Evening Moscow* (June 27, 1935) reported Eisler as saying: "I am extremely pleased to report a considerable shift to the left among the American artistic intelligensia. I don't think it would be an exaggeration to state that the best people in the musical world of America (with very few exceptions) share at present extremely progressive ideas. Their names? They are Aaron Copland . . . ."

Eight years later, when Hans Eisler was the subject of deportation proceedings in the United States, Aaron Copland repaid Eisler's tribute to his "extremely progressive ideas" and petitioned the United States Attorney General to halt the proceedings against Eisler.

The record of Copland's ties to the Communist Party can be traced back at least to 1935. Among Copland's affiliations have been: the American Committee for Democracy and Intellectual Freedom ("Communist, subversive" – "un-American"); the American Committee for Protection of Foreign Born [Americans] ("subversive and Communist" – "one of the oldest auxiliaries of the Communist Party in the United States" – under the "complete domination" of the Communist Party); the American League Against War and Fascism ("subversive and Communist"); the Artists Front to Win the War ("Communist front"); Citizens Committee for Harry Bridges ("Communist"); the Committee for Professional Groups for Browder and Ford ("Communist front"); the Coordinating Committee to Lift the Embargo ("Communist front"); the Friends of the Abraham Lincoln Brigade ("its officers and staff members were in the main [Communist] Party members and functionaries"); Frontier Films ("Communist front"); the Joint Anti-fascist Refugee Committee ("subversive and Communist"); the National Committee for People's Rights ("entirely under the control of the Communist Party"); the

National Council of American-Soviet Friendship ("subversive and Communist" — "specializing in pro-Soviet propaganda"); the National Council of the Arts, Sciences, and Professions ("a Communist front used to appeal to special occupational groups"); the Cultural and Scientific Conference for World Peace ("Communist front" — a propaganda front for Soviet foreign policy and "Soviet culture"); the National Federation for Constitutional Liberties ("under [Communist] Party domination and headed by responsible Party functionaries"); the Non-Partisan Committee for the Re-election of Congressman Vito Marcantonio ("Communist front"); the Open Letter in Defense of Harry Bridges ("Communist front"); the Reichstag Fire Trial Anniversary Committee ("Communist front"); and, the American Council on Soviet Relations ("established by Communist Party").

ANDREW CORDIER was born on March 3, 1901 in Canton, Ohio, son of Ida Anstine and Wellington Cordier. He married Dorothy Butterbaugh. He is an alumnus of Manchester College of Indiana (A.B., 1922) and the University of Chicago (A.M., 1923; Ph.D., 1926), where he was a teaching fellow in 1924 and 1925. He also studied at the Graduate Institute of International Studies in Geneva, Switzerland in 1930 and 1931.

From 1923 until 1944, Cordier was on the faculty at Manchester College as an associate professor of history (1923-1927) and chairman of history and political science (1927-1944). He also lectured in social science at Indiana University from 1929 until 1944.

From 1944 until 1946, Cordier was with the State Department as an "expert" on international security. He became a close working associate and admirer of Alger Hiss. Later, when Hiss was convicted of perjury for lying about his involvement with Communist espionage, Cordier would neither believe in Hiss' guilt nor think that Hiss was a security risk.

In the State Department Cordier was an active participant in the Department's and Hiss' contributions to the organizing of the United Nations. And, in 1946, Cordier went to work for the United Nations. For sixteen years, he was an advisor to all presidents of the UN General Assembly. He was also an executive assistant to the UN's Secretary General Trygve Lie and his successor Dag Hammarskjöld. Cordier represented Lie in Korea during the Korean War and Hammarskjöld during the UN's aggression in the Congo. In 1961 and 1962, Cordier was Under Secretary of the UN's General Assembly Affairs.

During Hammarskjöld's administration, Cordier played the major role in the hatchet job perpetrated on the Danish diplomat, Povl Bang-Jensen. In 1957, Bang-Jensen was the head of a UN committee investigating the Hungarian revolution of 1956. Anonymous Hungarian witnesses, during the course of the hearings, testified that the UN Secretariat was under the control of the Soviet Union and that American intelligence agencies were infiltrated by Soviet secret police. Soviet authorities demanded the names of the Hungarian witnesses, but Bang-Jensen refused to divulge them. Bang-Jensen was then fired for insubordination. And it was Cordier, in league with Hammarskjöld, who got rid of Bang-Jensen. In 1959, Bang-Jensen was found shot to death in a New York City park. There is overwhelming reason to believe that Bang-Jensen suffered a Soviet-style "natural death" — sometimes called the "perfect suicide."

In 1962, Cordier left the UN to become dean at Columbia University's Graduate School of International Affairs. He is a consultant to the Ford Foundation, which has been a horn of plenty for leftwingers and leftwing projects on every continent; a trustee of the leftwing, pacifist Carnegie Endowment for International Peace; a director of the leftwing Foreign Policy Association; and, a member of the Council on Foreign Relations, the informanl supra-State Department of the United States.

He remains a most ardent apologist and supporter for the United Nations. And he is most hopeful that his suggestion will be adopted for a UN permanent general military staff, drawn from small nations rather than from large powers, to make possible world peace-keeping chores for the UN.

NORMAN COUSINS was born on June 24, 1912 in Union Hill, New Jersey, son of Sara Miller and Samuel Cousins. He married Ellen Kopf. He studied for less than a year at Columbia University.

In 1934 and 1935 he was an educational writer for the *New York Post*. For the next five years, he was a literary editor and managing editor of *Current History* magazine. In 1940, he became an executive editor of *Saturday Review* magazine and, since 1942, has been editor of that most literate voice of the left. From 1943 until 1945, he was an editorial board member of the overseas bureau of Elmer Davis' Red-lined Office of War Information.

There have been occasions when Cousins has gone through the motions of being an ardent anti-Communist but these bursts of verbal fireworks have been more than offset during the past two decades by the rest of Cousin's

activities. He is America's leading "ban-the-bomb-boob," scaremonger, and pleader for co-existence with the Soviet Union's Communist regime. He has made his influence felt, not only through the impressive growth of *Saturday Review's* circulation, but in his active, high-ranking role in the United World Federalists and the World Association of World Federalists (both organizations' programs a very serious threat to American sovereignty and the sovereignty of all free nations); the National Committee for a Sane Nuclear Policy (leftwing, pacifist); Freedom House and the Willkie Memorial Foundation (centers for anti-anti-Communism); the Council on Foreign Relations (the informal supra-State Department of the United States); the Hiroshima Peace Center Associates (promoting emotional arguments to persuade Americans to work for nuclear disarmament); and, through his personal contacts with Soviet leaders. He has also served as a national officer of the American Civil Liberties Union, that motleyed collection of defenders of subversion, crime, and licentiousness. This latter affiliation probably explains Cousins' lavish endorsement ("one of the adornments of modern American literature") of Henry Miller's scatological *Tropic of Cancer*.

Cousins is a vice-president and director of McCall Corporation. He is on the board of directors of Educational Television and Radio Center and on the editorial board of *Encyclopedia Britannica*. Among his books are *The Democratic Chance; Man is Obsolete; Talks with Nehru; Who Speaks for Man?; The Last Defense in a Nuclear Age; In Place of Folly;* and *Present Tense: An American Editor's Odyssey*. In his publishing and writing efforts, Cousins is an unabashed proponent for an infinite expansion of Roosevelt's New Deal. He has implicit faith in the United Nations — "a strengthened United Nations is the best hope of man on earth." And he advocates an international legislative body with the power to enforce its decisions — in other words, a world police state.

WILLIAM J. CROCKETT was born on July 22, 1914 in Cimarron, Kansas, son of Ilda Furse and James Crockett. He married Verla Koelling. He is an alumnus of the University of Nebraska (B.S., 1942). From 1933 until 1941, he was an assistant cashier in a Hastings, Nebraska bank.

In 1946 and 1947, Crockett was an assistant to the director of administration for the U.S. Maritime Commission in Naples. In 1948, he returned to the Hastings bank as an assistant vice-president and remained there until 1951 when he entered the State Department. For ten years, Crockett served in minor State Department posts in Washington, Lebanon, Karachi, and Rome.

Then, under Secretary of State Dean Rusk, Crockett would serve for six years, first as assistant secretary for administration and then as deputy undersecretary for administration.

Crockett would be a prominent figure in the railroad job done on Otto Otepka, the evaluations division chief (security officer), who had committed a cardinal sin by testifying truthfully before the Senate Internal Security Subcommittee about the lack of security in the State Department. Otepka, as a security officer, labored to keep security risks out of the government. Such integrity went against Secretary Rusk's grain and he sent Crockett on the dirty errand of getting rid of Otepka. Recently, after a five year campaign, the Rusk-Crockett combination succeeded as Otepka was reprimanded, demoted, and re-assigned to a Siberia somewhere within the red walls of the State Department.

LAUCHLIN CURRIE was born on October 8, 1902 in West Dublin, Nova Scotia, son of Alice Eisenhauer and Lauchlin Currie. He was married to Dorothy Bacon. He is married to Elvira Wiesner. He is an alumnus of the London School of Economics (B.S., 1925) and Harvard University (Ph.D., 1931). He was naturalized as an American citizen in 1934.

From 1927 until 1934, Currie was an instructor and tutor in economics at Harvard University. In 1933 and 1934, he also worked as a professor of international economics at the Fletcher School of Law and Diplomacy of Tufts University.

In 1934, Currie was for a brief time a senior analyst with the U.S. Department of the Treasury. From 1934 until 1939, he was an assistant director of research for the Board of Governors of the Federal Reserve Board.

From 1939 until 1945, Currie was an administrative assistant to President Franklin Roosevelt. His special duties were in the field of economics and, during his White House years, Currie headed an economic mission to China (1941), went to China as Roosevelt's personal diplomatic representative (1942), served as deputy administrator of the Foreign Economic Administration (1943-1944), and headed an economic mission to Switzerland (1945).

After Franklin Roosevelt's death in 1945, Currie resigned from government service. For a brief time, he was president of the Council of American-Italian Affairs. Then he established Lauchlin Currie & Co., Inc., an export-import business.

On July 31, 1948, Elizabeth Bentley, a former Soviet espionage agent, was testifying before the House Committee on Un-American Activities. Miss Bentley testified that Lauchlin Currie had furnished United States government secrets to a Soviet spy ring. Two weeks later, Currie — accompanied by his friend and attorney Dean Acheson — appeared voluntarily before HCUA to make a vigorous and unequivocal denial of Miss Bentley's charges. In his defense under oath, Currie said: "I am not and never have been a Communist, a member of the Communist Party, a believer in the tenets or doctrines of communism and that I have never been affiliated with any organization or group sympathetic with the doctrines of communism or engaged in furthering that cause. I have never had any reason to believe that any friends of mine or even acquaintances or associates were Communists."

On November 8, 1945 — almost three years before the Bentley-Currie episode in the HCUA hearings — FBI Director J. Edgar Hoover had informed President Harry Truman, through the latter's military aide Brigadier General Harry Vaughan, that Currie was one of many persons within the federal government who "have been furnishing data and information to persons outside the Federal Government, who are in turn transmitting this information to agents of the Soviet Government." Along with Currie, Director Hoover mentioned Harry Dexter White, Nathan Silverman, and several individuals from the Office of Strategic Services.

In 1950, Currie was hired by the World Bank to make an economic study in Columbia. Soon after Currie arrived in Columbia, he was hired by that government — for a $150,000 fee — as a private consultant and given the task of reorganizing the Columbian government's administrative setup.

In 1951, the Senate Internal Security Subcommittee began to hold hearings in its monumental investigation of the Institute of Pacific Relations. The charges against Currie which had been made in 1948 before HCUA by Elizabeth Bentley were revived. This time, however, Currie would not rush to his own defense. He announced that he had decided to take up permanent residence in Columbia.

From testimony of Miss Bentley, from corroborative testimony of former Communists Whittaker Chambers and Louis Budenz, and from State Department archives, the truth about Currie has been gradually revealed. Miss Bentley and Chambers, both of whom testified from firsthand experience, insisted that Currie had been a member of the Silvermaster Communist cell of government officials. In addition to Currie, the Silvermaster cell membership included Solomon Adler, Frank Coe, William Taylor, William Ullmann, Nathan and Abraham Silvermaster, Norman Bursler, and Mr. and Mrs. Bela Gold.

Louis Budenz testified that Currie played a prominent role in the Communist Party's plans in 1942 to smear patriotic officials in the State Department. Budenz said that Earl Browder, then the boss of the Communist Party in the U.S.A., told him that Currie had helped to work out the propaganda used in the Communist press against the patriots.

From various sources, including State Department archives, it has been revealed that Currie, in addition to passing on government secrets to Soviet agents, was very busy aiding the Communist conspirators in one way or another. Indeed, he proved to be a very versatile character.

While serving as an administrative assistant to President Roosevelt, Currie was the Institute of Pacific Relations liaison with the White House. In 1951 and 1952, the Senate Internal Security Subcommittee found that the IPR was an "instrument of Communist policy, propaganda and military intelligence" and "a vehicle used by the Communists to orientate American far eastern policies toward Communist objectives."

When the Japanese government was interested in proposing peace overtures before Pearl Harbor, Currie was instrumental in having those overtures summarily rejected by President Roosevelt.

From his prestigious White House position, Currie was able to defend Communist Nathan Silvermaster against charges of being a security risk. Currie served as a character reference for Communist Irving Kaplan when the latter was a successful applicant for federal government employment. Currie hired Communist Michael Greenberg for a job in the Foreign Economic Administration as a specialist (!) on China. Currie had Owen Lattimore appointed as an advisor to Chiang Kai-shek. And, in 1945, Currie was directly responsible for preventing an important shipment of arms and ammunition from reaching Chiang Kai-Shek's forces. Currie even allowed his White House office to be used by Owen Lattimore, John Kenneth Fairbank, and Michael Greenberg — three men whose individual and collective efforts played a major role in the sell-out of China to the regime of Mao Tse-tung.

If Currie had any thoughts about leaving Columbia for a return to the United States, they must have been dispelled in 1953 when Attorney General Herbert Brownell released J. Edgar Hoover's 1945 report on Currie's contributions to Soviet espionage. At any rate, in 1955, Currie's American citizenship was cancelled because he had remained outside this country longer than the five years permitted by law for naturalized citizens. If Currie ever made protest of this cancellation, such a fact has never been published. And, in 1958, he became a citizen of Columbia.

In 1961, Currie's name was back in the news. President John F. Kennedy had instituted his socialist handout program for Latin America, the Alliance for Progress. From Columbia came the report that the Alliance's money in that nation would be spent under the planning supervision of Currie. Russell Freeburg of the *Chicago Tribune* tracked the story down: "Information received in the [U.S.] Commerce Department here [Washington, D.C.] from the Columbian-American Chamber of Commerce gives the details of Currie's plan, which he calls Operation Columbia. A Spanish language newspaper received here also outlines the plan in an interview with Currie.

"The former Roosevelt assistant is identified in both as a consultant of various Columbian planning and economic boards. No official word has been received at the Commerce Department from the American embassy in Bogota on Currie's role, however.

"The Currie plan presented to Columbian officials would combine land reform and industrialization. He recommended breaking up the land into small, highly mechanized farms operated by their owners. He suggested moving one and one half million people from rural areas into Columbia's four most populous cities to strengthen home building, public works and factory output."

Four months after Mr. Freeburg's story appeared in the *Chicago Tribune*, Richard Eder of the *New York Times*

(December 20, 1963), writing from Bogota, came to the defense of Currie and his Marxist plans for Columbia. It was a touching tribute to Currie who was portrayed as an innocent victim of congressional investigating committees. And Eder wrote that Currie had remained in Columbia because "he decided all his opportunities were here and let his naturalization lapse." Unmentioned by Eder were the chances that Currie, if he had not sought refuge in Columbia, faced potential charges of perjury and espionage if he did return to the United States.

After the brief flurry of publicity in 1963, Currie's name disappeared from the pages of the American press until 1967. At that time, it was announced that Currie had accepted a position as "visiting scholar" during 1967-1968 at the Simon Fraser University of British Columbia in Currie's native Canada. Currie was granted $6,000 and expenses for his visit by the Canada Council, a tax-supported agency. What has gone unexplained is why Currie would accept such a relative pittance since his income as an economist and dairy farmer in Columbia has been repeatedly and unchallengingly reported as in excess of $100,000 a year.

EDWIN DAHLBERG was born on December 27, 1892 in Tergus Falls, Minnesota, son of Christine Ring and Elof Dahlberg. He married Emilie Loeffler. He is an alumnus of the University of Minnesota (B.A., 1914) and Rochester Theological Seminary (B.D., 1917). He was ordained to the Baptist ministry, in 1918, and, until 1962, served in various pastorates. Since 1963, he has been preacher-in-residence at Crozer Theological Seminary in Chester, Pennsylvania.

From 1946 until 1948, Dahlberg was president of the Northern Baptist Convention. From 1948 until 1954, he was a member of the central committee of the World Council of Churches. From 1957 until 1960, he was president of the National Council of Churches of Christ, U.S.A.

Dahlberg has been affiliated with the National Committee for the Defense of Political Prisoners ("subversive and Communist"); the Citizens' Committee to Free Earl Browder ("Communist"); the National Committee to Repeal the McCarran Act ("a Communist front" – "subversive"); the Conference for Peaceful Alternatives to the Atlantic Pact ("initiated by Communists").

Dahlberg has been one of the leaders in the ban-the-bomb lobby and, as might be expected, is a national sponsor of the National Committee for a Sane Nuclear Policy (leftwing, pacifist). His bleedingheart scaremongering has been evident in his attitude toward the Vietnam War. In 1965, he was a sponsor of the pacifists' and racial agitators' March on Washington for Peace in Vietnam. In that same year he went on a clergymen's junket to Vietnam, sponsored by the radical pacifist Fellowship of Reconciliation. When he returned from Vietnam, Dahlberg announced that the Vietcong were "fighting a genuine revolutionary war against oppression, poverty, misery and ignorance." In 1966, he participated in the National Voters' Pledge Campaign, which was led by Socialist Norman Thomas, veteran Communist-fronter Reverend William Sloane Coffin, and Sanford Gottlieb, the political director of the National Committee for a Sane Nuclear Policy. The Voters' Pledge Campaign was designed to support "peace" candidates, who would work for a cease-fire in Vietnam and encourage negotiations in which the Vietcong would be participants.

JOHN PATON DAVIES JR. was born on April 6, 1908 in Kiating, China, son of U.S. citizens Helen MacNeil and John Davies. He married Patricia Grady. He attended the University of Wisconsin (1928-1929) and Yenching University (1930). He is an alumnus of Columbia University (B.S., 1931).

In 1931, Davies began a twenty-three-year career in the State Department. In 1932, he was a vice-consul in Windsor, Ontario. From 1933 until 1940, he was stationed in China as a vice-consul at Yünnanfu (Kunming), language officer at Peiping, and vice-consul at Mukden and Hankow. From 1940 until 1942, he was stationed in Washington, D.C. In 1942, he – along with John S. Service, Raymond Ludden, and John K. Emmerson – was assigned to the staff of the China Theater Headquarters, under the command of General Joseph Stilwell. (Technically, Davies held the position of second secretary of the U.S. mission in Chungking.) When General Albert C. Wedemeyer succeeded Stilwell, he inherited the four "China boys," whom Wedemeyer described as having given reports to Stilwell that "uniformly expressed strong disapproval of the National Government and invariably embodied favorable views of the [Chinese] Communists." (See, *Wedemeyer Reports,* 1958, page 303.)

Stilwell's undisguised hatred of Chiang Kai-shek and his total admiration for the Chinese Communists were encouraged – if not inspired – by Davies and his colleagues. According to Wedemeyer, "their sympathy for the Chinese Communists [was] obvious in their reports and in their recommendations that we back the Communists instead of the Nationalist Government" (*Reports,* page 312), and "they were either consciously or unwittingly disseminating exaggerated or false, Communist-inspired, reports concerning the Nationalist Government designed to stir up all manner of Sino-American distrust – as, for instance, when John Davies sent me long accounts of rumors or unsubstantiated reports that the Generalissimo [Chiang Kai-shek] was collaborating with the Japanese or had reached a tacit nonaggression pact with them." (*Reports,* page 313.)

Wedemeyer was astonished to find Davies very much concerned that a leading Communist general had "little faith in what the United States will do to help the Communists:" (*Reports,* page 314.) For his part, Davies certainly labored tirelessly to bolster the general's faith. In the midst of World War II, while Chiang Kai-shek was undeniably a staunch ally of the United States, Davies' strategy was that the United States "should not now abandon Chiang Kai-shek" because for the moment we would "lose more than we could gain." However, the United States should "have no qualms in ultimately abandoning him [Chiang Kai-shek] in favor of the progressive – Communist – forces in China." At another time, Davies described the Chinese Communists as "the most coherent, progressive and powerful force in China."

Without exception, every dispatch sent by Davies from China to the State Department adhered to the Communist line and there were times when Davies even outdid the Communists in misrepresentation ("They [the Chinese Communists] recognize that our strategic aims of a strong, independent and democratic China can jibe with their nationalist objectives.")

In the midst of the war in Asia, General Patrick Hurley was sent on an ambassadorial mission to China by President Franklin Roosevelt. Hurley's objective was to negotiate with the Chinese Communists to use their troops against Japan's forces. But Hurley found that his negotiations were being undermined by Davies and Service. Hurley became so incensed that he forced the recall of Davies from China. Hurley went so far as to charge that Davies was a Communist but Davies insisted that he had never accepted Communism as his philosophy. But his protestations notwithstanding, Davies was transferred to Moscow where he served as consul, second secretary, and first secretary at the U.S. Embassy from 1945 until 1947. He returned to the State Department in Washington, D.C. and, except for a brief stint in Germany, finished out his career there.

In 1951, Davies' pro-Communist conduct came under the scrutiny of the Senate Internal Security Subcommittee during its investigation of the Institute of Pacific Relations. (By that time, Davies was on the State Department's Policy Planning Staff.) As might be expected, the SISS found Davies to be quite unresponsive when he was interrogated as to his affiliations and activities with the pro-Chinese Communist clique, in and out of government circles, which had contributed so effectively to the sell-out of Free China. And, in the course of the hearings, the SISS found that Davies testified falsely with respect to his recommendations that the Central Intelligence Agency employ and utilize Edgar Snow, Wilma Fairbank, Benjamin K. Schwartz, John K. Fairbank, Agnes Smedley, and Anna Louise Strong – the latter three had been identified as Communists in sworn testimony before the SISS.

In the background, however, there were forces working determinately to protect Davies and he was "cleared" at least seven times by State Department loyalty boards. Finally, some of Davies' luck ran out and, in 1954, he was discharged from the State Department by Secretary of State John F. Dulles, who said: "The members of the Security Hearing Board unanimously found that Mr. Davies' lack of judgment, discretion and reliability raises a reasonable doubt that his continued employment in the Foreign Service of the United States is clearly consistent with the interests of national security. This is a conclusion which I am also compelled to reach as a result of my review of the case." Dulles did soften the blow by offering himself as a reference when Davies was searching for a new job. For his part, Davies took the setback with equanimity. He had been branded as a bad security risk but escaped all charges of disloyalty. And, instead of fighting for reinstatement to his old or some other government position, he repaired to Peru where he became a very successful furniture designer and manufacturer.

Davies has returned to the United States and for the past four years has resided in Washington, D.C. He has written *Foreign and Other Affairs,* a severe critique of the Kennedy-Johnson foreign policy. In his book, Davies demonstrates the pot-calling-the-kettle-black, particularly with regard to the current U.S. policy toward Communist China. (When the book appeared, *Newsweek* magazine wept over the return of the prodigal Davies as "one of the victims offered up to Sen. Joseph McCarthy's blood-lust." Ten years earlier, *Newsweek* had honestly recounted how Davies "reported from China that the Communists were 'agrarian reformers' interested in civil rights and friendly to the United States," and that Davies was fired by Secretary of State Dulles – not McCarthy – after extensive investigations by the SISS and the State Department's Security Board, neither of which could claim McCarthy as a member.) But Davies has now joined the ranks of elder liberal statesmen with particular expertise on China. And on April 3, 1966, when "Book Week" (*New York Herald Tribune* and *Washington Post*) had eight books on China to review, its editors called upon Davies to do the honors. He demonstrated that over the previous twelve years there had been no improvement in his "judgment, discretion and reliability."

JEROME DAVIS was born on December 2, 1891 in Kioto, Japan, son of U.S. citizens Frances Hooper and Jerome Davis. He married Mildred Rood. He is an alumnus of Oberlin College (A.B., 1913) and Columbia University (M.A., 1919; Ph.D., 1922). He also graduated from Union Theological Seminary in 1920.

Davis has divided his energies for fifty years between teaching (Columbia University, Dartmouth College, Yale University's Divinity School, Hiram College of Ohio, University of Colorado, Fisk University, International Christian University of Japan, and various theological seminaries); sociology; church work; pacificism; and, Communist fronts. He has done work for the Y.M.C.A., was president of the American Federation of Teachers, and has made many visits to the Soviet Union, beginning in 1927 when he went there with the late Edward A. Filene, a millionaire patsy for the Communists.

During his variegated career, Davis claims that E. Mandell House, Woodrow Wilson's alter ego, wanted him to become U.S. Ambassador to the Soviet Union.

Davis has written a great number of books, many of them extolling the glories of the Soviet Union, others preaching pacifism and the desirability of one world, and still others on the need for disarmament.

In 1956, the Senate Internal Security Subcommittee included Davis' name in its list of the eighty-two most active and typical sponsors of Communist front organizations. He has been affiliated with the American Committee for Democracy and Intellectual Freedom ("Communist front" – "subversive and un-American"); the American Committee for Protection of Foreign Born [Americans] ("subversive and Communist" – "one of the oldest auxiliaries of the Communist Party in the United States" – under the "complete domination" of the Communist Party; the American Council on Soviet Relations ("established by Communist Party"); the American Fund for Public Service ("a major source for the financing of Communist Party enterprises"); the American League for Peace and Democracy ("subversive and Communist"); the American League against War and Fascism ("subversive and Communist"); the American Peace Crusade ("Communist front"); the American Society for Cultural Relations with Russia ("Communist front"); the American Student Union ("Communist front"); the American Youth Congress ("subversive and Communist"); *Champion* ("Communist publication"); the Committee to Defend America by keeping out of War ("Communist-led"); Commonwealth College ("Communist"); the Coordinating Committee to Lift the Embargo ("Communist front"); the Council for Pan-American Democracy ("subversive and Communist"); the Friends of the Abraham Lincoln Brigade ("its officers and staff members were in the main [Communist] Party members and functionaries"); the Friends of the Soviet Union ("to propagandize for and defend Russia and its system of government" – "directed from Moscow"); the Galena Defense Committee ("Communist front"); International Labor Defense ("legal arm of the Communist Party"); the League of American Writers ("subversive and Communist"); the League for Mutual Aid ("Communist enterprise"); the Medical Bureau and North American Committee to Aid Spanish Democracy ("subversive and un-American"); the Methodist Federation for Social Action ("Communist front"); the Mid-Century Conference for Peace ("aimed at assembling as many gullible persons as possible under Communist direction and turning them into a vast sounding board for Communist propaganda" – "a Communist front"); the National Committee to Repeal the McCarran Act ("a Communist front" – "subversive"); the National Council of American-Soviet Friendship ("subversive and Communist" – "specializing in pro-Soviet propaganda"); the National Council of the Arts, Sciences and Professions ("a Communist front used to appeal to special occupational groups"); the National Emergency Conference ("Communist front"); the National Negro Congress ("subversive and Communist"); *New Masses* ("Communist periodical"); the New York Peace Institute ("Communist front"); the New York Tom Mooney Committee ("Communist front"); the Peace Information Center ("Communist front"); the *Protestant Digest* ("Communist Party line"); Russian Reconstruction Farms ("Communist enterprise"); *Social Work Today* ("Communist magazine"); and, Workers Library Publishers ("official Communist Party, U.S.A., publishing house"). He has also been an official of the socialist League for Industrial Democracy.

Incidentally, Davis insists that he is "opposed to Communism."

ARTHUR DEAN was born on October 16, 1898 in Ithaca, New York, son of William and Maud Dean. He married Mary Marden. He is an alumnus of Cornell University (A.B., 1921; LL.B., 1923).

He began the practice of law, in 1923, in the firm of Sullivan & Cromwell, where John Foster Dulles was a partner.

In 1953 and 1954, Dean was a special U.S. Ambassador to Korea to take part in the so-called peace negotiations with the Red Chinese at Panmunjom. Previously, Dean had been vice chairman of the Institute of Pacific Relations, at the very time that the IPR was under the control of Communists and pro-Communists who used the IPR as a vehicle to orientate U.S. foreign policy in the Far East toward Communist objectives. Dean, as late as 1947, had the gall to describe the IPR as lily-white. For Communist purposes, the choice of Eisenhower and Dulles to send Dean to Panmunjom could not have been more appropriate.

In the very period when Dean was the American negotiator for a Korean settlement, he was all but urging U.S. diplomatic recognition for Red China and its admission to United Nations membership. By 1955, the wraps were completely off as he wanted not only recognition for Red China but also U.S. trade with that nation.

Dean was brought back into government service by President Kennedy who made Dean the chairman of the U.S. delegation to the perennial Geneva disarmament conference where the disastrous nuclear test-ban treaty was concocted. And President Johnson has made Dean a member of his "peace panel."

Dean has been an official of the Council on Foreign Relations, the informal supra-State Department of the United States; a member of the Foreign Policy Association; and, an official of the extreme leftist United Nations Association which, in 1966, advocated not only membership in the UN for Red China but also membership on the UN security Council after a "probationary" period.

VERA MICHELES DEAN was born on March 29, 1903 in St. Petersburg, Russia, daughter of Alexander and Nadine Micheles. She was naturalized in 1925. She was married to the late William J. Dean. She is an alumna of Radcliffe College (A.B., 1925) and Yale University (M.A., 1926; Ph.D., 1928).

From 1928 until 1938, she was a research associate and editor of research publications for the Foreign Policy Association. From 1938 until 1961, she was the FPA's research director and editor. She has held teaching positions at Smith College, the University of Rochester, and New York University. She has written countless books, pamphlets, and articles.

Mrs. Dean is unquestionably the most prolific and certainly one of the most durable pro-Soviet apologists in this country. But she is also a leading member of the Red China lobby, an apologist for Tito, and a fanatic proponent for foreign aid boondoggles directed at any and all nations. And for all this, she has enjoyed richly deserved tributes in the Communist press. More than any other individual, Mrs. Dean deserves credit for making the Foreign Policy Association and its publications one of the most effective pro-Communist vehicles during her reign from 1931 until 1961. Yet, in 1961, Mrs. Dean was a guest lecturer at the United States Air Force War College. The Air Force Secretary Eugene Zuckert explained her appearance by saying that "considerable discretion is vested in the [War College's] Commandant to select those speakers who may best serve the needs of the school."!!!

[CLARENCE] DOUGLAS DILLON was born on August 21, 1909 in Geneva, Switzerland, son of U.S. citizens Anne Douglass and Clarence Dillon. He married Phyllis Ellsworth. He is an alumnus of Harvard University (A.B., 1931).

From 1931 until 1953, Dillon was in business as a member of the New York Stock Exchange; a director and president of U.S. & Foreign Securities Corporation; a director and president of U.S. & International Securities Corporation; vice president, director, and chairman of the board of Dillon, Read & Company. Dillon became active in New Jersey politics after World War II. Then, in 1948, he collaborated with John Foster Dulles in writing speeches for Thomas E. Dewey who was the Republican candidate for the presidency. In 1951, Dillon led a draft-Eisenhower movement in New Jersey, and, in 1952, he was a delegate to the Republican national convention.

In 1953, President Eisenhower sent Dillon as U.S. Ambassador to France. After four years in France, Dillon spent four years in the State Department as Under Secretary for Economic Affairs and as Under Secretary of State. In the State Department, it was Dillon's task to sell the merits of foreign aid programs to congressional committees. He did it well.

From 1961 until 1965, Dillon was Secretary of the Treasury. When the history of United States fiscal insanity is written, Dillon's activities as Secretary of the Treasury will be featured prominently. While he was in the Treasury, the American gold supply virtually disappeared. Printing press money, without deposits of silver in the Treasury, was foisted upon the American people. And for the first time in history, the U.S. mint counterfeited dates on coins. Meanwhile, Dillon, through his foreign aid advice to the Kennedy-Johnson Administrations, was pushing American money down foreign aid ratholes, such as Nasser's Egypt, Tito's Yugoslavia, Gomulka's Poland, and Nehru's India.

FRANK DONNER was born on February 25, 1911 in Brooklyn, New York. He is an alumnus of the University of Wisconsin (A.B. and M.A.) and Columbia University (LL.B.).

In the early 1940's, Donner was an attorney with the National Labor Relations Board when the NLRB staff had at least two separate cells of the Communist Party. From 1946 until 1948, he was assistant general counsel for the CIO. In 1948, he engaged in private law practice and, in 1956, he became general counsel of the United Electrical, Radio and Machine Workers.

On June 28, 1956, Donner – in testimony before the House Committee on Un-American Activities – pleaded the protection of the first, fifth, and sixth amendments to the U.S. Constitution when asked for his knowledge of Communists and their activities within the NLRB. He made the same pleas when asked about his own Communist Party membership. Before the HCUA on March 11, 1959, Donner refused to say if he had been a member of the Communist Party prior to June 28, 1956. Herbert Fuchs, Mortimer Reimer, and Harry Cooper testified under oath that they knew Donner as a comrade within the Communist Party.

In July of 1961, Ballantine Books published *The Un-Americans* a paper-

back written by Donner with the assistance of at least one Communist (Bertram Edises) and a number of other persons who had extensive records of Communist front activity.

Donner has been affiliated with the National Lawyers Guild ("the foremost legal bulwark of the Communist Party, its front organizations, and controlled unions"); the American Committee for Protection of Foreign Born [Americans] ("subversive and Communist" – "one of the oldest auxiliaries of the Communist Party in the United States" – under the "complete domination" of the Communist Party); and, the Emergency Civil Liberties Committee ("Communist front" – "subversive").

WILLIAM O. DOUGLAS was born on October 16, 1898 in Maine, Minnesota, son of Julia Fiske and William Douglas. He has had four wives: Mildred Riddle, Mercedes Hester, Joan Martin, and, presently, Cathleen Heffernan. He is an alumnus of Whitman College (B.A., 1920) and Columbia University (LL.B., 1925).

From 1920 until 1922, Douglas was a high school teacher in Yakima, Washington. He practiced law in New York City from 1925 until 1927. He was on the law faculties at Columbia University (1925-1928) and at Yale University (1928-1934). From 1929 until 1932, he was engaged in bankruptcy studies at the Yale Institute of Human Relations.

From 1934 until 1939, Douglas worked for the U.S. Department of Commerce as director – later commissioner and chairman – of a protective committee study of the Securities and Exchange Commission.

Since 1939, Douglas has been an Associate Justice of the Supreme Court. It was an appointment which best demonstrated President Franklin D. Roosevelt's utter contempt for the Supreme Court.

In his years on the Supreme Court, Douglas has proven to be one of the most obnoxious exhibitionists in the entire history of American public life. He has gained a great deal of notoriety as a world traveler, mountain climber, and conservationist. But his travels and advocacies of conservation are merely a front for his advocacy of the straight Communist line, which is unmistakably present in his judicial decisions, his writings, and his public speeches and lectures.

Douglas has been an unabashed apologist for the Soviet Union and for Communists at home and abroad; a lobbyist for U.S. diplomatic recognition of Red China, coupled with the disarming of Nationalist China; a lobbyist for Red China's admission to the United Nations; a virulent foe of business and free enterprise; an enemy of States' Rights and a pleader for the Welfare State; and, he has espoused world law, disarmament, and groveling accommodation between the United States and the entire Communist bloc. He has even gone so far as to hope that the Soviet Union could become the policeman for all Asia.

Douglas has made frequent visits to Communist nations where he has always been greeted with the friendliest of welcomes. He has seldom missed an opportunity to visit the Soviet Embassy in Washington when the Communists are celebrating some milestone in their history of bestiality. His voice on the Supreme Court is invariably on the side of Communists and criminals. He detests loyalty oaths or any investigations of subversives.

Douglas has long been associated with the leftwing Fund for the Republic's Center for the Study of Democratic Institutions. He has been a major fund raiser and consultant for the Center and chairman of its Board of Directors. As an official of the Center, Douglas — at least until recently — was receiving $12,000 a year through a subsidy from the tax-exempt Albert Parvin Foundation that derived much of its income from a mortgage on a Las Vegas hotel and gambling casino.

ROSCOE DRUMMOND was born about 1903 in Theresa, New York, son of Georgia Peppers and John Drummond. He married Charlotte Bruner. He is an alumnus of Syracuse University (B.S.J., 1924).

Drummond spent thirty years with the *Christian Science Monitor* in positions ranging from assistant city editor to executive editor. He was also the *Monitor's* chief editorial writer and head of its Washington news bureau.

In 1953, Drummond joined the now defunct *New York Herald Tribune* as head of that journal's Washington bureau and he inaugurated his syndicated column "Washington."

Drummond has been chairman of the board of trustees of Freedom House, a center for anti-anti-Communism; and, a non-resident member of the Council on Foreign Relations, the informal supra-State Department of the United States.

As a national columnist, Drummond really came into his own when he joined the liberal hyenas, yapping at the heels of the late Senator Joseph R. McCarthy. As recently as 1967, Drummond was equating McCarthyism with Nazism. It would be extremely difficult to place Drummond in the camp of either political party since he displays his adoration for the extreme leftists whether they are Republicans or Democrats. His heroes

308

are the likes of Lyndon Johnson, Bobby Kennedy, and George Romney while on the other extreme would be Barry Goldwater, Ronald Reagan, and anyone to the right of Americans for Democratic Action. Whether Drummond is writing on the United Nations, Kenya's President Jomo Kenyatta, Yugoslavia's Tito, or Vietnam, his column resembles nothing less than the latest political effusion of the Council on Foreign Relations and Americans for Democratic Action.

Drummond's forte has been his incredibly bad analyses of Communist machinations abroad. He has been in the forefront of those who have pushed Titoism as a less dangerous form of Communism. He has represented the Soviet Union's leaders as would-be peacemakers in Vietnam. And he has downgraded the continuing threat of Communist aggression and subversion whether it is Mao Tse-tung's, Brezhnev's, or Castro's brand.

DAVID DUBINSKY was born on February 22, 1892 in Brest-Litovsk, Poland, son of Shaine Wisingrad and Zallel Dubinsky. He joined the Bakers' Union in Russia in 1906. A year later, he was arrested for strike activities. He was arrested again in 1908 and served eighteen months in prison. In 1909, he was exiled to Siberia, but escaped from his banishment within five months. He came to the United States in 1911, and was naturalized in 1916. He married Emma Goldberg.

In 1911, Dubinsky went to work as a ladies' garment cutter and joined the Garment Workers Union. In 1919, he was on the executive board of a union local and, in 1920, was vice president and, in 1921, president of the local. In Poland, Dubinsky belonged to the Social Democratic Party and, during his first few years in the United States, he became active in the Socialist Party, the Jewish Socialist Federation, and the Jewish Socialist Verband. He became a supporter of the Communistic Brookwood Labor College and a sponsor of the Socialists' Trade Union Institute of the Rand School. During the 1930's, he raised over $100,000 for the red front in Spain.

In 1932, Dubinsky became president of the International Ladies Garment Workers Union. As virtual czar of the ILGWU, Dubinsky has been a politically active Socialist. In 1936, he founded the American Labor Party in New York. In 1944, he founded the Liberal Party in New York and, in 1947, he was a founder of Americans for Democratic Action. He has been affiliated with the socialist League for Industrial Democracy and is a resident member of the Council on Foreign Relations, the informal supra-State Department of the United States. Meanwhile, he has been active in international socialist union activities.

Dubinsky long ago adopted the posture of a non-Communist Socialist who battled against Communist control of ILGWU, but, as a radical political leader in the pivotal State of New York, Dubinsky has demonstrated that he is a class-conscious Marxist bent upon destroying all vestiges of conservatism in American politics. He has steadily but surely, with the help of other radical labor leaders, pushed the Democrat Party into socialism.

In 1966, Dubinsky retired as president-czar of ILGWU but his political power remains and he is an especial associate of the Johnson Administration. Vice President Hubert Humphrey has called Dubinsky "a great American citizen who has been in the forefront of American liberalism [!] ." President Johnson has described Dubinsky as his "teacher."

ANGIER BIDDLE DUKE was born on November 30, 1915 in New York City, son of Cordelia Biddle and Angier Duke. His third wife is Robin Chandler. He studied at Yale University but never graduated.

Duke has been president of Duke International Corporation, vice president of CARE, president of the socialist-lined International Rescue Committee, an active Democrat, and a member of the Council on Foreign Relations, the informal supra-State Department of the United States.

For reasons which defy rationalization, Duke entered the foreign service in 1949 as a second secretary with his first assignment in Buenos Aires. In 1951, he was made a special assistant to the U.S. Ambassador to Spain. In 1952 and 1953, he was U.S. Ambassador to El Salvador.

Duke served as the State Department's chief of protocol in the Kennedy and Johnson Administrations (1961-1965) and, in 1965, was appointed as U.S. Ambassador to Spain. In 1961, Duke was chairman of the sponsoring committee for a testimonial dinner given in honor of Adam Clayton Powell, Jr.

In 1955, Duke became head of American Friends of Vietnam which was basically a front of the International Rescue Committee. The AFV, itself, was nothing less than a propaganda agency for the late Ngo dinh Diem, who was presented to the American people by Duke and his leftwing cohorts as the answer to freedom's prayer in South Vietnam. At this stage of the game, it should be obvious that the purpose of AFV in its meddling in foreign policy was to impose a socialist dictatorship upon South Vietnam. Somewhere along the line Ngo dinh Diem outlived his usefulness to his American puppeteers and he was liquidated with the acquies-cence, if not the connivance, of American officials and the Central Intelligence Agency. While the dirty deeds were performed in South Vietnam, Duke remained on the national committee of AFV, which organization has remained squarely on the side of the Kennedy-Rusk-McNamara-Johnson team as it wages the perennial no-win war against the Communists. And the AFV has the gall to say that it is educating Americans as to the "essential facts" by "distinguishing real issues from red herrings" concerning the situation in South Vietnam. In truth, Duke and his AFV have been the biggest red herrings of them all.

CYRUS EATON was born on December 27, 1883 in Nova Scotia, son of Mary McPherson and Joseph Eaton. He came to the United States in 1900 and was naturalized in 1913. He was married to the late Margaret House and is married to Anne Jones. He is an alumnus of McMaster University of Toronto (A.B., 1905).

Eaton is a multi-millionaire who began his working career with John D. Rockefeller Sr. If Rockefeller was a teacher, then Eaton must be the best student he ever had because Eaton has been a successful tycoon in public utilities, steel, banking, railroading, mining, and the paint industry. Eaton's interests have included the Republic Steel Corporation, Otis & Company, the Sherwin-Williams Company, the Baltimore & Ohio Railroad, the Steep Rock Iron Mines, the Chesapeake and Ohio Railway, and various utility companies in this country and in Canada. (More recently, his son's Tower International Inc. has joined with the Rockefeller brothers' International Basic Economy Corporation to promote trade between the Communist bloc and the United States, Canada, and Latin America.)

Eaton became active in politics by supporting Franklin Roosevelt in 1932. Since then Eaton has progressed so far to the left that he is the most vocal mouthpiece for Communism outside the Communist bloc. Eaton's wife Anne is also a well-known fellow traveler, sometimes more brazen in her un-American outbursts than her elderly husband.

In 1954, Eaton dedicated his ancestral home at Pugwash, Nova Scotia as a retreat for intellectuals and, in 1954 and 1955, brief meetings of some of the world's outstanding leftwingers were held there. Then, in 1957, there developed the first formal Pugwash Conference, attended by more than twenty of the world's most publicized nuclear scientists. They came from the United States, Canada, Australia, France, Japan, Britain, Austria, Communist Poland, Communist China, and the Soviet Union. (The formal conference was inspired by two venerable Reds, Bertrand Russell and Albert Einstein, but Eaton has said that Einstein deserves most of the credit for the inspiration.) Since 1957, more than fifteen Pugwash conferences have been held at various locations, including several Communist nations. The overriding objective of the conferences, which have been attended by officials and others close to the Eisenhower-Kennedy-Johnson Administrations, has been the promotion of disarmament by the United States. And Americans who have taken part in the Pugwash conferences may accurately be described as this nation's surrender lobby — surrender to the Soviet Union.

Eaton's own personal love affair with the Soviet Union has been marked by his personal friendship with such notorious Soviet butchers as Khrushchev, Mikoyan, and Kosygin. Eaton has visited the Soviet Union and repaid Communist hospitality by entertaining hordes of Communist officials in this country. And for his efforts, he has received the Lenin Peace Prize, an award reserved only for those who have made a significant contribution to the Soviet Union.

In recent years, Eaton has labored tirelessly for U.S. diplomatic recognition of Red China.

DON EDWARDS was born on January 6, 1915 in San Jose, California. He is married. He is an alumnus of Stanford University (B.A., 1936; LL.B., 1938).

In 1940 and 1941, Edwards was a special agent in the Federal Bureau of Investigation. (He is now a critic of the FBI.)

In recent years, Edwards has been president of the Valley Title Company of San Jose. (Two individuals hired by Edwards include an identified Communist and a Fifth Amendment-pleader. Edwards has described them as "fine young men.")

Edwards is a Democrat. (At one time, he was a leader of the Young Republicans in California.)

In 1962, Edwards was elected to the U.S. House of Representatives. He was re-elected in 1964 and 1966. In the House, his main achievement has been a futile effort to abolish the House Committee on Un-American Activities. Not only did he lead a group of ultra-liberals in the abolition movement, but he proposed that HCUA's files be locked for fifty years.

In 1965, Edwards was elected to be national chairman of Americans for Democratic Action, the center of the radical left in American politics. He was an ideal choice for the job since he had been a defender of the ADA's program on the floor of the House — a program which mirrored his own principles.

311

Edwards' tenure as the ADA's national chairman had an auspicious beginning. The 1965 ADA convention was treated to an address by President Lyndon Johnson who heaped praises on the radicals — a far cry from 1960 when Mr. Johnson had spurned the support of the ADAers whom he characterized as odd balls on the left.

When Edwards assumed leadership of ADA, the organization presented a program for acceptance by the American people that could only be considered as pro-Communist and thoroughly anti-American. There was a demand for an immediate cease-fire by the United States in Vietnam, coupled with the United States holding out to the Vietcong "the prospect of a voice in the future political life of South Vietnam." To hasten negotiations, the ADA desired foreign pressures upon the United States government: "We urge Russia, India, Britain, and the rest of the world to press the United States to change its posture and to press Hanoi and Peking to agree to an early negotiated settlement."

For Red China, the ADA demanded U.S. diplomatic and trade relations, the removal of restrictions on travel to and from Red China, and the admission of Red China to the United Nations.

The ADA wanted the United Nations to develop a body of world law and, to support the UN, the United States should pursue policies that would create a UN Peace Force and a UN Peace Observation Corps recruited by and available to the Secretary General. The ADA further urged the U.S. and other nuclear powers to support UN peacekeeping operations by committing "a fraction of annual defense expenditures as evidence of sincerity." The U.S. Senate was urged to remove the Connally Reservation (which safeguards U.S. domestic interests from the World Court's jurisdiction) and to ratify UN conventions on genocide, slavery, forced labor, women's political rights, and racial discrimination.

On the European scene, the ADA favored de facto U.S. diplomatic recognition of East Germany, recognition of the Oder-Neisse boundaries for West Germany (a Soviet dictated settlement), and a U.S.-supported non-aggression pact between NATO and the Communist bloc's Warsaw Pact powers.

In further tribute to the United Nations, the ADA recommended that negotiations for disarmament and the non-proliferation of nuclear weapons be conducted under the aegis of the UN.

On African matters, the ADA condemned the Portuguese for maintaining their Overseas Provinces of Angola, Mozambique, and Portuguese Guinea. And the ADA urged a complete embargo against Rhodesia and economic sanctions against South Africa. The targets of ADA's program were, of course, the anti-Communist bastions in Africa. On the other hand, ADA recommended that the United States resume trade in "non-strategic" goods with Communist Cuba and lift passport restrictions on travel by American citizens to Cuba.

ADA did not neglect its socialist penchant for spending the United States into complete bankruptcy. It recommended a three-fold increase in foreign "aid" through long-term commitments and, on the domestic scene, a guaranteed annual income for every family, a doubling of social security "benefits," higher unemployment compensation, a federal monopoly on welfare programs, a higher minimum wage, a federal program to "create" five million jobs in five years, a tripling of funds for the Office of Economic Opportunity, an enlarged "soak-the-middle-class-and wealthy" tax program, a drastic increase of federal housing and urban renewal programs, and an increase of federal financing and control of elementary and secondary education.

Perhaps the most appreciated demand by ADA, in Edwards' eyes, was for the abolition of HCUA and the Senate Internal Security Subcommittee. But close upon this demand, for Edwards' appreciation, would be ADA's comprehensive program for federal legislation and enforcement of so-called civil rights. For his part, Edwards boasted of his financial support of the Student Non-violent Coordinating Committee, the revolutionary racist agitators who were heavily infiltrated by Communists. And when the anarchistic Free Speech Movement at the University of California's Berkeley campus was at its riotous height, Edwards protested the police action taken against the "student" and "non-student" mob.

Edwards did not interrupt his congressional career to lead ADA. Thus, his constituents and colleagues had the advantage of being able to predict with certainty how he would vote on every bill before the House – he simply followed the guidelines of ADA. And, after relinquishing his national chairmanship, he continued to be a 100 per cent ADAer.

MILTON EISENHOWER was born on September 15, 1899 in Abilene, Kansas, son of Ida Stover and David Eisenhower. He married Helen Eakin. He is an alumnus of Kansas State University (B.S., 1924).

From 1924 until 1926, Eisenhower was a vice consul in Edinburgh, Scotland. In 1926, he entered the Department of Agriculture where he remained until 1941. For two years, he was an assistant to the Secretary of Agriculture, then from 1928 until 1941, he was

Director of Information. Throughout most of the time that Eisenhower was in the Department, the Communists used it as the springboard to bigger and better things for subversion. Among Eisenhower's colleagues in Agriculture were such Communist luminaries as Harold Ware, John J. Abt, Nathan Witt, Lee Pressman, and Henry H. Collins Jr. – all of whom were members of the infamous Ware cell.

In 1942, Eisenhower, for a brief time, was director of the War Relocation Authority, which was the polite name for warden of Roosevelt's concentration camps where more than 100,000 American citizens or residents were imprisoned. In 1942 and 1943, he became associate director of Elmer Davis' Red-lined Office of War Information.

In 1943, Eisenhower began his first of three college presidencies. Until 1950, he was president of Kansas State University, where he had earned his only degree. He is not the only university president to hold just a bachelor's degree in modern times, but it is doubtful if any other individual with such a limited academic background has ever been president of three universities. At any rate, from 1950 until 1956, he was president of Pennsylvania State University and, from 1956 until 1967, he was president of The Johns Hopkins University.

While at Kansas State University, Eisenhower became prominent in the promotion and activities of UNESCO and, as chairman of the U.S. National Commission for UNESCO, Eisenhower went on record as advocating the sacrifice of U.S. sovereignty in the interests of world government. The Communists, of course, recognized UNESCO as an agency that could propagandize for world government through the corruption of educational processes of every member-nation of the United Nations.

Milton Eisenhower's presidential terms at Pennsylvania State and Johns Hopkins paralleled his brother Dwight's two terms in the White House. The President made Milton a member of the Commission on Government Organization and a special ambassador and personal presidential representative for U.S.-Latin American Affairs. But more important than the particular jobs he held was the overwhelming influence he exerted upon the entire Eisenhower Administration. The accelerated accommodation of the United States government with Communist regimes, the White House war against anti-Communist investigations, the rise of Castro, and the fragmentation of the Republican Party can all be attributed in great part to Milton Eisenhower, whose influence was constantly acknowledged by his brother, the President.

In the Johnson Administration, Milton has been one of a five-member team of advisers on the current sell-out of the United States' Panama Canal, a project which has long had a high priority position in the Communists' plans for world conquest.

Russell Kirk once quipped that Dwight Eisenhower was not a Communist. He was a golfer.

Milton is not noted for his golf.

ROBERT ELEGANT was born on March 7, 1928 in New York City, son of Lillie Sampson and Louis Elegant. He married Moira Brody. He is an alumnus of the University of Pennsylvania (A.B., 1946) and Columbia University (M.A., 1950; M.S., 1951).

In 1951 and 1952, Elegant was a Far East correspondent for the Overseas News Agency. In 1953, he covered the Korean War for International News Service. In 1954 and 1955, he was a correspondent in Singapore for the Columbia Broadcasting System, the North American Newspaper Alliance, and the McGraw-Hill News Service.

In 1956, Elegant went with *Newsweek* and, over the next eight years, he was that magazine's bureau chief in New Delhi, Hong Kong, and Bonn.

In 1965, Elegant began his present job as chief of the Hong Kong bureau of the *Los Angeles Times*. He has written several books on the Far East and has had at least two boosts from the left wing: a Pulitzer traveling fellowship and a Ford Foundation fellowship.

In 1966, *Time* magazine, in a very favorable appraisal of Elegant, described him as "a sympathetic but unsentimental observer of Communist China." *Time* explained further: "He stresses the fact that its rulers are not so very different from those of past regimes. Most of them, contends Elegant, have aspired to create a vigorously controlled utopia in China, whatever the cost.

"Mao [Tse-tung], he writes, is a 'man drunk with the foretaste of utopia.' " Equating Mao's barbarism with a search for utopia is not simply sympathetic, it is stupid. But Elegant usually seems eager to be accepted as a different breed of Red-Sinologist: neither fish nor fowl. However, in the past three years of writing from Hong Kong, the balance of Elegant's leanings are unmistakably on the side of U.S. diplomatic recognition of Red China. ("Communist China, 16 years after the regime's formal [*sic*] establishment, is neither the hell of starvation and oppression its bitter critics depict nor the paradise its enthusiastic friends [*sic*] praise. The truth, in this case, lies broadly in between.") Somehow Elegant uses 1958 as the turning point when Mao's regime began to mellow toward the peasants of the mainland. Elegant calls the transformation "Peking's new sanity."

Away from his dispatches on Red-Sinology, Elegant finds time to pass judgment on the Vietnam War (fought between the United States which is rich, expansive and technological "and North Vietnam which is poor, puritan and so primitive") and he leaves little doubt that he sympathizes with the North Vietnamese. He is not about to admit that the poor puritans of Ho Chi Minh's regime are in the war only because of the total support they receive from the Soviet Union and its satellites and "mellowing" Mao Tse-tung. Elegant is the Fulbright of the press.

THOMAS I. EMERSON was born on July 12, 1907 in Passaic, New Jersey, son of Wilhelmina Runft and Luther Emerson. Emerson was married to Bertha Paret (deceased) and is married to Ruth Calvin. He is an alumnus of Yale University (A.B. 1928; LL.B., 1931; M.A., 1946).

After a brief period of practicing law in New York City, Emerson entered federal government service in 1933. He served successively as assistant counsel in the National Recovery Administration, as attorney to the National Labor Relations Board and Social Security Board, as assistant and associate general counsel to the National Labor Relations Board, as special assistant to the Attorney General of the United States, as associate general counsel and deputy administrator for enforcement in the Office of Price Administration, and as general counsel in the Office of Economic Stabilization and the Office of War Mobilization and Reconversion.

While Emerson was with the National Labor Relations Board, he worked under his close and inseparable friend Nathan Witt. Emerson and Witt were among the founders and leaders of the extreme pro-Communist faction of the National Lawyers Guild, "the foremost legal bulwark of the Communist Party, its front organizations, and controlled unions." (Emerson has been vice president, president, and member of the executive board of the NLG.) Witt belonged to the notorious Harold Ware Communist cell which included in its membership Alger Hiss. Coincidentally, in 1958, Emerson endorsed Fred J. Cook's *The Unfinished Story of Alger Hiss*, a defense of Hiss.

In 1946, Emerson left the federal government and began his tenure as professor of law at the Yale University Law School. He has been a Guggenheim Fellow and a visiting professor at the London School of Economics and at Brookings Institution.

In 1956, the Senate Internal Security Subcommittee included Emerson's name in its list of the eighty-two most active and typical sponsors of Communist front organizations. He has been affiliated with the Civil Rights Congress ("subversive and Communist"); the National Committee of the International Juridical Association (an organization "which actively defended Communists and consistently followed the Communist Party line"); the Emergency Civil Liberties Committee ("Communist front" – "subversive"); the National Committee to Secure Justice for Morton Sobell ("Communist campaign"); the American Committee for Protection of Foreign Born [Americans] ("subversive and Communist" – "one of the oldest auxiliaries of the Communist Party in the United States" – under the "complete domination" of the Communist Party); and, the Cultural and Scientific Conference for

World Peace ("Communist front") – "a propaganda front for Soviet foreign policy and 'Soviet culture' "). Emerson is the advisor on Constitutional law to the National Committee to Abolish the Un-American Activities Committee ("to lead and direct the Communist Party's 'Operation Abolition' campaign").

In 1965, Emerson was a member of the Inter-University Committee for a Public Hearing on Vietnam, sponsors of the anti-Vietnam "teach-in" movement, which the Communist propaganda apparatus exploited for purely Communist purposes.

JOHN K. EMMERSON was born on March 17, 1908 in Canon City, Colorado, son of Margaretta Hitchcock and John Emmerson. He married Dorothy McLaughlin. He studied at the Sorbonne in Paris. He is an alumnus of Colorado College (A.B., 1929) and New York University (M.A., 1930). He also pursued graduate studies at Georgetown University in Washington, D.C.

Emmerson joined the State Department in 1935 after teaching social science for a year at the University of Nebraska and serving for two years as assistant director at the Berlitz School of Languages in Chicago. From 1935 until 1947, he held State Department positions in Japan, Washington, Peru, and China. From 1947 until 1949, he was stationed in Moscow as consul and first secretary at the U.S. Embassy. In 1949, he returned to Washington and was on detached service to the National War College. From 1950 until 1952, he was planning administrator for the Bureau of Far Eastern Affairs. Since 1952, he has held posts in Pakistan, Lebanon, France, Nigeria, Rhodesia and Nyasaland, and Japan. In 1967, he went on detached service to Stanford University as a senior fellow.

Emmerson, near the end of World War II, was a colleague of the China boys (John Paton Davies, John Stewart Service, Raymond Ludden) who worked feverishly and successfully to influence State Department policy makers to double-cross Chiang Kai-shek and support the Chinese Communists. In his *Wedemeyer Reports,* Lt. Gen. Albert Wedemeyer, who was Chief of Staff to Chiang Kai-shek and commander of American troops in the China theater, said of the four China boys: "Their sympathy for the Chinese Communists is obvious in their reports and in their recommendation that we back the Communists instead of the Nationalist Government."

In 1945, Emmerson was favorably impressed by the efficient indoctrination methods used on Japanese prisoners of war in China. The prisoners had been taken in tow by the Japanese People's Emancipation League, a group of Japanese prisoners in China that had been organized for wartime propaganda purposes, and for the ultimate purpose of leading a postwar Communist takeover in Japan. Emmerson recommended that Japanese prisoners in American stockades be turned over to Japanese Communists in the United States for indoctrination along the lines used by the Japanese People's Emancipation League.

In 1962, when Emmerson was being appointed to serve as U.S. Minister to Japan, Tetsuma Hashimoto, head of the Japanese Shiunso Society, protested the appointment in a letter to U.S. Ambassador Reischauer. Hashimoto recalled Emmerson's widely quoted statement while he served in Japan: "There is no person I can ever trust in Japan. The only people I believe in are the Communists imprisoned during the Pacific War. Let them be set free and have Japan reconstructed with those Communists taking leadership."

There has never been indications forthcoming from Emmerson that his admiration for Communists has lessened: But his State Department superiors evidently are somewhat timorous about letting Emmerson settle down very long in any one post, lest he focus attention upon himself with his pro-Communist utterances. Since the end of World War II, Emmerson has moved around like a shuttlecock in a championship badminton game.

MARK ETHRIDGE was born on April 22, 1896 in Meridian, Mississippi, son of Mary Howell and William Ethridge. He married Willie Snow. He studied at the University of Mississippi and Mercer University.

Ethridge began his life-long newspaper career in 1913. He was a reporter with the *Meridian Star* and the *Columbus (Ga.) Enquirer Sun,* and city editor and managing editor of the *Mason (Ga.) Telegraph.* He also worked for the *New York Sun,* the Consolidated Press, and the Associated Press.

In 1933 and 1934, he was assistant general manager of the *Washington Post.* From 1934 until 1936, he was president and publisher of the *Richmond (Va.) Times Dispatch.*

In 1936, Ethridge joined the *Louisville Courier Journal — Louisville Times.* Successively, he was general manager, vice president, publisher, and chairman of the board. From 1963 until 1965, he was editor of the Long Island (N.Y.) *Newsday,* from which he entered semiretirement as a consultant to that journal.

Ethridge has been affiliated with the Southern Conference for Human Welfare ("Commuist front") and the Civil Rights Congress ("subversive and Communist").

He has been a trustee for the Ford Foundation, which has been a horn of plenty for leftwingers and leftwing projects on every continent; a member of Clarence Streit's Atlantic Union, which is working towards a political merger of Western Europe and the United States, as a major step towards world government; a board member of the National Committee for an Effective Congress, a group which, since 1952, has campaigned for and financed ultra-leftist candidates for the House and Senate; a member of the American Civil Liberties Union, that motleyed collection of defenders of subversion, crime, and licentiousness; and, a member of the United World Federalists, an anti-American sovereignty group.

Ethridge made his major contribution to the liberal cause during his years with the *Louisville Courier Journal* and *Louisville Times.* The editorials in those journals might just as well have been written in Democratic National Headquarters, both as to domestic and foreign policy. Ethridge, as a bleeding-heart journalist, ranks right alongside such other leftwing stalwarts as Ralph McGill, Hodding Carter, Palmer Hoyt, the Sulzbergers, Erwin Canham, and Harry Ashmore.

JOHN K. FAIRBANK was born on May 24, 1907 in Huron, South Dakota, son of Lorena King and Arthur Fairbank. He married Wilma Cannon. He is an alumnus of Harvard University (A.B., 1929) and Oxford University (Ph.D., 1936), where he was a Rhodes scholar.

Fairbank became a member of Harvard University's history faculty in 1936 and, except for a leave of absence from 1941 until 1946, he has been there ever since. At present, he holds the Francis Lee Higginson chair in history and, since

317

1959, has been the director of Harvard's East Asian Research Center. He has been the recipient, in 1960 and 1964, of Guggenheim fellowships. His best known work is *The United States and China,* published in 1959.

In 1941 and 1942, Fairbank was the coordinator of information for the Office of Strategic Services in Washington, D.C. In 1942 and 1943, he was a special assistant to the U.S. Ambassador in China. In 1944 and 1945, he was back in Washington, D.C. where he was a sometime acting deputy director in charge of Far Eastern operations for Elmer Davis' Red-lined Office of War Information. In 1945 and 1946, he was the director of the U.S. Information Service in China.

From 1947 until 1951, Fairbank was a trustee and a member of the Institute of Pacific Relations, which – after extensive hearings in 1951 and 1952 – was described by the Senate Internal Security Subcommittee as "a vehicle used by the Communists to orientate American far eastern policies toward Communist objectives" and was an "instrument of Communist policy, propaganda and military intelligence." In that same period, he was also affiliated with such Communist-controlled organizations as *Amerasia* magazine, the American Committee in Aid of Chinese Industrial Cooperatives, and the China Aid Council.

During the course of the Senate Internal Security Subcommittee's hearings on the IPR, Louis Budenz testified under oath that, while he was managing editor of the Communists' *Daily Workers,* he learned from official Communist Party reports that Fairbank was a Communist. Fairbank, however, upon his own request, appeared before the SISS and swore under oath "that I am not now

and never have been a member of the Communist Party, that I do not now subscribe, believe in or adhere to the doctrines of Communism or Marxism-Leninism, that I have never done so in the past, and that I have never knowingly attended or participated in activities of the Communist Party." Fairbank described Budenz's testimony as slanderous and defamatory.

In the same hearings on the IPR, there was evidence presented that, when Fairbank was in government service, he had carried messages from Madam Sun Yatsen to the China Aid Council, a Communist organization, and from Chen Hanseng and Elsie Fairfax-Cholmeley to Israel Epstein. Fairbank acknowledged these actions but denied that he knew these persons were Communists.

Fairbank never denied his long-time professional and social association with those who were easily recognizable as the unofficial Red China lobby, both in and out of government. And Fairbank – despite his candid and all-inclusive denial of Communist ties – became, whether he wished it that way or not, one of the most articulate spokesmen and leaders of the lobby. As early as 1947, writing in the *New York Herald Tribune,* he urged opposition to Chiang Kai-shek and support for Mao Tse-tung. Fairbank was one of many so-called experts on China who wrote that the United States should not interfere with the "agrarian" revolution of the Chinese Communists.

On October 1, 1949, Mao Tse-tung proclaimed the inauguration of the Central People's Government of the People's Republic of China. With a remarkable burst of speed, Fairbank was into print (*The Reporter,* January 3, 1950), declaring: "The Chinese Communist regime shows promise on its record thus far of being the best government that modern China has had." This remarkable evaluation of a *three-month old* regime was coupled with Fairbank's recommendation that Red China be admitted to the United Nations. By way of justification, he argued: "The [Red] Chinese veto in the U.N. can have little more nuisance value than the present Russian veto." Of course, he did not mention that Red China's admission to the "peace-loving states" of the UN would be something more than a nuisance to the Chiang Kai-shek regime, the steadfast ally of the United States.

Ever since the Red takeover of China's mainland in 1949, Fairbank has been a consistent and persistent advocate of U.S. diplomatic recognition of Red China. As the years went by, however, and he came to realize that diplomatic recognition was not an entirely popular issue, he settled on the argument that a new type of recognition would be a good place to start: "Intellectual recognition of its [Red China's] existence, however, does not necessarily mean diplomatic recognition, which is a matter of expediency, something to bargain over — preferably before our bargaining power declines." (*The United States and China,* 1959, page 320.) Of course, there is no such thing in diplomacy as "intellectual recognition" but Fairbank was merely substituting his literary inventiveness for the cliché-ridden Red China lobbyists and their cries of "we can't ignore six hundred (or seven hundred) million Chinese." As late as 1966, Fairbank joined with such prominent Red China lobbyists as Doak Barnett, Oliver Edmund Clubb, Bayard Rustin, Anna Lord Strauss, Roger Hilsman, Clark Kerr, and Robert A. Scalapino to form the National Committee on United States-[Red] China Relations. This group, according to its organizers, was to sponsor public debate — as if it were needed —

on United States policy toward Red China, which simply meant to lobby and propagandize for a sellout of Nationalist China, and United States diplomatic recognition and United Nations membership for Red China.

In 1965, Fairbank became an organizer and leader of Americans for Reappraisal of Far Eastern Policy, with its headquarters at Yale University. With Fairbank in ARFEP were Socialist Party luminaries Michael Harrington and Norman Thomas. The ARFEP organized chapters on campuses, including Harvard, Yale, and the University of California at Berkeley, and ARFEP's member conducted "teach-ins," circulated petitions, organized committees, and distributed literature to promote the United States diplomatic recognition of Red China, U.S. support for Red China's admission to UN membership, and an end to U.S. restrictions on trade with Red China. (*Human Events,* May 21, 1966 reported that Owen Lattimore – a friend of Fairbank's for more than thirty years – spoke frequently at ARFEP functions.)

In 1965, when Chairman J. William Fulbright of the Senate Foreign Relations Committee was conducting hearings on U.S. policy in the Far East, Fairbank testified as an old China "expert." He used the well-publicized forum to promote U.S. diplomatic recognition of Red China and admission to UN membership for Red China. He admitted that the Chinese Communists would be "disruptive and extremely annoying" in the United Nations but he favored their membership "even if they said they would dynamite the place." (Three years later, writing "Steps to Coexistence with Red China" in the *Boston Globe,* January 6, 1968, Fairbank argued for diplomatic recognition by raising the bogies of nuclear warfare and Red Chinese military prowess. And paramount in Fairbank's worrisome mind was his query: "How can we coexist with Communist China?" Not should we or could we!)

As might be expected, Fairbank is extremely critical of U.S. participation in the Vietnam War. (" . . . The problem arises that it is not the [Red] Chinese whom we face in South Vietnam, but rather their model of revolution, Chairman Mao's idea. And how does one stop a revolutionary idea?) He argues against escalation by raising the bogey of Red Chinese military might and for negotiation by dealing directly with North Vietnam *and* Red China (a new twist: we must extend diplomatic recognition to Red China as a prerequisite to negotiations to end the war with North Vietnam).

There are discernible patterns in Fairbank's thinking processes: he argues on behalf of improved relations between the U.S. and China almost as if there were no longer a Free China, as if Red China were totally divorced from international Communism, as if nationalism were the dominant motive behind Mao Tse-tung's barbarism, and as if the Chinese people on the mainland were willing and satisfied subjects of a Communist regime.

Unquestionably, Fairbank's sworn disavowal of any and all conscious ties with Communism remains as one of the most candid statements of its kind ever made before a congressional committee. But his protestations notwithstanding, his position on Far East matters is certainly not offensive, but quite acceptable, to the Communists. Few Americans pleading the same causes as Fairbank can approach his obvious talent and he has been afforded the opportunity to carry his case to the American people through his writings in national publications such as *Atlantic* magazine, the *New York Times,* the *Washington Post,* and the *New York Review of Books.* His testimony before congressional hearings has been given wide publicity in the press. And, in 1966, he was named to a State Department advisory panel on Red China.

If Fairbank were only an ivory tower theorist, exercising his academic privileges to speak and teach the truth as he sees it, it would be unreasonable to be skeptical of his disavowal of Communist ties. But Fairbank is a public figure and an activist. Aside from his Red China lobby activities, in 1948, he was active as a member of the Committee of One Thousand, which had as its purpose an all-out attack upon the powers of the House Committee on Un-American Activities. In that same year, he petitioned the Congress to defeat the Mundt anti-Communist bill. This was also a project of a Communist lobby, the National Committee to Defeat the Mundt Bill.

One of the most curious facets of Fairbank's promotion of appeasement with Red China has been his reliance on and support of Edgar Snow's works. At best, such an association with Snow can only be attributed to a stubborn streak in Fairbank who cannot possibly be unaware that, for at least thirty years, Snow has been the No. 1 propagandist for Mao Tse-tung in the United States. When Snow's *Red Star Over China* was published in 1938, the most revealing and perceptive appraisal of that work was in a review by Victor A. Yakhontoff in the Communist weekly *New Masses:* "The value of this material [Snow's book] can be judged by the fact that most of it was supplied by Mao Tse-tung, head of the Soviet regime [in China], and that some of it was checked by personal observation of the author." Two former Communists confirmed that *Red Star Over China* was of more than passing interest to the Communists. Freda Utley, in her *The China Story*, wrote: "In the original edition of his best-selling book, *Red Star Over China*, Ed Snow has painted a most favorable picture of the Chinese Communist regime in the Northwest. But he had also included some passages critical of the Comintern and showing the subservience of the Chinese Communists to Moscow. My . . . impression of Snow as an honest journalist was altered when he eliminated in the second edition of his book, a number of passages distasteful to Moscow." Louis Budenz, a former Communist Party official, in testimony before the Senate Internal Security Subcommittee, identified Snow as a Communist and said that Snow "amended one edition of the book . . . . at the request of the Communist Party." In 1961, when Grove Press published *Red Star Over China* as a paperback, Fairbank wrote an Introduction in which he said that the book had "stood the test of time . . . as an historical record."

In 1962, Snow's *The Other Side of the River: Red China Today* was published. It was a virtual panegyric for Mao Tse-tung, whom Snow described "as a teacher, statesman, strategist, philosopher, poet laureate, national hero, head of the family, and greatest liberator in history. He is Confucius plus Lao-tzu plus Rousseau plus Marx plus Buddha." Communist Carl Marzani, who reviewed the book for the Communist weekly *National Guardian*, was so taken with Snow's outpourings that he had his firm of Marzani & Munsell publish seven chapters of *The Other Side of the River* under the title: *China, Russia and the U.S.A.* In their advertising copy, the

publishers of *Other Side* used tributes to Snow's propaganda by Felix Greene, the notorious British sycophant of Mao Tse-tung; Harrison Salisbury, the veteran *New York Times* apologist for Communists; Owen Lattimore, the original doyen of the Red China lobby; and, John K. Fairbank, who wrote: "No other volume on Communist China has covered so broad a range with so much perception . . . . Snow is neither an inexperienced traveler susceptible to the sheer enthusiasm of a fellow-traveler, nor on the other hand a Kremlinogist chiefly devoted to analyzing power relations as betrayed in Communist jargon. A field reporter, he tries to avoid the oversimplicity of the library researcher, who deals only with documents, not people."

The dramatic denial of Communist ties by Fairbank in 1952 would seem to have suffered a shock, at least to its spirit, by his deliberate support of those whose fellow-traveling is a matter of incontrovertible public record.

JAMES FARMER was born on January 12, 1920 in Marshall, Texas, son of Pearl Houston and James Farmer. His second wife is Lula Peterson. He is an alumnus of Wiley College (B.S., 1938) and Howard University (B.D., 1941). Farmer was never ordained to the ministry. He has offered two explanations for this: (1) There was racial segregation in the South; (2) The Church practiced discrimination.

From 1941 until 1945, Farmer was race relations secretary of the Fellowship of Reconciliation, one of the largest and oldest radical-pacifist organizations in the country. From 1946 until 1950, he was involved with labor as an organizer for the Upholsterer's International Union and as a lecturer on race and labor problems. From 1950 until 1954, he was field secretary for the socialist League for Industrial Democracy. (Later, he would serve as vice president of the LID and as a member of the LID's board of directors. In 1962, he received the LID's John Dewey Award, a tribute reserved for prominent radicals.) From 1954 until 1959, he was back in the labor movement as a representative for the State, County and Municipal Employees Union. From 1959 until 1961, he was program director for the National Association for the Advancement of Colored People, the fountainhead of Negro agitation for more than half a century.

In 1942, Farmer was a founder of the Congress of Racial Equality, which was allegedly organized to apply Gandhian techniques of non-violence to combat racial discrimination and segregation. From 1961 until 1966, Farmer was national director of CORE and, as such, he initiated the so-called freedom rides and plagued the entire country with sit-ins, picket lines, and demonstrations.

Over the years, Farmer did as much as any Negro agitator to make "police brutality" and "non-violence" nationwide bywords which accompanied riotous conditions wherever CORE decided to be Gandhian. As is the wont of so many Negro demagogues, Farmer has managed to have himself arrested and jailed. He has been quick to raise the cry of "police brutality" and has called for the establishment of civilian review boards.

In 1967, Farmer was scheduled to become the head of a so-called anti-poverty agency which was to be financed by private and federal funds under the aegis of the U.S. Office of Economic Opportunity. But, for reasons which have not been made clear, Farmer's sinecure was one of the very few boondoggles which the Johnson Administration was unable to foist on the American people. Farmer then turned to the academic world and accepted part-time teaching positions at Lincoln University and New York University. Campuses are not unfamiliar to Farmer. He has preached his demagoguery at Boston University, Harvard University, Brown University, Washington University of St. Louis, Monmouth College, and at numerous high schools.

In 1968, Farmer declared himself a candidate for Congress from Brooklyn on the Liberal Party ticket. (From 1954 until 1961, he was vice chairman of the Liberal Party in New York County.) Politics has been somewhat of an avocation for Farmer. He has often expressed the idea that black power could be attained by organizing Negroes into a political bloc, but he has made no serious attempts to do so. He has expended most of his energies organizing physical demonstrations against alleged discrimination. For his own part, however, he has spoken out strongly against presidential candidates Barry Goldwater, George Wallace, Richard Nixon, and Ronald Reagan. He has endorsed Nelson Rockefeller.

Aside from his CORE activities, Farmer has been a member and executive of the leftwing American Committee on Africa, a member of the radical American Civil Liberties Union, and a member of Americans for Democratic Action, the center of the radical left in American politics. He has been a close associate of such well-known agitators as Victor and Walter Reuther, John Lewis, James Forman, Bayard Rustin, and Martin L. King Jr.

JULES FEIFFER was born on January 26, 1929 in New York City, son of Rhoda Davis and David Feiffer. His second wife is Judith Sheftel. He studied art in New York City at the Art Students League and at Pratt Institute.

From 1946 until 1951, Feiffer was an assistant to the syndicated cartoonist Will Eisner. From 1949 until 1951, he drew his own syndicated cartoon, "Clifford," for six Sunday newspapers. From 1951 until 1953, he served in the U.S. Army Signal Corps, working in a cartoon animation unit. After his army service, he did odd jobs for the next five years betwen spells of unemployment.

In 1956, Feiffer began contributing cartoon strips to the avante-garde *Village Voice* of New York City. The exposure brought almost immediate success to him and within a short time his work was being syndicated in almost fifty newspapers and more than forty college papers. His cartoons have also appeared regularly in *Playboy* magazine and *The Observer* of London. They have also appeared from time to time in *Holiday* magazine and *Sports Illustrated* and on at least one occasion, in the Moscow *New Times*.

As well as publishing collections of his cartoons, Feiffer has written one novel and several plays. His first collection of cartoons (*Sick, Sick, Sick*) sold 150,000 copies within three years. His 1967 collection (*Feiffer on Civil Rights*) was published by the Anti-Defamation League. Many of his plays and skits are used as entertainment pieces at leftwing pacifist gatherings.

Feiffer is generally described as a satirist. His commentaries far outweigh his line drawings and it is the text rather than the artwork which has made him so popular. He admits to having undergone about eight years of psychoanalysis and bemoans the two years he spent in army service. As a matter of fact, he seems to dwell upon his attitude of insecurity.

There can be no denying that he is as much a scaremonger as a satirist since he has such an overwhelming preoccupation with the spectre of atomic bombs, nuclear testing, fallout, and air raid shelters. Away from his cartoon board, he is a longtime sponsor of the National Committee for a Sane Nuclear Policy (SANE), the most notorious collection of ban-the-bomb leftists in this country.

Feiffer's association with SANE is not his only relation to the left. On March 27, 1962, *The Worker* carried his name as a sponsor of fellow traveler Mark Lane's candidacy for Congress. In 1965, he appeared at a rally sponsored by the New York Council to Abolish the House Committee on Un-American Activities. One of his companions at the rally was the fellow traveler Pete Seeger.

In 1960, Feiffer supported the left-wing Hiroshima Day Parade to the United Nations. He supported the left-wing Turn Toward Peace "Washington Project" in 1962. He has participated in leftwing demonstrations against U.S. participation in the Vietnam War.

Feiffer makes strong pretensions to being an apolitical commentator on the American scene ("my obsession is with the uses and misuses of authority") but after a decade it becomes more and more evident that he is nothing less than a clever propagandist for the left and an apostle of doom finding little to admire in America or Americans – especially as long as the "bomb" exists.

THOMAS FINLETTER was born on November 11, 1893 in Philadelphia, Pennsylvania, son of Helen Grill and Thomas Finletter. He married Gretchen Damrosch. He is an alumnus of the University of Pennsylvania (A.B., 1915; LL.B., 1920).

Finletter began the practice of law in

1920. For more than forty years, he has been active in New York State's politics. He once described himself as an "Al Smith-Franklin D. Roosevelt-Herbert H. Lehman-Harry S. Truman Democrat" — a mongrelization which did not prevent him from becoming a close political associate of Eleanor Roosevelt.

Finletter has held a variety of appointive positions in government. From 1941 until 1944, he was a special assistant to the Secretary of State and, in 1945, he was a consultant to the U.S. delegation at the San Francisco organizing conference of the United Nations. In 1947 and 1948, he was chairman of the President's Air Policy Commission. In 1948 and 1949, he was minister-in-charge of the Economic Cooperation Administration in Britain. From 1950 until 1953, he was Secretary of the Air Force and, from 1961 until 1965, he was the U.S. Ambassador to the North Atlantic Treaty Organization.

He has written several books on law as well as *Can Representative Government Do the Job?*; *Power and Policy*; and *Foreign Policy: The Next Phase.* He has been an official of the Council on Foreign Relations, the informal supra-State Department of the United States; a member of Americans for Democratic Action, the center of the radical left in American politics; and, a trustee of the American Assembly, a Columbia University brainwashing project wherein American business executives are fed an up-to-date version of the State Department's soft-on-Communism, internationalist line. Finletter has been affiliated with Clarence Streit's one-world, anti-American sovereignty International Movement for Atlantic Union. He has also supported the United World Federalists, whose program is a very serious threat to American sovereignty and the

sovereignty of all free nations. Finletter advocates U.S. diplomatic recognition of Red China; a foreign aid program carried on through the North Atlantic Treaty Organization; and, disarmament without inspection. Said Finletter in his *Foreign Policy: The Next Phase:* "We must not expect the Russians to give up their closed society [sic] and the military secrecy it gives them without a *quid pro quo.*"

LOUIS FISCHER was born on February 29, 1896 in Philadelphia, Pennsylvania, son of Shifrah Kantzapolsky and David Fischer. He married Bertha Mark. He graduated in 1916 from the Philadelphia School of Pedagogy.

After a brief career as a teacher in Philadelphia's public schools, Fischer became a journalist, working first for the *New York Evening Post* as a European correspondent in 1921. In 1922, he went to the Soviet Union as a free-lance correspondent. In 1923, he began a twenty-one-year career as a correspondent for *The Nation* magazine. From 1923 until 1936, he was based in Moscow. It is academic if Fischer ever formally became a member of the Communist Party while in the Soviet Union. It is absolute that he was totally sympathetic to Communism (see, for example, his contribution to *The God That Failed*, Harper, 1950) and that he provided American readers with years of pro-Communist propaganda and misinformation from Moscow. In his *The Red Decade*, Eugene Lyons wrote: "Mr. Fischer was the least squeamish of the Kremlin's foreign favorites. Though he started his career as political litterateur as a Zionist, he could record the Soviet liquidation of Zionists with the same calmness that he reported liquidation of left or right deviationists, straying professors . . . . "

Among Fischer's better known works are *The Soviets in World Affairs; Men and Politics: An Autobiography; Gandhi and Stalin; Russia Revisited; The Life of Mahatma Gandhi; The Life of Lenin:* and *Russia, America and the World.*

After leaving Moscow in 1936, Fischer went to Spain and joined the Communists' International Brigade fighting in the Spanish Civil War. In 1942, he made his first visit to India, which accounts for his several books on Gandhi.

Fischer has lectured at the University of Washington and the New School for Social Research. In 1959, he became a member at the Institute for Advanced Study at Princeton, New Jersey, where Security Risk J. Robert Oppenheimer was the director.

Fischer has been affiliated with the American League for Peace and Democracy ("subversive and Communist"); the American Youth Congress ("subversive and Communist"); the Coordinating Committee to Lift the Embargo ("Communist front"); *Fight* ("a Communist front publication"); the Friends of the Abraham Lincoln Brigade ("its officers and staff members were in the main [Communist] Party members and functionaries"); the Friends of Soviet Union ("to propagandize for and defend Russia and its system of government" – "directed from Moscow"); the International Labor Defense ("legal arm of the Communist Party"); the League of American Writers ("subversive and Communist"); and, the North American Committee to Aid Spanish Democracy ("Communist").

Fischer has also been an official of the socialist League for Industrial Democracy; a founder of Americans for Democratic Action; and, a participant in Columbia University's American Assembly, a Columbia University brainwashing project wherein American business executives are fed an up-to-date version of the State Department's soft-on-Communism, internationalist line.

Fischer's writings are very popular references in high school and collegiate textbooks. And he is a frequent lecturer on the collegiate circuit. He is generally described as an anti-Communist liberal but his views must be regarded as no more than slightly outside the hard-core Communist line.

ADRIAN FISHER was born on January 21, 1914 in Memphis, son of Louise Sanford and Hubert Fisher. He married Laura Graham. He is an alumnus of Princeton Univeristy (A.B., 1934) and Harvard University (LL.B., 1937).

In 1938 and 1939, Fisher received a leftwing indoctrination that has been experienced by very few young lawyers. He was law clerk to two Associate Justices of the U.S. Supreme Court, Louis D. Brandeis and Felix Frankfurter. As did so many of Frankfurter's protégés, Fisher found a home for himself in the federal government.

From 1939 until 1941, he was an attorney in various government agencies and, in 1941 and 1942, he was briefly the assistant chief of the Foreign Funds Control Division in the Department of State. In 1942 and 1943, he was a navigator in the U.S. Army Air Force. In 1944, he became an assistant to the Assistant Secretary of War. In 1945, he was back on flying duty as a navigator. In 1946, he was a technical adviser to American judges at the Nuremberg trials. In 1947 and 1948, he was a solicitor in the Department of Commerce. In 1948 and 1949, he was general counsel to the Atomic Energy Commission. From 1949 until 1953, he was a legal adviser in the Department of State.

During the Eisenhower Administrations, Fisher was out of government service. From 1953 until 1961, he divided his time between private law practice, teaching international law and trade at Georgetown University, and serving as counsel and vice president to the left-wing *Washington Post*.

President Kennedy brought Fisher back into the government as a member of an advisory staff to the President on disarmament. And, since 1961, Fisher has been deputy director of the U.S. Arms Control and Disarmament Agency. Fisher and his immediate superior William C. Foster have worked efficently as a team to disarm the United States in keeping with the objectives of the infamous Pugwash Conferences which were instituted by Communists and have always been dominated by Communists. Fisher and Foster deserve a major share of the credit for concluding the infamous Nuclear Test Ban Treaty of 1963.

DORIS FLEESON was born about 1905 in Sterling, Kansas, daughter of Helen Tebbe and William Fleeson. She was married to the late John O'Donnell and is married to Dan Kimball. She is an alumna of the University of Kansas (A.B., c. 1927).

Fleeson began her career in journalism in 1927 with the *New York Daily News* and was a reporter and Washington correspondent for that newspaper until 1942. In 1943 and 1944, she was a war correspondent for *Women's Home Companion* magazine. Since 1945, she has been a Washington columnist for United Feature Syndicate and her column appears in such newspapers as the *Washington Star, Boston Globe, Chicago Daily News, Kansas City Star,* and *St. Louis Post-Dispatch.*

In the 1930's, Fleeson became infatu-

ated with Roosevelt's New Deal and since that time she has moved steadily leftward. She makes no apparent attempt to disguise her hostility toward what few conservatives remain in the ranks of the Republican Party or toward Southern Democrats. Her current Republican hero is George Romney but her columnar heart belongs to ADA-type Democrats.

DENNA F. FLEMING was born on March 25, 1893 in Paris, Illinois, son of Eleanor McCormick and Albert Fleming. He married Doris Anundsen. He is an alumnus of the University of Illinois (A.B., 1916; M.A. 1920; Ph.D., 1928).

During most of the years 1912-1922, Fleming was a high school teacher and principal in Washington and Illinois. From 1922 until 1927, he was on the faculty of Monmouth College in Illinois as an assistant professor, associate professor, professor, and departmental chairman of social science. In 1928 Fleming joined the faculty of political science at Vanderbilt University, where he served successively as assistant professor, associate professor, professor, departmental chairman, research professor, and professor emeritus. Recently he has been a professor of international relations at California State College in Los Angeles. Fleming has also lectured at Iowa State Teachers College, the University of Arizona, the University of California at Los Angeles, and has been a Fulbright lecturer at Cambridge University in England, and the School of International Studies in New Delhi, India.

From 1934 to 1937, Fleming was foreign news editor for the *Nashville Evening Tennessean,* and, from 1939 to 1947, he was a foreign news commentator on Radio Station WSM. From 1944 to 1946, Fleming was a radio commentator for the Woodrow Wilson Foundation and, from 1950 to 1955, he was director of that organization. In 1946, 1948, and 1949, he was a member of the Institute for Advanced Study at Princeton, New Jersey.

Fleming is the author of *The Treaty Veto of the American Senate; The United States and the League of Nations, 1918-1920; The United States and World Organization, 1920-1923; Can We Win the Peace?; While America Slept; The United States and the World Court;* and, a two-volume work, *The Cold War and its Origins, 1917-1960.* Fleming has also contributed articles to the Communist magazine *New World Review.*

For at least three decades Fleming's writings have been ardent advocacies of internationalism at the expense of United States sovereignty. And, in recent years, he has followed the Communist line so closely that his two-volume *The Cold War and its Origins,* published in 1961, was hailed in such Communist publications as *Political Affairs* and the *World Marxist Review.*

Fleming's pro-U.S.S.R. sympathies had their origin at least as early as 1933 when he petitioned for United States diplomatic recognition of the Soviet Union. In 1957, writing in the *Adult Student Sunday School Quarterly* of the Methodist Church, Fleming garnished a fulsome apologia for the Soviet Union with the proposition that the United States was obliged to organize a functioning world community with the Soviet Union and Red China.

Although Fleming has evidently refrained from joining Communist fronts, he has earned his leftwing credentials by urging the abolition of the House Committee on Un-American Activities; he has authored a vicious diatribe against the late U.S. Senator Joseph R. McCarthy; and, he provided his sympathies to Alger Hiss. ("Dear Mr. Hiss: This is just to record my indignation at the attempt to pin a red smear on you – and to wonder who is behind [Whittaker] Chambers. I earnestly hope that you never stop until he is convicted of perjury. That would be a national service of the first order, in addition to being your own best vindication. It is an intolerable situation that as between the two of you 'somebody has lied.' If a committee is formed to help with the prosecution, please let me know. With all good wishes, Cordially yours, D.F. Fleming.")

Fleming has been a member of a chapter of the leftwing, pacifist National Committee for a Sane Nuclear Policy (in 1946, he was an adviser to the atomic energy section of the State Department!). In 1965, Fleming was a sponsor of the Red-lined March on Washington for Peace in Vietnam, and a major participant in the anti-Vietnam "teach-in" movement, which the Communist propaganda apparatus exploited for purely Communists purposes. In 1966, he was a sponsor of the National Voters' Pledge Campaign, which was led by Socialist Norman Thomas, veteran Communist-fronter Reverend William Sloane Coffin, and Sanford Gottlieb, the political director of the National Committee for a Sane Nuclear Policy. The Voters' Pledge Campaign was designed to support "peace" candidates, who would work for a cease-fire in Vietnam and encourage negotiations in which the Vietcong would be participants.

ARTHUR FLEMMING was born on June 12, 1905 in Kingston, New York, son of Harriet Sherwood and Harry Flemming. He married Bernice Moler. He is an alumnus of Ohio Wesleyan University (A.B., 1927), American University (A.M., 1928), and George Washington University (LL.B., 1933).

Flemming was an instructor of government at American University from 1927 until 1930. During the next four years, he was on the editorial staff of *U.S. Daily* (now *U.S. News & World Report*). He returned to American University in the School of Public Affairs where he was director until 1939.

From 1939 until 1948, he was a member of the United States Civil Service Commission. In that same period, he did some work for the Office of Price Administration; the Navy Department; the War Manpower Commission; and, the Department of Labor. From 1948 until 1953, Flemming was president of Ohio Wesleyan University. In that same period, he was a member of the Commission on Organization of the Executive Branch of the Government; chairman of the advisory commission on personnel management for the Atomic Energy Commission; and, a member of the International Civil Service Advisory Board.

Flemming left Wesleyan in 1953 to become director of the Office of Defense Mobilization. In that position, he was a member of the National Security Council and a participant in presidential cabinet meetings. In 1957 and 1958, he was back as president of Wesleyan. But, in 1958, President Eisenhower appointed Flemming as Secretary of Health, Education and Welfare, a position he held throughout the remainder of the second Eisenhower Administration. In 1961, Flemming became president of the University of Oregon.

Flemming has been a very active official of the National Council of Churches of Christ, U.S.A. From 1950 until 1954, and from 1964 until 1966,

he was vice president of the NCC. In 1966, he was elected president of the NCC.

Flemming has been described as an arch bureaucrat which is an appropriate soubriquet for an individual who has been such a favorite of so many Administrations. The wonder is that he has not yet been tapped by the Johnson Administration for an important position. In the Kennedy Administration, he served as an adviser to the Peace Corps. During his long bureaucratic career, Flemming was a fanatic in his promotion of federal intervention in education and of socialized medicine. He was recognized as one of Washington's great spendthrifts. As Secretary of HEW, Flemming made some hysterical, unwarranted remarks linking cancer with cranberries. He came close to bankrupting the entire cranberry industry but the federal government would use taxpayer's money to compensate for Flemming's costly mistake.

When Flemming became president of NCC, he proved that his flip-flop mentality had not changed since his bureaucratic days. Said Flemming in his inaugural address: "People do not have any understanding of the role religion has played in the development of our civilization and the only way we can offset this is to offer courses about religion in the public schools. This is the great thing about the Supreme Court decision. It prohibited compulsory prayer and Bible reading in the public schools, but it also clarified the long-clouded issue of teaching about religion." It can only be supposed that Flemming expects the Supreme Court to look favorably upon religion courses in public schools – surely a millenium.

As for Flemming's role in the academic world, it is noteworthy that he received the Alexander Meiklejohn

Award for Academic Freedom, named in honor of a fellow-traveler who spent a lifetime trying his best to corrupt education in the name of radical permissiveness, designed to break down academic discipline. Meiklejohn, as a hero of the extreme left wing, received the Presidential Medal of Freedom in 1962 — Flemming had received the same award five years earlier.

JOSEPH F. FLETCHER was born on April 10, 1905 in Newark, New Jersey, son of Julia Davis and Joseph Fletcher. He married Forrest Hatfield. He is an alumnus of West Virginia University (A.B., 1925), Berkeley Divinity School (B.D., 1929), and Kenyon College (S.T.D., 1939). He also studied at Yale University and London University.

Fletcher was ordained to the Episcopalian ministry in 1929 and worked in various pastorates for the next ten years. Meanwhile, in 1936, he became dean of the Graduate School of Applied Religion in Cincinnati. In 1944, he joined the faculty of the Episcopal Theological Seminary in Cambridge, Massachusetts where he still is a professor of Christian ethics. He has lectured at the University of Cincinnati (1940-1944), the International Christian University in Tokyo (1963-1964), and at Harvard Divinity School (1964-1965).

Fletcher has been affiliated with the American Council on Soviet Relations ("established by the Communist Party"); the People's Institute of Applied Religion ("subversive and Communist"); the School for Democracy ("established by Communist teachers"); the National Free Browder Congress ("Communist front"); the Committee for Peaceful Alternatives to the Atlantic Pact ("a Communist front" — "part of Soviet psychological warfare against the United

States"); the World Peace Congress ("Communist front"); the National Committee to Repeal the McCarran Act ("a Communist front" — "subversive"); the Civil Rights Congress ("subversive and Communist"); the National Federation for Constitutional Liberties ("under [Communist] Party domination and headed by responsible Party functionaries"); the *Protestant* ("Communist"); the Abraham Lincoln School ("adjunct of the Communist Party"); the Citizens' Victory Committee for Harry Bridges ("Communist"); the National Council of American-Soviet Friendship ("subversive and Communist" — "specializing in pro-Soviet propaganda"); the National Committee to Win the Peace ("subversive and Communist"); the Samuel Adams School ("adjunct of the Communist Party"); the National Council of the Arts, Sciences and Professions ("a Communist front used to appeal to special occupational groups"); and, the National Committee to Abolish the House Un-American Activities Committee ("to lead and direct the Communist Party's 'Operation Abolition' campaign").

In testimony before the House Committee on Un-American Activities on July 6, 1953, while under oath, Herbert Philbrick, who had worked for the FBI within the Communist Party, said that he had known Joseph Fletcher as a Communist.

Fletcher has written at least six books, but he is best known for his *Situation Ethics: The New Morality*, published two years ago. The publisher's blurb on the jacket of Fletcher's book is an accurate summary of Fletcher's "situation ethics": "The sensational deductions which the author draws for this premise include the bold statement that any acts, even lying, premarital sex, abortion, adultery and murder could be right — depending on the situation. Because 'whatever is the most loving thing in the situation is the right and good thing. It is not excusably evil, it is positively good.' "

MARION FOLSOM was born on November 23, 1893 in McRae, Georgia, son of Margaret McRae and William Folsom. He married Mary Davenport. He is an alumnus of the University of Georgia (A.B., 1912) and Harvard University (M.B.A., 1914).

Since 1914, Folsom has been with Eastman Kodak Company, holding an executive position since 1935. During Roosevelt's New Deal, he was a member of the Presidential Advisory Council on Economic Security; a member of the Federal Advisory Council on Social Security; an executive of the National Advisory Defense Commission; and, staff director for the House of Representatives Special Committee on Postwar Economic Policy and Planning.

In the Eisenhower years, Folsom was Under Secretary of the Treasury (1953-1955) and Secretary of Health, Education and Welfare (1955-1958).

Folsom has been a non-resident member of the Council on Foreign Relations, the informal supra-State Department of the United States; a member of the Institute for American Democracy, hysterical successor to Larson's abortive NCCR; a member of Clarence Streit's Atlantic Union, working towards a political merger of Western Europe and the United States, as a major step towards world government; an official of the Committee for Economic Development, the major propaganda arm of the Council on Foreign Relations, in the important work of socializing the American economy; and, a member of the Business Advisory Council, virtually the CFR's patronage link to the federal government.

Folsom's tenure as Secretary of Health, Education and Welfare was marked by some of the most dramatic gains for federal intrusion, under the guise of federal aid, into public education. It was also a period when many of the traditional barriers against socialized medicine were broken down. Ironically, Folsom — a businessman and banker — proved to be a tireless lobbyist for the socialization of the United States.

HENRY FORD II was born on September 4, 1916 in Detroit, son of Eleanor Clay and Edsel Ford. He studied engineering and sociology at Yale University but never graduated.

In 1940, he joined the Ford Motor Company which his grandfather had established. Since 1960, Henry II has been chairman of the board and chief executive officer of the company.

In 1936, Henry Ford and his son Edsel (Henry II's father) established the Ford Foundation in order that control of the Ford Motor Company would remain in the Ford family. Almost from the beginning, the Ford Foundation was the greatest cornucopia ever directed towards the left wing. In its history, the Ford Foundation has spent literally hundreds of millions of dollars all over the world, financing one leftwing boondoggle after another. Yet, in 1966, the Foundation's assets were still more than three billion dollars. The Ford Foundation has spawned the ultra-leftwing Fund for the Republic, the socialistic Center for the Study of Democratic Institutions, as well as programs covering the entire span of education, sociology, science, engineering, journalism, economics, political science, and law.

For a few years, Henry II was chair-

330

man of the board of trustees which governs and controls the Ford Foundation's activities. And when some of the most outrageous, radical projects, financed by Ford money, were severely criticized, Henry made a few perfunctory remarks disavowing some of the more dubious projects. But never did Henry use his unmistakable influence to call a halt to the financing of socialistic, un-American – even pro-Communist – programs. Instead, he stepped down from the chairmanship to become merely a member of the board of trustees. And, for all practical purposes, the Ford Foundation and its offspring are merely financial angels for the benefit of the Council on Foreign Relations, the Americans for Democratic Action, internationalists, one-worlders, socialists, Marxists, racist agitators, and do-gooding planners.

ABE FORTAS was born on June 19, 1910 in Memphis, Tennessee, son of Ray Berson and William Fortas. He married Carolyn Agger. He is an alumnus of Southwestern College in Memphis (A.B., 1930) and Yale University (LL.B., 1933).

From 1933 until 1937, Fortas was an assistant professor of law at Yale. At the same time, he did legal work for the Agricultural Adjustment Authority and was assistant director of a corporate reorganization study for the Securities and Exchange Commission. After leaving Yale, he remained working for the federal government. From 1937 until 1939, he was a consultant and assistant director in the Public Utilities Division. From 1939 until 1941, he was general counsel for the Public Works Administration and for the Bituminous Coal Division. In 1941 and 1942, he was director for the Division of Power in the Interior Department. From 1942 until 1946, he was Under Secretary of the Interior. While in that position, he helped Soviet agents Alger Hiss and Harry Dexter White in their drafting of the United Nations charter.

In 1946 and 1947, Fortas returned to Yale as a visiting lecturer and also practiced law with the firm of Arnold, Fortas & Porter. He remained with that firm until 1965 when President Lyndon Johnson made him an Associate Justice of the Supreme Court of the United States.

Fortas was a long-time political crony of Johnson's. In 1948, when Johnson was involved in a Senate primary that was so tainted with fraud that a federal judge enjoined the printing of election ballots, Fortas represented Johnson before Supreme Court Justice Hugo Black, sitting as a one-man court. Black ruled in favor of Johnson. In later years, Fortas tried to have newspapers kill the first story of the Bobby Baker scandals. Baker was Johnson's protégé and close friend; Fortas was Baker's attorney, When the Walter Jenkins scandal broke, Fortas also tried to have the newspapers kill the story of Jenkins and his homosexual escapades. Jenkins was a member of the White House staff, a close friend and long-time political associate of Johnson's.

In the early 1940's, Fortas was a member of the Washington Committee for Democratic Action ("subversive and Communist"). In the 1930's, he was affiliated with the National Lawyers Guild ("the foremost legal bulwark of the Communist Party, its front organizations, and controlled unions"). Then there is Fortas' long time association with Owen Lattimore. The *Chicago Tribune* has noted: "He [Fortas] appeared as counsel for Lattimore when

331

that 'expert' on the Orient had to rush home from Afghanistan to face charges by the late Senator Joseph R. McCarthy that he had been promoting Communist objectives in Asia. Lattimore termed Fortas a 'solid rock' in helping him through his 'ordeal.' Fortas' services did not, however, save Lattimore from being indicted on seven charges of perjury arising from his testimony before the Senate Internal Security subcommittee, nor did it prevent the committee from pronouncing that from around 1930 Lattimore had been 'a conscious articulate instrument of the Soviet conspiracy.' Liberals, however, know their way around Washington, and a federal judge of that persuasion was easily induced to get Lattimore off the hook by finding that the indictment lacked 'clarity.' The Department of Justice had suggested that the judge disqualify himself for reasons of manifest bias, but the suggestion was spurned and the case never went to a jury to be heard on its merits. Fortas and his associates represented Lattimore."

Fortas was more than a lawyer to Lattimore. In Lattimore's book *Ordeal by Slander,* he quotes a letter he received from Fortas: "Again, I want to say for myself [and partners] . . . that we are glad to be in on the fight on your side."

When Lyndon Johnson appointed Fortas to the Supreme Court, he said that he regarded Fortas as "one of this nation's most able and most respected and most outstanding citizens." Representative John Ashbrook of Ohio, a Republican, felt that the only plausible explanation for the appointment was "that the President wants to make a moderate out of Chief Justice Warren."

WILLIAM C. FOSTER was born on April 27, 1897 in Westfield, New Jersey, son of Anna Chapman and Jed Foster. He married Beulah Robinson. He studied for a few months at Massachusetts Institute of Technology in 1918.

From 1922 until 1946, Foster was an officer and director of the Pressed and Welded Steel Products Company. In 1946, he began a two-year stint as Under Secretary of Commerce. For the next three years, he was with the Economic Cooperation Administration, eventually becoming administrator of that outfit.

From 1953 until 1955, Foster was president of the Manufacturing Chemists Association. In 1955, he became executive vice president and director of Olin Mathieson Chemical Corporation and remained with that organization until 1961.

Meanwhile, Foster had represented the United States at the Geneva Disarmament Conference in 1958. At the time *National Review* in an editorial entitled "An 'Incredible Appointment,' " commented: "Mr. Foster — it goes almost without saying of an Eisenhower appointment — began his career in public service as the choice of Democrats. President Truman just took him on, in 1946, acting on Averell Harriman's recommendation. Foster went from Harriman's staff in Europe to Paul Hoffman's, and succeeded him as Administrator of the Economic Cooperation Administration. Mr. Foster then had a brief whirl in the Pentagon, and left Washington in 1953, when the Republicans (it is said) moved in. Mr. Foster has yet to give evidence by word or deed that he has the slightest comprehension of Communism, or the will to stand firm against it. He has in public and private, fought — sometimes nastily — against a firm line. In recent months, he has used the inside track he gained as co-chairman of the secret 'Gaither report' to counter the rising demand that many of our military leaders have been making for stronger anti-Communist policies."

In 1961, Foster was named by President Kennedy to be director of the U.S. Arms Control and Disarmament Agency and he has been kept in that position by Lyndon Johnson. At every step down the road to disarmament, Foster has proven that he is a soft touch for the Communists. Along with his deputy, Adrian Fisher, he negotiated the one-sided Nuclear Test Ban Treaty of 1963 and while the United States is at war with the entire Communist world in Vietnam, Foster continues to talk of "peace" with our enemies in Geneva.

HENRY FOWLER was born on September 5, 1908 in Roanoke, Virginia, son of Bertha Browning and Mack Johnson. He married Trudye Hathcote. He is an alumnus of Roanoke College (A.B., 1929) and Yale University (LL.B., 1932; J.S.D., 1933).

From 1934 until 1939, Fowler was a counsel with the Tennessee Valley Authority. From 1939 until 1941, he did legal work in the Attorney General's office, the Federal Power Commission, and the Office of Production Management. Then, he spent two years with the War Production Board. In 1945, he was special assistant to the administrator of the Foreign Economic Administration.

From 1946 until 1951, Fowler practiced law in Washington, D.C. In 1951, he returned to government service, spending the next two years in the National Production Authority, the Defense Production Administration, and, finally, as director of the Office of Defense Mobilization. He then returned to private law practice until 1961. From 1961 until 1964, Fowler was Under Secretary of the Treasury. In 1964, he

returned to private practice until Lyndon Johnson named him to be Secretary of the Treasury, a position he still holds. As Secretary of the Treasury, Fowler has proven himself to be a complete Keynesian, believing that the taxpayers' pockets are bottomless wells. Fowler's creed seems to revolve around the idea that it is better to raise taxes rather than reduce government spending, no matter how ridiculous government boondoggles become. He has been the steward of Lyndon Johnson's inflationary spree of deficit spending coincidental with the utter dishonesty of printing worthless paper and calling it money.

JEROME D. FRANK was born on May 30, 1909 in New York City, son of Bess Rosenbaum and Jerome Frank. He married Elizabeth Kleeman. He is an alumnus of Harvard University (A.B., 1930; A.M. 1932; Ph.D., 1934; M.D., 1939).

In 1942, Frank joined the faculty at The Johns Hopkins Medical School, where he is presently a professor of psychiatry. He has done psychiatric work for the Veterans' Administration and has lectured at Harvard University and the Washington School of Psychiatry. He has been a director of clinical services at the Henry Phipps Psychiatric Clinic and the psychiatrist-in-charge of the psychiatric out-patient department of The Johns Hopkins Hospital.

Aside from his practice and teaching, Frank has been an activist in pacifist and political pressure groups. He is an official of the National Committee for a Sane Nuclear Policy Committee (leftwing, pacifist). He has been a member of the national advisory council of the leftwing Student Peace Union. In 1965, he was on the Inter-University Committee for a Public Hearing on Viet Nam sponsors of the anti-Vietnam "teach-in" movement, which the Communist propaganda apparatus exploited for purely Communist purposes. In 1966, he was a sponsor of the National Voters' Pledge Campaign.

Frank's most important political affiliation is with the Council for a Livable World. The Council, of which Frank is a director, lobbies for a ban on all underground nuclear tests; a drastic reduction in military spending; abolition of all restrictions on East-West trade; an end to travel bans that prevent Americans from visiting North Vietnam, Red China, and Communist Cuba; and, a "non-aligned" Vietnam. In 1966, the Council raised funds for the U.S.Senatorial campaigns of Clifford Case in New Jersey, Lee Metcalf of Montana, Thomas Adams of Massachusetts, Ralph Harding of Idaho, Roy Roper of Colorado, and Howard Morgan of Oregon – all "peace" candidates.

ORVILLE FREEMAN was born on May 9, 1918 in Minneapolis, son of Frances Schroeder and Orville Freeman. He married Jane Shields. He is an alumnus of the University of Minnesota (B.A., 1940; LL.B., 1946).

Freeman practiced law from 1947 until 1955. In that same period, he was chairman of the Minneapolis Civil Service Commission (1946-1949) and was secretary (1946-1948) and chairman (1948-1950) of Minnesota's Democratic-Farm Labor Party. He was an unsuccessful candidate for Attorney General (1950) and for Governor (1952).

From 1955 until 1961, he was Governor of Minnesota; he was defeated for re-election in 1960. He has been Secretary of Agriculture throughout the Kennedy and Johnson Administrations. He is a member of Americans for Democratic Action, the center of the radical left in American politics.

The farm program of the Kennedy Administration was the most radical ever offered to the Congress. Under the program, the federal government would have controlled and directed every phase of agricultural production, including the marketing of products and the processing of foods and fibers. Every farmer would become a thoroughly dependent ward of the federal government and every consumer would be at the mercy of the Secretary of Agriculture. The program was devised by University of Minnesota's Willard Cochrane, a professor of agricultural economics. For all practical purposes, Cochrane was the academic voice of the radically leftist National Farmers Union; but John F. Kennedy used Cochrane as his chief adviser on agriculture in the 1960 campaign. Freeman, who was also closely aligned to the National Farmers Union, bought the Kennedy-Cochrane program completely. The former Secretary of Agriculture the late Henry Wallace described the Kennedy-Cochrane-Freeman farm program as so radical that it would probably require "stricter control than they have in Communist countries." (And Wallace was once considered as being as far left in agriculture policies as anyone could be.)

The Kennedy-Cochrane-Freeman scheme envisioned total federal control of all food and feed production, agricultural finance, marketing subsidies, prices for agricultural products in domestic and foreign trade, and whatever monetary policies and banking practices were necessary to keep the rest of the program solely dependent upon the judgment of the Secretary of Agriculture, or more aptly titled – Dictator of Agriculture.

Fortunately, the entire Kennedy-Cochrane-Freeman scheme did not get by the Congress. But enough of it did to send food costs soaring consistently throughout Freeman's tenure, while farmers grumbled louder about their lot than at any time in the past thirty years.

Freeman, however, was popular in some places. He lobbied hard for agricultural trade with Communist Poland, Communist Yugoslavia, and went so far as to say that he favored selling the Communist bloc nations "anything they eat, smoke or drink."

At the time of the 1966 congressional election campaigns, however, even Freeman was admitting that he was not running the most popular department of government. At a confidential briefing of Democratic congressional candidates, Freeman told the hopefuls: "There is a reaction [from the farmers] far deeper and more bitter than I could ever have anticipated." Freeman advised: "Don't get caught in a debate over higher prices between housewives and farmers. If you do, and have to choose a side, take the farmer's side, and, besides, housewives aren't nearly as well organized." When asked about the increased cost of living, Freeman said: "I've been trying to figure out an answer to that question for six years. Slip, slide, and duck any questions on high consumer prices if you possibly can."

In October, 1966, Frank Le Roux resigned as general sales manager of the Department of Agriculture. Le Roux said that his disillusionment of Freeman and his associates began in 1961 and it grew so strong that he resigned in order to be able to present his views publicly. He charged that Freeman led a determined drive to sell the farmer down the river by contriving to lower prices on wheat, corn, pork, and other farm products. Le Roux further charged that Freeman's attitude was that the farmer was of little political significance but big city consumers were "the important political group to play with." Le Roux described the period, 1961 through 1965, as the worst five-year period for the American farmer in the history of modern American agriculture.

The farm program has not improved in the meantime.

ALFRED FRIENDLY was born on December 30, 1911 in Salt Lake City, son of Harriet Friendly and Edward Rosenbaum. He married Jean Ulman. He graduated from Amherst College in 1933.

Friendly began his journalism career in 1936 as a reporter for the *Washington Daily News*. In 1939, he became a reporter for the *Washington Post* and, since that time, he has been with that journal as assistant managing editor (1952-1955) and managing editor since 1955. Along the way, Friendly was director of overseas information for the Economic Cooperation Administration (1948-1949) and a Washington correspondent for the *London Financial Times* (1949-1952).

Friendly attained his initial national prominence by rushing to the attack of Senator Joseph McCarthy and the defense of Owen Lattimore in the August, 1950 issue of *Harper's* magazine. And, in the next few years, not even the Communist press could exceed the anti-McCarthy bias of the *Washington Post*. Friendly and his ultra-leftist *Post* colleagues, such as editorial cartoonist Herblock and writers Alan Barth and Murray Marder, were not content with their vicious attacks upon McCarthy's committee, they attacked any congressional committee, the FBI, or any other agency which was investigating subversives. At the same time, the leftwingers were treated with the utmost deference in the pages of the *Post*. Friendly, from his important editorial position, has contributed greatly toward the unmistakable recognition of the *Post* as one of the most pro-Communist sympathizing metropolitan newspapers in the nation.

CLAYTON FRITCHEY was born in Bellefontaine, Ohio, son of Elizabeth Shurr and Franklin Fritchey. He was married to the late Naomi Williamson.

From 1924 until 1950, Fritchey was a newspaperman: a reporter for the *Baltimore American* (1924-1927); assistant city editor of the *Baltimore Post* (1927-1929); night editor and assistant to the managing editor of the *Pittsburgh Press* (1929-1931); managing editor of the *Baltimore Post* (1931-1934); a special writer for the *Cleveland Press* (1934-1944); and, editor of the *New Orleans Item.*

In the Truman Administration, Fritchey became deeply involved in politics. From 1950 until 1952, he was an assistant to the Secretary of Defense and director of Public Information in the Defense Department. In 1952, he was a special assistant to President Truman. In that same period, he was editor of the *Democratic Digest* and he began a five-year period as deputy chairman of the Democratic National Committee.

From 1957 until 1961, Fritchey was back in the newspaper business as chairman of the *Northern Virginian Sun* in Arlington, Virginia. Then he spent two years as a special assistant to U.S. Ambassador Adlai Stevenson at the United Nations. Later, Fritchey would become director of public affairs for the U.S. mission to the UN.

At present, Fritchey is back in the newspaper business writing a column that appears in such newspapers as the *Boston Globe,* the *Detroit Free Press,* the *Cleveland Press,* and the *Pittsburgh Press* and other Scripps-Howard journals.

Fritchey's column is little more than a propaganda forum for the extreme left of the Democratic Party. He follows or even precedes the Americans for Democratic Action line on both foreign and domestic policy and he has a particular talent for downgrading the strength of Communism abroad and the influence of Communists within our own country.

ERICH FROMM was born on March 23, 1900 in Frankfurt, Germany, son of Rosa Drauss and Napthali Fromm. He married and was divorced from Frieda Reichmann. He was married to the late Henny Gusland. He is married to Annis Freeman. He is an alumnus of the University of Heidelberg (Ph.D., 1922).

Fromm is a psychoanalyst and has lectured in his field since 1929 at such institutions as the University of Frankfurt, New York City's International Institute of Social Research, Columbia University, Yale University, the American Institute of Psychoanalysis, Bennington College in Vermont, Michigan State University, and his two present affiliations — New York University and the National University of Mexico.

Fromm has written a number of books in his field, the most popular being *Escape from Freedom* which was first published in 1941 and has gone through at least two dozen printings. *Escape from Freedom* has become the bible of an ever-growing cult which accepts Fromm's up-dating of Sigmund Freud's psychology — the up-dating consists of Fromm's heavy interspersion of Marxian socialism. Fromm is an active member of the Socialist Party. He is also a very active member of the National Committee for a Sane Nuclear Policy (leftwing, pacifist). He has been affiliated with the National Committee to Abolish the House Un-American Activities Committee ("to lead and direct the Communist Party's 'Operation Abolition' campaign").

In 1965, Fromm sponsored the Redlined March on Washington for Peace in Vietnam. In 1966, he was on the national council of the National Conference for New Politics, a classical united front third party movement largely controlled by the Communist Party. And, also in 1966, he sponsored the National Voters' Pledge Campaign, which was led by Socialist Norman Thomas, veteran Communist-fronter Reverend William Sloane Coffin, and Sanford Gottlieb, the political director of the National Committee for a Sane Nuclear Policy. The Voters' Pledge Campaign was designed to support "peace" candidates, who would work for a cease-fire in Vietnam and encourage negotiations in which the Vietcong would be participants.

J. WILLIAM FULBRIGHT was born on April 9, 1905 in Sumner, Missouri, son of Roberta Waugh and Jay Fulbright. He married Elizabeth Williams. He is an alumnus of the University of Arkansas (A.B., 1925), Oxford University where he was a Rhodes scholar (B.A., 1928; M.A., 1931), and George Washington University (LL.B., 1934).

In 1934, Fulbright was admitted to the bar in Washington, D.C. and became an attorney in the anti-trust division of the Justice Department. He moved onto the staff of the National Recovery Administration but when the NRA was declared unconstitutional by the Supreme Court, Fulbright was out of a job. He stayed in Washington for another

year, lecturing on law at George Washington University.

From 1936 until 1939, Fulbright was a lecturer in law at the University of Arkansas and, from 1939 until 1941, he was president of the University. But then he was fired from that position by Governor Homer M. Adkins. For a short time, thereafter, Fulbright devoted most of his energies to the lumber business.

In 1942, Fulbright was elected to the House of Representatives, where he served one term. His two years in the House were distinguished by his vote against the continuance of the Special Committee on Un-American Activities (the Dies Committee). Fulbright said that the investigation of Communists in government or anywhere else was "unnecessary and moreover was not in the interests of maintaining good relations with our allies [the Soviet Union]." Also, as a freshman Representative, Fulbright succeeded in having the House adopt its first one-world resolution – the Fulbright Resolution by which the House went on record as favoring "the creation of appropriate international machinery, with power adequate to establish and maintain a just and lasting peace among the nations of the world, and [favoring] the participation of the United States . . . through its constitutional processes." The Senate followed the House in adopting the Resolution.

When some Congressmen suspected that the Fulbright Resolution could lead to a sell-out of American sovereignty, Fulbright began a career of invective against patriotic Americans: "The professional patriots beat their breasts and wave the flag and shout 'sovereignty,' hoping thereby to frighten us like sheep, into the corral of isolationism. In the minds of many, the word 'sovereignty' has some mystical connotation in some way associated with divinity."

Fulbright's stand against the investigation of Communists and his flair for internationalism made him a darling of the left and, since 1943, the Mahatma of American socialists and internationalists. Walter Lippmann has been Fulbright's tireless cheerleader.

In 1944, Fulbright did not run for re-election to the House but chose to run for the Senate. He was elected and has been re-elected three times. Two months after he took his seat in the Senate, Fulbright made his maiden speech and introduced what have become some of his favorite themes. He castigated those Americans who were anxious to preserve American sovereignty. According to Fulbright, such Americans were confused. They should be ready to sacrifice sovereignty and other of their "most cherished prejudices," in the interest of internationalism – a policy which would demonstrate "respect and consideration for a valiant ally [the Soviet Union] in peace as well as war."

Before Fulbright had completed his first year as a Senator, he established himself as one of that body's most fervent apologists for Soviet Dictator Stalin and his regime. Said Fulbright, in one of his most apologetic moments: "The Russian experiment [sic] in socialism is scarcely more radical for modern times than was the American Declaration of Independence in the days of George III."

Added to Fulbright's pro-Communist, pro-internationalist, anti-patriot rantings were his fulminations against the Constitution of the United States. Here Fulbright's Rhodes scholar heritage shone through as he stumped for a parliamentary system of government, modelled on Mother England's, to replace the American system. When both houses of Congress were held by Republican majorities in 1946, Fulbright went so far as to urge Democratic President Truman to resign since that is what a British Prime Minister would do in a similar situation.

Fulbright's contempt for the Constitution, which he has sworn "to support and defend," was never better demonstrated than in a speech he delivered to a Stanford University conference in 1961. Said Fulbright on that occasion: "The President is hobbled in his task of leading the American people to consensus and concerted action by the restrictions of power imposed on him by a constitutional system designed for an 18th century agrarian society far removed from the centers of world power.

"It is imperative that we break out of the intellectual confines of cherished and traditional beliefs and open our minds to the possibility that basic changes in our system may be essential to meet the requirements of the 20th century . . . .

"He [the President] alone, among elected officials can rise above parochialism and private pressures. He alone, in his role as teacher and moral leader, can hope to overcome the excesses and inadequacies of a public opinion that is all too often ignorant of the needs, the dangers, and the opportunities in our foreign relations . . . .

"Public opinion must be educated and led if it is to bolster wise and effective national policies. Only the President can provide the guidance that is necessary, while legislators display a distressing tendency to adhere slavishly to the dictates of public opinion . . . .

"I do not know whether the American people can be aroused in time from their current apathy and indifference and educated to the necessity for challenging tasks and policies that break sharply with the traditions of our past."

It was also in 1961 that Fulbright issued his infamous Memorandum which was designed to prevent military and naval officers from making public statements against Communism. Fulbright's excuse was his opinion that most military officers had neither the education, training, nor experience to make balanced judgments on the Communist menace nor the proper methods to combat it. But behind Fulbright's excuse was his fanatical hostility toward anti-Communists, genuine Americans. Fulbright's public ravings have been larded for a quarter of a century with his references to "super-patriots," "pseudo-patriots," "professional patriots," and, the most accursed, the "radical right extremists."

Fulbright's longevity in the Senate has brought him to the chairmanship of the powerful Senate Foreign Relations Committee. And he has taken advantage of his position to push hard for appeasement with the Soviet Union, recognition for Red China, and, most recently, for abject withdrawal of United States forces from the Vietnam War. So obvious is Fulbright's pro-Communist position that, in January, 1968, the Communist newspaper *Izvestia* in Moscow announced that it would translate and publish Fulbright's book *The Arrogance of Power,"* a bitter critique of an anti-Communist American foreign policy and a plea for accommodation with the Communists.

JOHN KENNETH GALBRAITH was born on October 15, 1908 in Iona Station, Ontario, son of Catherine Kendall and William Galbraith. He married Catherine Atwater. He is an alumnus of the University of Toronto (B.S., 1931) and the University of California (M.S., 1933; Ph.D., 1934).

From 1931 until 1934, Galbraith was a research fellow at the University of California. From 1934 until 1939, he was an instructor and tutor at Harvard University. From 1939 until 1942, he was an assistant professor of economics at Princeton University. While on the Princeton faculty, he also was an economic adviser to the National Defense Advisory Commission (1940-1941) and the assistant administrator in charge of the Price Division of the Office of Price Administration (1941-1942). In 1942 and 1943, he was deputy administrator of the Office of Price Administration.

From 1943 until 1948, Galbraith was a member of the editorial board of *Fortune* magazine. In that same period, he was a director of the U.S. Strategic Bombing Survey (1945) and director of the State Department's Office of Economic Security Policy.

In 1948, Galbraith returned to Harvard University as a lecturer of economics. In 1949, he became a professor of economics at Harvard, remaining there until he joined John F. Kennedy's presidential campaign in 1960. He was the chief architect of the Kennedy Administration's foreign and economic policies and Galbraith ties to the Kennedy dynasty remain down to the present time since Galbraith is a close adviser to Robert Kennedy.

President Kennedy appointed Galbraith to be U.S. Ambassador to India where he remained until 1963 when he returned to the Harvard faculty. During his tour of duty in India, Galbraith became a great admirer of India's Prime Minister, the late Jawaharlal Nehru, one of the world's most prominent Marxist leaders.

Galbraith has been a prolific contributor of articles on economics to newspapers and magazines and has written a number of books in the field, notably *The Affluent Society; The Liberal Hour,* and his most recent *The New Industrial State.* There is no doubt that Galbraith has proven in his writings that he worships at the altar of the queer John Maynard Keynes and his queerer economics. It is Galbraith's contentions that free enterprise, free competition, and small business are so outmoded that they should be relegated to the realm of nostalgia. He would prefer that the nation's economy be run by powerful cartels and monopolies.

Galbraith, in his writings, demonstrates repeatedly that he is a socialist of the Fabian breed. And away from the campus and government, Galbraith has been affiliated with the socialist League for Industrial Democracy. He was a founder of Americans for Democratic Action, the center of the radical left in American politics, and is presently national chairman of that organization. He is also a non-resident member of the Council on Foreign Relations.

Galbraith has been very outspoken on the Vietnamese War. He has stumped the country calling for a cessation of bombing by United States forces and stated that "we should have a coalition government in South Vietnam" – meaning, of course, that Communists should be given a role in that government.

Galbraith has called for U.S. diplomatic recognition of Red China, admission of Red China to the United Nations, and for the removal of Nationalist China from the UN's Security Council.

BUELL GALLAGHER was born on February 4, 1904 in Rankin, Illinois, son of Elma Poole and Elmer Gallagher. He married June Sampson. He is an alumnus of Carleton College of Minnesota (B.A., 1925), Union Theological Seminary (B.D., 1929), and Columbia University (Ph.D., 1939). He attended the London School of Economics in 1929 and 1930. He is the author of *American Caste and the Negro College* (1939); *Color and Conscience* (1946); and *Portrait of a Pilgrim* (1946).

In 1925 and 1926, Gallagher was an instructor at Doane College in Nebraska. In 1929, he was ordained to the ministry of the Congregationalist Church. In 1930 and 1931, he was secretary of the Interseminary Movement. From 1931 until 1933, he held a pastorate in Passaic, New Jersey.

From 1933 until 1943, Gallagher was president of Talladega College, a small Negro school in Alabama. From 1944 until 1949, he was a professor of Christian ethics at the Pacific School of Religion, a haven for leftwing clergy. In 1948, he was an unsuccessful candidate for the U.S. House of Representatives on the Democrat ticket in California. He sought and received the nomination of the Independent Progressive Party which was thoroughly dominated by Communists. At the same time, he was openly supported by individual Communists and by Americans for Democratic Action. Also, in 1948, he campaigned actively for presidential candidate Henry A. Wallace, a patsy of the Communists. (In California, Wallace's supporters were organized as the Independent Progressive Party, the same which endorsed Gallagher. The IPP, according to the House Committee on Un-American Activities, was "one of the largest and most successful fronts ever created by the Communists.")

In 1949, Gallagher worked as a consultant to the Federal Security Agency.

From 1950 until 1952, he was an assistant commissioner in the U.S. Office of Education. From 1952 until 1961, he was president of the City College of New York.

In 1961, California's Governor Edmund G. (Pat) Brown appointed Gallagher as the first chancellor of California's state colleges. Gallagher served only one year as chancellor. Then he returned to the presidency of CCNY, where he has since remained.

Gallagher's ultra-liberalism brought about a great deal of opposition when he was appointed to the chancellorship of the state colleges in California. He had been a staunch supporter of Alger Hiss whose investigation by the House Committee on Un-American Activities was described by Gallagher as a "red herring." Gallagher's antipathy for anti-Communist investigations by congressional committees naturally made him a vigorous critic of the late Senator Joseph R. McCarthy's efforts to uncover Communists and pro-Communists in the employ of the federal government.

Opposition to loyalty oaths for teachers and students and the right and freedom of Communists and other subversives to speak on college campuses were causes defended by Gallagher with his anti-anti-Communism. By the time he became chancellor, his penchant for the left was well established. In the early 1930's he was a founder and executive committee member of the Fellowship of Socialist Christians, which had scarcely hidden Marxist-Socialist objectives. The Communists' *Daily Worker* of April 13, 1936 carried Gallagher's name among the endorsees of the United Student Peace Committee which had been established by the American Student Union, a Communist front. The Communists' *People's World* of May 9, 1946 listed Gallagher as a sponsor of a rally for Claude Williams, a Communist by his own admission.

On various occasions Gallagher expressed his opposition to Communism but Communists did not seem to be offended since he invariably received favorable notices in the Communist press. Under no circumstances, however, was Gallagher active in his opposition. As president of CCNY in 1960, he stated: "Communists have spoken here – and continue to come – without any opposition from me." And, at the same time, he indicated that he certainly should be considered somewhere on the left: " . . . The political and social orientation of the great mass of our students and faculty is pretty generally between the center and the far left. I do not regard this as a bad thing – or a good thing either. It is just the way we are. And it should be therefore quite a congenial place for one who has the prejudices and predilections which your president has . . . . I have not changed my own position appreciably during my residence here. I am still the man who for over a quarter of a century has battled unremittingly for the rights of minorities, through the NAACP, but not exclusively there. I am still the man who ran for Congress on the invitation of united labor and with the backing of Americans for Democratic Action. I am still the man who has spoken uncompromisingly against nuclear warfare and the Balance of Terror. I am still the man who did his part in the fight against the McCarthy hysteria. I continue to condemn colonialism and imperialism in any form – whether by a capitalist nation or by a communist power. And I make no pretense of being unprejudiced. Indeed, there are very real judgments which I have just suggested – and every one of them can be called a prejudice."

Less than a year after Gallagher spoke of the "congenial" atmosphere of his presidency ("the great mass of our students and faculty is pretty general between the center and the far left"), he was awarded the U.S. Army's outstanding Civilian Service Medal and hailed as one of the nation's chief foes of Communism.

In 1966, during his second presidency at CCNY, Gallagher was faced with sit-in demonstrations by students who were demanding a greater voice in the college's administrative decisions. Gallagher charged that "a small group of Communist" students were trying to take over the college and reduce it to anarchy. He mentioned that the students belonged to the Progressive Labor Club, the W.E.B. DuBois Club, Students for a Democratic Society, the Marxist Discussion Club, and the Anarchist Discussion Club.

Sometime within twenty-four hours of leveling these charges, Gallagher had a change of heart. Now he confessed: "If I had had my wits about me, I should have replied at once [to questions about the political affiliations of the students] what I now in sober wisdom assert — that political affiliation was irrelevant to the issues of the sit-in."

When the sit-in began, Gallagher said that CCNY was "the No. 1 target of the American Communist Party" and had been since 1927. He even offered to release documents to substantiate his charges. But on the following day in his gesture of contrition, he said: "I do not charge that the sit-in is Communist-led or influenced, despite the fact that some individuals participating in the sit-in were reported to me by the media to have declared themselves to be Communists . . . . I continue to affirm my con-

fidence in the liberal idealism of these dedicated City College students, including the leadership and the vast majority of those involved in the sit-in."

Gallagher's rapid *volte-face* was explained away by the *New York Times* (November 12, 1966): " . . . Dr. Gallagher made a tactical error . . . by characterizing some sit-in leaders as Communists and left-wingers. Such lapses are exceedingly rare in a man known to be articulate and eloquent, who chooses his words carefully to make them say precisely what is on his well-trained mind."

JOHN W. GARDNER was born on October 8, 1912 in Los Angeles, son of Marie Flora and William Gardner. He married Aida Marroquin. He is an alumnus of Stanford University (A.B., 1935; A.M., 1936) and the University of California (Ph.D., 1938).

From 1936 until 1938, Gardner was a teaching assistant in psychology at the University of California. From 1938 until 1940, he was an instructor in psychology at Connecticut College. From 1940 until 1942, he was an assistant professor of psychology at Mount Holyoke College.

In 1942 and 1943, Gardner was with the Federal Communications Commission as head of the Latin American section of the Foreign Broadcast Intelligence Service. Then he joined the U.S. Marine Corps and, before World War II ended, he had served a stint on detached service with the Office of Strategic Services.

In 1946, Gardner joined the Carnegie Corporation in New York as a staff member. Later he became an executive associate, vice president, and, in 1955, president of the Corporation as well as president of the Carnegie Foundation for the Advancement of Teaching. Naturally, he was a member of the Council on Foreign Relations, the informal supra-State Department of the United States. From 1962 until 1964, he was chairman of the U.S. Advisory Commission on International Educational and Cultural Affairs. In 1965, he was chairman of the White House Conference on Education. Shortly after that conference ended, Gardner took a leave of absence from Carnegie to accept Lyndon Johnson's appointment of him to be Secretary of Health, Education and Welfare. There is no indication that Johnson knew much about Gardner more than a month before the White House Conference took place. But when making the announcement of Gardner's appointment, Johnson gushed that Gardner "has been all of his adult life an explorer in the search for excellence. As we near the outer edges of this century, the loss of quality and the discovery of excellence become the searing issues of the times. I know of no one who is better suited by temperament, by experience, and by intellectualism to confront these issues and bend them to the national desire." Gardner, however, as chairman of the White House Conference had rallied the educationist forces of this nation behind Johnson's $1.3 billion interference-with-education law. The Conference was nothing but a facade of educationist respectability to bolster Johnson's program to nationalize education.

Since he became Secretary of HEW, Gardner has proven to be one of the most revolutionary policy-makers in the so-called Great Society Administration. For leftwing educationists at home and abroad, Gardner is the best thing to come along since the days of John Dewey. If Gardner has his way, there won't be a classroom – from kindergarten through graduate schools – anywhere in the world that will be immune from direct or indirect federal government handouts.

JAMES M. GAVIN was born on March 22, 1907 in New York City, son of Mary Terrel and Martin Gavin. His first marriage ended in divorce and he is now married to Jean Duncan. He is an alumnus of the U.S. Military Academy (B.S., 1929).

In 1924, Gavin enlisted as a private in the U.S. Army. Within fifteen months, he entered West Point. He made a career out of the military service, rising through the ranks to become a lieutenant general. By 1958, Gavin was the chief of the Army's research and development program. In that year, while testifying before a Senate Preparedness subcommittee, Gavin was strongly critical of the Joint Chiefs of Staff system. Gavin recommended that the planning of overall military programs should be done by a planning group that did not specifically represent the various armed services. He charged that decisions were reached by compromise among the Joint Chiefs. At the time Gavin voiced his criticisms, he had a reputation for advocating more reliance upon the Army in the development of a missile program. And when his testimony before the subcommittee was concluded, Gavin retired from the service, explaining that in civilian life he could advance his ideas more freely.

In 1958, Gavin became executive vice president of Arthur D. Little Company, an industrial research organization in Cambridge, Massachusetts. Then, Gavin became a close political associate of Senator John F. Kennedy. When Kennedy became President of the United States, he appointed Gavin as U.S. Ambassador to France. In 1962, Gavin resigned his mission, claiming that he could not afford the post. But there was every indication that Gavin had come under the spell of the anti-American Charles de Gaulle and had thereby become a liability to the Kennedy Administration. Then, Gavin returned to the Little Company as president. He is now chairman of the board and chief executive officer.

In February, 1966, Gavin wrote a letter to *Harper's* magazine, presenting his views on the U.S. conduct of the Vietnam War. Shortly thereafter, Gavin testified before the Senate Foreign Relations Committee, under the benign eye of the committee's oh-so-soft-on-Communism chairman, J. William Fulbright. Gavin's letter and testimony were given wide publicity throughout the communications media and he became a hero of the doves, both in and out of the government. There was little or no clarity in Gavin's critique of the conduct of the war but he did raise the spectre of Red China somehow throwing its entire might against the United States and its allies. Other than that Gavin treated readers of his letter and listeners of his testimony to some rambling generalities, involving some vague political judgments and some equally vague military theories and suggestions which were apparently misinterpreted by everyone except Gavin.

Whatever Gavin tried to convey with his analysis, the net result was that he became a hero of the peaceniks. And Gavin seemed to assure them that they chose the right man when, in April, 1966, two months after he testified before Fulbright's committee, he called for U.S. diplomatic recognition of Red China, admission of Red China into the United Nations, increased American trade with Communist nations, and the sharing of U.S. scientific and technological advances with emerging nations – the same emerging nations, of course, which are generally wedded to international Communism.

In the past year, peaceniks in Massachusetts and a few other places have been trying to drum up a presidential candidacy for Gavin, whose disavowals of such efforts have not rung loud and clear.

WALTER GELLHORN was born on September 18, 1906 in St. Louis, Missouri, son of Edna Fischel and George Gellhorn. He married Kitty Minus. He is an alumnus of Amherst College (A.B., 1927) and Columbia University (LL.B., 1931).

In 1931, Gelhorn was a legal secretary to Associate Justice Harlan Stone of the U.S. Supreme Court. In 1932 and 1933, he was on the staff of the U.S. Solicitor-General. Since 1933, Gellhorn has been on Columbia University's faculty and has taught political science and law. He has also lectured at the University of Manchester in England, Tokyo University, and the University of Leyden in The Netherlands.

While on Columbia's faculty, Gellhorn was a regional attorney for the U.S. Social Security Board (1936-1938); an assistant general counsel and regional attorney in the Office of Price Administration (1942-1943); a special assistant to the Secretary of the Interior (1943-1944); and vice chairman (1944-1945) and chairman (1945) of the National War Labor Board. In 1957, he received the Sidney Hillman Award, a milestone in the career of leftists.

Gellhorn has been affiliated with the National Lawyers Guild ("the foremost legal bulwark of the Communist Party, its front organizations, and controlled unions"); the International Juridical

Association (an organization "which actively defended Communists and consistently followed the Communist Party line"); the National Emergency Conference for Democratic Rights ("Communist front"); and, the Non-Partisan Committee for the Re-election of Congressman Vito Marcantonio ("Communist front"). He has also been a long-time member of the American Civil Liberties Union, that motleyed collection of defenders of subversion, crime, and licentiousness.

Among Gellhorn's better known books are *American Rights; Individual Freedom and Governmental Restraits;* and *Security, Loyalty and Science.* His position in these books reflects the ACLU line against true liberty in favor of license. As might be expected, Gellhorn is a bitter critic of congressional investigating committees or any agency which is concerned with exposing subversives. He also is in complete sympathy with the licentious decisions of the Supreme Court whereby all manners of law enforcement have been attacked so that criminal elements may have more opportunities to violate law and order.

In the past few years, Gellhorn has emerged as a leftwing hero as an expert on the Ombudsman system especially through the publication of his two books on the system – *Ombudsman and Others* and *When Americans Complain*, both published by the Harvard University Press in 1966. The Ombudsman system is at work in Sweden, Norway, Denmark, Finland and New Zealand. Similar systems are in Japan, Yugoslavia, and the Soviet Union. Behind the system is the theory that, whenever citizens have personal complaints concerning government services, the aggrieved citizen can receive relief and satisfaction through the Ombudsman – a middleman be-

tween the citizen and the bureaucrat in government at any level.

Interest in the Ombudsman system perked up among the leftwingers when they suffered so many setbacks in trying to establish civilian review boards so as to harass and intimidate police officers. The leftwingers see the Ombudsman as a workable substitute for civilian review boards (the Communists' *Worker* liked this idea) and also as a means of harassing any government worker trying to do an honest job. Rushing to join the Ombudsman bandwagon have been such leftwingers as Senators Robert Kennedy of New York, Philip Hart of Michigan, Edward Long of Missouri, and Warren Magnuson of Washington. Also Franklin D. Roosevelt Jr., New York's Mayor Lindsay, and Representative Henry Reuss of Wisconsin.

GEORGE GILDER was born on November 29, 1939 in New York City, son of Anne Alsop and Richard Gilder. He is an alumnus of Harvard University (A.B., 1962).

While at Harvard in 1961 and 1962, Gilder was editor and co-founder of *Advance* magazine, which was described as "a journal of political thought." The magazine, financed by David and Nelson Rockefeller and other far-left Republicans, was merely one more vehicle used by self-styled moderates to prevent Barry Goldwater's nomination as the Republican Party's presidential candidate in 1964.

Gilder and his fellow collegian Bruce Chapman, who was *Advance's* publisher and co-founder, were sufficiently financed to send copies of their magazine to the members of the Republican National Committee, the leaders of the Young Republicans, and all state, county, and local leaders of the Republican

Party. And, early in its publishing life, *Advance* received a fulsome endorsement from former President Dwight Eisenhower.

The Gilder-Chapman heroes among the Republicans were Nelson Rockefeller, Jacob Javits, John Lindsay, Ogden Reid, Kenneth Keating, and John Roosevelt of New York; Edward Brooke and Bradford Morse of Massachusetts; George Romney of Michigan; William Scranton and Hugh Scott of Pennsylvania; Thomas Curtis of Missouri; Mark Hatfield of Oregon; Thruston Morton of Kentucky; Clifford Case of New Jersey; Robert Taft Jr., William Ayres, James Rhodes, and Ray Bliss of Ohio; and, Perkins Bass of New Hampshire. In effect, the collegians were publishing a Republican counterpart to the Americans for Democratic Action's *ADA World* and, except for the party labels, the heroes of *Advance* and *ADA World* were practically indistinguishable in their ideological positions. Villains in the eyes of Gilder-Chapman were Barry Goldwater of Arizona, Strom Thurmond of South Carolina, John Tower of Texas, Clarence Brown of Ohio, and, inexplicably, Everett Dirksen of Illinois and Charles Halleck of Indiana. But *Advance* seemed to be undecided somewhat as to the virtues of Richard Nixon.

After graduation from Harvard, Gilder and Chapman moved *Advance's* base of operations to Washington, D.C., where they labored in vain until 1964 to prevent Goldwater's nomination. Gilder even became a speech writer for his benefactor Nelson Rockefeller in that year.

Gilder's next stop was the Council of Foreign Relations where he was a junior fellow in 1964 and 1965. (Chapman gravitated to the *New York Herald Tribune* whose high officials had been financial angels to *Advance*. When the *Herald Tribune* went out of business, Chapman moved on to Seattle, Washington where he occupied himself as a free-lance author.) Then, in 1965, Gilder found his proper milieu at the trade unionist-socialist *New Leader* magazine where he was an associate editor until June, 1967.

Meanwhile, Gilder and Chapman co-authored *The Party that Lost its Head*, their version of how the "moderate" Republicans lost the 1964 Republican National Convention to the "fanaticism and duplicity" of rightists "by conspiracy, infiltration and subterfuge." Goldwater, according to the sour grapes of the two young would-be politicos, "was allowed to pass as a reputable conservative Republican" but, in reality, the Arizona Senator waged a campaign "designed to appeal to suspicion, xenophobia, fear, resentment, religiosity and barroom virility."

ROSWELL GILPATRIC was born on November 4, 1906 in Brooklyn, son of Charlotte Leavitt and Walter Gilpatric. He was married to, and divorced from, Margaret Kurtz and Harriet Heywood. He is married to Madelin Kudner. He is an alumnus of Yale University (A.B., 1928; LL.B., 1931).

From 1931 until 1951, Gilpatric practiced law in New York City. From 1951 until 1953, he was with the Air Force: first, as Assistant Secretary, then as Under Secretary. He returned to his law practice until 1961. From 1961 until 1964, he was Deputy Secretary of Defense. In 1964, Gilpatric left government service and joined the Corning Glass Works as a director.

Gilpatric has been an official of the soft-on-Communism Foreign Policy Association; a member of the Council on

Foreign Relations; and, a member of the Rockefeller Brothers Special Studies Project, which, in the Eisenhower Administration, produced one of the most hysterical clamors for U.S. disarmament and accommodation with the Soviet Union.

In 1965, Gilpatric and Jerome Wiesner were co-authors of a report issued by the White House Committee on Arms Control and Disarmament. They urged Lyndon Johnson to negotiate with the Soviet Union for a three-year moratorium on the production and deployment of anti-missile missile systems. Within months the Soviet Union's militarists were boasting that they had an anti-missile missile system deployed at Moscow and had plans to cover other cities in the Soviet Union. It can be seriously doubted that the Soviet Union's leaders were even approaching the truth with their boasts, but the fact remains that Gilpatric and his colleague Wiesner were dead set against the United States developing an up-to-date defensive system.

In the Defense Department, Gilpatric stood shoulder to shoulder with Defense Secretary Robert McNamara when McNamara — against the strong and unequivocal advice of military leaders — went ahead with his premature scrapping of manned bombers in favor of intercontinental ballistic missiles.

Since leaving government service, Gilpatric assumed a position of leadership in the disarmament lobby. He has all the scare-mongering clichés at his command: accepting all Soviet military claims at face value; raising the Red China bogey; breast-beating about the perils of an arms race; a third world war; and, shuddering over the thought that the U.S. détente with the Soviet Union might be in jeopardy — a détente alleged-

ly reached in the perennial disarmament conferences at Geneva. Naturally, Gilpatric has opposed the bombing of North Vietnam. He is very much opposed to up-to-date measures to defend the United States because expenditures for such programs would "forestall further financing of the Great Society programs such as antipoverty projects, Federal aid to education, demonstration cities and the like."

ROBERT GOHEEN was born on August 15, 1919 in Vengurla, India, son of American citizens Anne Ewing and Robert Goheen. He married Margaret Skelly. He is an alumnus of Princeton University (B.A., 1940; M.A., 1947; Ph.D., 1948). While pursuing his graduate studies, Goheen was a part-time teacher of classics. From 1948 until 1950, he was an instructor of classics. From 1950 until 1957, he was an assistant professor of classics.

In 1957, from his relatively obscure position in the classics department, Goheen was made president of Princeton and — for good measure — was promoted two grades to a full professorship.

As he presided over the first regular faculty meeting of his administration, Goheen dismissed the University's Catholic chaplain, Rev. Hugh Halton, O.P., M.A., Ph.D. — a Dominican priest. Father Halton had been at Princeton for five years. But from his campus pulpit and off-campus lecture platforms, Fr. Halton — as he candidly admitted — "exposed intellectual mediocrity, moral and political subversion, and intolerable nonsense in the groves of Princeton's academic wonderland."

But it was in June, 1956 when Fr. Halton committed an unpardonable crime in the eyes of Princeton's liberal establishment. Alger Hiss was invited to speak to Princeton's students. Fr. Halton, of the mind that such an appearance presented a moral crisis for the University, protested that, "In an academic community dedicated to a search for an enduring truth, an unrepentant perjurer has nothing to say." On the night before Hiss' scheduled appearance, Fr. Halton conducted an anti-Hiss meeting on the Princeton campus. The featured speaker at the meeting was the *Chicago Tribune's* veteran reporter Willard Edwards whose topic was "The Meaning of Alger Hiss." In his speech, Mr. Edwards simply outlined the facts of the celebrated Hiss case. In his introduction of Mr. Edwards, Fr. Halton expressed his opinion that having Hiss speak was tantamount to the logic of inviting a prostitute to address the students on "purity." Fr. Halton notwithstanding, Hiss spoke.

Within two weeks, Princeton's trustees voted to dismiss Fr. Halton from the campus as soon as Princeton's president, Harold W. Dodds, retired – which he did in June, 1957. Later, Goheen admitted that he "fully shared in the Trustees' decision to withdraw University recognition from Fr. Halton, and indeed I urged this decision."

With Dodds gone, Goheen became president. As Fr. Halton expressed it, Goheen was "like so many presidents of private schools, a puppet of Trustees. When they pull the strings, he could dance all night. Had he not promised to implement the Trustees' arbitrary decision . . . he might not have been invested as President of Princeton. He knows it, I know it, and that is all that really matters." Goheen remains as President of Princeton and – oh yes – Alger Hiss has been back to speak to the Princeton students. Fr. Halton has long since been relegated to that limbo where all effective, anti-Communists go.

ARTHUR GOLDBERG was born on August 8, 1908 in Chicago, son of Rebecca Perlstein and Joseph Goldberg. He married Dorothy Kurgans. He is an alumnus of Northwestern University (B.S.L., 1929; J.D., 1930).

In 1929, Goldberg began the practice of law and for the next thirty-two years he worked almost exclusively as a labor union representative. In 1948, he became general counsel for the Congress of Industrial Organizations and the United Steelworkers of America. In 1961 and 1962, Goldberg was President Kennedy's Secretary of Labor. The two men had become very close political associates. Nevertheless, the appointment was extraordinary in the sense that Goldberg had always been an extremely bitter critic of the Taft-Hartley Act, the federal law which necessarily had to be administered without bias by any Secretary of Labor.

In 1962, President Kennedy appointed Goldberg as Associate Justice of the Supreme Court. Goldberg had no judicial experience but he took the so-called Jewish seat on the Court, vacated by Felix Frankfurter. The appointment was obviously a cheap political ploy.

In 1965, President Johnson appointed Goldberg to his present position as U.S. Ambassador to the United Nations. Goldberg not only lacked experience in diplomacy but there is no evidence that he ever had the slightest interest in foreign policy.

At the United Nations, Goldberg has been a study in soft-on-Communism diplomacy. He has bent like a frail reed whenever the softest zephyr blew in from the Soviet Union. He has led the pro-Communist charge in the UN against the anti-Communist regimes of Rhodesia and South Africa. He has expressed his willingness and eagerness to have Red

China sit in on disarmament talks, since he feels that Red China should be "brought into the mainstream of world peace efforts." In 1967, at the very time when the United States was opposed by the might of Soviet Union weaponry and other war matériel in Vietnam, Goldberg was confidently predicting that the Soviet Union "may increasingly support" a peace-keeping role for the United Nations. Goldberg's line for the Vietnamese War has always been to assure the Communists that the United States is only waging a limited war effort and has no intention of upsetting the Communist regime of North Vietnam.

In years past, according to the House Committee on Un-American Activities documents, Goldberg was a sponsor of the Chicago Conference on Race Relations which had well-known and publicly avowed leaders of the Communist Party among its sponsors. Goldberg was president of the Chicago chapter of the National Lawyers Guild, "the foremost legal bulwark of the Communist Party." Goldberg was also a sponsor of the Conference on Constitutional Liberties in America and also for the National Emergency Conference – both Communist fronts.

Goldberg has also been affiliated with the leftwing, pacifist Carnegie Foundation for International Peace and the World Affairs Center; the Fund for the Republic (ultra-leftist); and, the Americans for Democratic Action (the center of the radical left in American politics).

RICHARD GOODWIN was born on December 7, 1931 in Boston, Massachusetts, son of Belle Fisher and Joseph Goodwin. He married Sandra Leverant. He is an alumnus of Tufts University (B.A., 1953) and Harvard University (LL.B., 1958).

In 1958 and 1959, Goodwin was a law clerk to Associate Justice Felix Frankfurter of the Supreme Court. In 1959, for a brief time, he was special counsel to the House Subcommittee on Legislative Oversight. From 1959 until 1961, Goodwin was an assistant to U.S. Senator John F. Kennedy and he campaigned for Mr. Kennedy in 1960.

In 1961, Goodwin was a special counsel to President Kennedy and, in that same year, he became Deputy Assistant Secretary for Inter-American affairs, despite the fact that he had never been in Latin America. But Goodwin became the Kennedy Administration's No. 1 expert on Latin America and he was the author of the text for the Alliance for Progress – the Administration's ambitious program for socialist handouts. Goodwin became somewhat of an embarrassment to the Kennedy Administration through his constant espousal of a policy of accommodation with Castro – a policy which was evidently discussed by Goodwin in a secretive meeting in 1961 with Castro's henchman Ché Guevara. At any rate, in 1963, Goodwin was eased out of the State Department back into the White House as an assistant to Peace Corps Director Sargent Shriver.

Goodwin remained in the White House with the advent of Lyndon Johnson and stayed there for two years as a speech writer for the Great Society. In 1965, Goodwin left the White House to become a fellow at the Center of Advanced Studies at Wesleyan University in Connecticut. According to columnists Allen and Scott, Goodwin, in his first few months at Wesleyan, continued working for the Johnson Administration on a private mission in an effort to unite leftwing college student movements behind the more revolutionary programs of the Great Society.

Somewhere along the line of 1966, Goodwin divorced himself from the Johnson Administration and hitched his wagon to Robert Kennedy's star. And he accompanied the New York Senator on the latter's famous tour when he brought red hot coals to red hot revolutionaries throughout Latin America.

Goodwin, as a close political crony of Robert Kennedy's, has not turned his back on the Great Society which is no more than an extension of the New Frontier in which Goodwin played such a major role. But Goodwin has become a critic of the Johnson policy in Vietnam. During the past two years, Goodwin has repeatedly spoken and written against increasing the American military effort. He has called for a peace settlement with North Vietnam – a settlement which will provide for a neutral South Vietnam; elections in South Vietnam, with the participation of the Communists; and perhaps, a role for the Communists in any interim government before such elections are held.

Goodwin has been on the national board of Americans for Democratic Action (the center of the radical left in American politics) but the unmistakable proof of his dedication to socialism may be found in abundance throughout his writings.

FELIX GREENE was born on May 21, 1909 in Berkhamsted, England, son of Eva Stutzer and Edward Greene. He married Elena Lindeman. He studied at the University of Cambridge for two years.

From 1931 until 1933, Greene did political work in the office of Britain's Prime Minister. From 1932 until 1940, he worked for the British Broadcasting Corporation in London and New York. Since 1940, Greene has been employed in the United States. He has worked at various times as a lecturer, a photographer for McGraw-Hill Book Company, and a free-lance radio and television commentator. He has always traveled on a British passport and has visited Red China at least four times. Among his writings are *Awakened China; A Curtain of Ignorance; What's Really Happening in China?;* and *Vietnam: The Case Against.* Green enjoys extremely favorable press notices throughout Communist publications in the United States.

Senator Milward L. Simpson (R.-Wyo.) presented his colleagues with a lengthy exposé of Greene's activities. In the course of his remarks, Mr. Simpson said: "Felix Greene can write on behalf of the People's Republic of China, he can produce films on behalf of the People's Republic of China, he can deliver speeches on behalf of the People's Republic, and he can exploit the public airways for radio broadcasts on behalf of the People's Republic. But because the Justice Department cannot produce a contract between Mr. Greene and Peiping, the Britisher is apparently beyond the scope of the Foreign Agents Act, which has been just recently amended.

"It is perhaps to the credit of the Department of Justice that Mr. Greene has been investigated at some length and that the Department at least finds his activities worthy of 'dislike.'

"In addition to the visible evidence of his unstinting devotion to Peiping, Mr. Greene is an unusual man in other ways. He is fast on his feet. He is a fast man with a nationality change. He is a fast man with his wife's passport. And apparently he has some pretty fast allies in the American bureaucracy.

"I call the Senate's attention to this most amazing sequence of events: In

August of 1963, Mr. Greene applied to the Department of State for permission to travel to Communist China. Permission was denied. And yet, 6 weeks later he was enroute to China. How? By the simple expedient of informing the Immigration and Naturalization Service that 'he' no longer considered himself a permanent resident of the United States.

"He wrote the Service, turned in his alien registration card, and, with an unfettered British passport, embarked for mainland China by way of London.

"After 4 1/2 months of trekking through the People's Republic, Mr. Greene applied for reentry to the United States as a new immigrant. He was given a visa at the American Embassy in London on January 29, 1964, and reentered the United States at New York on February 6, 1964. Our Embassy in London could have refused him a visa but obviously chose not to do so.

"Initial action to have kept Mr. Greene out of his sometimes country should have come from the State Department.

"This was Mr. Greene's third trip to China, but not his last. Reports reaching Washington late in 1965 told startled officials that their jolly Greene traveler was again in Communist China and again by way of England. This time he had a fellow traveler — his wife — who is an American citizen and who did not have a passport validated for travel in Red China. Greene had also been in North Vietnam.

"This time, Greene did not even go to the trouble of abandoning his permanent resident status in the United States. He summarily and without fanfare went to Communist China, and despite the fact that he was in patent violation of American law, which makes such conduct a felony, he was again allowed back into the United States.

"For reasons known only to the Department of State, Mr. Greene was given a visa by our embassy in London on December 30, 1965. He reentered the United States at New York as a permanent resident on January 3, 1966. To assuage his trepidation in this moment of consternation, his wife dutifully filed a petition declaring him an immediate relative.

"The State Department clamped down on the distaff side of the Greene team. Mrs. Greene's passport was withdrawn on March 17, 1966, and she will have a much more difficult time getting back into China. But even though Felix Greene is just as obviously in violation of law, no action has been taken against him.

"I should point out in this regard, Mr. President, that for her illegal entry into a restricted country, Greene's wife could have been prosecuted under regulations which make a felony of her conduct. The State Department simply lifted her passport.

"Mr. Greene is truly a most clever or fortunate man because the same agency of the Department of State which had denied him permission to travel to Communist China in August of 1963 turned around and approved his reentry into the United States only 4 months later and again 2 years later . . . .

"Felix Greene for the past decade has acted in the capacity of a foreign agent representing the People's Republic of China. That he is effective in that capacity, despite the lack of a 'contractual relationship' between himself and Communist China, cannot be disputed.

"Felix Greene willfully violated the intent of our laws in failing to secure in advance of his 1963 trip to China the necessary Treasury Department licenses to bring Communist Chinese film — a commodity – into the United States. He got such permission 'after the fact.'

"Felix Greene has egregiously abused the Government that has allowed him to be a guest of the United States for more than 25 years. He has used his unique status and his British passport to confuse and confound American laws and policy.

"And finally, Felix Greene is in patent violation of Federal laws and regulations which prohibit travel to a restricted country by an alien with permanent resident status in the United States. The law is clear in this matter, and the Departments of State and Justice ought to cooperate in initiating criminal prosecution proceedings.

"Felix Greene has been a guest of the United States. That he has misused the courtesies extended to him by his sometimes country, there can be no doubt. That he has no inherent right to residency in the United States, there can be no doubt.

"He has made no attempt to secure citizenship. He has been an alien leech in this country's jugular, proselytizing on behalf of our enemy, deprecating our policies, and inveighing against our objectives.

"He has made countless statements advocating the supremacy of a Communist Chinese hegemony; apologizing for the rapacious excesses of the Peiping regime.

"While our guest, he has been actively engaged in pursuits which have been detrimental to the interests of the United States. He has advocated and continues to advocate through lectures, motion pictures, books, radio broadcasts, and other means, the affirmative cause of a nation with which we have extremely hostile relations."

ERWIN GRISWOLD was born on July 14, 1904 in East Cleveland, Ohio, son of Hope Erwin and James Griswold. He married Harriet Ford. He is an alumnus of Oberlin College (A.B., A.M., 1925) and Harvard University (LL.B., 1928; S.J.D., 1929).

From 1929 until 1934, he did legal work for the federal government in the Solicitor General's office and as a special assistant to the Attorney General. In 1934, he joined Harvard University's faculty as an assistant professor of law. A year later, he became a professor of law and, in 1946, he was named dean of Harvard's Law School, a position he held until 1967 when he was appointed by President Johnson to be Solicitor General.

Griswold has written a number of books on law, his best known being *The Fifth Amendment Today,* published in 1957, thirty-five thousand of which were distributed by the leftwing Fund for the Republic. The book was not so much a defense of the Fifth Amendment as it was a defense of the Communists and their fellow travelers who took refuge behind the amendment rather than testify as to their knowledge of subversion within the United States. When C. Dickerman Williams wrote a brilliant refutation of Griswold's exercise in pedantry, the Fund for the Republic – with the merest nod in the direction of impartiality – distributed *one thousand* copies of Williams' work.

Griswold was a member of Arthur Larson's National Council for Civic Responsibility, an election year's drive by the Democrat Party against anti-Communists.

Johnson's appointment of Griswold as Solicitor General of the United States must rank as one of the worst that could have been conceived. Throughout the years, Griswold has been one of the most grovelling apologists for the Supreme Court. He vigorously denies that the

Court has trespassed upon States' rights or legislative matters. Naturally, Griswold has been a vigorous critic of congressional or state legislative committees investigating subversion. And he has been an enthusiastic supporter of any and all Supreme Court decisions which have rendered such committees harmless. Griswold has consistently downgraded threats of Communism and socialism, and in his bleeding-heart manner moans about the danger to academic freedom if an investigating committee has the temerity to question a fellow-traveling professor about his avocation within the Communist conspiracy.

Since the Solicitor General's duty is to represent the United States government before the Supreme Court in any case in which the government is interested, the leftwingers can rest assured that in Griswold they have a most reluctant prosecutor.

ERNEST GROSS was born on September 23, 1906 in New York City, son of Carolina Fleisher and Arnold Gross. He married Kathryn Watson. He is an alumnus of Harvard University (B.S., 1927; LL.B., 1931). He also studied at Oxford University of England and at the School of International Studies in Geneva, Switzerland.

From 1931 until 1933, Gross was an assistant legal adviser in the Department of State. From 1933 until 1936, he was a counsel to the National Recovery Administration. From 1936 until 1938, he was associate general counsel to the National Association of Manufacturers. From 1938 until 1943, he was associate general counsel to the National Labor Relations Board.

In 1944, he was an adviser to the U.S. delegates at the International Labor Organization.

From 1946 until 1952, he was with the State Department, serving successively as a deputy assistant secretary of state for occupied areas; a legal adviser in the State Department; an alternate delegate to the 3rd, 4th, 5th, and 6th General Assemblies of the United Nations; and, as deputy U.S. Representative to the Security Council of the United Nations. From 1953 until 1961, Gross was special counsel to the United Nations Secretary General, the late Dag Hammarskjöld.

In 1953, Gross was president of Freedom House, a center for anti-anti-Communism. He is the author of *The United Nations: Structure for Peace,* a propaganda tract on behalf of internationalism – UN style. He has been a resident member of the Council on Foreign Relations, the informal supra-State Department of the United States. He was a member of Arthur Larson's National Council for Civic Responsibility, an election year's drive by the Democrat Party against anti-Communists. In 1958, Gross was chairman of the Fifth World Order Study Conference, convened by the National Council of Churches, which resolved in favor of U.S. diplomatic recognition of Red China and Red China's admission to membership in the United Nations.

In 1957, Povl Bang-Jensen, a Danish diplomat, was the head of a U.N. committee investigating the Hungarian revolution of 1956. Anonymous Hungarian witnesses, during the course of the hearings, testified that the U.N. Secretariat was under the control of the Soviet Union and that American intelligence agencies were infiltrated by Soviet secret police. Soviet authorities demanded the names of the Hungarian witnesses but Bang-Jensen refused to divulge them.

The U.N. Secretariat investigated Bang-Jensen and heading the investigating committee was Ernest Gross, who proceeded to railroad Bang-Jensen out of the United Nations. In 1959, Bang-Jensen was found shot to death in a New York City Park. There is overwhelming reason to believe that Bang-Jensen was put to death by Soviet agents because he would not expose the Hungarian witnesses to Communist reprisals.

ERNEST GRUENING was born on February 7, 1887 in New York City, son of Phebe Fridenberg and Emil Gruening. He married Dorothy Smith. He is an alumnus of Harvard University (A.B., 1907; M.D., 1912). He is the author of *Mexico and Its Heritage; The Public Pays;* and *The State of Alaska.* In 1968, he was co-author with Herbert W. Beaser of *Vietnam Folly.*

Gruening did not pursue the medical profession despite his degree from Harvard's distinguished medical school. Instead, from 1912 until 1934, he worked in various reportorial and editorial capacities with the *Boston American, Boston Herald, Boston Traveler, New York Tribune, Portland* (Maine) *Evening News, New York Post,* and *Nation* magazine. During this period, he interrupted his journalistic career with brief service in the U.S. Army during World War I and with a stint as publicity director for Robert LaFollette's presidential candidacy in 1924 on the Progressive Party ticket.

From 1932 until 1936, Gruening was a director of the Foreign Policy Association when that organization and its publications were becoming most effective pro-Communist propaganda vehicles under the leadership of the notorious fellow traveler Vera Micheles Dean.

In 1934, Gruening became a New Dealer. From 1934 until 1939, he was in the U.S. Department of the Interior as director of the Division of Territories and Island Possessions. While in this position he also served, from 1935 until 1937, as administrator of the Puerto Rican Reconstruction Administration and as administrator, in 1935 and 1936, of the Federal Emergency Relief Administration for Puerto Rico. In 1939, Gruening was appointed governor of the Alaskan Territory. He was twice reappointed and served until 1953 in that office.

In 1955, Gruening was keynote speaker at Alaska's Constitutional Convention. From 1956 until 1958, he was U.S. Senator-elect, pending Alaska's statehood. When Alaska was admitted as a State into the Union, on January 3, 1959, Gruening began serving a four-year term as a Democrat in the Senate. He was re-elected for a six-year term in 1962.

During his years in the Senate, Gruening has voted — with very rare exceptions — the straight liberal line as befits the campaign support he has received from the ultra-leftist National Committee for an Effective Congress and from the AFL-CIO's Committee on Political Action, which is Socialist Walter Reuther's most important campaign weapon.

Gruening, however, is much more than a run-of-the-mill lackey for organized labor and the eggheaded liberals of the NCEC. Since 1964 his has been the most persistent voice in the Senate uttering the pro-Communist line on the Vietnam War. To Gruening, it is and has been a civil war with the United States — not North Vietnam — guilty of aggression. It is Gruening's contention that United States security cannot be jeopardized by anything that happens to South Vietnam. He likewise dismisses any danger to other South East Asian nations if South Vietnam falls to the Communists.

Gruening describes U.S. bombing strikes against North Vietnam as immoral, illegal, indefensible, and atrocious. Not only has he called for a cessation of such bombing strikes, but he has urged a complete withdrawal of U.S. forces from South Vietnam. He concedes that an American withdrawal would probably result in a Communist takeover of South Vietnam, but, as he explains: "Of course it is a source of regret whenever a new political entity appears to be falling behind the Iron or Bamboo Curtain. But why should we persist in seeking to prevent what is ultimately inevitable, in impossible terrain, for a people who care not, in the most distant spot on the globe?"

Gruening has frequently spoken at leftwing protest demonstrations against the Vietnam War. But his most widely publicized appearance was on December 10, 1965 at the Bill of Rights dinner, sponsored by the Emergency Civil Liberties Committee ("subversive" — "Communist front"). So highly regarded by the Communists and fellow travelers was Gruening, he was guest of honor at the dinner and his anti-Vietnam War address was reprinted in the Communist weekly *National Guardian.* Since that time, Gruening has been a particular hero in the Communist press.

Perhaps the most brazen contribution to the left made by Gruening was his suggestion that all of his Senatorial colleagues should read Wilfred Burchett's *Vietnam: Inside Story of the Guerilla War.* Burchett, an Australian Communist, was one of the guiding hands for the Chinese Communists as they brainwashed American POW's during the Korean War. And, in the course of the Vietnam War, Burchett has been openly propagandizing on behalf of Ho chi Minh.

Gruening's most recent contribution to the cause of Ho chi Minh is his *Vietnam Folly* written in collaboration with his legislative director, Herbert W. Beaser. This virulent anti-American polemic has been warmly endorsed by such distinguished leftists as Senator J. William Fulbright, fellow traveler I.F. Stone, and journalists Drew Pearson, Marquis Childs, and Clayton Fritchey.

JACK W. HALL was born on February 28, 1914 in Ashland, Wisconsin. He is married to a Nisei. (His wife Yoshiko has been identified as having been a member of the Communist Party by four persons who knew her in the Party. Yoshiko Hall invoked her constitutional privileges against self-discrimination by citing the Fifth Amendment when questioned about Communist activities by the Senate Internal Security Subcommittee in December 1956.)

In 1935, Harry Bridges, the Communist leader of the International Longshoremen's and Warhousemen's Union, sent Hall to Hawaii for the twofold purpose of carrying on labor union and Communist Party organizational activites. When Hall arrived in Hawaii, he went to work for the Communist newspaper *Voice of Labor,* which was edited by Communist Corby Paxton. Shortly thereafter Hall began to direct his Communist activities toward the unions in Hawaii. He became Harry Bridges' chief aide in Hawaii and a member of the executive board of Hawaii's Communist Party.

Ichiro Izuka, an ex-Communist labor leader in Hawaii, has recounted that, from his own personal experiences, he knew Hall as a Communist Party functionary from 1937 until 1946. When Izuka first encountered Hall, the latter was distributing Communist Party literature in the midst of a labor strike. Later,

Izuka and other labor leaders were taught by Hall how to control union meetings, parliamentary procedure tactics, and Communist principles which were to be applied to labor activities. In 1939, when Izuka belonged to an AFL-affiliated union, Hall successfully urged Izuka and his associates to leave the AFL and to join Bridges' ILWU, an affiliate of the CIO. Later that same year, Izuka was chosen by the Communist Party's Central Committee in Hawaii to attend a Communist Party school in San Francisco. Hall was not only a member of the Central Committee but he attended the San Francisco training school with Izuka. From 1939 until 1945, Izuka was a witness to Hall's direction of Hawaii's Communist Party as it followed the line laid down by Moscow. It was Hall who ordered the Party in Hawaii to go underground during the World War II years and it was under Hall that the Party was re-activated in 1945. Izuka, in 1945, was a member of the same Communist cell as were Hall and Hall's wife, and Hall paid his initiation fee and dues to Izuka who was treasurer of Hall's cell. Izuka left the Communist Party in 1946. (See, Izuka's pamphlet, "The Truth about Communism in Hawaii," published by the author in Honolulu in 1947.)

Hall was very successful as a union organizer for the Communist Party and he made the ILWU the most powerful single force in the political life of Hawaii. Even after the ILWU was expelled from the CIO in 1949, Hall maintained his influence in Hawaiian labor and politics. (After extensive investigations, CIO investigators, in 1949, reported: "The ILWU has consistently and without a single deviation followed the sharp turns and swerves of the Communist Party line and has sacrificed the economic and social interest of its membership to that line . . . . The ILWU leadership has made its own choice between the CIO and the Communist Party, and has chosen the Communist Party.")

The action of the CIO, if it did nothing else, brought Hall to the attention of the House Committee on Un-American Activities. And, along the way, Hall was identified, in sworn testimony, as a Communist by at least twelve persons who claimed to have known Hall within the Communist Party. When Hall was before HCUA and questioned about his Communist activities, he invoked his constitutional privileges under the Fifth Amendment. But he did volunteer the information that he had "filed with the National Labor Relations Board the customary non-Communist affidavit," as called for under provisions of the Taft-Hartley Labor Act. However, the HCUA voted unanimously to cite Hall for contempt of Congress, but Hall remained unscarred. And, for the benefit of his followers, Hall issued a statement: "My refusal to answer many questions on the ground that the answer might tend to incriminate me should not be misunderstood by our membership or level-headed, clear-thinking people. A 'yes' or 'no,' or 'don't know' answer could result in a perjury indictment with perjured witnesses against me." (*Honolulu Advertiser*, April 14, 1950.)

In 1953, it did appear for a time that Hall was finally going to be slowed down in his activities. In that year, he was one of seven Communist leaders convicted of violating the Smith Act by conspiring to teach and advocate the violent overthrow of the government. (In the course of the trial, Hall's Defense Counsel, A.L. Wirin, made a startling admission: "The Government claims that there is evidence in this case that every one of these defendants was a member of the Executive Board of the Territory of Hawaii. That is accepted. That means that they held office in the Communist Party in Hawaii . . . . They were officers of the Communist Party. They were officers and members of the Executive Board.") Hall's conviction was greeted in Hawaii by a labor walkout, participated in by fifty per cent of Hawaii's pineapple workers, ninety per cent of the sugar workers, and all 1,700 of the island's longshoremen.

Hall appealed his conviction and after four years the conviction was overthrown by Justice Richard M. Chambers of the Ninth Federal Court of Appeals. Judge Chambers explained that he had no choice in the matter since the Warren Court had made a "virtual shambles" out of the Smith Act.

Despite the publicity focussed upon his Communist activities and the overthrow of his conviction on a contrived technicality by the leftist Supreme Court, Hall has retained his power in Hawaii's political and economic life. He has been treated with all the deference ordinarily given to a respectable community leader and it is not unusual to read that in the *past* he did flirt with Communism. In 1960, Hawaii's Republican Governor William F. Quinn appointed Hall to his Traffic Advisory Committee. In 1962, the Democrat Governor John A. Burns appointed Hall to his Maritime Advisory Committee. In February, 1962, when the Regents of the University of Hawaii held a reception for the new University President, Hall and his wife were among a highly selective list of guests. In May, 1963, when Governor Burns gave an official reception for Astronaut Gordon Cooper, Hall and his wife were among the "specially screened" guests. In June, 1963, Hall

accepted an invitation to address Oahu County's Young Republicans. And, it is no secret that any Hawaiian who goes to Congress owes much of his political success to the support of Hall.

It is possible and even probable that for strategic reasons Hall's name has long been stricken from Communist Party rolls as a formal member. But there is no tangible evidence that his ideological coloration has ever faded from rosy red. He has kept his close association with his sponsor of thirty-three years' standing, Harry Bridges. Hall remains as Regional Director of Bridges' ILWU. In 1959, the two men attended the Communist-initiated and Communist-organized First All-Pacific and Asian Dockworker's Trade Union Conference in Tokyo, Japan. As recently as October, 1967, while Hall was addressing the biennial convention of ILWU in Hawaii, his boss Bridges was telling newsmen in Australia that he would set up a base in Hong Kong, aimed at furthering better relations with the Chinese Communists.

In July, 1962, when it was revealed that Hall's daughter, Michele, would attend the Communist World Youth Festival at Helsinki, Finland, Hall said: "I am happy she has made this decision as it should be a tremendous experience for her to meet with the youth of Socialist and neutralist countries and the progressive forces of practically every Western nation." As the daughter of Jack and Yoshiko, Michele must have been right at home with the "progressive forces" she met in Helsinki.

RALPH HARDING was born on September 9, 1929 in Malad City, Idaho, son of Kathryn Olson and Ralph Harding. He married Willa Conrad. He is an alumnus of Brigham Young University (B.A., 1955). He has worked

357

as an auditor and controller in private business.

In 1955 and 1956, Harding was a member of Idaho's House of Representatives. From 1961 until 1965, he was a Democrat member of the U.S. House of Representatives.

During his brief and unspectacular career in the Congress, Harding voted with the far left of his party and was especially noted for his perfect record on the side of organized labor. In 1964, Harding was defeated when he sought re-election – the only northern Democrat to lose his seat in the Johnsonian presidential landslide victory. In that year, Harding was the only candidate for the House to receive support from the Council for a Livable World, an ultra-radical pacifist group.

As consolation for his ignominious defeat, Harding was given a $25,000-a-year sinecure as a special assistant to the Secretary of the Air Force. In 1966, Harding resigned his position to run for the U.S. Senate against Idaho's incumbent Len Jordan. Despite campaign support afforded by the Council for a Livable World and the AFL-CIO's Committee on Political Education, Harding was defeated and retired to private life.

AVERELL HARRIMAN was born on November 15, 1891 son of Mary Averell and Edward Harriman. He was married to Kitty Lawrance. He is married to Marie Whitney. He is an alumnus of Yale University (B.A., 1913).

Harriman entered government service in 1934 and worked for the National Recovery Administration for two years. During Roosevelt's New Deal, he was a member and then chairman of the Commerce Department's Business Advisory Council.

During World War II, he worked in the Office of Price Administration; was a special representative of President Roosevelt in Britain, holding ministerial rank, and in Moscow, where he held ambassadorial rank; and, was a member, in London, of the Combined Shipping Adjustment Board.

From 1943 until 1946, he was U.S. Ambassador to the Soviet Union and, in 1946, was Ambassador to Britain.

From 1946 until 1948, he was Secretary of Commerce. He left the Cabinet to be the U.S. representative in Europe, holding ambassadorial rank, for the Economic Cooperation Administration.

In 1950, Harriman was a special assistant to President Truman. From 1951 until 1953, he was director of the Mutual Security Agency.

From 1955 until 1958, he was Governor of New York. In the Kennedy and Johnson Administrations he has been an Ambassador-at-Large. He also served the Kennedy Administration as Assistant Secretary of State for Far Eastern Affairs and he served the Johnson Administration as Under Secretary for Political Affairs.

In the Roosevelt-Truman-Kennedy-Johnson Administrations, Harriman has been a diplomatic catastrophe in any and all dealings with Communist leaders or their viceroys wherever he has traveled. Of course, in the liberal press Harriman has been hailed for his shrewd bargaining power when up against the likes of Stalin, Khrushchev, Brezhnev, Tito, or Nasser. But the fact remains that Harriman has been either naive or worse in every encounter that he has ever had with Communist leaders.

During World War II, Harriman, more than any other individual, was responsible for the U.S. policy of giving Stalin anything he asked for but with no expectation of anything in return. Harriman played a major role in the sell-out of Poland to the Soviet Union. He encouraged anti-Communist Rumanians to join in a coalition government with Communists, thereby sealing the doom of that country. In 1955, he suggested that Nationalist China relinquish its off-shore islands of Quemoy and Matsu in order to placate Mao Tse-tung. He has also gone very close to an outright suggestion that the United States should support Red China's admission to the United Nations.

In 1962, Harriman was the chief architect of the deal whereby Laos was forced by the United States to accept a coalition government.

In 1963, Harriman — more than any other American — was responsible for the disastrous Nuclear Test Ban Treaty. He was the perfect patsy for Khrush-chev. In an interview, published in *Family Weekly* (August 30, 1964), Harriman gave a most revealing account of his relationship with Khrushchev: "Russian people crave peace more than anything else. And, in spite of the fact that their leaders hold us up as imperialists, they also hold us up as the nation to emulate. 'Catch the United States' is a slogan in all their factories.

"The people want our friendship. I was very aware of this feeling when I sat with Khrushchev and his wife at a Soviet-American track meet. At the end of the meet, both teams walked arm in arm around the stadium carrying Soviet flags next to American ones. There was very good feeling between them. As the colors of our nations came by, Khrush-chev said, 'We must stand.' As we stood, the crowd applauded wildly. I saw tears in Khrushchev's eyes, and we all felt moved.

"It would be wonderful if someday there could be a real friendship between our people, but it isn't true today."

During the Johnson Administration, Harriman has been gadding about the world discussing "peace" with some of the bloodiest tyrants of our times. He is truly the clown prince of diplomacy but the tragic joke is always on the United States.

Harriman has been a member and director of the Council on Foreign Relations, the informal supra-State Department of the United States. He has been a member of the Business Advisory Council, which is virtually the CFR's patronage link to the federal government. He has been a trustee of the American Assembly, a Columbia University brain-washing project wherein American business executives are fed an up-to-date version of the State Department's soft-on-Communism, internationalist line.

DONALD HARRINGTON was born on July 11, 1914 in Newton, Massachusetts, son of Leita Hersey and Charles Harrington. He married Vilma Szantho. He is an alumnus of the University of Chicago (A.B., 1936) and Meadville Theological School in Chicago (B.D., 1938).

Since 1944, Harrington ·has been minister of the Community Church in New York City. And he is state chairman of New York's Liberal Party.

Harrington has been a national officer of the socialist League for Industrial Democracy; of the National Committee for a Sane Nuclear Policy (leftwing, pacifist); and of the United World Federalists (the most prestigious group of fellow-travelers and dupes working for the world government at the expense of American sovereignty). He has also been affiliated with the socialist Workers Defense League; the leftwing, pacifist Fellowship of Reconciliation; and the National Voters' Pledge Campaign of

1966, which was led by Socialist Norman Thomas, veteran Communist-fronter Reverend William Sloane Coffin, and Sanford Gottlieb, the political director of the National Committee for a Sane Nuclear Policy. The Voters' Campaign was designed to support "peace" candidates, who would work for a ceasefire in Vietnam and encourage negotiations in which the Vietcong would be participants. Apparently he has been affiliated with only one officially cited front, the National Federation for Constitutional Liberties ("Communist and subversive"). But Harrington has supported Communist projects: the clemency appeals for the A-Bomb spies, the Rosenbergs; commutation appeals for convicted Communist leaders; appeals to call off H-bomb tests; and, a petition against the McCarran-Walter Immigration Act.

MICHAEL HARRINGTON was born on February 24, 1928 in St. Louis, Missouri, son of Catherine Fitzgibbon and Edward Harrington. He married Stephanie Gervis. He is an alumnus of Holy Cross College (A.B., 1947) and the University of Chicago (M.A., 1949). He also studied at Yale Law School in 1947 and 1948.

In 1951 and 1952, Harrington was an associate editor of the leftwing, pacifist *Catholic Worker*. In 1953, he was organizing secretary for the leftwing Workers Defense League, a group that defended political undesirables who were subject to deportation. In 1954, he became a consultant to the ultra-leftist Fund for the Republic.

Harrington is one of the nation's most prominent Socialists. He is on the national board of Americans for Democratic Action, the center of the radical left in American politics. He is chairman of the board of directors of the League for Industrial Democracy (socialist). He helped to establish *New America*, a Socialist publication. He is on the board of directors of the American Civil Liberties Union, that motleyed collecton of defenders of subversion, crime, and licentiousness.

Since 1960, Harrington has been on the national executive committee of the Socialist Party. In 1959, he was a delegate to the International Union of Socialist Youth in Berlin. In 1960, he was a delegate to the Congress of the Socialist International in Amsterdam.

In 1963, Harrington wrote *The Other America* which became the chief inspiration for Lyndon Johnson's so-called war on poverty, and Harrington became a consultant to Sargent Shriver, the poverty war's director. Along the same lines, Harrington has been working with Walter Reuther in establishing a Citizens Crusade against Poverty.

Harrington is a master of the leftwing lexicon whether he is advocating abolition of the House Committee on Un-American Activities, fighting a belated battle against "McCarthyism," defending the rampaging beatniks at Berkeley, or praising the British welfare state – a system Harrington wants for this country.

In 1967, as the major speaker at the Third Annual Conference of Socialist Scholars, Harrington described the absolute necessity for creating a "reformist Liberal-Labor political and intellectual coalition for future success of the American Socialist Revolution." Said Harrington, "We ourselves [American Socialists] have to make a revolution for the entire society."

In 1966, Harrington was a sponsor of the National Voters' Pledge Campaign, which was led by Socialist Norman

Thomas, veteran Communist-fronter Reverend William Sloane Coffin, and Sanford Gottlieb, the political director of the National Committee for a Sane Nuclear Policy. The Voters' Pledge Campaign was designed to support "peace" candidates, who would work for a cease-fire in Vietnam and encourage negotiations in which the Vietcong would be participants.

VANCE HARTKE was born on May 31, 1919 in Stendal, Indiana, son of Ida Egbert and Hugo Hartke. He married Martha Tiernan. He is an alumnus of Evansville College (A.B., 1941) and Indiana University (J.D., 1948). In 1948, he was admitted to the Indiana bar and, from 1948 until 1958, he practiced law in Evansville.

In 1950 and 1951, he was a deputy prosecuting attorney for Vanderburgh County. From 1952 until 1958, he was chairman of Vanderburgh County's Democratic Party Central Commission. From 1956 until 1958, he was Mayor of Evansville. Since 1959, he has been in the U.S. Senate.

During his first senatorial term, Hartke was a rather obscure party hack. He was beholden to the AFL-CIO and the United Auto Workers for campaign support and he voted regularly as a pro-labor Democrat. The same degree of regularity was reflected in his support of legislation favored by Americans for Democratic Action. He was taken under the wing of the Senate Democratic Leader, Lyndon Johnson, and Johnson's alter ego, Bobby Baker. (So close was Hartke to Baker that in June 1961, he said: "If the time comes when I am asked where I stand in the estimation of my friends, I should like to say that I stand high in the friendship of Bobby Baker.")

During Hartke's second senatorial term, he decided to get away from Lyndon Johnson's shadow and make a name for himself as a leader of the pacifists in the Senate. His pacifism centered upon the Vietnam War as he cried for de-escalation, a cease-fire, and peace negotiations. As he promoted his newfound issue, Hartke became so extreme that he virtually portrayed President Johnson and Secretary of State Dean Rusk as warhawks. (Michael Pader of the *Indianapolis Star* on February 6, 1966 noted that Hartke "has now joined the rather 'select' group of American politicians and newspaper columnists who are quoted with approval by Radio Moscow and the Communist press in East Europe because of their opposition to President Johnson's Vietnam policy.")

The apogee of Hartke's pacifism came in June, 1968 when he introduced "a bill to establish an International Peace Institute that would train young men and women for leadership in the nonviolent revolution of international conflict and the expansion of socio-economic co-operation among nations." The bill provided that the Institute would be established under the direction of the Secretary of Health, Education and Welfare. Hartke hoped that the Institute would bear the name of Martin Luther King Jr.

On other matters of foreign policy, Hartke has been a leftwing conformist — voting for appeasement with the Communist bloc, supporting foreign "aid" programs, and paying utmost deference to the United Nations.

MARK HATFIELD was born on July 12, 1922 in Dallas, Oregon, son of Dovie Odom and Charles Hatfield. He married Antoinette Kuzmanich. He is an alumnus of Willamette University (A.B., 1943) and Stanford University (A.M., 1948).

In 1949, Hatfield joined the faculty of Willamette as a political science instructor. In 1950, he became dean of students and, by 1956, he served as assistant professor and associate professor of political science.

From 1951 until 1955, Hatfield was a State Representative, elected as a Republican. From 1955 until 1957, he was a State Senator. From 1957 until 1959, he was Secretary of State and, from 1959 until 1967, he was Governor of Oregon. In 1966, he was elected to the U.S. Senate.

At various times, Hatfield has indicated that his Republican heroes have been Herbert Hoover, Nelson Rockefeller, Wendell Wilkie, and Dwight Eisenhower. At any rate, during his two four-year terms as Governor, he earned the reputation as a progressive administrator. In the language of Oregon politics, this meant that Hatfield had been an ultra-liberal, beholden to organized labor, welfare statists, and civil rights fanatics.

While in the gubernatorial office, Hatfield became a nationally known political figure. In 1960, he made a nominating speech for presidential candidate Richard Nixon at the Republican National Convention. In 1964 he was temporary chairman and the keynote speaker of the Convention. In 1965, at the annual Governor's Convention, Hatfield and Michigan's Governor George Romney cast the only two votes against a resolution supporting the Johnson Administration's Vietnam policy. In the 1966 Governor's Convention, Hatfield cast the only vote against the other governors' affirmation of "support of our global commitments, including our support of the military defense of South Vietnam against aggression."

Hatfield has not allowed his unmistakably dovish stance to go unexplained. For several years, he has been insistent that the conflict in Vietnam is basically a civil war. He insists that Johnson Administration leaders and those who seek a victory against North Vietnam are guilty of confusing Ho chi Minh and North Vietnamese "nationalism" with Communism.

Hatfield refuses to acknowledge that Communism or Communist aggression are issues in Vietnam ("Ho chi Minh has been fighting since before the end of the Second World War and always under the primary cause of *nationalism* − not Communism."). Consequently, Hatfield has called repeatedly for a halt to any and all bombing of North Vietnam and to any build-up of the American military effort in the Vietnam War.

Aside from the issue of the Vietnam War, Hatfield's approach to foreign policy is centered upon his mawkish attitude toward the United Nations for which he advocates more financial support and a strengthening of its "peacekeeping" functions as an international police agency. Otherwise, his suggestions for the conduct of foreign policy are a continuation of foreign handouts in better managed programs; a continuation and intensification of the Peace Corps approach ("we must expose other nations to the idealism of our young people"); an increase in the understanding of private organizations and individuals of their responsibilities in foreign relations ("we should consider whether there should be a formal orientation program that would broaden the perspective and understanding of personnel sent abroad by American firms"); consideration for a decentralization of our efforts to assist economic development ("I would only suggest that we ought to explore the possibility that quasi-governmental economic development corporations might provide a useful device to enhance the effectiveness of the choices we must make"); and reconsideration of our military assistance programs ("conceivably, we could make the acceptance of United Nations rather than U.S. troops a condition prerequisite to the availability of economic or technical assistance from this nation").

Long active in church affairs, Hatfield is a lay preacher in the Baptist Church. He has been associated with Youth for Christ, World Vision, Campus Crusade, and International Christian Leadership. His speeches — even on political issues — invariably contain a religious theme. But at times piety is merely a handmaiden of his demagoguery. Says Hatfield: "When you substitute the gospel of anti-Communism for the Gospel of Jesus Christ, you betray the Church." If Hatfield ever had a good word for any anti-Communists, this would only be an indictment of fanatics. But in the context of his unequivocal anti-anti-Communism, he brands anti-Communists as anti-Christian.

Then there is Hatfield on Vietnam: "The war in Vietnam has eroded our concept of the sacredness of human life. There is no provision in the Department of Defense cost analysis system that reflects the value of a human life." Why anyone's concept of the sacredness of human life should be different under conditions of war or peace, Hatfield does not explain except by his cute irrelevancy about the cost analysis system in the Defense Department.

And finally another Hatfield admixture of inferences: "We must rationally decide if our goal of preserving liberty is better served through huge expenditures to beat the Russians — or

through developing methods to feed a hungry world." No qualification is forthcoming from Hatfield that our liberty to do anything in the world is constantly threatened by the Russians.

As the keynote speaker of the Republican National Convention, Hatfield expressed his faith "that the American nation and system will prevail against the Communist menace that stalks and threatens to bury us." In light of Hatfield's Senatorial record after two years, the words ring hollow. His votes and utterances on Vietnam and other issues directly related to the Communist menace ("that stalks and threatens to bury us") give no indication that he is other than willing to appease and "co-exist" with Communists everywhere.

GABRIEL HAUGE was born on March 7, 1914 in Hawley, Minnesota, son of Anna Thompson and Soren Hauge. He married Helen Resor. He is an alumnus of Concordia College (A.B., 1935) and Harvard University (M.A., 1938; Ph.D., 1947).

In 1938, Hauge was a budget examiner for the State of Minnesota. From 1938 until 1942, he was an instructor of economics at Harvard University (1938-1940) and at Princeton University (1940-1942).

From 1947 until 1950, Hauge worked in the New York State Banking Department. From 1950 until 1952, he was an editorialist for *Business Week* magazine and a member of the executive committee of McGraw-Hill publishers. In that same period, Hauge became research director of Citizens for Eisenhower and a research director on Eisenhower's campaign staff.

From 1953 until 1958, Hauge was on the White House staff as an administrative assistant and special assistant on economic affairs to Eisenhower. Since he left government service in 1958, Hauge has been with the Manufacturers Trust Company and the Manufacturers Hanover Trust Company. Out of the government, Hauge has become a critic of the very same fiscal policies he helped foist on the suffering American taxpayer during the Eisenhower Administration when he was a Keynesian economist in the garb of a modern Republican.

Hauge has been a member of the leftwing, pacifist Carnegie Endowment for International Peace; a member of the Committee for Economic Development, the major propaganda arm of the Council on Foreign Relations, in the important work of socializing the American economy; a member of the Council on Foreign Relations, the informal supra-State Department of the United States; and, a director of the Atlantic Council of the United States, an organization which stresses the need for closer cooperation, especially economic, between the United States and the socialist nations of Western Europe.

ROBERT J. HAVIGHURST was born on June 5, 1900 in De Pere, Wisconsin, son of Winifred Weter and Freeman Havighurst. He married Edythe McNeely. He is an alumnus of Ohio Wesleyan University (A.B., 1921) and Ohio State University (Ph.D., 1924).

In his early academic career, Havighurst served on the science faculties of Harvard University, Miami University of Ohio, the University of Wisconsin, and Ohio State University. In 1934, he joined the General Education Board of the Rockefeller Foundation, serving as assistant director and director for general education until 1941. In 1941, Havighurst began a twenty-four-year tenure as professor of education at the University

of Chicago. After leaving Chicago, he became a professor of education at the University of Missouri and later joined the faculty of Fordham University as the John Mosler Professor of Urban Education. He has also served (1956-1958) as co-director of the Brazil Government Center for Educational Research at Fordham University. Havighurst is the author or co-author of a score of books on education, sociology, and social history.

In 1956, the Senate Internal Security Subcommittee included Havighurst's name in its list of the eighty-two most active and typical sponsors of Communist front organizations. As recently as 1965, the Subcommittee reported that Havighurst's affiliations have included the National Council of American-Soviet Friendship ("subversive and Communist" — "specializing in pro-Soviet propaganda"); the Chicago affiliate of the National Council of the Arts, Sciences and Professions ("a Communist front used to appeal to special occupational groups"); the Committee for Peaceful Alternatives to the Atlantic Pact ("a Communist front" — "part of Soviet psychological warfare against the United States"); the National Committee to Defeat the Mundt Bill ("a Communist lobby"); the Mid-Century Conference for Peace ("a Communist front" — "aimed at assembling as many gullible persons as possible under Communist direction and turning them into a vast sounding board for Communist propaganda"); the American Committee for Protection of Foreign Born [Americans] ("subversive and Communist" — "one of the oldest auxiliaries of the Communist Party in the United States" — under the "complete domination" of the Communist Party); the National Committee to Repeal the McCarran Act ("a Communist front" — "subversive"); and the National Committee to Abolish the Un-American Activities Committee ("to lead and direct the Communist Party's 'Operation Abolition' campaign").

On separate occasions Havighurst has signed a petition in defense of Communist schools; a statement supporting the teaching of Marxism in institutions; a statement against an attack on the Communists' Jefferson School of Social Science; a protest against the Subversive Activities Control Board's adverse ruling on Communist schools; a protest against the 1948 anti-Communist film *The Iron Curtain;* a telegram to the Immigration and Naturalization Department, demanding the release of Goldie Davidoff, a Communist, who was held for deportation; a telegram to President Truman against the Subversive Activities Control Act of 1950, creating the Subversive Activities Control Board; and, a petition for executive clemency for Carl Braden and Frank Wilkinson, Communists. Havighurst was also a sponsor of the Labor Committee for Peace, which demanded United States diplomatic recognition and trade with the Communist governments of China and Eastern Europe.

In 1965, Havighurst was a major participant in the anti-Vietnam "teach-in" movement, which the Communist propaganda apparatus exploited for purely Communist purposes. In 1966, Havighurst was co-chairman (with the Negro "civil rights" agitator Dick Gregory) of the Chicago conference of the Committee for Independent Political Action. The CIPA has as its objective the formation of a new political party, and the conference was attended by radical pacifists, violent racists, representatives of the so-called "new left," and known members of the Communist Party. In

1966, Havighurst was also a sponsor of the National Voters' Pledge Campaign, which was led by Socialist Norman Thomas, veteran Communist-fronter Reverend William Sloane Coffin, and Sanford Gottlieb, the political director of the National Committee for a Sane Nuclear Policy. The Voters' Pledge Campaign was designed to support "peace" candidates, who would work for a cease-fire in Vietnam and encourage negotiations in which the Vietcong would be participants.

AUGUST HECKSCHER was born on September 16, 1913 in Huntington, New York, son of Louise Vanderhoef and Gustave Heckscher. He married Claude Chevreux. He is an alumnus of Yale University (B.A., 1936) and Harvard University (M.A., 1939).

From 1939 until 1941, Heckscher was an instructor in government at Yale University. During World War II, he was with the Office of Strategic Services. From 1946 until 1948, he was editor of the *Auburn* (N.Y.) *Citizen-Advertiser.* From 1948 until 1956, he was chief editorial writer for the *New York Herald-Tribune.*

In 1962 and 1963, Heckscher was a special consultant on the arts to President John F. Kennedy — or more accurately to Mrs. John F. Kennedy, when she was on her culture binge in the White House. Later Heckscher would join the Fun City Administration of New York City's leftwing Mayor John Lindsay. He is now New York City's commissioner of parks. His major concern seems to be making the grass greener for the hippies, who look upon Heckscher as one of their own.

Heckscher has been a member of the Council on Foreign Relations, the informal supra-State Department of the

United States; an official of the American Civil Liberties Union, that motleyed collection of defenders of subversion, crime, and licentiousness; a trustee and vice chairman of the ultra-radical New School for Social Research; and, a board member of the Atlantic Council of the United States, an organization which stresses the need for closer cooperation, especially economic, between the United States and the socialist nations of Western Europe.

HUGH HESTER was born on August 5, 1895 in Hester, North Carolina, son of Marietta Bullock and William Hester. He married Paula Green. He is an alumnus of the University of North Carolina (A.B., 1916; LL.B., 1917). In 1917, he was commissioned as a second lieutenant in the U.S. Army. In 1951, he retired as a brigadier general, saying that he "was fed up with it [the Army]."

During World War II, Hester served in the Southwest Pacific Theater on quarter-master duty. From 1945 until 1947, he was director of the Food and Agriculture Office of Military Government in Germany. (The *Omaha Herald,* commenting on this phase of Hester's career, said: "His principal claim to fame in 30 years of service came . . . in 1946 when he proposed world wide rationing of food, an idea which for sheer nonsense on a global scale was probably unmatched up to its time.") In 1947 and 1948, he was a military attaché with the U.S. diplomatic mission in Australia. From 1948 until his retirement in 1951, he was commanding general of the Philadelphia Quartermaster Depot.

In his army retirement, Hester began a career of frenetic leftwing activities. He became affiliated with the National Council of American-Soviet Friendship ("subversive and Communist"); the Emergency Civil Liberties Committee ("Communist front" — "subversive"); the Fair Play for Cuba Committee (Castro-subsidized); various Communist publications including *The Worker, National Guardian, New World Review,* and *Political Affairs;* various pro-Communist publications including *Minority of One* and *The Churchman*; and, various leftwing-pacifist groups including the American Friends Service Committee, Women's International League for Peace and Freedom, the Katherine Van Orden Fund for Freedom, and the National Committee for a Sane Nuclear Policy. He addressed a convention of the National Lawyers Guild ("the foremost legal bulwark of the Communist Party, its front organizations, and controlled unions"). He was co-author with the veteran Communist fronter Jerome Davis of *On the Brink,* an appeasement tract in which the authors urged their readers to promote coexistence with Communists by joining "peace" organizations and supporting "peace" movements. He associated with notorious Communists and fellow travelers. In 1962, he urged American youths to attend the Communist World Youth Festival in Helsinki. He became active in the pro-Communist ranks of those working to abolish the House Committee on Un-American Activities.

Hester visited the Soviet Union. Upon his return, he sang the praises of Lenin, Stalin, and Khrushchev. He urged summit meetings between American and Soviet leaders in order to achieve coexistence. He called for expanded trade and travel agreements between the Soviet Union and the United States. At every turn, he encouraged accommodation with the Soviet Union on grounds that an American defense against Communism was impossible. How far he would carry appeasement was demonstrated when he suggested "every time that the Russians or anybody else restricts the movement of our people in their country, let us extend the movement of their people in ours." On a grander scale of concessions to the ambitions of the Soviet leaders, he recommended that the United States discontinue nuclear weapons testing, scrap all of its military defenses, and work for the unification of a neutralized Germany.

The sympathy displayed by Hester for the Soviet Union was matched when he turned his attention toward Red China. He called for U.S. diplomatic recognition and support of United Nations membership for Red China. He defended Red China's genocidal conquest of Tibet.

The Vietnam War, of course, has been anathema to Hester. He has portrayed the United States as waging a war of aggression in Vietnam in order to control Asia. Consequently, he has called for the withdrawal of all U.S. forces from Asia. He has been a participant in pro-Communist "teach-ins" and marches against the United States continuance in the Vietnamese struggle.

On at least two occasions, Hester has gone to Communist Cuba. In the winter of 1959-1960, his visit was sponsored by the Castro-financed front, the Fair Play for Cuba Committee. In letters-to-the-editor of *Progressive* magazine, he expressed his reactions: "I was in Cuba . . . and the Cuban Government was not a Communist government then, and I don't believe it is now. I know of no informed person who really believes that Castro is a Communist or is controlled by the Communists."

In 1961, writing in *The Churchman* magazine, Hester insisted that Cuba was not Communist. In the same year, however, he began to concede that Cuba might be Communist. To the *Kansas City Star's* editor, he wrote: "Castro, like Tito, is only guilty of trying to survive the power of a very strong neighbor [the United States]." And to the *Progressive* magazine's editor, he said: "The Soviet Union has learned to live with Tito and the United States will have to learn to live with Castro. Castro offers the West a great opportunity to get moving again. Any monopoly softens up those exercising it. Communism has challenged and broken the capitalist monopoly in this hemisphere. It offers an alternative which must be met through economic competition, not military competition."

Hester, writing in the Communists' *New World Review* (April, 1961), recommended that the United States surrender its Cuban naval base at Guantánamo Bay, that the U.S. repeal its embargo on Cuban sugar, that U.S. financial aid be extended to the Castro regime, that normal diplomatic relations be restored between Cuba and the United States, and that American authorities hand over Cuban refugees in the United States to Castro.

In 1962, Hester went to Cuba as an accredited correspondent for the North American Newspaper Alliance. He reported that "it is simply not true that Cuba is now a Communist satellite." While tens of thousands of Cubans were doing everything in their power to escape from their native land, Hester reported: "This year the [Cuban] people are healthy, happy and busy. Engaging in sports and dancing, playing on the beaches . . . often supplying labor for some of the projects where they themselves will live."

ROGER HILSMAN was born on November 23, 1919 in Waco, Texas, son of Emma Prendergast and Roger Hilsman. He married Eleanor Hoyt. He is an alumnus of the United States Military Academy (B.S., 1943) and Yale University (M.A., 1950; Ph.D., 1951).

From 1945 until 1947, during his army service, Hilsman was with the Office of Strategic Services in the Far East. In the early days of the Central Intelligence Agency, Hilsman was a special assistant to the executive officer of the CIA. Between 1950 and 1953, he saw service with the Joint American Military Advisory Group in London as a planning officer and with the Headquarters of the U.S. European Command as an adviser on international politics.

From 1953 until 1955, Hilsman was a research fellow and research assistant at Princeton University's Center for International Studies. From 1956 until 1958, he worked in the legislative reference service of the Library of Congress.

In 1958, he returned to Princeton as a research associate and lecturer. In that same year, he lectured on international relations at Columbia University and also began working for the State Department.

In the State Department, Hilsman was deputy director for research (1958-1961), director of the bureau of intelligence and research (1961-1963), and Assistant Secretary of State for Far Eastern Affairs (1963-1964).

From 1957 until 1961, Hilsman was a research associate at the Washington Center for Foreign Policy Research and he also lectured, in this same period, on international affairs at the School for Advanced International Studies of The Johns Hopkins University.

In 1964, Hilsman joined the faculty at Columbia University as a professor of government.

Since he left the Johnson Administration, Hilsman has been a very vocal critic of American involvement in the Vietnam War. He keeps insisting that the United States is on a collision course with Red China. His solution: (1) The United States and Red China should get together and discuss arms control; (2) the United States should lift all travel restrictions to Red China; (3) the United States should re-examine its trade policies with Red China; and (4) the United States should recognize Outer Mongolia (!).

Hilsman has urged that bombing of North Vietnam should be halted. His reason: "the use of airpower in almost any form is to Asians a weak response." Whatever Asians have ever said that have gone unmentioned by Hilsman.

PAUL HOFFMAN was born on April 26, 1891 in Chicago, Illinois, son of Eleanor Lott and George Hoffman. He was married to the late Dorothy Brown. He is married to Anna M. Rosenberg. He studied at the University of Chicago for about a year.

From 1911 until 1956, Hoffman was in the automobile business with Studebaker and Studebaker-Packard. From 1948 until 1950, he was administrator of the Economic Cooperation Administration. In 1956 and 1957, he was a member of the U.S. delegation to the United Nations, and since 1959, he has been the head of the United Nations Special Fund.

Although Hoffman made his reputation in a capitalistic environment, he has been a leftwing socialist for at least twenty-five years. During that time, he was a trustee for the Committee for Economic Development, the major propaganda arm of the Council on Foreign Relations, in the important work of socializing the American economy; a trustee of the Ford Foundation, which has been a horn of plenty for leftwingers and leftwing projects on every continent; an official of the Advertising Council, which propagandizes for socialism at home and abroad; a trustee of the Institute of Pacific Relations, the "instrument of Communist policy, propaganda and military intelligence"; a nonresident member of the Council on Foreign Relations, the informal supra-State Department of the United States; a member of such one-world outfits as the UN Association of the United States, the American Committee on United Europe, and Americans United for World Government.

The United Nations Special Fund (now the UN Development Program) was created and began its operations on January 1, 1959. The UNSF was first suggested by Paul G. Hoffman, then a U.S. delegate to the UN, and, since its origin, the only Managing Director which the Fund has had.

In May, 1961, Paul Hoffman and the Governing Council of the UNSF approved a grant to finance expansion of the Central Agricultural Experimental Station in Santiago de las Vegas, Cuba. The total cost of the project was estimated at $3,000,000 − $1,157,600 to be given by the UNSF, the remainder to be raised by Castro's government. The UN's Food and Agriculture Organization (FAO) was selected as the "administering agency."

It was late in 1962 before Castro would allow the FAO's agents to enter Cuba to sign agreements that were necessary before aid could be given. On February 13, 1963, Paul G. Hoffman announced that UNSF would make the grant to Communist Cuba, despite formal objections made in the UN by the U.S. delegation.

Representative Durwood G. Hall (R.-Mo.), disturbed at the UN grants to Communist Cuba, addressed the House of Representatives and reviewed the history of UNSF in February, 1963. Mr. Hall produced facts to prove that the Communist-bloc nations were the profiteers: "I call your attention to the fact that [since 1959] while the total contribution of the Communist bloc has increased less than 5 percent, and the contribution of Soviet Russia has remained constant over a 5-year period; the U.S. contribution to the U.N. Special Fund has increased 300 percent in that same period.

"Not a single year has gone by since 1959 that we have failed to increase the U.S. contribution by a substantial amount. None of the funds are spent on projects in the United States which contributes 40 percent of the Special Fund, while the Communist-bloc countries are sure that almost all of their funds will be spent in Communist nations because they do not permit conversion of their moneys, except to a very restricted degree.

"Here is what one finds when one traces the history of contributions: In 1959, the United States contributed $10,300,000 while the U.S.S.R. contributed $1 million and the total Communist-bloc contribution was $1,593,000. In 1960, the United States contributed $15,900,000 − a 50-percent increase. The U.S.S.R. contribution remained steadfast at $1 million and the total Communist-bloc contribution was only $1,625,425. In 1961, the United States increased its contribution again, this time to $19,900,000. The U.S.S.R. contribution remained at $1 million and the total Communist-bloc contribution was $1,637,425. In 1962, the United States again increased its contribution to $25,300,000. The U.S.S.R. contribution

369

once more remained steadfast at $1 million and the total Communist-bloc contribution also remained relatively static at $1,685,000. In 1963, the U.S. contribution jumped to $29 million. The U.S.S.R. contribution remained at $1 million and the total Communist-bloc contribution remained at $1,685,000.

"Now, even these astounding ratios do not tell the full story. The Communist-bloc figures include a $30,000 pledge from Cuba which as of November 1962 had not been paid. Presumably, now that Cuba has been given a large grant she will not mind keeping her word. After all, who would not give a nickel to get a dollar?

"Furthermore, contributions from the Communist nations are made in the currency of the donor with only a very insignificant provision of conversion. Yugoslavia allows 20 percent convertibility. The three Russian members of the U.N. limit convertibility to 25 percent and then only to cover travel expenses, salary payments to experts – usually their own – and freight and transportation charges on equipment shipped from the U.S.S.R.

"In other words, the Communist-bloc nations make sure that any money they contribute to the fund will be expended in Communist countries or countries which can only spend their assistance in rubles.

"How have the Communists fared under this arrangement? Yugoslavia, which has contributed a total of $957,000 over the 5 years, is on the receiving end of three projects totaling $2,627,000. Poland, which has contributed the meager sum of $625,000 over a 5-year period, is on the receiving end of two projects totaling $1,837,000. Mr. Speaker, even the tiny country of Switzerland contributes more to the U.N. fund than Soviet Russia.

"The Members will be interested to know that only one identified nuclear research project is being carried out under the auspices of the U.N. Special Fund. It is going on in Yugoslavia – a Communist-bloc nation – and is labeled 'Nuclear Research and Training in Agriculture,' and is a 3-year project approved only last May – 1962."

Hoffman's Development Program has continued to spend American money at a fearful pace and today he is handing out American dollars to one hundred and fifty countries and territories. He maintains that "an awful lot of countries are just plain fearful about taking aid" from the United States. But evidently this fear melts away when American money is channeled through his hands in the Development Program.

AMORY HOUGHTON was born on July 27, 1899 in Corning, New York, son of Adelaide Wellington and Alanson Houghton. He married Laura Richardson. He is an alumnus of Harvard University (A.B., 1921).

Since 1921, Houghton has been with the Corning Glass Works and an officer of the company after 1926. He is now honorary chairman of the board.

During World War II, Houghton did some work in the Office of Price Administration and War Production Board. He was also deputy chief of the mission for economic affairs in the State Department.

From 1957 until 1961, Houghton was U.S. Ambassador to France.

He has been a non-resident member of the Council on Foreign Relations, the informal supra-State Department of the United States; an official of the Atlantic Council of the United States, an organization which stresses the need for closer cooperation, especially economic, between the United States and the socialist nations of Western Europe; and, a trustee of the Committee for Economic Development, the major propaganda arm of the Council on Foreign Relations, in the important work of socializing the American economy.

In the late 1940's when the House Committee on Un-American Activities found that Dr. Edward U. Condon was one of "the weakest links in our atomic security," Condon was Director of the U.S. Bureau of Standards. The FBI and HCUA had amassed a mountain of evidence showing that Condon and his wife had been in frequent association with Communist espionage agents and other Communists.

In 1951, Condon resigned from the Bureau of Standards and went to Houghton's Corning Glass Works as director of research and development.

It is probably only a coincidence, but when former Ambassador Robert Murphy ended his career in the State Department where he had been a harbinger of bad tidings for anti-Communist regimes, he wound up as president of Corning Glass International and a director of the Corning Glass Works.

HAROLD HOWE II was born on August 17, 1918 in Hartford, Connecticut, son of Margaret Armstrong and Arthur Howe. He married Priscilla Lamb. He is an alumnus of Yale University (B.A., 1940) and Columbia University (M.A., 1947).

In 1940 and 1941, and from 1947 until 1960, Howe was a teacher and principal in secondary schools in Ohio, Massachusetts, and New York. From 1960 until 1964, he was superintendent of schools in Scarsdale, New York. Then, for eighteen months, he was executive director of the Learning Institute of

North Carolina where he was concerned with the integration of schools and other innovations in that State's education system. Since 1965, Howe has been the U.S. Commissioner of Education.

Howe has made no secret of the fact that he considers himself to be the czar of public education. He said early in his administration that the federal government needs to be a "stronger partner in the educational enterprise." But how strong a partner? Howe despises local control of schools because, as he explains, it "gives the communities the right to have both good and bad schools, and the right has been liberally exercised in both directions. What the federal government [meaning Howe's office] is now about . . . is to curtail the right to have bad schools."

Howe seems to feel that his primary mission as czar of public education is to end alleged *de facto* segregation in public schools — not an insurmountable object as far as he is concerned. He feels his mission can be accomplished by rezoning school districts, bussing children from one district to another, and shifting pupils from one school to another. There seems to be no limit to his imagination: "We could, for example, alter political boundaries to bring social, economic and intellectual strength of the suburbs to bear on the problems of the city schools. Building programs for the future could be planned so that new schools would break up, rather than continue, segregation of the racial and economic sort . . . and if I have my way the Office [of Education] will provide construction funds before long."

Perhaps Howe's wildest exhibition took place at a National Student Association conference in the summer of 1967. The NSA (long financed by the Central Intelligence Agency) conference de-

371

nounced the war in Vietnam, made plans to promote resistance to the draft, and agreed to support Black Power "by any means necessary." This all prompted Howe to express his concern that NSA agitators, as they grow older, "may lose the sharpness of your viewpoints and the determination to put those viewpoints to work." He also told the students that he believed it might be best for students "to have curricula which revolve around such problems as poverty, or peace or urban planning."

Howe put himself on record as favoring more student control of colleges and universities. He expressed his admiration for the Free University Movement in San Francisco where most of the faculty are students whose "course offerings are intriguing: Nonviolence in a Violent World, Black Writers . . . Obscure Literature, Sex Education for a Changing Society and Technology and Human Emotions." Howe also appreciated another course: "Dance of Joy Seminar in the Ecstatic Style of Cosmic consciousness."

QUINCY HOWE was born on August 17, 1900 in Boston, son of Fanny Quincy and Mark Howe. He married Mary Post. He is an alumnus of Harvard University (A.B., 1921).

From 1922 until 1928, he was on the staff of *Atlantic Monthly* magazine. From 1929 until 1935, he was editor of *Living Age* magazine. From 1935 until 1942, he was with Simon & Schuster publishers.

From 1942 until 1963, Howe was a news analyst for Columbia Broadcasting System, Station WILL, and the American Broadcasting Company. In 1961, he became editor of *Atlas* magazine, which brought thunderous ovations from such distinguished leftwingers as Walter Lipp-

mann, Edward R. Murrow, and Warren Magnuson.

Howe has been an official of the American Civil Liberties Union, that motleyed collection of defenders of subversion, crime and licentiousness; and, for two years, was on the board of directors of the socialist League for Industrial Democracy.

PALMER HOYT was born on March 10, 1897 in Roseville, Illinois, son of Annie Tendler and Edwin Hoyt. He was married to and divorced from Cecile DeVore. He is married to Helen Taber. He is an alumnus of the University of Oregon (A.B., 1923).

From 1923 until 1926, Hoyt was telegraph and sports editor of the *Pendleton Oregonian*, beginning as a copy reader, working through the ranks, and eventually becoming editor and publisher.

Since 1946, he has been publisher-editor of the *Denver Post*.

In 1943, Hoyt was domestic director of Elmer Davis' rosey red Office of War Information. He has been a non-resident member of the Council on Foreign Relations, the informal supra-State Department of the United States. He has been a national official of the American Civil Liberties Union, that motleyed collection of defenders of subversion, crime, and licentiousness. He was a founder of the Americans for Democratic Action, the center of the radical left in American politics.

With his *Denver Post*, Hoyt has managed to give his Rocky Mountain readers about the same extreme leftwing journalism as readers get in the nation's capitol from the *Washington Post*.

EMMET HUGHES was born on December 26, 1920 in Newark, New Jersey, son of Grace Freeman and John Hughes. He is an alumnus of Princeton University (A.B., 1941).

During World War II, Hughes was a press attaché at the U.S. Embassy in Madrid.

From 1946 until 1949, Hughes was a correspondent and bureau chief for *Time-Life* magazines in Rome and Berlin. From 1949 until 1952, he was an articles editor for *Life*. In 1952, he was a speech writer for presidential candidate Dwight Eisenhower. In 1953, he was an administrative assistant to President Eisenhower and also worked for Eisenhower in the 1956 presidential campaign.

In 1956 and 1957, Hughes was on *Fortune* magazine's board of directors. From 1957 until 1960, he was chief foreign correspondent for *Time-Life* magazines. From 1960 until 1963, he was senior adviser on public policy and public relations to the Rockefeller family.

Since 1963, Hughes has been a columnist and editorial consultant for *Newsweek* magazine and the *Washington Post*.

Hughes has written several books, the most important by far being *The Ordeal of Power*. In that book, Hughes (who describes himself as oriented toward the Christian Democratic Left of Western Europe) more or less apologizes for having once been a part of a Republican Administration. Hughes describes his experience as "a most uncertain, occasionally heartening, often troubling journey." Somehow Hughes found Eisenhower to be too conservative, John Foster Dulles too anti-Communist, Eisenhower too soft on the late Senator Joseph R. McCarthy (perhaps, Hughes would have been satisfied if McCarthy had been hung from atop the Washington Monument), and Eisenhower too timid about making accommodation gestures for peace and disarmament towards the Soviet Union. Hughes did like Eisenhower's sharp and alert mind!

H. STUART HUGHES was born on May 7, 1916 in New York City, son of Marjorie Stuart and Charles Hughes. He was married to, and divorced from, Suzanne Rufenacht. He is married to Judith Markham. He is an alumnus of Amherst College (A.B., 1937) and Harvard University (M.A., 1938; Ph.D., 1940).

In 1940 and 1941, Hughes was an instructor at Brown University. During World War II, he went from private in the field artillery to lieutenant colonel in the Office of Strategic Services.

From 1946 until 1948, Hughes was in the State Department as chief of the division of research for Europe.

From 1948 until 1952, he was an assistant professor at Harvard University.

From 1952 until 1956, he was an associate professor, professor, and head of the history department at Stanford University.

Since 1957, Hughes has been a history professor at Harvard. In 1950, he was a visiting member at the Institute for Advanced Study in Princeton, New Jersey.

Hughes has been a member of the American Civil Liberties Union. He has been national co-chairman of the National Committee for a Sane Nuclear Policy (leftwing, pacifist). He has been a sponsor of the National Committee to Abolish the House Un-American Activities Committee ("to lead and direct the Communist Party's 'Operation Abolition' campaign"). In 1965, he was on the Inter-University Committee for a Public Hearing on VietNam, sponsors of the anti-Vietnam "teach-in" movement, which the Communist propaganda apparatus exploited for purely Communist purposes. Also, in 1965, he was a sponsor of the red-lined March on Washington for Peace in VietNam.

In 1966, he was on the national council of the National Conference for New Politics, a classical united front third party movement largely controlled by the Communist Party. Also, in 1966, he was a sponsor of the National Voters' Pledge Campaign, working for a ceasefire in Vietnam and encouraging negotiations in which the Vietcong would be participants.

Hughes has recommended membership for Red China in the United Nations; American contributions of men and weapons to a United Nations peacekeeping force; foreign aid to Communist nations; technical assistance and Peace Corps workers to Communist nations; and, a renunciation of our nuclear weapons "in order to show our good faith" to the Communists.

In 1965, Ho chi Minh, the President of Communist North Vietnam, let loose one of his anti-United States propaganda barrages by means of a letter addressed to Hughes.

Hughes insists that he is only a democratic Socialist who has neither been a strenuous anti-Communist nor has he remotely thought of becoming a Communist. But he concedes that he left the State Department because he wanted to maintain friendly relations with the Soviet Union and he feared that the State Department was hardening its position against Communism.

HUBERT HUMPHREY was born on May 27, 1911 in Wallace, South Dakota, son of Christine James and Hubert Humphrey. He married Muriel Buck. He studied at the Denver College of Pharma cy in 1932 and 1933. He is an alumnus of the University of Minnesota (A.B., 1939) and the University of Louisiana (A.M., 1940).

From 1933 until 1937, Humphrey was a pharmacist. From 1939 until 1941, he was an assistant instructor of political science at the University of Louisiana and the University of Minnesota. From 1941 until 1943, he worked for the Minnesota branch of the War Production Administration. In 1943 and 1944, he was a visiting professor of political science at Macalester College.

From 1945 until 1948, Humphrey was Mayor of Minneapolis. From 1948 until 1964, he was U.S. Senator from Minnesota. Since 1965, he has been Vice President of the United States.

Humphrey has been a non-resident member of the Council on Foreign Relations, the informal supra-State Department of the United States. He was a founder and vice chairman of the socialist Americans for Democratic Action, the center of the radical left in American politics. In 1960, he was a chief beneficiary, as a Senatorial candidate, of campaign support from the ultra-leftwing National Committee for an Effective Congress, a group which, since 1952, has campaigned for and financed ultra-leftist candidates for the House and Senate.

On any and all domestic issues throughout his career in Washington, Humphrey has gone right down the line with the socialist Americans for Democratic Action. On matters of foreign policy, he has been a flaming evangelist of one-worldism and extremely soft on Communism. Perhaps his greatest contribution to the left was his long and successful sponsorship for the establishment of the U.S. Arms Control and Disarmament Agency, and the subsequent Nuclear Test Ban Treaty of 1963.

CHET HUNTLEY was born on December 10, 1911 in Cardwell, Montana, son of Blanche Tatham and P.A. Huntley. He was married to Ingrid Rolin. He is married to Lewis Stringer. He is an alumnus of the University of Washington (B.S., 1934). He also studied at Montana State College and the Cornish School of Arts.

From 1934 until 1936, he was on the staff of radio station KPCB in Seattle. From 1936 until 1939, he was a news broadcaster on local radio stations KHQ in Spokane, KGW in Portland, Oregon, and KFI in Los Angeles. From 1939 until 1951, he was a news broadcaster for CBS in Los Angeles. From 1951 until 1955, he was a news broadcaster for ABC in Los Angeles. Since 1955, he has been a news broadcaster for NBC in New York City.

In 1956, during the national political conventions, Huntley first teamed up with David Brinkley. And the two have covered the conventions in 1960 and 1964. Along the way, they began a five-night-a-week news program on NBC-television.

Perhaps the best summation of Huntley's ideological bent may be found in a book published in 1966, *Chet Huntley's News Analysis.* In his writings, there are no surprises for those who have listened to his commentaries over the years. He has absolute scorn for political conservatism. Consequently, his recent American heroes are the late John F. Kennedy and Lyndon Johnson except on those rare occasions when either individual seemed to deviate slightly backward from their drive to the left. Much of Huntley's infatuation for the past two Administrations is traceable to his enthusiasm for so-called civil rights legislation.

In contrast to his wisecracking teammate Brinkley, Huntley assumes the posture of an elder statesman, not unlike Eric Sevareid or the late Edward R. Murrow. But his pronouncements are merely the clichés of the far left Liberal Establishment: the threat of worldwide Communism is lessened as what might have been a monolith is breaking up (i.e. the phony polycentrism theory, as propounded tirelessly by George F. Kennan, Robert M. Hutchins, and assorted echoes in the State Department and "think" factories); and, there has been a real change in the Soviet Union since nasty Khrushchev was ousted, so that today under the benevolent butchers, Kosygin and Brezhnev, the magic word is "caution."

On the domestic scene, Huntley can find excuses for the most obnoxious and revolutionary campus and street demonstrators: "We who are the product of three wars and one big depression could use a bit of their vitality and enthusiasm in our struggle to bridge the gap between the horse and buggy and the space craft, between the telegraph key and the laser, between the mustard plaster and chemotherapy."

SOL HUROK was born on April 9, 1888 in Poger, Russia, son of Israel and Naomi Hurok. He came to the United States in 1905. He was naturalized in 1915. His second wife is Emma Runitch.

Since 1915, he has been an impresario of ballets and concerts. Among others, he has been impresario for the Russian Ballet, the Bolshoi Ballet, the Maryinsky Ballet, and Moiseyev Folk Ballet.

Bringing performers from the Soviet Union to the United States is an old experience for Hurok. He had been doing this intermittently since 1920, but since 1958, it has become a habit — a bad habit — which has served the interests of the Soviet Union. And it was planned that way.

When the first U.S.-U.S.S.R. cultural exchange agreement was signed, the motives of the Soviet government were spelled out in the pages of *Pravda* by the Soviet Minister in charge of cultural relations, G. Zhukov. He said it was planned to have pro-Soviet propaganda implanted in the American visitors to the U.S.S.R. and the same propaganda would be disseminated by Russian groups visiting the United States.

In 1958 and 1959 under Hurok's auspices, dance companies and a ballet group were brought to the United States. Zhukov's plans were realized: "The first buds of cultural exchange – guest performances in the United States of Igor Moiseyev's Folk Dance Company, the Beryozka Dance Company, and the Bolshoi Ballet – dissipated the myth current among Americans about 'forced' labor in the U.S.S.R. Even the most obtuse of businessmen had it brought home to him that such pearls of world art can be produced only by people inspired by supreme freedom." (A. Ajubei and others, *Face To Face With America,* Moscow: Foreign Languages Publishing, 1960.)

The Senate Internal Security Subcommittee tried to warn the American people that more than propaganda was being imported by Hurok and others involved in the cultural exchange programs: "Soviet hoaxters are playing us, individually and nationally, for suckers. In the interest of realism and commonsense, a plain statement of certain cold facts seems called for . . . . Every member of a Soviet cultural mission is an observer for Soviet military intelligence. Each such member is thoroughly screened to assure political reliability."

In 1964, during an interview, Hurok summed up his experiences: "The exchanges have certainly been in our favor . . . . We have had five to six thousand artists here. It has done more good for us than all the speakers and ambassadors have done. The artists bring back to Russia the message that the American people are not hungry for war. They report on our culture. This is one important factor in cementing goodwill."

In that same year, Natalie Anna Beinstock, a Cornell University graduate student, admitted to the Justice Department that she had spied for the Soviet Union, giving information about potential defectors among Soviet artists on tour in the U.S. to Soviet agents. Miss Beinstock said she had been trained for her espionage duties in Moscow, while there in the employ of Sol Hurok.

This was not the first time that Hurok's name had come under a cloud in connection with Soviet artists. In 1958, the House Committee on Un-American Activities interrogated Arthur Lief who had been employed by Hurok as a conductor for the Moiseyev dancers.

In less than five pages of testimony Lief invoked the first and fifth amendments sixteen times. He refused to tell the Committee if he was a Communist, whether he discussed his Communist Party membership with Sol Hurok, the impresario who hired him, whether Communists obtained the job for him, whether he attended meetings with the ballet members outside the professional sessions of the ballet, or if he knew of other Americans working with the ballet who were Communists.

ROBERT M. HUTCHINS was born on January 17, 1899 in Brooklyn, son of Laura Murch and William Hutchins. He was married to, and divorced from, Maude McVeigh. He is married to Vesta Orlick. He is an alumnus of Yale University (A.B., 1921; A.M., 1922; LL.B., 1925). He also studied at Oberlin College.

From 1921 until 1923, he was a secondary school English and history teacher in Lake Placid, New York. From 1923 until 1927, he was a secretary at Yale University. From 1925 until 1927, he lectured at Yale University Law School. From 1927 until 1929, he was a professor of law, simultaneously serving as acting dean (1927-1928) and dean (1928-1929).

From 1929 until 1945, Hutchins was president of the University of Chicago and chancellor from 1945 until 1951.

From 1951 until 1954, he was associate director of the Ford Foundation, which has been a horn of plenty for leftwingers and leftwing projects on every continent. In 1954, he became president of the Fund for the Republic. He is also president of the Fund's Center for the Study of Democratic Institutions (ultra-leftist).

He has also been a director (since 1943) and a member of the board of editors (since 1946) of the Encyclopedia Brittanica.

He is a columnist for the *Los Angeles Times.*

Hutchins has been affiliated with the American Civil Liberties Union, that motleyed collection of defenders of subversion, crime, and licentiousness. In 1965, he was a member of the Inter-University Committee for a Public Hearing on Vietnam, sponsors of the anti-Vietnam "teach-in" movement, which the Communist propaganda apparatus exploited for purely Communist purposes. In 1959, he won the Sidney Hillman Award, a coveted memento among leftwingers.

The monumental eggheadism of Robert Maynard Hutchins is exceeded only by his stature in the ranks of anti-anti-Communists. But it is virtually inconceivable that Hutchins has followed any planned methodology during his past thirty-five years as the most ridiculous apologist for Communism in the entire non-Communist world. He makes the ordinary hammer and sickle fellow traveler appear to be an arch-conservative. He has made statements on behalf of Communists and Communism that would make Gus Hall choke with embarrassment.

When Hutchins became president at the University of Chicago, he was hailed as the boy wonder of the academic world. But, during his tenure, he allowed that campus to become one of the most hospitable havens for Communists and fellow travelers in America. He abolished football at Chicago evidently as a clear and present danger to education but he didn't think Communism was a clear and present danger or that membership in the Communist Party should disqualify an individual from a position on his faculty. Hutchins' test for membership on a university's faculty, even for a Communist, was the individual's "competence and integrity."

When Hutchins became president of the Fund for the Republic, he had $15,000,000 to spend in support of "activities directed toward the elimination of restrictions on freedom of thought, inquiry and expression in the U.S., and the development of policies and procedures best adapted to protect these rights." Hutchins wasted no time in exposing the federal government's loyalty security program (the Fund decided that there should be no effective program). The Fund studied the blacklisting of Communists and fellow travelers in the entertainment business (the Fund decided that the un-Americans had as much right to be entertainers as Communists had to be on Hutchins' faculty). The Fund studied the nature of Communism in the United States and the degree of its threat to freedoms (naturally, Communism was merely an exercise in free thought and the ones who thought otherwise were the real threats to freedom).

A few years earlier, Hutchins was chairman of the Commission on Freedom of the Press. Under Hutchins, the Commission recommended that a continuing private agency should report periodically on the performance of the press — sort of a "blacklisting" agency. Fortunately, Hutchins and his Commission were not taken seriously especially after veteran *Chicago Tribune* reporter Frank Hughes wrote a 642-page book, *Prejudice and the Press,* which exposed the Commission's work as an attempt to shackle the press in the name of freedom.

Another ambitious program undertaken by Hutchins concerned world government and he was a founder and president of the Committee to Frame a World Constitution. As he explained, in the age of the atomic bomb "our only salvation lies in establishment of international morality, a mutual acceptance of the futility of further warfare and a mutual avowal to keep the peace." Those idiotic platitudes were written in 1947.

Since 1959, Hutchins has probably made his greatest contributions to the left through the Center for the Study of Democratic Institutions. With a generous budget, Hutchins and his ultra-leftwing cohorts produce a steady stream of socialist tracts which, if they emanated from the Kremlin, could not be more anti-American or pro-Communist.

Hutchins' column in the *Los Angeles Times* is a repetitious effusion of his favorite theme: there is no Communist world conspiracy because Communists are not conspirators and, even if they were, they would be conspiring for peace and brotherhood.

JACOB JAVITS was born on May 18, 1904 in New York City, son of Ida Littman and Morris Javits. He married Marion Borris. He is an alumnus of New York University (LL.B., 1926).

Javits has practiced law in New York since 1927. From 1947 until 1954, he was a member of the House of Representatives. From 1954 until 1956, he was Attorney General of the State of New York. Since 1956, Javits, a Republican, has been a U.S. Senator.

In 1937, Javits first became active in politics when he campaigned for the late Fiorello La Guardia who was the Republican-fusion candidate for mayor of New York City. In 1940, Javits campaigned to get President Franklin D. Roosevelt re-elected to a third term. In 1945, he campaigned for Jonah Goldstein, a Democrat running as the Republican Liberal-fusion candidate for mayor of New York.

In 1946, leftwing labor leaders Alex Rose, David Dubinsky, and Morris Shapiro — all Liberal Party leaders — encouraged Javits to run for Congress. In 1956, the Congressional campaign of 1946 became a subject for the Senate Internal Security Subcommittee in its hearings on the "Scope of Soviet Activity in the United States." Javits sought the opportunity to testify and to refute what he described as "vicious" rumors about his past political associations. The subcommittee had heard sworn testimony from Dr. Bella Dodd, a former member of the National Committee of the Communist Party. Dr. Dodd testified that, in 1946, she was in charge of the Communist Party's election activities in New York. She said that Javits came to her office seeking political advice which she gave to him and that the Communist Party supported Javits in his successful 1946 Congressional campaign.

In the course of the subcommittee hearings, Javits was asked about earlier and later associations with Communists. The Javits hearings ended inconclusively and, although further hearings were scheduled, the Chairman of the subcommittee, Senator James O. Eastland (D.-Miss.) called them off. Willard Edwards, a Washington correspondent for the *Chicago Tribune,* later reported that the Javits hearings were called off at the request of Mayor Robert Wagner, Javits' Democrat opponent in the senatorial campaign. Wagner, according to Edwards, feared that the Democrat-controlled subcommittee was making a martyr out of Javits. Nevertheless, Javits was elected to the Senate. And Javits received support from on high. President Eisenhower, who remembered Javits as one of his original supporters in the Congress, said that he "wants and needs Jack Javits in the United States Senate."

In 1964, Javits wrote *Order of Battle: A Republican's Call to Reason.* In a review of the book, William A. Rusher (*National Review,* June 30, 1964) commented: "In the early chapters of his book, Senator Javits treats us to a lot of historical hoo-hah to explain 'Why I Am a Republican'; but, while he trims the turkey with a great deal of parsley about Tammany Hall and the Ku Klux Klan, it takes no very sophisticated reader to deduce that, man and boy, he was simply a partisan of that pseudo-Republican school of thought wherewith Fiorello La Guardia, heading a coalition of Italians and Jews, smote the Irish-Democratic Philistines who had theretofore dominated New York. And his record as a candidate for elective office from 1946 to the present bears out the conclusion: here is one of the most accomplished practitioners of the religious bullet-vote that has ever graced the polyglot New York scene. Such a man may be hard to beat, but he is not necessarily worth listening to . . . . Yet it would be idle to pretend that Senator Javits and his viewpoint can be written off as wholly outside the internal Republican dialogue. His is not a popular viewpoint within the GOP, but it has its devotees. Substantially, he proposes to adopt the entire Liberal credo, and then to best the Democrats by a more slavish adherence to its imperatives. Whatever we may think of such a proposal, it has the merit of a robust, if rather cynical, practicality. In the years-long struggle that now clearly lies ahead for possession of the soul of the GOP, it will probably outlast the empty bombast of the Eisenhower-Nixon centrists. But if the Republican Party is to survive at all, the Javits philosophy will surely succumb to the advocates of a Republicanism that truly opposes the Liberal domination of America."

It is not enough to say that Javits is the most unlikely "Republican" to sit in the U.S. Senate. That he is in that body under any party label seems incredible.

PHILIP C. JESSUP was born on January 5, 1897 in New York City, son of Mary Stotesbury and Henry Jessup. He married Lois Kellogg. He is an alumnus of Hamilton College (A.B., 1919), Yale University (LL.B., 1924), and Columbia University (A.M., 1924; Ph.D., 1927).

From 1925 until 1961, Jessup was on the faculty of Columbia University where he lectured on international law and diplomacy. Away from the campus, Jessup served (1924-1953) as a legal adviser to federal government officials, and was a legal adviser (1948-1952) at various international conferences, embassies, and to U.S. delegations at the United Nations.

From 1949 until 1953, Jessup was U.S. Ambassador-at-Large. Since 1961, he has been a judge on the International Court of Justice.

Jessup was a top official, in the 1930's and 1940's, of the Institute of Pacific Relations when that "instrument of Communist policy, propaganda and military intelligence" was at its efficient best, influencing the State Department to betray China to the Communists and, with that accomplished, to do likewise for Korea and Formosa. In the State Department, Jessup was a protégé of Dean Acheson and such a close friend of Alger Hiss that he appeared as a character witness for him at both of the Hiss trials. (Even Mrs. Jessup got into the act. After Whittaker Chambers identified Hiss as a Communist, Mrs. Jessup importuned Henry Luce to fire Chambers from his position on *Time* magazine's editorial staff.) Jessup would later rush to the defense of Owen Lattimore when that "conscious, articulate instrument of the Soviet conspiracy" was being exposed by the late Senator Joseph R. McCarthy.

Jessup, however, always seemed to land on his two feet. In 1951, Jessup's nomination to be on the American delegation at the United Nations was before the Senate Foreign Relations Committee. After stormy hearings, the Senate adjourned without taking action on Jessup. President Truman appointed him anyway. When Soviet Foreign Minister Andrei Vishinsky heard of Jessup's travails, he was at a U.N. conference in Paris. Said Vishinsky: "I learned the other day with some dismay that 37 Senators [there were actually 38] had asked the United States Government if it would dismiss Mr. Jessup from here because he was rather sympathetically inclined toward an un-American way of thought . . . . I must express my sympathy for Mr. Jessup."

In 1960, when Jessup was nominated to be a Judge on the International Court of Justice, the nominating committee was appointed by President Eisenhower on advice from Secretary of State Dulles. But then Eisenhower and Jessup had been close friends for years, especially at Columbia where Eisenhower was president while Jessup held the distinguished chair as Hamilton Fish professor of international law and diplomacy.

JOSEPH E. JOHNSON was born on April 30, 1906 in Longdale, Virginia, son of Margaret Hilles and Joseph Johnson. He married Catherine Abbott. He is an alumnus of Harvard University (A.B., 1927; A.M., 1932; Ph.D., 1943).

In 1934 and 1935, Johnson was a history instructor at Bowdoin College. From 1936 until 1950, Johnson was on the faculty at Williams College.

From 1942 until 1947, Johnson, on leave of absence from Williams, was in the State Department. He became chief of the division of International Security Affairs and was on the policy planning staff. Johnson also attended the Dumbarton Oaks Conference, the San Francisco organizing conference of the United Nations, and the United Nations General Assemblies in London and New York.

Since 1950, Johnson has been a trustee and president of the Carnegie Endowment for International Peace, where he succeeded his old friend and working associate Alger Hiss.

Johnson has been a trustee of the leftwing, pacifist World Peace Foundation. He has been a director of the Council on Foreign Relations, the informal supra-State Department of the United States, and of the soft-on-Communism Foreign Policy Association.

Freda Utley in her *The China Story* probably offers the most useful summary of how Johnson fits into the leftwing picture: "It is important here to call attention to the manner in which the members of the 'progressive' group in Washington and New York managed to replace each other in important positions inside and outside the Administration. For instance, after Alger Hiss resigned from the State Department to become Director of the Carnegie Endowment for International Peace, Dean Acheson recommended Dean Rusk to take Hiss' place as Director of the Office of Special Political Affairs. Rusk had formerly served under Joseph E. Johnson who, as Chief of the Division of International Security Affairs, under the Special Political Affairs Office, had been chief assistant to Alger Hiss. In 1949, Rusk stepped higher up the ladder of preferment, becoming First Assistant, and then Deputy Under Secretary of State. Today Johnson, who resigned from the State Department in 1947 to return to teaching at Williams College, holds the position with the Carnegie Endowment held by Alger Hiss when he was indicted for perjury."

Johnson is still at the head of Carnegie Endowment, dispensing more than a million dollars a year to advance the day when this will all be one great big red world. One of the Endowment's most recent projects was the financing of a 170-page study which blueprinted a United Nations military invasion and conquest of the Republic of South Africa. This "peace" gesture, according to the study, would only take about four months to accomplish – not surprising since the "Endowment for International Peace" suggested that the U.S. and Soviet Union would be supporting the "massive direct military intervention."

LYNDON B. JOHNSON was born on August 27, 1908 near Stonewall, Texas, son of Rebekah Baines and Sam Johnson. He married Claudia Alta Taylor. He is an alumnus of Southwest Texas State Teachers College (B.S., 1930).

While still in college, Johnson was an elementary school teacher for one year. From 1932 until 1935, he was a secretary to Representative Richard M. Kleberg, a Democrat from Texas. From 1935 until 1937, he was director in Texas of the National Youth Administration, one of the New Deal's agencies.

In 1937, Johnson won a special election to the House of Representatives and was re-elected in 1938, 1940, 1942, 1944 and 1946. He made an unsuccessful bid for a U.S. Senate seat in 1941.

In 1948, Johnson won a runoff primary for a Senate seat by 87 votes. The election was marked by charges of fraud by Johnson's opponent, but the matter was settled by the U.S. Supreme Court in Johnson's favor. He was re-elected to the Senate in 1954. In his years as Representative and Senator, Johnson was thoroughly schooled in socialist legislation by his mentor Franklin D. Roosevelt. At the same time, Johnson became an accomplished political wheeler-dealer under the tutelage of Representative Sam Rayburn of Texas, who, from 1937 until his death in 1961, was majority leader, minority leader or Speaker of the House.

From 1937 until 1960, Johnson, in the Congress, was – with one major exception — a Democrat wheelhorse in his voting record, right down the line on liberal legislation for domestic and foreign policy. The one exception was in the area generally described as "civil rights." From 1937 through 1956, Johnson voted one hundred per cent with the Southern bloc on civil rights measures. He voted against federal anti-lynch laws; against proposals to abolish state poll taxes by federal law; against the so-called Fair Employment Practices Commission being instituted; and, against anti-discrimination features of measures dealing with federal housing, federal school-lunch programs, federal aid-to-education, and federal railway-labor laws. He supported filibusters against cloture. He voted for an amendment to a home-rule bill for the District of Columbia which would have, in effect, prolonged segregation in the District.

While campaigning in 1948, Johnson said: "This civil rights program, about which you have heard so much, is a farce and a sham — an effort to set up a police state in the guise of liberty. I am opposed to that program. I fought it in Congress. It is the province of the state to run its own elections. I am opposed to the anti-lynching bill because the Federal Government has no more business enacting a law against one kind of murder than another. I am against FEPC [Fair Employment Practices Commission] because if a man can tell you whom you must hire, he can tell you whom you cannot employ. I have met this head on."

On the floor of the Senate, in 1949, Johnson said: "I say frankly that the Negro — as the minority group involved in this discussion of civil rights — has more to lose by the adoption of any resolution outlawing free debate [that is, the cloture rule] in the Senate than he

stands to gain by the enactment of the civil rights bills as they are now written." At the same time, Johnson opposed federal anti-poll tax measures as "wholly unconstitutional." FEPC legislation, he said, was "the least meritorious proposal of the whole civil rights program . . . . Such a law would necessitate a system of federal police officers such as we have never before seen. It would require the policing of every business institution, every transaction made between an employer and employee, and, virtually every hour of an employer's and employee's association while at work . . . . We in the Senate should learn the facts of life. We cannot legislate love. We can find the fair and permanent answers to our problems of housing, education, medical care, income — and all other domestic issues — without reducing government to an absurdity by attempting to police the most intimate thoughts of our populace."

Not until Johnson was twenty-one years in Congress did he cast his first vote for a "civil rights" bill. But, by that time, he was willing to forget the sentiments of the voters back home; he had his eyes set on the presidency of the United States, and there were more northern and western votes to woo than southern. When Johnson did become president, two years later than his target date, he made up for lost time by becoming a fanatical civil-rights promoter, through his creation of the police state he once maligned. And he went overboard in his promotion of socialist programs, "reducing government to an absurdity by attempting to police the most intimate thoughts of our populace."

For those who had followed Johnson's voting record over the years, it was readily apparent that it was no idle boast when he said that he was more liberal than Eleanor Roosevelt — through twelve consecutive Congresses, the liberals did not have a more reliable leader and voter than Johnson. And, in his tenure as president, Johnson has advanced the cause of socialism more and faster than all of his four White House predecessors put together.

In the field of foreign policy, Johnson has always been an internationalist and, although he cast an occasional vote in Congress in favor of national security, his soft-on-Communism attitude became fixed once he became a likely candidate for national office. (In years gone by, he also cast an occasional anti-Communist vote on internal security legislation but once the spectre of "McCarthyism" was raised by the Communists and their patsies throughout the entire liberal camp, Johnson ranged himself irrevocably on the side of the anti-anti-Communists.)

The most prominent features of Johnson's foreign policy have been his no-win policy in the Vietnam War, coupled with his frantic and grovelling "peace" missions, and the trade-bridges-to-the-East program wherein he is virtually begging for trade with the nation's Communist enemies.

Johnson may also take credit for making the phrase "credibility gap" a part of our everyday language. Willard Edwards of the *Chicago Tribune* has called the gap "the result of a long series of administration misstatements, contradictions, evasions, and not a few deliberate deceptions which have served to befog the picture of what is happening at home and abroad." The progress of the war in Vietnam has been one of the principal subjects for deception in the statements of Johnson, Secretary of State Dean Rusk, and Defense Secretary

Robert McNamara. The deception has been evident in press conferences and interviews, messages to Congress, and testimony before congressional committees. But it is not just on the Vietnam War where the American people are deceived and lied to by the Administration. The same situation holds true for the entire span of foreign policy, the budget, the farm program, the war on poverty, the civil rights agitation, and Johnson's previous voting record. ("I have always opposed the poll tax," said Johnson on April 27, 1965. The truth was something else. During his congressional career, he voted against the poll tax twice out of sixteen roll calls. And Mr. Johnson, as a southerner, was not likely to forget how he voted on that issue, which was so very sensitive to every southern politician.)

For those who were once beguiled by Johnson's synthetic reputation as a conservative, the most startling development in his presidency has been the eventual realization that he is a captive of the left — leftwing labor leaders, leftwing racial agitators, leftwing internationalists, leftwing educationists, leftwing lawyers and justices, leftwing economists and sociologists, and leftwing scientists. They are the ones who have been appointed to positions in the federal government or to advisory and consultant roles. They are the ones who are feted and rewarded in well publicized functions at the White House. They are the ones whose programs are promoted through legislation, executive orders, bureaucratic rules and regulations, and judicial decisions.

U. ALEXIS JOHNSON was born on October 17, 1908 in Falun, Kansas, son of Ellen Forsse and Carl Johnson. He married Patricia Tillman. He is an alumnus of Occidental College (A.B., 1931).

He also studied at Georgetown University.

Johnson entered the State Department in 1935. From 1935 until 1945, he held minor posts in Japan, Korea, China, Manchuria, and Rio de Janeiro. In 1945, he was U.S. Consul in Manila and, in 1946, held the same position in Yokohama. From 1947 until 1950, he was U.S. Consul-General in Yokohama.

From 1950 until 1953, he was at the State Department in Washington, where he was director for Northeast Asian Affairs, then deputy assistant secretary of state for Far Eastern Affairs. From 1953 until 1958, he was U.S. Ambassador to Thailand.

From 1961 until 1964, he was deputy under secretary of state for political affairs. Briefly in 1964, he was deputy ambassador to South Vietnam. In 1965 and 1966, he was deputy under secretary of state for political affairs. In 1966, he became U.S. Ambassador to Japan.

From 1955 until 1958, Johnson was the U.S. representative for ambassadorial level talks with Red Chinese representatives at Geneva. Johnson participated in more than seventy of these talks which never were more than diplomatic rituals that gave Red China – in the eyes of the world – a stature as a sovereign equivalent to the United States or any civilized nation. And while the U.S. official policy was non-recognition of Red China, Johnson was involved in the most widely publicized diplomatic tête-á-têtes in the world. If Johnson learned anything about Communist intransigence at the meetings, he has long since forgotten it. When he was appointed as Ambassador to Japan, he prattled about how Red China may be moving toward "live-and-let-live" policies, and how Red China "stands in growing isolation even within the international Communist movement." And once the Red Chinese moderated their Communism, Johnson suggested "nothing would be more welcomed by the American Government and people than an opportunity to renew the bonds of friendship with the people of mainland China."

HOWARD MUMFORD JONES was born on April 16, 1892 in Saginaw, Michigan, son of Josephine Miles and Frank Jones. He was married to Clara McLure. He is married to Bessie Zabar. He is an alumnus of the University of Wisconsin (B.A., 1914) and the University of Chicago (M.A., 1915).

From 1919 until 1936, Jones taught English, successively, at the University of Texas, the University of North Carolina, and the University of Michigan. In 1936, Jones joined Harvard University's faculty as a professor of English and became professor emeritus of humanities in 1962. He also served as dean of Harvard's Graduate School of Arts and Sciences in 1943 and 1944. He has lectured at the Hebrew University of Jerusalem and was a Guggenheim fellow in 1964 and 1965. As well as a teacher, Jones has been an author, editor, poet, and playwright over the past half century.

In 1965, Jones reaped national publicity when he resigned a visiting professorship at the University of Texas in protest against the University's required loyalty oath. Texas law requires all teachers to swear that they were not nor ever had been members of the Communist Party, or for five years had not been members of subversive organizations. Jones had taken the same stand against a loyalty oath in 1950 when he had the opportunity to teach at the University of California. He then became a sponsor in California of the Federation for Repeal of the Levering Act [Loyalty Oath], an organization which received the complete support of the Communists since the Federation was riddled with Communist fronters and notorious apologists for the Communist Party.

Jones has been affiliated with the Joint Anti-Fascist Refugee Committee ("subversive and Communist"); the National Council of American-Soviet Friendship ("subversive and Communist" – "specializing in pro-Soviet propaganda"); and, the National Council of the Arts, Sciences and Professions ("a Communist front used to appeal to special occupational groups"). He has petitioned on several occasions to abolish the House Committee on Un-American Activities. He has supported Fifth Amendment pleaders who appeared before investigating committees and he petitioned on behalf of Carl Marzani, who was convicted and imprisoned on perjury charges when he denied that he was a Communist.

MATTHEW JOSEPHSON was born on February 15, 1899 in Brooklyn, son of Sarah Kasindorf and Julius Josephson. He married Hannah Geffen. He is an alumnus at Columbia University (A.B., 1920).

He was editor of *The Broom* (1922-1924); of *Transition* (1928-1929); and, assistant editor of *New Republic* (1931-1932). In 1933 and 1934, Josephson was a Guggenheim Fellow.

Since 1923, Josephson has written more than a dozen books, the best known of which are *The Politicos; The Robber Barons; The President Makers;* and *Sidney Hillman: Statesman of American Labor.* Josephson's anti-capitalistic, leftwing writings are favorite bibliographical references in the textbooks foisted upon high school and college students in their history, government, and political science classes.

Josephson has been affiliated with Book Union ("distributors of Communist literature"); the Golden Book of American Friendship with the Soviet Union ("Communist enterprise"); the League of American Writers ("subversive and Communist"); the National Institute of Arts and Letters ("Communist front"); the Cultural and Scientific Conference for World Peace ("Communist front" – "a propaganda front for Soviet foreign policy and 'Soviet culture' "); the American Committee for Democracy and Intellectual Freedom ("Communist front" – "subversive and un-American"); Consumers Union (when characterized as "subversive"); the American Friends of Spanish Democracy ("subversive"); the Committee of Professional Groups for Browder and Ford ("Communist front"); the National Emergency Conference for Democratic Rights ("Communist front"); the Nonpartisan Committee for the Re-election of Congressman Vito Marcantonio ("Communist front"); the Civil Rights Congress ("subversive and Communist"); and, the National Committee to Abolish the House Un-American Activities Committee ("to lead and direct the Communist Party's 'Operation Abolition' campaign").

Josephson has supported Communist candidates in election campaigns, and has contributed to the *New Masses* ("Communist periodical") and the *Daily Worker* ("chief journalistic mouthpiece of the Communist Party").

In 1965, Josephson was a prominent supporter of the anti-Vietnam "teach-in" movement, which the Communist propaganda apparatus exploited for purely Communist purposes.

ROBERT W. KASTENMEIER was born on January 24, 1924 in Beaver Dam, Wisconsin, son of Lucille Powers and Leo Kastenmeier. He married Dorothy Chambers. He is an alumnus of the University of Wisconsin (LL.B., 1952). In 1952, he was admitted to the Wisconsin bar and began his law practice in Watertown.

From 1956 until 1958, Kastenmeier was a justice of the peace (elective) in Jefferson and Dodge Counties.

Since 1959, Kastenmeier, a Democrat, has been in the U.S. House of Representatives. Throughout his congressional career, he has served on the House Judiciary Committee where he has displayed virtual fanaticism on so-called civil rights and so-called civil liberties legislation. He ranks as one of the most extreme agitators in the Congress for federal discrimination on behalf of Negroes. In every session of his congressional career, he has worked to abolish the House Committee on Un-American Activities. He has opposed any and all wiretapping under all conditions, even on matters of subversion and espionage. He is a vigorous defender of the U.S. Supreme Court's decisions and maintains that laws of Congress cannot overturn the Court's decisions.

Kastenmeier has served on the national board of Americans for Democratic Action, the center of the radical left in American politics. By the ADA's standards, in his twelve sessions of Congress, he has a perfect voting record. The political arm of the AFL-CIO, the Committee on Political Education, rates Kastenmeier as having a perfect pro-labor voting record.

In 1960, Kastenmeier announced that he was chairman of a newly formed House Liberal Project, a group of twelve ultra-liberal Representatives. He further announced that the Congressmen would join with scientists, scholars, and experts to formulate new domestic and foreign policies for the United States. The work of the Liberal Project resulted in the 1962 publication of *The Liberal Papers,* edited by Representative James Roosevelt of California, a far-left Democrat. Contributors to the volume included such well-known leftists as Stuart Hughes, Walter Millis, Vera Micheles Dean, Arthur Waskow, Quincy Wright, .David Riesman, and James Warburg. The papers were devoted exclusively to foreign policy and reflected abject appeasement with Communist powers, extravagant extensions of foreign "aid" programs, reckless disarmament proposals, and grovelling obeisance to the United Nations.

On the Vietnam War, Kastenmeier has been one of the foremost leaders in the House in opposition to United States involvement. There have been times, however, when Kastenmeier's opposition has taken some rather eccentric twists. In 1960, he used the "letters-to-the-editor" column in the *New York Times* to call for a pledge by the United States not to resort to biological warfare unless the enemy did so first. If any such type of warfare was being contemplated by any American in governmental authority, Kastenmeier omitted to identify him. In 1962, Kastenmeier wrote to President Kennedy to stop U.S. military advisers in Vietnam from condoning tortures against Communist guerilas. The basis for Kastenmeier's complaint was a single, brief account in *Time* magazine. In 1965, Kastenmeier and a group of his fellow doves in the House tried to persuade the House Foreign Affairs Committee to hold hearings on U.S. involvement in Vietnam. When persuasion failed, Kastenmeier held his own hearings in a Madison, Wisconsin church. He listened to about fifty witnesses, most of whom were as dove-like as he, and published the transcript of their testimony under the title: *Vietnam Hearings: Voices from the Grass Roots.*

Under ordinary circumstances, Kastenmeier's opposition to the Vietnam War has followed orthodox ultra-liberal lines: no increase of American troops; no bombing of North Vietnam; a unilateral cease-fire by the United States; and the United States should sue for peace and invite the Vietcong to the peace table.

NICHOLAS KATZENBACH was born on January 17, 1922 in Philadelphia, son of Marie Hilson and Edward Katzenbach. He married Lydia Stokes. He is an alumnus of Princeton University (B.A., 1945) and Yale University (LL.B.,1947). He was a Rhodes scholar at Oxford University (1947-1949).

From 1950 until 1952, Katzenbach did legal work in the office of the General Counsel to the Air Force. During the next four years this legal work became a part-time chore as he was an associate professor of law at Yale University. From 1956 until 1960, he was a professor of law at the University of Chicago. In 1960 and 1961, he was a fellow of the Ford Foundation, which has been a horn of plenty for leftwingers and leftwing projects on every continent.

From 1961 until 1966, Katzenbach was in the Department of Justice as an assistant, then deputy, under Attorney General Robert Kennedy, whom Katzenbach succeeded in January, 1965.

Since September, 1966, Katzenbach has been Under Secretary of State. When Robert Kennedy was Attorney General, Katzenbach was the errand boy sent to do the dirty work of using federal power in the South to enforce so-called civil rights laws. Katzenbach was such an excellent patsy that when Kennedy resigned from the cabinet, he urged President Johnson to appoint Katzenbach as Attorney General. Within a few months, Johnson did just that.

In his tenure as Attorney General, Katzenbach was faced with the problem of the racial revolutionaries who were rioting in cities across the country. Katzenbach made one headlong rush after another to deny that "Communists or black nationalists and terrorists" were fomenting the riots. And he lapsed into a pseudo-sociological explanation of how the real agitators were "named disease and despair, joblessness and hopelessness, rat-infested housing and long-impacted cynicism" and "generations of indifference by all the American people to the rot and rust and mold which we have allowed to eat into the core of our cities." (Martin L. King could not have embellished Katzenbach's fantasies.)

And when the revolutionaries adopted their rallying cry of "black power," Katzenbach had an excuse for them: "If we think of 'black power' as merely an assertion by Negroes of rights, dramatizations of some of their injustices, then it is not very different from other kinds of powers. Not very different from the real estate lobby's power in Congress, today, or from the doctor's power in fighting the Medicare program." Of course, those shouting "black power" were something other than lobbyists since they didn't restrict themselves to one slogan; they followed their cries of "black power" with shouts of "burn, baby, burn" and "kill Whitey" – and they burned and killed.

In other areas as Attorney General, Katzenbach's performance was just as incredible. While the Great Society leaders, including himself, moaned and groaned continually about the sizeable ranks of the unemployed, Katzenbach proposed that Congress pass a law allowing selected federal prisoners to take jobs outside penitentiaries before they had completed their sentences. Katzenbach explained that this was one way to combat crime!

One of Katzenbach's most memorable performances took place in March, 1965 when Negroes conducted a sit-in demonstration in a Justice Department hallway outside his office. The Negroes claimed that they had come from Alabama seeking promises of federal protection. Katzenbach approached the Negroes on his hands and knees and pleaded with the sit-inners to "have the courtesy" to leave the building. Naturally photographers were on hand to record this grovelling spectacle for the benefit of front-page treatment in the nation's newspapers.

As Under Secretary of State, Katzenbach has found it quite easy to adapt himself to the State Department's aggressive appeasement of the Communists. A few months after he became Under Secretary, he was singing the praises of the "bridges to the East" theme. Trade with the Soviet Union and the Communist bloc in eastern Europe is "good business, good policy, and good sense," said Katzenbach. He then explained that through such trade "we can increase their [the Communists'] stake in peaceful relations with the West" and demonstrate our faith in "the strength of the free society." For those who urged a boycott of Communist slave labor goods and opposed sending American goods to our Communist enemies, Katzenbach had the utmost scorn. Their "patriotism exceeds their understanding." Well, at least he did concede that it was patriotism that motivated them.

In the spring of 1967, Katzenbach made an eleven-nation junket in Africa. He took time out to describe the veteran Communist President of Kenya, Jomo Kenyatta, as "surely one of the really great leaders of Africa." On the same day, when asked why the Johnson Administration rejected a Rhodesian offer to send troops to fight the Communists in Vietnam, Katzenbach said: "We had doubts they were coming in on our side." A more malicious libel against the staunchly anti-Communist regime of Rhodesia would be impossible to imagine.

From all indications, Katzenbach's attitude toward the Vietnam War is nothing more than the "no-win" policy which has been the Johnson-Rusk-McNamara position. In an adulatory appraisal of Katzenbach in the *New York Times* magazine (December 24, 1967), Victor S. Navosky has written that Katzenbach "is by nature a civilian predisposed to distrust military solutions." And Navosky quotes Mrs. Katzenbach as saying: "If Nick were allowed to talk about what he is doing, a lot of our friends would be heartened." In the context of Navosky's piece, this simply means that Katzenbach would like nothing better than to set speed records, rushing to a "peace" table where he could flap his dove-like wings before the vulturous Communists of North Vietnam.

EDWARD KEATING was born on April 17, 1925 in New York City, son of Harriet Martin and George Keating. He married Helen English. He is an alumnus of Stanford University (A.B., 1948; LL.B., 1950).

Keating has practiced law; developed

real estate; lectured; written a book (*The Scandal of Silence*); taught a year, as an instructor in English, at the University of Santa Clara; studied playwriting; and lived as a "gentleman farmer" in Virginia. He inherited substantial wealth. In 1962, he founded *Ramparts* magazine. From 1962 until 1967, he was publisher and editor-in-chief of *Ramparts*.

In the beginning, *Ramparts* was represented as a Catholic journal, edited by Catholic laymen. Keating, a convert to Catholicism, has claimed that he started the magazine "to create a platform for Catholic writers. I found there were few Catholic writers and intellectuals around, so we started inviting other people — Protestants, Jews and agnostics — to contribute. We began as a Catholic magazine with a capital 'C' and now we're catholic with a lower-case 'c.'" In its promotional literature, in 1967, *Ramparts* claimed that Keating began to publish *Ramparts* as a needed gadfly for "ghetto Catholicism" and as "a challenge to the hierarchy of the Roman Catholic Church in America: Get off the ball. You preach social justice and love for fellow men. But on racism, on poverty, on nuclear war, the Catholic Church stays comfortably silent, does little. You just don't rock the boat."

Most of *Ramparts'* religious pieces were of a decidedly negative character. Attacks were made against Francis Cardinal McIntyre of Los Angeles, the late Francis Cardinal Spellman of New York City, the Jesuit order, and Catholic clerics and laity who opposed drastic and revolutionary changes in Catholic liturgy and doctrine. But any focus on religious matters was discarded early in *Ramparts'* history. The magazine ranged far beyond religion and soon bore no resemblance to a Catholic journal. Under Keating's leadership, the magazine became just another far-left periodical. Its targets were the same as could be found in the regular Communist and pro-Communist press: Barry Goldwater, the Federal Bureau of Investigation, the House Committee on Un-American Activities, active anti-Communists, American military leaders, and United States involvement in the Vietnam War. The magazine's heroes have included such internationally notorious Communists as Jean Paul Sartre, Ché Guevara, Bertrand Russell, Ho chi Minh, and Mao Tse-tung.

Ramparts has advertised in the Communist journal *National Guardian* and used the *Guardian's* stencils in the solicitation of subscriptions. Advertisements in *Ramparts* have been carried for the DuBois Clubs (a Communist front) and the Progressive Labor Party (a Communist group which propagandizes for Red China). Leftwing groups which have advertised in *Ramparts* include Americans for Democratic Action, United World Federalists, and Women Strike for Peace. Articles in *Ramparts* have glorified such dignitaries of the left as J. William Fulbright and Stokely Carmichael, as well as hippies, pacifists, and draft dodgers in general.

Once Keating had shunted aside the fiction that *Ramparts* was a religious publication, his editors and contributors resembled a cross-section of the far left's literary world. Identified Communists who became part of the *Ramparts* family included Don Rothenburg, Jessica Mitford (Decca Treuhaft), and Carl Marzani. Leftwingers included Fred Cook, Judy Stone, Ralph Gleason, Gene Marine, Gerald Feigen, John Beecher, Thomas Merton, Rex Stout, Warren Hinckle III, Robert Scheer, Marcus Raskin, Arthur Waskow, Paul Jacobs, Benjamin Spock, Julian Bond, William A. Williams, Carlton Goodlett, Howard Zinn, and Jules Feiffer.

Keating has not been secretive about his anti-anti-Communist convictions. As he expressed it: "If anything marks American political orientation and direction, it is its paranoia over Communism. If our policy-makers had their way, we would not only contain communism, we would destroy it." Away from the magazine, Keating has lectured scores of times at anti-Vietnam rallies. In 1966, he ran for Congress, from California, as a peacenik candidate. He directed the west coast version of Spring Mobilization, a Vietnik activity instituted by Communists and pro-Communists.

In 1967, the board of directors of *Ramparts* voted to unseat Keating as publisher and editor-in-chief of the magazine. There was no ideological dispute between Keating and the other directors. Keating insisted that, since he had invested $860,000 in the magazine, he should be able to have a larger voice in its budgeting program which he charged had been one of fiscal irresponsibility. On the other hand, the editors of *Ramparts* insisted that there was a "generation gap" between them and Keating. Whatever the truth behind the internecine quarrel, Keating has remained as *Ramparts'* major stockholder. The magazine has flourished (at the end of 1967, it had more than 200,000 paid circulation; it had been only 15,000 in January, 1965). The pro-Communist stance which Keating introduced when he was publisher and editor-in-chief has continued unabated – at least there was no "ideological gap" between Keating and his colleagues.

GEORGE F. KENNAN was born on February 6, 1904 in Milwaukee. He is an alumnus of Princeton University (A.B., 1925).

Kennan began his career with the State Department in 1927 and, during his first eighteen years, held relatively minor posts in Hamburg, Tallin, Berlin, Riga, Vienna, Moscow, Prague, Washington, Lisbon, and London.

In 1945, he was minister-counselor at the U.S. Embassy in Moscow. Kennan had been to Moscow in 1933 when he accompanied U.S. Ambassador William C. Bullitt there. And, in 1935 and 1936, he was second secretary in Moscow. In 1946, he was deputy for foreign affairs at the National War College. In 1947 and 1948, he was on the State Department's policy planning staff. In 1949 and 1950, he was department counselor and adviser to the Secretary of State.

From 1950 until 1952, Kennan was at the Institute for Advanced Study at Princeton, New Jersey. In 1952, he was U.S. Ambassador to the Soviet Union. In 1953, he returned to the Institute in Princeton and, since 1956, he has been a permanent professor at the Institute. In the meantime, he was U.S. Ambassador to Yugoslavia from 1961 until 1963.

Kennan has written extensively on Soviet-American relations and on Soviet history. His book *Realities of American Foreign Policy,* published in 1954, is the most callous presentation of pragmatic diplomatic principles ever offered by an American diplomat. But his most influential writings appeared in *Foreign Affairs* magazine ("The Sources of Soviet Conduct," July, 1947; and, "America and the Russian Future," April, 1951). It was in these two articles that Kennan produced his Containment Policy. In its essentials, Containment meant that the United States (and the free world) would acquiesce in Soviet conquests and usurpations, including those made during the course of World War II by military means or through the simple expedient of violating treaties to

390

which the United States was a signatory nation. Having uttered the pious warning – thus far, and no farther – the United States and other free world nations would then build a moral wall of righteous indignation around the Soviet Empire to discourage future conquests and usurpations. The example of righteousness would eventually make the Russians see the error of their ways and lead them into peaceful coexistence. (The most notable dissent to Kennan's policy came from Walter Lippmann who felt that Kennan was being too tough on the Soviet Union.)

But with the promulgation of the Containment Policy, the entire Liberal Establishment rose up to foist Kennan on the American public as *The* expert on Soviet-American relations – a cruel hoax that has survived to the present time. And Kennan has helped the hoax along by his protestations that he is a pillar of anti-Communism, but at the same time he has insisted that anti-Communism is an unsatisfactory approach for coping with Communism.

Somewhere along the line, Kennan introduced the theory of polycentrism. According to this theory, there have been and are all kinds of Communism – that of Marx, of Lenin, of Mao Tse-tung, of Gomulka. And these various kinds are often in conflict with one another; consequently, the United States must treat with each kind of Communism in a different manner. Then, as a natural corollary to his polycentrism theory, Kennan has been one of the pioneers in selling the American public the fiction that there is a genuine rift between Tito's Yugoslavia and the Soviet Union, and that the Red Chinese and the Kremlin leaders are irrevocably separated. Under such circumstances, according to

Kennan, it is feasible and it behooves the United States to cultivate genuine friendship with each and every Communist nation on an individual basis. Fundamental to Kennan's diplomatic advice is his contention that the domestic behavior of Communist regimes is none of our business as long as the internal practices and institutions of the Communist regimes do not damage our interest. He is resolute in his refusal to acknowledge that the Communist leaders who inflict barbarism on the peoples within their own countries would behave the same way in their relations with peoples of the free world. Kennan concedes that the Communists might have done so in the past but they are mellowing more and more all the time. Not all, of course. He admits that, "some Communists are brutal, dangerous and treacherous" – who or where they are, he doesn't mention – "but often I have had more respect for them than for pillars of American society, vegetating in smugness, superficiality and philistinism."

If Kennan was merely an ivory-tower theorist, he would be no danger. Unfortunately, he held ambassadorial positions in the Soviet Union and Yugoslavia where, despite all that he did to help Stalin and Tito, he acquired his phony prestige as an expert who must be heeded no matter how wrong he has been proven in the past. He has added to his phony prestige by taking up a position at the Institute of Advanced Study in Princeton, New Jersey. He was brought there by his very close friend, the notorious security risk, the late J. Robert Oppenheimer. And the Institute, in the eyes of the Liberal Establishment, is the modern day Olympus from which Kennan, the appeasement deity, smiles down on his cult in the State Department.

EDWARD M. KENNEDY was born on February 22, 1932 in Brookline, Massachusetts, son of Rose Fitzgerald and Joseph Kennedy. He married Virginia Bennett. He is an alumnus of Harvard University (A.B., 1954) and the University of Virginia (LL.B., 1959).

For a few months in 1961 and 1962, he was one of many assistants to the District Attorney of Suffolk County in Massachusetts. In 1962, he was elected to the U.S. Senate from Massachusetts. He had campaigned on the slogan that he could do "more for Massachusetts" – an obvious reference to the fact that one of his brothers was President of the United States, another was Attorney General of the United States.

In the Senate, Edward has been one more vote for the left – a perfect stooge for Americans for Democratic Action, organized labor, the pro-United Nations fanatics, the racial agitators, and the anti-Vietnam War lobby promoting appeasement. He has come out unequivocally for admission of Red China to the United Nations. He has called for negotiations with the Vietcong. His solution for Vietnam is to neutralize North and South Vietnam which, he says, "could lead to a confederation of North and South Vietnam under a truly neutral government." There have been times when Edward seems to be waging all-out war against the Saigon government but he is always anxious to protect North Vietnam against American military action.

Castro's Cuba has not been overlooked by Edward. In 1964, against even public evidence offered by Fidel Castro, Edward said: "There has been an almost complete termination of the utilization of Cuba for training Communist agents to go out to other countries in Latin America. There also has been a severe decline in Cuba as a base for sending out Communist propaganda. And I think because of our activity and the direction of our policy, we have almost halted any kind of movement of Communist agents with the cooperation of the Latin American countries." Of course, Edward did not offer the slightest bit of evidence to prove a single item of his estimate of the Cuban situation.

Edward's willingness to cooperate with Communists was never better demonstrated than in 1965, just fifteen months after his brother was assassinated. Luigi Nono, a notorious and active member of the Italian Communist Party, had applied for a visa to visit the United States. Nono, a composer, wanted to attend the American premiere in Boston of his opera *Intolleraza 1960*. When he applied for a visa, Nono admitted his Communist Party membership and a visa was automatically and legally denied him. Edward intervened with the State Department and Nono was granted his visa and came to America. Two months later, Nono displayed his gratitude by writing a vicious anti-Boston, anti-American diatribe in *Rinacita*, the Italian Communist weekly.

Since Edward became a Senator, he has shown a hitherto well-concealed sympathy for Negroes. He has become one of the Senate's most dedicated integrationists. One of his principal targets is the neighborhood school system whereby schools, because of their location within communities, have either a preponderance of white or Negro children. Edward, as egalitarian as any socialist, would bus children from one neighborhood to another, or from one community or municipality to another community or municipality, to accomplish racial balance in schools. In his pursuit of Negro votes, Edward has rushed to the defense of Negro rioters and supported every bit of welfare-state handout legislation designed to give preferential treatment to Negroes. One of his own proposals was a bill to create a federal teacher corps — one of the most ambitious and expensive boondoggles ever suggested as a means to curry favor with Negroes and, of course, to increase federal control of education.

On another occasion, Edward proposed a federal law academy where college graduates could get a "free' education in this federally financed and administered academy. But six months later, Edward had the gall to say that it is "important to improve our federalist system and make it possible for people to administer more effectively in the states so they are not always coming to Washington."

ROBERT F. KENNEDY was born on November 20, 1925 in Boston, Massachusetts, son of Rose Fitzgerald and Joseph Kennedy. He married Ethel Skakel. He is an alumnus of Harvard University (B.A., 1948) and the University of Virginia (LL.B., 1951).

In 1951 and 1952, he was an attorney in the criminal division of the Justice Department. From 1953 until 1955, he was a counsel, then general counsel and staff director, of the U.S. Senate permanent subcommittee on investigations. From 1957 until 1960, he was chief counsel to the U.S. Senate select committee on improper activities in labor and management.

From 1961 until 1964, he was Attorney General of the United States. Since 1965, he has been U.S. Senator from New York.

Kennedy first came into national prominence as a counsel with the McCarthy Committee where he sulked in the shadow of Roy Cohn, the general counsel. Kennedy's main preoccupation was to serve as hatchet-man for the Democrats on the Committee who were angry that McCarthy's exposures of Communists and fellow travelers were reflecting upon the Democrat Administrations of Roosevelt and Truman.

The next national spotlight fell on Kennedy when he was counsel to the McLellan Labor Rackets Committee. In that job, Kennedy whitewashed Walter Reuther and the United Auto Workers and waged a personal vendetta against Jimmy Hoffa, head of the Teamsters Union. When the whitewash of Reuther was accomplished, the Kennedy dynasty's reward was the complete support of the UAW in the 1960 presidential campaign. The vendetta against Hoffa was partially successful but the U.S. Constitution took a fearful beating at the hands of Kennedy as he ignored constitutional processes to get Hoffa. Before he left committee work, Kennedy reaped headlines but no results in a frantic search for the Mafia.

In the 1960 presidential campaign, Kennedy was his brother's campaign manager. He distinguished himself by promoting issues of religious bigotry and racism to help his brother to the White House. And, of course, his brother was elected despite Robert's management.

Shortly before the 1960 election, John F. Kennedy stated that "nepotism is dangerous to the public interest and to our national morality." Robert echoed his brother's sentiments by saying that if he were appointed to a cabinet post, it would be "nepotism of the worst sort." Public interest and national morality notwithstanding, Robert Kennedy was appointed Attorney General.

As Attorney General, Robert Kennedy launched an invasion of federal forces into Mississippi for the coercive enrollments of a Negro agitator into the University of Mississippi. In a well-rehearsed performance, the Governor of Mississippi played the role of stooge to the Attorney General. In the circumstances of the Mississippi farce, Major General Edwin T. Walker was seized and incarcerated in a mental ward of a federal penitentiary at the express orders of the Attorney General. Walker had committed no crime. He had been a disgusted spectator of the police-state tactics at the University. But Walker had established himself as a vigorous anti-Communist military leader who would not be muzzled. (By the time of the Mississippi invasion, Robert Kennedy was already obeying directives of Walter Reuther to muzzle outspoken anti-Communist military leaders. Walker had resisted Kennedy.)

Robert Kennedy throughout his Attorney Generalship had a soft spot for Communists. As the nation's top law-enforcement officer, he lifted the ban on unsolicited propaganda coming into this country from the Communist bloc; he was the most important individual behind the successful move to get Otto Otepka because Otepka in the State Department's security division was conscientiously concerned with keeping security risks out of government; he opposed travel restrictions for U.S. citizens who wanted to visit Red China, Albania, and Cuba; and, he talked tough against Communists but in his tenure as Attorney General he did absolutely nothing against them.

Robert Kennedy was not content with being Attorney General. He was also the chief dispenser of patronage in the Kennedy Administration. He served as an ambassador without portfolio, dabbling in diplomacy. As a pseudo-diplomat he managed to sell out Dutch West New Guinea to the Communist regime of Indonesia's Sukarno. By rewriting history, he re-opened century old wounds in U.S.-Mexican relations. He was his brother's closest adviser in the Bay of Pigs fiasco which solidified Castro's hold on Cuba. Then, as a follow-up to that abortive invasion, Robert Kennedy conducted the ignominious ransom of prisoners held by Castro after the Bay of Pigs. To raise funds, Robert arm-twisted the American business community. If the Kennedy millions were ever tapped to pay for part of the ransom, it is a closely guarded secret.

As Attorney General and Senator, Kennedy has traveled the world in spectacular displays of exhibitionism. He has deliberately sought out Communists in Asia, Africa, Europe, and Latin America and given them reams of publicity through his friendly chats or phony debates with them. He has consistently downgraded the United States during his encounters with the Communists but always has a kind word for the social revolutionaries wherever he goes.

On the home front, Robert Kennedy is the complete welfare-stater: voting right down the socialist line for any and all expansion of big brother government, with especial attention toward Negro voters. The brazenness of Negro agitators has had tremendous encouragement from Robert Kennedy ever since 1960 when, as a gesture of cheap politics, he arranged to get Martin L. King out of an Atlanta jail where he had been placed legally for invading a department store and staging a "sit-in." And Kennedy has been a leader of the leftwing forces who believe that the way to reply to Negro revolutionaries is to give them all that they demand plus a little bit more.

On the Vietnam War, Robert Kennedy

has been one of the sword-carriers for Ho chi Minh. He has gone so far as to say that "to give blood to the North Vietnamese would be in the oldest traditions of this country. I'm willing to give blood to anybody who needs it." Without a day's combat activity to his credit, Robert hasn't been the least bit bashful about uttering the most absurd statements on military matters. He has a pathological fear of American military victory in Vietnam and says that "victory in a revolutionary war is not won by escalation but by de-escalation." He has long urged peace negotiations with the North Vietnam regime, the National Liberation Front, and the Vietcong as if they were three separate entities instead of the unified command of Ho chi Minh.

Kennedy's activities since 1960 have made him a hero to the revolutionaries in this country and abroad. His wooing of the leftists, especially the young, has been done not only through his world junkets and platform appearances with revolutionaries from Harlem to Tokyo but also in his frantic attempts to display himself as a vigorous, never-grow-old dare-devil on ski-slopes, on mountains, in swimming pools, on Harlem streets, atop automobiles making speeches — complete with mod clothes and a beatnik hair-do.

His closest associates have been paragons of leftism: William O. Douglas, Arthur M. Schlesinger Jr., Martin L. King, Thurmond Arnold, Ralph Bunche, Theodore Sorenson, Robert S. McNamara, and organized labor's Walter Reuther, Alex Rose, and David Dubinsky.

ROBERT W. KENNY was born on August 21, 1901 in Los Angeles, son of Minnie Carleton and Robert Kenny. He married Sara McCann. He is an alumnus of Stanford University (A.B., 1921).

From 1920 until 1923, Kenny was a correspondent for the United Press association, working in San Francisco, Los Angeles, and London, England. In 1923, he was a correspondent for the *Chicago Tribune* in Paris, France. From 1924 until 1927, he was a reporter with the *Los Angeles Evening Herald.*

In 1926, Kenny was admitted to the California bar and, since that time, with brief interruptions, he has practiced law in Los Angeles. In 1931 and 1932, he was a municipal court judge in Los Angeles. From 1932 until 1938, he was a superior court judge in Los Angeles.

From 1939 until 1942, Kenny was a member of the California Senate, representing Los Angeles County. From 1943 until 1947, he was Attorney General of California.

As a member, sponsor, or officer, Kenny has had an extraordinarily active career as a fellow traveler. He has been affiliated with Mobilization for Democracy ("a Communist-inspired and dominated organization, carefully window-dressed and directed" and "engaged in inciting riots, racial hatred, and disrespect for law and order"); the California Labor School ("a subversive and Communist organization"); American Youth for Democracy ("subversive and Communist"); the Hollywood Community Radio Group ("Communist inspired and directed"); Progressive Citizens of America ("Communist front"); Hollywood Writers Mobilization ("subversive and Communist"); the Independent Progressive Party ("one of the largest and most successful fronts ever created by the Communists"); the American League for Peace and Democracy ("subversive and Communist"); the International Labor Defense ("legal arm of the

Communist Party"); Friends of the Abraham Lincoln Brigade ("its officers and staff members were in the main [Communist] Party members and functionaries"); the Hollywood Anti-Nazi League ("Communist front"); the Hollywood Independent Citizens Committee of the Arts, Sciences and Professions ("Communist front"); the Hollywood League for Democratic Action ("Communist front"); the International Juridical Association (an organization "which actively defended Communists and consistently followed the Communist Party line"); the United Negro and Allied Veterans of America ("subversive and among the affiliates and committees of the Communist Party, U.S.A."); the Civil Rights Congress ("subversive and Communist"); the Independent Citizens Committee of the Arts, Sciences and Professions ("Communist front"); the Cultural and Scientific Conference for World Peace ("Communist front"); the American Slav Congress ("subversive and Communist"); the Joint Anti-Fascist Refugee Committee ("subversive and Communist"); the Coordinating Committee to Lift the [Spanish] Embargo ("Communist front"); the American Committee for Democracy and Intellectual Freedom ("Communist front" – "subversive and un-American"); the American Continental Congress for Peace ("another phase in the Communist 'peace' campaign, aimed at consolidating anti-American forces throughout the Western Hempishere"); the American Society for Cultural Relations with Russia ("Communist front"); the Los Angeles Committee for Protection of Foreign Born [Americans] ("one of the oldest and most active Communist front organizations in California"); the Emergency Civil Liberties Committee ("Communist front" – "subversive");

American Friends of the Chinese People ("Communist front"); the California Legislative Conference ("characterized by complete subservience to the twists and turns of the Communist Party line"); the American Committee for Spanish Freedom ("Communist"); the American Russian Institute of Los Angeles ("Communist"); the Los Angeles Committee to Secure Justice in the Rosenberg Case ("Communist campaign"); the American Committee for Yugoslav Relief ("subversive and Communist"); the Motion Picture Artists' Committee ("Communist front"); the North American Committee to Aid Spanish Democracy ("Communist"); and, the American Labor Party ("Communist political front").

Kenny, as a lawyer, has defended Communists. He was general counsel and fund-raiser for the notorious Hollywood Ten. He was president of the National Lawyers Guild, "the foremost legal bulwark of the Communist Party, its front organizations, and controlled unions." He has been praised in the pages of the Soviet Union's *Pravda* as one of the "friends of the Soviet Union." He was a character witness for the Red labor leader Harry Bridges when Bridges was on trial for perjury and conspiracy in 1950.

In 1964, Kenny was a featured speaker at the *People's World's* (West Coast Communist daily) twenty-sixth anniversary celebration. In 1964, Kenny visited Portugal, ostensibly as a tourist in company with three other lawyers. Within a short time, Kenny and his three companions were expelled from Portugal on grounds that they had meddled in Portuguese internal matters, attempted to disturb public order, and abused the hospitality guaranteed to them as tourists. At least one of Kenny's companions, Robert Treuhaft of San Francisco, has been repeatedly identified as a member of the Communist Party.

In 1965, Kenny was the honor guest at a banquet sponsored by the Los Angeles Committee for the Defense of the Bill of Rights and the Protection of Foreign Born [Americans], a Communist front.

In 1966, Kenny became honorary chairman of the Lawyers Committee on American Policy toward VietNam, a group organized to seek a legal basis for halting U.S. resistance to the aggression of Communist North Vietnam. It was also in 1966 that the incredible Governor Edmund (Pat) Brown of California, during his lame-duck period, named Kenny to be a superior court judge in Los Angeles County — a post that Kenny held for six years in the 1930's.

CLARK KERR was born on May 17, 1911 in Stone Creek, Pennsylvania, son of Caroline Clark and Samuel Kerr. He married Catherine Spaulding. He is an alumnus of Swarthmore College (B.A., 1932), Stanford University (M.A., 1933), and the University of California (Ph.D., 1939). He also attended the London School of Economics in 1936 and 1939.

In 1935 and 1936, he was a traveling fellow for the leftwing American Friends Service Committee. In 1936 and 1937, he was an economics instructor at Antioch College. From 1937 until 1939, he held fellowships at the University of California. In 1939 and 1940, he was an acting assistant professor of labor economics at Stanford University. From 1940 until 1945, he was an assistant professor and associate professor at the University of Washington. From 1945 until 1952, he was an associate professor and professor at the University of California (Berkeley). In that same period, he founded and became director of the University's Institute of Industrial Relations. From 1952 until 1958, he was the chancellor and, from 1958 until 1967, the president of the University of California (Berkeley).

In 1942, Kerr was a senior analyst with the War Manpower Commission. In that same year, he worked for the Office of Price Administration in Seattle. From 1943 until 1945, he was a consultant to the Hawaiian Territorial War Labor Board and for the Twelfth Regional War Labor Board. In 1945 and 1946, Kerr worked for the Office of Wage Stabilization in San Francisco.

In its Thirteenth Report (1965), the California Senate Fact-finding Subcommittee on Un-American Activities commented on Kerr's off-campus activities: "It was inevitable that he was brought into close contact with the many Communists who were also working in these agencies . . . . We make no implication that there was any guilt by association, but we do make clear that many of Kerr's most intimate colleagues during these years were at the same time teaching at the Communist school [in San Francisco] and participating in a wide variety of pro-Communist activities. Some of them came to work at the Berkeley campus after Kerr became its Chancellor, and some found places with the Institute of Industrial Relations, which he headed."

In September, 1964, demonstrations erupted on the Berkeley campus under the name of the Free Speech Movement. Students and non-students, Communists and fellow travelers, dupes and radicals of various sorts, were engaged in the FSM. Kerr refused to punish those students who took part in the demonstrations and who were among the almost eight hundred persons arrested on the campus. Kerr came under considerable criticism for the manner in which he handled the situation. When the criticism continued, Kerr – in February, 1965 – asked for a vote of confidence from the University's Regents. They refused to grant it.

In March, 1965, demonstrations again broke out at Berkeley – this time as the Filthy Speech Movement. The Regents demanded that Kerr discipline the students involved in the outbreak. Kerr refused to do so and, instead, tried to pass off his responsibility to the Academic Senate of the University. Then Kerr, in what he admitted was a dramatic gesture, submitted his resignation from the presidency. Four days later, before the Regents had an opportunity to accept the resignation, Kerr withdrew it. Throughout Kerr's troublous reign at Berkeley, he was under the benevolent protection of California's Governor Edmund G. (Pat) Brown. But, in 1966, Brown was defeated for re-election by Ronald Reagan.

In an effort to forestall any move by the new governor to ease him out of the presidency, Kerr – in January, 1967 – demanded a vote of confidence from the Regents. The Regents by a vote of 14 to 8 decided to terminate Kerr's services as president.

The *Santa Monica Evening Outlook* commented on Kerr's dismissal: "In the nine years that he was president, the university went through unprecedented growth and expansion, and attracted outstanding professors to its far-flung campuses. But Kerr was no more responsible for this than former Governor Brown was for the state's growth in the same years . . . .

" . . . The growth [of the University] was spurred by the traditional generosity and responsiveness of the taxpayers and legislators to higher education in the state – and to their confidence in the university developed during the fine administration of Dr. Kerr's predecessor, Dr. Robert Gordon Sproul.

"No, Dr. Kerr should not be remembered as the architect of the university's growth, for he wasn't. He should be remembered, rather, as the architect of its internal deterioration, decay and divisiveness. For it was during his administration that the university's Berkeley campus became the greatest concentration of Communists and ultra-leftists in the nation.

"It was during his tenure as president that: The university's security system was abolished and longtime Communist associates hired as professors; the Free Speech Movement, under the guidance of Communists and ultra-leftists erupted and some 800 students and nonstudents seized Sproul Hall; a policy of buying peace on the campuses through appeasement with the activists was instituted; the Vietnam Day Committee [pro-Communist] staged massive protests originating on the campus at Berkeley; the state and nation were treated to the spectacle of a university opening its doors to a national 'Black Power' rally."

Four days after Kerr was fired, the Carnegie Foundation for the Advancement of Teaching announced that Kerr was to head a major study of the future structure and financing of American higher education. It was also announced that Kerr had accepted the assignment for the project (the Carnegie Study of Higher Education) *before* he was fired by the Regents.

Although Kerr had lost his presidential post, he still remained a faculty member at Berkeley. And, in April, 1967, University officials announced that Kerr would teach on a part-time basis. He would conduct a seminar in labor-management problems and policies and a seminar in advanced labor economics. He would also do research in the Institute of Industrial Relations.

Kerr retained one souvenir from his presidency. In 1964, he received the Alexander Meiklejohn award for academic freedom from the American Association of University Professors. The "academic freedom" consisted of Kerr's defense of students' "rights" to invite controversial (that is, Communist) speakers to the University's campuses. (The award was appropriate. Meiklejohn, a notorious and obnoxious Communist fronter, was one of education's all-time champions of licentiousness.)

JAMES R. KILLIAN JR. was born on July 24, 1904 in Blacksburg, South Carolina, son of Jeannette Rhyne and James Killian. He married Elizabeth Parks. He is an alumnus of Massachusetts Institute of Technology (B.S., 1926).

From 1926 until 1939, Killian was with *The Technology Review* as managing editor and editor.

In 1939, he became executive assistant to the president of MIT. Over the years since then, he became executive vice president, president, and, in 1954, chairman of the MIT Corporation – his present position. In 1963, he was named to the board of directors of the Corporation.

Away from the campus, Killian has seen government service. From 1951 until 1957, he was a member of the science advisory committee in the Office of Defense Mobilization. From 1957 until 1961, he was on President Eisenhower's Science Advisory Committee and, during the Kennedy Administration, he was a consultant to President

Kennedy's Science Advisory Committee and a trustee of the President's Foreign Intelligence Advisory Board.

The appointment of Killian to positions in the Eisenhower Administration caused very little commotion, despite his soft-on-Communism record. In 1947, he was a vigorous opponent of a Massachusetts Un-American Activities Investigating Committee and was indignant that Massachusetts' Attorney General had published a list of subversive organizations. The next year, Killian came out against legislation that would have barred Communists from teaching in Massachusetts. Killian had some personal interests at stake. One of MIT's faculty members, Dirk Struik, had been indicted for sedition by the Commonwealth of Massachusetts. Struik had a long and notorious record as a supporter of Communist causes, activities, and organizations. And when called to account for his activities, Struik pleaded protection under the Massachusetts Constitution's provisions against self-incrimination (similar to the U.S. Constitution's Fifth Amendment). The indictment against Struik was dropped when the U.S. Supreme Court decided that States had no authority in sedition cases. But Killian decided to keep Struik on the MIT faculty.

When J. Robert Oppenheimer was branded a security risk by the federal government, Killian went out of his way to defend Oppenheimer. As Eisenhower's chief scientific adviser, Killian was responsible for the United States suspending all nuclear weapons testing in 1958 – a suspension that lasted throughout the rest of the Eisenhower Administration. When Killian had been appointed, *National Review* (November 23, 1957), in an editorial, said that the appointment was "an augury of the enlightened day when the Scientist-kings will be in full command of our national strategy and policy." The augury was realized within months after Killian took over. General Nathan Twining, Chairman of the Joint Chiefs of Staff, categorically endorsed nuclear weapons testing as vital to the safety of the United States and its allies. But Killian's inspired unilateral moratorium on testing gave the Soviet Union the opportunity to make up for lost time.

Killian went into the Kennedy Administration as the coordinator and monitor of the government's intelligence agencies, especially the CIA which was given the blame for the fiasco at Cuba's Bay of Pigs. In retrospect there was irony in having Killian baby-sit for the CIA, since that agency was swarming all over the MIT campus where it had established and financed the Center for International Studies.

If nothing else tipped off the incredibility of Killian's position, an item in the Moscow *New Times* should have done so. In its issue of September, 1958, the dean of Soviet apologists in America, Cyrus Eaton, said he was glad Killian was back in the government because he is a "positive man. His voice is pitched for peace."

As recently as January, 1967, Killian let it be known that his voice is pitched for a one-world idiocy as "the entire human community is being made into a global neighborhood and an interacting whole." Which probably meant that the carnage in Vietnam was merely a sign of a neighborly spat.

MARTIN LUTHER KING was born as Michael Luther King (he and his father changed their names when Michael Jr. was six) on January 15, 1929 in Atlanta, Georgia, son of Alberta Williams and Michael Luther King. He married Coretta Scott. He is an alumnus of Morehouse College (A.B., 1948), Crozer Theological Seminary (B.D., 1951), and Boston University (Ph.D., 1955). He has worked at Baptist pastorates in Alabama and Georgia.

In 1964, FBI Director J. Edgar Hoover described King as the "most notorious liar in the country." On October 4, 1967, Representative John M. Ashbrook (R.-Ohio), as an extension of remarks in the *Congressional Record,* used forty columns of eight- and/or nine-point type to summarize King's character. He found King to be an apostle of violence and lawlessness, a racist, a power-hungry tyrant, an associate of "the most radical elements in our society," an individual who "has done more for the Communist Party than any other person of this decade." Ashbrook described King's methodology as "criminal conduct and conspiracy, not civil disobedience." He also said that King's disregard for the law is deplorable, but his disregard for the laws of God is almost inconceivable."

Mr. Ashbrook, in the concluding portion of his remarks, said: "Mr. [J. Edgar] Hoover is privy to many confidential reports on Mr. King's activities just as I am, and while their nature cannot be disclosed, I can say without equivocation that Martin Luther King does not want nor can he stand a public airing of his record. I can rest my case against King with the public utterances and actions of this man and any revelation of confidential matter is entirely unnecessary.

"Why has he been immune for so many years and, in the parlance of the day, 'allowed to get by with murder?' There is a peculiar double standard which the liberal community consistently applies. If any prominent person, particularly a conservative, were to identify with or share a speakers' platform with a member of the John Birch Society or some group the liberals might currently be attacking, he would be maligned forever. Let Martin Luther King openly identify with Communists and radicals, have a Communist as an adviser, engage in criminal activity, appear at the most way-out meetings in the Nation and advocate racism, revolution, or civil disobedience and these same people look the other way."

It would be belaboring the point to add much to Mr. Ashbrook's remarks. King's immunity, however, is not difficult to understand. King's friendship with the late President John F. Kennedy and the President's brothers, Senators Robert and Edward, along with President Johnson, have made King a political sacred cow. He has taken shelter behind a clergyman's cloth which, in this era, has become a license for King to preach anarchism and racism, and – when it suits his purpose – the straight Communist line. He is the self-anointed spokesman for all Negro Americans and draft dodgers. He has adopted the posture of a Christian leader of nonviolence (following the example of the non-Christian Gandhi) but his preachments of non-violence for more than ten years have been followed invariably by violence. He has repeatedly disrupted the routine of government – local, state, and federal – in total disregard of the law or the people who live peaceably under that law.

Neither King's Nobel Peace Prize, nor his man-of-the-year award from *Time* magazine, nor his entree to the White House diminish the fact that he is alien to the interests of Negro Americans and all other Americans.

ROBERT KINTNER was born on September 12, 1909 in Stroudsburg, Pennsylvania. He married Jean Rodney. He is an alumnus of Swarthmore College (B.A., 1931).

From 1933 until 1937, he was with the *New York Herald Tribune* as a reporter and a member of that journal's Washington bureau. For the next four years, he was a columnist partner of Joseph Alsop.

After military service in World War II, Kintner joined the American Broadcasting Company. From 1950 until 1957, he was president of ABC. In 1957, he switched networks and became vice president of the National Broadcasting Company. From 1958 until 1965, Kintner was president of NBC and, in 1965, became chairman of the board and chief executive officer. In his ABC career, Kintner presided over a system that was called "planned programming" that might better have been described as brainwashing by the left, since ABC's headline features were the commentaries of Drew Pearson, Walter Winchell, and Elmer Davis. Kintner, in his pre-War newspaper career, was an ardent devotee of Rooseveltian policies – the commentary triumvirate of Pearson, Winchell, and Davis could be counted upon to perpetuate the myth of Roosevelt's greatness.

As head of NBC, Kintner placed great stress upon sex and violence in his television presentations. And his "news" team was distinctly to the left: Chet Huntley, David Brinkley, Frank McGee, Elie Abel, Sander Vanocur, Edwin Newman, Herb Kaplow, and Richard Harkness.

In 1966, Kintner left NBC to join the White House staff as a special assistant to President Johnson. It has never been clear as to what Kintner's duties were supposed to be. Joseph Kraft, a leftwing admirer of Kintner's, wrote in his syndicated column that Kintner was calling and presiding over White House staff meetings and recruiting top executives from private business to take important jobs in the government.

FREDA KIRCHWEY was born about 1894 in New York City, daughter of Dora Wendell and George Kirchwey. She married Evans Clark. She is an alumna of Barnard College (A.B., 1915), where, from 1912 until 1915, she served, successively, as secretary and president of the Intercollegiate Socialist Society.

In 1915 and 1916, Freda was a reporter for the *New York Morning Star Telegraph*. In 1917 and 1918, she was on the editorial staff of *Every Week* and, briefly in 1918, she was on the staff of the *New York Sunday Tribune*.

In 1918, Freda began a thirty-seven-year career with *The Nation* magazine, becoming vice president and managing editor in 1922, literary editor in 1928, editor in 1932, and, from 1937 until 1955, publisher-editor. Under Freda's guidance *The Nation* became one of the most influential fellow-traveling magazines in the country. Its editorial staff and contributors were representative of the most notorious Socialists, Fabian Socialists, fellow travelers, and pro-Communist apologists on the American scene.

In 1956, the Senate Internal Security Subcommittee included Freda's name in its list of the eighty-two most active and typical sponsors of Communist front organizations. Her affiliations have included the All-America Anti-Imperialist League ("Communist enterprise"); the American Committee for Democracy and Intellectual Freedom ("Communist front" — "subversive and un-Ameri-can"); the American Committee for Yugoslav Relief ("subversive and Communist"); the American Friends of the Chinese People ("Communist front"); the American Friends of Spanish Democracy ("subversive"); the American Fund for Public Service ("a major source for the financing of Communist Party enterprises"); the American Student Union ("Communist front"); the Committee for a Democratic Far Eastern Policy ("Communist"); the Coordinating Committee to Lift the [Spanish] Embargo ("Communist front); the Descendants of the American Revolution ("Communist front — "subversive and un-American"); Films for Democracy ("Communist front"); Film Audiences for Democracy ("Communist front"); The Greater New York Emergency Conference on Inalienable Rights ("Communist front"); the League of Women Shoppers ("Communist-controlled front"); the National Emergency Conference for Democratic Rights ("Communist front" — "subversive and un-American"); the National People's Committee against Hearst ("subsidiary" organization of the American League for Peace and Democracy — "subversive and Communist"); the National Federation for Constitutional Liberties ("subversive and Communist" — "under [Communist] Party domination and headed by responsible Party functionaries"); *New Masses* ("Communist periodical"); the North American Committee to Aid Spanish Democracy ("Communist"); the Schappes Defense Committee ("Communist"); the Union of Concerted Peace Efforts ("Communist front"); *Women Today* ("Communist front magazine"); the Southern Conference for Human Welfare ("Communist front"); the Spanish Refugee Relief Campaign ("Communist front"); the World Congress of Intellectuals ("Communist"); the Metropolitan Music School ("controlled by Communists"); the Committee for a Boycott against Japanese Aggression ("Communist front"); the National Citizens Political Action Committee ("Communist front"); and, the National Committee to Abolish the House Un-American Activities Committee ("to lead and direct the Communist Party's 'Operation Abolition' campaign").

Freda worked on behalf of the convicted Communist spies, Julius and Ethel Rosenberg. She intervened on behalf of the German Communist Hanns Eisler when he was being deported by U.S. authorities. She has been involved with leftwing movements for world disarmament. She has been affiliated with the leftwing, pacifist Women's International League for Peace and Freedom. She has been affiliated with the leftwing International League for the Rights of Man.

In the 1920's, Freda was in the Socialist Party. She has been a member of the socialist League for Industrial Democracy. She was a member of the Union for Democratic Action, the ultra-leftwing predecessor of Americans for Democratic Action. And, she has also found time to be active in the American Civil Liberties Union, the National Association for the Advancement of Colored People, and the League of Women Voters. It all adds up to more than a half century of leftwing activity by the daughter of George Washington Kirchwey, a Socialist and pacifist of some renown.

GRAYSON KIRK was born on October 12, 1903 in Jeffersonville, Ohio, son of Nora Eichelberger and Traine Kirk. He married Marion Sands. He is an alumnus of Miami University of Ohio (B.A., 1924), Clark University (M.A., 1925), and the University of Wisconsin (Ph.D., 1930).

From 1929 until 1949, Kirk was on the government faculties of the University of Wisconsin and Columbia University. In 1949, he became provost at Columbia and, in 1953, he became the University's president. In 1959, he assumed the chair of Bryce professor of history of international relations.

In 1944, Kirk was on the secretarial staff at the Dumbarton Oaks Conference. In 1945, he was an executive on the staff of Alger Hiss at the San Francisco organizing conference of the United Nations.

Kirk is an exponent of the theory that it is nationalism, not Communism, which has caused upheavals throughout the new nations of the world. The influence of Communist propaganda and subversion is greatly overrated according to Kirk.

At the same time, it should be noted that Kirk at Columbia would have to look no further than his faculty to see that the attraction of Communism has not been insignificant. The Communist fronters at Columbia are legendary.

HENRY KISSINGER was born on May 27, 1923 in Fuerth, Germany, son of Paula Stern and Louis Kissinger. He was naturalized in 1943. He married Ann Fleischer. He is an alumnus of Harvard University (A.B., 1950; M.A. 1952; Ph.D., 1954).

Since 1951, Kissinger has been at Harvard University serving as executive director of the International Seminar of the Harvard Summer School — a seminar he established to bring together young leaders from various countries for informal discussions. He has been in Harvard's government department and has held a professorship since 1962. In 1955 and 1956, Kissinger was the director for nuclear weapons and foreign policy studies in the Council on Foreign Relations. From 1956 until 1958, he was director of a special studies project for the Rockefeller Brothers Fund. In 1963, he was an adviser to Nelson Rockefeller on military and foreign policy when Rockefeller was campaigning for the U.S. presidency. In 1965, Ambassador Henry C. Lodge appointed Kissinger to make a study of Vietnam.

At the tender age of twenty-seven, Kissinger began a career as a consultant on defense and foreign policy and propaganda warfare to the federal government. (Between the ages of twenty and twenty-three, Kissinger had served in the army. After that he was at Harvard in pursuit of his three academic degrees.) But notwithstanding his lack of practical experience, he became involved in the highest levels of policy making, involving the State and Defense Departments, the CIA, the National Security Council, and the U.S. Arms Control and Disarmament Agency. And, as a consultant, he served the Truman, Eisenhower, and Kennedy Administrations.

Through articles in *Foreign Affairs* quarterly and, especially through two of his books (*Nuclear Weapons and Foreign Policy* and *The Necessity for Choice: Prospects of American Foreign Policy*), Kissinger has gained a great following throughout the appeasement community (for example, J. Robert Oppenheimer, the security risk, was most enthusiastic over *Nuclear Weapons and Foreign Policy*). At the same time, Kissinger is highly regarded by those who consider themselves to be conservatives. They take comfort in the fact that Kissinger, in his erudite military and diplomatic

pronunciamentos, does not advocate abolition of nuclear weapons, unilateral disarmament, or outright overtures for peaceful coexistence with the Soviet Union. As a matter of fact, he isn't a bit bashful about describing the Soviet Union as hostile to the United States and a threat to the whole world. But – and it is a big But – Kissinger is an advocate of limited nuclear warfare because, according to his estimates, the United States could not possibly be victorious in all-out war against the Communists. Therefore, the United States should concentrate on building its defenses against an all-out nuclear war (evidently as a means of discouraging the Soviet Union from an attempt to destroy the U.S.), and be content to fight limited wars indefinitely in hopes that we never lose one of these limited wars. All the while, we can hope that, through some miracle, any and all limited wars will end in a peaceful settlement when the Communists get tired of waiting for us to surrender. In brief, Kissinger's theory is that a substitute for victory is an indefinite struggle toward a piecemeal death.

FOY KOHLER was born on February 15, 1908 in Oakwood, Ohio, son of Myrtle McClure and Leander Kohler. He married Phyllis Penn. He is an alumnus of Ohio State University (B.S., 1931).

Kohler began his career in the State Department in 1931 and, for the first sixteen years, held minor posts in Canada, Rumania, Yugoslavia, Greece, Washington, and London.

From 1947 until 1949, he was at the U.S. Embassy in Moscow, serving successively as first secretary, counsellor, and minister plenipotentiary.

From 1949 until 1953, he was in Washington. There he served as head of the State Department's International

Broadcasting Division, director of Voice of America broadcasts, assistant administrator of the International Information Administration, and on the policy planning staff of the Department.

From 1953 until 1956, Kohler was counsellor at the U.S. Embassy in Ankara. From 1956 until 1958, he was with the International Cooperation Administration. From 1958 until 1962, he was, successively, deputy assistant and assistant secretary of state for European affairs.

From 1962 until 1966, Kohler was U.S. Ambassador to the Soviet Union. In 1967, he was Deputy Under Secretary for Political Affairs. He retired from his position as the highest-ranking career diplomat in the foreign service on December 31, 1967. He has accepted a position as professor at Miami University's Center for Advanced International Studies.

The departure of Kohler from Moscow in 1966 must have been a severe blow to the Kremlin leaders. During his tour of duty there, the Communists might just as well have given their propaganda machines a holiday. During his first tour of duty in Moscow (1947-1949), Kohler certainly did not learn anything about Communist duplicity or, if he did, he concealed his knowledge very well. At the time of his appointment, in 1962, to be Ambassador, he was interviewed by Robert T. Hartmann, the *Los Angeles Times* Washington bureau chief. Mr. Hartmann asked Kohler: "Do you think the classic rules of diplomacy can be used when dealing with Russian Communists?" Kohler replied: "I think their basic elements are the same but for their application in every single different country you need a profound knowledge and appreciation of their makeup, history, traditions and

psychology. When I was in Moscow before, one thing I did was to read their official grammar school readers right from kindergarten through the seventh grade. This was useful to me in learning the language but it also gave me a sense of what goes on in the mind of the average Russian citizen – this is the kind of understanding you have to seek." Any American diplomat who goes to the Soviet Union thinking he is going to cope with "the mind of the average Russian citizen" should be forced to swim and walk from Washington to Moscow.

As Ambassador, Kohler regaled the American public with one fantasy after another: mutual understanding between the Soviet Union and the United States has improved; the people of the Soviet Union "are getting a much more objective picture" of the United States; "Russian society [sic] ... wishes to develop closer contacts with the United States" and "participate [sic] in Western civilization." Kohler, in 1966, announced that the Soviet Union had won its battle to isolate Red China in the Communist movement and in the world. With the main enemy isolated, the Soviet leaders, according to Kohler, were genuinely interested in improving relations with the United States.

In 1964, columnists Allen and Scott reported that Kohler was sending "almost frantic messages from Moscow pleading with Secretary Rusk to oppose any more crackdowns on Soviet spies [in the United States]. Since taking over his present diplomatic post, Kohler has bombarded the State Department with urgent pleas, contending that spy trials and expulsions of Communists were making it extremely difficult for his staff to function." (Naturally, Kohler's pleas were heeded. Through the connivance of

Secretary Rusk, Acting Attorney General Nicholas Katzenbach, and Deputy Under Secretary of State Llewellyn Thompson two Soviet spies [Alexsandr Sokolov and Joy Garber Baltch] had their espionage charges dropped after a federal jury had already been sworn to hear testimony from FBI agents. The two spies had gathered information on U.S. missile sites and atomic weapon shipments and were linked with an espionage ring involving Soviet officials at the United Nations and in Washington.)

Kohler was an ideal mouthpiece for the Great Society as he propagandized for "building bridges" of trade with the Soviet Union and its satellites for purposes of "peaceful engagement" – not, Kohler emphasized, to subvert the satellites or make them hostile to Moscow. According to Kohler, Communism is dying in the Soviet Union and its satellites: "The revolution of rising expectations which has already affected so much of the world has penetrated the Soviet Union and is producing profound effects." Which means, according to Kohler, that the Russian people are pushing the Soviet regime toward a state of peaceful togetherness with the United States and the West.

ROBERT W. KOMER was born on February 23, 1922 in Chicago. His second wife is Geraldine Peplin. He is an alumnus of Harvard University (B.S., 1942; M.B.A., 1947).

From 1943 until 1946, Komer served in Army intelligence. After World War II, he joined the Central Intelligence Agency. His fourteen-year career in the CIA ended in 1961 when he joined the White House staff as an assistant to McGeorge Bundy who was President Kennedy's and President Johnson's special assistant for national security affairs.

President Kennedy gave Komer a great deal of notoriety by describing the Yemeni-Egyptian conflict as "Mr. Komer's war." The background for Mr. Kennedy's reference was outlined in *Human Events* (April 1, 1967): "On Sept. 26, 1962, anti-American, pro-Nasser revolutionaries expelled Yemen's pro-Western royal ruler from the capital and plunged the country into a chaotic civil war which has yet to be resolved.

"The revolution, carefully nurtured by Egyptian President Gamal Abdel Nasser, soon required Nasser's direct intervention and by December no less than 13,000 Egyptian troops had invaded Yemen to help the rebels flatten the royalists who were now receiving supplies from Saudi Arabia.

"On December 19, three months before the Soviet-equipped Egyptian Army could even capture some of the important central eastern towns, the United States – to the consternation of the Western-aligned Arab powers – recognized the pro-Nasser revolutionaries as the Yemeni Arab Republic.

" 'The act was appeasement of Nasser, pure and simple,' noted one observer, who added that it had the same shock effect on the pro-Western Arabs as 'one might expect the Asians to feel if we suddenly recognized the Viet Cong as a nation.'

"It was largely due to Komer's urging that the United States recognized the pro-Nasser, anti-Western revolutionaries.

"Acknowledging Komer's part in U.S. recognition of the revolutionaries, the *New York Times* noted last week that this act 'created considerable confusion and dismay among the pro-Western monarchies of the Middle East and appeared to encourage rather than neutralize the aggrandizing instincts of President Gamal Abdel Nasser . . . . '

"In 1966, as Bundy left the White House staff to become President of the Ford Foundation, Lyndon Johnson named Komer to be his special assistant for 'peaceful reconstruction' in Vietnam, the Great Society's euphemism for CIA-socialism imposed upon South Vietnam. In May 1967, Komer was accorded rank as deputy ambassador as an aide to the commander of the U.S. forces in South Vietnam, General William Westmoreland. This all meant that Komer was then the No. 2 American diplomat in Saigon — No. 1 was Ambassador Ellsworth Bunker, an old acquaintance of Komer's and a long-time harbinger of bad news for non-Communists and victims of Communist aggression throughout the world. (Bunker had a hand in the sell-out of Yemen to Nasser by drawing up 'the Jiddah peace agreement, which was signed by Nasser and King Faisal of Saudi Arabia in 1965. Under this agreement, Faisal was to stop sending supplies to the royalists if Nasser would withdraw his troops, which now numbered 50,000. Under U.S. pressure, Faisal's supplies have stopped, but Nasser's troops remain, still fighting the royalists.')"

In July, 1967, Komer was given rank as Ambassador and he is the chief of the "pacification" program in South Vietnam. Komer's deserved reputation as a blowhard during his years at the White House and his abrasiveness which has alienated him from American and Vietnamese officials and the press corps in Saigon would indicate that his diplomatic position is merely a front for his apparent position as the CIA boss in Saigon. Part of Komer's "pacification" program seems to involve the character assassination of Nguyen Cao Ky, the anti-Communist Vice President of South Vietnam whose desire for victory against North Vietnam runs counter to the "no-win" policy of the Johnson Administration.

JOSEPH KRAFT was born on September 4, 1924 in South Orange, New Jersey, son of Sophie Surasky and David Kraft. He married Polly Winton. He is an alumnus of Columbia University (A.B., 1947). He did a year of postgraduate study at Princeton University and spent a year in residence at the Institute for Advanced Study in Princeton, New Jersey.

In 1951 and 1952, Kraft was an editorial writer for the ultra leftwing *Washington Post*. For the next four years, he was a staff writer for the *New York Times*. Kraft's first big splash in journalism, however, came in 1957 and 1958. At that time, Kraft — under the auspices of the Communist Forces of National Liberation — went to Algeria to write an account of the French-Algerian struggle. Kraft had a well guided tour. The Communist terrorists — the FLN — who would come into contact with Kraft were given explicit orders and instructions as to how to play Kraft for a sucker. ("Say that you are against Communism, that Communism has no influence on the Algerian people.")

Kraft's experiences appeared as a two-part article in the *Saturday Evening Post* (January 11 and 18, 1958) and, as might be expected, the article was a glorification of the Communist revolution in Algeria. "These nationalists," wrote Kraft of the Communist FLN, "I thought, harbored a virulent strain of hatred for the Communists." (For his trip to Wonderland, Kraft received from the Overseas Press Club an award for the Best Magazine Reporting of Foreign Affairs in 1958.)

In 1962, Kraft became Washington correspondent for *Harper's* magazine. Then, in 1963, he began writing his syndicated column "Insight and Outlook" which appears in about eighty American newspapers. In 1964, Kraft traveled to Communist Poland with his close friend Senator Robert F. Kennedy (Kraft had been a speech writer for the late President John F. Kennedy) and Kraft's column generally seems to be inspired by the junior Senator from New York.

In the last few years, Kraft has written a considerable amount in his columns on Vietnam. He believes that the United States should sponsor a civilian government in Saigon that could and would negotiate with the Vietcong. According to Kraft, the wardogs are in Washington and Saigon — not in Hanoi, Moscow, and Peking. And the reason why peace overtures have been rejected by Hanoi is that Ho chi Minh's regime and the Vietcong have a "genuine suspicion of American trickery." Kraft looks kindly upon Ho chi Minh of whom he wrote: "All his life he seems to have exuded what Ruth Fisher, an ex-Communist who knew him in Moscow, calls 'a note of goodness.'"

But whether Kraft writes of North Vietnam or Red China or the Soviet Union, he constantly downgrades the Communist threat. He follows the tiresome line that the Communist world has broken up. If any Communist regime is really hostile toward us, it would be Red China and, if such is the case, then the United States, advises Kraft, should do all in its power to achieve a détente with the Soviet Union.

A couple of years ago, British journalist Henry Fairlie said that Kraft was Walter Lippmann's "only visible successor." And Lippmann conceded that Kraft "is the most promising commenta-

tor of his generation." With an endorsement like that, Kraft can rest assured that there is nothing too inane he can write for the edification of the Liberal Establishment.

THOMAS KUCHEL was born on August 15, 1910 in Anaheim, California, son of Lutetia Bailey and Henry Kuchel. He married Betty Mellenthin. He is an alumnus of the University of California (A.B., 1932; LL.B., 1935). He was admitted to the California bar in 1935 and, until 1946, he practiced law in Anaheim.

From 1937 until 1946, Kuchel served two terms each in the California Assembly and California Senate. In February, 1946, Governor Earl Warren appointed Kuchel as Controller of the State of California. Kuchel was elected as Controller in November, 1946, and re-elected in 1950. In 1952, Governor Warren appointed Kuchel as U.S. Senator, replacing Richard Nixon who had resigned. Kuchel was elected Senator in 1954, and re-elected in 1956, and 1962. Since 1959, Kuchel has been the assistant Republican leader in the Senate.

When Kuchel first entered the U.S. Senate, he described himself as a "middle-of-the-road Eisenhower Republican." By the end of the second Eisenhower Administration, Kuchel's voting record indicated that he was keeping company with a handful of leftwing "Republicans," including Jacob Javits of New York, Clifford Case of New Jersey, Hugh Scott of Pennsylvania, George Aiken of Vermont, Margaret Chase Smith of Maine, and John Sherman Cooper of Kentucky.

During the Kennedy and Johnson Administrations, Kuchel virtually dropped all pretenses of being a Republican in any part of the road — left, right, or the middle. And, in the 90th Congress (his last), Kuchel's voting companions on the Republican side included only Javits of New York, Cooper of Kentucky, and Hiram Fong of Hawaii. This select group of Republicans was in perfect harmony with the ultra-leftist Democrats in the Senate: Edmund Muskie of Maine, Edward Kennedy of Massachusetts, Gale McGee of Wyoming, Eugene McCarthy of Minnesota, George McGovern of South Dakota, Birch Bayh of Indiana, and Joseph Tydings of Maryland.

Kuchel's years in the Senate were made possible only by the support he received from Democrats in California. And since 1962, he has been practically divorced from other Republican leaders in California. In 1962, he ignored Richard Nixon's campaign for Governor. In 1964, he ignored George Murphy's campaign for U.S. Senate and, in that same year, he actively campaigned against Barry Goldwater's candidacy for the presidency of the United States. (For a brief time in 1964, Kuchel was Nelson Rockefeller's campaign manager in California as the New York Governor made a futile bid for the Republican presidential nomination.) In 1966, Kuchel kept his record of consistency by refusing to support the gubernatorial candidacy of Ronald Reagan.

On the domestic scene, Kuchel has been an effective pork barrel specialist. His rubber-stamp vote for the liberals has been rewarded with federal spending in California. He has been quick to pay homage to a "successful free and private enterprise system," but has been even quicker to vote for every conceivable bit of legislation to hamper and to interfere with the "free and private enterprise system." In 1966, when the nation was becoming increasingly aware of the fraudulent nature of Johnson's "War on Poverty," Kuchel's remedy was to move private enterprise into the anti-poverty program in partnership with the government. But liberal remedies and liberal clichés have been Kuchel's stock-in-trade. In the summer of 1967, as cities across the nation were being rocked by remarkably similar demonstrations and riots, Kuchel insisted that the riots were not organized but stemmed from discontent caused by impoverished conditions, aggravated by the summer heat.

In foreign affairs, Kuchel is a complete internationalist. He does talk a great deal against Communism but, when it comes to a showdown, he votes consistently on the side of appeasement. He has tremendous faith in the United Nations and, as a solution to the Vietnam situation, he wanted the UN to establish a collective guarantee of the territorial integrity of the borders of North and South Vietnam. Otherwise, Kuchel has supported the "no-win" policy of the Johnson Administration all the way in the Vietnam War.

In 1968, Kuchel was defeated by Max Rafferty when he sought the Republican nomination for his re-election to the U.S. Senate.

CORLISS LAMONT was born on March 28, 1902 in Englewood, New Jersey, son of Florence Corliss and Thomas Lamont. He was married to, and divorced from, Margaret Irish. He is married to Helen Lamb. He is an alumnus of Harvard University (A.B., 1924) and Columbia University (Ph.D., 1932). He also did graduate work at Oxford University in England.

Lamont, the son of the multi-millionaire financier Thomas W. Lamont, has avoided the business and banking world for a lifetime of extreme radicalism. Between 1928 and 1949, Lamont lectured on occasions at Columbia University, Harvard University, Cornell University, and the New School for Social Research. But most of Lamont's energies in that period were expended on books that he wrote extolling the virtues of humanism, Socialism (the Marxian variety), and the Soviet Union. For diversion, Lamont busied himself promoting Communist causes and projects and joining Communist fronts.

By 1944, the House Special Committee on Un-American Activities described Lamont as "probably the most persistent propagandist for the Soviet Union to be found anywhere in the United States. No matter what the fluctuations of Soviet foreign policy, and no matter what the corresponding shifts in the line of the Communist Party in the United States, Lamont has been found for many years a subservient fellow traveler of the Communists." Twelve years later, the Senate Internal Security Subcommittee included Lamont's name in its list of the eighty-two most active and typical sponsors of Communist front organizations.

There is no public evidence that Lamont has ever been formally inducted into the Communist Party. But it would be much easier to enumerate the Communist causes and enterprises and Communist fronts which he has not supported than to detail a blow-by-blow account of his fellow traveling career during the past three and a half decades.

What is of especial interest, however, is that Lamont — while he was habitually in close association with Communists — was a director of the American Civil Liberties Union from 1932 until 1954. He has been vice chairman of the Emergency Civil Liberties Committee and a member of the National Association for the Advancement of Colored People, the American Humanist Association, the American Association for the United Nations, and the Foreign Policy Association. It is difficult not to imagine that, in Lamont's opinion, this latter group of organizations (ACLU, ECLC, NAACP, AHA, AAUN, and FPA) serves his ambition to advance the same types of causes and attain the same sort of objectives as the myriad of Communist fronts which he has supported down through the years.

MILLARD LAMPELL was born on January 10, 1919 in Paterson, New Jersey, son of Bertha Unger and Charles Lampell. He married Elizabeth Whipple. He is an alumnus of the University of West Virginia (B.S., 1940).

In 1940 and 1941, Lampell was with the folk-singing group, the Almanac Singers, which he helped to form in company with the notorious Communists, the late Woody Guthrie and Pete Seeger. In 1941, he began a career writing scripts for radio. His work included scripts for Station WMCA and the U.S. Navy, Columbia Broadcasting System's program "Green Valley, U.S.A.," the National Safety Council's program "Men, Machines, and Victory," the Prudential Insurance Company's "Family Hour," various programs for the U.S. Army Air Corps, the U.S. Steel Corporation's program "Theater Guild of the Air," and several programs for the United Nations on the networks of the National Broadcasting Company and the American Broadcasting Company.

Lampell's other work has included two cantatas ("The Lonesome Train" and "Morning Star"), a novel (*The Hero*), films ("Chance Meeting," "The Idol," "The Whistle," "The Victims," and "A Walk in the Sun"), and many plays including "The Inheritance," "The Wall," "Jacob and the Angel," and "Hard Travelin' " (part of which was presented at the 1966 White House Festival of the Arts).

In 1964, Lampell wrote "No Hiding Place" for David Susskind's television series *East Side, West Side*. For that effort, Lampell received the leftwing Sidney Hillman and Anti-Defamation League awards. In 1965, he wrote "Eagle in a Cage" for Hallmark's Hall of Fame television series. For that drama, Lampell received an Emmy Award.

At the 1966 Emmy presentation ceremonies, Lampell stunned the audience when he remarked: "I think I ought to mention that I was blacklisted for ten years."

Shortly thereafter, in a full-page article for the *New York Times* (August 21, 1966), Lampell explained what he meant by his statement: "By 1950, I had been a professional writer for eight years, including the time spent as a sergeant in the Air Force . . . . I had published poems, songs and short stories, written a novel and adapted it as a motion picture, authored a respectable number of films, radio plays and television dramas, collected various awards . . . . Then, quietly, mysteriously and almost overnight, the job offers stopped coming . . . . It was about three months before my agent called me in, locked her door, and announced in a tragic whisper, 'You're on the list.' It seemed that there was a list of writers, actors, directors, set designers, and even trapeze artists, choreographers and clowns who were suspected of Communist leanings and marked by all the film studios, networks and advertising agencies as unemployable . . . . What made it all so cryptic was the lack of accusations or charges."

Lampell claimed that, in the next few years, he was forced to resort to a pseudonym in order to get his work produced. He wrote "a few radio broadcasts for the Government of Israel, an educational film for the Government of Puerto Rico, a few scripts for benefits given by charitable organizations." But, as time went on, work became more and more available and throughout the latter half of the 1950's Lampell kept busy writing under his pseudonym. And, in 1962, his name appeared on a film for a major Hollywood studio. Then, in 1964, he was finally rehabilitated from the alleged blacklist by David Susskind.

Along the way, in 1952, Lampell had appeared before the Senate Internal Security Subcommittee during its investigation of the subversive infiltration of radio, television, and the entertainment industry.

In writing of his appearance before the SISS, Lampell recalled that his pre-1952 career was "haphazardly reported and presented as evidence that I had taken part in a subversive plot to bring riot and ruin to my native land. I was ordered to account for my life and to give the names of everyone I could ever remember having seen at those bygone benefits. Considering privacy of belief to be a constitutional right of all Americans, I refused." (The benefits to which Lampell referred, he earlier described as part of his experience with the Almanac Singers when they performed in the early 1940's at "union meetings and left-wing benefits for Spanish refugees, striking Kentucky coal miners and starving Alabama sharecroppers.")

There is no quarrel with the fact that Lampell made his one and only appearance before a congressional investigating committee in 1952 when he was subpoenaed by the Senate Internal Security Subcommittee. But the SISS displayed no interest in Lampell's experiences at "benefits" with the Almanac Singers.

411

Furthermore, Lampell did not plead his constitutional right of "privacy of belief." Rather, within thirteen pages of testimony, Lampell invoked the Fifth Amendment *eighty* times on grounds that if he answered he might incriminate himself.

By 1952, Lampell had such an extraordinary background of affiliations, that the interest by SISS in his career was not remarkable. Lampell had been affiliated with the Voice of Freedom Committee ("subversive"); Veterans Against Discrimination ("subversive and Communist"); the National Council of the Arts, Sciences and Professions ("a Communist front used to appeal to special occupational groups"); *Mainstream* ("Communist publication"), the China Conference Arrangements Committee ("Communist front"); the Freedom from Fear Committee ("Communist front"); the National Committee to Win the Peace ("subversive" – "Communist"); the United Negro and Allied Veterans of America ("subversive" – "Communist front"); People's Songs, Inc. ("subversive"); the *Daily Worker* ("Communist Party publication"); the Civil Rights Congress ("subversive and Communist"); the Cultural and Scientific Conference for World Peace ("Communist front" – a propaganda front for Soviet foreign policy and "Soviet culture"); the American Labor Party ("Communist political front"); Contemporary Writers ("subversive and Communist"); the People's Institute of Applied Religion ("subversive and Communist"); the Progressive Citizens of America ("political Communist front"); Stage for Action ("subversive"); the Committee to Defend Don West ("Communist front"); the Committee for Free Political Advocacy ("Communist front"); *New Masses* ("Communist periodical); *Masses and Mainstream* ("Communist periodical"); the American Youth Congress ("subversive and Communist"); the American Continental Congress for Peace ("another phase in the Communist 'peace' campaign"); and, the People's Radio Foundation ("subversive and Communist organization").

Lampell was interrogated about many of these specific affiliations when he appeared before the SISS. He was also asked about his participation in the Communists' May Day celebration of 1947, his sponsorship of the Communists' World Youth Festival of 1947, his relationship with such notorious Communists as John Stapp, Jack Stachel, Gregory Duncan, and Ella Reeve Bloor, his activities on behalf of convicted Communists, and his membership and duties within the Communist Party. It was in response to such items that Lampell stubbornly invoked the Fifth Amendment.

In 1956, the Senate Internal Security Subcommittee included Lampell's name in its list of the eighty-two most active and typical sponsors of Communist front organizations. But ten years later when Lampell received his Emmy Award, he speculated: "It seemed that I had at last come in from the cold." And today he has no need of pseudonym, nor has he ever repudiated his Red-lined past.

ARTHUR LARSON was born on July 4, 1910 in Sioux Falls, South Dakota, son of Anna Huseboe and Lewis Larson. He married Florence Newcomb. He is an alumnus of Augustana College (A.B., 1931) and Oxford University of England where he was a Rhodes Scholar (B.A. and M.A. in Jurisprudence, 1935 and 1938, respectively).

From 1935 until 1939, Larson practiced law in Milwaukee. From 1939 until 1941, he was an assistant professor of law at the University of Tennessee. During World War II, he was with the Office of Price Administration and the Foreign Economic Administration. From 1945 until 1953, Larson taught law at Cornell University.

In 1954, Larson joined the Eisenhower Administration as Under Secretary of Labor. While in that job, Larson wrote a book – *A Republican Looks at his Party*. It was not an ordinary book since there were countless reports that President Dwight Eisenhower had actually read it. The book, in effect, was a disavowal of the Republican Party that Americans had known from Lincoln's day down to Robert A. Taft's era. There was a "new Republicanism" with Modern Republicans, best personified by the Eisenhower Administration. The new breed was determined to improve upon and expand the socialist New Deal of Franklin Roosevelt by fusing the insane economics of John Maynard Keynes with the principles of free enterprise. It all added up to a managed economy made more palatable when done by Modern Republicans rather than by Democrats.

Of course, Larson with his book virtually read out of the Republican Party all those in Congress who had labored for years against the encroachment of the federal government upon free enterprise. As Larson described it, the Republican Party represented the "authentic American center" where could be found Adlai Stevenson and Dean Acheson.

The book may not have done much for old guard Republicans but it did a lot for Larson who was promoted to be director of the United States Information Agency. Then, in 1957 and 1958, he was a special assistant to President Eisenhower.

In 1958, Larson became director of the World Rule of Law Center at Duke University. (He did not sever his ties completely with the government. He was a consultant to the State Department throughout the remainder of the Eisenhower Administration and held the same position in the Kennedy Administration. Later in the Kennedy Administration, he was a consultant to the Department of Health, Education and Welfare and, in the Johnson Administration, he became a member of the President's Panel of Distinguished Citizens to Consult on Major International Problems. Larson campaigned for Johnson in 1964.) At the World Rule of Law Center, Larson has worked strenuously and specificially for repeal of the Connolly Reservation so that the World Court can assume jurisdiction over United States domestic affairs.

Larson is an unabashed internationalist, professing implicit faith in the United Nations. He insists that most of the world's problems are merely legal questions and can be decided by impartial jurists such as those found on the UN's World Court. Larson has great faith in the goodwill of the Soviet Union's leaders. In 1961 and again in 1964, in company with a famous ban-the-bomb-boob, Norman Cousins, Larson went to the Soviet Union leading a delegation of American peaceniks to meet with alleged peaceniks of the Soviet Union.

It was also in 1964 that Larson announced the formation of the National Council for Civic Responsibility, with himself as chairman. The genesis of the NCCR can be traced back to 1961 when the ultra-leftist labor leaders Walter and Victor Reuther dictated a memorandum to their friend Attorney General Robert Kennedy. The Reuthers called for Kennedy to bring federal government pressure down upon rightists — that is to say, squelch the conservatives and anti-Communists. The Reuthers suggested that private agencies could be utilized to make the initial attacks upon the radical right (the conservatives and anti-Communists). Within a short time, Group Research Inc. was formed. This outfit began looking for right wingers under the bed, over the bed, and between the covers. It was a pretty awkward operation especially when they discovered that Dwight Eisenhower was a member of the right.

By 1964, the Reuthers and the Democrat Party decided that The John Birch Society and Barry Goldwater's campaign had to be destroyed and so Larson rallied together the NCCR, composed mostly of Democrats. The remainder were Modern Republicans. And the members of Larson's Council among themselves represented just about every Communist front, Communist project, and Communist enterprise of the past thirty or thirty-five years. (*The Worker* was enthusiastic in its editorial praise for the formation of Larson's group.)

Once the presidential elections were over in 1964, the NCCR dwindled out of the spotlight, claiming they lacked funds to carry on their campaign. And Larson, pleading he didn't have time to work for NCCR, went back to his World Center where he could concentrate on selling out American sovereignty to the interests of the one-worlders.

In the past couple of years, Larson has been stumping for disarmament, calling for U.S. diplomatic recognition of Red China, and urging cessation in the bombing of North Vietnam and a U.S. agreement to recognize the right of the Vietcong to attend peace negotiation talks. Larson is constantly wringing his hands over the fact that

the Vietnam question was not given to the United Nations for settlement.

In 1966, Larson joined Franklin Littell's Institute for American Democracy which is taking up the dirty work left incomplete by Larson's NCCR.

Along the way, Larson has been deeply involved in one of the most prestigious organizations in the entire left-wing peace movement — the Peace Research Institute. Larson was a founder and served as president of this outfit which has been financed in great part by its contracts with the U.S. Arms Control and Disarmament Agency, the Department of Health, Education and Welfare, and the Air Force Office of Behavioral Science Research.

Larson is also on the board of sponsors of the monthly *War/Peace Report,* one of the far left publications in the disarmament-peacenik lobby.

JOSEPH P. LASH was born on December 2, 1909 in New York City, son of Mary Avchin and Samuel Lash. He married Trude Wenzel. He is an alumnus of the City College of New York (A.B., 1931) and Columbia University (M.A., 1932).

While a junior in college, Lash joined the Socialist Party in which he became quite active until his resignation in 1937. From 1933 until 1935, he worked for the socialist League for Industrial Democracy. From 1935 until 1939, he was executive secretary of the American Student Union which was formed in 1935 in Columbus, Ohio when young Socialists and Communists joined in a united front. In 1940, he became general secretary of the International Student Service — a move which Lash claimed was an effort on his part to create an anti-Communistic youth movement.

In 1939, Lash became somewhat of a

national celebrity when he testified before the Special Committee on Un-American Activities (Dies Committee). His activities with the Communist-dominated American Student Union and American Youth Congress had been well publicized. He had attended "two or three" board meetings of the Young Communist League. He had gone to Spain to support the Reds in the Civil War. (He did no fighting there but instead lectured to "youth" groups.) He had been affiliated with the American League against War and Fascism ("subversive and Communist"); the American League for Peace and Democracy ("subversive and Communist"); *Champion* magazine ("Communist publication"); the North American Committee to Aid Spanish Democracy ("Communist"); *New Masses* magazine ("Communist periodical"); and, Veterans of the Abraham Lincoln Brigade ("subversive and Communist").

At the Dies Committee hearings, Lash and his fellow fronters proved to be uncooperative and hostile witnesses as they did their best to disrupt the hearings. Lash, especially, was brazen in his conduct – an attitude explainable in great part because he was a dear protégé of Eleanor Roosevelt. While Lash and his colleagues performed their juvenile antics at the hearings, the President's wife sat chortling in appreciation of their obstreperous conduct. And while the hearings were in progress, Lash lived at the White House and was driven to the hearing room in a presidential automobile.

In 1942, Lash made a second appearance before the Dies Committee, at his own request. He attempted – and with some success – to convince the Committee that he had renounced his Communist friends and was now engaged in the International Student Service "to break the influence of the Communists over American young people." At the same time, Lash told the Committee quite bluntly that he would not divulge information about individuals he had met during his united front days. Lash was allowed to do this – it was not the Committee's finest hour.

During the course of Lash's testimony, he mentioned that he had applied for a commission with Naval Intelligence but he surmised that it had not been forthcoming because of his earlier ties with the American Student Union and the American Youth Congress. (Later, Lash did become a second lieutenant in the U.S. Army. A visit to Lash on Guadalcanal during World War II by Eleanor Roosevelt, garbed in a Red Cross uniform, brought unfavorable publicity to these dear friends.)

After World War II, Lash became a director for Americans for Democratic Action, the center of the radical left in American politics. He left this position in 1949 and, in 1950, he joined the leftwing *New York Post* as a United Nations correspondent. From 1961 until 1966, he was assistant editor of the *Post's* editorial page. Since 1966, he has been a free lance writer.

In 1961, Lash wrote an adulatory study, *Dag Hammarskjöld: Custodian of the Brushfire Peace.* And, in 1965, he memorialized an old friendship with *Eleanor Roosevelt: A Friend's Memoir.* At the present time, he is preparing a "definitive" biography of Mrs. Roosevelt, at the request of her family.

OWEN LATTIMORE was born on July 29, 1900 in Washington, D.C., son of Margaret Barnes and David Lattimore. He married Eleanor Holgate.

From 1920 until 1937, Lattimore

spent most of his time in the Far East, in business, and writing and traveling. He also did research work and was financed by the Social Science Research Council, the Harvard-Yenching Institute, the Guggenheim Foundation, and the Institute of Pacific Relations. From 1934 until 1941, he was editor of *Pacific Affairs,* a publication of the Institute of Pacific Relations in which Lattimore held membership. In 1952, after more than a year and a half of study, investigations, and hearings, the Senate Internal Security Subcommittee concluded that the IPR was "considered by the American Communist Party and by Soviet officials as an instrument of Communist policy, propaganda and military intelligence ... [and the IPR] disseminated and sought to popularize false information including information originating from Soviet and Communist sources."

In 1938, while still with *Pacific Affairs,* Lattimore joined the faculty of The Johns Hopkins University, and he remained on the faculty until 1963. From 1939 until 1953, he was director of the Walter Hines Page School of International Relations at Johns Hopkins. During World War II, Lattimore was deputy director for Pacific Operations in Elmer Davis' rosy red Office of War Information. Over the years, Lattimore had written a considerable number of books on the Far East, particularly dealing with Manchuria, China, Mongolia, and Turkestan.

In 1950, Lattimore ran up against the late Senator Joseph R. McCarthy. McCarthy had charged that Lattimore was a top Soviet spy. The charge was heard in a whitewash committee under the chairmanship of Senator Millard Tydings (D.-Md.). The Tydings hearings turned out to be a love-feast with Lattimore as the guest of honor.

But, in 1952, Lattimore was a witness before the Senate Internal Security Subcommittee which was investigating the IPR. When Lattimore was through testifying, the Subcommittee reported that Lattimore "was from some time in the middle 1930's a conscious, articulate instrument of the Soviet conspiracy." In its Report, the Subcommittee went into detail on Lattimore's pro-Communist activities in the IPR, in the pages of *Pacific Affairs,* and in State Department circles where Lattimore had considerable influence. The SISS recalled testimony of former Communist Louis Budenz who swore to five separate personal experiences within the Politburo of the Communist Party in the United States when Lattimore was involved as a full participant in the Soviet conspiracy. The SISS also recommended that the Justice Department take grand jury action on questions of perjured testimony given by Lattimore. A jury indicted Lattimore on seven charges. Through a strange chain of circumstances, Lattimore was never tried in open court before a jury of any of the perjury charges. And he returned to his faculty position at Johns Hopkins.

In 1961, Lattimore was back in the news. The Soviet Union was driving to get Outer Mongolia — one of the very first Soviet satellites — admitted to the United Nations. The main opposition to this maneuver was coming from Nationalist China. Then Lattimore took a trip to Outer Mongolia and upon his return talked in private to officials in the State Department. The Kennedy Administration decided to make a deal.

Mauritania — a new African nation — was seeking admission to the UN, a move that the Kennedy Administration supported as part of its "emerging nations" policy. The Soviet Union threatened to block Mauritanian membership unless

Outer Mongolia was let into the UN. The Kennedy Administration submitted to the Communist blackmail, applied pressure on Nationalist China to refrain from its opposition, and Outer Mongolia was admitted to the UN.

In 1963, Lattimore resigned from Johns Hopkins and went to England where he joined the faculty of Leeds University as head of a Chinese studies department. In 1965, he sponsored the Society for Anglo-[Red] Chinese Understanding, which was the brain-child of Dr. Joseph Needham, a biochemist, who gained world-wide notoriety by charging that Americans had waged germ warfare in Korea.

In 1967, Lattimore was a major speaker at the Third Annual Conference of Socialist Scholars in New York City. He was back on the familiar red line, calling the Chinese Communist Party "nationalistically patriotic."

EMIL LENGYEL was born on April 26, 1895 in Budapest, Hungary, son of Joan Adam and Joseph Lengyel. He married Livia Delej. He is an alumnus of the Royal Hungarian University (Utriusque Iuris Doctor, 1919).

During World War I, Lengyel served in the Austro-Hungarian Army and was a prisoner of war in Siberia for twenty months. After World War I and after completing his university studies, he began a career in journalism and wrote for newspapers in Budapest and Vienna. In 1921, he came to the United States and, until 1930, he was a United States correspondent for European newspapers. During this period, he became an American citizen.

In 1931, Lengyel began his prolific career of writing books. And he is the author or co-author of at least two dozen works in addition to countless pamphlets, book reviews, newspaper feature pieces, and articles in magazines and learned journals. Subject matter of Lengyel's writings has included Germany of the Nazi era, the Soviet Union, India, the Middle East, Central Europe, Africa, and Israel.

From 1935 until 1942, Lengyel was an adjunct professor of history and economics at Brooklyn Polytechnic Institute. Meanwhile, in 1939, he joined New York University's faculty as a staff lecturer in history and, until 1960, he served, successively, at NYU as assistant professor, associate professor, professor, and professor emeritus. In 1960, he became professor of history at Fairleigh Dickenson University. Since 1963, he has been chairman of FD's social science department. While at NYU, Lengyel lectured to U.S. armed forces during World War II, and also lectured from 1950 until 1955 at the New School for Social Research. From 1942 until 1954, he was a correspondent for *The Star Weekly* of Toronto, Canada. And, he has been a book reviewer for *Saturday Review* magazine.

Lengyel has been affiliated with the American Committee for Democracy and Intellectual Freedom ("Communist front" – "subversive and un-American"); the American Committee for Protection of Foreign Born [Americans] ("subversive and Communist" – "one of the oldest auxiliaries of the Communist Party in the United States" – under the "complete domination" of the Communist Party); the American Committee to Save Refugees ("Communist enterprise"); the Joint Anti-Fascist Refugee Committee ("subversive and Communist"); American Friends of Spanish Democracy ("subversive"); the American Council on Soviet Relations ("established by Communist Party"); the Coordination Committee to Lift the [Spanish] Embargo ("Communist front"); the American-Russian Institute ("subversive" – "Communist" – "specializing in pro-Soviet propaganda"); the American Slav Congress ("subversive and Communist"); the Greater New York Emergency Conference on Inalienable Rights ("Communist front"); the League of American Writers ("subversive and Communist"); the North American Committee to Aid Spanish Democracy ("Communist"); the National Council of American-Soviet Friendship ("subversive and Communist" – "specializing in pro-Soviet propaganda"); the National Federation for Constitutional Liberties ("subversive and Communist" – "under [Communist] Party domination and headed by responsible Party functionaries"); the National Council of the Arts, Sciences and Professions ("a Communist front used to appeal to special occupational groups"); *Soviet Russia Today* ("Communist front publication"); *Equality* ("a Communist Party enterprise"); *New Masses* ("Communist periodical"); and, the Reichstag Fire Trial Anniversary Committee ("Communist front").

As well as his extensive front activity and his participation in Communist projects, Lengyel's writings have been consistently pro-Communist in content. His bibliographical references are replete with Communist and/or pro-Communist sources. He is unmistakably an apologist for the Soviet Union and an idolatrous biographer of Krishna Menon, the notorious anti-American, pro-Communist Indian leader.

When Vera Micheles Dean, the notorious fellow traveler, was the Foreign Policy Association's research director and editor, she was especially ardent in promoting Lengyel's leftwing writings in the FPA's Headline Series of pamphlets, particularly through the Great Decisions programs that have become so widespread and popular among would-be culture seekers in the past decade.

SIDNEY LENS was born on January 28, 1912 in Newark, New Jersey. His real name is Sidney Okun and, while testifying under oath on February 15, 1965 before the Senate Internal Security Subcommittee, said that he could not remember if he had ever changed his name legally. Lens-Okun married Shirley Ruben.

Since 1941, Lens-Okun has been director of Local 329, of the United Service Employees Union, AFL-CIO. He has been a faculty member at Columbia College of Chicago, and has lectured on foreign affairs and labor at the University of Chicago, Roosevelt University, and De Paul University. He has been an unsuccessful candidate for election to the Illinois legislature and to the United States House of Representatives. He has been a member of the board of directors of the Chicago Council for Foreign Relations.

Lens-Okun's pro-Marxism-Leninism is evident in his writings which include *Left, Right and Center; The Counterfeit Revolution; A World in Revolution; The Crisis of American Labor; Working Men; Africa – Awakening Giant; The Futile Crusade;* and *A Country is Born.* He has also written for newspapers, syndicates, and such magazines as *Commonweal* and *Harvard Business Review.* He is editor of *Liberation* magazine, the masthead of which features a representative list of pacifists, Socialists, "civil rights" agitators, and notorious Communist-fronters, including Dorothy Day, Waldo Frank, Bayard Rustin, Lewis Mumford, Staughton Lynd, Michael Harrington, James

Peck, and Martin Luther King Jr.

Lens-Okun's activities as an original sponsor of the Castro-subsidized Fair Play for Cuba Committee caused the Senate Internal Security Subcommittee to call him as a witness. Lens-Okun invoked the protection of the first and fifth amendments to the Constitution when asked whether he had been a member of the Revolutionary Workers League ("subversive and Communist") from the mid-1930's until late 1947. He declined to answer when asked if he had ever been a Trotskyite or a member of any splinter group of Trotsky-ites. He did admit to having held offi-cial positions in the now defunct American Forum for Socialist Educa-tion. He did admit writing a pamphlet for the Mine, Mill and Smelters Union, ten years after that union was expelled from the C.I.O. for being dominated by Communists. He did admit to signing an appeal to the 86th Congress, calling for the United States to abandon uni-laterally all nuclear weapons tests, calling for admission of Red China to the United Nations, and calling for all U.S. foreign aid to be channeled through agencies of the United Nations. He did admit that he had petitioned at various times for amnesty for Commu-nist Party leaders who were convicted under the Smith Act; for the convicted Communist spy, Morton Sobell; and, for Communists Henry Winston and Gil Green.

Lens-Okun has been a sponsor of the National Committee to Abolish the House Un-American Activities Commit-tee ("to lead and direct the Communist Party's 'Operation Abolition' cam-paign"). In 1965, he was a prominent supporter of the anti-Vietnam "teach-in" movement, which the Communist propaganda apparatus exploited for purely Communist purposes. In 1966, he was a member of the national coun-cil of the Committee for Independent Political Action, and a main speaker at the CIPA's Chicago conference. The CIPA has as its objective the formation of a new political party, and the Chica-go conference was attended by radical pacifists, violent racists, representatives of the so-called "new left," and known members of the Communist Party.

MAX LERNER was born on Decem-ber 20, 1902 in Minsk, Russia, son of Bessie Podel and Benjamin Lerner. He came to the United States when he was five years old. He was married to, and divorced from, Anita Marburg. He later married Edna Albers. He is an alumnus of Yale University (A.B., 1923), Wash-ington University of St. Louis (A.M., 1925), and the Robert Brookings Graduate School of Economics and Government in Washington, D.C. (Ph.D., 1927). He also studied law, in 1923 and 1924, at Yale University.

In 1927, Lerner was an assistant edi-tor of the Encyclopedia of the Social Sciences. Later he was managing editor. From 1932 until 1935, he was on the social science faculty at Sarah Lawrence College. From 1933 until 1935, he was faculty chairman at the Wellesley College Summer Institute. From 1935 until 1938, he was a lecturer in the department of government at Harvard University, and a professor of govern-ment, from 1939 until 1941, at the Harvard Summer School. From 1936 until 1938, he was an editor of *The Nation* magazine. From 1938 until 1943, he was a professor of political science at Williams College. From 1943 until 1948, he was a radio commenta-tor and editorial director for the daily *PM*. In 1948 and 1949, he was a columnist for the *New York Star* and, since 1949, has been a syndicated columnist for the *New York Post*. Since 1949, he has been a professor of American Civilization at Brandeis University, where he also served, from 1954 until 1956, as dean of the Graduate School. In 1959 and 1960, he was a Ford Foundation professor of American Civilization at the school for international studies at the University of Delhi in India.

Among Lerner's better known books are *The Mind and Faith of Justice Holmes; America as a Civilization; The Age of Overkill;* and *Education and a Radical Humanism.*

Lerner has been affiliated with Allied Voters against Coudert ("Communist front"); the American Committee for Anti-Nazi German Seamen ("Communist front"); the American Committee for Democracy and Intellectual Freedom ("Communist front" – subversive and un-American"); the American Committee for Protection of Foreign Born [Americans] ("Subversive and Communist" – "one of the oldest auxiliaries of the Communist Party in the United States" – under the "complete domination" of the Communist Party); the American Council on Soviet Relations ("established by Communist Party"); the American Friends of Spanish Democracy ("subversive"); American Investors Union ("Communist front"); the American League for Peace and Democracy ("subversive and Communist"); the American Student Union ("Communist front"); the California Labor School ("a subversive and Communist organization"); the Citizens Committee for Harry Bridges ("Communist"); the citizens Committee to Free Earl Browder ("Communist"); the Council for Pan-American Democracy

("subversive and Communist"); Frontier Films ("Communist front"); the Harry Bridges Defense Committee ("Communist front"); the Independent Citizens Committee of the Arts, Sciences and Professions ("Communist front"); the League of American Writers ("subversive and Communist"); the Michigan Civil Rights Federation ("a subversive and Communist organization"); the National Citizens Political Action Committee ("Communist front"); the National Emergency Conference ("Communist front"); the National Emergency Conference for Democratic Rights ("Communist front"); the National Federation for Constitutional Liberties ("under [Communist] Party domination and headed by responsible Party functionaries"); *New Masses* ("Communist periodical"); the Non-Partisan Committee for the Re-election of Congressman Vito Marcantonio ("Communist front"); and, *Soviet Russia Today* ("Communist front publication"). Lerner has also been a frequent signer of petitions which were Communist enterprises.

Lerner has been on the national board of Americans for Democratic Action, the center of the radical left in American politics; on the national board of the American Civil Liberties Union, that motleyed collection of defenders of subversion, crime, and licentiousness; and, has been affiliated with the League for Industrial Democracy and the Student League for Industrial Democracy, both socialist.

In recent years, Lerner has apparently veered away from participation in Communist fronts and enterprises. But his radical views are presented with unbroken regularity in his syndicated column and in his frequent appearances before collegiate audiences across the country. One of the most brazen pro-Soviet Union statements he has ever made concerned his attitude toward the Vietnam War. Writing in his syndicated column, Lerner said: "The American problem is not to end the [Vietnamese] war but to end it so that Russia, rather than [Communist] China, emerges as the force in North Vietnam and the surrounding area. That is complex but war is complex because life is." This consignment of more than eleven millions of people to an existence in a Soviet satellite, complete with famines, concentration camps, broken families, terrorism, purges, and religious persecution is nothing less than an all-time low of callousness in American journalism.

SOL M. LINOWITZ was born on December 7, 1913 in Trenton, New Jersey, son of Rose Oglenskye and Joseph Linowitz. He married Evelyn Zimmerman. He is an alumnus of Hamilton College (A.B., 1935) and Cornell University (LL.B., 1938).

In 1938, he began practicing law in Rochester, New York. From 1942 until 1944, he was assistant general counsel to the Office of Price Administration. In 1946, he joined the Xerox Corporation, eventually becoming chairman of the board.

In 1966, Linowitz was named by President Johnson to be United States Representative, with the rank of Ambassador, to the Organization of American States. In that same year, Senator Robert F. Kennedy of New York had tried and failed to promote Linowitz as the Democratic candidate for governor of New York. Linowitz has been a close friend of the Kennedy dynasty, especially Senator Robert, Mrs. John F. Kennedy, and Sargent Shriver. Other

close friends of Linowitz include Hubert Humphrey, David Rockefeller, Lyndon Johnson, and UN Secretary General U Thant.

Linowitz, away from his business responsibilities, has been vice-chairman of the trustees of the John F. Kennedy Center which is being developed in Washington. He has been an ardent promoter of the United Nations through his work as an officer of the leftwing American Association for the United Nations. As head of Xerox, he sponsored a series of television programs glorifying the United Nations in 1964. The programs were such awkwardly and blatantly leftwing propaganda pieces that even television critics, who normally praised such presentations, couldn't refrain from panning them. After the first such program, however, *People's World* – the Communist daily on the west coast, said of the Xerox presentation: "A sermon on humanity and its responsibilities is precisely what is necessary. It's not a little horrifying that in our country at this time a pitch is needed for the United Nations and for peace but that is the case, and we're all for figuratively hitting people over the head with the message. The program did that."

Linowitz ingratiated himself with Lyndon Johnson by supporting the Administration's foreign aid program as well as Johnson's "building bridges of trade to the East" obsession. And when Linowitz was appointed Ambassador to the OAS, he had absolutely no diplomatic experience. But Linowitz had the liberal jargon at the tip of his tongue and was ready to export socialism to Latin America through the "Alliance for Progress" program instituted in the Kennedy Administration.

In 1967, at the Overseas Press Club

in New York, Linowitz posed a question: "What should our attitude then be if and when a democratic government in the hemisphere is occasionally overthrown by force?" And Linowitz answered his own question: "Obviously, nothing is more crucial to the success of the Alliance [for Progress] than courageous and progressive political leadership in the nations striving for modernization. It is not going too far to say that the Alliance will stand or fall on the capacity of the progressive democratic governments, parties and leaders of Latin America."

South of the border, the leftwingers know enough to interpret Linowitz' support of "progressive democratic governments" as encouragement for red hot socialists (Marxist or otherwise) to take over any non-socialist regime, especially an anti-Communist regime led by the military.

WALTER LIPPMANN was born on September 23, 1889 in New York City, son of Daisy Baum and Jacob Lippmann. His first wife was Faye Albertson. He is married to Helen Armstrong, He is an alumnus of Harvard University (A.B., 1909).

During World War I, he was an assistant to the Secretary of War. During the course of the post-War peace conferences and negotiations, he was secretary to the Woodrow Wilson-Edward M. House "Inquiry."

Lippmann has written about twenty-five books; the best known include *A Preface to Politics* (1913), *A Preface to Morals* (1929), and *The Public Philosophy* (1955).

In his early years of journalism, he was an editor with *New Republic* magazine and the *New York World*. He was one of the first syndicated daily columnists in America and for most of his career wrote for the *New York Herald-Tribune*. In recent years, he has been a regular columnist for *Newsweek* magazine.

In his college days, Lippmann was president of Harvard's Socialist Club and he was one of the earliest members of the Intercollegiate Socialist Society which changed its name to the League for Industrial Democracy and to which Lippmann belonged.

The most important fact about Lippmann which seems to be obscured whenever he is discussed by friend or foe is that he has been throughout his adult life a dedicated and active Fabian Socialist. Admittedly, there can be pinpointed throughout his career instances and even long periods when any one of the three traditional labels of political position — conservative, moderate, liberal — could serve as an accurate characterization of his ideology. Equally true, there have been countless times when Lippmann was so confused that no single label or even a combination of labels could be applied to him. The *Herald Tribune,* when Lippmann was its star performer, used to advertise him as the "Clarifier" — nothing could have been more inappropriate. In the complete context of his entire life's output of punditry, Lippmann has been the Grand Confuser — on men, on events, on principles which were the objects of his analysis, his criticism, his praise, his scorn whether in his books, his columns, or his public utterances. He has been a model of inconsistency, contradiction, ambiguity, and eccentricity. Yet, he has been taken seriously as an erudite, objective observer by world and national leaders. He has been the confidant and adviser of the high and mighty, in and out of government, and throughout most of the fourth estate he has been regarded as Superman.

As befits a Fabian Socialist, Lippmann is a fanatical internationalist who dismisses with a sneer any and all who consider the freedom and sovereignty of civilized peoples' nations incompatible with the Communist world conspiracy. And he is just as intolerant with those who see the dangers to American security from Communist subversion or who see the impossibility of retaining the American constitutional republic when its entire political, economic, and social structure is interlaced vertically, horizontally, and diagonally with socialism.

FRANKLIN LITTELL was born on June 20, 1917 in Syracuse, New York, son of Lena Hamlin and Clair Littell. He married Harriet Lewis. He is an alumnus of Cornell College (B.A., 1937), Union Theological Seminary (B.D., 1940), and Yale University (Ph.D., 1946).

From 1940 until 1942, Littell was minister of youth at Central Methodist Church in Detroit. From 1944 until 1949, he was director of Lane Hall at the University of Michigan. In 1948 and 1949, he lectured at McCormick Theological Seminary.

From 1951 until 1953, Littell was dean of chapel at Boston University. From 1953 until 1958, he was senior representative at the Franz Lieher Foundation. From 1958 until 1960, he taught church history in the Candler School of Theology at Emory University. From 1960 until 1962, he taught history at the Perkins School of Theology at Southern Methodist University.

In 1962, he became a professor of church history at the Chicago Theological Seminary. More recently, Littell has been president of Iowa Wesleyan College.

Littell signed a statement of the University of Michigan Academic Freedom Committee, condemning attacks on academic freedom and on the organization known as American Youth for Democracy. The statement was contained in a leaflet published by the American Youth for Democracy entitled "Facts on the Current Widespread Campaign Against Academic Freedom" and released February, 1947.

On March 29, 1944, a Special Committee on Un-American Activities of the House of Representatives cited American Youth for Democracy as the new name under which the Young Communist League operated and which also largely absorbed the American Youth Congress. According to U.S. Attorney General Francis Biddle, the American Youth Congress had "originated in 1934 and . . . has been controlled by Communists and manipulated by them to influence the thought of American youth."

A letterhead of the Methodist Federation for Social Action, dated April 12, 1946, listed Franklin H. Littell as a member of the Executive Committee of the organization. He was nominated for Member-at-large on the ballots of the Methodist Federation for Social Action in 1945 and 1947 elections of the organization.

In 1956, the Senate Internal Security Subcommittee said: "With an eye to religious groups, the Communists have formed religious fronts such as the Methodist Federation for Social Action."

On January 13, 1953, the Communists' *Daily Worker* carried a list of clergymen who were petitioning for clemency on behalf of the convicted spies Julius and Ethel Rosenberg. Dr. Littell's name was among the signatories, who included such warhorses of the radical left as Rev. Harry Ward, Rev. Willard Uphaus, Rev. Stephen Fritchman, Rev. Abraham J. Muste, Rev. Donald Harrington, and Rev. Dana McLean Greeley.

In July of 1953, Benjamin Gitlow, former general secretary of the Communist Party, gave testimony before the House Committee on Un-American Activities concerning three articles written by Franklin H. Littell in the February, March, and April, 1945 issues of the *Social Questions Bulletin,* the official publication of the Methodist Federation for Social Action. The articles were entitled "A Cell in Every Church," "Protestantism is a 'Success,' " and "Formation of the Group." Mr. Gitlow's analysis of these articles included these comments: "Mr. Littell's organizational proposals on the infiltration of religion follow closely the cell techniques on infiltration described in the thesis on organization of both the Communist Party and the Communist International. In his second article, 'Protestantism is a "Success" ' − note, success in quotation marks − his views put him in favor of planned economy and in the camp of the Communists who like to call themselves liberals . . . .

"To carry out aggressively and boldly a program to win support among church people for a system of planned economy and to build up opposition to the American economic system, Littell strongly advocates the cell concept of organization, developed by the Communists, as the most important element in the formation of the group . . . .

"The driving force of the Methodist Federation for Social Action, is the small cell that knows where it is going, that is disciplined and the driving force in the organization. The record will show that the cell in the federation consistently follows the Communist Party line. Mr. Littell describes the cell as follows:

" 'The cell is a face-to-face group without turnover in membership.' He elaborates: 'This working unit in our time is usually called "the cell," a term describing a living thing which subdivides and becomes a whole body.'

"That is precisely the theory behind the Communist strategy of infiltration, the Communist cell to eventually become the whole body, the dominant force in the organizations, institutions infiltrated. That Mr. Littell knows he is writing about the Communist concept of organization is clear from the following words of his article, 'A Cell in Every Church': 'There are some progressive movements today which have rediscovered the importance of keeping the basic unit small if much is to happen.'

"The only so-called progressive movements that are consciously built on the cell concept of organization is the Communist Party, the Communist-front organizations and the trade unions and other organizations in which the Communist cells have gained control."

This testimony of Benjamin Gitlow can be found in the HCUA hearing, entitled "Investigation of Communist Activities in the New York City Area − Part 6," July 7, 1953, pp. 2120-2121.

In November, 1966, Littell announced the formation of the Institute for American Democracy, with himself as chairman. He said at that time that the institute "grows out of the concern of informed Americans over the rising volume of extremist activity, particularly by organizations in the John Birch Society orbit."

In reality, Littell's IAD was nothing less than a revival of Arthur Larson's National Council for Civic Responsibility of 1964 and 1965. The NCCR had been formed in response to Walter and Victor Reuther's dictates to have the federal government squelch conservatives and anti-Communists. The Reuthers suggested that private agencies could be utilized to make the initial attacks upon the "radical right." Within a short time, Group Research Inc. was formed. It was utilized by Larson's outfit to collect names and records of conservatives and anti-Communists. Among others Group Research uncovered was Dwight Eisenhower.

In 1964, the Reuthers and the Democrat Party decided to muddy the water of that year's presidential campaign and destroy The John Birch Society once and for all time. It was then that Larson organized the NCCR, composed mostly of Democrats, with a few Modern Republicans and some nondescript characters thrown in for good measure. The NCCR represented just about every Communist front, Communist project, and Communist enterprise of the past thirty or thirty-five years.

Once the presidential elections of 1964 were over, the NCCR faded out of sight, claiming a lack of funds. Larson said that he couldn't spare the time to work for NCCR, and he went back to his World Rule of Law Center at Duke University.

Littell, in 1966, gathered together the same sort of people that Larson had in 1964. Even Larson was an original member of IAD, along with Dore Schary; Roy Wilkins; Walter Reuther; Senators Clifford Case, Gale McGee, and Frank Moss; Marion Folsom; Francis Biddle; Thurmond Arnold; James Patton; Jacob Potofsky; John C. Bennett; George C. Lodge; Harry Ashmore; Ralph McGill; Hodding Carter; and, Louis Untermeyer. All in all, Littell was able to amass an elite representative group of the leftists who had specialized in anti-anti-Communist activities and utterances.

Unsurprisingly, Littell's intelligence agency is, of course, Group Research Inc. as a facade, Littell does also claim to be concerned with the far left – he did mention the Communists. But since IAD was formed, its vilification has been reserved for anti-Communists.

HENRY CABOT LODGE was born on July 5, 1902 in Nahant, Massachusetts, son of Mathilda Davis and George Lodge. He married Emily Sears. He is an alumnus of Harvard University (A.B., 1924).

From 1933 until 1936, Lodge was a legislator in Massachusetts. He was in the U.S. Senate from 1936 until 1943 and from 1947 until 1953.

In 1952, Lodge was campaign manager for Dwight Eisenhower. From 1953 until 1960, he was U.S. Ambassador to the United Nations. In 1960, he was the Republican party's nominee for vice president, and he proved to be nothing but an anchor around presidential candidate Richard Nixon's neck.

In 1961, he was a general consultant to *Time, Life,* and *Fortune* magazines. In 1961 and 1962, he was director-general of The Atlantic Institute, an internationalist organization formed to coordinate U.S. economic policies with Canada and the socialist and other nations of Western Europe.

In 1963 and 1964, Lodge was U.S. Ambassador to South Vietnam. He rushed home in 1964 to make an attempt to get the Republican party's presidential nomination but this try failed miserably. He returned to that post in 1965 and remained there until 1967.

Lodge has been a non-resident member of the Council on Foreign Relations, the informal supra-State Department of the United States. He has been an official of the soft-on-Communism

425

Foreign Policy Association, and an official of The Atlantic Council of the United States.

In the pre-World War II days in the Senate, Lodge was pretty much of a New Dealer on domestic issues but voted on foreign policy with some regularity with the Republican leadership. However, after World War II, Lodge became a full blown internationalist and a welfare-stater on domestic issues. He was a leader of the dirty fight against the Robert A. Taft forces in the 1952 presidential campaign. Lodge, in 1951, had somehow discovered that Dwight Eisenhower was a Republican — much to the surprise of most veteran Republican leaders and certainly a surprise to Eisenhower. Then Lodge became the leader of the phony "draft Eisenhower" movement for the presidency. Once Lodge had sold the "draft" bill of goods to the press and public, he became a leader of the Eisenhower campaign. In 1952, however, Lodge was not re-elected to the Senate from Massachusetts — an extraordinary development for a three-term Senator anywhere. Lodge's reward for his anti-Taft, pro-Eisenhower machinations was the U.S. Ambassadorship to the United Nations.

For eight years, Lodge regaled television audiences and tourists at the UN with blustery oratory which he directed against the Communists. But it was only oratory and in his eight-year tenure, the Communists ignored Lodge's papier-mâché thunderbolts and ran the United Nations as if it were the Kremlin's annex. Along the way, Lodge took time out from his UN duties to be a leader in the "get-Joe McCarthy" cabal. Lodge was disturbed that McCarthy was uncovering too many unsavory characters in government.

Lodge more than once has proved himself to be a staunch anti-anti-Communist. In the United Nations, he always ridiculed the idea that Communists and fellow travelers might use their jobs in the United Nations to do anything harmful to the United States. And when the Danish diplomat Povl Bang-Jensen heard testimony from Hungarian refugees that Communists were in the UN Secretariat and U.S. intelligence agencies, Lodge supported Secretary General Dag Hammarsköld in railroading Bang-Jensen out of the UN. Bang-Jensen would then die in the usual manner of Soviet victims.

Lodge was perhaps most obvious in his soft-on-Communism attitude when he chaperoned the Soviet butcher Nikita Khrushchev around the United States in 1959. Millions of Americans were treated to the spectacle of a smiling Khrushchev upbraiding anything and everything American while a grinning Lodge stood by his side.

Lodge's first ambassadorial mission to South Vietnam coincided with the assassination of Ngo dinh Diem, the President of South Vietnam. The President, who had been the product and pride of the U.S. Liberal Establishment, had outlived his usefulness. The complete and true circumstances surrounding his assassination are still hidden in the recesses of the CIA files and Lodge's memory. But enough of the story has been revealed to show that Lodge shed no tears at Diem's fate.

Throughout both of his missions to South Vietnam, Lodge was an echo of the misleading optimism which the Kennedy-Rusk-Johnson-McNamara team perpetuated as to the progress of that eternal Vietnam War.

JAMES LOEB was born on August 18, 1908 in Chicago, son of Viola Klein and James Loeb. He married Ellen Katz. He is an alumnus of Dartmouth College (A.B., 1929) and Northwestern University (M.A., 1931; Ph.D., 1936).

From 1930 until 1936, he taught Romance languages at Northwestern University. From 1937 until 1941, he taught Romance languages in a New York City high school.

In 1945, Loeb became a national director of the Union for Democratic Action. When that Red-lined outfit dissolved in 1947, Loeb became a founder and national director of Americans for Democratic Action. In 1951 and 1952, he was a consultant on the White House staff and, also in 1952, he was executive assistant to Averell Harriman who was, at that time, in the foreign aid program.

In 1953, Loeb became the editor and co-publisher of the *Adirondack Daily Enterprise* of Saranac Lake, New York. He became co-publisher of the *Lake Placid* [N.Y.] *News* in 1960.

In the Kennedy Administration, Loeb was U.S. Ambassador to Peru and to Guinea.

HELEN MERRELL LYND was born in 1896 in La Grange, Illinois, daughter of Mabel Waite and Edward Merrell. She married Robert S. Lynd. She is an alumna of Wellesley College (B.A., 1919) and Columbia University (M.A., 1922; Ph.D., 1944).

From 1924 until 1929, Mrs. Lynd was a research associate at the Lincoln School in New York City. From 1924 until 1929, she was a research associate of the Middletown Study in Muncie, Indiana. She lectured at Vassar College in 1929 and 1930. Since 1928, she has been a faculty member at Sarah Lawrence College and is presently in the college's philosophy department.

Mrs. Lynd is the author of *England in the 1800's; Toward a Social Basis for Freedom; Essays in Teaching; On Shame and the Search for Identity;* and, *Toward Discovery.* Better known than these works, however, are two books (*Middletown* and *Middletown in Transition*) in which she shared authorship with her husband Robert. These collaborative studies, written in 1929 and 1937, respectively, are still highly recommended as bibliographical references by the ultra-liberal authors of textbooks and teachers of sociology and political science in high schools and colleges.

Although Mrs. Lynd is the wife and mother of two notorious fellow-travelers (Robert and Staughton, respectively), she has compiled an impressive front record in her own right. She has been affiliated with the American Committee to Save Refugees ("Communist enterprise"); the American Committee for Protection of Foreign Born [Americans] ("subversive and Communist" – "one of the older auxiliaries of the Communist Party); the American League for Peace and Democracy ("subversive and Communist"); the League of American Writers ("subversive and Communist"); the League of Women Shoppers ("Communist-controlled front"); the National Committee to Abolish the House Un-American Activities Committee ("to lead and direct the Communist Party's 'Operation Abolition' campaign"); the National Council of American-Soviet Friendship ("subversive and Communist" – "specializing in pro-Soviet propaganda"); the National Council of the Arts, Sciences and Professions ("a Communist front used to appeal to special occupational groups"); the National Federation for Constitutional Liberties ("under [Communist] Party domination and headed by responsible Party functionaries"); the Veterans of the Abraham Lincoln Brigade ("subversive and Communist"); and, the World Peace Appeal ("subversive").

In 1965, Mrs. Lynd was a sponsor of the Inter-University Committee for a Public Hearing on VietNam, organizers of the anti-Vietnam "teach-in" movement, which the Communist propaganda apparatus exploited for purely Communist purposes. Mrs. Lynd has also held an honorary position on the Academic Freedom Committee of the American Civil Liberties Union, that motleyed collection of defenders of subversion, crime, and licentiousness.

ROBERT S. LYND was born on September 26, 1892 in New Albany, Indiana, son of Cornelia Day and Staughton Lynd. He married Helen Merrell. Lynd is an alumnus of Princeton University (A.B., 1914), Union Theological Seminary (B.D., 1923), and Columbia University (Ph.D., 1931).

From 1914 to 1918, Lynd was managing editor of *Publisher's Weekly,* and, from 1923 to 1926, he was, successively, director of a small city study for the Institute of Social and Religious Research in New York City; assistant director in the educational research division of the Commonwealth Fund; and, permanent secretary of the Social Science Research Council. In 1931, Lynd joined the faculty of Columbia University's Graduate School as a professor of sociology. He is now professor emeritus. His most famous books, written in collaboration with his wife, *Middletown* (1929) and *Middletown in Transition* (1937) are still highly recommended as bibliographical references by the ultra-liberal authors of textbooks and teachers of sociology and political science in high schools and colleges.

In 1956, the Senate Internal Security Subcommittee included Lynd's name in its list of the eighty-two most active and typical sponsors of Communist front organizations. He has been affiliated with the American Committee for Democracy and Intellectual Freedom ("Communist front" – "subversive and un-American"); the American Committee for Friendship with the Soviet Union ("subversive"); the American Committee for Protection of Foreign Born [Americans] ("subversive and Communist" – "one of the oldest auxiliaries of the Communist Party in the United States" – under the "complete domination" of the Communist Party); the American Committee for Yugoslav Relief ("subversive and Communist"); the American Friends of Spanish Democracy ("subversive"); the American Investors Union ("Communist front"); the American-Russian Institute ("subversive" – "Communist" – "specializing in pro-Soviet propaganda"); the Bill of Rights Conference ("subversive"); the Committee for Peaceful Alternatives to the Atlantic Pact ("a Communist front" – "part of Soviet psychological warfare against the United States"); the Conference on Constitutional Liberties in America ("subversive"); the Council for Pan-American Democracy ("subversive and Communist"); the Federation of Architects, Engineers, Chemists & Technicians ("in which Communist leadership was strongly entrenched"); Frontier Films ("Communist front"); the Golden Book of American Friendship with the Soviet Union ("Communist enterprise"); the Joint Anti-Fascist Refugee Committee ("subversive and Communist"); the League of American Writers ("subversive and Communist"); the National Committee to Repeal the McCarran Act ("a Communist front" – "subversive"); the National Council of American-Soviet

Friendship ("subversive and Communist" – "specializing in pro-Soviet propaganda"); the National Council of the Arts, Sciences and Professions ("a Communist front used to appeal to special occupational groups"); the National Emergency Conference ("Communist front"); the New York Conference for Inalienable Rights ("Communist front"); Progressive Citizens of America ("subversive"); the Spanish Refugee Appeal ("subversive"); Veterans of the Abraham Lincoln Brigade ("subversive"). Lynd has written for *Science and Society* ("Communist publication"), has petitioned on behalf of Communist leaders, and has petitioned for the abolition of the House Committee on Un-American Activities. He is a member of the American Civil Liberties Union and has been a trustee of the Twentieth Century Fund, which, in its 48-year history, has been a financial boon to leftwing researchers in the fields of economics, political science, and sociology.

In 1965, Lynd was a member of the Inter-University Committee for a Public Hearing on VietNam, sponsors of the anti-Vietnam "teach-in" movement, which the Communist propaganda apparatus exploited for purely Communist purposes.

STAUGHTON C. LYND was born on November 22, 1929 in Philadelphia, son of Helen Merrell and Robert Lynd. He married Alice Niles. He is an alumnus of Harvard University (B.A., 1951) and Columbia University (M.A., 1959; Ph.D., 1962). He has also studied at the University of Chicago.

In 1953, Lynd told his draft board that he was a conscientious objector and he was sworn into the U.S. Army as a non-combatant. In 1954, he was given an undesirable discharge from the army because of his past political activities, including his membership – while at Harvard – in the Communists' John Reed Club. (Later, Lynd joined the Trotskyite Socialist Workers Party.) Lynd fought the "undesirable" discharge in the courts and eventually the U.S. Supreme Court directed the army to give him an honorable discharge. Lynd then used the G.I. Bill to finance his doctoral studies.

After his stint in the army, Lynd and his wife moved to a Communist-type cooperative farm in Georgia where they remained until 1957 when they moved to a cooperative community in Glen Gardner, New Jersey. It was there that Lynd met Dave Dellinger, editor of the radical, pacifist *Liberation* magazine. Lynd became a member of *Liberation's* editorial board. From Glen Gardner, Lynd moved to New York City where he organized tenant councils and rent strikers on the lower East Side.

From 1961 until 1964, Lynd was an assistant professor of American History at Spelman College (a school for Negro women) in Atlanta, Georgia. While in Atlanta, Lynd became affiliated with the pro-Red Chinese Progressive Labor Movement and wrote for its publication *Freedom*. At the same time, he joined the editorial boards of the far-left publications, *Studies on the Left* and *Viet-Report*.

In 1964, Lynd joined the faculty of Yale University as an assistant professor of history. In the summer of 1964, he directed the agitators in the Mississippi Freedom Schools, organized by the Council of Federated Organizations. In the fall of 1964, Lynd helped to raise funds for the Communist-line journal *National Guardian*, which he described as telling "the truth about issues which mean a lot to me."

In 1965, Lynd was a stellar attraction at the "teach-ins" which were directed against U.S. participation in the Vietnam War. He advocated obstructionist methods to prevent American troops from fulfilling their mission and he called upon young Americans to go to North Vietnam where they could help rebuild "non-military" structures destroyed by American bombs. In 1965, Lynd also led the anti-Vietnam War rally in Washington, D.C. which was held under the auspices of the Assembly of Unrepresented People. It was evident that Lynd was a spokesman at the rally for young Communists and other so-called New Left activists. And Lynd said of his ralliers "nothing could have stopped that crowd from taking possession of its government. Perhaps next time we should keep going." The police, however, took possession of Lynd and arrested him.

It was also in 1965 that he became an international celebrity. Ho chi Minh, the Communist President of North Vietnam, invited the American Communist Herbert Aptheker to bring two non-Communists to Hanoi. Aptheker chose Thomas Hayden, founder of Students for Democratic Action, and Lynd, whose trip would be sponsored by *Viet-Report* magazine. The three men, in defiance of U.S. passport regulations, traveled to Hanoi where they talked with Ho chi Minh and other Communist leaders. Lynd reaped world-wide headlines from Hanoi as he delivered anti-American diatribes and branded U.S. policy as "immoral, illegal and anti-democratic." En route home, Lynd and his fellow travelers visited Peking and Moscow.

Lynd's trip to Hanoi evidently upset some of Yale's alumni and Yale's President Kingman Brewster even criticized the young assistant professor as having done "a disservice to the causes of freedom of dissent, freedom of travel and conscientious pacifism." Finally, the State Department decided to revoke the passports of Lynd and his companions. But, before such action was taken, Lynd flew to England at the request of the British Broadcasting Corporation and he appeared on a BBC television panel show to denounce U.S. involvement in Vietnam. At a rally in Trafalgar Square, Lynd called U.S. policy "as ruthless to the truth as it is ruthless to human beings." Lynd also told his British listeners "that American bombing and the use of chemical warfare was worse than the disemboweling and decapitation done by the Vietcong."

Upon his return from England, Lynd's passport was canceled by the State Department. But he was not quieted down by any means. He continued preaching the Communist line, telling a "teach-in" audience that in Hanoi he learned that "the rhetoric of both the National Liberation Front and the government of North Vietnam runs far more in terms of nationalism than in terms of Communism."

In February, 1966, Lynd announced that he had been granted a year's leave of absence, beginning in September, to do research for a book, using a Morse Fellowship to finance the project. But throughout 1966, Lynd continued his anti-war activities. He journeyed to Canada and called upon the Canadian Government to join its colleagues in the International Control Commission for Vietnam in an investigation of United States misconduct in Vietnam. He announced that he had joined the Communist-organized W.E.B. DuBois Clubs. He signed an advertisement in which he said he would not voluntarily pay his federal income tax. He spoke at a encouraged student demonstrations against the draft.

In May, 1967, Yale's history department announced that Lynd had been granted a second year's leave of absence. Lynd, by this time, was working for the Chicago Organizing Group of political agitators and teaching a course on the history of radicalism in America at the New Center for Radical Research, and conducting a graduate history seminar at Roosevelt University. A few months later, it became known that Lynd had applied for teaching positions at the University of Illinois and at Northern Illinois University but he was rejected at both institutions. Then Lynd was accepted for a position as associate professor of history at Chicago State – salary $14,000-a-year – but this job was obtained only after Lynd had brought a breach-of-contract suit against the Illinois Board of Governors of State Colleges and Universities.

Lynd has said: "I see myself as a product of Marxist and pacifist thought, neither of one school nor of the other, but influenced by both."

ARCHIBALD MacLEISH was born on May 7, 1892 in Glencoe, Illinois, son of Martha Hillard and Andrew MacLeish. He married Ada Hitchcock. He is an alumnus of Yale University (A.B., 1915) and Harvard University (LL.B., 1919). He has been a poet and playwright for fifty years.

In 1939, MacLeish began a five-year term as Librarian of Congress, but while holding that position he was director of the U.S. Office of Facts and Figures (1941-1942) and assistant director of Elmer Davis' Red-lined Office of War Information (1942-1943). In 1944 and 1945, he was Assistant Secretary of State and, in that job, he is given credit for having masterminded the formation of UNESCO, which became a nesting place for international Reds and radicals who wanted to subvert traditional educational norms and principles. Whether MacLeish deserves so much credit or not, the fact remains that he was on the American delegation to the UN concerned with UNESCO from 1945 until 1947.

From 1949 until 1962, MacLeish was Boylston Professor at Harvard University and, in 1963, he went to Amherst College as Simpson Lecturer.

MacLeish's fellow-traveling career began at least thirty years ago. In one way or another, he has been affiliated with the American Committee for Protection of Foreign Born [Americans] ("subversive and Communist" – "one of the oldest auxiliaries of the Communist Party in the United States" – under the "complete domination" of the Communist Party); the American Friends of Spanish Democracy ("subversive"); the American Pushkin Committee ("Communist front"); the American Youth Congress ("subversive and Communist"); the Committee for the First Amendment ("Communist front"); the Coordinating Committee to Lift the Embargo ("Communist front"); Friends of the Abraham Lincoln Brigade ("its officers and staff members were in the main [Communist] Party members and functionaries"); Independent Citizens Committee of the Arts, Sciences and Professions ("Communist front"); International Labor Defense ("legal arm of the Communist Party"); the League of American Writers ("subversive and Communist"); the Spanish Refugee Appeal ("subversive" – "Communist front"); *New Masses* (Communist periodical"); and, *Soviet Russia Today* ("Communist front publication"). He has also been a national officer of the American Civil Liberties Union, that motleyed collection of defenders of subversion, crime, and licentiousness, and a member of Arthur Larson's National Council for Civic Responsibility, an election year's drive by the Democrat Party against anti-Communists.

MacLeish desecrated the Coolidge Auditorium in the Library of Congress on December 4, 1956 by delivering a eulogy on behalf of Laurence Duggan, one of the most notorious Communist spies ever to infiltrate the State Department.

MacLeish has been affiliated with the National Committee for an Effective Congress, a group which, since 1948, has campaigned for and financed ultra-leftist candidates for the House and Senate. For the 1968 elections, MacLeish has been soliciting political funds as a one-man campaign committee for the re-election of leftwing Senators including Church of Idaho, McGovern of South Dakota, Fulbright of Arkansas, Clark of Pennsylvania, Gore of Tennessee, Nelson of Wisconsin, Morse of Oregon, and Gruening of Alaska.

As Russell Kirk has commented: "Almost any left-wing outfit can count on the endorsement of Mr. Archibald MacLeish, since he suspects practically everybody this side of Gus Hall as being reactionary."

WARREN MAGNUSON was born on April 12, 1905 in Moorhead, Minnesota, son of Emma Anderson and William Magnuson. His second wife is Jermaine Peralta. In 1923 and 1924, he attended the University of North Dakota and North Dakota State College. He is an alumnus of the University of Washington (LL.B., 1929). He was admitted to the Washington bar in 1930.

In 1930 and 1931, Magnuson was secretary of the Seattle Municipal League. From 1931 until 1933, he was a special prosecutor for King County. In 1933 and 1934, he was a Representative in Washington's legislature. In 1934, he was an assistant U.S. district attorney. From 1934 until 1936, he was prosecutor for King County. From 1937 until 1944, he was in the U.S. House of Representatives. Since 1944, as a Democrat, he has been in the U.S. Senate.

Throughout his years in the Congress, Magnuson has been a persistent ultra-liberal. He has enjoyed campaign support from organized labor. He has long been a favorite of the International Longshoremen's and Warehousemen's Union, led by Harry Bridges who has been identified many times under oath as a Communist. (In 1967, when Communist Jeff Kibre, an ILWU leader, died, Magnuson Wired his sympathy to the ILWU: "Impact of Jeff Kibre loss felt as keenly here [Washington, D.C.] as there [Los Angeles]. So many of the statutes on the books in the field of maritime labor will stand as a monument to his work and his beliefs in these programs he helped to build.")

Magnuson is also a favorite of the AFL-CIO's political arm, the Committee on Political Education which has contributed financially to his campaigns. In return, Magnuson has seldom voted contrary to COPE's wishes. His voting record is also near perfect by the standards of Americans for Democratic Action, the center of the radical left in American politics.

During the Kennedy and Johnson Administrations, Magnuson's left-wingism has been especially notorious in foreign affairs. He has been a champion of U.S.-Red China trade relations. He has been one of the strongest supporters of Lyndon Johnson's "trade bridges to the East" policy. Magnuson went so far as to introduce a bill which would lower tariffs on all goods imported by the U.S. from the entire Soviet bloc.

In 1966, President Johnson entrusted his good friend Magnuson with a mission to Moscow. The announced purpose was to the effect that Magnuson would seek to have Soviet Union officials persuade North Vietnam officials to go to a "peace" table to settle the Vietnam War. In turn, the United States would offer increased trade and long-term credits to the Soviet bloc and — when peace was restored in Vietnam — economic and financial aid to North Vietnam. Of course, neither Soviet nor North Vietnamese officials gave Magnuson's mission serious consideration but the Washington Senator served a useful purpose to the Johnson Administration by performing the "peace" charade.

Magnuson's influence in the Senate was never better dramatized than in 1962 when Maine's Senator Edmund Muskie, who was campaigning for his ultra-liberal colleague in Washington, said that he "stood in awe of Maggie's ability to separate funds from the U.S. Treasury for the state of Washington."

THOMAS C. MANN was born on November 11, 1912 in Laredo, Texas, son of Ida Moore and Thomas Mann. He married Nancy Ayneworth. He is an alumnus of Baylor University (B.A., 1934; LL.B., 1934).

In 1942 and 1943, Mann was a special assistant at the U.S. Embassy in Montevideo, Uruguay. From 1943 until 1947, he was in Washington at the State Department. In 1947 and 1948, he was at the U.S. Embassy in Caracas, Venezuela. In 1949, he was back in the State Department.

From 1950 until 1952, he was deputy assistant secretary of state for Inter-American affairs. From 1953 until 1955, he was deputy chief of the U.S. mission in Athens, Greece. In 1955, he was counselor at the U.S. Embassy in Guatemala City. From 1955 until 1957, he was U.S. Ambassador to El Salvador. From 1957 until 1960, he was assistant secretary of state for economic affairs.

In 1960 and 1961, Mann was Assistant Secretary of State for Inter-American Affairs (he also held this post in 1964). From 1961 until 1963, he was U.S. Ambassador to Mexico. In 1965, he became Under Secretary of State for economic affairs. In 1966, he resigned from government service to become a visiting scholar at The Johns Hopkins University.

Mann's career was most important in those positions he held with relation to Latin America. Although Mann spoke strongly against Communism and Communists in Latin America, he supported the idea that the United States should fight Communism with Socialism through the Alliance for Progress and agrarian reforms. To Mann, American economic aid was the panacea for Latin America and he placed great faith in the so-called non-Communist left of Latin America to serve as an effective bulwark against the growth of Communism. As for Latin Americans, Mann advised them to practice agrarian reform, family planning, and make tax reforms to bring their taxes more in line with the confiscatory nature of the U.S. tax structure. It is no wonder that the *New York Times* expressed its editorial disappointment at Mann's departure from government service.

MICHAEL J. MANSFIELD was born on March 16, 1903 in New York City, son of Josephine O'Brien and Patrick

Mansfield. He married Maureen Hayes. While still in his teens, he had the unusual experience of serving as a seaman in the U.S. Navy (1918-1919), a private in the U.S. Army (1919-1920), and a private first class in the U.S. Marines (1920-1922).

From 1922 until 1931, Mansfield was a miner and mining engineer in Montana. He never finished elementary school but, in 1927 and 1928, he attended the Montana School of Mines. Then he enrolled at Montana State University, where he earned two degrees (A.B., 1933; A.M., 1935).

From 1933 until 1942, Mansfield was on the faculty at Montana State University, teaching Latin American History, Far Eastern History, and political science. In 1943, he was elected to the House of Representatives where he served continuously from the 78th through the 82nd Congress. In 1952, he was elected to the U.S. Senate from Montana. He was re-elected in 1958 and 1964. From 1957 until 1961, he was assistant majority leader in the Senate (Lyndon B. Johnson was the majority leader) and, since 1961, he has been majority leader.

As long as he has been in the Congress, Mansfield has been a rubber-stamp ultra-liberal, voting down the line for the socialist program of organized labor and Americans for Democratic Action. In his role as majority leader in the Kennedy and Johnson Administrations, he has conducted himself as a lackey for the White House.

Because of long service on the House Foreign Affairs Committee and the Senate Foreign Relations Committee, Mansfield has acquired a reputation as an expert on foreign policy. His expertise, however, breaks down under analysis. He is an uncritical devotee of the United Nations. To him it can do no wrong and he has always been in favor of strengthening that international body. He has been in the van of the appeasers in Washington who have conducted the relentless drive toward the disarmament of the United States and for years, with little or no provocation, Mansfield has repeatedly raised the spectre of a third world war.

In recent years, Mansfield's two primary concerns have been the Vietnam War and Red China. His concern with Red China is directly related to his fear-ridden alarms about a third world war. He insists that the United States should take the initiative in seeking an accommodation with Red China so as to insure a "civilized survival" for the world. And, as an important prerequisite for a Red China-United States reconciliation, Mansfield has called for a U.S. withdrawal from Vietnam and the rest of Southeast Asia because "we have no vital interest there and . . . it is not necessary to the security of the United States." To buttress his suggestions, Mansfield holds to the ridiculous theory that the Vietnam War is a civil war. His reasoning? It is a civil war "because the Vietcong are South Vietnamese."

To be sure, Mansfield's views on the Vietnam War are not exceptional among peaceniks, both in and out of government. But he departs from even most of his ultra-leftist soulmates when he questions whether the Vietcong are Communists. ("As far as the allegations being made that the Vietcong is a Communist organization, I think that is very questionable." *Honolulu Star-Bulletin,* April 18, 1968.) From this display of monumental ignorance or deliberate rejection of contrary evidence, Mansfield's logic carries him on to advocacy of a coalition government —

including Communists, of course – for South Vietnam.

In 1967, Mansfield, in his role as Senate majority leader, suggested that the Vietnam War be the subject of an "open debate" in the United Nations Security Council. And he hoped that the Security Council's members (the United States, the Soviet Union, Britain, India, and Canada) would be joined in the "debate" by Communist Poland, Red China, South Vietnam, North Vietnam, the National Liberation Front (the Vietcong's political facade), and "any other government or group whose presence might be of some relevance to negotiations." (By the simple matter of finding a distinction between the National Liberation Front and the North Vietnam regime of Ho chi Minh, Mansfield was, in effect, proposing that Ho have two voices in the "debate." Furthermore, by including the Soviet Union and Red China in the "debate," he was making certain that Ho would not lack for friends at court since these two powers are and have been the chief military supporters of Ho's Communist aggression. And, in a display of unbridled fanaticism or absolutely hopeless naiveté, he insisted that such a gathering of Communists was no reason even to suspect that the United Nations would be used as a propaganda forum or that there would be criticism which would embarrass the United States.)

Mansfield's implacable concern for peace-at-any-price in Vietnam is coupled with his antagonism toward any and all U.S. military leaders who advocate an honest military effort against Communist aggression in Vietnam. As he raises the bogey of militarism, he places bombing high among his bugaboos as he firmly opposes any and all bombing attacks upon North Vietnam. (Mansfield has gone so far as to charge the United States with indiscriminate bombing of North Vietnam – the very line so widely disseminated by Communists and fellow travelers throughout the world.)

While the Johnson Administration has pursued its Vietnam strategy of "limited" warfare as a part of its no-win policy, Mansfield has played the role of a critic by insisting that the Administration is too hawkish and should accept his program of a speedy withdrawal from all of Southeast Asia – no warfare and no victory. It is not that Mansfield wishes to be harsh on the Administration. He simply wants to give the impression of a possibility that the Administration's civilian leaders could be tempted to follow sound military advice and pursue victory over the Communists in Vietnam – all of which would incense the Chinese Communists and precipitate a third world war. As long as Mansfield remains in the Senate, especially as majority leader, the Communist regimes of China and North Vietnam may be assured that their propaganda line on the Vietnam War is parroted by him, whether out of ignorance or otherwise.

HERBERT MARCUSE was born on July 19, 1898 in Berlin, Germany. In 1940, he became a naturalized United States citizen. He is an alumnus of the University of Freiburg (Ph.D., 1922). He is the author of *Reason and Revolution* (1941), *Eros and Civilization* (1955), *One Dimensional Man* (1964), and *Negations* (1968).

Upon completion of his graduate studies at Freiburg, Marcuse became a co-founder of the radical-socialist Institute of Social Research in Frankfurt, where he developed and taught a Marxian brand of sociology.

With the rise of Hitler, Marcuse left

Germany and went to Geneva, Switzerland where, in 1933 and 1934, he was a research fellow at the Institut de Recherches Sociales. In 1934, he came to the United States.

From 1934 until 1942, Marcuse was a research associate at Columbia University. In 1942 and 1943, he was a senior analyst in the Office of War Information. From 1943 until 1945, he was an analyst with the Office of Strategic Services. From 1945 until 1950, he was in the State Department's Office of Intelligence Research as a senior analyst and chief of the European Division.

After leaving the State Department, Marcuse took up residence at Harvard University's Russian Research Center. From 1954 until 1965, he was a professor of politics and philosophy. Since 1965, he has been a professor of philosophy at the University of California (San Diego). In 1967, he lectured at the Free University of Berlin.

Marcuse readily admits that he is a Marxist but insists that he is not a Communist. His writings which lean heavily on Hegel, Marx, Lenin, and Freud are extremely abstruse, but in whatever lucid passages he has produced, there emerges a blend of Marxism, nihilism, and anarchism. His central thesis is an absolute detestation of modern industrial civilization. He preaches that the civilization's social and political structure should be destroyed and replaced by a society and government of the elite — a totalitarian system in which dissenters would be repressed. The precise standards by which Marcuse's elite would govern are not detailed in any positive manner (he prefers negative rather than positive thinking). But some idea of his standards can be gleaned from his warm endorsement of the political revoluton and sexual revolution sweeping university and college campuses throughout the world.

In 1968, Marcuse became internationally famous as the philosopher of the "new left" or guru of the "student" rioters at Columbia University, in West Berlin and Rome and Paris. Marcuse, himself, was on the scene in Paris when the riots took place at the Sorbonne. He was attending a UNESCO symposium on Marx simultaneously with the riots. And, he took advantage of the situation to confer with the North Vietnamese delegates to the interminable Paris "peace" talks. In Rome, Berlin, and Paris Marcuse's name was bracketed by the rioters with Mao Tse-tung, Ché Guevara, and Marx.

In the United States, Marcuse has not been an activist. (He did, however, serve on the national council of the Communist-dominated National Conference for New Politics.) But he is a familiar sight on college and university lecture platforms. And he is far from being an unknown in other quarters. There have been extensive notices of his work published in *Time, Newsweek,* the *New York Times Book Review,* and other large circulation journals. When he wrote his most famous book, *One Dimensional Man,* he was subsidized by the American Council of Learned Societies, the Louis M. Rabinowitz Foundation, the Rockefeller Foundation, and the Social Science Research Council.

LEONARD MARKS was born on March 5, 1916 in Pittsburgh, son of Ida Lewine and Samuel Marks. He married Dorothy Ames. He is an alumnus of the University of Pittsburgh (B.A., 1935; LL.B., 1938).

From 1938 until 1955, Marks taught law at the University of Pittsburgh

(1938-1942) and at National University (1943-1955). In the same period, he was assistant to the general counsel of the Federal Communications Commission (1942-1946) and began a law practice in Washington, D.C. in 1946. In 1958 and 1961, he lectured for the State Department on administrative and constitutional law in India, Iran, Turkey, Pakistan, and Afghanistan.

In 1965, he was named director of the U.S. Information Agency. Marks has long been an intimate friend of Lyndon Johnson. In the 1940's, Marks represented the Johnson's radio-television station KTBC of Austin, Texas – the center of the Johnson's broadcasting empire. And, Marks was the chief planner of the Johnson inauguration festivities in 1965. As head of the USIA, Marks has not let his friend Lyndon down. Not long after he became propaganda chief, it was discovered that the USIA bought and distributed 214,830 copies of *The Lyndon Johnson Story* by Booth Mooney, a long-time political crony of Johnson's who had been on Johnson's Washington staff for six years.

In May, 1968, Marks invited the Chinese Communists to send journalists to the United States to cover the 1968 presidential election campaign. Not content with letting the Communists be treated as other foreign journalists, Marks said "The Voice of America [an expense of the American taxpayers] will make prime listening time available daily to these journalists for broadcast to their homeland."

In total disregard of the fact that the Chinese Communists were involved in war against the United States in Vietnam, Marks was eager to give the Communists constitutional privileges: "In our tradition of free speech, we in the United States will not attempt in any manner to censor these broadcasts. The Chinese can express themselves as they wish in any language .... We would expect Chinese observers to be critical and to look for the worst but I am confident that any observer [in Communist China] will find in our election processes the true flavor of a free society." Why Marks could expect anything but the most distorted and virulent anti-American propaganda to emanate from such an unprecedented patronizing gesture to the enemy, he left unexplained. He could only resort to the banal and befuddled outburst of a farout liberal: "If people can know the facts, if they can exchange ideas, if they can use words so that there is a communication of thought – then the peoples of the world may find understanding. That is our best hope in this very troubled world."

THURGOOD MARSHALL was born on July 2, 1908 in Baltimore, son of Norma Williams and William Marshall. He was married to the late Vivian Burey. He is married to Cecilia Suyat. He is an alumnus of Lincoln University (A.B., 1930) and Harvard University (LL.B., 1933).

From 1933 until 1936, Marshall was in private law practice. From 1936 until 1961, he was with the National Association for the Advancement of Colored People as assistant special counsel (1936-1938), special counsel (1938-1940), and director and counsel for the legal defense and educational fund (1940-1961). In 1962, Marshall was appointed by President Kennedy to be U.S. Circuit Court Justice for the Second Judicial Circuit. In 1965, President Johnson appointed him to be Solicitor General of the United States.

In 1967, Marshall became an Associate Justice of the Supreme Court, an appointment that was viewed as a political ploy on behalf of Negro votes.

When Marshall was nominated for the federal bench by President Kennedy in 1961, opposition to the nomination was strong enough to delay confirmation in the Senate for more than a year. In 1965, when President Johnson named Marshall to be Solicitor General of the U.S., there was opposition but confirmation was speedily granted by the Senate.

In both instances, Marshall's qualifications were called into question with particular attention devoted to his earlier affiliations with Communist fronts. But Marshall had been especially anointed by the Liberal Establishment, and even his opponents, realizing the futility of it all, only went through the motions of opposing his appointment when Lyndon Johnson appointed him to the Supreme Court.

Representative Joe Waggoner (D.-La.) said at the time: "I suppose we should be thankful it was not Stokely Carmichael who got the job.

"The appointment of Mr. Marshall would not have much of an effect one way or the other on the Court's philosophies, but it does point out just how far we are removed from the ideas our Founding Fathers had of an unbiased court serving the law. What we have now is a top-heavy group of social philosophers picked, not for judicial impartiality, but for their proven tendencies to interpret laws not on the basis of two centuries of wisdom, but rather in line with current social fads and their own personal theories on how to create the perfect society."

Marshall's background supported Waggoner's appraisal of him and his future role in the Court. From 1938 to 1961, as counsel for the NAACP, he had

represented that organization thirty-two times before the Supreme Court, and won twenty-nine of the cases. But the connection was more than a lawyer-client relationship, since Marshall was an active devotee of the NAACP's program, in and out of court rooms.

His most notable achievement before the Supreme Court came in 1954, when he successfully argued the *Brown v. Board of Education* case with the resultant revolutionary decision by the Court that segregation in public schools was unconstitutional. Both Marshall and the Supreme Court Justices emerged from that decision with a completely tarnished view of the law and of the Court's function.

Seven years later, Dr. Alfred H. Kelly, an historian who served as an aide to Marshall in the preparation of a brief for the segregation case, revealed that Marshall set out to deceive the Court with dishonest historical arguments. As Kelly described it: "It is not that we were engaged in formulating lies; there was nothing as crude and naive as that. But we were using facts, quietly ignoring facts and, above all, interpreting facts in a way to do what Marshall said we had to do — 'get by those boys down there.' There was one optimistic element in all this, as Marshall pointed out: It was obvious that the Court was looking for a plausible historical answer."

In 1966, Marshall admitted that the favorable ruling he received in the 1954 segregation case from the Supreme Court "initiated and required social change." He explained that the Supreme Court involved itself in social reform because the executive and legislative branches of the federal government and other representative institutions had refused to act.

At times Marshall seems to have extended himself deliberately in derogating the law. Before the Senate Judiciary Committee, he was quoted as saying: "I want you to understand that when the colored people take over, every time the white man draws a breath, he'll have to pay a fine." On another occasion, he said, with reference to Negroes: "We've negotiated too quietly and too reasonably for too long. We've made up our minds to harass the legal hell out of the school boards. From here on out, we're going to be unreasonable, undecent, and uneverything else.

The conclusions are inescapable: to Marshall, the Supreme Court is nothing more than a social reform group. If Negroes believe that the merits of their cause are not appreciated, then they should twist and stretch and distort the law – even use it to punish the white man.

Lyndon Johnson is quoted as saying of Marshall: "I didn't appoint him because he is a Negro, but that fact didn't disqualify him." This was too much for even the very liberal Joseph Kraft of the *Washington Post* to swallow. Said Kraft: "Beyond any doubt, Mr. Marshall was appointed because he is a Negro; not just any Negro, not even the best qualified Negro. He was appointed because he is a Negro well known to the Negro community for action on behalf of Negro causes. He was appointed, in other words, on the outmoded principle of ethnic representation, and for years to come his seat on the Court will probably be a Negro seat." Kraft also said that "Mr. Marshall will not bring to the Court penetrating analysis or distinction of mind."

Marshall brought to the Court more than a quarter of a century's total commitment to the NAACP's partisan program, at least a modicum of racism, and an undisguised impatience and contempt for legal processes.

The possibility is infinitely remote that Marshall, while on the Supreme Court, will disqualify himself in every or any case before the Court which concerns Negroes. Marshall must be aware that his appointment is a calculated political gesture on the part of Lyndon Johnson, who can appreciate the impact of Negro votes, especially in northern cities, in the 1968 presidential election. And the Marshall appointment was a cheap political gimmick to pacify impatient civil rights agitators and keep them within the ranks of the Democrat Party.

A few years ago Lyndon Johnson explained to the veteran Negro civil rights lobbyist Clarence Mitchell, that in his early senatorial years he held the theory that civil rights action would have to come from the executive and judicial branches of the government. It could not come from the legislative branch because this would divide the Democrat Party. And if it were divided, it would kill legislation for the common man.

But, in one dramatic move, Johnson brought about civil rights action through the executive and judicial branches. As he explained in announcing the appointment: "I believe it is the right thing to do, the right time to do it, the right man and the right place."

The *New York Times* described Marshall's appointment as "rich in symbolism. Since he will be the first Negro to serve on the nation's highest tribunal, this twentieth-century Mr. Justice Marshall will be an historic figure before he even casts a vote or drafts an opinion." It was symbolic all right – symbolic of the personal and political commitments Lyndon Johnson had made to the social, economic, and political ambitions of an agitating minority who have assumed leadership of all American Negroes. Even the *Times* admitted that Marshall's qualifications left something to be desired: "There are judges in the state and Federal courts whose judicial work has been far more outstanding than Mr. Marshall's record during his brief service on the Second Circuit. Nor as Solicitor General did he demonstrate the intellectual mastery of Archibald Cox, his predecessor."

KIRTLEY F. MATHER was born on February 13, 1888 in Chicago, son of Julia King and William Mather. He married Marie Porter. He is an alumnus of Denison University (B.Sc., 1909) and the University of Chicago (Ph.D., 1915).

From 1911 until 1914, Mather was, successively, an instructor and assistant professor of geology. In 1914 and 1915, he was a fellow at the University of Chicago. From 1915 until 1918, at Queen's University in Ontario, he was, successively, an associate professor of geology and a progessor of paleontology. From 1918 until 1924, he was a professor of geology at Denison University. From 1924 until 1954, he was at Harvard University, successively, as an associate professor of physiography and a professor of geology. In 1954, he became professor emeritus at Harvard.

Since his retirement from the classroom, Mather has kept busy in YMCA activities. From 1946 until 1948, he was president of the national council of the YMCA. From 1947 until 1955, he was a member of the executive committee of the World's Alliance of YMCA's and, from 1957 until 1960, he was the Alliance's representative at the United Nations. He has written three books on geology in the past seven years.

In 1956, the Senate Internal Security Subcommittee included Mather's name in its list of the eighty-two most active and typical sponsors of Communist front organizations. Mather has been affiliated with the American Committee for Democracy and Intellectual Freedom ("Communist front" – "subversive and un-American"); the American Committee for Protection of Foreign Born [Americans] ("subversive and Communist" – "one of the oldest auxiliaries of the Communist Party in the United States" – under the "complete domination" of the Communist Party); the American Council on Soviet Relations ("established by Communist Party"); American Friends of Spanish Democracy ("subversive"); the American League for Peace and Democracy ("subversive and Communist"); the American League against War and Fascism ("subversive and Communist"); the American Relief Ship for Spain ("Communist Party front enterprise"); the American Rescue Ship Mission ("Communist"); the American Slav Congress ("subversive and Communist"); American Youth for Democracy ("subversive and Communist"); the Citizens' Committee to Free Earl Browder ("Communist"); the Civil Rights Congress ("subversive and Communist"); the Committee for a Democratic Far Eastern Policy ("Communist"); the Committee of One Thousand ("Communist created and controlled front organization"); the Council for Pan-American Democracy ("subversive and Communist" – "Communist front"); the Council of United States Veterans ("Communist front"); Friends of the Abraham Lincoln Brigade ("its officers and staff members were in the main [Communist] Party members and functonaries"); the International Labor Defense ("legal arm of the Communist Party"); the Joint Anti-Fascist Refugee Committee ("subversive and Communist"); the League of American Writers ("subversive and Communist"); the Mid-Century Conference for Peace ("aimed at assembling as many gullible persons as possible under Communist direction and turning them into a vast sounding board for Communist propaganda" – "a Communist front"); the National Committee to Repeal the McCarran Act ("a Communist front" – "subversive"); the National Council of American-Soviet Friendship ("subversive and Communist – specializing in pro-Soviet propaganda"); the National Council of the Arts, Sciences and Professions ("a Communist front used to appeal to special occupational groups"); the National Emergency Conference for Democratic Rights ("Communist front" – "subversive and un-American"); the National Federation for Constitutional Liberties ("subversive and Communist" – "under [Communist] Party domination and headed by responsible Party functionaries"); the *Protestant* ("Communist front"); the Reichstag Fire Trial Anniversary Committee ("Communist front"); *Science and Society* ("Communist publication"); *Soviet Russia Today* ("Communist front publication"); the Spanish Refugee Appeal ("subversive" – "Communist front"); Veterans of the Abraham Lincoln Brigade ("subversive and Communist"); the World Youth Congress ("Communist conference").

Beyond his formal Communist front activities, Mather has been a longtime opponent of congressional anti-Communist investigating committees. He has been a very active petitioner on behalf of convicted Communists. He has a special penchant for peace groups, especially of the ban-the-bomb variety. He has been an official of the Civil Liberties Union of Massachusetts. And, from 1957 until 1961, he was president of the American Academy of Arts and Sciences. He has denied being a Communist.

HERBERT MATTHEWS was born on January 10, 1900 in New York City, son of Frances Lewis and Samuel Matthews. He married Edith Crosse. He is an alumnus of Columbia University (A.B., 1922).

From 1922 until 1967, Matthews was with the *New York Times.*

Matthews' best known books are *The Yoke and the Arrow,* a dishonest history of the Spanish Civil War which, at the same time, eulogizes the Communists who joined in that struggle from all over the world; *The Cuban Story* (1961) and *Cuba* (1964) in which Matthews reaffirms that he, as much as any individual, was responsible for the thoroughly dishonest treatment that the *New York Times* gave its readers with the Castro story, beginning in 1957.

Matthews began his tub-thumping for Castro in 1957 when he wrote three front-page articles for the *New York Times.* As the former U.S. Ambassador to Cuba, Earl E.T. Smith, has written, Matthews "served to inflate Castro to world stature and world recognition. Until that time, Castro had been just another bandit in the Oriente Mountains of Cuba, with a handful of followers who had terrorized the peasants. After the Matthews articles which followed an exclusive interview ... in Castro's mountain hideout and which likened him to Abraham Lincoln, he was able to get followers and funds in Cuba and in the U.S. From that time on arms, money and soldiers of fortune abounded. Much of the American press began to picture Castro as a political Robin Hood . . . . "

In July, 1959, Matthews – seven months after Castro seized power in Cuba – filed a dispatch from Havana, reporting that there were no Communists in any position of influence within Castro's government and that Castro was not only anti-Communist but would resist the Communists if they made any attempt to gain power in Cuba. This dispatch forced the *New York Times* to put Matthews into relative obscurity and, until his retirement in 1967, his writings generally appeared anonymously as editorials in the *Times*. Occasionally, his by-line did appear with some pro-Communist punditry on Latin America, but to the very end of his stay with the *Times,* Matthews never did admit that Castro was anything but a nice idealist who was forced to become a Communist (not an orthodox Communist – but a unique one) because the U.S. tried to destroy his "social" revolution.

BENJAMIN MAYS was born on August 1, 1895 in Epworth, South Carolina, son of Louvania Carter and Hezekiah Mays. He married Sadie Gray. He is an alumnus of Bates College (A.B., 1920) and the University of Chicago (M.A., 1925).

From 1921 until 1924, Mays taught mathematics at Morehouse College and held a pastorate at Shiloh Baptist Church in Atlanta, Georgia. In 1925 and 1926, he was an instructor in English at the State College of South Carolina. From 1926 until 1928, he was executive secretary of the Urban League of Tampa, Florida. From 1928 until 1930, he was national student secretary of the YMCA. From 1930 until 1932, he was director for a study of Negro churches in the United States for the Institute of Social and Religious Research. From 1934 until 1940, he was dean of the school of religion at Howard University. In 1940, Mays became president of Morehouse College.

Mays has been affiliated with the American Committee for Protection of Foreign Born [Americans] ("subversive and Communist" – "one of the oldest auxiliaries of the Communist Party in the United States" – under the "complete domination" of the Communist Party); the Civil Rights Congress ("subversive and Communist"); the National Council of American-Soviet Friendship ("subversive and Communist" – "specializing in pro-Soviet propaganda"); the National Federation for Constitutional Liberties ("under [Communist] Party domination and headed by responsible Party functionaries"); the Southern Negro Youth Congress ("subversive"); the Mid-Century Conference for Peace ("aimed at assembling as many gullible persons as possible under Communist direction and turning them into a vast sounding board for Communist propaganda" – "a Communist front"); the Southern Conference Educational Fund (the financial backbone of racial agitators including the "black power" revolutionaries); the Southern Conference for Human Welfare ("Communist front"); and the National Committee to Repeal the McCarran Act ("a Communist front" – "subversive").

Mays has been a member of the U.S. advisory committee for the United Nations. He has been a member of the national advisory council to the Peace Corps. He has been a member of the U.S. national commission for UNESCO.

EUGENE McCARTHY was born on March 29, 1916 in Watkins, Minnesota, son of Anna Baden and Michael Mc-Carthy. He married Abigail Quigley. He is an alumnus of St. John's University of Minnesota (A.B., 1935) and the University of Minnesota (A.M., 1938). He is the author of *Frontiers in American Democracy* (1960), *Dictionary of American Politics* (1962), *A Liberal Answer to the Conservative Challenge* (1964), and *The Limits of Power* (1967). (His *Limits of Power* was reviewed most favorably in the *New Times,* a Moscow weekly magazine.)

From 1935 until 1940, McCarthy was a high school teacher in Minnesota and North Dakota. In this period, he also spent ten months as a novice in the Benedictine monastery at St. John's. From 1940 until 1943, he was a professor of economics and education at St. John's. In 1944, he was a civilian technical assistant in the Military Intelligence Division of the War Department. In 1945, he returned to teaching in a high school. From 1946 until 1949, he was an instructor in sociology and economics at St. Thomas College in Minnesota.

From 1949 until 1959, McCarthy served in the U.S. House of Representatives as a Democrat from Minnesota. Since 1959, he has been in the U.S. Senate. His political fortunes have been promoted by the Democrat Farmer-Labor Party of Minnesota, Walter Reuther's Committee on Political Education, the ultra-leftist National Committee for an Effective Congress, and the socialist Americans for Democratic Action.

In the House and Senate, McCarthy has been a bulwark of ultra-liberalism in domestic and foreign affairs. He has voted straight down the line for organized labor, so-called civil rights legislation, and any and all welfare-state programs. His political hero was Adlai Stevenson and McCarthy has striven valiantly to equal Stevenson's record for appeasement. He has been a staunch supporter of foreign aid programs. He has advocated expanded trade with the Soviet Union. He has recommended that the U.S. extend diplomatic recognition to and begin trade relations with Red China.

McCarthy is on the steering committee of Members of Congress for Peace Through Law which has as its goal "peace through general and complete disarmament under enforceable world law." When the group was formed in 1966 (Senators Joseph Clark, Robert Kennedy, Jacob Javits, and George McGovern; Representatives Jonathan Bingham, Bradford Morse, Robert Kastenmeier, Donald Fraser, James Fulton, Patsy Mink, Richard Schweiker, and Benjamin Rosenthal), it announced as its specific objectives, peace with honor in Vietnam; an international treaty to prevent the spread of nuclear arms to nations without them; extension of the 1963 test-ban treaty to cover underground nuclear explosions – thus, a total ban; a consular treaty between the United States and the Soviet Union; agreement on a treaty governing space; establishment of a permanent peace force in the United Nations; a general strengthening of the United Nations; and, increased East-West trade. (In his *Limits of Power,* McCarthy's chief recommended reform for foreign policy was that it should be conducted as much as possible through international agencies.)

In his congressional career, McCarthy has received extensive notoriety for his dovish position on the Vietnam War. As late as 1964, Lyndon Johnson described McCarthy as "my counselor, my colleague, and my friend." But within a short time after the President had delivered this tribute, McCarthy had become one of the severest critics of the Administration's policy in Vietnam. Despite the Johnsonian no-military-victory policy in the conduct of the war, McCarthy insisted that this was not enough and that there should neither be a political nor diplomatic victory in the war. He recommended that a compromise settlement be negotiated, conditioned upon U.S. recognition of the Vietcong and U.S. acceptance of Communists in any South Vietnamese government which emerged from the negotiations.

McCarthy has reasoned that there is no indication that the South Vietnamese know what they want or if they do, there is no indication that they are willing to fight for it. He advocates a U.S. withdrawal from Vietnam but insists that the U.S. should remain a significant presence in Asia – a puzzlement since he also insists that the major power in Asia, Red China, is not expansionist there.

In 1968, McCarthy became a national political phenomenon when he campaigned for the Democratic presidential nomination in the New Hampshire primary. To the astonishment of most political observers, he obtained forty-two per cent of the votes. Encouraged by his victory, McCarthy made an all-out effort to capture the liberal-leftist voting bloc. Socialists, pacifists, and leftists – including Communists – rallied to his cause. The national board of Americans for Democratic Action endorsed him. Prominent liberals joined his campaign: George F. Kennan, Jerome Wiesner, George Kistiakowsky, Richard Goodwin, Arthur Schlesinger Jr., Allard Lowenstein, John K. Galbraith, Thomas Finletter, Mrs. Drew Pearson, Max Lerner, Mrs. Don Edwards, Mrs. Henry Reuss, and Mrs. Philip Hart.

McCarthy was the perfect demagogue for the amalgamated left. He had something for everybody: a federal government guarantee of a minimum income for all; a federal government-subsidized health insurance program for all; a federal home building program of six million units for low and moderate income families; federal government subsidized on-the-job training programs and special vocational schools and adult literacy courses; and, for the Negroes, he would lift them out of their "colonial" status. He promised that, if elected, he would remove J. Edgar Hoover from his position as Director of the FBI, General Lewis Hershey from his position as Director of Selective Service (McCarthy favored granting amnesty to draft dodgers who fled to Canada), and Dean Rusk from his position as Secretary of State.

At one time, McCarthy said that Dean Rusk should be replaced by Senator Mike Mansfield. Later, as he speculated on his cabinet, McCarthy mentioned as possibilities for the State Department Senators J. William Fulbright, John Sherman Cooper, and Thruston Morton; for Secretary of Defense, he named only John W. Gardner; for Housing and Urban Development a choice between Nelson Rockefeller and New Jersey Governor Richard Hughes; for Treasury a choice between IBM's Thomas B. Watson and CBS's Frank Stanton; for Health, Education and Welfare only Walter Reuther; and Mrs. Martin L. King Jr. as U.S. Ambassador to the United Nations.

Although McCarthy did not attain his party's nomination for the presidency, he did rally the leftists to his cause as no other candidate has since the Communists thrust Henry Wallace upon the political scene in 1948. Open support by easily identified Communists was given to McCarthy and he never repudiated such support. Black and white revolutionaries, old and young, joined his cause and he welcomed them. And there is every indication that in 1972 the McCarthy-leftwing coalition will rise again since he has intimated that he will lead a separate party in quest of the presidency. He gave only reluctant and belated endorsement to Hubert Humphrey's candidacy in 1968 and, at the same time, announced that he would not seek re-election to the Senate in 1970.

JOHN McCLOY was born on March 31, 1895 in Philadelphia, son of Anna Snader and John McCloy. He married Ellen Zinsser. He is an alumnus of Amherst College (A.B. 1916) and Harvard University (LL.B., 1921). He was admitted to the New York bar in 1921 and, for the next four years, he practiced law with the firm of Cadwalader, Wickersham, and Taft.

From 1925 until 1940, McCloy was with Cravath, de Gersdorff, Swaine, and Wood, a law firm which was instrumental in manipulating the United States diplomatic recognition of the Soviet Union in 1933.

In 1940, McCloy became a consultant to Secretary of War Henry L. Stimson. From 1941 until 1945, McCloy was Assistant Secretary of War. In this latter position in 1944, he approved of an order permitting Communists to be officers in the U.S. Army. And, in 1945, he was a member of the U.S. delegation to the United Nations organizing conference in San Francisco.

In 1946 and 1947, McCloy returned to the practice of law. From 1947 until 1949, he was president of the World Bank. From 1949 until 1952, he was U.S. High Commissioner for Germany. In 1953 he became chairman of the board of the Chase National Bank and retained that position when Chase merged with the Bank of Manhattan to become the Chase Manhattan Bank.

In 1961, McCloy — although well-known as an active member of the Republican Party — became President Kennedy's adviser on disarmament. Within a few months, McCloy's advice resulted in the Kennedy Administration's creation of the United States Arms Control and Disarmament Agency. McCloy became chairman of the Agency's general advisory committee and was retained in that position in the Johnson Administration. Every disarmament maneuver carried out by the Kennedy and Johnson Administrations had the complete and active support of McCloy. (So anxious was McCloy to appease the Soviet Union on disarmament that, in 1962, he recommended that the United States increase its cultural and trade relations with the Soviet Union to provide an atmosphere of trust in order that the United States and the Soviet Union get together on disarmament treaties.)

Aside from his activities within the federal government, McCloy has played a very prominent role in some of the more prestigious leftist internationalist institutions of the Liberal Establishment.

In 1950, McCloy was a founding official of World Brotherhood (now known as the Council on World Tensions) which was organized at the suggestion of the ubiquitous leftist Paul Hoffman. (Other founders included Eleanor Roosevelt, Adlai Stevenson, William Benton, and Herbert Lehman — all prominent members of the Democratic Party's far left: rather strange company for prominent Republican McCloy.) The 1958 meeting of World Brotherhood was reported by the veteran Arthur Krock in the *New York Times* (November 21, 1958.) Dan Smoot in his *The Invisible*

Government has summarized Krock's article on the conclusions of the World Brotherhood conclave: "We must recognize that the communist countries are here to stay and cannot be wished away by propaganda. All is not bad in communist countries. Western nations could learn from communist experiments. We should study ways to make changes in both systems – communist and western – in order to bring them nearer together. We should try to eliminate the stereotype attitudes about, and suspicion of, communism. We must assume that the communist side is not worse than, but merely different from, our side."

While he served in the Kennedy and Johnson Administrations, McCloy held the very lucrative chairmanship of the Ford Foundation's board of trustees. The multi-billion dollar Foundation has been the greatest cornucopia ever directed toward the left wing. It has spawned the ultra-leftwing Fund for the Republic, the socialist Center for the Study of Democratic Institutions, and leftwing boondoggles all over the world in such areas as education, sociology, science, engineering, journalism, economics, political science, and law. For all practical purposes, the Foundation and its offspring are merely financial angels for the benefit of the Council on Foreign Relations, Americans for Democratic Action, internationalists, one-worlders, Marxists, racist and campus agitators, and do-gooding planners.

No sooner had McCloy relinquished his board chairmanship of the Ford Foundation than he became, in February 1966, the chairman of the Atlantic Institute's board of governors. The Institute was founded in 1961 and has been financed by the Ford Foundation, various corporations and trade unions, and several governments. It operates under the fiction that it is a private organization but, in reality, it is quasi-governmental. Officials and members of the Institute are drawn from the NATO nations and invariably they are or have been government officials or have very close ties to their respective governments. The Institute's literature describes its function as promoting "unified action by those nations on both sides of the Atlantic which are willing to cooperate regarding their own development and the discharge of their world responsibilities." But by an appraisal of the statements and activities of the Institute's members and from the Institute's publications, it is evident that the real function of the Institute is to promote political unity at the expense of national sovereignty of the NATO nations as a preliminary step toward world government.

From his chairmanship of the Atlantic Institute's governing board, McCloy became chairman of the board of directors of the Council on Foreign Relations, of which he has been a longtime member as well as a member of the editorial advisory board of the CFR's quarterly *Foreign Affairs.*

For the CFR, McCloy was an instant success in his chairmanship. For a new endowment fund, McCloy and his directors were able to raise $4.3-million in pledges from foundations and private benefactors, before asking CFR members to contribute $700,000 so as to reach the endowment fund's goal of $5-million. At the same time, the Ford, Rockefeller, and Carnegie Foundations contributed $2.9-million for the CFR's normal research and administrative costs through 1974.

McCloy's chairmanship in the CFR coincided with a major drive by the CFR to give the Red China lobby a massive dose of encouragement with the CFR's publication of Robert Blum's *The United States and China in World Affairs*. (Blum died before the book was completed but Doak Barnett, a veteran Red China lobbyist, completed Blum's work.) The Blum-Barnett volume recommended U.S. diplomatic recognition and United Nations membership for Red China; U.S. cultural exchanges with Red China; and, the abolition of the U.S. trade embargo against Red China. (The CFR, through chairman Allen W. Dulles of its China study project, denied that the Blum-Barnett book was a statement of policy by the CFR. But, as Dulles explained, the book presented "what we consider a useful set of conclusions, useful knowledge to inform people . . . [and] will prove to be a very important book in the history of our relations with [Red] China.")

McCloy's background in the Ford Foundation, World Brotherhood, the Disarmament Agency, and the Atlantic Institute made him an ideal leader for the CFR. For several decades, it has been obvious that the saturation of federal government policy-making positions by CFR members has driven U.S. foreign policy in the direction of appeasement for the Communist bloc, disarmament of U.S. defenses, betrayal of anti-Communist allies, loss of American sovereignty, and measures designed to achieve a one-world order dominated by Socialists and Communists. As an advisory editor of CFR's *Foreign Affairs,* McCloy must bear the responsibility of offering an influential and prestigious forum to ultra-liberal American and foreign internationalists as they propagandize for anti-United States policies.

The Public Policy Committee of the Advertising Council has also been served by McCloy. A major part of the Coun-

cil's efforts has been the promotion of a socialized America in a collectivist one-world. And, as usual, McCloy would be affiliated with some of the nation's more prominent leftwingers on the Policy Committee, including Sarah Blanding, Ralph Bunche, Henry Wriston, and Eugene Meyer. (One of McCloy's earliest indications of his affinity for leftwingers was in his defense of J. Robert Oppenheimer *after* Oppenheimer had been branded as a security risk.)

Among other tasks which McCloy has performed in his busy career was his participation in a three-man coordinating committee assigned by President Kennedy to work out a final "settlement" of the Cuban problem in 1962. With McCloy on the committee were Adlai Stevenson and George Ball. If they settled anything favorable to American interests, the American people have yet to be informed.

In the very early days of the Johnson Administration, McCloy was appointed to the President's Commission on the Assassination of President Kennedy – the so-called Warren Commission whose report created more questions than it ever answered.

GALE McGEE was born on March 17, 1915 in Lincoln, Nebraska, son of Frances McCoy and Garton McGee. He married Loraine Baker. He is an alumnus of Nebraska State Teachers College (A.B., 1936), the University of Colorado (M.A., 1939), and the University of Chicago (Ph.D., 1947).

From 1936 until 1940, McGee was a high school teacher. From 1940 until 1946, he was a history instructor at Nebraska Wesleyan University, Iowa State College, the University of Notre Dame, and the University of Chicago. From 1946 until 1958, he was a history professor at the University of Wyoming. In 1952 and 1953, he made a study of Soviet intentions for the Council on Foreign Relations, the informal supra-State Department of the United States. In 1956, he was director of a tour to the Soviet Union.

Since 1958, McGee has been in the United States Senate as a Democrat from Wyoming. He is a non-resident member of the Council on Foreign Relations. In 1964, he was a member of Arthur Larson's National Council for Civic Responsibility and, in 1966, he joined Franklin Littell's Institute for American Democracy, hysterical successor to Larson's abortive NCCR. He is a member of Clarence Streit's Atlantic Union, which is working towards a political merger of Western Europe and the United States, as a major step toward world government.

McGee as a Senator has made a career out of anti-anti-Communist activity.

His particular targets have been members of The John Birch Society. In his seven-year fight against the anti-Communists, McGee has displayed little imagination and has been content to repeat the tiresome clichés of the Anti-Defamation League, the Communist press, and the minions of Walter Reuther. McGee starts out with the theory that there is little difference between the Communist Party and The John Birch Society, and parlays this bit of nonsense with one extreme statement after another into his conclusion – bolstered by not one whit of evidence – that The John Birch Society is seeking totalitarian control of the United States. As for McGee's Senatorial activities, he is predictably a super-liberal on both foreign and domestic affairs, and, in bald political terms, he is in Bobby Kennedy's back pocket.

RALPH McGILL was born on February 5, 1898 in Soddy, Tennessee, son of Lou Skillern and Benjamin McGill. He studied at, but did not graduate from, Vanderbilt University.

From 1923 until 1928, McGill was a reporter and sports editor for the *Nashville Banner*. Since 1929, he has been with the *Atlanta Constitution*. He was sports editor (1929-1938), executive editor (1938-1942), editor (1942-1960), and, since 1960, has been publisher.

He has been a director of the socialist Ford Fund for Advancement of Education. He has been a trustee of the leftwing pacifist Carnegie Endowment for International Peace. In 1964, he belonged to Arthur Larson's National Council for Civic Responsibility and, in 1966, he joined Franklin Littell's Institute for American Democracy, hysterical successor to Larson's abortive NCCR. He has been affiliated with the Southern Conference for Human Welfare ("Communist front"), and the ultra leftwing National Committee for an Effective Congress. In 1964, he received the Presidential Medal of Freedom.

It is entirely possible that McGill was a competent sports writer in his early days. He is capable of competence. He has been over the years one of the most competent anti-anti-Communists to be found in American journalism. It matters little whether McGill writes on congressional investigating committees, civil rights, The Congo, China (Free or Red), Cuba, politics, Kenya, Vietnam, the United Nations, the Soviet Union, the Supreme Court, or riots in the streets, he epitomizes the hysterical bleeding-hearts who ignore logic and history to prove that anti-Communists are the scourge of the 20th Century, while the Communists – if not completely on the side of the angels — are really not too difficult to get along with.

How far McGill will go not to offend Communists was demonstrated in a recent piece he did for *Saturday Evening Post* ("Hate Knows no Direction"). In the piece, McGill wrote a plaintive account of President Kennedy's assassination. The assassin was not named — the deed was performed by a "psychopathic hater. So hate triumphed. And hate remains." Lee Harvey Oswald, the self-described Marxist, was dismissed by McGill as "the first suspect at Dallas . . . a typical product of the furnaces of madness . . . not alone in his hate. His deed brought out the glee of the right-wing extremists." How the Communists reacted to theirr comrade's deed, McGill never mentioned.

GEORGE McGOVERN was born on July 19, 1922 in Avon, South Dakota, son of Frances McLean and Joseph McGovern. He married Eleanor Stegeberg. He is an alumnus of Dakota Wesleyan University (B.A., 1945) and Northwestern University (M.A., 1949; Ph.D., 1953).

From 1948 until 1950, McGovern held a teaching assistantship and fellowship at Northwestern University. From 1950 until 1953, he was a professor of history and political science at Dakota Wesleyan University.

From 1953 until 1966, McGovern was executive secretary of the South Dakota Democratic Party. In that same period, he was a member of the advisory committee on political organization of the Democratic National Committee. (In 1948, McGovern was a staunch supporter of presidential candidate Henry A. Wallace, the Communists' patsy.)

From 1957 until 1961, McGovern was in the U.S. House of Representatives where his voting record established him as one of the great spendthrifts of that era. In 1960, he made a vain attempt to unseat U.S. Senator Karl Mundt but as a consolation prize he became a special assistant to President John F. Kennedy and, in 1961 and 1962, he became the first director of the so-called Food-for-Peace Program.

In 1962, McGovern was elected to the U.S. Senate. There he continued his tradition of voting for one federal boondoggle after another. But of more importance has been his stand on foreign policy. He is an out-and-out peacenik and a scaremonger. On domestic issues, he has been a vigorous anti-anti-Communist and, in foreign affairs, he has been extremely soft on Communism, going so far as to advocate that foreign aid be extended to Red China and that Red China be invited by the United States to sit in on discussions of nuclear weapons control and other disarmament measures.

A few years ago, McGovern was quite incensed over what he felt was an American obsession with Fidel Castro whom McGovern described as a second-rate Communist whose barbarous regime in Cuba and whose exporting of subversion to Latin America was not worth our worry.

On the Vietnam War, McGovern has been a close ally of J. William Fulbright. He considers the conflict a civil war. He shuns the idea of a military victory and wants the Vietcong at the peace table and to be represented in any provisional government that might emerge from peace negotiations.

McGovern could serve as the archetype of ultra-liberals in the Congress. He has been supported by the leftist National Farmers Union, Walter Reuther's

Committee on Political Education, the radical-leftist Americans for Democratic Action, Jimmy Hoffa's opportunistic Teamsters Union, and the ultra-leftist National Committee for an Effective Congress.

In 1968, McGovern made two dramatic moves into the headlines. On August 10 – just a few days before the Democratic National Convention – he announced that he was a candidate for the U.S. presidency, committed to "the goals for which Robert Kennedy gave [sic] his life . . . an end to the war in Vietnam and a passionate commitment to heal the divisions in our life here at home." Three days after his announcement (which made scarcely a ripple in Democrat Party politics), McGovern joined a picket line of grape strikers and praised their pro-Communist leader Cesar Chavez.

FLOYD B. McKISSICK was born on March 9, 1922 in Asheville, North Carolina, son of Magnolia Thompson and Ernest McKissick. He married Evelyn Williams. He is an alumnus of North Carolina College (A.B., 1951; LL.B., 1952). He also attended Morehouse College and he was the first Negro to attend the University of North Carolina's Law School.

In 1952, McKissick was admitted to the North Carolina bar and he began the practice of law in Durham as senior partner in the firm of McKissick & Burt.

In 1960, McKissick became general counsel for the Congress of Racial Equality. Subsequently, in 1963, he became CORE's national chairman and, in 1966, its national director, succeeding James Farmer.

McKissick became an active agitator in 1947 when he joined in demonstrations with James Farmer. In 1961, he organized and defended sit-in demonstrators in Durham. In 1963, he was a leading figure in the March on Washington.

In the past few years, McKissick has become the most vocal and literate advocate of black power – a power to be achieved through revolutionary means. His utterances are perhaps the key to understanding his inflammatory position: "The Negro people have dictated the course of this revolution. We shall proceed by carrying out this revolution." – "Forget about civil rights. I'm talking about black power." – "Negroes are not geared to nonviolence."

For the white man, McKissick has this advice: "If you want to help, keep your mouth shut and get out of my way." He has stated bluntly that nonviolence and integration are "dead and gone. You turn your right cheek and you turn your left cheek, and when you run out of cheeks you pick up a two by four."

As is the case with other Negro demagogues, McKissick has portrayed the Vietnam War as a conspiracy against colored people: "This is a war to extend our [U.S. military] bases, and the poor colored peoples over there are fighting for the same thing that we're fighting for [in the U.S.]. I was there and I talked with them and I know how they think. They see the U.S. as an aggressor.

"This is truly a war of neo-colonialism, a method to control people. We say we need Vietnam as protection against Chinese Communists, and we classify anybody who wants to be free of oppression as a Communist. If I'm here in New York City and a man has got his foot on my neck and is beating me on the head and I say, 'Take your foot off my neck, I want my freedom.' They say, 'You're a Communist.' "

McKissick, despite his legal training, is not above resorting to hyperbole and even outright lies to promote his racist cause as he slanders America and Americans: "The true bastion of white supremacy, that country which makes it all possible, is the United States of America. The cry of the racist white man is: 'Threaten not our system, or you will be annihilated by our National Rifle Association, the Ku Klux Klan, the White Citizens Councils — which we fund; by the Minuteman, Birchers and vigilantes, whom we condone; and by our National Guard, which is integrated, our state militia, our state, city and county police forces, which are also integrated. The system of exploitation is far more important — and far more precious — than human lives . ' ... Would America destroy the lives of millions of blacks whose forebears, as slaves, made and developed this economic-political system by their blood, sweat and free labor? ... Would America systematically destroy 22 million blacks? My answer is: Look at the record! More specifically, I believe they can. I believe they will."

In the aftermath of Martin L. King's assassination, President Lyndon Johnson summoned a number of Negro leaders to the White House. McKissick was among them. But when he arrived at the White House he considered himself to be the only militant there. ("I didn't see Stokely [Carmichael], Rap [Brown], Elijah Muhammad or any other black brothers.") Deprived of his leftwing soul mates for company, McKissick refused to meet with President Johnson.

In the past, McKissick has expressed his admiration for the ultra-leftist former Congressman Adam Clayton Powell. He has worked with the Communist agitator Jesse Gray. He was a key figure in 1967 at the National Conference for New Politics, which was nothing less than a classical united front third party move-

ment largely controlled by the Communist Party. And when he assumed the national directorship of CORE in 1966, he all but invited the Communists to join him in his agitation: "CORE has many friends. Some might be Black Muslims or the Communists. I am interested in working only for the interest of the people, no matter who the people are."

McKissick, at times, presents an elaborate facade of an enlightened program for Negroes. For example, in 1967, he took a brief leave of absence from CORE to work with the Metropolitan Applied Research Center, which was financed by a $500,000 grant from the Ford Foundation. Ostensibly, McKissick's method was to transfer power from whites to blacks by stressing Negro education and participation in politics, economics, leadership training, consumer cooperatives, and the strict enforcement of existing laws.

Such lofty sentiments may deserve the largesse of the Ford Foundation but McKissick's real methodology is better understood in the language he uses to exhort his black followers ("pick up a two by four") and how he would intimidate the white man ("keep your mouth shut and get out of my way").

ROBERT S. McNAMARA was born on June 9, 1916 in San Francisco, son of Clara Strange and Robert McNamara. He married Margaret Craig. He is an alumnus of the University of California (A.B., 1937) and Harvard University (M.B.A., 1939).

From 1940 until 1943, McNamara was an assistant professor of business administration at Harvard University. From 1946 until 1961, he was an executive of the Ford Motor Company.

From 1961 until 1968, he was Secretary of Defense. He announced his resignation, effective March 1, 1968, and he will become head of the World Bank.

Clark Mollenhoff, the veteran Washington correspondent, wrote in his book *The Pentagon,* published in 1967: "Periodically, an authoritarian trend becomes apparent in the comments or actions of a highly placed civilian official or military officer. But such glimpses of the danger are fleeting, and few take the time to examine the evidence of the total power potential accumulated in the Office of Defense Secretary.

"Viewed in its totality, the power centralized in the Office of Defense Secretary could be used to impose a dictatorship on the nation. There are still occasional challenges to the Office of Defense Secretary, but they have appeared to be futile in most instances."

Mr. Mollenhoff obviously had Robert McNamara in mind when he made these comments. In eight years as Secretary of Defense, McNamara certainly did impose a dictatorship upon the military. For in those eight years, strategic and tactical warfare were not under the direction of military men but rather under the guidance of McNamara who, before he entered the Kennedy cabinet, had been no closer to combat than the Pentagon building where he spent a couple of years during World War II working on statistical control for supplies in the Army Air Corps.

After he became Defense Secretary in 1961, McNamara displayed an almost pathological distrust of competent military men and, with respect to the Vietnam War, he has shown a marked obsession against victory. As Secretary of Defense, McNamara has accomplished a total fiasco in Communist Cuba with the abortive invasion at the Bay of Pigs; he has intimidated military leaders into virtual silence on the matter of public utterances about the Communist enemies of this nation; he has utilized his power in the Defense Department to promote the sociological idiocies of the New Frontier and Great Society, and to implement the equally idiotic sociological excursions of the Supreme Court; he has lobbied for disarmament along the very lines advocated by the pro-Communist Pugwashers; he has revamped the Air Force defense mechanism in direct contradiction to the most experienced advisors in the Air Force; he has given the Congress and the American people a mountain of mis-information on Defense Department budgets and on the progress of the Vietnam War; and, he has bedeviled the greatest military establishment in the world with computers to replace human ingenuity and the will to win so as to prolong the Vietnam War against a foe that couldn't care less as to how long American lives and resources are expended in Southeast Asia.

CAREY McWILLIAMS was born on December 13, 1905 in Steamboat Springs, Colorado, son of Harriet Casley and Jerry McWilliams. He married Iris Dornfeld. He is an alumnus of the University of California (LL.B., 1927).

From 1927 until 1938, McWilliams practiced law in Los Angeles. From 1938 until 1942, he was Commissioner of Immigration and Housing for the State of California.

In 1945, McWilliams joined the staff of *Nation* magazine as a contributing editor. In succeeding years, he became an associate editor, editorial director, and, since 1955, has been editor. Among his better known books are *Brothers under the Skin; Prejudice; A Mask for Privilege: Anti-Semitism in America;* and *Witchhunt: The Revival of Heresy.*

In 1956, the Senate Internal Security

Committee included McWilliams' name in its list of the eighty-two most active and typical sponsors of Communist front organizations. McWilliams has been identified under oath as a Communist. McWilliams (not under oath) has denied this.

McWilliams has been affiliated with the American Committee for Protection of Foreign Born [Americans] ("subversive and Communist" – "one of the oldest auxiliaries of the Communist Party in the United States" – under the "complete domination" of the Communist Party); the American Committee for Spanish Freedom ("Communist"); the American Council on Soviet Relations ("established by the Communist Party"); the American League against War and Fascism ("subversive and Communist"); the American Peace Crusade ("Communist front"); American Peace Mobilization ("subversive and Communist"); American Slav Congress ("subversive and Communist"); American Writers Congress ("subversive"); American Youth for Democracy ("subversive and Communist"); *Black and White* ("Communist-controlled publication"); Citizens Committee for Better Education ("Communist front"); Citizens' Committee to Free Earl Browder ("Communist"); the Civil Rights Congress ("subversive and Communist"); the Committee for a Democratic Far Eastern Policy ("Communist"); the Committee of One Thousand ("Communist created and controlled front organization"); Consumers Union ("subversive and un-American"); the Emergency Conference to Halt the Black-out of Civil Liberties in California ("Communist-inspired conference"); Friends of the Abraham Lincoln Brigade ("its officers and staff members were in the main [Communist] Party members and functionaries"); the Hollywood Community Radio Group ("Communist inspired and directed"); the Hollywood Independent Citizens Committee of the Arts, Sciences and Professions ("Communist front"); the International Juridical Association (an organization "which actively defended Communists and consistently followed the Communist Party line"); the International Labor Defense ("legal arm of the Communist Party"); the International Workers Order ("subversive and Communist"); the Joint Anti-Fascist Refugee Committee ("subversive and Communist"); Lawyers Committee on American Relations with Spain ("Communist lawyers' front organization"); the League of American Writers ("subversive and Communist"); the Los Angeles Emergency Committee to Aid the Strikers ("Communist front"); Mobilization for Democracy (one of the "key Communist fronts in California" – "engaged in inciting riots, racial hatred, and disrespect for law and order"); the National Emergency Conference ("Communist front"); the National Emergency Conference for Democratic Rights ("Communist front" – "subversive and un-American"); the National Federation for Constitutional Liberties ("subversive and Communist"); the National Free Browder Congress ("Communist front"); the National Lawyers Guild ("the foremost legal bulwark of the Communist Party, its front organizations, and controlled unions"); *New Masses* ("Communist periodical"); *Pacific Weekly* ("Communist publication"); *People's Daily World* ("official organ of the Communist Party"); People's Educational Center ("a Communist Party school"); People's Institute of Applied Religion ("subversive and Communist"); Progressive Citizens of America, California ("political Communist front"); the Schneiderman-Darcy Defense Committee ("Communist"); *Science and Society* ("Communist publication"); the Simon J. Lubin Society (Communist front"); the Sleepy Lagoon Defense Committee ("Communist front"); *Social Work Today* ("Communist magazine"); the Southern Negro Youth Congress ("subversive" – "Communist front"); the Spanish Refugee Appeal ("Communist front"); Veterans of the Abraham Lincoln Brigade ("subversive and Communist"); Western Writers' Congress ("Communist front"); the Yanks Are Not Coming Committee (the Communist Party was "the principal agent" in the movement); the American Continental Congress for Peace ("another phase in the Communist 'peace' campaign, aimed at consolidating anti-American forces throughout the Western Hemisphere"); an Open Letter to American Liberals (published by "a group of well-known Communists and Communist collaborators" in defense of the Moscow purge trials); and, the National Committee to Abolish the House Un-American Activities Committee ("to lead and direct the Communist Party's 'Operation Abolition' Campaign").

McWilliams was an early member of Americans for Democratic Action, the center of the radical left in American politics. In 1966, McWilliams was a member of the National Council of the National Conference for New Politics (a classical, united front, third party movement largely controlled by the Communist Party).

MARGARET MEAD was born on December 16, 1901 in Philadelphia, daughter of Emily Fogg and Edward Sherwood. She is an alumna of Barnard College (B.A., 1923) and Columbia University (M.A., 1924; Ph.D., 1929).

In 1925 and 1926, Mead was a fellow of the National Research Council, working in Samoa. Since 1926, she has been associated with the American Museum of Natural History as assistant curator (1926-1942), associate curator (1942-1964), and, since 1964, as curator of ethnology. Since 1954, she has been adjunct professor of anthropology at Columbia University. In 1954, she was a visiting professor of psychiatry at the University of Cincinnati. She has written numerous books on anthropology, including one with the notorious fellow traveler Ruth Benedict.

Mead has become widely known through her writings in such popular magazines as *Redbook* and *Parents'* and her appearances before lecture audiences. No subject seems to be beyond her expertise: patriotism, religion, nuclear warfare, international law, mental health, population control, peaceful coexistence, labor, and education. Her stance on any issue is invariably far to the left, and she reveals herself as an anti-anti-Communist, a ban-the-bomb pleader, and a complete one-worlder.

SEYMOUR MELMAN was born on December 30, 1907 in New York City, son of Pauline Kozdan and Abraham Melman. He married Clarice Danielsson. He is an alumnus of the College of the City of New York (B.S.S., 1939) and Columbia University (Ph.D., 1949).

In 1944 and 1945, Melman was a research assistant to the National Industrial Conference Board in New York City. Since 1948, he has been a professor at Columbia University. He has written *Dynamic Factors in Industrial Productivity; Decision-Making and Productivity; Inspection for Disarmament;* and *The Peace Race.*

Melman is an official of the National

Committee for a Sane Nuclear Policy (leftwing, pacifist.) He has been affiliated with the socialist League for Industrial Democracy. In 1966, he was a sponsor of the National Voters' Pledge Campaign, which was led by Socialist Norman Thomas, veteran Communist-fronter Reverend William Sloane Coffin, and Sanford Gottlieb, the political director of the National Committee for a Sane Nuclear Policy. The Voters' Pledge Campaign was designed to support "peace" candidates, who would work for a cease-fire in Vietnam and encourage negotiations in which the Vietcong would be participants. In 1966, he became an officer of the National Conference for New Politics (a classical united front third party movement largely controlled by the Communist Party).

Melman is usually described as an industrial management expert. His expertise consists of setting up the mythical military-industrial complex as a straw man, knocking it down, and converting it to a useful "industrialization of Latin America, Asia and Africa." He has the typical Marxist disdain for free enterprise industrial development and preaches that industrial production should serve "a larger social purpose" by allowing trade unions to decide how and to which nations industrial products will be given away.

Melman is also a leading advocate of a no-win policy in the Vietnam War. But his real forte is his campaign for disarmament. It is his plan that the United States should halt its missile production, close down all military research laboratories and facilities, and abandon all factories which operate under the Atomic Energy Commission. He believes that total disarmament should be administered through a United Nations police force but that only self-inspection

of disarmament procedures should take place in those nations involved in disarmament agreements.

By himself, with his fanatical pacifism, Melman could be ignored; but unfortunately he has the powerful SANE organization as a platform and he is no stranger to eggheads in the Johnson Administration. His well-publicized pleas for unilateral disarmament were praised in the Communists' *Worker* as "constructive, involving no concessions to imperialist [i.e., American] objectives which are the actual cause of international tension."

LEE METCALF was born on January 28, 1911 in Stevensville, Montana, son of Rhoda and Harold Metcalf. He married Donna Hoover. He is an alumnus of Stanford University (A.B., 1936) and Montana State University (LL. B., 1936). In 1936, he was admitted to the Montana bar and began the practice of law. In 1937, he was a Representative in the Montana Legislature. From 1937 until 1941, he was an assistant attorney general of Montana. From 1946 until 1952, he was an associate justice (elected) of the Montana Supreme Court.

From 1953 until 1961, Metcalf was a Representative to the U.S. Congress. Since 1961, he has been in the U.S. Senate.

In the Senate, Metcalf has been a rubber-stamp hack for the Kennedy and Johnson Administrations, voting without deviation for welfare state legislation. He is an especially ardent supporter of federal "aid" to education, the Job Corps, and legislation dictated by organized laborr. He is an extremist on gun control legislation and has advocated the *complete* prohibition of the sale of hand guns. He votes the ultra-liberal line on foreign affairs. On the matter of Vietnam, he has slavishly followed the dovish example of Montana's senior Senator Mike Mansfield, particularly on the matter of placing the Vietnam question in the hands of the United Nations Security Council.

Metcalf is a favorite of the ultra-leftist National Committee for an Effective Congress for which he has solicited funds and, in return, he has received the NCEC's endorsement along with such other ultra-liberals as Frank Church of Idaho, Ernest Gruening of Alaska, Clifford Case of New Jersey, George McGovern of South Dakota, and Wayne Morse of Oregon.

Metcalf was a favorite candidate of Eastern liberals, including the Kennedy dynasty. Organized labor has given him its complete backing and, in 1966, the Communist journals of the east coast and west coast (*The Worker* and *People's World*) were quite concerned about his chances for re-election. The Mine, Mill and Smelter Workers Union, so prominent in the mining State of Montana and which was expelled from the CIO in 1950 because it was Communist-controlled, threw its support to Metcalf in 1966.

ARTHUR MILLER was born on October 17, 1915 in New York City, son of Augusta Barnett and Isidore Miller. He was married to and divorced from Mary Slattery and Marilyn Monroe. He is married to Ingeborg Morath. He is an alumnus of the University of Michigan (A.B., 1938).

After his graduation from Michigan, Miller worked briefly for the Federal Theater Project. He wrote scripts for several radio network programs and then settled down to a career as author and playwright. His books include *Situation Normal* and *Focus*. His plays include *The Man Who Had All the Luck; All My Sons; Death of a Salesman; Enemy of the People; The Crucible; A View from the Bridge; After the Fall; The Price;* and, *Incident at Vichy.* He has written a film script, "The Misfits," which is included in a collection of his short stories, *I Don't Need You Any More.* Miller's writings have brought him numerous honors, including the New York Drama Critics Circle Award on two occasions, the Pulitzer Prize for Drama, the Antoinette Perry Award, and the Gold Medal for Drama from the National Institute of Arts and Letters.

Miller has been affiliated with the World Peace Congress ("Communist front"); American Youth for Democracy ("subversive and Communist"); the Civil Rights Congress ("subversive and Communist"); Progressive Citizens of America ("subversive") Contemporary Writers ("subversive"); Stage for Action ("subversive"); the Voice of Freedom Committee ("subversive"); the National Council of the Arts, Sciences and Professions ("a Communist front used to appeal to special occupational groups"); *Jewish Life* ("Communist front" publication); *New Masses* ("Communist periodical"); the National Committee to Defeat the Mundt Bill ("a Communist lobby"); the American-Russian Institute ("subversive" – "Communist"); and, the National Council of American-Soviet Friendship ("specializing in pro-Soviet propaganda").

In 1956, Miller was called upon to testify before the House Committee on Un-American Activities when the HCUA was investigating the unauthorized use of United States passports. Throughout the greater part of his testimony, Miller was evasive and argumentative and, to many questions, he reacted with a remarkable loss of memory. This latter point was dramatically demonstrated when he said that he couldn't remember if, in 1939 or 1940, he had signed an application for membership in the Communist Party.

During the course of his testimony, Miller swore that he had never been under Communist Party discipline nor had he ever written anything in his life that followed the Communist line. However, he did admit that, in 1947, he attended five or six meetings of Communist Party writers. But, when pressed by the HCUA staff and committee to reveal the names of those whom he had encountered in the Communist Party meetings, he refused to do so and was cited and convicted for contempt of Congress. On appeal to the U.S. Court of Appeals, his conviction was overturned on a technicality.

Beyond his long history of affiliations with Communist fronts, Miller was active in defending Communists who had been convicted or were threatened with conviction for being in violation of U.S. security laws. He has also been, during the past three decades, vigorous in his opposition to congressional investigating committees and anti-Communist legislation. And his opposition has been expressed not only through his front activities but also in his writings.

Though Miller has denied that he writes along the Communist line, his most popular themes have been directed against alleged witch hunts, capitalism, and free enterprise. He also raises the bogey of anti-Semitism and neo-Nazism. And, despite his disclaimer, Miller's writings are quite acceptable to the Communists who have given Miller extremely warm and favorable treatment in their publications.

Miller received nationwide, even international, attention in 1965, when, in a well-publicized letter, he refused an invitation to attend a White House signing of the Federal Arts and Humanities Act. Miller's letter was his form of protest against the United States' conduct of the war in Vietnam. Miller was grieved that the United States had not accepted Hanoi's peace proposals which, if accepted, would have meant virtual surrender on the part of the Americans. (The Communist publications *The Worker* and *National Guardian*, reveled in Miller's cheap histrionics.)

In the wake of the Robert F. Kennedy assassination, Miller was in the van of the hysterical breast-beaters blaming the murder on the American people ("a people of violence") and the Congress ("face to face with an army of poor people pleading for some relief of their misery – a Congress whose reply is a sneer, a smirk and a warning to keep order"). And, in a flight from all that is reasonable and logical, Miller somehow confused the act of assassination with Negroes' difficulties and the conduct of the war in Vietnam.

CLYDE MILLER was born in 1888 in Columbus, Ohio, son of Sarah Ketter and Charles Miller. He married Lotta MacDonald. He is an alumnus of Ohio State University (A.B., 1911). He is the author of *Process of Persuasion; What Everyone Should Know about Propaganda;* and, *The Seven Common Propaganda Devices.* He is co-author, with Fred Charles, of *Publicity and the Public School.*

In 1911 and 1912, Miller was a public school teacher in Mt. Vernon, Ohio. From 1912 until 1915, he was an assistant advertising manager for a department store in Columbus. From 1915 until 1920, he was a reporter for the *Ohio State Journal* and the *Cleveland Plain Dealer.* From 1920 until 1928, he was in charge of community relations for Cleveland's public school system. In this latter period, he lectured on public opinion, school administration, journalism and education at Harvard University, Ohio State University, Western Reserve University, New York University, and Columbia University. From 1928 until 1948, Miller was an administrator and teacher at Columbia University's Teachers College.

In 1937, Miller founded the Institute for Propaganda Analysis, an outlet for his own writings on propaganda and race relations. Since 1950, he has been an educational consultant to the leftwing-pacifist American Friends Service Committee. In recent years, he has been a visiting lecturer to New York University, Pennsylvania State University, Roosevelt University, and Southern Illinois University.

Miller was a founder of the National Committee to Repeal the McCarran Act, a Communist front. He was a founder of Protestants and Other Americans United for Separation of Church and State, which for twenty years has been a hotbed of anti-Catholicism under the leadership of Glenn Archer.

Miller was a founder of the Emergency Civil Liberties Committee, a Communist front. He was founder of Consumers Union, a Communist front. In 1956, the Senate Internal Security Subcommittee included Miller's name in its list of eighty-two most active and typical sponsors of Communist front organizations. Among his affiliations have been the American Committee for Democracy and Intellectual Freedom ("Communist front" – "subversive and un-American"); the American Committee for Protection of Foreign Born [Americans] ("subversive and Communist" – "one of the oldest auxiliaries of the Communist Party in the United States" – under the "complete domination" of the Commu-

nist Party); the American Council on Soviet Relations ("established by Communist Party"); the American League for Peace and Democracy ("subversive and Communist"); the Conference on Pan-American Democracy ("Communist front"); the Descendants of the American Revolution ("Communist front"); Associated Film Audiences ("Communist front"); Film Audiences for Democracy ("Communist front"); the League of American Writers ("subversive and Communist"); the National Emergency Conference ("Communist front"); the National Emergency Conference for Democratic Rights ("Communist front"); the People's Institute of Applied Religion ("subversive and Communist"); *Protestant Digest* ("the Communist Party line under the guise of being a religious journal"); the National Conference on American Policy in China and the Far East ("Communist"); the American Continental Congress for Peace ("another phase in the Communist 'peace' campaign, aimed at consolidating anti-American forces throughout the Western Hemisphere"); the Jefferson School of Social Science ("adjunct of the Communist Party"); the National Federation for Constitutional Liberties ("under [Communist] Party domination and headed by responsible Party functionaries"); and, the Scientific and Cultural Conference for World Peace ("Communist front").

Miller has been a staunch defender of the Communist Party and individual Communists. He has worked to abolish the House Committee on Un-American activities.

MAX MILLIKAN was born on December 12, 1913 in Chicago, Illinois, son of Greata Blanchard and Robert Millikan. He married Jeanne Thompson. He is an alumnus of Yale University (B.S., 1935; Ph.D., 1941). He also studied at California Technological Institute (1931-1933) and Cambridge University in England (1935-1936).

From 1938 until 1946, Millikan was on the faculty at Yale University as an instructor, assistant professor, and research associate. While on leave of absence from Yale during the war years, Millikan was a senior business specialist in the Office Price Administration (1942); the principal economist in the War Shipping Administration (1942-1944); and, assistant director of the division for ship requirements in the War Shipping Administration (1944-1946).

In 1946, Millikan was the chief economist in the intelligence branch of the division of research for Europe in the State Department. In 1947, he served, successively, as the assistant executive secretary of the President's Committee on Foreign Aid and as a consultant to the House of Representatives Select Committee on Foreign Aid.

In 1949, Millikan became a member of the faculty at Massachusetts Institute of Technology as an associate professor (1949-1951). In 1951 and 1952, Millikan, on leave of absence from MIT, became an assistant director of the Central Intelligence Agency. Upon his return to MIT in 1952, he became a professor and the director of the Center for International Studies, a CIA front. In 1956, he became president of the leftist World Peace Foundation and, in 1964, a trustee of the pacifist Carnegie Endowment for International Peace. He is a member of Clarence Streit's International Movement for Atlantic Union, which is working towards a political merger of Western Europe and the United States, as a major step towards world government. He is a non-resident member of the Council on Foreign Relations, the informal supra-State Department of the United States.

In 1957, Millikan collaborated with Walt W. Rostow in writing *A Proposal — Key to a More Effective Foreign Policy*, a product of the CIA's front, the Center for International Studies at MIT. The book was subsidized $200,000 by the United States Senate's Foreign Relations Committee. Millikan and Rostow called for a permanent foreign aid program for so-called underdeveloped nations which needed a "sense of progress." No strings were to be attached to the handouts. The entire book wasn't worth two cents — never mind $200,000 — but at least the CIA hoaxed some overhead expenses out of the Foreign Relations Committee and the unwitting American taxpayers.

WALTER MILLIS was born on March 16, 1899 in Atlanta, Georgia, son of Mary Raoul and John Millis. He was married to Norah Thompson. He is married to Eugenia Sheppard. He is an alumnus of Yale University (A.B., 1920).

From 1920 until 1954, Millis was a newspaper man as an editorial writer for the *Baltimore News* (1920-1923) and *New York Sun and Globe* (1923-1924), and as an editorial and staff writer for the *New York Herald Tribune* (1924-1954).

Since 1954, Millis has been staff director for the Fund for the Republic (ultra-leftist). He is on the staff of the Center for the Study of Democratic Institutions.

Millis was a sponsor of the National Committee to Abolish the House Un-American Activities Committee ("to lead and direct the Communist Party's 'Operation Abolition' campaign"). He has been a national official of the American Civil Liberties Union, that motleyed collection of defenders of subversion, crime, and licentiousness. He has been a non-resident member of the Council on Foreign Relations, the informal supra-State Department of the United States. He has been a sponsor of the National Committee for a Sane Nuclear Policy (leftwing, pacifist).

Millis has long been a leading member of the Surrender Lobby. Ten years ago, writing in the *New York Times* magazine, Millis said: "The establishment of Communist regimes in China, North Korea, North Vietnam and in Central Europe is the result of historic processes which, whether good or ill, cannot be undone . . . we should accept the situation and learn to live with it . . . . " In 1964, in a pamphlet ("Permanent Peace"), published by the Center for the Study of Democratic Institutions, he wrote: "If the price of avoiding all-out thermonuclear war should prove to be acquiescence in the 'Communist domination of the world' or any of the other unpleasant imaginings against which we cling futilely, to the war system, to preserve us, it seems possible that the price will be paid."

Millis is generally described as a "military historian" but he is, in reality, a pleader for a "better-Red-than-dead" approach to Communism. He is a scaremonger who adopted the utterly phony thesis that an American military-industrial complex is on the brink of leading this nation and the rest of the world into a nuclear holocaust. Here is the curious pseudo-psychoanalytical basis for his fears: "No one can doubt the sincerity with which the American professional declares his abhorrence of war – yet he is still a professional soldier. From the beginning of his career, war has provided his only [*sic*] reason for existence; he

has been deeply trained to think of war as the be-all [*sic*] and end-all [*sic*] of international relations and the only [*sic*] ultimate solution for the problems which international politics presents." It is no wonder that when James Roosevelt edited *The Liberal Papers* (the American leftwing manifesto of 1962), Millis was chosen to write on *A Liberal Military-Defense Policy*. At that time, he stated bluntly that U.S. foreign policy was founded upon the institution of war to the same extent as that of Red China and the Soviet Union.

In 1967, when the Consular Treaty between the U.S. and the Soviet Union was under consideration, Millis said, in a letter to the *New York Times:* "No one seems to have pointed out that even if the treaty enabled the Soviet Union to double or triple its espionage agents in the United States it would have little practical effect. Soviet espionage is like our own, all-pervasive and irritating; but it seems unlikely that all the secret activities of all the intricate 'intelligence communities' can have much effect on the destinies of nations in times of peace . . . .

"Mr. J. Edgar Hoover, having spent his career in combating Communist espionage, cannot admit that Communist espionage is a matter of very minor importance in the contemporary international world.

"I doubt that the treaty will actually be of much assistance to Russian espionage. But I am sure that, if it is, it will make very little practical difference."

JESSICA MITFORD was born on September 11, 1917 at Batsford, Gloucestershire, England, daughter of Sydney Bowles and David Mitford (Lord Redesdale).

At the age of eighteen, Jessica married

Esmond Romilly, a Communist. The newlyweds then went to Spain to fight alongside the Reds in the Civil War. In 1939, the Romillys moved to the United States. During World War II, Esmond Romilly was killed in action. (Depending on the whim of the moment, Jessica, in the course of interviews, sometimes says that her husband died while in the Royal Canadian Air Force. At other times, she says he was killed while serving in the British Army.)

In 1941, Jessica went to work for the Office of Price Administration in Washington, D.C. After her husband's death, she moved to San Francisco where she continued working for the OPA. In 1944, she married Robert Treuhaft, an attorney with the OPA. (In later years, Treuhaft would become notorious for his legal work on behalf of individual Communists, the Communist Party, and Communist fronts. On several occasions, he was identified in sworn testimony as a Communist but when given the opportunity to contradict such testimony, he pled his privilege against self-incrimination under the Fifth Amendment.)

While still with the OPA in 1944, Jessica became financial director of the California Labor School, which was subversive and Communist. By 1945, the Treuhafts' home became a popular meeting place for Communists. In 1946, Jessica was a successful fund-raiser as a county financial director for the Communist Party.

From 1949 until 1955, Jessica was secretary of the East Bay Civil Rights Congress. In a recent interview (*Boston Globe,* June 4, 1968), she described that outfit as "jolly subversive. It wanted to overthrow all sorts of segregation laws." On the other side of the coin, the House Committee on Un-American Activities, the Senate Internal Security Subcommit-

tee, and the Attorney General of the United States also cited the East Bay Civil Rights Congress as subverrsive – no jollity involved.

In 1956, Jessica worked a few months for the *San Francisco Chronicle.* She was fired from the Chronicle and shortly thereafter Jessica and her husband traveled to Communist Hungary in the wake of the Freedom Fighters' revolution which was crushed so barbarously by Khrushchev & Company. The Treuhafts, in an article for the Communist *People's World* (February 17, 1957), wrote a glowing account of life in Budapest. In 1958, Jessica went off on what appeared to be, at first glance, an unusual tangent. She launched an attack in *Frontier* magazine against undertakers. Meanwhile, in 1955, her husband had organized the Bay Area Funeral Society, a co-operative plan to finance burials. The set-up of the Society was socialistic and its directorship was studded with Communist fronters.

Five years later, Jessica hit the bestseller lists with a major attack on the undertakers with her full-length book, *The American Way of Death* – a hodgepodge of truth, half truths, innuendoes, and erroneous assertions. The left wing showered praises upon Jessica for her battle against the "capitalistic" villains of the undertaking profession. Even such prestigious Communist publications as the *New World Review* and the Moscow *New Times* spared space to hail Jessica's anti-capitalist crusade. And with the publication of her book, Jessica's name became a familiar by-line in popular magazines.

Jessica really did not need her book to win the favor of the extreme left. Over the years, she had labored tirelessly for Communist causes: clemency for the convicted atom spies, the Rosenbergs and Morton Sobell; clemency for convicted Communist Carl Braden; a petition against the Internal Security Act of 1950; a defense in *Nation* magazine of the anti-House Committee on Un-American Activities riots of 1960 in San Francisco; and, service in 1961 and 1962 as northern California representative for the Southern Conference Educational Fund, the financial backbone of the black power revolutionaries.

In 1966, Jessica became an associate editor of the far leftist *Ramparts* magazine. In 1968, she covered the Benjamin Spock trial when the baby doctor, turned ban-the-bomb-boob, was found guilty of conspiring to counsel, aid, and abet young men to evade the draft. Jessica represented the *Ladies Home Journal* at the trial and she is under contract to write a book about the proceedings.

On many occasions under sworn testimony, Jessica Mitford (or as she is also known, Decca Treuhaft) has been identified as a Communist Party member and functionary, but when given the opportunity to confirm or deny either status, she has invoked the protection of the Fifth Amendment against possible self-incrimination.

HANS MORGENTHAU was born on February 17, 1904 in Coburg, Germany, son of Frieda Bachmann and Ludwig Morgenthau. He came to the United States in 1937 and was naturalized in 1943. He married Irma Thormann. He studied at the University of Berlin, the University of Frankfurt, and the University of Munich, receiving academic degrees from Frankfurt and Munich. He did graduate work at the Graduate Institute for International Studies at Geneva, Switzerland.

From 1927 until 1930, Morgenthau practiced law in Germany. In 1931, he was an assistant to the law faculty at the University of Frankfurt. From 1932 until 1935, he was a political science instructor at the University of Geneva. In 1935 and 1936, he was a professor of international law at the Institute of International and Economic Studies in Madrid, Spain. From 1937 until 1939, he was an instructor in government at Brooklyn College. From 1939 until 1943, he was an assistant professor at the University of Kansas, teaching law, history, and political science.

Since 1943, Morgenthau has been on the faculty of the University of Chicago, teaching political science and modern history. He has been a visiting professor at the University of California, Harvard University, Northwestern University, Columbia University, Yale University, the Washington Center of Foreign Policy Research, and the Institute for Advanced Study in Princeton, New Jersey.

Morgenthau has been a sponsor of the National Committee for a Sane Nuclear Policy (leftwing, pacifist); a non-resident member of the Council on Foreign Relations (the informal supra-State Department of the United States); a national board member of Americans for Democratic Action (the center of the radical left in American politics); a member of Clarence Streit's Atlantic Union (working towards a political merger of Western Europe and the United States, as a major step towards world government); a member of Arthur Larson's National Council for Civic Responsibility (an election year's drive by the Democrat Party against anti-Communists); and, a member of the Inter-University Committee for a Public Hearing on VietNam (sponsors of the anti-Vietnam "teach-in" movement, which the Communist propaganda apparatus exploited for purely Communist purposes).

Morgenthau was a consultant to the Department of State in the Truman and Kennedy Administrations and a consultant to the Defense Department in the Kennedy Administration.

Morgenthau has become quite prominent nationally through his widely-publicized opposition to the Vietnam War. His solution is simple enough: let Ho chi Minh win the war. If that is not acceptable, then Morgenthau offers these alternatives: "A face-saving agreement which would allow us to disengage ourselves militarily in stages spaced in time; restoration of the status quo of the Geneva Agreement of 1954, with special emphasis upon all-Vietnamese elections; cooperation with the Soviet Union in support of a Titoist all-Vietnamese Government, which would be likely to emerge from such elections." The Communist editors of *New World Review* appreciate Morgenthau's views on the Vietnam situation so much that, on at least two occasions, they have reprinted his opinions in a totally favorable light. Morgenthau has also made quite a name for himself with his incredible observations on Red China. He insists that Red China is not and will not be a military threat to Asia but that its expansive ambitions are to be realized by its political and cultural preponderance. He has said that all the policies that Red China has pursued, even the rape and genocidal slaughter of Tibet, are part of Red China's traditional nationalist and imperialist policies. And Morgenthau is impressed by the "very great restraint and very limited aims the [Red] Chinese government has tried to pursue by military means."

WAYNE L. MORSE was born on October 20, 1900 in Dane County, Wisconsin, son of Jessie White and Wilbur Morse. He married Mildred Downie. He is an alumnus of the University of Wisconsin (Ph.B., 1923; M.A., 1924), the University of Minnesota (LL.B., 1928), and Columbia University (J.D., 1932).

In 1924, Morse was an instructor on the University of Wisconsin's faculty. From 1924 until 1928, he was an assistant professor at the University of Minnesota. In 1928 and 1929, he was a teaching fellow at Columbia University. From 1929 until 1944, he was on the faculty at the University of Oregon, serving successively as assistant professor of law (1929), associate professor (1930), and professor and dean of the law school (1931-1944), While on the Oregon faculty, Morse also served Roosevelt's New Deal in various capacities for the Justice Department, the Department of Labor, the President's Railway Emergency Board, the National Defense Mediation Board, and the National War Labor Board.

In 1944, Morse was elected as a Republican to the United States Senate and was re-elected in 1950. In his first term, Morse revealed himself to be wildly eccentric. He entered the Senate as a Republican but a fervent disciple of Franklin Roosevelt. In the Senate, he attacked Roosevelt and supported the Republican presidential candidacy of Thomas E. Dewey. Morse turned on Dewey and almost simultaneously turned on Harry Truman. Then Truman became Morse's "peerless leader." In his second term, Morse was a very early supporter of Dwight Eisenhower's presidential candidacy but, a week before the presidential elections of 1952, Morse switched his allegiance to the Democrats' presidential candidate, Adlai Stevenson. Shortly thereafter, Morse switched parties and finished his second term in the Senate as a Democrat. In 1956 and 1962, Morse was reelected to the Senate as a Democrat.

In his senatorial years, Morse has made more speeches and inserted more extraneous material in the *Congressional Record* than any other Senator in history. His speeches are invariably delivered before a minimum number of his colleagues, especially when he undertakes one of his frequent filibusters. When he is not speaking on the Senate floor, Morse is seldom present and, instead, spends a considerable amount of time traveling about the country on his very lucrative lecture circuit.

It would be easy to dismiss Morse as a harmless windbag or to explain his behavior as did former Ambassador Clare Boothe Luce. (After Morse had cast doubts on Mrs. Luce's mental stability and made inquiries as to whether she had been under psychiatric care, Mrs. Luce remarked that Morse's troubles were traceable to an occasion when he had been kicked in the head by a horse.) It is true that on domestic issues, Morse is completely unpredictable and there is no discernible pattern to his voting record, even though he is a member of Americans for Democratic Action. But on foreign policy, Morse is consistently on the side of Communist and pro-Communist regimes and against pro-American and anti-Communist regimes. He is unalterably opposed to any and all attempts to uncover subversive activities. He was one of the first Congressmen to advocate withdrawal from South Vietnam and his activities in this regard have received warm notices of approval in the Communist press throughout the world.

TEODORO MOSCOSO was born on November 26, 1910 in Barcelona, Spain, son of U.S. citizens Alejandrina Mora and Teodoro Moscoso. He married Gloria Vilella. He is an alumnus of the University of Michigan (B.S., 1932).

From 1932 until 1938, Moscoso was in private business in Puerto Rico. From 1938 until 1942, he was, successively, vice-chairman and executive director of the Ponce, Puerto Rico Housing Authority. From 1942 until 1950, he was president and general manager of the Puerto Rico Industrial Development Company. From 1950 until 1960, he was administrator of the Economic Development Administration in Puerto Rico.

In 1961 and 1962, Moscoso was U.S. Ambassador to Venezuela. While in Venezuela and visiting the University of Caracas, Moscoso left some classified intelligence documents in a parked automobile. He was decoyed away from the car and when he returned to the car, a mob was sacking and burning it. A few weeks later Ché Guevara, Castro's hatchet-man, displayed the documents at an Inter-American conference, in a successful move to embarrass the United States. From 1962 until 1964, Moscoso was the U.S. coordinator, with the rank of Ambassador, for the Alliance for Progress, the Kennedy Administration's program for handouts for socialism in Latin America. In 1964, he was a special advisor on Inter-American affairs to the Secretary of State. Since 1965, Moscoso has been a banker and businessman in Puerto Rico but, in 1966, New York City's Mayor John Lindsay appointed Moscoso to be a special consultant on the problems of the Puerto Ricans in Lindsay's Fun City.

Moscoso was never anything but completely sympathetic to leftwing regimes and absolutely hostile toward anti-Communist regimes in Latin America. And the nature of the Alliance for Progress and Moscoso's sympathies were revealed when Felipe Pazos was appointed as a director of the Alliance for

464

Progress. Pazos had been the treasurer of Fidel Castro's 26th of July Movement, was appointed by Castro to be president of Cuba's National Bank, and served as Castro's economic ambassador to Europe.

[MORRIS] STANLEY MOSK was born on September 4, 1912 in San Antonio, Texas, son of Minna Perl and Paul Mosk. He married Edna Mitchell. He is an alumnus of the University of Chicago (Ph.B., 1933).

Mosk studied law at the University of Chicago and was admitted to the California bar in 1935. From 1935 until 1939, he practiced law in Los Angeles. From 1939 until 1942, he was executive secretary to California's Governor Culbert L. Olson. From 1943 until 1958, he was a superior court judge in Los Angeles County. From 1959 until 1964, he was Attorney General of California. On August 14, 1964, Governor Edmund (Pat) Brown appointed him Justice of California's Supreme Court.

Mosk has affiliated himself with American Youth for Democracy ("subversive and Communist") and the National Lawyers Guild ("the foremost legal bulwark of the Communist Party, its front organizations, and controlled unions"). According to the west coast Communist publication *People's World*, he has been affiliated with the American Committee for Yugoslav Relief ("subversive and Communist"); the International Workers Order ("subversive and Communist"); Citizens' Committee to aid Locked-Out Hearst Employees ("Communist inspired and dominated group"); and, according to the *Los Angeles Examiner*, the California Conference for Democratic Action ("Communist front").

Mosk became an early member of Americans for Democratic Action, the center of the radical left in American politics. He has been very active in the American Civil Liberties Union, that motleyed collection of defenders of subversion, crime, and licentiousness. He has been a member of the ultra-leftist California Democratic Council.

Mosk, as Attorney General, displayed an obvious pro-Communist, anti-anti-Communist bias in his attitude toward legislative committees investigating subversion. He constantly downgraded the real and provable presence of organized Communist activity in California. He has allowed the prestige of his name and public office to be used in support of leftwing pacifists, pro-Communists, and civil rights agitators. On the other hand, his name and public office have been used offensively against anti-Communists.

FRANK MOSS was born on September 23, 1911 in Salt Lake City, son of Maud Nixon and James Moss. He married Phyllis Hart. He is an alumnus of the University of Utah (B.A., 1933) and George Washington University (J.D., 1937). In 1938, he was admitted to the Utah bar.

In 1938 and 1939, Moss was an attorney for the U.S. Securities and Exchange Commission. From 1939 until 1942, he practiced law in Salt Lake City. From 1940 until 1950, he was a judge (elective) in the City Court of Salt Lake City — a period interrupted by four years' service in the armed forces. In 1951, he resumed his Salt Lake City law practice. From 1951 until 1958, he was county attorney (elective) of Salt Lake. Since 1958, he has been in the U.S. Senate.

As a Democrat in the Senate, Moss has had an almost impeccable ultra-liberal voting record on both domestic and foreign issues. He is a very strong supporter of the United Nations. He is a member of the ultra-liberal appeasement group: "Members of Congress for World Peace through Law." On Vietnam, he is a follower of Senator J. William Fulbright, the leading agitator for peace negotiations.

Although Utah has had almost no racial strife, Moss is a fiery supporter of so-called civil rights legislation. But on gun-control laws, he has broken away from his liberal colleagues, deferred to his constituents, and taken a strong stand against restrictive gun legislation.

Moss is a sponsor of Franklin Littell's Institute for American Democracy, an elite representative group of leftists who have specialized in anti-anti-Communist activities and utterances.

DANIEL MOYNIHAN was born on March 16, 1927 in Tulsa, son of Margaret Phipps and John Moynihan. He married Elizabeth Brennan. He is an alumnus of Tufts University (B.A., 1948; M.A., 1949; Ph.D., 1961). He was a Fulbright fellow at the London School of Economics in 1950. He is on the national board of Americans for Democratic Action.

In 1953, Moynihan entered politics, campaigning for New York City's Mayor Robert Wagner. From the Wagner mayoralty campaign, Moynihan went to the International Rescue Committee and served that socialist-lined outfit as a director of public relations. From 1955 until 1958, he was on the staff of New York Governor Averell Harriman. During the next two years, he was a member of the New York State Tenure Commission and director of a New York State research project at Syracuse University.

In 1960, Moynihan worked in John F. Kennedy's presidential campaign, writing position papers on urban renewal and traffic safety. President Kennedy appointed Moynihan to the Department of Labor. He remained there until mid-1965 when he ran an unsuccessful campaign for the presidency of New York City's city council. In 1964, while in the Labor Department, Moynihan was a co-author (with Adam Yarmolinsky, Sargent Shriver, and James Sundquist) of the Economic Opportunity Act of 1964 – the legislative basis for Lyndon Johnson's so-called war on poverty. Also, while in the Labor Department, Moynihan wrote his famous *The Negro Family: The Case for National Action.*

Moynihan propounded the thesis – so familiar among racist agitators – that "three centuries of sometimes unimaginable mistreatment have taken their toll on the Negro people ... the circumstances of the Negro American community in recent years has probably been getting worse, not better ... [and] a national effort is required that will give a unity of purpose to the many activities of the Federal government in this area, directed to a new kind of national goal: the establishment of a stable Negro family structure." The "Moynihan Report," as it became popularly known, was just one of many of Moynihan's salvoes for making the Negroes, in their family life, the objects of "social legislation" (Moynihan's phrase).

When Moynihan left the Johnson Administration in mid-1965, he accepted a fellowship at Wesleyan University's Center for Advanced Studies to do further writing on the Negro family. And, since 1966, Moynihan has been director of the M.I.T.-Harvard Joint Center for Urban Affairs, where he is still concentrating on his pet theme.

In its full context, Moynihan's plan for social legislation on behalf of the

Amerian Negroes would make it appear that the federal government existed for the sole purpose of applying socialist measures to give the Negroes economic equality. For example, Moynihan proposes that the federal government guarantee jobs whenever the national unemployment rate is above three per cent. The federal government would create baby bonuses or as Moynihan expresses it: "a family or children's allowance." Moynihan suggested that the Post Office Department revive the two-deliveries a day system (not for the convenience of the public) so as to create 50,000 jobs which could help solve the problem of Negro unemployment. Other federal jobs could be "created" for hundreds of thousands in public services such as work in hospitals or street and building repair.

Moynihan, oddly enough, has been criticized bitterly by liberals and racial agitators. They have no objections to his socialist proposals. They do not care that he has no regard for the cost of the programs he suggests. They do object, however, to the fac that he has not placed one hundred per cent of the blame on the white people for whatever plight Negro families have. And some critics are unhappy that Moynihan's plans for federal social legislation to create family stability seem to be directed only at Negroes — which the critics insist is an insult to Negroes.

LEWIS MUMFORD was born on October 19, 1895 in Flushing, New York, son of Elvina Baron and Lewis Mumford. He was married to the late Sophia Wittenberg. He studied at the College of the City of New York, Columbia University, New York University, and the New School for Social Research.

In his early years, Mumford combined his prolific authorship with some teaching assignments. He was an associate editor of the *Fortnightly Dail* (1919); acting editor of the *Sociological Review* of London (1920); an editor of *The American Caravan,* a year book (1927-1936); and, a contributing editor of *New Republic* magazine. He lectured at the New School for Social Research (1925); at the School for International Studies at Geneva (1925); and, was a visiting lecturer at Dartmouth College from 1931 until 1935. From 1935 until 1937, he was a member of New York City's Board of Higher Education. He held a Guggenheim Fellowship in 1932 and 1938.

In more recent years, while continuing an enormous output of books, Mumford has been a professor of humanities at Stanford University (1942-1944); a professor of city and regional planning (1951-1959) and a research professor (1959-1961) at the University of Pennsylvania; a visiting professor at Massachusetts Institute of Technology (1957-1960); and, a senior fellow at the Center for Advanced Studies at Wesleyan University.

Mumford has been affiliated with the American Committee for Anti-Nazi German Seaman ("Communist front"); the American Committee for Anti-Nazi Literature ("Communist front"); the American Committee for Democracy and Intellectual Freedom ("Communist front" — "subversive and un-American"); the American Friends of Spanish Democracy ("subversive"); the American League for Peace and Democracy ("subversive and Communist"); the American Youth Congress ("subversive and Communist"); Book Union ("distributors of Communist literature"); the Coordinating Committee to Lift the Embargo ("Communist front"); the Lawyers Committee on American Relations with Spain

("Communist lawyers' front organization"); the National Committee for People's Rights ("entirely under the control of the Communist Party"); the Washington Committee to Lift the Spanish Embargo ("Communist front"); the Council for Pan-American Democracy ("subversive and Communist"); the League of American Writers ("subversive and Communist"); *New Masses* ("Communist periodical"); the National Committee to Repeal the McCarran Act ("a Communist front" — "subversive"); the Committee of One Thousand ("Communist created and controlled front organization"); the John Reed Clubs of the United States ("Communist front"); the American Society for Technical Aid to Spanish Democracy ("Communist front"); the Citizens Committee for Better Education ("Communist front"); and, the National Committee to Abolish the House Un-American Activities Committee ("to lead and direct the Communist Party's 'Operation Abolition' campaign").

Mumford has also been affiliated with the socialist League for Industrial Democracy; the United World Federalists, whose program is a very serious threat to American sovereignty and the sovereignty of all free nations; the American Civil Liberties Union, that motleyed collection of defenders of subversion, crime, and licentiousness; the National Committee for a Sane Nuclear Policy, leftwing, pacifist; the National Council for Civic Responsibility, an election year's drive by the Democrat Party against anti-Communists; and, Rex Stout's leftwing Society for the Prevention of World War III.

Mumford has petitioned for amnesty for Communists and for the atom spies — Sobell and the Rosenbergs. He is a non-resident member of the Council on Foreign Relations, the informal supra-State Department of the United States.

In 1964, President Lyndon Johnson presented Mumford with the Presidential Medal of Freedom.

EDMUND MUSKIE was born on March 28, 1914 in Rumford, Maine, son of Josephine Czarnecki and Stephen Muskie. He married Jane Gray. He is an alumnus of Bates College (B.A., 1936) and Cornell University (LL.B., 1939). In 1939, he was admitted to the Massachusetts bar. In 1940, he was admitted to the Maine bar and in that year he began the practice of law in Waterville.

Muskie served three terms in Maine's House of Representatives (1947, 1949, and 1951). In 1947, he was an unsuccessful mayoralty candidate in Waterville. In 1951 and 1952, he was district director in Maine for the Office of Price Stabilization. From 1952 until 1954, he was Maine's Democratic National Committeeman. In 1954, he was city solicitor for Waterville.

In 1954, after being unopposed in the Democratic gubernatorial primary, Muskie defeated the incumbent Republican Governor Burton Cross. Muskie was re-elected in 1956.

Since 1959, Muskie has been in the U.S. Senate. During his freshman year as a Senator, Muskie voted for cloture (anti-filibuster) against the expressed wishes of the Senate Majority Leader Lyndon Johnson. For his nonconformity, Muskie was exiled to the obscurity of three minor committees. The object lesson made an impression upon Muskie who from that day forward became a party hack. (Muskie evidently had some additional tutelage. In 1961, speaking of Lyndon Johnson's alter ego, Bobby Baker, Muskie admitted that Baker had been "a tremendous source of learning for me.")

When Muskie was elected Maine's Governor in 1954, he said that he was "neither a New Deal nor a Fair Deal Democrat, but a Maine Democrat." His party heroes were the late Franklin D. Roosevelt and Adlai Stevenson. But as a Governor and Senator, Muskie certainly conformed to the New Deal and Fair Deal, as well as the New Frontier and Great Society. His political fortunes have been supported lavishly by the United Auto Workers and other unions and his voting record has been 100 per cent pro-organized labor. His adherence to the program of Americans for Democratic Action is not perfect but is far superior to that of most of his Senatorial colleagues.

In 1968, Muskie's liberal credentials were so unmistakably established that he was chosen by the ultra-liberal presidential candidate Hubert Humphrey to be his vice presidential partner.

FRED WARNER NEAL was born on August 5, 1915 in Northville, Michigan, son of Bertha Frendt and Frank Neal. He married Grace Repine. He is an alumnus of the University of Michigan (B.A., 1937; Ph.D., 1955). He was a Nieman fellow at Harvard University in 1942 and 1943, a graduate student at the University of Karlova (Prague, Czechoslovakia) in 1949, and held Fulbright fellowships in 1950 and 1961.

Neal has written editorial columns for the *Detroit Free Press* (1953-1954) and the *Los Angeles Times* (1956-1958). He has contributed articles to the *Saturday Evening Post, Atlantic Monthly, Harper's, Current History, Nation,* and scholarly journals. He is the author of *The Politics of War* (1943), *Titoism in Action: The Reforms in Yugoslavia after 1948* (1958), *U.S. Foreign Policy and the Soviet Union* (1961), and *War and*

Peace and Germany (1962). With George W. Hoffman, he is co-author of *Yugoslavia and the New Communism* (1962).

In 1938, Neal was a Washington correspondent for United Press. From 1939 until 1943, he was a Washington and foreign correspondent for the *Wall Street Journal.* From 1943 until 1946, he saw service with the U.S. Navy. From 1946 until 1948, he was with the State Department as chief of foreign research and as a consultant on Russian affairs. In this latter capacity, "he presided over this country's first 'cultural relations' with the U.S.S.R. – a visit to the United States in 1946 by Russian writers Ilya Ehrenburg, Konstantin Simonov, and General Mikhail Glaktionov, military editor of *Pravda* – and organized the Voice of American broadcasts to the Soviet Union." (See, "Biographical Note" in Neal's *U.S. Foreign Policy and the Soviet Union.*)

In 1948 and 1949, Neal was assistant to the commissioner of the New York State Department of Education at the time when the State University of New York was being established.

In 1950, Neal was in France at the University of Paris as a Fulbright fellow. From 1951 until 1956, he was an assistant professor of political science at the University of Colorado. In 1956 and 1957, he was an associate professor at the University of California. From 1957 until 1960, he was an associate professor of international relations at the Claremont Graduate School in California and, since 1960, he has been a professor at the same institution. He has also been a visiting lecturer at the University of Michigan and a member of American University's Field Staff.

Neal has been a co-director of the Twentieth Century Fund's study on Yugoslavia. He has been a member of the foreign policy committee of the ultra-leftist California Democratic Council, a board member of the leftwing pacifist National Committee for a Sane Nuclear Policy, a member of the board of directors of the leftist Los Angeles Association for the United Nations, and a member of the Council on Foreign Relations (the informal supra-State Department).

In 1961, Neal became a consultant to the ultra-leftist Fund for the Republic's Center for the Study of Democratic Institutions. It was the Center that published Neal's *U.S. Foreign Policy and the Soviet Union,* and, as of 1967, there had been five printings of this brazen pro-Soviet tract. Neal's basic theme is that the Soviet Union has always been justifiably suspicious of the United States motives and that the United States must at least share the blame for the Cold War. Neal even offers the probability that the United States initiated the Cold War. As background for this muddled logic, Neal says: "A reasonable case can be made . . . for saying that the Russians gave as much as they got at Yalta." Exactly what they gave is not mentioned but obviously Neal believes that U.S. dissatisfaction with the Yalta deal brought about bad relations between the U.S. and the Soviet Union.

To Neal, the Soviet Union can do and has done no wrong. For example, he explains away the Soviet takeover of Eastern Europe in this fashion: "When Americans talk today about 'Soviet aggression,' they are likely to have in mind Soviet actions in Eastern Europe. In one sense these actions did constitute a type of aggression. But one does not have to approve of what the Russians did to see that it was not physical, military aggression, in the sense of one state simply initiating a war against another for the purpose of territorial aggrandizement. This point has been overshadowed by our emotional opposition to the Soviet Union."

Neal goes to great lengths in defense of Stalin who, says Neal, had a foreign policy that was purely defensive from 1921 until 1952. By a fantastic misreading of history, Neal insists that Stalin opposed the 1947 Communist revolution in Greece and advised Mao Tse-tung not to proceed with his Communist revolution in China. (Neal's pro-Communist apologetics is not confined to the Soviet Union. He has described North Korea's 1950 invasion of South Korea as not without "defensive overtones." And, in his two books on Yugoslavia, he applies the whitewash liberally to Tito.)

The purpose behind Neal's rewriting of history is to recommend a U.S. foreign policy saturated with compromise and appeasement so as to compensate the Soviet Union for the years of bad behavior on the part of the United States. And, if Neal's recommendations are to be followed, the United States will be completely cooperative in following the Soviet Union down the road to disarmament: "All Soviet proposals for disarmament are not necessarily propaganda and . . . there is little doubt about the earnestness and sincerity of the Soviet desire to limit and control arms production and to eliminate thermonuclear weapons and the deadly dangers for everybody that their existence creates." The United States, therefore, has no choice but to cooperate with the peace-loving Soviets as Neal indicates when he insists that "compromises [with the Soviet Union] are both possible and necessary."

The continuous distribution of Neal's tract by the influential Center for the Study of Democratic Institutions indicates clearly that the Center's officials, led by Robert Maynard Hutchins, are determined to propagandize for the total surrender of the United States to the Communist World. And the guidelines for the surrender which have been laid down by Neal seem remarkably close to the trend of U.S. diplomacy at the present time.

SCOTT NEARING was born on August 6, 1883 in Morris Run, Pennsylvania, son of Minnie Zabriskie and Louis Nearing. He married Nellie Seeds. He is an alumnus of Temple University (B.O., 1904) and the University of Pennsylvania (B.S., 1905; Ph.D., 1909).

From 1906 until 1915, Nearing taught economics – as an instructor and assistant professor – at the University of Pennsylvania and Swarthmore College. From 1915 until 1917, he was a professor of social science and dean of the College of Arts and Sciences at Toledo University. In that same period, he became a lecturer at the extremely radical Rand School of Social Science in New York City.

In 1919, Nearing was a candidate for Congress on the Socialist Party ticket in New York City. Nine years later he campaigned for the governorship of New Jersey on the Communist Party ticket. In 1924, he was the leader of a group which began the Communist infiltration of the New York Teachers Union.

In 1908, Nearing began a prolific writing career. His books, pamphlets, and brochures number in the hundreds. As recently as 1965, he wrote *The Conscience of a Radical,* a book which was singled out for special praise in the Communists' *The Worker.*

In recent years, Nearing has confined most of his activities to the lecture platform, usually on college and univer-sity campuses. He is billed as a peace movement leader, an advocate of world federation, and a world traveler. (In 1960, he traveled to Communist Cuba and, in 1959, to Communist China.)

In June, 1956, Chairman Francis Walter of the House Committee on Un-American Activities described Nearing as an identified member of the Communist Party. In November, 1964, while speaking in Miami, Florida, Nearing was asked: "Are you a card-carrying Communist?" He replied: "I am not now a card-carrying Communist but I am a Communist." For public consumption, Nearing was expelled from the Communist Party for publishing a book without obtaining previous permission from Party officials.

If Nearing held hard feelings toward the Communist Party over his expulsion, his activities and affiliations afterwards did not reflect this. He has been affiliated with the All-America Anti-Imperialist League ("Communist enterprise"); the American Committee for Struggle Against War ("Communist front"); the American Fund for Public Service ("a major source for the financing of Communist Party enterprises"); the American League for Peace and Democracy ("subversive and Communist"); the Federated Press ("Communist-controlled" news syndicate); Friends of the Soviet Union ("to propagandize for and defend Russia and its system of government" – "directed from Moscow"); the International Labor Defense ("legal arm of the Communist Party"); the John Reed Clubs ("Communist front"); the League of American Writers ("subversive and Communist"); the *Liberator* ("Communist magazine"); the American Committee for Protection of Foreign Born [Americans] ("subversive and Communist" – "one of the oldest auxiliaries of the Communist Party in the United States" – under the "complete domination" of the Communist Party); the National Student League ("Communist front"); People's Peace ("Communist front"); *Soviet Russia Today* ("Communist front publication"); the Student Congress against War ("controlled by the Communists"); the World Congress against War ("sponsored by the Communist International"); the Scientific and Cultural Conference for World Peace ("Communist front"); the International Workers Order ("subversive and Communist"); *New Masses* ("Communist periodical"); the American Continental Congress for Peace ("another phase in the Communist 'peace' campaign"); and, the World Peace Congress ("Communist front").

Since about 1955, Nearing has been director of the Social Science Institute at Harborside, Maine, which is nothing more than a launching pad for his radicalism.

REINHOLD NIEBUHR was born on June 21, 1892 in Wright City, Missouri, son of Lydia Hosto and Gustave Niebuhr. He married Ursula Keppel-Compton. He is an alumnus of Yale University's Divinity School (B.D., 1914; A.M., 1915).

In 1915, Niebuhr was ordained in the Evangelical Synod of North America. From 1915 until 1928, he held a pastorate in Detroit. In 1928, he joined the faculty of the Red-riddled, Red dominated Union Theological Seminary. He became professor emeritus in 1960.

Niebuhr has been with the American Committee for Protection of Foreign Born [Americans] ("subversive and Communist" – "one of the oldest auxiliaries of the Communist Party in the United States" – under the "com-

plete domination" of the Communist Party); the American Friends of the Chinese People ("Communist front"); the American Friends of Spanish Democracy ("subversive"); the American League for Peace and Democracy ("subversive and Communist"); the American League against War and Fascism ("subversive and Communist"); the American Student Union ("Communist front"); the China Aid Council ("Communist-controlled"); the Consumers' National Federation ("Communist front"); the Coordinating Committee to Lift the Embargo ("Communist front"); the National Citizens Political Action Committee ("Communist front"); the *Protestant Digest* ("Communist Party line"); and, the National Committee to Abolish the House Un-American Activities Committee ("to lead and direct the Communist Party's 'Operation Abolition' campaign").

Niebuhr has also been a founder and vice chairman of Americans for Democratic Action, the center of the radical left in American politics (he had been with the Red-lined Union for Democratic Action in the 1940's); a resident member of the Council on Foreign Relations, the informal supra-State Department of the United States; an official of the socialist League for Industrial Democracy; a supporter of the ultra-leftist National Committee for an Effective Congress; a consultant to the socialist Center for the Study of Democratic Institutions; a committeeman for the leftwing American Committee on Africa; and, a sponsor of Negotiation Now!, an ad hoc committee led by leftwing luminaries for appeasement in Vietnam, including Martin Luther King Jr., Joseph L. Rauh Jr., Victor Reuther, Arthur Schlesinger Jr., and John Kenneth Galbraith.

In 1964, Lyndon Johnson awarded Niebuhr the Presidential Medal of Freedom.

PAUL NITZE was born on January 16, 1907 in Amherst, Massachusetts, son of Anina Hilken and William Nitze. He married Phyllis Pratt. He is an alumnus of Harvard University (A.B., 1928).

In 1929, he joined the investment banking firm of Dillon, Read & Co. During World War II, he worked for the Coordinator of Inter-American Affairs, the Board of Economic Warfare, the Foreign Economic Administration, the War Department, and was vice chairman of the U.S. Strategic Bombing Survey.

In 1946, he began seven years of service in the State Department, serving successively as deputy director for International Trade Policy, deputy to the assistant secretary of state for economic affairs, and director of the policy planning staff.

Nitze left the State Department in 1953 and became president of the Foreign Service Educational Foundation which subsidizes (and administers jointly with The Johns Hopkins University) the School of Advanced International Studies in Washington.

During the Eisenhower Administration, Nitze was on the Gaither Committee which issued a scaremongering report on alleged military developments and progress of the Soviet Union, and the Gaither conclusion pointed toward the necessity of a peaceful accommodation with the Communists.

In the Eisenhower Administration, Nitze was named to be Assistant Secretary of Defense for International Security Affairs, but the appointment was rejected in the Senate. Nitze's reputation was enough to alarm anyone seriously concerned with national security.

In 1958, Nitze was chairman of a study commission at the National Council of Churches World Order Study Conference. The committee of which Nitze was chairman issued a report ("The Power Struggle and Security in a Nuclear-Space Age") which was nothing short of an out-and-out plea for accommodation and coexistence with the Soviet Union. The report recommended that U.S. foreign policy should move in the direction of diplomatic recognition for Red China and support membership for Red China in the United Nations. Other parts of the report included recommendations for unilateral cessation by the United States of nuclear testing; discontinuance of the military draft; and the use of military force only if such use received the sanction of the United Nations. Nitze would later object that the report was not his, but that of a committee. Nevertheless, he was the chairman and his disavowal came only after his critics caught up to him.

In 1960, Nitze was presidential candidate John F. Kennedy's chief advisor on national security policy. In that same year, while speaking to a seminar at Monterey, California, Nitze proposed that the United States Strategic Air Command be turned over to NATO and that later SAC and NATO be placed under the authority of the United Nations General Assembly.

Nitze's pay-off for his work during the 1960 presidential campaign was the same job that had been denied him in the Eisenhower Administration by the Senate − Assistant Secretary of Defense for International Security. Nitze was in the Defense Department until 1963, when he became Secretary of the Navy. In 1967, Nitze became the No. 2 man in the Defense Department when Lyndon Johnson named him to be Deputy Secretary of Defense.

CHARLES OSGOOD was born on November 20, 1916 in Somerville, Massachusetts, son of Ruth Egerton and Merrill Osgood. He married Cynthia Thornton. He is an alumnus of Dartmouth College (B.A., 1939) and Yale University (Ph.D., 1945).

In 1945 and 1946, Osgood was a research associate at Yale University. From 1946 until 1949, he was an assistant professor of psychology at the University of Connecticut. Since 1949, he has been on the faculty of the University of Illinois. In 1949, he became an associate professor and, in 1952, a professor of psychology. In 1957, he became the director of the University's Institute of Communications Research and a professor of communications and psychology. He has held fellowships from the Guggenheim Foundation and from the Center for Advanced Study in Behavioral Sciences. He has been president of the American Psychological Association. He has been a member of the behavioral science study section of the National Institute for Mental Health. He has been a visiting professor at the University of Hawaii.

Osgood has been a member of the science advisory panel of the Peace Research Institute (now known as the Institute for Policy Studies). The PRI-IPS was founded in 1961 as a clearing house for research scholars and those institutions and individuals interested in financing such scholars in the quest for world peace through disarmament and other measures. (In the PRI-IPS, Osgood joined a stellar group of leftists including: Marcus Raskin, Hans Morgenthau, James Warburg, Arthur Waskow, Thurman Arnold, Arthur Larson, Anna Rosenberg Hoffman, Victor Reuther, Margaret Mead, Jerome Frank, and Clark Clifford.)

While Osgood was in the Peace Research Institute, the organization's litera-

ture stated that "scholars and highly placed government people have worked with us on off-the-record projects." In effect, the PRI launched trial balloons which were much too revolutionary to *originate* as official government policies. The PRI explained its strategic role: "In general, there are many approaches to be explained which run counter to long and short run government policy and as such would embarrass present policy proponents and their offices if it were discovered that the government were supporting such studies."

Osgood proved to be an excellent trial balloonist. In 1962, he contributed an article ("Reciprocal Initiative") to *The Liberal Papers* which were edited by James Roosevelt. (*The Liberal Papers* were a result of the work done by the House Liberal Project, a group of twelve ultra-liberal members of the House of Representatives. They were led by Representative Robert W. Kastenmeier, Democrat from Wisconsin. Contributors to *The Liberal Papers* included such well-known leftists as Stuart Hughes, Walter Millis, Vera Micheles Dean, Arthur Waskow, Quincy Wright, David Riesman, and James Warburg. The papers contributed by this crowd, including Osgood's, were devoted exclusively to foreign policy. They reflected abject appeasement with Communist powers, extravagant extensions of foreign "aid" programs, reckless disarmament proposals, and grovelling obeisance to the United Nations.)

In his "Reciprocal Initiative," Osgood's major theme was that some form of world government was absolutely essential if our civilization were to survive. He proposed that the United States take unilateral steps in a "deliberate 'peace offensive' designed to induce reciprocation by an enemy." Fully aware that the American people would not support what amounted to a virtual and instantaneous surrender, Osgood suggested a subtle approach: "Unilateral acts must be planned in sequences and continued over considerable periods regardless of reciprocation by an opponent."

Osgood had a wide-ranging set of unilateral actions which the United States could take in its 'peace offensive,' which was only designed to *induce* — not force — reciprocation by an enemy. Many of his tempting morsels dealt with Red China: the United States would extend formal diplomatic recognition to Red China; the United States would lift all trade and travel bans between the United States and Red China; the United States would support Red China's admission to membership in the United Nations (Red China would replace Free China on the United Nations Security Council); and, the United States would work for the demilitarization of Free China's offshore islands, Quemoy and Matsu.

In the area of disarmament, Osgood suggested that the United States institute a unilateral ban on the testing of all nuclear weapons; the United States would remove all nuclear weapons from American bases in Japan (as a sign of good faith, the United States would invite inspection teams from the Soviet Union and the United Nations to see that the Japan-based weapons were removed); and, the United States would be thrown open to inspection so that United Nations teams could be assured that nuclear weapons-testing was abolished.

For American space programs, Osgood suggested that all United States space flights be supervised by a United Nations agency and that any medical or other scientific information, gathered in the course of the space flights, be shared with the Soviet Union. He proposed that the United States DEW (early warning system against enemy attack) be made "bi-directional," by inviting the Soviet Union to "plug in" on the American system (so that the Soviet Union would be warned of an American attack!).

If the United States followed Osgood's designs, student exchanges would be very extensive with the Communist bloc powers and America's surplus crops — with prices adjusted downward — would be offered for sale to anyone, including the Communist bloc countries.

The American public would have to be brainwashed before agreeing to the Osgood-designed sell-out of our security. But Osgood hoped that the United States government and the American mass communication media could come to some agreement whereby Soviet propaganda would appear in special sections of Sunday newspapers and on television and radio programs.

Osgood did try to leaven the impact of his suggestions by noting that' the "deliberate 'peace' offensive" through a unilateral sell-out by the United States was only hypothetical. This plea for understanding of a scholar's conjectural scheme, however, is offset by Osgood's personal conviction that the danger to the United States from the Communists is greatly overdrawn. Furthermore, Osgood is convinced that the Communists will react humanely to strong moral pressures exerted by the United States.

HARRY OVERSTREET was born on October 25, 1875 in San Francisco, son of Julia Detje and William Overstreet. He was married to Elsie Burr. He is married to Bonaro Overstreet. He is an alumnus of the University of California (A.B.,

1899) and Oxford University of England (B.Sc., 1901).

From 1901 until 1911, Overstreet taught philosophy at the University of California. From 1911 until 1939, he was a professor of philosophy at the College of the City of New York. He became professor emeritus in 1939. He has also lectured at the University of Michigan and the New School for Social Research. Overstreet has been on the national council of the socialist League for Industrial Democracy and on the national advisory board of the leftwing, internationalist United World Federalists.

In 1953, Overstreet, in an effort to clear up his record, told the House Committee on Un-American Activities that, with regard to organizations with which he had been affiliated, "I did not know at the time of my affiliation that I was serving Communist ends by lending my name or by becoming a member." Overstreet had something to worry about. He had a socialist pacifist record going back more than thirty years. He had been a member of the John Reed Club, as much a part of the Communist Party as anything could be. And Overstreet had been found without question to have belonged to a number of Communist fronts, supported Communist projects, and engaged in Communist enterprises just about as long as anybody in America.

By 1958, Overstreet had been quite prolific writing on psychology, philosophy, and related fields. Perhaps, his best known book by that time was *The Great Enterprise*. Russell Kirk, writing in *National Review* (May 23, 1959), had some pertinent observations on that book: "A general thesis . . . runs through his writings: that whatever Harry (or Bonaro) Overstreet says is the Scientific Real McCoy, and that you must be stupid, crazy, or wicked if you dissent from

Pure Overstreet Doctrine. That hundreds of thousands of people seem to have taken Mr. Overstreet seriously is one symptom of the shallowness of American education.

"I take my text from Holy Writ, New Style: that is, *The Great Enterprise*, by Dr. Harry Overstreet; and I am charmed by this passage: 'A man, for example, may be angrily against racial equality, public housing, the TVA, financial and technical aid to backward countries, organized labor, and the preaching of social rather than salvational religion . . . . Such people may appear "normal" in the sense that they are able to hold a job and otherwise maintain their status as members of society; but they are, we now recognize, well along the road toward mental illness.'

"Mr. Overstreet is a vulgarizer; and this concept that people who are not Guaranteed Liberals must be candidates for a straight jacket is derived from the writings of certain American 'behavioral social scientists' — who, however, usually disguise this blunt conclusion in jargon. As a way of injuring the reputation of persons who oppose your ambitions or disagree with your brand of politics, this 'you're mentally sick' strategy has been much employed in recent years by members of Communist cells and fellow-traveling groups on American campuses."

Then, in 1958, Overstreet and his wife wrote *What We Must Know About Communism*, which was greeted enthusiastically by the entire Liberal Establishment as the last word on the subject. In a very short time, the book became a best seller — a situation aided and abetted by Secretary of State John Foster Dulles, who was so entranced by the Overstreets' wisdom that he recommended the book to President Dwight Eisenhower. Then a publisher's dream came true. News photographers snapped pictures of Ike holding the book — whether Ike ever read it remains one of his scholarly secrets.

Former Communist Frank Meyer, reviewing the Overstreets' book in *National Review* (February 28, 1959), said: "The Overstreets' best-seller on psychological problems, shallow though they were, have probably harmed no one seriously. The shallowness of this book, however, with its half-digested parroting of the ignorances of fashionable Soviet 'experts' and its one-world sentimentality out of Carl Sandburg and Norman Cousins, can be very harmful indeed."

Former Communist Louis Budenz called the book "fragmentary and partially inadequate" and said it did "not live up to its title." Budenz further said: "In the main, the Overstreet 'anti-Communist' work is open to criticism not so much on what it says or how the whole complex and ramified problem of Communism is treated, but what it fails to mention we should know about Communism. Communism is a loathsome and generally fatal spiritual and mental disease. It is propagated by trained disease-carriers. Discussing the disease, no matter how brilliantly and extensively, without saying much about the disease-bearers and how they operate, is obviously doing only half a job, if not less than that."

But Overstreet was not going to be denied his reputation as an expert. In 1961, he wrote *The War Called Peace* and, in 1963, *The Iron Curtain*. Neither book was any better than *What We Must Know About Communism* but that didn't matter. The Liberals had taken Overstreet to their hearts.

Then, in 1964, Overstreet — again with his wife collaborating — wrote *The Strange Tactics of Extremism*. The Over-streets had finally discovered the "radical right," especially The John Birch Society, and they used well-honed hatchets in as vicious an exhibition of slaughtering scholarship as could be imagined. Their analysis of The John Birch Society and other anti-Communist groups bore no resemblance to truth. As M. Stanton Evans wrote in *National Review* (January 26, 1965): "The Over-streets are not above a little smear of their own. They constantly equate the people they are discussing with the Communists, making the asserted 'similarity' of the Bolshevik and the right-wing positions the major premise of their discussion. This cavalier stroke of the tarbrush tells as much by what it omits as by what it says. It equates loyal and law-abiding citizens with conspirators pledged to deceit, violence and treason; it also neatly ignores the whole spread of far-out-non-Communist Left organizations and individuals who have wielded so baleful an influence on America's destiny."

JAMES G. PATTON was born on November 8, 1902 in Bazar, Kansas, son of Jane Gross and Ernest Patton. He married Velma Fouse.

From 1921 until 1926, Patton was an athletic director and physical education instructor in Colorado and Nevada. From 1927 until 1929, he was an assistant business manager at Western State College of Colorado. In 1931, he became a general agent for life insurance in Colorado. From 1932 until 1934, he was an organizer for cooperative insurance for the Colorado Farmers Union and, from 1934 until 1937, he served that union as executive secretary.

In 1937, Patton became the director of the National Farmers Union and, from 1940 until recently, he was president of that union. He is now president emeritus.

Patton has been affiliated with the National Committee to Abolish the Poll Tax ("Communist front"); the Civil Rights Congress ("subversive and Communist"); the American Slav Congress ("subversive and Communist"); the National Citizens' Political Action Committee ("Communist front"); the National Federation for Constitutional Liberties ("under [Communist] Party domination and headed by responsible Party functionaries"); the National Council against Conscription ("Communist front"); the Union of Concerted Peace Efforts ("Communist front"); and, *In Fact,* ("Communist publication").

Patton has also been affiliated with the Workers Defense League, a group that defended political undesirables who were subject to deportation; the American Civil Liberties Union, that motleyed collection of defenders of subversion, crime, and licentiousness; the United World Federalists, the most prestigious group of fellow-travelers and dupes working for world government at the expense of American sovereignty; Americans for Democratic Action, the center of the radical left in American politics; the leftwing, pacifist National Committee for a Sane Nuclear policy; Arthur Larson's National Council for Civic Responsibility, an election year's drive by the Democrat Party against anti-Communists; the Institute for American Democracy, hysterical successor to Larson's abortive NCCR; the Atlantic Union, which is working towards a political merger of Western Europe and the United States, as a major step towards world government; and, the Council for a Livable World, an ultra-leftwing pacifist and political pressure group making an especial appeal to the scientific community.

Patton has advocated unrestricted agricultural trade with Red China and other Communist-bloc countries; the development of a give-away world food policy, administered by the United Nations; and, a federal governmental guarantee of a $5,000 annual *net income* for every efficient (*sic*) American farm family.

Patton's philosophy seems to be nothing less than a crude paraphrase of Marxism: "I say that what the individual can offer no longer can or should determine the measure of his reward. His reward should and must be measured by his need . . . . In years past, it was considered immoral not to work a long, hard day and not to save. Now I say it is becoming immoral to overwork and oversave."

Patton's leadership of the National Farmers Union has been hailed by President Lyndon Johnson, Vice President Hubert Humphrey, and Secretary of Agriculture Orville Freeman. Patton certainly earned the gratitude of the Johnson Administration when he campaigned against Barry Goldwater with such flamboyancy as: "Ladies and gentlemen, if you call a corporate Fascist-police state, sprinkled with brinkmanship and rash moves, a peaceful existence then vote for General Goldwater."

DREW PEARSON was born on December 13, 1897 in Evanston, Illinois, son of Edna Wolfe and Paul Pearson. He was married to, and divorced from, Felicia Gizycka. He is married to Lucie Moore. He is an alumnus of Swarthmore College (A.B., 1919).

From 1919 until 1921, Pearson was director of the American Friends Service Committee (Quakers) in Serbia, Montenegro, and Albania. From 1921 until 1923, he was a lecturer, a newspaper reporter, and an instructor of industrial geography at the University of Pennsylvania. In 1924, he lectured on commercial geography at Columbia University.

From 1925 until 1927, Pearson was a reporter for Consolidated Press, and, from 1926 until 1933, he was a staff reporter for *United States Daily*. In that same period (1929-1932), he was a staff reporter for the *Baltimore Sun.*

Pearson began writing his syndicated feature "Washington Merry-Go-Round" in 1931. His early partner was Robert Allen. In recent years, his partner has been Jack Anderson. Pearson has also been a radio and television commentator.

In the history of American journalism, no individual has been the object of more justifiably contemptuous remarks by public figures than Pearson. Reasons for contempt of Pearson vary from one individual to another. Some have taken offense at his malicious innuendoes, reflecting upon their personal integrity. Others resent Pearson's soft spot for Communism and for home-grown and foreign Communists. Still others resent his long history of publishing highly classified information which action can only serve to undermine national security, but for unknown reasons Pearson has remained immune to any punishment for his anti-American behavior. Over the years, Pearson's particular heroes have included Franklin Roosevelt, Harry Truman, Fidel Castro, Tito, Nikita Khrushchev, and, the one held highest in Pearson's esteem, Earl Warren. The Pearson-Warren friendship has been well publicized through their numerous trips to visit Communist tyrants.

The victims of Pearson's dirty hatchet have included all chairmen of the House Committee on Un-American Activities and just about every other Congressman who has ever tried to do an effective job of investigating Communists; Francis Cardinal Spellman; Douglas MacArthur; James Forrestal; Thomas Dodd; Richard Nixon; J. Edgar Hoover; and – most of all – Joseph R. McCarthy.

It is not merely coincidental that while Pearson has been particularly vicious against anti-Communists, he has received exceptionally favorable press notices in the Communist journals in this country and abroad.

CLAUDE PEPPER was born on September 8, 1900 in Dudleyville, Alabama, son of Lena Talbot and Joseph Pepper. He married Irene Webster. He is an alumnus of the University of Alabama (A.B., 1921) and Harvard University (LL.B., 1924).

In 1924, Pepper was admitted to the Alabama bar and, in 1924 and 1925, he was a law instructor at the University of Arkansas. In 1925, he moved permanently to Florida where he was admitted to the bar and began to practice law. During the intervening years his law practice has been carried on in Perry, Tallahassee, Miami Beach, and Cocoa, Florida.

Pepper became active in politics during the presidential campaign of 1928 when, as a member of the Florida State Democratic Executive Committee, he stumped for Alfred E. Smith's candidacy. In 1929 and 1930, he served as Representative from Taylor County in Florida's legislature. He did not seek re-election.

In 1934, Pepper made an unsuccessful bid for the Democrat nomination for United States Senator. However, when the incumbent died in 1936, Pepper – running unopposed – was elected to the unexpired term in the U.S. Senate. (He was re-elected for full terms in 1938 and 1944.)

When Pepper went to the Senate in

1936, he embraced Franklin D. Roosevelt's New Deal program so completely that he soon became widely known as "F.D.R.'s errand boy," and, as the *New York Herald Tribune* commented in 1940: "It has long been suspected that when the White House has an important balloon to send up, it invites Senator Pepper to supply the necessary oratorical helium for the occasion." Earlier, *New Republic* magazine noted that Pepper's "utterances in the Senate . . . are for the most part simply the voice of Hyde Park in the drawling accents of northwest Florida." How close Pepper was to Hyde Park was markedly demonstrated in 1938 when James Roosevelt, son of the President, campaigned actively for Pepper's re-election to the Senate.

Just as there was no New Deal program too extreme or too radical for Pepper's support, so also was he a totally committed devotee of FDR's internationalism and intervention in the European war. And Pepper was a trial balloonist for FDR's escapades in foreign policy as well as in domestic matters. So well did Pepper serve his master that, in 1944, when the Senator was faced with a probable defeat for re-election, FDR personally intervened on his behalf, using some brazen, but effective, pork-barrel chicanery.

Sometime during the World War II years, Pepper developed a heavy infatuation for the Soviet Union, its leaders, and its Communist Party and stooges in this country. And, before his service in the Senate ended, he became affiliated with the American Committee for Protection of Foreign Born [Americans] ("subversive and Communist" – "one of the oldest auxiliaries of the Communist Party in the United States" – under the "complete domination" of the Communist Party); the American Slav Congress ("subversive and Communist"); American Youth for Democracy ("subversive and Communist"); the American Russian Institute ("subversive" – "Communist" – "specializing in pro-Soviet propaganda"); the Committee for the First Amendment ("Communist front"); the Independent Citizens Committee of the Arts, Sciences and Professions ("Communist front"); the International Labor Defense ("legal arm of the Communist Party"); the International Workers Order ("subversive and Communist"); the National Committee to Win the Peace ("subversive and Communist"); the National Council of American-Soviet Friendship ("subversive and Communist" – "specializing in pro-Soviet propaganda"); the Joint Anti-Fascist Refugee Committee ("subversive and Communist"); the National Citizens Political Action Committee ("Communist front"); and, the Southern Conference for Human Welfare ("Communist front").

Pepper's fellow-traveling was not confined to Communist fronts even though his activity in such a variety of them has never been matched before or since by any United States Senator. In the aftermath of World War II, he became one of the most outspoken pro-Communist apologists in any walk of life in this country except for a few top-ranking Communist Party leaders.

On September 14, 1945, Pepper spent an hour in the Kremlin chatting with the Soviet Union's Dictator Stalin. When Pepper returned to this country, he extolled Stalin and the Soviet Union from public platforms, from the floor of the Senate, and in print.

From his Kremlin visit, Pepper recalled: "Stalin told me Russia does not want to waste her substance on war or preparation for war, and she is not thinking of aggression upon the nations of the world." Taking Stalin's word as his own premise, Pepper became a vigorous opponent of the few anti-Communist measures undertaken by the Truman Administration. And no Communist could have improved upon Pepper's portrayal of a bullied Soviet Union: " . . . Russia is beset with many fears . . . believing that her philosophy is such that she will never be accepted by nations dominated by cartelists, reactionaries, or Russophobes . . . . Russia's fear is aggravated by her memory of the past . . . . Russia remembers the Red-baiting, the articulated and open conspiracy against her among the major capitalistic powers of the world." To Pepper, the United States was one of the "major capitalistic powers" that was "dominated by cartelists, reactionaries, or Russophobes.

What wrongs existed in the relationship between the Soviet Union and the United States were clearly not the former's, as Pepper made clear in an introduction he wrote for a book in 1946: "I do not know of a great contribution which has been made to world peace through better international understanding of Russia, her present as influenced by her past, than Albert E. Kahn and Michael Sayers have made through their great book, *The Great Conspiracy against Russia.*

"If there can be real understanding between Russia on one hand, Great Britain and the United States on the other, there can be a true lasting peace. We of the Western world know our own past and see it in terms of our own experience, of course. But so few of us know what has been the experience of the people of Russia and, therefore, most of us do not realize why they happen to have their present opinions.

"What the authors of this book have done is to take the period beginning with the Revolution in Russia and let us see the world a bit through Russia's experience. In short, they have bestowed the rare gift for which the poet Burns yearned by letting us see ourselves as the Russians see us — out of their experience.

"A continuation of the disastrous policies of anti-Soviet intrigue so vividly described in this book would inevitably result in a third world war.

"That is why this book should be read and studied by all those eager to see peace durably established in the world. This work is required reading for every American and British statesman, and, for that matter, required reading for every citizen of both countries.

"Surely, if the major nations and peoples of the earth can look upon each other with sympathy and genuine understanding, we have the brightest hope for an enduring peace mankind has ever had in its heart."

The book which received such a panegyrical offering from Pepper was a product of a now-defunct Communist publishing house, Boni and Gaer. One of the authors, Kahn, was unmistakably a Communist at the time. Further light on the book came from Colonel Igor Bogolepov, who defected from the Soviet Union in 1942 and testified before the Senate Internal Security Subcommittee in 1952 that he had seen the Kahn-Sayers book in manuscript form in the Soviet Union and that the largest part of the book was written in the Soviet Union by a high official in the Soviet Union's Foreign Office. Yet this Communist propaganda is what Pepper recommended as required reading to guide U.S. and British statesmen.

In 1946, in a preface he wrote for a pamphlet published by the National Council of American-Soviet Friendship,

Pepper said: "Men, wittingly or unwittingly, are contributing toward an hysteria which is the fuel of war. It will not stop until this whole red-baiting campaign, either by the embittered or the ignorant, is stifled in the indignation of the people who want peace. Russia is our friend in the future as she has been in the past. Let us resolve, that we will let nothing stop us or distract us from building a world of prosperity and abiding peace."

It was also in 1946 that Pepper in his frantic pursuit of appeasement with the Soviet Union called upon the United States government to "destroy every atomic bomb which we have, and smash every facility we possess which is capable of producing only destructive forms of atomic energy." Pepper insisted that Communism and the goals of Communists were objects of wide misunderstanding: "I made a careful inquiry in every capitol to which I went, including American military and civilian representatives, if they had any proof which would stand up in an American court that the Communist parties of the world, within their knowledge, were directed from Moscow . . . . I have not met one yet who was able to tell me that he had the proof which in his opinion would stand up in an American court of law. I have yet to see a credible witness who could convince a fair jury that that is true.

"I could astonish the American people by telling you the witnesses whom I have heard say that Moscow does not direct or dominate the Communist Party of China in Manchuria . . . . "

Pepper was prone to call upon anonymous high-level witnesses to support his pro-Communist utterances: "I have it from the lips of most responsible statesmen that Communism in every country in Europe today where it exists is a patriotic indigenous movement of that country."

Pepper's overt fellow-traveling brought him widespread publicity in the Communist and non-Communist press: "Claude Pepper has broken so many lances in radical causes that his colleagues now call him Red Pepper. But the pro-Communist left returns his affection." (*Newsweek,* January 20, 1947) — "The communist press whoops it up for [Pink] Pepper, because he has been taking Russia's side in international disputes." (*Saturday Evening Post,* August 31, 1946) — "Senator Claude Pepper, a foremost advocate of a go-easy-with-Russia policy, is emerging as the forthright leader of America's more extreme or radical liberals." (*U.S. News & World Report,* September 27, 1946) — Ralph McGill described Pepper as "Pinko Senator Pepper" and "left-wing, long-in-office Pepper." (*Saturday Evening Post,* April 22, 1950) — William S. White called Pepper one of the "leaders of the far left wing." (*New York Times,* September 21, 1946) — Articles on Pepper were entitled "Red Pepper" in *Time* magazine of April 1, 1946 and *Newsweek* magazine of April 7, 1947.

In the campaign year of 1948, Pepper endorsed Dwight Eisenhower for the Democrat presidential nomination. When Eisenhower declined that nomination, Pepper threw his own name out front. It was not received with enthusiasm except by Drew Pearson, who was taking a brief fling as a president-maker. Then Pepper was willing to settle for the vice presidential nomination but his generous offer was studiously ignored by his Democrat colleagues.

In 1950, Pepper lost his fourteen-year seat in the Senate when he was defeated by George Smathers in Florida's Democratic primary. Years later, Pepper brooded: "All I got was my head bruised. What a price I paid! They hung the red smear around my neck . . . . I was the first victim of McCarthyism." (Willard Edwards in the *Los Angeles Times*, March 31, 1963.)

In 1958, Pepper made a vain attempt to return to the Senate. But, in 1962, after Florida was given four new congressional seats as a result of the 1960 census, Pepper was elected from that State's third congressional district. His biggest boost came from President John F. Kennedy, who, in a well-publicized letter to Pepper, said: "During your many years in Congress, the people of Florida and of the nation had an outstanding and valiant fighter on behalf of the public interest."

Since taking his seat in the 88th Congress, Pepper has found himself right at home voting for the socialist measures of the Kennedy and Johnson Administrations. He has expressed no recantation of his pro-Communist stance of earlier years. He is still willing to defend his high estimation of Stalin as a peacemaker, deserted by British and American statesmen. For the benefit of his Floridian constituency, however, Pepper takes a dim view of the Soviet occupation of Cuba and feels that Nikita Khrushchev betrayed the ideals of Stalin. He is even willing to concede that there is a "Communist threat" abroad in the world, but when it comes to a showdown in the Congress, Pepper still votes on the side of appeasement and accommodation with the international Communist order.

CHARLES H. PERCY was born on September 27, 1919 in Pensacola, Florida, son of Elizabeth Hartings and Edward Percy. He was married to the late Jeanne Dickerson. He is married to Loraine Guyer. He is an alumnus of the University of Chicago (A.B., 1941).

In 1938, Percy went to work for Bell & Howell. He became president of the company in 1949 and chairman of the board in 1961.

Percy became active in Republican party politics as a fund-raiser in Illinois. From 1957 until 1959, he was the vice chairman of the Republican National Finance Committee. Percy and President Dwight Eisenhower formed a mutual admiration society which led Percy to suggest that what the Republican Party needed was a long-range program of objectives. Eisenhower agreed and Percy had a group of political hack-writers put together a book, *Decisions for a Better America*, which was published in 1959. The book was the basis for the Republicans' platform in 1960, and Percy served as chairman of the platform committee.

In 1964, Percy was an unsuccessful gubernatorial candidate in Illinois. And, in his campaign, he reluctantly supported Barry Goldwater's presidential candidacy. In 1966, Percy was elected to the U.S. Senate – his election attributable in great part to the death of the leading Republican contender for high office in the midst of the 1964 campaign, and to the fact that the aging (74) Paul Douglas had obviously worn out his welcome after three terms in the Senate.

Since he became a Senator, Percy has been widely touted as a presidential candidate in 1968, although he insists that Nelson Rockefeller is the best qualified Republican for the presidency. (Martin L. King, the agitator, has cited Robert Kennedy and Percy as the best possible presidential candidates "from a civil rights standpoint.")

Percy, even though he is still a freshman Senator, has had his views on major issues widely publicized. He favors the diplomatic recognition of Red China by the United States. He is not only in favor of Lyndon Johnson's "building trade bridges to the East" program, but wants to speed up such trade with the Communist bloc. He has been frantic in his demands that the United States reduce its bombing strikes in North Vietnam. Percy has repeatedly called for full participation of the Vietcong in peace negotiations. He envisions and welcomes a coalition government for South Vietnam: "I think you have to invite them [the Vietcong] into the government, into the civil service, and even into the ministry." Percy can evidently separate "good" from bad Communists since he has stated: "We cannot wage holy wars of anti-Communism . . . . Let us deal with the real world, not with a world of make-believe in which all Communists are equally villainous and America is presumed to be 99 and 44/100 per cent pure."

On the domestic scene, Percy has made a great deal of noise by introducing legislation for a nation-wide housing program as a means of discouraging riots in the cities. Ostensibly the program would be privately financed and, when Percy introduced it, it was greeted enthusiastically by conservatives and liberals. But when its provisions are studied closely, it becomes apparent that Percy has simply proposed another federal housing scheme.

JACOB S. POTOFSKY was born on November 16, 1894 in Radomisl, Russia, son of Rebecca and Simon Potofsky. He was married to Callie Taylor. He is married to Blanche Zetland.

From 1908 until 1914, he was a clothing worker in Chicago. In 1914, he became an active union official with the Amalgamated Clothing Workers of America and has been president of the ACW since 1946.

Potofsky has long been a major power in radical politics, along with his socialist labor leader colleagues Alex Rose and David Dubinsky. As early as 1925, he was an official of the socialist League for Industrial Democracy. In 1964, he was a member of Arthur Larson's National Council for Civic Responsibility and, in 1966, he joined Franklin Littell's Institute for American Democracy. Both outfits were loaded down with Communist fronters who were following Walter Reuther's dictates to crush anti-Communists in this country. Potofsky has been president of the Sidney Hillman Foundation which honors the memory of one of the most notorious Reds ever in the ranks of American labor.

Potofsky is a close confidant and supporter of Lyndon Johnson. Aside from his radical labor leadership, Potofsky dabbles in public affairs on occasion. In 1966, Potofsky unequivocally endorsed Red China's admission to the United Nations, the expulsion of Nationalist China from the UN's Security Council, and a seat for Red China on the Security Council after a probationary period.

WILLIAM PROXMIRE was born on November 11, 1915 in Lake Forest, Illinois, son of Adele Flanigan and Theodore Proxmire. He married Ellen Hodges. He is an alumnus of Yale University (B.A., 1938) and Harvard University (M.B.A., 1940; M.P.A., 1948).

In 1949, Proxmire was a political and labor reporter for *The Capital Times* of Madison, Wisconsin. In 1950, he was a reporter for the *Madison Union Labor News*. In 1951 and 1952, he was an assemblyman in the Wisconsin legislature. From 1953 until 1957, he was president of Artcraft Press in Waterloo, Wisconsin. In 1952, 1954, and 1956, he was an unsuccessful gubernatorial candidate in Wisconsin. Since 1957, he has been in the U.S. Senate.

As a Democrat in the Senate, Proxmire has been consistently on the far left wing of his party. On foreign affairs, he is relatively quiet although he is probably unequaled in the Senate as a devotee of the United Nations.

On domestic matters, Proxmire has been conspicuous for his support of so-called civil rights legislation, and he is an organized labor hack. In his early senatorial career, most of Proxmire's notoriety stemmed from his sponsorship of ludicrous spending measures. In recent years, however, he periodically has disarmed his conservative critics by affording token opposition to some of John F. Kennedy's and Lyndon Johnson's spending programs. But the opposition is only a token and, in the overall picture, Proxmire has been one of the most reliable voters for the New Frontier's and the Great Society's spending sprees.

ISIDOR I. RABI was born on July 29, 1898 in Austria, son of Jennie Teig and David Rabi, who brought Isidor to the United States when he was an infant. He married Helen Newmark. He is an alumnus of Cornell University (B. Chem., 1919) and Columbia University (Ph.D., 1927). He also did graduate work in Munich, Copenhagen, Hamburg, Leipsig, and Zurich.

From 1924 until 1927, Rabi was a tutor in physics at the City College of New York. From 1929 until 1949, Rabi was on the physics faculty at Columbia University, eventually becoming the executive officer of the physics department. In that same period, he lectured at the University of Michigan and Stanford University. He was also a staff member and associate director of the radiation laboratory at Massachusetts Institute of Technology.

From 1952 until 1956, Rabi was chairman of the general advisory committee of the Atomic Energy Commission. In that same period, he was chairman of the scientific advisory committee of the Office of Defense Mobilization and a member of the Naval Research Advisory Committee. In 1957, he became a member of President Eisenhower's Science Advisory Committee. In the Kennedy Administration, Rabi was on the general advisory committee of the U.S. Arms Control and Disarmament Agency.

When Rabi was appointed to Eisenhower's Science Advisory Committee, an Editorial entitled "Unseeing Eyes" in *National Review* (November 2, 1957) called attention to many alarming features of Rabi's background: (1) Rabi was "especially enthusiastic" over [J. Robert] Oppenheimer's "moral character." (2) Rabi was a leading opponent of the proposal to develop an H-Bomb. (3) Rabi (along with Oppenheimer, Jerrold Zacharias, and Charles Lauritsen) belonged to "the notorious ZORC cabal, exposed in 1953 by *Fortune* [magazine]. ZORC tried to promote passive continental air defense and its distant radar warning lines at the expense of the Strategic Air Command and offensive striking power . . . . " (4) Rabi "succeeded Oppenheimer as Chairman of the AEC General Advisory Committee. Before his defense of Oppenheimer and his involvement in ZORC he became known to a wide public when, in 1946, he, Philip Jessup . . . and others signed a letter to the *New York Times* calling on the United States to stop nuclear bomb production and to dump all U-235 into the ocean." (5) "Less known to the public has been Rabi's service as a scientific consultant to the State Department. His conduct in that post led certain other agencies of the government, when setting up a highly confidential project, to include an entire special security procedure to cut off all lines of communication to Rabi."

When J. Robert Oppenheimer, the security risk, died in 1967, Rabi was moved by the glowing obituary which appeared in the *New York Times* and he wrote, in a letter to the *Times:* "Your Feb. 19 obituary of Dr. Robert Oppenheimer concentrated, very naturally, on the tragic events of 1954 when a misguided Government rejected one of its most famous citizens to the great loss to the country and to the world . . . .

"It is to be hoped that in future years the nation will more deeply understand the depth of its loss in the untimely death of this vital and gifted man who justly deserved its highest honors."

EUGENE RABINOWITCH was born on April 27, 1901 in St. Petersburg, Russia, son of Zinaida and Isaac Weinlud. He married Anna Mejerson. He is an alumnus of the University of Berlin.

Rabinowitch, a physical chemist, was a research associate at the University of Göttingen (1929-1933), at the University College of London (1934-1938), at Massachusetts Institute of Technology (1939-1944), and on the Manhattan Project for the construction of the A-bomb (1944-1946). Since 1947, he has been a research professor at the University of Illinois. He is the author of *Minutes to Midnight* and *Dawn of a New Age.*

Since 1949, Rabinowitch has been the editor of the *Bulletin of the Atomic Scientists,* which has been and is the propaganda outlet for the Pugwash Conferences which began in 1957, subsidized by the notorious Russophile Cyrus Eaton. Rabinowitch used his influence upon the American scientific community to support the Pugwash Conferences. Almost every American who has attended these conferences is either on the masthead of Rabinowitch's *Bulletin* or has contributed articles to it.

In 1955, Rabinowitch was the only American participating in the international conference of scientists held under the auspices of the Parliamentary Association for World Government in London. The conference was called upon the initiative of Bertrand Russell, Britain's advocate of a "better-Red-than-dead" policy. Russell and his fellow travelers in the scientific community had become discouraged when some of their colleagues, notably Klaus Fuchs and Alan Nunn May, had been caught giving atomic secrets to the Soviet Union. In order to avoid the sordid trappings of cloak-and-dagger espionage, scientists were now going to be encouraged to make overt personal contacts with scientists from the Communist bloc. And the Pugwash Conferences would be the meeting place.

In 1965, the Senate Internal Security Committee concluded that the Pugwash activities served as an organic part of the Soviet Union's strategy in promoting Communist policies and aims. The bulk of the specific proposals emanating from the Pugwash Conferences calls for concessions or changes of policy on the part of the United States and its Western allies, with no substantive demands for changes in the Soviet Union's policies. And the entire history of Pugwash serves to agitate and propagandize for the disarmament and demilitarization of non-Communist governments. There are consistent calls for restraint on the part of the United States with regard to advancing weapons technology or increasing overall strategic power, but no similar demands on the Soviet Union.

Over the years, Rabinowitch's *Bulletin* has gone hand-in-hand with the Pugwash movement. The major advocacies of the *Bulletin* have included the elimination of all secrecy and security surrounding the development of U.S. atomic bombs and other devices. An earlier policy of the *Bulletin* was to oppose the development of the H-bomb. The *Bulletin* has called for international control of atomic energy without inspections. It has called for disarmament based upon mutual trust of the various national scientific communities, whose members are expected to take an active political role in their respective governments. And, of no little moment, the *Bulletin* provides a forum for Soviet Union propagandists to reach American scientists.

The *Bulletin,* under the guidance of Rabinowitch, has given its pages over to the world's most famous pleaders for appeasement, surrender, and coexistence as the desirable relationship between the Communist bloc and free nations. The *Bulletin* has featured calls for world government and unilateral disarmament by the United States. And the contributors to the *Bulletin* represent pacifists, security risks, Communists, fellow travelers, and the most notable opponents of any law or group which is working to protect the security of the United States.

The names on the masthead of the *Bulletin* have included J. Robert Oppenheimer, the security risk; Edward U. Condon, who, in 1958, was found to be one of the "weakest links" in atomic security; Isidor I. Rabi, one of the strongest opponents of development of the H-bomb and a defender of Oppenheimer's "moral" character; Harold C. Urey, one of the most prominent scientists who has consistently joined Communist fronts and supported Communist projects; disarmament advocates such as Ralph E. Lapp, Willard Libby, David Riesman, Hubert Humphrey, and Linus Pauling; and, the late Leo Szilard who was probably the most outspoken "no victory" advocate in the entire American scientific community. He organized the Council for a Livable World as a peace lobby and political campaign chest to support members of the no-victory bloc such as Senators Wayne Morse, Joseph S. Clark, George McGovern, and Gale McGee.

Rabinowitch has also welcomed to the pages of the *Bulletin* a rather representative collection of American and foreign leftwingers, including Adlai Stevenson, Quincy Wright, Fred Warner Neal, Bertrand Russell, Harrison Salisbury, Orville Freeman, Brock Chisolm, P.M.S. Blackett, and Alfred Friendly.

ASA PHILIP RANDOLPH was born on April 15, 1889 in Crescent City, Florida, son of Elizabeth Robinson and James Randolph. He married Lucille Campbell.

In 1925, Randolph organized the Brotherhood of Sleeping Car Porters in New York City, and he has been the head of that Brotherhood's union since that time. In 1941, he organized and directed the March on Washington Movement which so terrified President Franklin Roosevelt that he created the Fair Employment Practices Committee.

Since 1957, Randolph has been a vice president of the AFL-CIO and is on the executive council of that organization.

Randolph has been affiliated with the American League against War and Fascism ("subversive and Communist"); the American League for Peace and Democracy ("subversive and Communist"); the American Youth Congress ("subversive and Communist"); the China Aid Council ("Communist-controlled"); Commonwealth College ("Communist"); the Consumers' National Federation ("Communist front"); the Coordinating Committee to Lift the Embargo ("Communist front"); the Council for Pan-American Democracy ("Communist front"); the Greater New York Emergency Conference on Inalienable Rights ("Communist front"); the International Labor Defense ("legal arm of the Communist Party"); the National Emergency Conference for Democratic Rights ("Communist front"); the National Negro Congress ("subversive and Communist"); the Southern Conference for Human Welfare ("Communist front"); and, the United May Day Committee ("Communist front").

Randolph has also been affiliated with the Red-lined Union for Democratic Action and the socialist League for Industrial Democracy. He has been co-chairman of the leftwing American Committee on Africa and a sponsor of the National Committee for a Sane Nuclear Policy. He has been a national officer of the American Civil Liberties Union.

In recent years, Randolph has acquired stature as elder statesman of racial agitators. Randolph's most dramatic fling in recent years was the March on Washington which he planned in 1963. Marjorie Shearon in her *Challenge to Socialism* (September 5, 1963) described the scene: "On [Wednesday] August 28 there was the 'March on Washington for Jobs and Freedom.' It was certainly not a march in the accepted sense of the term. Approximately one percent of the Negroes of the country sauntered a distance of about half a mile from the Washington Monument to the Lincoln Memorial. There were no bands, few sidewalk viewers. Normally when there are parades and marches, Government workers are urged to line the walks and are often given leave to do so. This time such workers were asked to take annual leave and to stay at home for the day.

"Many merchants closed their shops. Department stores were empty and reported losses in sales up to 90 percent of their usual receipts. Liquor stores and all bars were closed. Restaurants, unable to serve drinks, closed voluntarily. It was like Sunday in most of downtown Washington.

"The 1,500 chairs reserved for VIPs were only partly occupied. Some 75 Members of Congress joined the ceremony for 15 minutes, but did not make speeches. TV and radio stars, who had said they would attend, failed to show up. The leaders of the 'March' were entertained at the White House by the President [Kennedy] and then went to a party given by Senator and Mrs. Jacob Javits."

Whether Americans realized it or not, Randolph's intimidation of the nation's capital and federal government leaders was merely a prelude to what can be expected in every major city in the country when a Randolph decides to make an all-out effort to bring the entire governmental machinery to a complete standstill. Randolph learned his lessons well as he rubbed elbows with Communists over the past three decades.

JOSEPH L. RAUH JR. was born on January 3, 1911 in Cincinnati, Ohio, son of Sara Weiler and Joseph Rauh. He married Olie Westheimer. He is an alumnus of Harvard University (B.S., 1932; LL.B., 1935).

From 1936 until 1939, he was a law clerk to Associate Justices of the U.S. Supreme Court Felix Frankfurter and Benjamin Cardozo. Between 1935 and 1942, Rauh did legal work for various agencies of the New Deal. Since 1946, he has had a private law practice in Washington, D.C. In 1946, he was the legal representative for Communist Poland.

Rauh was a founder of Americans for Democratic Action and has been a top official of that outfit since it was established in 1947. He was national chairman of ADA from 1955 until 1957. He is vice chairman at the present time and is also general counsel to Walter Reuther's United Auto Workers. In 1957, Rauh, while taking part in a panel discussion at the Federal Bar Association's annual convention, insisted that lawyers and the American people in general wanted anti-Communist investigations to be halted. Rauh, for his part, said: "What we must now do is abolish the committees." When asked if all congressional investigating committees should be abolished, Rauh replied that only those that investigate Communism should be because such a cessation of investigations "would signal at home and abroad the true end of McCarthyism."

No lawyer in America had gone to greater lengths to discredit Joe McCarthy than had Rauh. Brent Bozell told a fascinating story in *National Review* (July 13, 1957): "In January 1954, Rauh testified in the case of *U.S. v. Hughes* he was approached by one Paul Hughes who represented himself as a confidential investigator on the staff of the McCarthy Subcommittee on Investigations. Hughes told him, Rauh said, that he was in a position to furnish documentary evidence of the 'illegal activities' of Senator McCarthy and his committee. Shortly thereafter, Hughes produced a 94-page 'black book' of miscellaneous data relating to the committee's and McCarthy's personal affairs, very little of which even purported to demonstrate 'illegal activities,' but all of which substantiated the Liberal picture of McCarthy as a dark and dangerous scoundrel. What is more, there was valuable information concerning the confidential activities of the McCarthy Committee – e.g., the names of McCarthy informants, including his informant in the White House; references to other informants whose identity Hughes had not yet learned (such as the one who kept phoning in from the *Louisville Courier Journal* and another who Hughes thought was the cooking editor of the *New York Post*); intra-committee memoranda; a number of investigators' reports that were, apparently, to be used in forthcoming investigations; a secret correspondence between Eisenhower and McCarthy; transcripts of executive session testimony that invariably revealed browbeating of witnesses by Cohn and McCarthy.

"Rauh licked his chops, told Hughes to keep up the good work. He also made the first of several payments to his spy that were, before the year was out, to total $8,500.

"All of his 'information,' Hughes later confessed, was fraudulent. Rauh claimed he had been hornswoggled – as did both Fritchey, who earlier paid out $2,300 for the same stuff, and Friendly, who arranged for an additional $2,000 after the *Washington Post* had become interested in publishing the story. Hughes, however, said that he believed Rauh was aware of the hoax all along. For that statement, among others, he was indicted for perjury; at the trial, eleven of twelve jurors acquitted Hughes of lying on that count."

It is difficult to call one mud pie dirtier than another. Nevertheless, over the past twenty years, Rauh typifies the worst of the Americans for Democratic Action.

For the present Rauh is concerned with urging a "peace" candidate for the Democratic presidential nomination in 1968. He explains that this should intimidate Lyndon Johnson to implement speedily the ADA's surrender policy for South Vietnam.

NORMAN REDLICH was born on November 12, 1925 in New York City, son of Pauline Durst and Milton Redlich. He married Evelyn Crobow. He is an alumnus of Williams College (A.B., 1947), Yale University (LL.B., 1950), and New York University (LL.M., 1955). He was admitted to the New York State bar in 1951 and his law practice is in New York City.

From 1960 until 1962, Redlich was an associate professor and, since 1962, has been a professor of law at New York University. In 1963 and 1964, he was an assistant counsel to the President's Commission on the Assassination of President Kennedy (the Warren Commission). In 1966, Mayor John Lindsay appointed him as Executive Assistant Corporation Counsel of New York City.

Representative Gerald R. Ford (R.-Mich.), a member of the Warren Commission, made a motion that Redlich's employment be terminated as counsel to the Commission. Ford's motion was rejected by the Commission on grounds that there was no evidence that Redlich was actually a member of the Communist Party.

In Redlich's background, however, there was a great deal of evidence that indicated he was an unusual choice to work on a Commission which was investigating an assassination, of which the alleged prime suspect was a self-styled Marxist and known Communist fronter.

At the time of his appointment to the Warren Commission, Redlich was a member of the national council (the governing body) of the Emergency Civil Liberties Committee. Relich had been a member of the ECLC for more than ten years and continued to hold his position on its national council while working with the Warren Commission. In 1958, the House Committee on Un-American Activities reported: "The Emergency Civil Liberties Committee is an organization . . . whose avowed purpose is to abolish the House Committee on Un-American Activities and discredit the FBI . . . . The committee finds that the Emergency Civil Liberties Committee, established in 1951, although representing itself as a non-Communist group, actually operates as a front for the Communist Party. It has repeatedly assisted, by means of funds and legal aid, Communists involved in Smith Act violations and similar legal proceedings. One of its chief activities has been and still is the dissemination of voluminous Communist propaganda material." The Senate Internal Security Subcommittee and FBI Director J. Edgar Hoover also found the ECLC to be a Communist front.

Redlich was not merely a letterhead figure in the ECLC. In 1955, he spoke at an ECLC forum in New York City. In 1961, he spoke at a meeting sponsored by the ECLC in New York City. In 1962, he signed an ECLC endorsement of Justice Hugo Black's dissent of the Supreme Court's decision requiring the Communist Party to register with the Justice Department. In 1964, while he was counsel to the Warren Commission, Redlich's name was on a *New York Times* advertisement which lauded the work of the ECLC and solicited funds for its support.

In December, 1961, Redlich spoke at a New York City rally, sponsored by the New York Council to Abolish the House Un-American Activities Committee, a branch of the National Council to Abolish the House Un-American Activities Committee. In 1962, the New York Council circulated a form letter, appealing for manpower and funds to be used to elect Congressmen who would vote to abolish the HCUA. Redlich was listed on the form letter as a member of the Advisory Committee of the New York Council. While Redlich was on the staff of the Warren Commission, the *Abolition News* (February 21, 1964), the bulletin of the HCAHUAC, carried his name as one of NCAHUAC's sponsors. The NCAHUAC was established in 1960 to lead and direct the Communist Party's 'operation abolition' against the HCUA. Seven of its national leaders were identifiable as Communists.

In February, 1962, Norman Redlich's name was on a petition to the President of the United States, seeking executive clemency for two Communists who were convicted and imprisoned on the charge of contempt of Congress.

While Redlich was on the Warren Commission staff, his name appeared in advertisements, published in *Nation* magazine (December 21, 1962) and *Frontier* (February, 1964), soliciting funds for the defense of three "students" who had been indicted for illegal travel to Castro's Cuba.

Despite demands from Congress that the circumstances surrounding the hiring and retaining of Redlich by the Commission be investigated, no action was ever taken.

EDWIN REISCHAUER was born on October 15, 1910 in Tokyo, Japan, son of U.S. citizens Helen Oldfather and August Reischauer. He was married to Adrienne Danton. He is married to Haru Matsukata. He is an alumnus of Oberlin College (A.B., 1931) and Harvard University (A.M., 1932; Ph.D., 1939). He also studied at the University of Paris from 1933 until 1935.

From 1938 until 1942, Reischauer was on Harvard University's faculty as an instructor of Far East languages. In 1941, he was appointed to be Senior Divisional Assistant of the State Department's division of Far Eastern affairs. In 1942 and 1943, he was a senior research analyst in the War Department. After a brief tour of duty in the U.S. Army as a lieutenant colonel, Reischauer returned to the State Department as an assistant to the director of Far Eastern affairs. And, in 1946, Reischauer returned to Harvard's faculty of Far Eastern languages. While holding a professorship at Harvard, he also served as director (1956-1961) of the Harvard-Yenching Institute.

In 1961, President Kennedy appointed Reischauer to be U.S. Ambassador to Japan, an appointment that was greeted with praise by Japan's Socialist Party. When Reischauer's appointment was being considered by the Senate Foreign Relations Committee, he declared that he had never been connected with the Institute of Pacific Relations ("an instrument of Communist policy, propaganda and military intelligence") in any way. The facts were that Reischauer had had one book published by the IPR and he had contributed articles to two IPR publications. Furthermore, the former Executive Vice Chairman of the IPR, William L. Holland, said that Reischauer was a member of IPR from 1944 until 1948.

While Ambassador to Japan, Reischauer constantly played down the threat of Communism in the Far East. This has long been a favorite theme of his. As early as 1949, Reischauer saw nothing wrong with U.S. diplomatic recognition of Red China. He had the same degree of contempt for Nationalist China as did the IPR crowd whose activities were a major factor in the sellout of China to the Reds.

Reischauer was one of the earliest proponents of the theory that Red China and the Soviet Union were genuinely parted. To make the separation permanent, Reischauer suggested that it would be a good idea for the United States to get rid of its nuclear weapons. By his logic, as long as the United States was superior to the Soviet Union in atomic weapons, Red China would be dependent on the Soviet Union; therefore, if the United States relinquished its superiority, the Red Chinese would be drawn closer to us. (No atomic weapons make strange bedfellows!)

Another Reischauer suggestion was to the effect that Japan should increase her trade relations with Red China. Japan would grow stronger. Red China would grow stronger and might split irrevocably from the Soviet Union. Reischauer also thought the United States should give up its "colonial rule" over Okinawa and the Ryukyu Islands, and should not oppose "neutralism" in India, Indonesia, and Japan because "neutralism" is one of Communism's "most dangerous enemies." (!)

While Ambassador in Japan, Reischauer could easily have been regarded as Lyndon Johnson's personal publicity chief. On March 7 and 8, 1966, in a Japanese newspaper *Yomiuri Shimbun*, Reischauer wrote a two-part article "What Is The Great Society?" After worshipful obeisance to Roosevelt's New Deal and Kennedy's New Frontier, Reischauer went into a rhapsodic eulogy of the Great Society and its Great Big Daddy, Lyndon Johnson. Needless to say, Reischauer did not drop the slightest hint to his Japanese readers that the Roosevelt-Kennedy-Johnson socialism was not appreciated by all Americans.

Since retiring from his Ambassadorship in 1966 when he returned to Harvard's faculty, Reischauer has received a fair share of publicity, speaking out against victory in the Vietnam War and the need to reduce bombing. Unlike most of the soft-on-Communism clique, Reischauer preaches that there is nothing to fear from Red China which, at worst, is only "somewhat of a problem" to its Asiatic neighbors – and, besides, Red China will mellow in time.

JAMES RESTON was born on November 3, 1909 in Clydebank, Scotland, son of Johanna Irving and James Reston, who came to the United States in 1910. He married Sarah Fulton. He is an alumnus of the University of Illinois (B.S., 1932).

In 1932 and 1933, he was on the staff of the *Springfield* [Ohio] *Daily News.* In 1933, he did publicity work for Ohio State University and, in 1934, he was publicity director for the Cincinnati Reds Baseball Club. From 1934 until 1937, he was a reporter for the Associated Press. Since 1939, Reston has been with the *New York Times,* serving successively as a reporter, chief Washington correspondent, and associate editor.

In 1967, he wrote a book, *The Artillery of the Press.* Eliot Fremont-Smith who knows who carries the butter for his bread, reviewed Reston's book in the *Times* and began: "James Reston, associate editor of *The New York Times* and one of America's most knowledgeable and acute political journalists . . . ." The truth is something else again. In more than a quarter of a century of writing from Washington, Reston has been nothing but a political trumpeter, heralding the glories of the Liberal Establishment.

Reston was such an idolatrous worshipper of Franklin Roosevelt that he described the tragic sellout to Communists at the Yalta conference as "a great Roosevelt victory and a compromise by Stalin." So brazen was the sellout, that the Truman and Eisenhower Administrations spared no efforts to cover up the details of Roosevelt's Yalta perfidies.

The late Whittaker Chambers in his *Witness* provided an interesting chapter in Reston's Washington career. When John Foster Dulles was seeking to find a lucrative pasture for his friend Alger Hiss, he thought of the Carnegie Endowment presidency. Chambers recounted how Dulles "consulted two eminent evangelists of the cosmic New Order, James Reston of the *New York Times* and the late Bert Andrews of the *New York Herald Tribune,* and they agreed that Hiss would be a superlative choice." Naturally, no newspaper rallied its forces stronger than the *New York Times* on the side of Hiss when he was caught lying about his Communist espionage activities — activities that were common knowledge to every competent newsman in Washington at the very time Reston was calling Hiss "a superlative choice" for the Carnegie job.

In 1964, less than two months after Nikita Khrushchev was ousted from the Kremlin, Reston wrote from Moscow: "This is a more generous city because he [Khrushchev] controlled the police. It is a more flexible capital because of his willingness to experiment with policy at home and abroad. Conversation is freer now. It moves always along rigid lines, like a railroad train, but within the bounds of Communist ideology, it is easy, courteous, and even friendly. The Kremlin is no longer a symbol of fear and death . . . and whatever his shortcomings, he [Khrushchev] has clearly made life a little more pleasant for a great many people."

In his book *The Artillery of the Press,* Reston wrote: "The credit of the American newspapers with the American people for accuracy and good judgment is not high." Reston must have taken a good look in the mirror.

HENRY REUSS was born on February 22, 1912 in Milwaukee, Wisconsin, son of Paula Schoellkopf and Gustave Reuss. He married Margaret Magrath. He is an alumnus of Cornell University (A.B., 1933) and Harvard University (LL.B., 1936). He was admitted to the Wisconsin bar in 1936 and began his practice of law in Milwaukee.

In 1941 and 1942, he was assistant general counsel in the Office of Price Administration in Washington, D.C. From 1948 until 1952, he was on the advisory committee of the U.S. National Resources Board. In 1949, he was a deputy general counsel for the Marshall Plan in Paris, France. Since 1954, he has been in the U.S. House of Representatives. In 1960, he was an unsuccessful mayoralty candidate in Milwaukee.

Since he first entered Congress, Reuss has been one of the most dependable votes for ultra-liberalism. He has been a fanatic in the promotion of so-called civil rights legislation and "soak-the-rich" taxation. As a self-annointed expert on finances, he introduced legislation in 1965 to repeal completely the twenty-five percent minimum gold support for the dollar. To attract European tourists to America, he offered a bonus plan for such tourists (he suggested $100) to help defray their travel expenses in the United States. The bonus would be financed equally by the U.S. government and the American travel industry. As an answer to the racial riots in American cities, he suggested federal subsidies for police forces. But that has always been typical of his approach to domestic problems — the expenditure of federal funds.

On the foreign scene, Reuss is a devotee of the United Nations. He is a typical peacenik, who breast-beats about an arms race and nuclear holocaust and favors any and all disarmament talks with the Soviet Union. He is a member of the ultra-liberal appeasement group: "Members of Congress for World Peace through Law." He is also a member of the highly secretive liberal group in the House of Representatives: the Democratic Study Group, which is allied with the ultra-leftist National Committee for an Effective Congress and the AFL-CIO's Committee on Political Education, the most powerful political arm of organized labor.

VICTOR REUTHER was born on January 1, 1912 in Wheeling, West Virginia, son of Anna Stoker and Valentine Reuther. He studied at, but did not graduate from, the University of West Virginia and Wayne University.

From 1932 until 1935, Reuther traveled and worked abroad, where he spent some time in the Soviet Union with his brother Walter. In 1935 and 1936, he was an assembly line worker in Detroit. Since 1937, he has been an official of the United Auto Workers and a henchman of his brother Walter.

Reuther has been affiliated with the socialist Student League for Industrial Democracy and the socialist League for

Industrial Democracy. He has been a director and counsel for the leftwing, pacifist National Committee for a Sane Nuclear Policy. He has been a national board member of Americans for Democratic Action. He has been on the advisory council of the leftwing, internationalist World Affairs Center. He has been on the executive board of the leftwing American Committee on Africa. He is an official of Clarence Streit's Atlantic Union, which is working towards a political merger of Western Europe and the United States, as a major step toward world government. He has sponsored Negotiation Now!, an ad hoc committee led by leftwing luminaries for appeasement in Vietnam, including Martin Luther King Jr., Joseph L. Rauh Jr., Arthur Schlesinger Jr., Reinhold Niebuhr, and John Kenneth Galbraith.

Victor has been at his brother Walter's side for thirty-five years as the two have worked unceasingly to Sovietize America. Since socialism is, by its nature, internationalist, Victor's particular specialty has been the international machinations of the United Auto Workers.

WALTER REUTHER was born on September 1, 1907 in Wheeling, West Virginia, son of Anna Stoker and Valentine Reuther. He married May Wolf. He attended Wayne University for a brief time.

From 1924 until 1927, Reuther worked as a tool and die maker in Wheeling. From 1927 until 1932, he worked in Detroit at Briggs Manufacturing, General Motors, and Ford Motor Company.

From 1932 until 1935, Reuther traveled and worked abroad, where he spent some time in the Soviet Union with his brother Victor.

In 1935, Reuther organized the automobile workers of the United States. Since 1946, he has been president of the United Auto Workers. He became president of the Congress of Industrial Organizations in 1952 and, since 1955, he has been president of the CIO's division of the AFL-CIO.

Reuther has been a national sponsor of the leftwing, pacifist National Committee for a Sane Nuclear Policy. He has been a member of the socialist Student League for Industrial Democracy. He has been a vice president of the leftwing, internationalist United World Federalists. He has been affiliated with the ultra-leftwing National Committee for an Effective Congress and with Clarence Streit's Atlantic Union, which is working towards a political merger of Western Europe and the United States, as a major step towards world government.

He was a founder and has been a top official of Americans for Democratic Action. He has been a member of Arthur Larson's National Council for Civic Responsibility and Franklin Littell's Institute for American Democracy, hysterical successor to Larson's abortive NCCR.

More than a decade ago, Arthur M. Schlesinger Jr. wrote: "Walter Reuther, the extraordinary able and intelligent leader of the United Auto Workers, may well become in another decade the most powerful man in American politics." Schlesinger's prediction came about twenty years too late. It should have been made shortly after Reuther returned from his eighteen-month stay in the Soviet Union back in the early 1930's. Reuther returned from the Soviet Union determined to Communize America. He began with his successful organizing of the United Auto Workers and brought that union into complete collaboration with the Communists as they went all-out with force and violence during the sit-down strikes of the 1930's. The automobile industry and all America, for that matter, were impressed with Reuther's violent methods to impose a labor dictatorship on America — a Workers' Republic was the phrase used by his brother Roy.

Since Reuther first came into power with the aid of the Communists, he has become the most tyrannical labor leader in the world. He is today the virtual boss of the Democrat Party on federal and state levels. He has spent millions of dollars of union funds either to elect or defeat candidates for governorships, mayoralties, state legislatures, the Congress of the United States, and the Presidency. In blunt terms, Walter Reuther has the Democrats in his back pocket along with the leftwing of the Republican party. He is not a Fabian socialist. He is in a hurry. He is not an ivory tower or parlor chair pink. He is a street fighter whose methodology has brought rave notices from the Communists who appreciate the large gains made by Reuther over the past thirty years in achieving their goal of a Workers' Republic.

How far Reuther has gone into the hierarchy of power was perhaps best demonstrated in 1961 when he dictated orders directly to the Attorney General of the United States, and indirectly to the President of the United States, to take drastic measures to silence anti-Communist military leaders and civilians. The Justice Department and the White House heeded the orders. Those orders are still being carried out by Franklin Littell's Institute for American Democracy, a successor to Arthur Larson's earlier version of a Reuther anti-anti-Communist front, the National Council for Civic Responsibility.

CHARLES RHYNE was born on June 23, 1912 in Charlotte, North Carolina, son of Mary Wilson and Sydneyham Rhyne. He married Sue Cotton. He attended Duke University in 1928 and 1929, and from 1932 until 1935. He is an alumnus of George Washington University (LL.B., 1937) and has practiced law in Washington, D.C. since 1937. He lectured on aviation law at George Washington University from 1948 until 1953.

During the Eisenhower Administration, Rhyne served at various times as a member of the Federal Communications Commission, a member of the Federal Power Commission, a consultant to the President's science advisor, general counsel to the Federal Commission on Judicial and Congressional Salaries, and consultant to President Eisenhower.

Rhyne has been an especially active member and official of the International Bar Association and the American Bar Association. While serving as president of the latter group, Rhyne began to promote a theme of "world peace through law." His promotion finally reaped benefits on July 6, 1963 in Athens, Greece where the First World Conference on World Peace through the Rule of Law adopted a declaration of general principles. The conference was attended by members of the legal profession from more than one hundred nations.

Among the general principles adopted by the conferees were: (1) All States and persons must accept the rule of law in the world community. In international matters, individuals, juridical persons, states and international organizations must all be subject to international law, deriving rights and incurring obligations thereunder. (2) International obligations, including decisions of international tribunals, must be enforced by appropriate international community action. (3) The United Nations organization is the world's best hope for international peace under the rule of law and must be supported and strengthened by all possible means, and to this end we reaffirm our support of the principles of the Charter of the United Nations.

Out of the Athens Conference, there came an agreement to establish a World Peace through Law Center, with Rhyne as its chairman. At the end of its first year, the Center had more than 1500 dues-paying members from 114 nations. Subsequently, other conferences have been held and Rhyne has traveled the world speaking on behalf of "world peace through law." Central to his spiel are his glowing tributes to the United Nations, the Supreme Court of the United States, and the World Court. He dwells heavily on generalities – "in nearly every nation on earth dramatic law reforms are under way to provide economic, social and other progress" – "many nations are ahead of us in new law ideas, new legal institutions and reforms." What nations he has in mind go unmentioned and, as a matter of fact, he contradicts his own rosy picture of the advances of law throughout the world – "less than 20 of the some 125 nations of the world have a fairly up-to-date printed law code or a recent compilation of their laws" – "less than 20 nations have up-to-date printed volumes of their high court decisions."

Basic to Rhyne's drive for a world law for a world community is his antagonism toward the Connally Reservation which allows the United States to determine whether an issue in which it is involved is a proper one for adjudication by the World Court. Rhyne, if he had his way, would allow the World Court to make the decision for the United States. And, as a means of abolishing the Connally Reservation, Rhyne was instrumental in establishing the Rule of Law Center at

Duke University where Arthur Larson — the original "new" Republican — labors tirelessly against the Connally Reservation.

On many occasions, Rhyne has emphasized that he is not utopian in his quest for world peace through law. He professes to believe that all nations can be counted upon to agree on a world code and to abide by it. As long ago as 1962, he said: "The Soviet [Union] is for some as yet unclear reason moving toward acceptance of more law." This naïve — or whatever it is — view of the Soviet Union squares with Rhyne's unwarranted faith in the idea that obedience to law will be the rule rather than the exception once nations adopt a world code.

The most alarming feature of Rhyne's work has been his willingness to downgrade law as it exists in the United States, but, at the same time, to treat with deference the legal systems of other nations, irrespective of their utter contempt for justice. He is markedly silent on the abuses suffered by millions of individuals under the so-called law of Communist and other totalitarian regimes.

In 1967, Rhyne was re-elected to his perennial role as president of the World Peace through Law Center when more than 2,000 lawyers from all over the world met at Geneva, Switzerland where the Center's permanent headquarters were established in 1966. Among the resolutions adopted at the 1967 meeting was one calling for the United Nations General Assembly to assume "jurisdiction and control" over the mineral resources of the high seas and the ocean bed underneath. Another resolution called for all governments to accept the compulsory jurisdiction of the World Court. While still another suggested that all nations adhere to a convention (sponsored by Rhyne's Center), establishing machinery for the settlement of investment disputes between a state and nationals of another country.

In 1968, during the presidential campaign, Rhyne served as one of Richard Nixon's closest advisers and took a leading role in Republican campaign strategy sessions.

DAVID RIESMAN was born on September 22, 1909 in Philadelphia, son of Eleanor Fleisher and David Riesman. He married Evelyn Thompson. He is an alumnus of Harvard University (A.B., 1931; LL.B., 1934).

In 1934 and 1935, he was a research fellow at Harvard. In 1935 and 1936, he was a law clerk to associate Justice Louis Brandeis of the U.S. Supreme Court. In 1936 and 1937, he practiced law.

From 1937 until 1941, Riesman was a professor of law at the University of Buffalo. During World War II, he was a research fellow at Columbia University Law School, a deputy assistant district attorney in New York County, and assistant to the treasurer of Sperry Gyroscope Company.

In 1946 and 1947, he taught social sciences at the University of Chicago. In 1948 and 1949, he was at Yale University as director of a research project on mass communications. He returned to Chicago's faculty in 1949.

Since 1958, Riesman has been the Henry Ford II professor of social sciences at Harvard University. He has also lectured at The Johns Hopkins University.

Among his best known books are *The Lonely Crowd* and *Faces in the Crowd*. He was a contributor to James Roosevelt's *The Liberal Papers* in 1962 — a virtual manifesto of America's far left for the guidance of peaceniks, internationalists, and ban-the-bombers. Riesman is a sponsor of the National Committee for a Sane Nuclear Policy (leftwing, pacifist).

Riesman is a bleeding-heart sociologist, an attitude that places him squarely in the socialist camp. He is a leftwing pacifist which causes him to downgrade Communism as a threat to world peace or a subversive force within the United States. His detestation for anti-Communists is great, and when he turns his scorn on them, his legal training seems to give way to his sociological theories. In *The Liberal Papers*, he and his collaborator Michael Maccoby deplored the lack of influence of Fabian socialism in this country.

In 1965, he belonged to the Inter-University Committee for a Public Hearing on Vietnam, sponsors of the anti-Vietnam "teach-in" movement, which the Communist propaganda apparatus exploited for purely Communist purposes. In 1966, he joined in the National Voters' Pledge Campaign, which was led by Socialist Norman Thomas, veteran Communist-fronter Reverend William Sloane Coffin, and Sanford Gottlieb, the political director of the National Committee for a Sane Nuclear Policy. The Voters' Pledge Campaign was designed to support "peace" candidates, who would work for a ceasefire in Vietnam and encourage negotiations in which the Vietcong would be participants.

He was a member of Arthur Larson's Natonal Council for Civic Responsibility, the anti-anti-Communist political pressure group sponsored by Walter Reuther and the Democratic Party in 1964 and 1965. When the NCCR didn't destroy The John Birch Society as it set out to do, Riesman must have been very disappointed.

CHALMERS ROBERTS was born on November 18, 1910 in Pittsburgh, son of Lillian McGeagh and Franklin Roberts. He married Lois Roberts. He is an alumnus of Amherst College (A.B., 1933).

From 1933 until 1939, Roberts was a reporter, successively, with the *Washington Post,* the *Associated Press,* the *Toledo News Bee*, and the *Japan Times* of Tokyo. From 1939 until 1941, he was an editor for the *Washington Daily News* and the *Washington Times-Herald.* From 1941 until 1943, he was on the staff of Elmer Davis' rosy Red Office of War Information. After two years of military service, he worked for *Life* magazine (1946-1947) and the *Washington Star* (1947-1949).

Since 1949, Roberts has been with the *Washington Post* as a reporter and, since 1959, head of the *Post's* national news bureau. In 1958, he wrote *Can We Meet the Russians Half Way?* The title had to be rhetorical since Chalmers certainly knew that "we" had gone more than half way in the pages of the *Post.*

In the early 1950's, it was often wryly remarked by anti-Communists that the nation's capital didn't need the *Daily Worker,* it had the *Washington Post.* It remains a question as to whether the *Post's* international coverage or national coverage is the more obviously soft-on-Communism. It could be a dead heat and Chalmers, with his responsibility for the *Post's* national news bureau, can rest assured that he has done his part to present the strongest case for anti-anti-Communism over the years.

JOHN P. ROCHE was born on May 7, 1923 in Brooklyn, New York, son of Ruth Pearson and Walter Roche. He married Constance Ludwig. He is an alumnus of Hofstra College (A.B., 1943) and Cornell University (A.M., 1947; Ph.D., 1949).

From 1949 until 1956, he was on the political science faculty at Haverford College as an instructor, assistant professor, and professor. From 1956 until 1966, he was on the faculty of Brandeis University as a professor politics, chairman of the department of politics, dean of the arts and sciences faculty, and chairman of the graduate committee on American Civilization. He has also lectured at Columbia University, Massachusetts Institute of Technology, Cornell University, Swarthmore College, and the University of Chicago. He has held fellowships from the Rockefeller Foundation and the Foundation for the Advancement of Educatiiion.

Roche has been a consultant to Vice President Hubert Humphrey and to the Department of State. He has been a member of the executive committee of the Massachusetts Civil Liberties Union. He has been an executive of the socialist Student League for Industrial Democracy and on the national board of directors for the socialist League for Industrial Democracy. He has been affiliated with the National Committee for a Sane Nuclear Policy (leftwing, pacifist).

Roche has been national chairman and vice chairman of Americans for Democratic Action, the center of the radical left in American politics.

Roche has been a particular favorite of President Lyndon Johnson. In 1966, Mr. Johnson sent Roche to South Vietnam to advise that nation's governing regime on constitutional government. On September 8, 1966, Mr. Johnson appointed Roche as a special consultant in the White House, succeeding Roche's liberal soulmate Eric Goldman as "intellectual-in-residence." The position is of a liaison nature — keeping the President in touch with the academic egghead community.

Roche carried to the White House his views against the bombing of North Vietnam, his vigorous opposition to the House Committee on Un-American Activities, his admiration for Britain's Socialism, and his predilection (almost unequivocal) for unilateral disarmament by the United States.

NELSON ROCKEFELLER was born on July 8, 1908 in Bar Harbor, Maine, son of Abby Aldrich and John Rockefeller Jr. He was married to and divorced from Mary Clark. He is married to Margaretta Murphy. He is an alumnus of Dartmouth College (A.B., 1930).

From 1931 until 1958, Rockefeller's basic occupation was as an executive of Rockefeller Center, Incorporated.

In 1940, Harry Hopkins — the pro-Soviet occupant of the White House and Franklin Roosevelt's alter ego — persuaded the President to bring Rockefeller into the Administration. Roosevelt created a job for Rockefeller as Coördinator of Inter-American Affairs. In an editorial, the *Richmond News Leader* (May 6, 1963) has provided an able summary of Rockefeller's accomplishments in the position: "The Coördinator's office was answerable to no department and meddled with all. The result was that Rockefeller made many enemies among the old-line diplomats who later brought his downfall. In five years he managed to spend $140 million building up his agency from scratch! But he frequently had to call in his good friends Henry Wallace and Anna Rosenberg (now Mrs. Paul Hoffman) to intercede with the President to spare the axe.

"Rockefeller's bureau-building is hardly exceptional in Washington. What counts for the record is his curious impulsiveness to act without a complete understanding of a given situation. Two examples are fairly typical. Impressed by two operators of a South American news service, he hired them for important positions in his agency. Long afterwards he discovered that their efficient news contacts came from the network of South American Communist agents. Another mistake, which almost caused Roosevelt to kill the agency, was Rockefeller's idea for an extensive advertising campaign in the South American press to sell U.S. good will. He worked up a series of ads that portrayed a pair of Latin tourists discovering the good life in North America. But wartime made travel impossible and the ads ridiculous – and the net effect was a handsome subsidy for pro-Nazi Latin newspapers."

Rockefeller's job as a Coördinator came to an end in December, 1944. Later, as a candidate for the U.S. presidency, he would claim that he saved Latin America from the Communists and Nazis during World War II.

In December, 1944, Rockefeller became Assistant Secretary of State for Latin American Affairs. In this position, he had the ambition of promoting hemispheric unity – an ambition that could not be fulfilled because the Argentinian military regime, in which Juan Perón was now the real power, was not recognized by the United States. Rockefeller settled upon a strategy to have the Latin American nations act in concert against Argentina. He persuaded Roosevelt to support a meeting of hemispheric diplomats in Mexico. The meeting was held but unattended by Argentina and El Salvador. The nineteen other American republics, by signing the Act of Chapultepec, agreed to act collectively in defense of the Western Hemisphere, whether aggression came from a non-American or American state. (Hemispheric defense had been a singularly and traditionally United

States responsibility under the Monroe Doctrine but neither Roosevelt nor Rockefeller respected the 122-year-old policy.)

Rockefeller decided to apply "moral pressure" upon the Argentinians. He exacted promises from Perón that free elections would be held in Argentina and thus Argentina could join the Chapultepec signatories. Perón made the promises (which he didn't keep) and Argentina became a signatory. Rockefeller had his unity in March, 1945.

In April, 1945, Rockefeller attended the organizing conference of the United Nations at San Francisco. He was not a member of the official U.S. delegation. The *Richmond News Leader* (May 7, 1963) has described his activities at the conference: " . . . Mr. Rockefeller was engaged in lining up the Latin American diplomats to vote in a bloc for and against U.S. motions, as Rockefeller chose. In retrospect one can think of plenty of reasons for opposing the policy of Alger Hiss, but Rockefeller's reasons more often served Latin American interests than ours.

"The State Department originally opposed Rockefeller's presence in San Francisco. Soon, however, the Russians were lining up Soviet satellites into a bloc, and it was plain that the Latin American votes would turn the tide. Secretary of State Stettinius gave in, and told Rockefeller to come as an unofficial observer.

"The Conference had scarcely begun, when [Vyacheslav] Molotov began his gambit. He said that if the Lublin government were recognized in Poland, then Russia would vote to seat Argentina in the UN. Now, U.S. recognition of the Lublin Communists would mean direct repudiation of the Yalta agreement. On the other hand, if the obnoxious Perón government were not seated, then the Latin Americans would feel that the Act of Chapultepec was disintegrating at its first test.

"Rockefeller had succeeded so well at forging Latin American unity, that the Latin Americans were arrayed against us in full body. While Stettinius pondered the dilemma, Molotov came up with a compromise: He would drop his Polish demands. He would be happy to seat Argentina if Byelorussia and the Ukraine were included in the motion. It was preposterous that two member states of the U.S.S.R. should have seats — and votes — in addition to the U.S.S.R. as a whole. It was preposterous, but not as obnoxious as the Polish demands. All three of the anti-U.S. countries were voted in by the Conference. And, of course, as time went on, the Polish Communists got into the UN anyway.

"While all this maneuvering was going on, Rockefeller seemed to think that the admission of Argentina was a triumph for American unity. When members of the official U.S. delegation declined to take his advice, he intervened directly with Senators Vandenberg and Connally. At one point he was supporting the Latin American bloc in its demands to do away with the Big Powers' veto. Only when Vandenberg intervened — pointing out that the Senate would never approve — did Rockefeller relent. But the Latin Americans were by no means unanimous in following the sudden reversal of their leader." Later, as a candidate for the U.S. presidency, Rockefeller would claim that he inflicted defeats upon the Soviet Union at the UN's organizing conference in San Francisco.

In 1950 and 1951, Rockefeller was chairman of the International Development Advisory Board of President Truman's "Point-4" foreign aid program. The program was born in Truman's 1949 inaugural address. Later, as a candidate for the U.S. presidency, Rockefeller would claim that he planned the program — a claim that stamped him as an internationalist-socialist Fair Dealer.

In 1953 and 1954, Rockefeller was Under Secretary of Health, Education and Welfare during the Secretaryship of the ultra-leftwing Oveta Culp Hobby. Rockefeller's main contribution in this office consisted of his support for an enlargement of the Social Security program and his opposition to "pay-as-you-go" proposals which were an attempt to bring some semblance of fiscal responsibility to the Social Security program. Organized labor and the entire liberal community opposed "pay-as-you-go" proposals and Rockefeller followed the liberals' leadership.

In 1953, Rockefeller, Milton Eisenhower, and Arthur Flemming — none of whom had a day's military experience — were delegated by President Eisenhower to reorganize the Defense Department. Their instructions were to increase civil control of the military establishment — which they did.

In 1954 and 1955, Rockefeller became a special assistant for foreign affairs to President Eisenhower. In this position, he sat in on cabinet and national security council meetings. Later, as a candidate for the U.S. presidency, Rockefeller would claim to have been Eisenhower's cold war strategist.

In 1958, Rockefeller was elected Governor of New York. He has been re-elected for successive terms in 1962 and 1966. In his governorship, his administration has been so extravagant that New Yorkers pay the highest taxes (federal, state, and local) in the entire nation.

While Governor of New York, Rockefeller has been a candidate for the U.S. presidency in 1960, 1964, and 1968. When he was summarily rejected by the

Republican Party in those years, he virtually sabotaged the chosen candidate – Nixon in 1960 and 1968; Goldwater in 1964.

In his quest for the U.S. presidency, Rockefeller has occasionally made statements, especially on foreign policy, which would suggest to the unwary that he might be a moderate or even a conservative Republican. But over the long haul of his public career, he has demonstrated in both domestic and foreign affairs an ultra-liberalism that is at home only on the extreme left of both major parties.

Rockefeller is totally committed to welfare statism in agriculture, transportation, housing, and education. He has advocated national compulsory health insurance, medicare, medicaid, higher minimum wage laws, rent controls, and compulsory unionism. He supported Lyndon Johnson's phony "war on poverty" as if he devised it himself.

On the matter of civil rights, Rockefeller has been a fanatic. He was a major financial supporter of the late Martin Luther King Jr. He is a life-member of the National Association for the Advancement of Colored People. He has taken part in black racist demonstrations and fraternized with some of the nation's most notorious black revolutionaries.

In the summer of 1967, as cities throughout the United States were being racked with riots, Rockefeller rushed to the defense of the black revolutionaries: "There have been a lot of changes recently in the racial situation and a number of forces have been unleashed, but they're part of the forces of progress . . . I'm very optimistic." In 1968, Rockefeller's reward for these apologetics was support for his presidential ambitions by black revolutionaries.

In the field of foreign policy, Rockefeller has long been a one-worlder. This posi-

tion has not always been boldly stated. But eventually he blurted out: "I used to see a series of regional unions – an Atlantic union, an African union, a Latin American union – and I'm talking political union now; NATO is military. But now I think the time has passed for that kind of solution. Now I think the answer is some free-world supranational political being with the power to tax, especially for aid for underdeveloped countries, public health and roads." In his book *The Future of Federalism,* he expanded on his theme of surrendering American sovereignty to a supranational political being. (The book has been a major promotion of Clarence Streit's Atlantic Union Committee. Streit has planned far beyond an alliance of free-world nations and has moved into a position where he advocates a world government which would include even Communist nations.)

Rockefeller has not stopped at his advocacy of a free-world alliance. He is in total sympathy with Streit's position and he has constantly worked to break down distinctions between free-world nations and the Communist bloc. He has proposed an extension of cultural and scientific exchanges and other cooperative measures with the Soviet Union. He has suggested that the United States institute trade and diplomatic relations with Red China. And, as part of his push for co-existence with the Communists, he has been a fanatical supporter of the Red-dominated United Nations. Disarmament proposals, favorable to the Communist bloc, are always given Rockefeller's blessing, as are foreign handouts in the "aid" programs directed toward the support of Socialist and Communist regimes throughout the world.

The most brazen overture Rockefeller has made in the direction of co-existence with the Communists occurred in 1967.

At that time, the International Basic Economy Corporation, which he organized in 1947, announced that it was making an alliance with Tower International, headed by Cyrus Eaton Jr., son and namesake of the notorious Communist apologist. The Tower organization has a special entree to Soviet-bloc nations because of the elder Eaton's extremely close comradeship with Soviet Union officials. The merger of the Rockefeller-Eaton efforts was made to promote trade between the Soviet empire and the United States, Canada, and Latin America. A Rockefeller spokesman explained that IBEC's objective was "to improve the standard of living of the people of the world." More to the point would have been an observation that IBEC was looking for profits by trading with the enemy.

Rockefeller's alliance with the Eatons is not inconsistent with his pattern of associations. He has been a longtime intimate of Communist Romulo Betancourt, the former president of Venezuela. His political cronies, supporters, and admirers have included such leftists and liberals as Jacob Javits, Anna Rosenberg, James Wechsler, Walter Lippmann, Roscoe Drummond, George Romney, Thomas Kuchel, Jacob Potofsky, Thruston Morton, Arthur Schlesinger, Walter Reuther, William Miller, William Scranton, and J. Irwin Miller. When Rockefeller made his futile bid for the Republican presidential nomination in 1968, he called upon Emmet Hughes, an old friend, for campaign guidance. Hughes has admitted in print that he is a liberal Democrat in the fashion of European Socialists.

There have been times when Rockefeller has appeared willing to go to any lengths to ingratiate himself with Communists. In 1959, when Khrushchev visited the United States, Rockefeller went through preliminary motions of opposing the visit. But when the Soviet butcher arrived, news photographers caught Rockefeller and Khrushchev in a playful pose generally associated with two fraternity brothers greeting each other after a long absence.

In one of his more inane moments, Rockefeller offered his solution to the Cuban problem. He said it was his belief that the United States could make a profitable swap with the Soviet Union on Cuba: the Soviets would stop training saboteurs in Cuba; American restraints would be placed on anti-Castro freedom fighters.

For the Vietnam problem, Rockefeller advised an acceptance of the fact (?) that "total military victory in Vietnam" is impossible and thus the United States should work for a live-and-let-live agreement with the Communists. "We're going to have to live with the Communists," he further explained, "but we want to live too, and they've got to recognize this." He feared that North Vietnam would receive as much help from the Soviet Union and Red China as would be needed to match any increase of U.S. military efforts in the war. To forestall and pacify the Communists, he felt the U.S. should "open communications" with Red China, because such a move "would introduce an entirely new element for everyone – including the Soviets. We would open up the options and the fluidity of the situation . . . . You can't tell what might happen once you start opening doors."

Much of the Rockefeller family's money has financed the Rockefeller Foundation and the Rockefeller Brothers Fund. Much of the money has been expended on genuinely good philanthropic and charitable causes. But Nelson and his several brothers have also allowed enormous sums to be used to finance insidious causes, of which the two most notorious have been the Institute of Pacific Relations ("a vehicle used by the Communists to orientate American far eastern policies toward Communist objectives" – an "instrument of Communist policy, propaganda, and military intelligence") and the Council on Foreign Relations. The CFR, in which Nelson and at least two of his brothers have held active membership, long ago adopted the U.S. Department of State as its own vehicle by which CFR leftist-internationalist policies could be promoted under the aegis of the United States government. It is not merely coincidental that the views of Nelson Rockefeller have been activated for at least three decades by a CFR-dominated State Department, hell-bent for surrender to a Communistic one-world.

GEORGE ROMNEY was born on July 8, 1907 in Chihuahua, Mexico, son of Anna Pratt and Gaskell Romney (U.S. citizens). He married Lenore LaFount. He attended, but did not graduate from, the University of Utah and George Washington University.

In 1927 and 1928, Romney was a Mormon missionary in England and Scotland. In 1929 and 1930, he was a clerk in the office of U.S. Senator David I. Walsh (D.-Mass.). In 1930, he went to work for the Aluminum Company of America (Alcoa). From 1932 until 1938, he was Alcoa's lobbyist in Washington, D.C. From 1939 until 1941, he was the Detroit manager of the Automobile Manufacturers Association (AMA). From 1942 until 1948, he was the AMA's general manager. From 1956 until 1958, he was AMA's president. From 1941 until 1945, he was the managing director of the Automotive Council for War Production.

In 1948, Romney joined the Nash-Kelvinator Corporation as assistant to the president. In 1953 and 1954, he was the Corporation's executive vice president. From 1954 until 1962, with the American Motors Corporation, he was general manager, president, and chairman of the board.

Since 1963, Romney has been Governor of Michigan. When Romney campaigned for governor in 1962, it was his first attempt to gain political office. Although he ran on the Republican ticket, his campaign literature studiously avoided any use of the word "Republican." In 1964, he refused to support Barry Goldwater, the Republican presidential nominee.

Romney's partisanship has long been a speculative question. Among his quotations on the subject are: "I am neither a Republican nor a Democrat." (*Detroit News,* December 5, 1958) – "I am not a Republican . . . . I was a Republican, but I am an independent now." (*Detroit Free Press* January 30, 1960) – "I am a Republican . . . I have been a Republican all my life. I have never been anything else." (*Detroit Free Press* January 8, 1964). But when Romney began to display aspirations for the presidency, his supporters included Republican leftwingers Nelson Rockefeller, William Scranton, and Jacob Javits. From the liberal press, he had Roscoe Drummond, Doris Fleeson, and Jack Anderson on his side. And, among his staff members were George Gilder and Bruce Chapman, two ultra-liberals whose introduction to the American political scene was financed by Nelson Rockefeller.

As Governor of Michigan, Romney has been notable as a spendthrift, a persistent advocate for a state income tax, an opponent of right-to-work laws which would preclude compulsory unionism, and a marcher for "civil rights." He has repeatedly evangelized about the evils of federal government spending and the centralization of power in Washington but, at the same time, he has welcomed any and all federal handouts to Michigan and has stumped for a federal open-housing law and federal "aid" to education.

In 1966, Romney began to behave in the fashion of a candidate for the presidency of the United States. And, in November, 1967, he was the first major party politico to announce his candidacy. Although his candidacy suffered a quick collapse, his views on foreign affairs were broadcast, somewhat hazily but nevertheless revealing enough to indicate that his thinking was definitely on the side of the internationalists.

On the Vietnam War, Romney was most confusing. In July, 1965, he seemed to give his unqualified endorsement to the Administration's conduct of the war. In October and November, 1965, he visited Vietnam and upon his return he still appeared to endorse the Administration. In June, 1966, during an amazing performance on the television program "Face the Nation," Romney assumed several positions and neither hawks, doves, nor in-betweens could be either satisfied or dissatisfied with his statement. On July 5, 1966, in a rambling discourse, he could not seem to make up his mind whether he should support or oppose the Administration but he offered no hint of any specific point of agreement or disagreement with the Johnsonian policy. Less than a week later, he was urging the U.S. to bomb installations around the North Vietnamese port of Haiphong. He assured his audience that there was no danger of Red China becoming involved in the war.

Shortly after Romney appeared to be an unmistakable hawk, he held a press conference where he said: "Well, look

...I...I think it should...oh.... If, if this conflict really involves the question of our stopping Communism, the international Communist conspiracy, and stopping it in South Vietnam – if this conflict is really supported by the Red Chinese and the Russians – if this really is naked Communism, international conspiracy, then I think we have to weigh the question of how far... how much we can escalate without their continuing to escalate if they... if they agree that's the real issue in South Vietnam."

In April, 1967, in what was described in advance as Romney's definitive statement on Vietnam, he endorsed Johnson's "no-win" policy and Johnson's pursuit of "peace" negotiations. In September, 1967, Romney's confounding vacillation took a turn for the worse when he claimed that on his 1966 trip to Vietnam, he had been brainwashed by American diplomats and military leaders on the scene. Now he believed that it was never "necessary for the U.S. to become involved in South Vietnam to stop Communist aggression in Southeast Asia." Two months later, Romney said that on Vietnam he was "a dissenter on our Government's policy" and "I'm looking for an alternative, not merely a more popular or devastating criticism of the way things are going."

In December, 1967, Romney set out on a 25,000 mile trip through Europe and Asia, including a visit to South Vietnam. In January, 1968, while campaigning for the presidency, he said that if elected he would end the Vietnam War by seeking a "guaranteed neutralization" of Southeast Asia. There was no more confusion as to where Romney stood; he was on the left with the peaceniks as he explained: "I mean that North and South Vietnam, Laos, and Cambodia would be defused from cold war conflict, liberated from the destructive presence of a so-called 'war of national liberation,' and relieved of the use or threat of force as a way of resolving disputes or pursuing political goals on their territory. There would be the removal of foreign military troops or bases in the area, and there would be no alliances by nations in the area with outside blocs, either eastern or western." To achieve this Utopian situation, Romney said, would require "an international settlement in South Vietnam . . . worked out by Saigon and the National Liberation Front [Vietcong]," and with provisions for "open participation in the political processes of the South for members of the Vietcong . . . an agreement among the great powers," including Red China, that would prohibit political or military involvement by outside powers in the neutralized area; and, "a carefully coordinated system of international community supervision, control, and implementation of the agreement . . . perhaps under the aegis of the United Nations."

In other areas of foreign policy, Romney favors building trade bridges between the United States and the Communist bloc; he looks forward to having Red China in the United Nations (when they qualify!); he is an advocate of foreign aid programs which he believes would be better administered by Republicans; and, he relies heavily on the United Nations as a vehicle for peace.

Romney's criticism of the welfare state generally centers on the size of the federal government's role in socialistic programs. He would share the role more with state and local governments. But perhaps his most notable contribution to national dilemmas was his suggestion that there be a national "tithe of time" − "four hours − ten per cent of the 40-hour week − spent in well conceived voluntary effort at the local level could reshape America faster than Federal programs ever will." Romney even claimed to have found a national survey showing more than 61 per cent of adult Americans willing to tithe their time.

JAMES ROOSEVELT was born on December 23, 1907 in New York City, son of Eleanor and Franklin D. Roosevelt. He graduated from Harvard University in 1930.

Between 1930 and 1937, Roosevelt was an insurance broker in Boston, Massachusetts. From 1938 until 1940, he was in the motion picture business. After World War II, he went back to the insurance business and settled in California.

In 1946, Roosevelt supported Representative Hugh DeLacy (D.-Wash.) who was a member of the Communist Party. Roosevelt served as an executive officer of the Communist-dominated Hollywood Independent Citizens Committee of the Arts, Sciences and Professions. From 1948 until 1952, he was a national committeeman of the Democrat party. In that same period, he was a close supporter of the notorious patsy of the Communists, Henry Wallace. Roosevelt's soft-on-Communism attitude easily matched Wallace's. Roosevelt was delighted when the Red Chinese took over China's mainland, and he began advocating limited United Nations membership for Red China in 1950.

From 1955 until 1965, Roosevelt was in the House of Representatives. Most of his energies in the House were directed toward the abolition of the House Committee on Un-American Activities.

In 1962, Roosevelt edited *The Liberal Papers,* a manifesto of the far left. In that same year, he supported Soviet

Dictator Khrushchev's demands that the United States remove its missile bases from Europe.

Roosevelt has served on the national board of Americans for Democratic Action. He has been a national committeeman of the leftwing American Committee on Africa. And he was the first national chairman of the ultra-leftist National Committee for an Effective Congress.

ELMO ROPER was born on July 31, 1900 in Hebron, Nebraska, son of Coco Malowney and Elmo Roper. He married Dorothy Shaw. He attended the University of Minnesota and the University of Edinburgh.

Roper achieved fame as a public opinion pollster. In his civilian career, he has been a marketing consultant, a radio commentator, newspaper columnist, editor-at-large for *Saturday Review* magazine, and research director of *Fortune* magazine's Survey of Public Opinion.

During World War II, Roper was in government service with the Office of Price Administration, the Office of Facts and Figures, with the U.S. Navy and U.S. Army Air Force as a consultant, and, from 1942 until 1945, as deputy director of the Office of Strategic Services.

During the past twenty years, Roper has worked tirelessly for world government in one world. He has promoted his objectives through his affiliations with the Council on Foreign Relations; the Atlantic Council, of which he is a director; Clarence Streit's Atlantic Union; Freedom House, where he is a trustee; the Fund for the Republic and its Center for the Study of Democratic Institutions, in both of which he has been a top official; and, the National Committee for a Sane Nuclear Policy.

ALEX ROSE was born on October 15, 1898 as Olesh Royz in Poland, son of Faiga Halpern and Hyman Royz. He came to the United States in 1913. He married Elsie Shapiro.

Rose was a millinery worker and joined the Millinery Workers Union in 1914. Shortly afterwards, he joined the Labor Zionist movement. In 1918, he volunteered for the Jewish Legion — special battalions of Jews who were recruited into the British Army to drive the Turks out of Palestine.

After World War I, Rose was very active in Union activities. In 1927, he became vice president of the Millinery Workers International. In 1936, he was a founder of the American Labor Party which became a device whereby the Communists could run their candidates without the inconvenience and stigma of a Communist label. Rose was an official of the ALP until 1944 when he was a founder, along with David Dubinsky, of the Liberal Party of New York. Rose has been an official of the LP since its beginning and is vice chairman today. Since 1950, Rose has been president of the Millinery Workers International Union. Because of his influence in the Liberal Party, Rose has been very influential in Democrat Party politics, and his support has been given to his close political cronies John F. Kennedy and Lyndon Johnson, just as it was given to Franklin Roosevelt through the American Labor Party and Harry Truman in the early years of the Liberal Party. Most recently, Rose supported the candidacy of New York City's ultra-liberal mayor, John Lindsay.

EUGENE V. ROSTOW was born on August 25, 1913 in Brooklyn, son of Lillian Helman and Victor Rostow. He married Edna Greenberg. He is an alum-

507

nus of Yale University (A.B., 1933; LL.B., 1937; A.M., 1944). He also studied, in 1933 and 1934, at King's College in England.

Rostow practiced law in New York City in 1937 and 1938. In 1938, he joined the law faculty at Yale University, eventually serving as dean of the Law School, from 1955 until 1965.

During World War II, Rostow was a special assistant to Assistant Secretary of State Dean Acheson. In 1949 and 1950, following in the footsteps of his brother Walt, he was an assistant to the executive secretary (who was the notorious Swedish Marxian-Socialist Gunnar Myrdal) of the Economic Commission for Europe in Geneva. While still on the Yale faculty, Rostow lectured at the University of Chicago, the University of Michigan, Northwestern University, Brown University, Brandeis University, the University of Utah, the University of Colorado, and King's College in Cambridge, England. He was a Guggenheim fellow in 1959 and 1960.

Rostow has made little attempt to hide his commitment to socialism. He has complete contempt for free enterprise. Back in the 1950's, he recommended that the United States adopt proposals that would place all American business under UN control. In 1953, Attorney General Brownell established a National Committee to Study the Anti-trust Laws. Rostow served on the committee which issued its report two years later. The majority of the committee found that American business had been hurt by too much antitrust activity on the part of the Justice Department. Rostow said that there had been too little antitrust activity, and he urged the Justice Department to increase its antitrust prosecutions, choosing those cases (regardless of merits, of course) that would be most widely publicized.

In 1961, Rostow was welcomed into the Kennedy Administration as a member of the Peace Corps' advisory council and as a consultant in the State Department.

In 1964, Rostow – with his prestige as Yale Law School dean behind his public utterances – campaigned vigorously against Barry Goldwater, charging that Goldwater "is the first candidate of a major party in American history who is seeking to encourage racial tension and conflict among our people rather than to pacify them. He is doing his best to bring conflict to society, not peace, and this is something only a demagogue or a Fascist would do."

Rostow did not raise the spectre of fascism in vain. In September, 1966, Rostow became Under Secretary of State for Political Affairs. In October, 1967, he expressed his complete acquiescence in his brother Walter's no-win policy in Vietnam: "Neither South Viet Nam nor the United States wants to conquer North Vietnam, or to overturn its Communist regime . . . . We are in Viet Nam because we are obliged to be there specifically by the SEATO Treaty and generally by the U.N. Charter itself." In that same speech he said that U.S. policy is to have "respect for the vital interests of the other side." What is the other side? He described it in the same speech: "ambitious and energetic Communist regimes." Not, of course, ruthless and barbaric regimes. Evidently, by Rostow's standards, the war in Vietnam will go on until the Communists indicate that they are flagging in ambition and energy.

WALT W. ROSTOW was born on October 7, 1916 in New York City, son of Lillian Helman and Victor Rostow. He married Elspeth Davies. He is an alumnus of Yale University (B.A., 1936;

Ph.D., 1940). He was a Rhodes scholar at Balliol College of Oxford University from 1936 until 1938.

In 1940 and 1941, Rostow was an economics instructor at Columbia University. During World War II, Rostow served with the Office of Strategic Services. In 1945 and 1946, he was assistant chief in the State Department's German-Austrian Economic Division. In 1946 and 1947, he taught American history at Oxford University. From 1947 until 1949, he was an assistant to the executive secretary of the Economic Commission for Europe in Geneva (who was the notorious Swedish Marxian-Socialist Gunnar Myrdal). In 1949 and 1950, he taught American history at Cambridge University in England.

During the Eisenhower Administration, Rostow was being considered for work on a psychological warfare project of the State Department's Operations Coordinating Board. Rostow could not obtain a security clearance. At least once before, Rostow had a similar difficulty; he was the subject of an adverse security finding by the Department of the Air Force.

From 1950, Rostow was at Massachusetts Institute of Technology as a professor of economic history and, from 1951 until 1960, he was on the staff of MIT's Center of International Study which was nothing less than a Central Intelligence Agency center.

By 1960, Rostow had become a part of the Kennedy team and, in November 1960, President-elect Kennedy sent Rostow and his MIT colleague Jerome Wiesner to Moscow to attend the Sixth Pugwash Conference on Disarmament and World Security. The Pugwash Conferences had been initiated by Communists and prominent fellow-travelers for the purpose of selling out United States

security and advancing the world conquest designs of international Communism.

While attending the Pugwash Conference in Moscow, Rostow held a secret conference with the Soviet Union's First Deputy Minister Vasily V. Kuznetsov at the Soviet Union's Foreign Office. Frank Kluckhohn, in his *Lyndon's Legacy,* has commented on the Rostow-Kuznetsov meeting: "According to a *Chicago Sun-Times* report of Rostow's *tête-a-tête* with the Soviet official, Rostow agreed with the Soviet-advanced thesis that the United States should curtail our 'first-strike weapons, including the B-70' bomber. Kuznetsov is reported to have told Rostow that America's scrapping of our first-strike weapons 'would ease world tensions.' "

Rostow has denied that he relayed this Soviet advice to President Kennedy when he served in the White House as a Presidential adviser for National Security Affairs, from January to December, 1961. Nevertheless, four months after the Soviet official proposed the plan to Rostow, President Kennedy, on March 11, 1961, ordered scrapping of all U.S. first-strike weapons.

As Kluckhohn further noted: "Accordingly, our intercontinental bombers (one of our major war deterrents) are no longer being produced; the Skybolt missile has been abandoned; the Dyna-Soar orbital winged flight has been scrapped; and military space programs are not being developed."

Despite Rostow's denials, he had already gone on record in opposition to the development of first-strike weapons, even prior to his Moscow trip. In his book, *The United States in the World Arena,* published earlier in 1960, Rostow had written: "The United States must continue to develop and protect its nuclear *retaliatory* capacity by a substantial and persuasive margin . . . the maintenance of an effective and persuasive *retaliatory* capacity in the next several years will demand an imaginative and determined effort to maintain the capacity to penetrate Soviet defenses with *less advanced weapons systems.*" (Emphasis ours.)

After talking only about retaliatory weapons of a "less advanced" variety, Rostow − later on in his book (page 549) − wrote that it would not be necessary for the United States to develop any nuclear capacity, retaliatory or otherwise. Instead, he urged that the United States disarm and place its military power under the "effective international control" of a "federalized world organization."

In 1961, Rostow went to work for President Kennedy as a deputy special assistant for national security affairs. Less than a year later, he became counselor and chairman of the State Department's policy planning staff.

In June, 1962, Willard Edwards of the *Chicago Tribune* revealed the existence of a foreign policy paper which Rostow had prepared for President Kennedy. Rostow based his suggestions on the absolutely unprovable assertion that Soviet Union leaders were mellowing. Mr. Edwards summarized Rostow's suggestions: "Russia's leaders are beginning to realize that neither the United States nor the Soviet Union can defeat the other in the world of the future.

"Both the United States and Russia are losing power and authority in their respective area and an area of 'overlapping interests' is developed in which mutually profitable agreements may be negotiated.

"The Chinese Communists can be encouraged to 'evolution' into a peaceful state by showing them we have no aggressive intentions.

"Any idea of the United States contemplating a 'first strike' is ruled out. Planning in that direction is not relevant since the United States does not plan to initiate a nuclear attack on Communist nations.

"Despite all rebuffs to date, strenuous efforts should be continued to get an agreement on limited arms control. [This was accomplished on September 24, 1963 when the United States Senate ratified the Moscow Treaty, banning nuclear testing in space, in the atmosphere, and under water.]

"General and complete disarmament is a goal which must never be obscured. [The October 19, 1964 issue of the American Security Council's *Washington Report* pointed out that in the disarmament section of this Paper, Rostow called for 'the reduction and eventual elimination of national military capabilities except those required for maintaining internal order and for an international police force.' This is just an echo of the view expressed on page 549 of *The United States in the World Arena.*]

"Rising tensions or the pleas of our allies or of the American public must be ignored in any crisis with Russia. The temptation must be avoided to prolong or expand any crisis in an effort to degrade or embarrass the Soviets in the eyes of the world.

"Gentle treatment of the satellite nations is advocated. No official attacks should be made against their regimes, whatever the provocation, and even criticism should be softened. Western Europe, at the same time, must be encouraged to closer relationship with the satellites and urged to furnish aid to them.

"East Germany, the policy draft says, cannot be forever insulated from dealings with the United States and business must be transacted with them.

"Above all, no encouragement or support must be given to armed uprisings in eastern Europe."

One year later, veteran reporters Robert Allen and Paul Scott revealed the existence of a new policy paper which had been prepared by Rostow and McGeorge Bundy (special foreign policy adviser to the President). This key document stated, among other things: "We should welcome temporary and partial accommodations or détentes with the U.S.S.R. We should seek to develop the basis for these agreements by further expanded contacts and exchanges between President Kennedy and the top Soviet leadership which would – unlike formal summit meetings – be viewed by the public as a form of communications while actually involving negotiations."

On June 28, 1961, in a speech to the graduating class of the U.S. Army's Special Warfare Center at Fort Bragg, North Carolina, Rostow stated that the United States would not seek victory over the Communists "in the usual sense." Rostow went on to blueprint the "no-win" policy that would be adopted by the Kennedy and Johnson Administrations: "The victory we seek will see no ticker tape parades down Broadway – no climactic battles nor great American celebrations of victory. It is a victory which will take many years and decades of hard work and dedication – by many peoples – to bring about. This will not be a victory of the United States over the Soviet Union. It will not be a victory of capitalism over socialism. It will be a victory of men and nations which aim to stand up straight over the forces which wish to entrap and to exploit their revolutionary aspirations of modernization. What this victory involved – in the end

– is the assertion by nations of their right to independence and by men and women of their right to freedom as they understand it. And we deeply believe this victory will come – on both sides of the Iron Curtain.

" ... For Americans the reward of victory will be simply this: It will permit American society to continue to develop along the old humane lines which go back to our birth as a Nation – and which reach deeper into history than that – back to the Mediterranean roots of Western life. We are struggling to maintain an environment on the world scene which will permit our open society to survive and to flourish."

One of the greatest hoaxes of recent years has been the characterization in the liberal press of Walt Rostow as the hawk leader in the White House. For today Rostow is at the side of Lyndon Johnson as the president's special assistant for national security affairs – the mastermind of the U.S. strategy in the Vietnam War.

RICHARD ROVERE was born on May 15, 1915 in Jersey City, New Jersey, son of Ethel Roberts and Louis Rovere. He married Eleanor Burgess. He is an alumnus of Columbia University (A.B., 1937).

In 1938 and 1939, Rovere was an associate editor of *New Masses*, a weekly publication, officially controlled by the Communist Party. From 1940 until 1943, he was an assistant editor on the radically leftist *Nation* magazine. He was also active in the American Labor Party, which was Communist in all but its name. At that time, the ALP was being wracked by an internecine struggle for power. On one side were Sidney Hillman and Vito Marcantonio. (Hillman was one of the most despicable Reds in the entire

American labor movement. Marcantonio was the Communists' spokesman in the U.S. Congress.) On the other side of the spat were David Dubinsky and Alex Rose. (They had been founders in 1936 of the ALP which became a device whereby the Communists could run their candidates without the inconvenience and stigma of a Communist label.) Rovere sided with Dubinsky and Rose but they lost control of the ALP anyway, and the two old radicals founded a new vehicle, the Liberal Party. (The alleged net result was staunch anti-Communists [the good guys] had lost to the obviously Red duo of Hillman and Marcantonio [the bad guys].)

In 1943 and 1944, Rovere was editor of the venerable, radical leftist *Common Sense* magazine which catered to contributions from the likes of Stuart Chase and Owen Lattimore. In 1944, Rovere became a staff writer for the *New Yorker* magazine. Over the years, he has retained his connection with this publication as a contributor and, in recent years, has written the *New Yorker's* feature "Letter from Washington." In 1949, he began a five-year stint as a book critic and contributing editor of *Harper's* magazine. From 1954 until 1962, he was a United States correspondent for the *London Spectator*. (An Editorial in *National Review,* September 27, 1958, provides an apt commentary on the type of thing Rovere was offering his British readers: "Mr. Richard Rovere, who is retained by *The* [London] *Spectator* to keep its readers informed about what goes on in this country, thus illuminates the constitutional crisis caused by the Supreme Court's intervention in the educational affairs of the Southern states: 'Governor Faubus, who was campaigning for re-election this summer, addressed a crowd in an Arkansas town and ranted against the President, the Supreme Court, the NAACP and just about everything else. When he had done, a great shaft of light pierced the roof of the meeting hall, and, lo, Jesus Christ appeared. He said that He was the resurrection and the life, that those who set man against man shall not enter the kingdom of Heaven, that the meek and the peacemakers are blessed. The mob was quiet while He spoke; when He finished, there was a great shout through the hall — "Nigger-lover." Another contribution by Mr. Rovere to the public understanding of great issues.") On at least one occasion (August 25, 1963), Rovere wrote a feature story for *The Sunday Times* of London. The feature's title was "How Right is America?" Rovere could see a tremendous increase in "rightist" activity but, as he psychoanalyzed it, the increase was only a "manic phase following a depressive phase, a mere thrashing about of the previously somnolent and still." Rovere was trembling at the thought of a Barry Goldwater presidential candidacy in 1964, but he assured his British readers that, unless Goldwater took some giant steps to the left, he could never be elected because "Presidential candidates of both parties are most commonly found . . . near the safe centre."

In 1951, Rovere collaborated with Arthur M. Schlesinger Jr. in the writing of *The General and the President* — purporting to be an account of the controversy between President Harry S. Truman and the late General Douglas MacArthur. It was not history. It did not resemble history. It was, and remains, a thoroughly dishonest hatchet-job on MacArthur. The two authors committed just about every known sin against objective scholarship in their attempt to bury the truth surrounding the circumstances that led to the catastrophic Korean War.

Rovere has demonstrated an enormous talent for hateful and spiteful attacks upon Republicans. In recent years, two of his favorite targets have been Barry Goldwater and Richard Nixon. But the most splenetic of his writings have been directed at Senator Joseph R. McCarthy. During the past fifteen years, in the pages of *The Reporter, Esquire, New York Times,* and *New Yorker* magazines, and in a full-length book (*Senator Joe McCarthy*), Rovere has compared McCarthy — unfavorably, of course — to Hitler, Huey Long, Mao Tse-tung, Castro, and Stalin. There have been few avenues of malice unexplored by Rovere as he has reviled McCarthy's political, ideological, and personal character: prince of hatred, seditionist, bum, cheap politician, guttersnipe, crook, political thug, foul-mouthed liar, mucker, ogre, rattlesnake, master of the scabrous and the scatalogical, con man, foul-mouthed, base-born, demagogue.

McCarthy's most grievous sin — in the eyes of Rovere — was his attempt to do something effective against Communists and Communism and Rovere, who rubbed elbows with Communists in his earliest working days, has retained a sympathetic approach to Communism and the behavior of Communists. When Soviet troops encamped ninety miles from our shores, Rovere reflected that "from the point of view of our over-all policy in Latin America and the rest of the world, the present occupation of Cuba by Russian troops is not entirely a bad thing." He detests what he calls "the simplistic anti-Communist ideology" which he alleges is the basis of U.S. foreign policy and claims that all history argues against the view that "every square mile dominated by Communists would increase Soviet power and diminish the power of the 'free world.' "

Rovere has been particularly incensed at U.S. participation in the Vietnam War. If he had his way, South Vietnam and other nations would be abandoned to the Communists because after all "a few more Communist governments in Southeast Asia might be no threat to us and might, in fact, dilute some of Peking's power." (Rovere's woeful ignorance of history and his uncivilized attitude toward victims of Communism are strange credentials for his part-time position, since 1957, as an associate in American civilization at Columbia University.)

In 1968, when Walter Goodman's *The Committee* (an ultra-liberal attack upon the House Committee on Un-American Activities) was published, it was only fitting that the glowing introduction came from the pen of Richard Rovere.

CARL ROWAN was born on August 11, 1925 in Ravenscroft, Tennessee, son of Johnnie Bradford and Thomas Rowan. He married Vivien Murphy. He attended Tennessee State University and Washburn College. He is an alumnus of Oberlin College (A.B., 1947) and the University of Minnesota (M.A., 1948). He is the author of *South of Freedom* (1953); *The Pitiful and the Proud* (1956); *Go South to Sorrow* (1957); *Wait till Next Year* (1960); and *No Need for Hunger* (1962).

From 1948 until 1961, Rowan was with the *Minneapolis Tribune* as a copywriter (1948-1950) and as a staff writer (1950-1961).

From 1961 until 1963, Rowan was a deputy assistant secretary of state for public affairs. In that position, he was used as a speech writer and traveling companion for Vice President Lyndon B. Johnson. His major achievement for the

State Department, however, was to serve as the Kennedy Administration's efficient hatchetman against Moise Tshombe of the Congo's Katanga Province. When Tshombe's anti-Communist regime seceded from the rest of the chaotic Congo, Rowan branded Tshombe as an "international Uncle Tom" who was nothing more than a hand-picked stooge for Belgian businessmen.

In 1963 and 1964, Rowan was U.S. Ambassador to Finland. In 1964 and 1965, he was Edward R. Murrow's successor as director of the United States Information Agency. While in that position, he traveled to Europe, promoting Lyndon Johnson's "bridge building" between the United States and the Communist bloc of eastern Europe. He went out of his way to assure Communist leaders that the United States government had placed its permanent seal of approval on Europe's Communist regimes. To an audience in Belgrade, Yugoslavia, Rowan said that Americans were acutely aware of revolutionary changes sweeping the world. He elaborated: "We emphasize that we believe in change because we were born of it, we have lived by it, we prospered and grew great by it. So the status quo has never been our god and we ask no one else to bow down before it."

In 1965, Rowan resigned his directorship and became a columnist for the *Chicago Daily News* and Publishers Newspaper Syndicate. He is also a regular contributor to *Reader's Digest* magazine and a radio and television commentator for the Westinghouse Broadcasting System.

Throughout his several careers, Rowan has demonstrated that he is a liberal and has been recognized as such by his peers. He has received the Sidney Hillman award for news reporting, the Contributions to American Democracy award from Roosevelt University, the Golden Ruler award from the Philadelphia Fellowship Commission, the Liberty Bell award from Howard University, the Communications Award in Human Relations from the Anti-Defamation League, and the National Brotherhood award from the National Conference of Christians and Jews. These tributes are almost invariably reserved for those who are actively promoting leftist-liberal causes.

When the Kennedy Dynasty discovered the value of Negroes' votes and began to place Negroes in high government positions, Rowan was one of the show pieces. In 1962, an application for membership to the famous Cosmos Club of Washington, D.C. was submitted on behalf of Rowan. The application was rejected. Within a few days, leading figures in the Kennedy Administration — many of them longtime members of the Cosmos Club — suddenly became color conscious and resigned their membership.

Alexander Jones, executive editor of the *Syracuse Herald-American,* rushed to the defense of the Cosmos Club officers: "I say this incident is a planned political effort in which the Kennedy forces are trying to make Negro capital, using Rowan as a sort of Freedom Rider in the National Capital on the club front.

"I have been a member of the fine old Cosmos Club for more than 20 years and I believe I can speak with some slight knowledge of how it operates.

"I say that there are people who think Carl Rowan is a bumptious, self-enamored and tasteless fellow.

"And that estimate completely discounts the color of his skin. He could be platinum blond and the people I am thinking about would still turn thumbs down on him.

"Many men have been blackballed in application for membership by the Cosmos Club committee, as they have in most private clubs.

"The only one I have ever heard of who ever made a public issue of it is this same Carl Rowan, who is giving every indication of becoming a professional racist."

Rowan has the normal prejudices of a modern liberal. He detests political conservatives and anti-Communist investigations. He is a staunch admirer of the United Nations and its Red hierarchy. He fancies himself an expert on foreign affairs but in reality he is no more than a parrotting apologist for the appeasement-toward-Communism policy that has prevailed for so long in the White House and the State Department.

In 1966, Rowan was convinced, or at least let his readers think he was convinced, that the Soviet Union's leaders were trying very hard to effect a peaceful settlement of the Vietnam War.

Rowan has long championed the idea that the United States should make friendly overtures to Red China – something which would have been done a long time ago, he contends, if only the "purges and inquisitions of the late Sen. Joseph McCarthy" had not had a stifling effect on public debate of U.S. policy toward Red China. (When and where this alleged stifling took place, Rowan has never mentioned.)

One curious fact of Rowan's work remains unexplained. On radio and television and in his writings, he is a persistent and dedicated defender of the Central Intelligence Agency – so much so, that it is not unreasonable to suspect that he is or has been a CIA agent.

DEAN RUSK was born on February 9, 1909 in Cherokee County, Georgia, son of Frances Clotfelter and Robert Rusk. He married Virginia Foisie. He is an alumnus of Davidson College (A.B., 1931) and St. John's College of Oxford University in England (B.S., 1933; M.A., 1934). He was a Rhodes scholar at St. John's.

From 1934 until 1938, Rusk taught government in the leftwing atmosphere of Mills College, a college for women in California. In 1938, Rusk became dean of the faculty.

In 1940, Rusk, an army reservist, was called to duty with rank of captain. He became chief of the British Empire section of the War Department's military intelligence. Next, Rusk moved to the War Department's Far East Section of military intelligence.

In 1943, Rusk – by this time a colonel – was assigned to the staff of General "Vinegar Joe" Stilwell, commander of the China-Burma-India theater of operations. Stilwell, at the time, was doing everything he could to arm a million Red Chinese in order that they could seize China from Chiang Kai-shek. Rusk became Deputy Chief of Staff for the CBI theater. On Stilwell's staff, when Rusk was climbing to military glory, were such pro-Red Chinese stalwarts as John Paton Davies, John Stewart Service, John K. Emmerson, and Raymond Ludden.

In 1945, Rusk was back in Washington as Assistant Chief in the Operations Division of the War Department's General Staff. He left the service in 1946 as a colonel. Rusk did not return to the academic world. Instead, he began a fifteen-year stay – with one brief interruption – in the State Department.

In 1946, Rusk was for a few months Assistant Chief of the State Department's Division of Internal Affairs. He then moved to the War Department for about a year as a special assistant to Secretary of War Robert Patterson. In 1947, Rusk was back in the State Department where he succeeded Alger Hiss as Director of the Office of Special Political Affairs. Rusk took this job upon the specific request of Secretary of State George Marshall who was in the midst of selling out China to the Communists. Rusk would be at Marshall's side when the coup de grâce was administered to the Chiang Kai-shek regime.

The Office of Special Affairs became the Office of United Nations Affairs and, in 1949, Rusk became the first Assistant Secretary for UN Affairs. In that position, Rusk continued Alger Hiss' tradition of letting American Communists be hired to work for the UN without protest from the State Department. In 1949, Rusk received another quick promotion to become Deputy Under Secretary of State to coordinate State Department policy. He was the choice of Dean Acheson.

In March, 1950, Rusk became Assistant Secretary for Far Eastern Affairs. Rusk remained in this position long enough to help persuade President Truman to send American troops into the Korean War, to fight under the United Nations flag – it was a "precious opportunity . . . to intervene through the United Nations." Rusk also bears responsibility for providing the Red Chinese with a privileged sanctuary in Manchuria, which allowed the Red Chinese to launch a massive invasion upon Korea without any chance of American troops blocking it. General MacArthur's bitter criticism of Rusk's strategy led to the loss of his command when Harry Truman compounded his original mistake in listening to Rusk by firing MacArthur. Rusk then moved out of the State Department, in 1952, and, until 1960, was

president of the Rockefeller Foundation. While Rusk headed the Rockefeller Foundation, he waged war on congressional committees investigating Communists. He was particularly aggressive toward the late Joseph R. McCarthy whose charges that Communist influences were rife in government were followed by Senator Pat McCarran's investigation of the Institute of Pacific Relations. McCarran's work touched a sensitive spot on Rusk who not only had been a member of the IPR but had solicited several millions of dollars of foundation money for IPR activities.

In 1961, Rusk was appointed Secretary of State by John F. Kennedy, and he has remained there to the present time. Since the State Department and the White House have been so infested with appeasement and surrender lobbyists during Rusk's tenure, it is impossible to estimate how much of the disastrous foreign policy since 1961 is directly traceable to him. But during his stewardship of the No. 1 cabinet post, the United States has been in a steady retreat toward accommodation with the Communists throughout the world. Beyond accommodation has been the headlong rush toward disarmament and the simultaneous drive to place American security under the United Nations tent. During Rusk's secretaryship, the United States has been savage in its hostility toward the anti-Communist regimes of Katanga, Rhodesia, and Portugal. The United States betrayed West New Guinea into the hands of the Communist tyrant Sukarno of Indonesia. The United States has exported socialism throughout Latin America and built up Communist regimes with financial handouts in Europe, Asia, Latin America, Eastern Europe, and Africa. And Rusk has been a leading deceiver in his utterances on the Vietnam War.

When Rusk appeared at the Soviet Embassy in Washington, D.C. to help the Communists celebrate the fiftieth anniversary of their revolution and their fifty years of tyranny, he should have been their most honored guest. While he was exchanging toasts with the enemy, more than a half million American troops were committed to a perennial "no win" war in Vietnam — the Johnson-McNamara-Rusk war.

BAYARD RUSTIN was born in 1913 in West Chester, Pennsylvania. He attended Wilberforce University in Ohio, Cheyney State Teachers College in Pennsylvania, and the College of the City of New York. He spent a total of three years at Wilberforce and Cheyney; four more at CCNY. He has no degree.

In a friendly biographical article ("The Lone Wolf of Civil Rights," *Saturday Evening Post*, July 11, 1964), Martin Mayer described Rustin's experiences at CCNY: " . . . Rustin wandered into the Communist Party, and when he came to New York in 1938, it was as an organizer for the Young Communist League. He enrolled at City College [CCNY], where for three years 'I did just enough work to stay matriculated'; his real job was recruiting evening-school students for the [Communist] party . . . . Those first years in New York Rustin gave most of his earnings to the [Communist] party . . . . Hatred for the social system that creates [sic] Harlems kept Rustin in the Communist Party through the Trotsky trials and the Hitler-Stalin pact, which shook out much of the membership. What drove him away was the event that made Communism respectable [sic] for other Americans, the German attack on Russia in 1941."

Mayer quoted Rustin on this alleged break: "I was brought up a Quaker, you know, by my grandmother, and the Communists had become the great peace party. I was working on the campaign against segregation in the armed forces, and the Communists were all for it. Then Hitler attacked, and they became a war party. The line was, 'Everybody in the armed forces. People's war. Second front. No domestic issues; forget about discrimination in the Army.' "

After the alleged break with the Communist Party, Rustin sought another job through the good offices of the late Abraham J. Muste. (Muste had long been an influential and inveterate supporter of Communist fronts, projects, and causes. At one time, he had been the National Chairman of the now-defunct Workers Party, a Communist party. Muste, however, found that he could serve the Communists quite effectively by using a "pacifist" gimmick, and, under the banners of "peace" and "non-violence," he acquired a reputation for respectability among those too stupid or too unwilling to see through his hoax. The Communists, however, never ceased to regard Muste as one of their own. In 1957, when they held their 16th National Convention, the Communists hand-picked Muste to be present as an "impartial observer" and Muste rewarded his comrades by issuing a flattering report of the proceedings. In 1966, Muste was still so committed to his comrades that he endorsed the congressional candidacy of Communist Herbert Aptheker — a fact widely publicized in the Communist press.)

At the time Rustin approached Muste, the latter was the Executive Secretary of the Fellowship of Reconciliation. The FOR was one of the oldest and certainly the largest leftwing, pacifist group in the United States and its members were urged to join "political movements which aim at the replacement of private capitalism by a system of collective ownership" — which could be reasonably interpreted as a recruiting call for the Socialist and Communist Parties. Muste gave Rustin a job as Race Relations Director for FOR. Then Muste moved Rustin into the Congress of Racial Equality (CORE), a demonstrative group of racial agitators which was organized under the auspices of FOR. Rustin became the organizer of CORE's New York branch, but he soon came to grief as a conscientious objector. Not only was he a "conshie" but he refused to report for "work of national importance" as required by the Selective Service law and he served twenty-eight months in prison.

After World War II, Rustin busied himself in racial agitation. In 1947, he organized the first so-called Freedom Ride through the South. The ostensible purpose was to test compliance with the Supreme Court's 1946 ban on segregation in interstate travel. For his efforts, Rustin was arrested eighteen times on what he called the Journey of Reconciliation. In that same year, he traveled to India, allegedly to study the Gandhian tactics of nonviolence for national independence. And he prolonged this trip by going to Africa where he met with "nationalist" agitators. In 1948 and 1949, he was arrested several times and he served at least two short jail sentences in New York City and Washington, D.C. in connection with his racial-pacifist demonstrations.

In 1952, Rustin became Executive Secretary of the War Resisters League — a position he still maintains. (The WRL was organized in 1923, mainly through the efforts of World War I conscientious objectors. The WRL is affiliated with the War Resisters International which is active in more than sixty countries. The WRL claims its inspiration is drawn from "the Judeo-Christian sense of justice, from the anarchist and socialist resistance to human exploitation, from Gandhian nonviolence, from the many American efforts for a better human community [i.e. various leftwing, pacifist and racial organizations]."

While on a lecture tour in 1953, Rustin was arrested by Pasadena, California police for vagrancy and lewdness. He pleaded guilty to a charge of sex perversion and was sentenced to sixty days in jail. In that same year, Rustin traveled to South Africa and did some racial agitating there.

In 1955, Rustin began a five-year period as a secretary to Martin Luther King Jr. and he helped to organize King's Southern Christian Leadership Conference. Rustin continued to hold his position as Executive Secretary to the War Resisters League.

While in the service of King, Rustin, in 1957, attended the 16th National Convention of the Communist Party as an "impartial observer" in the company of his old benefactor Abraham J. Muste. (At that time, Rustin was also a member of the American Forum for Socialist Education, which — in 1957 — was called a Communist front by the Senate Internal Security Subcommittee.)

In 1958, Rustin organized M.L. King's march on Washington which the Communists, in *The Worker*, boasted was one of their projects. Also, in 1958, Rustin organized a "peace march" to the Soviet Union, under the sponsorship of the leftwing, pacifist Nonviolent Action Committee against Nuclear Weapons. In connection with this spectacle, Rustin organized the Aldermaston Ban-the-Bomb protest in Britain. In 1960, he led a group of his soul-mates in a march across the Sahara Desert in a vain attempt to halt the first French nuclear-test explosion.

His flair for international activity has been further demonstrated by his establishment of a Center for Nonviolence in Tanganyika. On another occasion he apologized to the Japanese people for the continuance of United States atomic tests. He has worked with the leftwing, pacifist World Peace Brigade and has been active in the Medical Aid to [Castro's] Cuba Committee.

Perhaps Rustin's most spectacular achievement was his direction of the 1963 March on Washington. He was assigned to this task by A. Philip Randolph, a veteran fellow traveler and racial agitator. The March was an effective pressure tactic upon the Congress and the Administration for passage of so-called civil rights legislation. In 1963, Rustin also found time to lead the first school boycott in New York City and he opened up a New York office of the radical leftist Student Nonviolent Coordinating Committee. His activities in 1963 gave Rustin unprecedented national publicity. His past was raked over and he was subjected to some criticism in the press and in Congress. But Rustin defended his pacifist activities as a natural consequence of his earlier Quaker environment. He denied – not under oath – that he had been a member of the Communist Party. As for judgment of his arrest and conviction for perversion, Rustin said: "This must be done by my peers who as you know are the Christian ministers of the Negro communities and the civil rights leaders. They have the responsibility for the moral and Christian leadership of the Negro people." Two of Rustin's peers – M.L. King and A. Philip Randolph – rushed to his defense, and since that time Rustin's reputation has been more or less sacrosanct from criticism. In 1964, when Rustin attended a private cocktail party given by the Soviet Union's Ambassador to the UN, Nikolai Federenko, there was scarcely a flurry of criticism. And Rustin blandly explained that he had been invited to the Soviet Union's UN Mission because of his pacifist activities in the Committee for Nonviolent Action and his concern and preoccupation with artistic freedom in the Soviet Union.

In the past few years, Rustin has been in great demand as a lecturer. His general theme is to call for a "social and political revolution" in the United States. He has spoken at such campuses as Harvard University and Mt. Mercy College in Pittsburgh. At Stanford University he lectured to two hundred and fifty educators and city officials who were attending a conference on urban school problems. There he offered one of his favorite solutions – those who attend school should not only have tuition, books, and incidental expenses paid for by the government but should also be given a salary while in school. On several occasions, he has called for a nation-wide minimum wage scale of two dollars an hour.

Before two thousand at a convention of the American Institute of Planners in Washington, D.C., Rustin called for a party of the left which would be a coalition of labor, civil rights and other groups within the Democratic Party.

It would be futile for Rustin to deny that he is at least a Socialist. In 1964, he solicited funds for the socialist League for Industrial Democracy. In that same year, the LID honored him by reprinting, as the first in a series of occasional papers, an article Rustin had written for *Contemporary* magazine. He has served on the national Board of Directors for the socialist Americans for Democratic Action. He has been actively involved with *Liberation* magazine, a Socialist publication. He has offered as a dictum: "The great task before the Negro of the future will require him to hammer at the basic contradictions of our society and work towards its socialization."

Rustin's pacifist activities have been further expressed in his affiliations with the Peace Information Center and the Women's International League for Peace and Freedom. Of course, he is a vigorous critic of U.S. participation in the Vietnam War, thereby following in the footsteps of his old mentor, Muste, who twice visited Ho chi Minh on missions of "peace and sympathy." (Ho was distraught at the news of Muste's death in 1967.) There can be no doubt that Rustin has acquired a national recognition accorded few other racial agitators. He has been called a "dynamic social reformer" (*Ebony* magazine), an "organizing genius" (*New York Times*), "enough of a realist and enough of a philosopher to fill the bill for the Negroes" (columnist Mary McGrory — who also described Rustin as a rangy, handsome, graying 53-year-old ex-football player), "the most electric man in the civil rights movement" (*Boston Herald*), "character integrity, and extraordinary ability . . . dedication to high human ideals" (A. Philip Randolph), "brilliant, efficient and dedicated organizer and one of the best and most persuasive interpreters of nonviolence" (M.L. King Jr.).

In his deliberately cultivated and affected British accent, Rustin calls himself a political actionist and a lonely genius who believes "in social dislocation and creative trouble." He is obviously not too happy being an American: "I tell you, brother, I fought it for years, against being American — in my speech, my manner, everything . . . It's a hard thing for a Negro to accept, being American, but you can't escape it." Rustin's fight against being American is not over.

WILLIAM FITTS RYAN was born on June 28, 1922 in Albion, New York, son of Harriet Fitts and Bernard Ryan. He married Priscilla Marbury. He is an alumnus of Princeton University (A.B., 1944) and Columbia University (LL.B., 1949). In 1949, he was admitted to the bar and began the practice of law in New York City. From 1950 until 1957, he was an assistant district attorney of New York County.

Since 1961, Ryan has been in Congress, representing the 20th Congressional District of New York. At every session of Congress, he has been in the vanguard of the ultra-liberals seeking to abolish the House Committee on Un-American Activities.

Ryan's bitter and hysterical anti-HCUA activities are only the beginning of his ultra-liberalism. He is the complete welfare statist. He has voted straight down the line for New Frontier and Great Society socialistic legislation. He is a fanatic on so-called civil rights and took pride in his participation in Ralph Albernathy's 1968 "Poor People's March" in Washington, D.C. He has called for the registration of every firearm in the United States. He has urged that the Peace Corps be placed under international control. He wants the federal government to provide a guaranteed annual income for everybody.

In foreign affairs, he is a rabid supporter of foreign aid programs, the United Nations, and disarmament proposals. On Vietnam, he is a peacenik and, as recently as 1967, he somehow concluded that the military was in ascendance over the civilians in the Department of Defense.

In 1965, Ryan made a futile bid for the mayoralty nomination on the Democratic ticket in New York City. His candidacy attracted the support of the Communists' *The Worker* and leftwingers who endorsed him included Ossie Davis, Ruby Dee, Robert Ryan, Theodor Bikel, and Pete Seeger.

HARRISON SALISBURY was born on November 14, 1908 in Minneapolis, son of Georgiana Evans and Percy Salisbury. He married Mary Hollis. He is an alumnus of the University of Minnesota (A.B., 1930).

Salisbury began his journalistic career, in 1928, as a reporter for the *Minneapolis Journal*. In 1930, he joined the United Press and, during the next twelve years, he was a correspondent, successively, in St. Paul, Chicago, Washington, D.C., and New York. In 1943, he became the manager of UPI's London bureau and, in 1944, he assumed the same position in UPI's Moscow bureau. He then returned to the United States and was UPI's foreign news editor from 1944 until 1948.

In 1949, Salisbury joined the staff of the *New York Times* as its Moscow correspondent. He remained in Moscow until 1954, when he returned to New York City as a staff correspondent for the *Times*. In 1964, he assumed his present position as assistant managing editor.

In 1946, Salisbury began writing what became a series of books, based upon his experiences and observations on the Soviet Union. His first such work was *Russia on the Way,* published in 1946 — a superficial and banal tribute to our recent "allies" in war and future "partners" in peace. Many such books were being produced by the bleeding-heart fraternity in the aftermath of World War

II and, if Salisbury had stopped there, his contribution to the post-war hysteria of accommodation with the Communists would not have been exceptional. However, Salisbury had merely begun his career as a pro-Communist apologist. And his big opportunity arrived when he went to the Soviet Union as the *Times'* Moscow correspondent in 1949. Then, for almost six years, he sent a steady stream of misinformation in his dispatches to the *Times*. Even *Time* magazine admitted that Salisbury's "reports often read more like Red propaganda than accounts of what was really going on inside Russia." The way Salisbury told it: the Russian people could not have been happier than they were under Stalin. At home and abroad, the Soviet Union was on the way to peace and prosperity.

When Salisbury returned to the United States, he wrote a curious book, *An American in Russia*. It was curious inasmuch as he admitted that his dispatches from Moscow had not been altogether accurate; he had gilded the Soviet lily a little bit. It was not a complete recantation by any means. But the Soviet authorities were miffed enough by even this slight deviation by one they had considered to be completely sympathetic that they made a wrist-slapping gesture and banned Salisbury from revisiting the Soviet Union. Salisbury quickly made amends and struggled valiantly in his American-based dispatches to the *Times* to lavish praise on the Khrushchevian era. Finally, in 1959, all was forgiven and Salisbury once again possessed a Soviet visa. His crowning touch of atonement had come when Anastas Mikoyan, the first deputy premier of the Soviet Union, visited the United States. Salisbury was assigned by the *Times* to report on the veteran

Communist butcher's tour and Salisbury wrote such ingratiating and flattering accounts that Mikoyan intervened personally to allow Salisbury's return to the Soviet Union. And so Salisbury made his own tour — of six months duration — which is perpetuated in his 1960 book, *To Moscow and Beyond.*

Eugene Lyons, whose disillusionment with the Soviet Union had come through his own journalistic career there, reviewed *To Moscow and Beyond* in *National Review,* May 7, 1960. Lyons recognized that Salisbury's main thesis in the book was that "unless we support Khrushchev without delay we may have to deal with a resusciated Stalinism." This was not a new idea of Salisbury's. Lyons recalled that "in a political essay disguised as a Washington news dispatch Salisbury made the identical threat several years ago. That does not in itself invalidate the argument, but it does make his eye-witness testimony rather suspect. The truth is that this rationale for 'playing ball with Khrushchev' has in recent years been common forensic currency among those eager to stake all on the rhetoric of 'peaceful coexistence.' And that, in fact, is what makes the new Salisbury book potentially mischievous. It provides for piecemeal surrender to Moscow. Salisbury bids fair to become for the 1960s what his long-ago predecessor in the Soviet post, Walter Duranty, was for the 1930s: the authority for self-delusion rooted in half-truth and wishful hoping."

Mr. Lyons could reasonably have dealt more harshly with Salisbury. *To Moscow and Beyond* was certainly more than "potentially mischievous" — it was prestigious pro-Communist propaganda. Examples? — "Khrushchev's look is not just a false face for the old Stalin treachery." — "No one who listens to

Nikita Sergevich [Khrushchev] long can doubt that he was reared in a good God-fearing Russian orthodox household." — "Khrushchev, I felt, had cast himself in the role in which he hoped history would cloak him. He was the man of peace." — "I had a strong suspicion that it [the Korean War] had been initiated as a blow by Stalin at Mao Tse-tung." — "If there was a crime to be charged against Truman and Acheson, it was not for the failure of their China policy in the years before 1948. It was their failure to establish diplomatic relations immediately with the Chinese Communist regime." — "You could not find in the communist society of 1959 any stronger motivation than those very motivations to a more comfortable way of life. This was what Russia was straining for."

Salisbury's paeans for the Soviet Union continued in his dispatches and books (*Moscow Journal,* 1961; *A New Russia,* 1962; *Russia,* 1965 [heartily endorsed by the Communist magazine *New World Review* in its issue of January 1967]; *The Soviet Union: The Fifty Years,* 1967). And his admiration for Khrushchev seemed limitless. As late as April 25, 1965, Salisbury wrote in the *New York Times Magazine:* "Six months after the forced departure of Nikita S. Khrushchev from Soviet leadership, it is becoming clear that history will remember him best for deeds of the spirit rather than material accomplishment." (The ungrateful Russians evidently could not share Salisbury's appreciation of Khrushchev as "the man of peace.") In the *New York Times* (September 17, 1967), Salisbury, while reviewing Mark Frankland's *Khrushchev,* wrote: " 'He [Khrushchev] left his country a better place than he found it, both in the eyes of the majority of his own people and of the world.' This is Mark Frankland's verdict on Nikita Khrushchev, an epitaph on the rambunctious career of the zestful Soviet politician . . . . Khrushchev won for himself and his country a kind of grudging affection and respect. Today it is not uncommon for Americans to say, a little puzzled: 'You know, it's a funny thing, but I miss old Khrushchev.' . . . For all his faults – and Mr. Frankland's able study presents an ample catalogue – he has left both his countrymen and the world his debtors."

In December, 1966, Salisbury became the first accredited American journalist to visit Hanoi, North Vietnam in twelve years. Not content with handpicking Salisbury as the perfect patsy for its propaganda purposes, Ho chi Minh's regime had Wilfred Burchett accompany Salisbury in North Vietnam. (Burchett is a veteran Communist propagandist. He achieved international prominence during the Korean Way by circulating charges that the United States was waging germ warfare. He is an especial hero to the Chinese Communists whom he helped in the brainwashing of American prisoners of war. Burchett has written for such Communist publications as the *National Guardian,* Moscow's *New Times,* the *Moscow Daily News,* and *New World Review.* His books have been published by Communist publishing houses and *The Worker* offered Burchett's *Vietnam – Inside Story of Guerrilla War* as a subscription premium.)

In late December, 1966 and early January, 1967, Salisbury's dispatches from North Vietnam were printed not only in the *New York Times* but in newspapers throughout the world. Ho chi Minh had scored his greatest propaganda coup as Salisbury portrayed American bombing efforts in North Vietnam as deliberate attacks on purely civilian

targets – the very line which Ho chi Minh had been trying ineffectively to sell to the world. But where Ho failed, the *New York Times'* assistant managing editor succeeded. Salisbury's implications were plain enough: the United States was perpetrating genocide and Salisbury had the Communist quotations and statistics to prove it. And never did the American doves flutter higher. From a hundred American colleges, student leaders used Salisbury's dispatches to demand an end to the bombing attacks on North Vietnam. Chairman J. William Fulbright of the Senate Foreign Relations Committee suffered a recurrence of television fever and threatened to hold a new round of TV-hearings. The Communist press throughout the world reprinted Salisbury's anti-American diatribes as did much of the non-Communist press. It was painfully evident that Ho chi Minh had made the perfect choice in Salisbury to set off a world-wide demand that the United States cease its strategic bombing of North Vietnam.

In June, 1966, it appeared for a while that Salisbury would not be taken seriously anymore as an observer of the war zone in the Far East. At that time, he was on a trip through Southeast Asia, Japan, Outer Mongolia, and the eastern parts of the Soviet Union. While in Pnompenh, Salisbury was told by Cambodian officials that there was probably no such thing as a "Sihanouk trail" used by Ho chi Minh to transport supplies to his forces in South Vietnam. Salisbury duly quoted his informants in his dispatch to the *Times.* A week later, the *Times'* Far East correspondent Seymour Topping reported that the "Sihanouk trail" was very real and was being used by Ho chi Minh to supply his troops in South Vietnam. (Salisbury's trip of 1966 has been perpetuated in his *Orbit of*

China, a book so bad that it was reviewed quite unfavorably in the *New York Times.*)

When Salisbury returned to the United States from his junket to North Vietnam, his efforts on behalf of Ho chi Minh did not cease. On February 1, 1967, he appeared before the Senate Foreign Relations Committee and its Chairman J. William Fulbright. In the course of the hearing, it was obvious that Fulbright, Salisbury, and Senate Majority Leader Mike Mansfield had formed a mutual admiration society. According to Salisbury, North Vietnam had been unified as never before because of U.S. bombing attacks; Hanoi was ready to begin peace talks; there was a strong possibility that Communist China and the Soviet Union might withdraw their support from Ho chi Minh if the Peking-Moscow "split" widened or the "civil war" in Communist China intensified; "the people of [North Vietnam] have . . . rallied around the national cause on the basis of patriotism rather than Communism"; if the Americans stopped bombing North Vietnam, world opinion would force North Vietnam to take some reciprocal steps to match our move; and, to Fulbright's query as to "why doesn't North Vietnam give up?" – Salisbury replied: "They don't trust us . . . they have a feeling that we have evil intentions toward them." This was the language that the doves could understand and appreciate and publicize. Fulbright did not bother to call military experts or victory-minded diplomats in rebuttal.

Salisbury, if anything, has gained prestige as a result of his pro-North Vietnam mission. (Perpetuated in his 1967 book, *Behind the Lines – Hanoi.*) And, his dispatches in the *Times* have continued to be scarcely veiled pleas for "peaceful"

coexistence with the Communists of the Soviet Union, Red China, and North Vietnam. The wonder is that he has not become Secretary of State. But he has had his share of rewards for his pro-Communist reporting: a Pulizer Prize for international correspondence; the Distinguished Achievement medal from his alma mater the University of Minnesota; the George Polk Memorial Award for foreign reporting; the Sigma Delta Chi Award for foreign correspondence; and, in 1967, the Asia Reporting Award from the Overseas Press Club.

PAUL SAMUELSON was born on May 15, 1915 in Gary Indiana, son of Ella Lipton and Frank Samuelson. He married Marion Crawford. He is an alumnus of the University of Chicago (B.A., 1935) and Harvard University (M.A., 1936; Ph.D., 1941). From 1935 until 1937, he held a pre-doctoral fellowship granted by the Social Science Research Council. From 1937 until 1940, he was a member of Harvard University's Society of Fellows. In 1948 and 1949, he held a Guggenheim Fellowship; in 1958 and 1959, he held a Ford Foundation fellowship.

In 1940, Samuelson joined the economics faculty at Massachusetts Insitute of Technology as an assistant professor. In 1944, he became an associate professor. Since 1947, he has been a professor of economics. From 1941 until 1943, he was a consultant to the National Resources Planning Board. In 1944 and 1945, he did work for MIT's Radiation Laboratory where he helped to develop computers for tracking aircraft. In 1945, he was a consultant to the War Production Borad and to the Office of War Mobilization and Construction. Also in 1945, he lectured on international economic relations at the Fletcher School of

Law and Diplomacy of Tufts University. He has been a consultant to the U.S. Treasury Department (1945-1952); the Bureau of Budget (1952); the research advisory panel to President Eisenhower's National Goals Commission (1959-1960); the National Task Force on Economic Education (1960-1961); the RAND Corporation (since 1949); and, the President's Council of Economic Advisors (in the Kennedy Administration).

Samuelson was an economic adviser to John F. Kennedy as senator, presidential candidate, and president-elect. In December, 1960, Mr. Kennedy appointed Samuelson to be head of an economic task force which would recommend measures to counter what Mr. Kennedy described as a serious business slump. Within a few weeks, Samuelson reported to Mr. Kennedy that the nation needed increased federal spending programs in such areas as unemployment compensation, defense programs, urban renewal, various health and welfare programs, highway construction, depressed area programs, and housing programs. In effect, Samuelson's report became the outline for the New Frontier's spending orgy. In October, 1964, Samuelson was chairman of President Johnson's Task Force on Maintaining Prosperity.

Samuelson has been a prolific author of books and articles. In 1966, he began writing an economics column for *Newsweek* magazine. He is frequently called upon for interviews by newspapers and magazines. He appears frequently on radio and television panel and interview programs. But his greatest fame and most rewarding financial windfall has been due to his textbook *Economics: An Introductory Analysis*, first published in 1948. As of 1965, it was in its sixth edition, having sold more than

one million copies in the United States, and was used by an estimated forty per cent of all American collegians who were studying introductory economics. The book has been translated into fourteen languages. (In 1965, a Russian translation of the book was published in Moscow.)

If Samuelson's brand of economics can be placed in a single category, it would be that of Keynesianism, which — when its contradictions, obscurities, and confusions are scraped away — remains as Socialism, not too far removed from the tenets of Marx and Engels.

Samuelson did his graduate work at Harvard under the tutelage of Alvin Hansen, one of the leading Keynesian theorists in the academic world. John Maynard Keynes, the British economist, advocated that the central government should manage the nation's economy in good times and bad. He despised a free market economy; he distrusted an economic system wherein the individual was free to save or to invest his money; he had no respect for the property rights of an individual; and, he believed that the central government should have the power to redistribute income.

Over the wide expanse of his writings, Samuelson adheres to the general Keynesian principles. He believes that the goal of government is full employment to be achieved by pump priming and credit expansion. He favors the federal government's tax power as a means to curb private spending on consumer and producer goods. He would have the Congress delegate wide discretionary power to the President so that he could manipulate the tax power more readily. (As Samuelson has written: "Along with being Commander in Chief of the armed forces, the President is architect of our economic destiny.")

To make his socialistic recommendations more palatable to his readers and listeners, Samuelson sets up the straw man of laissez-faire economy. With the mythical evil established, Samuelson promotes government intervention in all phases of economic activity through the use of fiat money, deficit spending, taxes, manipulation of interest and mortgage rates, price and wage controls, rationing, domestic welfare handouts, so-called foreign aid programs, and a myriad of public works programs.

The details of Samuelson's economics vary from time to time so that in totality he reveals inconsistencies and contradictions, but essentially, his program for government intervention in the economy is in perfect harmony with socialism.

ROBERT A. SCALAPINO was born on October 19, 1919 in Leavenworth, Kansas, son of Beulah Stephenson and Anthony Scalapino. He married Dee Jessen. He is an alumnus of Santa Barbara College (A.B., 1940) and Harvard University (M.A., 1943; Ph.D., 1948).

In 1948 and 1949, Scalapino was an instructor at Harvard University. In 1949, he joined the faculty of the University of California (Berkeley) where he has served, successively, as assistant professor (1949-1951), associate professor (1951-1956), professor (1956-1968), and chairman of the political science department (1962-1968). He is the author of *Democracy and the Party Movement in Pre-War Japan; Parties and Politics in Contemporary Japan; North Korea Today;* and *The Communist Revolution in Asia.* Since 1962, he has been editor of *Asian Survey.*

Scalapino's ultra-liberal credentials for extra-curricular activities are impeccable. He has been an active member of Americans for Democratic Action and on the board of directors of San Francisco's ADA. He has been a non-resident member of the Council on Foreign Relations. He has been a consultant to the Rockefeller Brothers Fund, the Ford Foundation, and San Francisco's World Affairs Council. He has held a fellowship from the Social Science Research Council and a grant from the Rockefeller Foundation.

In November, 1956, Scalapino, as an "expert" on Japan, presented a paper to the American Assembly, Columbia University's prestigious brainwashing seminar for gullible American business executives. It was Scalapino's contention that Americans were taking too strong a moral position against Communism in contrast to the pragmatic attitude of Europeans and Asians. Consequently Scalapino urged that U.S. policy makers encourage increased trade between Japan and Red China. This was "one of the areas where Japanese concepts of economic priority come into conflict with American concepts of political requirements," as he admitted, but he was quite willing to sacrifice American principles which, after all, were tiresome traditions.

On November 1, 1959, the U.S. Senate's Foreign Relations Committee received the Conlon Report to which Scalapino was one of three major contributors. (The Conlon Report was a product of Conlon Associates of San Francisco, consultants on foreign trade and headed by Richard P. Conlon, formerly of the State Department and the Central Intelligence Agency. Conlon had been a protégé of John Paton Davies Jr., one of the earliest and more influential promoters of Mao Tse-tung and his "agrarian reform" barbarism. Conlon became head of San Francisco's Asian Foundation and, for a brief period [June, 1958 to June, 1959], his Conlon Associates "consulting firm" was an agent for Ngo dinh Diem's South Vietnamese regime.) In the Conlon Report, Scalapino recommended that Free China should become the Republic of Taiwan, a protectorate of the United States and any other powers that wished to assume such a guardianship. As for Red China, the United States should prepare for a gradual establishment of good relations since trade with Red China was bound to be profitable in the future. Red China was becoming an economic giant. Who said so? The Red Chinese, of course. Chairman J. William Fulbright of the Senate Foreign Relations Committee received Scalapino's sell-out of Free China in favor of Red China as a welcome echo of his own sentiments.

Not long after his smashing success with Fulbright, Scalapino used his ADA colleagues to circulate his pamphlet ("New Perspective on Northeast Asia") in which he called for U.S. diplomatic recognition of Red China, immediate admission of Red China to the United Nations and expulsion of Free China from the UN. Free China would be further humiliated and betrayed by being "neutralized" as a UN trusteeship. Then the UN would supervise a plebiscite in Free China. Scalapino also recommended the abandonment of Free China's islands of Quemoy and Matsu to Red China and U.S. diplomatic relationship with Outer Mongolia — a Soviet Union stronghold since 1924.

During the "teach-in" craze of 1965, Scalapino used discussions on the Vietnam War as a means of promoting his pro-Red Chinese views. (Incredible as it may seem, Scalapino was widely publicized as a defender of the Johnson Administration's Vietnam policy.) He expressed his satisfaction over the Soviet Union's presence in Hanoi — a presence which through some convolutions of Scalapino's logic was proving beneficial to the United States. As for the Vietnam War, Scalapino's solution was easy: the United States would call for a "neutral, non-aligned Asia," since — he was happy to observe — neutralism was no longer considered immoral.

In 1966, Scalapino was again a "witness' before Chairman J. William Fulbright and the Senate Foreign Relations Committee. If Fulbright expected Scalapino to put in a good word for Red China, he was not disappointed. By this time, however, it was becoming difficult to fathom whether Scalapino was prompted more by his hatred of Free China or by his admiration of Red China. Early in 1966, Scalapino appeared as the author of a foreword to George H. Kerr's *Formosa Betrayed* — an expansion of two articles Kerr had written for the pro-Communist Institute of Pacific Relations' *Far Eastern Survey* in 1947. Kerr's premise was that the return of Formosa to Free China at the end of World War II was a betrayal of the island and its people. From this beginning, Kerr wrote a vicious attack upon the Free Chinese regime. And Scalapino's foreword was an endorsement of Kerr's diatribe.

It was also in 1966 that Scalapino became chairman of the National Committee on United States-China Relations. This outfit had as its ostensible purpose the sponsorship of public debate on United States relations with Red China. Of course, there had been no lack of public debate ever since 1949 when Mao Tse-tung seized the Chinese mainland from the betrayed and abandoned regime of Chiang Kai-shek. And the real purpose of Scalapino and his leftwing cohorts (John K. Fairbank, Doak Barnett, Clark Kerr, Roger Hilsman,

Oliver Edmund Clubb, and Anna Lord Strauss) was to inspire a large-scale demand for diplomatic relations between the United States and Red China.

The persistency of Scalapino over the years certainly entitles him to recognition as one of the leaders of the Red China lobby, and this undoubtedly was a factor in his appointment to a State Department advisory panel on Red China in 1966. The wonder is that Chiang Kai-shek's regime has survived the past two years.

THOMAS C. SCHELLING was born on April 14, 1921 in Oakland, California, son of Zelda Ayres and John Schelling. He married Corinne Saposs. He is an alumnus of the University of California (A.B., 1943) and Harvard University (Ph.D., 1951).

From 1948 until 1953, Schelling was an economist for the U.S. government, working in Copenhagen, Paris, and Washington. From 1953 until 1958, he was a professor of economics at Yale University and, since 1958, has held the same position at Harvard University. In 1958 and 1959, he was a senior staff member of the RAND Corporation.

Schelling has written *National Income Behavior; International Economics;* and *The Strategy of Conflict.* He is co-author of *Strategy and Arms Control.* He has been on the editorial board of the *American Economic Review,* the *Journal of Conflict Resolution,* and *World Politics.* He is a non-resident member of the Council on Foreign Relations, the informal, supra-State Department of the United States.

Schelling is an ideal example of that new breed of "think factory" habitués who are subsidized by the government to play paper war games which inevitably conclude with appeasement of our Com-munist enemies and surrender of American independence.

Mrs. Alice Widener, in her publication *U.S.A.* January 13, 1961, pin-pointed accurately the theme which has prevailed in Schelling's writing. Said Mrs. Widener: "The December 1960 issue of the magazine *Air Force and Space Digest* carried a major article by Dr. Thomas C. Schelling, a Pugwash participant, which was entitled 'Meteors, Mischief, and War.' This article used *On the Beach* as a point of intellectual departure and declares it gives a picture 'of human error and impotence.' Dr. Schelling eloquently puts forth the hold-back SAC line, the 'accident' theory given such 'priority' by the Soviets at Pugwash, and calls for all kinds of military safety measures which – to a civilian – seem to be appeasement measures. Even, Dr. Schelling goes so far into appeasement that *he calls for only 'measured doses' of retaliation by our Strategic Air Command in case of Soviet attack on the United States!*

"Thus, Dr. Schelling's 'measured doses' theory synchronizes in a tailspin of creeping defeatism with editor [of *The Bulletin of the Atomic Scientists*] Eugene Rabinowitch's 'spare the Soviets from destruction' argument.

"Dr. Schelling writes in a literary style full of the moderate, understated negative that is so confusing to all but the properly initiated or to the brainwasher, 'Even for the "pre-war deterrence" it is not obvious that the most effective threat (by the United States Strategic Air Command) is instant punitive destruction without regard to ourselves. To deter or forestall the unpremeditated attack (as if attack on us by the Soviets or Red Chinese would be a sudden thought or "accident only"!) or the "accidental," "false-alarm," or mischief-inspired attack – we ought to cultivate the enemy's belief that we shall respond to what may be the opening moves in a general war with deliberate care and control and sensitivity to what is going on, not with an instant, all-out indiscriminate effort to destroy all the enemies who may have been involved.'

"Now what does that mean? Doesn't it mean that we should hold back SAC from destruction of an enemy who might kill millions of Americans merely for mischief or by accident or false alarm? How would you feel if you were a maimed survivor of such an attack and SAC held back from punishment with the 'sensitive' excuse, 'Oh, you mustn't mind them, it was only a bit of Khrushchev's or Mao's mischief!'

"In other words, the Soviets and Red Chinese can be 'indiscriminate' but not us, not even if it means the life or death of America!

"Dr. Schelling's own sensitivity seems to be on the left side only. He makes faint motions with the right side and sometimes talks out of the right side of his mouth, but not nearly with the same 'sensitivity.' "

ARTHUR M. SCHLESINGER JR. was born on October 15, 1917 in Columbus, Ohio, son of Elizabeth Bancroft and Arthur Schlesinger. He married Marian Cannon. He is an alumnus of Harvard University (A.B., 1938).

From 1939 until 1942, Schlesinger was a fellow at Harvard. During the war years, he was with Elmer Davis' Redlined Office of War Information (1942-1943), the Office of Strategic Services (1943-1945), and did a brief stint in the U.S. Army (1945). Schlesinger then returned to Harvard as an associate professor (1946-1954) and professor (1954-1962). While on the Harvard faculty, he was also a consultant to the Eco-

nomic Cooperation Administration (1948), a consultant to the Mutual Security Administration (1951-1952), and a member of Adlai Stevenson's staff in the presidential campaigns of 1952 and 1956. In 1960, he was a member of John F. Kennedy's campaign staff and served as a special assistant to the president throughout the Kennedy Administration and briefly in the Johnson Administration.

Among Schlesinger's books are *The Age of Jackson* (which was more a defense of Roosevelt's New Deal than a history of our seventh president's administration, but it received the Pulitzer Prize for history in 1945); *The Vital Center; The Crisis of the Old Order; The Coming of the New Deal; The Politics of Upheaval; Kennedy or Nixon; The Politics of Hope; A Thousand Days* (about the Kennedy Administration without mentioning Lee Harvey Oswald, but nevertheless *Time* magazine honored Schlesinger and his book with a five-page cover story); and *The Bitter Heritage: Vietnam and American Democracy, 1941-1966* (which received a most laudatory review in Moscow's *New Times*). He was co-author with Richard Rovere of *The General and the President*.

In 1966, Schlesinger assumed the Albert Schweitzer chair in the humanities at the City University of New York. In 1967, he became president of University-at-Large Programs, Inc., which will produce "educational" films for high school and college curricula. The films will feature outstanding leftists such as Arnold Toynbee, Lionel Trilling, Aaron Copland, Robert Lowell, Isidor Rabi, and John Kenneth Galbraith.

Schlesinger has been a founder and official of Americans for Democratic Action, the center of the radical left in American politics; an official of the

American Civil Liberties Union, that motleyed collection of defenders of subversion, crime, and licentiousness; a member of Clarence Streit's Atlantic Union Committee, working towards a political merger of Western Europe and the United States, as a major step towards world government; and, a nonresident member of the Council on Foreign Relations, the informal supra-State Department of the United States. In 1967, Schlesinger sponsored Negotiation Now!, an ad hoc committee led by leftwing luminaries for appeasement in Vietnam, including Martin Luther King Jr., Joseph L. Rauh Jr., Victor Reuther, Reinhold Niehbuhr, and John Kenneth Galbraith.

When Schlesinger resigned from the Johnson Administration, Mr. Johnson wrote to him: "As one who has written so much political history, you should take great pride in now having helped make it."

If Schlesinger had any talent as an historian, it has never been evident in his writings. No matter what the book may be, he is a master of the diatribe or of sycophancy. His special heroes are Franklin D. Roosevelt, Harry S. Truman, John F. Kennedy, Robert F. Kennedy, Adlai Stevenson, Juan Bosch, Fidel Castro, labor demagogues, and just about any leftwing social and/or political revolutionist. His villains are first and foremost the late Senator Joseph R. McCarthy, Richard M. Nixon, General Douglas MacArthur, anti-Communists, Republicans in general, businessmen in particular, and just about anyone who ranges on the side of free enterprise, conservatism, traditional constitutionalism, and national security.

Whether Schlesinger writes on the Jackson, Roosevelt, or Kennedy Administrations, or whether it is simply a campaign document (*Kennedy or Nixon* or his privately circulated *The Big Decision*), or on Vietnam or American politics or the Latin American scene, he is making a special plea for socialism, for planned economy, for fallacious Keynesian economics, for the welfare state, for judicial usurpation of legislative powers and judicial sociological and economic reforms, and for people's democracy. He has received honorary degrees from university trustees who should know better, and academic awards from organizations in a rank betrayal of scholarship.

DAVID SCHOENBRUN was born on March 15, 1915 in New York City, son of Lucy Cassirer and Max Schoenbrun. He married Dorothy Scher. He is an alumnus of the College of the City of New York (B.A., 1934). He is the author of *As France Goes* (1957) and *The Three Lives of Charles de Gaulle* (1965).

From 1934 until 1936, Schoenbrun was a secondary school language teacher. From 1936 until 1940, he was a labor relations adjustor for the Dress Manufacturers Association. In 1940 and 1941, he was a free-lance writer. His work appeared in such publications as the *Chicago Sun, Click* magazine, and the pro-Communist newspaper *PM*.

In 1942 and 1943, Schoenbrun was the chief of the European propaganda division of Elmer Davis' Red-lined Office of War Information. In 1945, he was manager of the Overseas News Agency in Paris. In 1946, he joined the Columbia Broadcasting System's staff as a special correspondent. He became a regular correspondent in 1947 and remained with CBS until 1963. From 1946 until 1962, he was based in France and, in 1962 and 1963, he was the CBS bureau chief in Washington, D.C. Since 1964, he has been a correspondent for Metromedia

Network. In 1965 and 1966, he held a Carnegie Foundation fellowship at Columbia University's Graduate School of Journalism. He has taught a graduate course on Vietnam at Columbia.

In the summer of 1967, Schoenbrun went to North Vietnam for a six-week visit as guest of Ho chi Minh whom Schoenbrun had befriended in 1946. An account of this trip appeared in the *Saturday Evening Post* (December 16, 1967) — "Journey to North Vietnam" by David Schoenbrun. From beginning to end, the article is undeniably pro-North Vietnam and anti-United States. Schoenbrun received a very warm welcome from his Communist hosts and they were amply repaid in the *SEP* article which bears remarkable resemblance to the straight Communist line on the Vietnam situation.

Before Schoenbrun made his mission to Hanoi, his sympathies for North Vietnam and its Dictator Ho chi Minh had been expressed in an article which he wrote for the *Columbia University Forum*. Senator J.W. Fulbright (D.-Ark.) was so impressed with Schoenbrun's pro-Communist views ("one of the most succinct and penetrating analyses of the problem that has come to my attention") that he inserted it in the *Congressional Record* (January 19, 1967).

According to Schoenbrun, his old friend Ho chi Minh was "the Tito of Asia. That is, a national Communist, at the head of a small state, trying to keep independent of an enormous Communist neighbor . . . China." To carry this "independent" theme further, Schoenbrun wrote: "In Vietnam, only the Communists represent revolution and social change. The Communist Party is the one truly national organization that permeates both North and South Vietnam. It is the only group not dependent on

foreign bayonets for survival." (Not a hint appeared in Schoenbrun's article, nor was there any corrective contribution from Fulbright, that North Vietnam's war machine was totally dependent for arms and ammunition upon the Soviet Union, Red China, and Communist bloc nations throughout Europe and Asia.)

In July, 1968, at a meeting of the ultra-leftist Clergy and Laymen Concerned about Vietnam, Schoenbrun described "my friend Ho chi Minh" as a "Communist George Washington." According to Schoenbrun, Ho — a highly moral character — was struggling against "American imperialism." In pure Marxist style, Schoenbrun remarked that "the main struggle is the rich-poor struggle." And against poor North Vietnam the United States was waging an "imperialist war in Vietnam, using blacks as mercenary troops."

Schoenbrun's solution for Vietnam, unsurprisingly, was a call for "an immediate cease-fire in Vietnam and formation of a coalition communal government." This is the message — the sell-out of South Vietnam — which he continues to bring to audiences throughout the United States by film, by radio and television commentaries, and by his writings in the popular press. No American journalist has done more to bolster the cause of Ho chi Minh's Communist aggression than has Schoenbrun.

FREDERICK L. SCHUMAN was born on February 22, 1904 in Chicago, Illinois, son of Ella Schulze and August Schuman. He married Lily Abell. He is an alumnus of the University of Chicago (Ph.B., 1924; Ph.D., 1927).

From 1927 until 1936, Schuman was on the faculty at the University of Chicago, successively, as an instructor and assistant professor of political science. Since 1936, he has been a professor of political science and government at Williams College. He has been a visiting professor at Harvard University, the University of California, Cornell University, Columbia University, Stanford University, Central Washington College, the University of Chicago, and Portland State College.

In 1956, the Senate Internal Security Subcommittee included Schuman's name in its list of the eighty-two most active and typical sponsors of Communist front organizations. He has been affiliated with the American Slav Congress ("subversive and Communist"); the American Committee for Protection of Foreign Born [Americans] ("subversive and Communist" — "one of the oldest auxiliaries of the Communist Party in the United States" — under the "complete domination of the Communist Party); the American Council on Soviet Relations ("established by Communist Party"); the American League against War and Fascism ("subversive and Communist"); the American League for Peace and Democracy ("subversive and Communist"); the China Aid Council ("Communist-controlled"); the Civil Rights Congress ("subversive and Communist"); the Committee for a Boycott against Japanese Aggression ("Communist front"); the Committee for a Democratic Far Eastern Policy ("Communist"); the Friends of the Soviet Union ("to propagandize for and defend Russia and its system of government" — "directed from Moscow"); the International Workers Order ("subversive and Communist"); the Interprofessional Association for Social Insurance ("Communist front"); the Jefferson School of Social Science ("adjunct of the Communist Party"); the Lawyers Committee on American Relations with Spain ("Communist lawyers' front organization"); the League of Professional Groups for Foster ("Communist front"); the National Citizens Political Action Committee ("Communist front"); the National Committee to Win the Peace ("subversive and Communist"); the National Conference on American Policy in China and the Far East ("Communist"); the National Council of American-Soviet Friendship ("subversive and Communist" — "specializing in pro-Soviet propaganda"); the National Student League ("Communist front"); the Scientific and Cultural Conference for World Peace ("Communist front"); the Student Congress against War ("controlled by the Communists"); the United States Congress against War ("completely under the control of the Communist Party"); Workers Library Publishers ("official Communist Party, U.S.A., publishing house"); the World Peace Congress ("Communist front"); and, the Jan Wittenber Defense Committee ("Communist front").

Schuman has also been affiliated with Clarence Streit's Atlantic Union, which is working towards a political merger of Western Europe and the United States, as a major step towards world government; the American Civil Liberties Union, that motleyed collection of defenders of subversion, crime, and licentiousness; and, in 1942 and 1943, he was a political analyst (!) for the foreign broadcast intelligence service of the Federal Communications Commission.

Schuman has been a staunch advocate of United States diplomatic recognition of Red China and Red China's admission to membership in the United Nations. By any reasonable standards, Schuman must be recognized as one of the foremost apologists for Communism in the entire American academic community.

ABBA P. SCHWARTZ was born on April 17, 1916 in Baltimore, Maryland, son of Fannie Berman and Harry Schwartz. He is an alumnus of Georgetown University (B.S., 1936) and Harvard University (LL.B., 1939).

In 1938, while a student, Schwartz was sent to the White House by Harvard's Law School dean James M. Landis to recruit President Franklin Roosevelt in a program that Landis was leading to provide aid to German refugees. Schwartz had been an enthusiastic supporter of his dean's program back at Harvard. The President received Schwartz cordially but suggested that Eleanor Roosevelt was a more likely recruit for the refugee program. Mrs. Roosevelt did cooperate with the Schwartz-Landis program and thus began a long and close friendship between Schwartz and Eleanor Roosevelt. (Schwartz, according to one of his friends, was "almost by adoption, Mrs. Roosevelt's boy.") Two decades later, it was Schwartz who advised and convinced Eleanor to climb down from Adlai Stevenson's bandwagon and campaign in 1960 for presidential candidate John F. Kennedy. Schwartz accompanied her on a campaign-for-Kennedy tour.

In 1940, Schwartz was admitted to the bar in Washington, D.C. For a brief time he worked in a law office in New York City, then entered wartime service, first in the Merchant Marine, then in the U.S. Navy. In 1946 and 1947, for a period of about nine months, he was an assistant to the director of the Intergovernmental Committee on Refugees in London. In 1947 and 1948, he was director of the Reparations Division of the International Refugee Organization in Geneva.

In 1949, Schwartz began practicing law in Washington, D.C. Then, from 1950 until 1962, he was a member of a law firm headed by his former law school dean James M. Landis. The Landis firm had close ties with the Kennedy dynasty.

From 1951 until 1962, Schwartz represented the Landis firm as a legal consultant to the Intergovernmental Committee for European Migration. Then, in 1962, Schwartz's campaign activities of 1960 reaped dividends. President John F. Kennedy asked Schwartz to become Administrator of the State Department's Bureau of Security and Consular Affairs. Schwartz had been highly recommended for the position by two personal friends, David Rockefeller of Chase Manhattan Bank and Felix Frankfurter, Associate Justice of the Supreme Court.

In his appointive position, Schwartz had supervisory responsibilities over the State Department's passport and visa offices, the office of special consular services, and the office of refugee and migration affairs. He was also charged with enforcement of the immigration laws. But a few months after Schwartz took office, it became evident to his State Department colleagues, members of Congress, and the Washington, D.C. press corps that most of his energies would be devoted to getting rid of Miss Frances Knight, who had been director of the Passport Office since 1955. Miss Knight had made the Passport Office a model of efficiency — a rare commodity in the federal bureaucracy. Furthermore, Miss Knight, whose governmental career began in 1934, had acquired a much deserved reputation as an anti-Communist. She was firmly opposed to Communist infiltration in the government and, as head of the Passport Office, she had worked effectively to make it extremely difficult for Communists to travel from or to the United States.

The Schwartz vendetta against Miss Knight was waged through a series of harassments by which Schwartz curtailed Miss Knight's duties and authority, reduced the personnel and budget for her office, restricted the operations of the Passport Office, interfered directly with Miss Knight's work, and proposed to State Department higher-ups that Miss Knight be transferred out of her position. In the course of his guerrilla warfare, Schwartz caused changes in the physical appearance of a U.S. passport — changes which added positive and substantial risks against the national security in matters of subversion and espionage.

During Schwartz's three and a half years as Administrator, Communists found it quite a simple matter to reach the United States from Asia, Europe, and Latin America with American visas or in the guise of political refugees. American Communists had little or no difficulty traveling abroad with a U.S. passport, as virtually all anti-Communist barriers against immigration and migration policies and practices were broken down.

There was nothing subtle about Schwartz's activities and he was called to account by several congressional committees. And before these committees, Schwartz demonstrated an evasiveness and arrogance which harvested bad and widespread puboicity for the Kennedy and Johnson Administrations. Eventually Schwartz was forced to resign from the government. As might be expected, the Liberal Establishment elevated Schwartz to martyrdom — an alleged victim of an anti-Communist "witch-hunt." The *New York Times*, the *Washington Post*, and the *New Republic* led the parade of bleeding-hearts which included Senators Wayne Morse and Bobby Kennedy and Representatives Henry Reuss of Wisconsin and Leonard Farbstein of New York. Attorney Joseph L. Rauh Jr. spoke for Americans for Democratic Action as he described his long-time ADA colleague Schwartz as a victim of the "loyal [Joe] McCarthy underground in the State Department." But Schwartz returned to his law practice until March, 1968, when it was revealed that he had been hired by the Department of Defense to help in the negotiations for the release of the *Pueblo* prisoners held by the Communists in North Korea. At about the same time, William Morrow & Co., book publishers, announced the forthcoming appearance of Schwartz's *The Open Society* — introduced by his ADA colleague Arthur M. Schlesinger Jr.

HUGH SCOTT was born on November 11, 1900 in Fredericksburg, Virginia, son of Jane Lewis and Hugh Scott. He married Marian Chase. He is an alumnus of Randolph-Macon College (A.B., 1919) and the University of Virginia (LL.B., 1922). He was admitted to the Pennsylvania bar in 1922 and began the practice of law in Philadelphia.

From 1926 until 1941, Scott was an assistant district attorney in Philadelphia County. From 1941 until 1945, he was a Representative to the 77th and 78th Congresses. He was an unsuccessful candidate for the 79th Congress. From 1947 until 1959, he was again a Representative to Congress. Since 1959, he has been in the U.S. Senate.

A few years ago, Scott said: "I was born a conservative and have become increasingly liberal." Such an evolutionary process would be an accurate characterization of Scott's voting pattern since he first took his seat in Congress in 1941. From a relatively conservative position, he has moved inexorably leftward. The real turning point in his career was in 1950 when he became a charter member of Republican Advance along with such ultra-liberals as Henry Cabot Lodge, Wayne Morse, Christian Herter, Clifford Case, and Jacob Javits. Within two years of its founding, Republican Advance spearheaded the dirty political maneuver that cost Ohio's Senator Robert A. Taft the Republican presidential nomination in favor of Dwight Eisenhower.

With Eisenhower elected, Scott and his Republican Advance colleagues proceeded to assault congressional investigating committees and measures designed to preserve national sovereignty. They led the frenzied anti-anti-Communist hordes against Senator Joseph R. McCarthy. They led the fight against the Bricker Amendment which was simply designed to include in the U.S. Constitution the proposition that treaties and executive agreements do not make domestic laws except by legislation within the constitutional powers of the Congress. They voted on welfare state measures in consonance with the ultra-liberals of the Democrat Party, who followed the dictates of Americans for Democratic Action and of the socialist leaders of organized labor.

Republicans to the right of Scott he describes as Bourbons who had an "execrable 1964 platform." Since 1964, Scott has moved further and further left in his voting behavior. He is a confirmed spendthrift for handouts to foreign powers and for domestic welfare statism. He is a bleeding heart on federal open-housing and other so-called civil rights legislation. He wrings his hands over the menace of Communism yet has supported such measures of appeasement with the Soviet Union as the Consular Treaty and the Moscow Test Ban Treaty. He has described the Republicans' role as the loyal opposition on foreign policy yet he has firmly committed himself to the Johnsonian no-win policy in Vietnam and, when the Averell Harriman-conducted Paris "peace" talks began, he literally gushed with enthusiasm.

When Associate Justice Abe Fortas was nominated to be Chief Justice of the United States, Scott declared he would support the nomination. He warned Fortas' opponents that if Fortas' nomination were blocked, Earl Warren would remain on the Court to the exclusion of Homer Thornberry, another Johnson nominee, whom Scott described as a moderate – a characterization, considering its source, that could only mean that Thornberry was not quite as left as Scott himself.

PETE SEEGER was born on May 3, 1919 in New York City, son of Constance Edson and Charles Seeger. He married Toshi Ohta. He attended Harvard University from 1936 until 1938.

After his brief stay at Harvard, Seeger worked for awhile as an assistant to the curator of the Archives of American Folk Songs in the Library of Congress. In 1940, he organized the Almanac Singers, whose folk-singing repertoire assiduously followed the Communist Party line.

After traveling with the Almanac Singers for about a year, Seeger joined Woody Guthrie, a veteran Communist and a folksinger whose name has been revered with memorials by Secretary of the Interior Stewart Udall. Seeger and Guthrie – protégé and teacher – became prolific collaborators, writing folk songs with Communist messages. And, during World War II, Seeger sang on overseas broadcasts for the Office of War Information.

In 1945, Seeger became the national director of People's Songs, Inc. A few years later, the California Senate Fact-finding Committee reported "that People's Songs is a vital Communist front ... one which has spawned a horde of lesser fronts in the fields of music, stage entertainment, choral singing, folk dancing, recording, radio transcriptions and similar fields. It especially is important to Communist proselyting and propaganda work because of its emphasis on appeal to youth and because of its organization and technique to provide entertainment for organizations and groups as a smooth opening wedge for Marxist-Leninist-Stalinist propaganda."

On August 18, 1955, Seeger appeared before the House Committee on Un-American Activities. He was asked about his activities in the Communist Party and with Communist fronts. Seeger declined to answer. On July 25, 1956, he was cited for contempt of Congress. On March 29, 1961, he was convicted on ten counts of contempt in a New York federal court. On May 18, 1962, his conviction was overturned on a technicality by the U.S. Court of Appeals. The HCUA never sought another indictment.

A few years ago U.S. Ambassador Chester Bowles welcomed Seeger to India as a "true representative of the United States of America." The "true representative," Seeger, has been affiliated — as an entertainer, member, sponsor, instructor, or contributor — with the American Peace Mobilization ("subversive and Communist"); American Youth Congress ("subversive and Communist"); the Communist Party; American Youth for Democracy ("subversive and Communist"); the Council on African Affairs ("subversive and Communist"); the American Committee for Yugoslav Relief ("subversive and Communist"); the National Council of American-Soviet Friendship ("subversive and Commu-

nist" — "specializing in pro-Soviet propaganda"); the Civil Rights Congress ("subversive and Communist"); the American Committee for Protection of Foreign Born [Americans] ("subversive and Communist" — "one of the oldest auxiliaries of the Communist Party in the United States" — under the "complete domination" of the Communist Party); the Committee for a Democratic Far Eastern Policy ("Communist"); the National Council of the Arts, Sciences and Professions ("a Communist front used to appeal to special occupational groups"); the Nature Friends of America ("subversive and Communist"); the Jefferson School of Social Science ("adjunct of the Communist Party"); the Metropolitan Music School ("controlled by Communists"); Veterans against Discrimination of Civil Rights Congress ("subversive and Communist"); *New Masses* ("Communist periodical"); *Daily World* ("Communist publication"); the Labor Youth League ("Communist organization"); California Labor School ("a subversive and Communist organization"); the National Lawyers Guild ("the foremost legal bulwark of the Communist Party, its front organizations, and controlled unions"); Veterans of the Abraham Lincoln Brigade ("subversive and Communist"); the Committee for the First Amendment ("Communist front"); the American Peace Crusade ("Communist front"); the Emergency Civil Liberties Committee ("Communist front" — "subversive"); and, the National Committee to Abolish the House Un-American Activities Committee ("to lead and direct the Communist Party's 'Operation Abolition' campaign").

Seeger has participated in fund-raising benefits for the Communist Party and for individual Communists. He has participated in many May Day Parades run by the Communists. He has traveled extensively throughout the world (*The Worker* has described him as an "Ambassador with a Guitar"). He has been a favorite in Communist countries where his anti-American ditties are very popular. He has appeared on many concert stages and at folk singing festivals, privately and/or publicly sponsored. He is a familiar entertainer on university and college campuses, at high schools, and at church gatherings. In recent years, he has brought his anti-American, pro-Communist line to all sorts of peacenik gatherings. He has appeared in motion pictures, on radio and television programs, in night clubs and theaters, and on recordings made for Decca, Folkways, and Columbia. His most enduring fame, however, may come from the fact that he is one of the lyricists for the racial agitators' anthem "We Shall Overcome."

For many years, Seeger was excluded from television appearances on major networks. But he is now a familiar sight on programs carried by the Columbia Broadcasting System and his indefatigable propagandizing of the Communist line receives rave reviews from the left-wing and liberal press.

WHITNEY NORTH SEYMOUR was born on January 4, 1901 in Chicago, son of Margaret Rugg and Charles Seymour. He married Lola Vickers. He is an alumnus of the University of Wisconsin (A.B., 1920) and Columbia University (LL.B., 1923).

In 1923, Seymour began his practice of law in New York City. From 1925 until 1931, he was an instructor of law at New York University. From 1931 until 1933, he was an assistant to the Solicitor-General of the United States. From 1935 until 1945, he lectured in law at Yale University.

From 1954 until 1959, and in 1964, Seymour was chairman of the board of Freedom House, which was organized in 1941 allegedly "to advance the goals of a free society and oppose all forms of totalitarianism." (In actuality, Freedom House has been a curious collection of Socialists, Communist fronters, anti-anti-Communists, do-gooders, dupes, and out-and-out trouble makers. Its luminaries have included Ralph Bunche, Jacob Javits, Ralph Sockman, Rex Stout, John Lindsay, Roy Wilkins, Roscoe Drummond, Paul Hoffman, Bonaro Overstreet, and Eric Sevareid. Annual Freedom House Awards have gone to James B. Conant, Walter Lippmann, Pablo Casals, Paul Hoffman, David Lilienthal, Willy Brandt, Jean Monnet, Lyndon Johnson, Roy Wilkins and Dean Acheson.)

In 1960 and 1961, Seymour was president of the American Bar Association. The choice of Seymour for this high office was most unusual in light of his previous record which was known to the members of the ABA's House of Delegates who elected Seymour.

In 1937, Seymour became a director of the American-Russian Institute and, during World War II, a director of Russian War Relief. Seymour, in 1953, explained that "without approving Communism in the slightest, many years ago I was optimistic enough to hope that some cultural exchange with Russia and later that sending medical supplies in the early days of World War II might create friendship between the Russian and American peoples. Many wise and good citizens felt the same way. Events have proved them wrong but certainly the world would look brighter today if their hopes had been realized. This view led me to become a director for a short time of the American Russian Institute which seemed to have a representative board and was supposed to facilitate interchange of students and other cultural representatives. I cannot recall the details of the termination of my relationship because it was so brief and I went to so few meetings, but it is my impression that it was shortly before the Nazi-Soviet Pact in August, 1939 which, of course, ended temporarily any hope of understanding [Seymour became a director in 1937]. I joined a very notable board for Russian War Relief after the Nazis attacked Russia .... I have an impression from something I read somewhere that perhaps the Institute may have come under Communist control at some later date but I feel reasonably sure that this was after all the Republicans had left."

In 1931, the House Special Committee to Investigate Communist Activities had cited the American-Russian Institute as a Communist Party operation. In 1948, the California Committee on Un-American Activities reported that the American-Russian Institute was "a direct agent of the Soviet Union, engaged in traitorous activities under the orders of Stalin's consular service in the United States." In 1952, the Senate Subcommittee on Internal Security described the American-Russian Institute as a "Communist controlled organization, intimately linked with the Institute of Pacific Relations," which in turn the SISS described as "an instrument of Communist policy, propaganda and military intelligence."

Russian War Relief, which Seymour remembered as "a sort of counterpart of the American Red Cross and, I think, had its blessing," was reported on by the House Special Committee on Un-American Activities in 1944: "The present Board of Directors [of Russian War Relief] includes the following: Edward C. Carter, President [secretary-general of the Institute of Pacific Relations]; Frances Adams Gumberg ["a trusted worker for the Communists"]; C.C. Burlingham; Harriet Moore [a Communist]; Raymond Robbins [well-known apologist for the Soviet Union]; Whitney North Seymour; Henry E. Sigerist [well-known Communist fronter]; Vilhjahmur Stefansson [well-known Communist fronter]; and, Allen Wardwell [on the advisory board of Russian Reconstruction Farms, run by Harold Ware, the notorious boss of Alger Hiss' Communist cell]. A review of the background of this controlling group will reveal the fact that the organization is firmly in the hands of those who have a history of close cooperation with the Soviet Union, the Communist Party, or its satellite front organizations. It is not an organization like the American Red Cross, in pro-American hands."

On two occasions, Seymour was retained by the International Labor Defense, "the legal arm of the Communist Party." In 1935, Seymour successfully defended Angelo Herndon, an organizer for the Communist Party, by having Herndon's conviction in Georgia overthrown. In 1939, Seymour defended Joseph Strecker, a Communist, by preventing Strecker's deportation. Associated with Seymour in Strecker's defense was Carol Weiss King, general counsel for the Communist Party. Both the Herndon and the Strecker cases were very important victories for the Communist Party.

In 1936, Seymour signed a letter of transmittal which accompanied a memorandum to the U.S. Department of Commerce sent by the International Juridical Association. The International Juridical Association "actively defended Communists and consistently followed the Communist Party line."

In 1953, Seymour was chairman of the American Bar Association's Special Committee on Individual Rights as Affected by National Security. The Special Committee was financed by $50,000 granted by the leftwing Fund for the Republic, which had been organized less than a year before when the Ford Foundation granted the Fund $15,000,000. The Seymour Report, which emerged from the Special Committee, was nothing less than an attack upon congressional investigating committees, especially those investigating subversive activities. By coincidence, the Ford Foundation, the source of the Seymour Committee's finances, was at the very time being investigated by a congressional committee.

From 1954 until 1956, Seymour served on the Special Committee on the Federal Loyalty-Security Program of the Association of the Bar of the City of New York. The Special Committee was financed by $100,000 granted by the Fund for the Republic. Seymour was not only a member of the Special Committee but also president of the New York City Bar Association. The report of the Special Committee recommended that the federal loyalty-security program be concentrated on clearance of only those jobs with access to information classified as secret or top secret. This would reduce the number of so-called sensitive jobs by seventy-five per cent. Also recommended was the abolition of the Port Security Program and the International Organizations Employees Program, which, in effect, would remove merchant seamen, longshoremen, and United Nations employees from any federal loyalty-security qualifications.

In 1958, Seymour was a member of an American Bar Association subcommittee of three which recommended that past or present membership in the National Lawyers Guild ("the foremost legal bulwark of the Communist Party") would not automatically disqualify an applicant for membership in the ABA.

Seymour has been chairman of the board of trustees of the Carnegie Endowment for International Peace, the most heavily endowed leftwing-pacifist organization in the world. For many years, he was a director and member of the national board of the American Civil Liberties Union, a motleyed collection of defenders of subversion, crime, and licentiousness.

Seymour has described himself as having "always been a Republican with fairly conservative views . . . opposed to tyranny, totalitarianism in any form, and of course against it in the form of Communism."

HARLOW SHAPLEY was born on November 2, 1885 in Nashville, Missouri, son of Sarah Stowell and Willis Shapley. He married Martha Betz. He is an alumnus of the University of Missouri (A.B., 1910; A.M., 1911) and Princeton University (Ph.D., 1913).

From 1914 until 1921, Shapley was an astronomer at the Mount Wilson Observatory in California. From 1921 until 1952, he was director of the Harvard University Observatory. From 1952 until 1956, he was a professor of astronomy at Harvard and, since 1956, he has been professor emeritus. He was a research professor at Smith College in 1956 and 1957 and, in 1958, he was a Phi Beta Kappa resident lecturer at several American colleges. He has also lectured at foreign universities.

In 1956, the Senate Internal Security Subcommittee included Shapley's name in its list of the eighty-two most active and typical sponsors of Communist front organizations. Shapley's affiliations have included the American Committee for Democracy and Intellectual Freedom ("Communist front" – "subversive and un-American"); the American Russian Institute ("subversive" – "Communist" – "specializing in pro-Soviet propaganda"); the Citizens Committee to Free Earl Browder ("Communist"); the Committee of One Thousand ("Communist created and controlled front organization"); the Congress of American Women ("subversive and Communist"); the Council for Pan-American Democracy ("subversive and Communist" – "Communist front"); the Freedom from Fear Committee ("Communist front"); the Greater New York Emergency Conference on Inalienable Rights ("Communist front"); the Hollywood Writers Mobilization for Defense ("subversive and Communist"); Independent Citizens Committee of the Arts, Sciences and Professions ("Communist front"); the Joint Anti-Fascist Refugee Committee ("subversive and Communist"); the League of American Writers ("subversive and Communist"); the National Emergency Conference ("Communist front"); the National Emergency Conference for Democratic Rights ("Communist front" – "subversive and un-American"); the National Federation for Constitutional Liberties ("subversive and Communist" – "under [Communist] Party domination and headed by responsible Party functionaries"); the Progressive Citizens of America ("political Communist front"); the Scientific and Cultural Conference for World Peace ("Communist front"); Veterans of the Abraham Lincoln Brigade ("subversive and Communist"); the World Congress of Intellectuals ("Communist"); the National Committee to Abolish the House Un-American Activities Committee ("to lead and direct the Communist Party's 'Operation Abolition' campaign"); the American Continental Congress for World Peace ("another phase in the Communist 'peace' campaign, aimed at consolidating anti-American forces throughout the Western Hemisphere"); New Masses ("Communist periodical"); and, the Mid-Century Conference for Peace ("aimed at assembling as many gullible persons as possible under Communist direction and turning them into a vast sounding board for Communist propaganda" – "a Communist front").

Shapley is famous in the world of astronomy for proving that our solar system is at the outer fringe of the Milky Way. In the world of fellow travelers, he is famous not only for his front activities but also for his active support of Communist projects and enterprises, individual Communists, and a pro-Communist foreign policy. He has also been affiliated with the radical-pacifist Women's International League for Peace and Freedom and the United World Federalists, the most prestigious group of fellow travelers and dupes working for world government at the expense of American sovereignty.

WILLIAM L. SHIRER was born on February 23, 1904 in Chicago, son of Bessie Tanner and Seward Smith Shirer. He married Theresa Stiberitz. He is an alumnus of Coe College (A.B., 1925).

In 1925, Shirer entered upon his career in journalism as a reporter for the Paris edition of the *Chicago Tribune.* From 1926 until 1933, he was a foreign correspondent for the *Tribune* and, from 1929 until 1932, he was chief of the *Tribune's* Central European bureau in Vienna. In 1934, he was a reporter for the Paris edition of the *New York Herald.* From 1935 until 1937, he became a correspondent for the University News Service.

In 1937, Shirer became the continental representative in Europe of the Columbia Broadcasting System and during the next eight years he became one of the most famous American radio correspondents of that era. In that same period (1942-1948), he added to his fame by writing a column for the *New York Herald Tribune* and that journal's syndicate. From 1947 until 1949 when he began devoting full-time to a writing career, he was a commentator for the Mutual Network.

In 1945, Shirer was chairman of the Friends of the Spanish Republic when that group petitioned President Truman to intervene in an attempt to restore to power the defeated Communist regime in Spain. In 1950, he was affiliated with the subversive Voice of Freedom Committee. In that same year, he petitioned the Supreme Court to review the conviction of the infamous Hollywood Ten, who had tried to cover up their Red associations by pleading, vainly, protection under the First Amendment.

Shirer has been a member of the Council on Foreign Relations (the informal supra-State Department of the United States) and the Foreign Policy Association (one of the most effective pro-Communist propaganda vehicles of the past three decades in the United States).

Far more important than Shirer's affiliations have been his writings, the most notable of which are: *Berlin Diary; End of a Berlin Diary; Stranger Come Home;* and, *The Rise and Fall of the Third Reich.* Aside from *Stranger Come Home* (which is a bitter indictment in fictional form of congressional investigating committees), these books are representative of Shirer's chief stock-in-trade: Germanophobia. Old Nazis never die, they live on in Shirer's pages. By Shirer's

standards, the entire German people were *and remain* collectively guilty of everything atrocious connected with Hitler and his Nazi colleagues.

Shirer's fanatical hostility toward Germany, Germans, and German culture and mores was evident — though not overwhelmingly so — in his earlier works: *Berlin Diary* and *End of a Berlin Diary.* Unquestionably, he was an all-out interventionist who propagandized that the United States as well as Europe was faced with the singular threat of Nazi Germany. If Shirer viewed the Soviet Union with even a fraction of such trepidation, he kept such fear well concealed. But, as the years went by, his Germanophobia became more and more evident in his radio commentaries and in his writings for popular magazines. Then, in 1960, he produced his monumental *The Rise and Fall of the Third Reich: A History of Nazi Germany.* As Michael F. Connors wrote a few years ago in his brilliant pamphlet, "The Development of Germanophobia," Shirer embodies "the very worst features of the Germanophobic propaganda of 1933-1945, contributes very little to an honest understanding of German history."

Despite its sub-title, *Rise and Fall* is not history. It is a very bitter diatribe in which Shirer releases his fanatical anti-German prejudices to the point of absurdity. But *Rise and Fall* became a best seller at a time when it was quite difficult to see any books beyond the swastika-covered volumes on book stands across the country. No such attention as has been given to Nazism in the past few years has ever been focused on the real threat to civilization — Communism. And Shirer, as much as any author, can take credit for diverting attention away from live Communists to dead Nazis.

SARGENT SHRIVER was born on November 9, 1915 in Westminister, Maryland, son of Hilda Shriver and Robert Shriver. He married Eunice Kennedy. He is an alumnus of Yale University (B.A., 1938; LL.B., 1941).

Shriver practiced law briefly before World War II. After service in the U.S. Navy, Shriver was an assistant editor of *Newsweek* magazine. In 1946, he joined his future father-in-law's operations, the Joseph P. Kennedy Enterprises and, from 1948 until 1961, he was assistant general manager of Kennedy's Merchandise Mart in Chicago. In 1960, Shriver campaigned for his brother-in-law, John F. Kennedy, the Democrat Party's presidential candidate. Shriver's pay-off was the directorship of the Peace Corps, which socialists had been promoting for years, but which became a reality by an executive order issued by President Kennedy on March 1, 1961. Then the Congress passed enabling legislation "to promote world peace and friendship through a Peace Corps."

In his five years as Peace Corps director, Shriver recruited a mélange of young and old idealists and do-gooders, along with draft-dodgers, racial agitators, pacifists, thrill-seekers, and socialists of varied hues, running from pink to rosy red. Perhaps the best selling job done by Shriver was to call these individuals "volunteers." It struck up an image of bravery and dedication but what distinguished them from anyone else who applied for and received a government job, Shriver never mentioned. Letter carriers, typists, file clerks, or anyone else who worked for the government were just as much "volunteers" as Shriver's peace corpsmen and corpswomen.

Shriver's brigade was completely supported by the left wing in this country. He insured this support by sending his corps throughout the world, not overlooking socialist nations anywhere. And when the "volunteers" returned to this country they revealed themselves to be mostly a group of bleeding-heart whiners, critical — even resentful — of America's self-accomplished affluence, and they naturally gravitated toward anti-Vietnam War protests in one form or another. In 1965, Shriver tipped his hand completely as to what types he wanted in the Peace Corps when he went all-out to recruit members of the Students for a Democratic Society, which Communist leader Gus Hall had boasted was working for the Communist Party. In Hall's words: "We've got . . . Students for a Democratic Society going for us."

In 1964, while still director of the Peace Corps, Shriver was appointed by Lyndon Johnson to be director of the Office of Economic Opportunity, headquarters for the so-called war on poverty. The whole thing was just a further extension of the socialist schemes of handouts to bribe voters in the cities, especially Negroes. It had worked for Franklin Roosevelt, and Johnson more than once boasted of how much he learned from the original New Dealer. Not since the days of Harry Hopkins has any Washington bureaucrat thrown money around with less regard for the taxpayers than has Shriver as czar of the OEO.

As part of Shriver's war, the Job Corps was created and in its first two years of operation, the average job "created" cost American taxpayers $128,182. The saddest feature was that those who had been trained in the Job Corps were so poorly trained that they had difficulty holding jobs once they were out of Shriver's clutches.

As might be expected, various facets of Shriver's program proved to be a bonanza for agitators, including Communists, who found jobs in Shriver's Mobilization for Youth. And, in the long hot summer of 1967, more than one city riot was financed and staffed out of OEO offices.

Representative Phil Landrum (D.-Ga.), who was the floor manager in the House for Lyndon Johnson's war on poverty legislation in 1964, reviewing the first three years of Shriver's directorship, accused the OEO's hierarchy of "monstrous mismanagement" and "stupid judgment."

STEPHEN SMALE was born on July 15, 1930 in Flint, Michigan. He is an alumnus of the University of Michigan (B.S., 1952; M.S., 1953; Ph.D., 1956).

From 1956 until 1958, Smale was a mathematics instructor at the University of Chicago. From 1958 until 1960, he was at the Institute for Advanced Study in Princeton, New Jersey, where J. Robert Oppenheimer, the notorious security risk, was the director. In 1960 and 1961, Smale was an associate professor at the University of California (Berkeley.) From 1961 until 1964, he was a professor at Columbia University. In 1964, he returned to the Berkeley campus as a professor.

In 1965, Smale was co-chairman of the Berkeley Vietnam Day Committee which planned the nation-wide "get out of Vietnam" demonstration for October 15 and 16, 1965. In 1951, Smale began his leftist involvements when, as a student at the University of Michigan, he joined the Labor Youth League ("Communist front" – "youth section of the Communist Party"). He was also connected with the Michigan Council of Arts, Sciences and Professions, an affiliate of the National Council, which was a Communist front. In 1961, at Berkeley,

he was faculty adviser to the University of California's Fair Play for Cuba Committee, which was subsidized by Fidel Castro. (See, "On the Left," *National Review Bulletin,* September 28, 1965.)

Columnists Ralph de Toledano and James Jackson Kilpatrick have been among the few newsmen who have attempted to keep the American taxpayers abreast of their generosity toward Smale. "In the summer of 1966, Prof. Stephen Smale received $1,000 for a round-trip jet ticket to the Soviet Union, plus $2,778 a month. Once in Moscow, the professor . . . called a press conference at which he denounced the United States and its Vietnamese policy. The NSF grant to Prof. Smale will be a total of $13,000 when he does this summer's junketing at the American taxpayer's expense. What he will say to the world in the next months is anybody's guess. His Moscow remarks, delivered to Communist newspapermen from North Viet Nam, painted the United States as horrible and brutal." (de Toledano, "National Science Foundation Subsidizes Anti-U.S. Attacks," *Human Events,* July 22, 1967.)

"The National Science Foundation now has settled upon the boyish head of Stephen Smale a new grant of $87,500 in public funds. For another two years, the taxpayers of America thus will be subsidizing the summer vacations of this peacenik mathematician whose abiding avocation is to give aid and comfort to America's enemies in Viet Nam. It is, in truth, a lunatic world we live in . . . . In his capacity as a co-chairman of the Vietnam Day Committee, he proposed in May 1965 that thousands of students and others block the gates of the Oakland army terminal. Also, 'we might consider the en masse breaking of the Espionage Act of 1917 and the Selective Service Act.'

"In August 1965 Smale led a company of demonstrators who attempted to block troop trains at the Santa Fe Station in Berkeley. Earlier, Smale had urged that 'we must put our bodies on the line,' but when the train came down the tracks he chickened . . . . Smale's demonstration of grantsmanship began early in 1965, when he was named principal investigator on an NSF grant totaling $58,900; his share, for two months' summer salary, was $4,800. In 1966 he won a two-year grant for $91,500, including $12,112 for his summer salary and for travel. The new grant is for $87,500, of which $17,868 is to go to Smale directly for summer work in 1968 and 1969. This adds up to $238,900 put under the gentleman's thumb. His own take, for a total of 10 months' research and travel, is $34,780.

"The ultimate irony is that Smale probably can ride this gravy train forever. A few months ago the NSF exuded some skepticism that Smale really had spent two months in the summer of 1966 in actual research; they suspected he was junketing. The NSF also complained mildly of Smale's loose administration of the grant money. Whereupon a terrible clamor arose within the groves of academe, and the NSF was accused of trying to punish Smale because of his political views.

"Meanwhile, Indiana's Congressman Dick Roudebush was raising hell at the prospect of giving Smale another dime. In the end, NSF caved in, invoked the holy name of academic freedom, and gave Smale the money." (Jackson, "Why More Tax Money to Stephen Smale?" *Human Events,* December 16, 1967.)

Smale's political views, which are of so much concern to the National Science Foundation, are clearly discernible in an interview he granted in 1965: "We want the Vietcong to defeat the United States for international reasons. If the United States is defeated in Southeast Asia, this will help break American power elsewhere in the world. This would give new impetus to revolutionary social change – wars of liberation – in such places as Africa and Latin America. And if surrounded by revolutionary change, it will make it easier to achieve radical change in the United States."

Among his mathematician colleagues, Smale is considered brilliant for his achievements in differential topology.

EDGAR SNOW was born on July 19, 1905 in Kansas City, Missouri, son of Anna Edelmann and James Snow. He was married to Nym Wales. He is married to Lois Wheeler. He attended Kansas City College and the University of Missouri but did not graduate from either school.

Until 1941, Snow was a journalist with the *Kansas City Star,* the *China Weekly Review* of Shanghai, the *Chicago Tribune,* the *Consolidated Press* Association, the *New York Sun,* and the *London Daily Herald.* He also lectured at Yenching University of Peiping in 1934 and 1935. It was in this same period that Snow wrote his famous *Red Star Over China.* In the Communist weekly, *New Masses* of January 25, 1938, Victor A. Yakhontoff wrote: "The value of this material [Snow's book] can be judged by the fact that most of it was supplied by Mao Tse-tung, the head of the Soviet regime [in China], and that some of it was checked by personal observation of the author."

Two former Communists confirmed that *Red Star Over China* was of more than passing interest to the Communists. Freda Utley, in her *The China Story,* wrote: "In the original edition of his best-selling book, *Red Star Over China,* Ed Snow has painted a most favorable picture of the Chinese Communist regime in the Northwest. But he had also included some passages critical of the Comintern and showing the subservience of the Chinese Communists to Moscow. My ... impression of Snow as an honest journalist was altered when he eliminated, in the second edition of his book, a number of passages distasteful to Moscow."

Louis Budenz, in testimony before the Senate Internal Security Subcommittee, identified Snow and Snow's wife (Nym Wales) as Communists, and said that Snow "amended one edition of the book ... at the request of the Communist Party."

From 1942 until 1951, Snow was associated with the *Saturday Evening Post,* first as a correspondent, then as an associate editor. In that period, Snow contributed sixty-one articles on China, the Soviet Union, Asia in general, and Europe. Individually and collectively, Snow's contributions were a massive barrage of pro-Communist propaganda. He also had contributed pro-Communist pieces to the publications of the Institute of Pacific Relations and had been affiliated with the China Aid Council ("Communist controlled") and the Committee for a Democratic Far Eastern Policy ("Communist").

Since he left the *Saturday Evening Post,* Snow has been a special research consultant at Harvard University, and a correspondent for *Look* magazine and for *Le Nouveau Candide* of Paris. He has continued to write pro-Communist books, the most important being his *The Other Side of the River: Red China Today,* published in 1962. It was a virtual panegyric for Mao Tse-tung, whom Snow described as "a teacher, statesman, stra-

tegist, philosopher, poet laureate, national hero, head of the family, and greatest liberator in history. He is Confucius plus Lao-Tzu plus Rousseau plus Marx plus Buddha."

Communist Carl Marzani, who reviewed Snow's book for the Communist weekly, *National Guardian,* was so impressed with Snow's outpourings that he had his firm, Marzani & Munsell, publish seven chapters of *The Other Side of the River,* under the title: *China, Russia and the U.S.A.* Bennett Cerf's Random House, publishers of Snow's 1962 book, in its advertising, cited endorsements of Snow's Red Chinese propaganda from John Gunther, Harrison Salisbury, John K. Fairbank, *Newsweek,* the *New York Herald Tribune,* Felix Greene, *Harper's* magazine, the *Christian Science Monitor,* and − last but not least − Owen Lattimore.

Snow, who now lives in Switzerland, lectured at the University of Hartford in March, 1967. He was still acting as Mao Tse-tung's favorite mouthpiece in America.

RALPH SOCKMAN was born on October 1, 1889 in Mt. Vernon, Ohio, son of Harriet Ash and Rigdon Sockman. He married Zellah Endly. He is an alumnus of Ohio Wesleyan (B.A., 1911; D.D., 1916), Columbia University (M.A., 1913; Ph.D., 1917), and is a graduate of Union Theological Seminary (1916).

From 1916 until 1961, Sockman served Christ Church (formerly the Madison Avenue M.E. Church) of New York as associate minister and minister, and is now minister emeritus. He has also been an associate professor of practical theology and director at the leftwing Union Theological Seminary, and Lyman Beecher lecturer at Yale University.

Sockman has been an active member,

vice president, and president of the leftwing Church Peace Union and, since 1928, has been chairman of the World Peace Committee of the Methodist Church, one of religion's most influential groups for accommodation with Communism and Communists. He has also been chairman of the Interfaith Committee of the American Society for Russian Relief and, in 1947, was a delegate to the Soviet Union representing that Society.

Sockman has been affiliated with the American Committee for Spanish Freedom ("Communist"); the American-Russian Institute ("subversive" – "Communist" – "specializing in pro-Soviet propaganda"); the Methodist Federation for Social Action ("Communist front"); the National Committee for a Sane Nuclear Policy (leftwing, pacifist); the World Youth Congress ("Communist conference"); the *Protestant* ("Communist front"); and, the United World Federalists (the most prestigious group of fellow-travelers and dupes working for world government at the expense of American sovereignty).

Sockman has also been affiliated with the leftwing American Committee on Africa and, in 1966, he sponsored the National Voters' Pledge Campaign, which was led by Socialist Norman Thomas, veteran Communist-fronter Reverend William Sloane Coffin, and Sanford Gottlieb, the political director of the National Committee for a Sane Nuclear Policy. The Voters' Pledge Campaign was designed to support "peace" candidates, who would work for a cease-fire in Vietnam and encourage negotiations in which the Vietcong would be participants.

THEODORE SORENSEN was born on May 8, 1928 in Lincoln, Nebraska, son of Annis Chaikin and Christian Sorensen. He was married to, and divorced from, Camilla Palmer, and married to, and separated from, Sara Elbery. He is an alumnus of the University of Nebraska (B.S., 1949; LL.B., 1951).

In 1948, Sorensen was registered for the draft as a conscientious objector, available only for non-combatant military service. After the outbreak of the Korean War, Sorensen was re-classified as 3-A (he had been married and became a parent). In 1952, he was again re-classified as a conscientious objector, ordered to report for a physical examination, but was found physically unfit.

In 1951 and 1952, Sorensen was an attorney with the Federal Security Agency and, in 1952, was on the staff of the United States Senate's subcommittee on railroad retirement. In 1953, he became an assistant to Representative John F. Kennedy (D.-Mass.) and remained as an assistant to Mr. Kennedy during his years in the Senate and the White House. Sorensen resigned from the White House staff on February 29, 1964, three months after Lyndon Johnson succeeded Mr. Kennedy. Sorensen spent the next eighteen months writing *Kennedy* an idolatrous book which reflects Sorensen's devotion to the late president and his scorn for historical accuracy. (Earlier Sorensen had written *Decision Making in the White House,* a flattering tribute to the Kennedy administration.)

Since he completed his *Kennedy,* Sorensen has taken up the practice of law in New York City. One of his clients is the savage dictator Joseph Mobutu of the Congo. Sorensen has also become an editor-at-large for *Saturday Review,* that most literate voice of the left. He is active in the Democratic Party of New York, and a close political associate of Senator Robert F. Kennedy. Sorensen's parents were ardent pacifists and liberals.

He has not betrayed his heritage.

Terence Smith ("The New Frontier of Ted Sorensen," *New York Times Magazine,* March 26, 1967) quotes a friend of Sorensen and Robert Kennedy as saying: "Bobby and Ted got along in the White House but they were rivals for the President's ear. Sorensen was the staff liberal while Bobby was the pull to the right." If there really is a position to the left of Bobby, then Sorensen certainly has the credentials to fulfill it. He advocates admission of Red China to the United Nations. He advocates a strong permanent peace-keeping force for the United Nations. Since his collegiate days, he has been an activist in Americans for Democratic Action, the center of the radical left in American politics. In 1967, while the Soviet Union was far and above the major supplier of war material to North Vietnam, Sorensen was in Moscow talking to Communist trade officials about a "major high-level policy change" for the United States (where Sorensen got such authority for those discussions remains a mystery). At the same time, Sorensen urged that the United States cease bombing North Vietnam and agree to negotiations with the Communists that would provide for a coalition government in which the Vietcong would have a position.

BENJAMIN SPOCK was born on May 2, 1903 in New Haven, Connecticut, son of Mildred Stoughton and Benjamin Spock. He married Jane Cheney. He is an alumnus of Yale University (B.A., 1925). He studied at Yale's Medical School from 1925 until 1927, and received his M.D. from Columbia University's College of Physicians and Surgeons in 1929.

From 1929 until 1931, Spock practiced general medicine. Since 1931, he has specialized in pediatrics, psychiatry, and pediatric-psychiatry. From 1951 until 1967, he taught his medical specialties at the University of Pittsburgh and Western Reserve University.

Until 1962, Spock was best known as the author of the best-selling book, *Baby and Child Care,* published in 1946. In its first twenty years, the book had gone through one hundred and thirty printings in twenty-six languages, and more than seventeen million copies had been sold. Then, in 1962, Spock joined the National Committee for a Sane Nuclear Policy. In October, 1962, Spock explained: "Like most people, I had evaded and denied the dangers of nuclear explosions in the atmosphere since Hiroshima. I read reports in journals but I didn't face the issue. The turning point came last March. Then the President said though we still were ahead, we must test to stay ahead. There was no quitting while we were ahead and the hopeless lack of logic in the race on both sides was apparent. Both of us, the United States and Russia, are scared to death that the big bombs sooner or later will go off, especially as new countries get the bomb. The danger ever increases."

Since there was a seventeen-year span between Hiroshima and the time when Spock's guilt-complex caught up to him, he wasted no time in going crazy over SANE. A month after Spock joined SANE, his picture was featured in a full-page SANE ad in the *New York Times.* He had a hang-dog look and appeared much older than his fifty-nine years. In large bold type, the ad said: "Dr. Spock is worried." Then followed a brief ban-the-bomb message from Spock. Below Spock's picture was a roll-call of a truly representative and international cross-section of socialists, pro-Communists, racial agitators, and leftwing pacifists, including: Pablo Casals, Brock Chisholm, Gunnar Myrdal, Gordon Allport, James Baldwin, Edward Condon, Edwin Dahlberg, Erich Fromm, Hugh Hester, H. Stuart Hughes, Martin L. King, Lewis Mumford, Walter and Victor Reuther, Dore Schary, Ralph Sockman, Norman Cousins, Donald Harrington, Elmer Rice, and Norman Thomas. A year later Spock became co-chairman, with H. Stuart Hughes, of SANE.

Since 1962, Spock has become one of the all-time heroes of the leftwing. He has roamed widely carrying his message of doom. His writings have appeared with regularity in popular magazines. From a practicing and teaching pediatrician, Spock has become an "expert" on just about every issue promoted by the left. He stumped for medicare (socialized medicine) and federal-aid-to-education (socialized education). Occasionally, he has been more to be pitied than scorned (in 1965, he warned parents not to take their children to see "a live Santa Claus" because the experience is "quite upsetting"). And Spock, the greatest scaremonger of our age, wrote in 1962 of "how I think we can help our children to take the cold war in their stride" – his suggestions: "We can refrain from talking in a pessimistic or alarmist manner" – "We can say with a grin, 'We're all alive, aren't we?' "

Since 1962, Spock has jumped headlong into leftwing activities. He has sponsored the National Committee to Abolish the House Un-American Activities Committee ("to lead and direct the Communist Party's 'Operation Abolition' campaign"). He has joined the national advisory board of the leftwing, one-world United World Federalists. He sponsored the National Voters' Pledge Campaign, which was led by Socialist Norman Thomas, veteran Communist-fronter Reverend William Sloane Coffin, and Sanford Gottlieb, the political director of the National Committee for a Sane Nuclear Policy. The Voters' Pledge Campaign was designed to support "peace" candidates, who would work for a cease-fire in Vietnam and encourage negotiations in which the Vietcong would be participants. He sponsored the 1965 March on Washington for Peace in Vietnam when 15,000 leftwing demonstrators gathered at the Washington Monument demanding a cessation of the war against the Vietcong. He became a committee member of Negotiation Now!, an ad hoc committee led by leftwing luminaries for appeasement in Vietnam including Martin Luther King Jr., Joseph L. Rauh Jr., Victor Reuther, Arthur Schlesinger Jr., Reinhold Niehbuhr, and John Kenneth Galbraith. He went on the executive board of the ultraleftwing National Conference for New Politics.

In 1965, Spock entered into an exchange of correspondence with Communist North Vietnam's President Ho chi Minh. Although in clear violation of federal law (The Logan Act provides a $5,000 find and/or 3 years imprisonment for any U.S. citizen who without authorization "commences or carries on any communication" with any foreign government "with intent to influence" that government in any dispute with the United States), Spock has yet to be called to justice. However, in January, 1968, Spock was indicted by a federal grand jury for conspiring to counsel young men to violate the draft laws. Spock, in the past few years, has become a familiar figure at anti-Vietnam War demonstrations, standing shoulder to shoulder with the most prominent leftwingers in America.

548

MAXWELL S. STEWART was born on July 4, 1900 in Johnstown, Pennsylvania, son of Maud Slutz and John Stewart. He married Marguerite McKlveen. He is an alumnus of Allegheny College (A.B., 1921) and Columbia University (M.A., 1926). He also studied at Northwestern University (1921) and Boston University (1922-1923).

In 1921 and 1922, Stewart was an instructor at Columbia College in Oregon. From 1923 until 1930, he was in China as an instructor at Shanghai's American School (1923-1925) and at Yenching University (1926-1930). In 1935, he lectured at the radical New School for Social Research. From 1938 until 1941, he was a lecturer at the College of the City of New York.

From 1931 until 1934, Stewart was a research economist for the Foreign Policy Association. At that time, the pro-Soviet apologist Vera Micheles Dean was the editor of the FPA's research publications and, under the direction of Mrs. Dean who reigned until 1961 at the FPA, the Association — through its publications — was one of the most effective pro-Communist vehicles in the United States.

From 1934 until 1947, Stewart was an associate editor of the leftwing *Nation* magazine which was, at that time, under the editorship of Freda Kirchwey. (In 1956, the Senate Internal Security Subcommittee included Kirchwey and Stewart in its list of the eighty-two most active and typical sponsors of Communist front organizations.)

In 1936, Stewart began his present occupation as editor of Public Affairs Pamphlets which, since 1937, have been published by Public Affairs Committee, a non-profit organization incorporated in New York. In its issue of September 1, 1960, the *American Legion Firing Line* newsletter recounted: "In a comprehensive report released on April 27, 1960, PAC disclosed that a total of nearly 30,000,000 Public Affairs Pamphlets have been distributed during the period from 1936 thru 1959 to persons representing 'every segment of the Nation's population.' Appropriately titled 'The Story of Thirty Million Pamphlets,' the PAC report revealed that the 'majority of readers are professional and business leaders — teachers, physicians, ministers, officers in community organizations, counselors, social workers, public officials, and other key persons in the community. But a very large proportion of the orders for single pamphlets come from just people — housewives, parents, retired persons, and school children. A surprising proportion of the letters from readers about specific pamphlets are from people who have obviously had few educational advantages; some are virtually illiterate. Yet at the same time tens of thousands of Public Affairs Pamphlets are used each year by our colleges and universities as a basis for classroom work .... Experience has shown that organizations, large and small, constitute the major channel for pamphlet distribution. A glance at past records indicate that for many years close to half of the total distribution of Public Affairs Pamphlets was in orders of 10,000 copies or more. A large proportion of these orders came from state and national health and welfare agencies. Another large share was taken by the voluntary health organizations.'

"With reference to 'indirect distribution' of PAC literature, PAC claims that 'the influence of the Public Affairs Pamphlets is by no means limited to the readers of the million and a half pamphlets distributed each year. Millions of persons, who may never see one of the pamphlets, read more or less extended digests in newspapers, magazines, and textbooks. The (Public Affairs) Committee has long placed great emphasis on this method of disseminating the contents of its pamphlets because it has recognized that this was the only way of reaching a mass audience. Recent years have witnessed a sharp increase in the amount of space devoted to the pamphlets in other media. Although estimates of lineage are notoriously incomplete owing to the shortcomings of the various clipping services, there can be no question that substantial gains have been achieved. The total lineage of the clippings received during 1959 was 1,768,000 as compared with 1,095,000 in 1958 and 958,000 in 1957. A large portion of this total – and the most significant portion in terms of pamphlet sales – was in the form of favorable review of various pamphlets by syndicated columnists.' PAC recently reported that 'a distinguishing feature of the Public Affairs series as compared with the publications of most organizations is the wide range of acceptance by individuals and groups that would not normally be reached by a parochial publication.' In addition to the numerous segments of our society which have been exposed to PAC literature, certain librarians are also included among those who utilize Public Affairs Pamphlets.

"An important factor to be considered in evaluating the apparent success of PAC's publishing activities is the organization's 'long-standing policy of working closely with the research departments of health, welfare, and business groups in the preparation of manuscripts and in promotional planning.' According to the PAC, 'a very large proportion of the pamphlets that have been published in the past 24 years have been coopera-

tive projects with a variety of national organizations' including the American Heart Association, American Cancer Society, National Health Council, National Association for Mental Health, National Tuberculosis Association, Twentieth Century Fund, Brookings Institution and the Institute for Consumer Education."

Many of the PAC's pamphlets issued under the editorship of Stewart have been unobjectionable from an ideological perspective. But these items merely served as bait to acquire a large readership for other PAC outpourings which were indisputably Communist propaganda – a fact recognized by Communists and fellow travelers who warmly endorsed and even wrote PAC's pamphlets. During World War II, Public Affairs Pamphlets were widely used in the armed forces – especially in the U.S. Army's Information-Education program.

In 1942 and 1943 and from 1946 until 1948, Stewart expanded his activities as a propagandist by serving as an editor for a pamphlet series published by the Institute of Pacific Relations, "a vehicle used by the Communists to orientate American far eastern policies toward Communist objectives." (Stewart's wife, Marguerite, worked as secretary for the IPR.) As an editor and author of IPR pamphlets, Stewart was an outspoken apologist for the Soviet Union and propounded the thesis that Chinese Communism had no parallel elsewhere. To Stewart the forces of Mao Tse-tung were nothing more than agrarian radicals similar to the populists of 19th century American history. (In 1952, the Senate Internal Security Subcommittee concluded that Stewart "knowingly and deliberately used the language of books and articles which . . . [he] wrote or edited in an attempt to influence the American public by means of pro-Communist or pro-Soviet content of such writings.")

Stewart has been affiliated with the American Committee for Democracy and Intellectual Freedom ("Communist front" – "subversive and un-American"); the American Committee for Protection of Foreign Born [Americans] ("subversive and Communist" – "one of the oldest auxiliaries of the Communist Party in the United States" – under the "complete domination" of the Communist Party); the American Council on Soviet Relations ("established by Communist Party"); the American Committee to Save Refugees ("Communist enterprise"); the American Friends of Spanish Democracy ("subversive"); the American Friends of the Chinese People ("Communist front"); *China Today* ("Communist-controlled publication"); the American League against War and Fascism ("subversive and Communist"); the American League for Peace and Democracy ("subversive and Communist"); the China Aid Council ("Communist-controlled"); the American Youth Congress ("subversive and Communist"); the Book Union ("distributors of Communist literature"); the Committee for a Democratic Far Eastern Policy ("Communist"); the Conference on Pan-American Democracy ("Communist front"); the Coordinating Committee to Lift the Embargo ("Communist front"); *Fight* magazine ("a Communist front publication"); Friends of the Soviet Union ("to propagandize for and defend Russia and its system of government" – "directed from Moscow"); the Greater New York Emergency Conference on Inalienable Rights ("Communist front"); Labor Research Association ("direct auxiliary of the Communist Party"); the League of American Writers ("subversive and Communist"); the National Committee for

People's Rights ("entirely under the control of the Communist Party"); the National Committee for the Defense of Political Prisoners ("subversive and Communist"); the National Committee to Win the Peace ("subversive and Communist"); the National Council of American-Soviet Friendship ("subversive and Communist" – "specializing in pro-Soviet propaganda"); the National Emergency Conference ("Communist front"); the National People's Committee against Hearst ("subsidiary" organization of the American League for Peace and Democracy – "subversive and Communist"); *New Masses* ("Communist periodical"); the Non-Partisan Committee for the Reelection of Congressman Vito Marcantonio ("Communist front"); the North American Committee to Aid Spanish Democracy ("Communist"); *Soviet Russia Today* ("Communist front publication"); *Moscow News* (Communist publication); the United American Spanish Aid Committee ("Communists"); the Committee for Peaceful Alternatives to the Atlantic Pact ("a Communist front" – "part of Soviet psychological warfare against the United States"); and, *Amerasia* ("Communist controlled magazine"). Stewart has also been affiliated with the socialist League for Industrial Democracy.

A former Communist Party official, Louis Budenz, testified under oath that he knew Stewart to be a member of the Communist Party. Stewart denied under oath that he was a Communist.

ISIDOR F. STONE was born on December 24, 1907 in Philadelphia, Pennsylvania, son of Katherine Novack and Bernard Stone. Stone married Esther Roisman. He is an alumnus of the University of Pennsylvania.

In 1922, Stone was editor of *The*

Progress in Haddonfield, New Jersey. From 1923 to 1933, he was a reporter, successively, for the *Haddonfield Press,* the *Camden* (N.J.) *Courier-Post,* the *Philadelphia Record,* and the *Philadelphia Inquirer.* In 1933, he was an editorial writer for the *Philadelphia Record* and, from 1933 to 1939, held the same position with the *New York Post.* From 1938 to 1946, he was on the staff of *The Nation* magazine as an associate editor and Washington editor. From 1942 to 1952, he was a reporter, columnist, and editorial writer for the *New York Star, PM,* the *New York Post* and the *New York Compass.*

In 1953, Stone became the publisher and editor of his own *I.F. Stone's Weekly.* He is the author of *The Court Dis Poses; Business As Usual; Underground to Palestine; This is Israel; The Hidden History of the Korean War; The Truman Era; The Haunted Fifties;* and *In Time of Torment.* Stone's *This is Israel* was favored with a listing in the catalog of Workers Book Shops, the headquarters for a chain of Communist book stores. His *The Hidden History of the Korean War* received laudatory reviews in such Communist publications as *Masses and Mainstream* and the *Daily Worker.* The latter listed it as one of the "best book buys for 1952."

In 1956, the Senate Internal Security Subcommittee included Stone's name in its list of the eighty-two most active and typical sponsors of Communist front organizations. He has been affiliated with the American Committee for Democracy and Intellectual Freedom ("Communist front" – "subversive and un-American"); Artists' Front to Win the War ("Communist front"); Citizens' Committee for Harry Bridges ("Communist"); League of Women Shoppers ("Communist-controlled front"); the Na-

tional Federation for Constitutional Liberties ("under [Communist] Party domination and headed by responsible Party functionaries"); *New Masses* ("Communist periodical"); Council for Pan-American Democracy ("subversive and Communist"); Friends of the Abraham Lincoln Brigade ("its officers and staff members were in the main [Communist] Party members and functionaries"); the National Council of the Arts, Sciences and Professions ("a Communist front used to appeal to special occupational groups"); the National Committee to Secure Justice for the Rosenbergs and Morton Sobell ("Communist front"); Emergency Civil Liberties Committee ("Communist front" – "subversive"); Citizens' Committee to Free Earl Browder ("Communist"); the National Council of American-Soviet Friendship ("subversive and Communist" – "specializing in pro-Soviet propaganda"); the American Committee for Protection of Foreign Born [Americans] ("subversive and Communist" – "one of the oldest auxiliaries of the Communist Party in the United States" – under the "complete domination" of the Communist Party); the National Committee to Defeat the Mundt Bill ("a Communist lobby"); the Fair Play for Cuba Committee ("Castro-subsidized"); the National Committee for the Abolition of the House Committee on Un-American Activities ("to lead and direct the Communist Party's 'Operation Abolition' campaign"); and, the Student League for Industrial Democracy (socialist).

Stone's obvious Marxism and his long history of defending Communists and their causes has not prevented him from lecturing on college campuses or from having his writings quoted in non-Communist newspapers and magazines.

REX STOUT was born on December 1, 1886 in Noblesville, Indiana, son of Lucetta Todhunter and John Stout. He married and divorced Fay Kennedy. He married Pola Hoffmann.

Stout has written dozens of detective stories which, since 1934, have featured the hero Nero Wolfe. Stout's most notable departure from the novel was his *The Illustrious Dunderheads,* a diatribe against those in public life who opposed Roosevelt's fanatical drive for intervention in World War II.

By 1965, Stout's fame as a novelist seemed to be in a decline, but in that year he published a novel, *The Doorbell Rang,* which was an unbridled attack upon the Federal Bureau of Investigation. The novel was highly praised by the Communists in their *Worker* in two separate issues – October 26 and November 30.

Stout's first claim to notoriety might well be dated as of 1926 when he was one of the original publishing team of *New Masses,* a Communist weekly which dealt principally with problems in the arts and sciences from the Communist Party's point of view. The leading editorial of *New Masses,* hailing the Soviet Union, set the tone: "In millions of proletarian hearts in every corner of the world the workers' republic [Soviet Russia] is still enshrined as fresh and new and beautiful as first love."

Stout remained as a contributing editor (his wife was business manager) of *New Masses* until 1930. But he did not turn his back on the Communist Party. While he developed a career as a novelist, he was affiliated with the Joint Anti-fascist Refugee Committee ("subversive and Communist"); the League of American Writers ("subversive and Communist"); and, the Hollywood Writers Mobilization for Defense ("subversive and Communist").

Along the way, Stout became Chairman of the Board of the malodorous Friends of Democracy where his partner in defamation was the so-called "Reverend" Leon M. Birkhead. One of their more ambitious projects was to assassinate the character of the great American patriot, Colonel Charles A. Lindbergh.

The most spectacular undertaking of Friends of Democracy was the subsidization of *Under Cover,* written by Avedis Boghos Derounian, alias John Roy Carlson. The book was enthusiastically promoted by Walter Winchell, various Communist fronts, and the Communist press. The publishers sold about 700,000 copies. Eventually the book became the object of libel suits. Federal Judge John P. Barnes, who presided over one of these suits, said: "I think this book was written by a wholly irresponsible person who would write anything for a dollar. I think this book was published by a publisher who would do anything for a dollar."

During World War II, Stout was made head of the War Writers' Board by the infamous anti-anti-Communist Elmer Davis, who was Director of the Office of War Information, a propaganda outfit that was a haven for American and alien Communists. Then, in 1944, Stout and his friend Leon Birkhead became chairman of the board and president, respectively, of the Society for the Prevention of World War III, where they were joined by some of the better known Communist front veterans in this country (Algernon Black, Norman Cousins, Lewis Mumford, Mark Van Doren, Ben Hecht, Quentin Reynolds, Emil Lengyel, Guy Shipler, and William L. Shirer).

In recent years, Stout has been an official of Freedom House, a curious collection of liberals, Socialists, do-gooders, Communist fronters, and an occasional innocent. Then, in 1964, Stout joined at least two dozen Communist fronters in

Arthur Larson's National Council for Civic Responsibility – a short-lived campaign weapon for the Democratic Party, aiming principally at anti-Communists.

Stout has a strong penchant for one-worldism and has associated himself with such anti-American-sovereignty groups as Students for World Government, Student Federalists, United World Federalists, Writers Board for World Government, and Action for World Federation.

CLARENCE STREIT was born on January 21, 1896 in California, Missouri, son of Emma Kirshman and Louis Streit. He married Jeanne Defrance. He is an alumnus of Montana State University (A.B., 1919). He also studied at the Sorbonne in Paris and, as a Rhodes Scholar, at Oxford University.

From 1920 until 1939, Streit was a correspondent for the *Philadelphia Public Ledger* (1920-1924) and for the *New York Times* (1925-1939). From 1929 until 1939, Streit covered the League of Nations in Geneva for the *Times.*

In 1939, Streit gave up journalism to become president of Federal Union which has evolved into the Atlantic Union Committee and the International Movement for Atlantic Union.

Streit is the author of *Union Now; Union Now with Britain; Freedom against Itself;* and *Freedom's Frontier: Atlantic Union Now.* He has also been editor of *Freedom and Union* magazine since it was founded in 1946.

For almost thirty years, beginning with his book *Union Now,* Streit has propagandized for the end of American independence. In the beginning, Streit seemed content with the incorporation of the United States and European "democracies" into the British Empire, as the basis for a world government. But when the North Atlantic Treaty Organi-

zation was formed, he began to strive for a political union of the NATO nations into an Atlantic Union. Now Streit has planned far beyond an alliance of NATO nations and writes of a world government which would include even the Communist nations.

Streit uses a mixture of pacifism, scare-mongering, patriotism, political scientism, and virulent anti-nationalism to promote his program which has attracted the support of an impressive roster of internationalists, not only from the United States but from all the NATO nations. His supporters include academicians, businessmen, religious leaders, government officials, scientists, jurists, military leaders, artists, labor leaders, journalists, and theatrical personalities. If name-dropping were the key to success, Streit would have erased national boundaries and made us all world citizens years ago.

LYLE STUART was born on August 11, 1922 as Lionel Simon, in New York City, son of Theresa and Alfred Simon. He did not complete high school. He married Mary Strong. He changed his name legally in 1952.

In 1942, Stuart was indicted by a grand jury in New York City for extortion. He pleaded guilty to the charge, receiving a suspended sentence and being placed on two years probation. During World War II, he saw service with the merchant marine and the Air Transport Command.

In 1945, he was a reporter for International News Service for a few months. Then he worked for about six months on *Variety* magazine. Between 1946 and 1950, he edited a music magazine, *Music Business,* and a women's wear trade paper, *Ready to Wear Scout.* In 1950, he wrote radio scripts for the Voice of

America, wrote some magazine articles, and – according to his sworn testimony before the Senate Internal Security Subcommittee – was a ghostwriter for some Congressmen, not identified.

From 1953 until 1956, Stuart was general manager of E.C. Publications, publisher of *MAD* magazine.

In 1951, Stuart began publishing *Independent* magazine under its original name, *Exposé*. The publishing house of *Exposé-Independent* is Exposé, Inc., of which Stuart is the majority stockholder. In 1956, Stuart formed a publishing corporation of which he owns all the stock.

Stuart's publishing output has included such anti-Catholic works as Emmet McLoughlin's *American Culture and Catholic Schools* and *Crime and the Catholic Church;* such sex books as Armando Meoni's *Strange Lovers* and Nathan Shiff's *Diary of a Nymph;* and such pro-Communist books as Robert Taber's *M-26: The Biography of a Revolution,* Juan Jose Arevalo's *The Shark and the Sardines,* and Fidel Castro's *History Will Absolve Me.* Stuart has written: "I am opposed to Communism as I am opposed to Fascism and as I am opposed to Catholicism or to any totalitarian system."

In 1960, Stuart joined the Fair Play for Cuba Committee, which was exposed as a Communist front to promote the interests of Fidel Castro's Communist regime. Stuart became treasurer of the New York chapter of the FPCC and traveled to Castro's Cuba in 1960, 1961, and 1962. His activities with the FPCC and his trips to Castro's Cuba caused the Senate Internal Security Subcommittee to hear his testimony. He proved to be an obstreperous witness.

Stuart is still publishing *Independent* and the same flavor of books. His ads have appeared with regularity in the *New York Times* and, on at least one occasion, in the Communist *National Guardian.*

ARTHUR SYLVESTER was born on October 21, 1901 in Montclair, New Jersey, son of Natasha Victorson and Arthur Sylvester. He married Kathryn Ferguson. He is an alumnus of Princeton University (A.B., 1923).

In 1924, Sylvester joined the reportorial staff of the *Newark* N.J.) *Evening News.* From 1929 until 1944, he held various editorial positions and, from 1944 until 1961, he was the *News'* Washington, D.C. correspondent.

In January, 1961, Sylvester was appointed as Assistant Secretary of Defense for Public Affairs. He held that position until February, 1967 when he was given the Pentagon's Distinguished Public Service Medal by Secretary of Defense Robert McNamara. In view of Sylvester's six-year work in the Defense Department, such an award had to be a travesty on reality.

In general, Sylvester's responsibility was to explain the purpose and meaning of the Military Establishment, in terms of both a home audience and a world audience. As part of his responsibility, he reviewed speeches by both military and civilian personnel in the Defense Department. For work on these speeches, Sylvester had a staff of fifteen and in 1961 – his first year on the job – more than two thousand speeches were "reviewed" by Sylvester and his group. Sylvester described their work as "a service to Defense personnel which makes them more effective in supporting our national objectives."

In 1962, a Special Preparedness Subcommittee of the Senate's Armed Services Committee held extensive hearings on "Military Cold War Education and Speech Review Policies." Sylvester was a key witness at the hearings. From Sylvester's testimony and that of numerous military and civilian personnel, it became apparent during the course of the hearings that Sylvester had become a leading figure in censoring and muzzling of military men. As their speeches came under the scrutiny of Sylvester and his aides, overtones of victory were softened, the aggressive intent of the Soviet Union and Red China was downgraded, and references which characterized the Communists as hostile were deleted. As justification for his actions, Sylvester said: "The reviewer must try to protect against expressions which unwittingly might provide the unscrupulous Communist propaganda machine with material to be used against us, thus producing confusion among our allies, and suspicion among the uncommitted nations." (Unmentioned by Sylvester was any proof that "the unscrupulous Communist propaganda machine" ever needed inspiration to concoct material against the United States in order to create confusion and suspicion throughout the world.)

Sylvester's unwillingness to allow the American public to hear the hard truth about Communist perfidy was demonstrable during the Cuban crisis when he played a major role in the manipulation of news by the Kennedy Administration. While the Soviet Union established a strong military garrison in Cuba, Sylvester decided to deceive the American public as to Soviet actions and American counter-actions.

Willard Edwards, the *Chicago Tribune's* Washington correspondent, remarked on Sylvester's explanation for his behavior on the matter of Cuba: "A great deal of shocked indignation was expressed in the newspaper world . . . when Arthur Sylvester . . . voiced an astounding confession of manipulation of news by the Kennedy Administration during the Cuban crisis. It is essential that the full meaning of his words be explored, so I read them: 'News generated [mark the word "generated" which means to create, to make news] by actions of the government as to content and timing are part of the arsenal of weaponry that a President has in the application of military force and related forces.' To what end? Sylvester says the end is the solution of political problems and the application of international political pressure. 'In the kind of world we live in [he continued] the generation [and mark the word again] of news by actions taken by the government becomes one weapon in a strained situation. The results, in my opinion, justify the methods we used.'

"Five weeks later . . . Sylvester, in another statement, got down to earth and made his meaning crystal clear. The government, despite the storm of criticism about his first statement, he said, would continue its policy of 'generating' news because 'information is power.' And then he added, defiantly, perhaps, but very, very firmly: 'I think the inherent right of the government to lie — to lie to save itself when faced with nuclear disaster — is basic.'

"There we had it. The government has both an inherent and basic right to falsify news in the name of self-preservation . . . . "

Twice in 1963, the journalism fraternity Sigma Delta Chi, to which Sylvester belonged, criticized him. On the first occasion, the fraternity said: "Arthur Sylvester has become something of a liability to the Defense Department and the Administration. It is difficult to see how anyone now can have much confidence in what he has to say." On the second occasion, Sylvester and Defense Secretary Robert McNamara were criticized for having created an "oligarchy of control" over the news.

During the course of the Vietnam War, Sylvester's propensity for a totalitarian-like censorship was further demonstrated when he decided to deceive the American public as to what was taking place between the United States and its allies vis-à-vis the Communist enemy. It was Sylvester's contention that American war correspondents had an obligation to defend the Johnson Administration's conduct of the war. He made this clear during a confrontation with four correspondents in Saigon.

Morley Safer, a CBS correspondent who was one of the four, wrote of the encounter with Sylvester in the 1966 issue of *Dateline*, a publication of the Overseas Press Club of New York City. "There was general opening banter," wrote Safer, "which Sylvester quickly brushed aside. He seemed anxious to take a stand — to say something that would jar us. He did: 'I can't understand how you fellows can write what you do while American boys are dying out here,' he began. Then he went on to the effect that American correspondents had a patriotic duty to disseminate only information that made the United States look good.

"A network television correspondent said, 'Surely, Arthur, you don't expect the American press to be the handmaidens of government.'

" 'That's exactly what I expect,' came the reply.

"An agency man raised the problem that had preoccupied Ambassador [Maxwell] Taylor and [Minister-Counselor in Saigon] Barry Zorthian — about the credibility of American officials. Responded the Assistant Secretary of Defense for Public Affairs: 'Look, if you think any American official is going to tell you the truth, then you're stupid. Did you hear that? — stupid.'

"One of the most respected of all the newsmen in Vietnam — a veteran of World War II, the Indochina War and Korea — suggested that Sylvester was being deliberately provocative. Sylvester replied: 'Look, I don't even have to talk to you people. I know how to deal with you through your editors and publishers back in the States.' "

At this point, Walter Trohan of the *Chicago Tribune* furnishes an epilogue to Safer's story: "Not long after the publication of the article, the editors of *Dateline* received a phone call from Sylvester. The editors wrote: 'Like the original incident described by Safer, it had to be experienced to be believed. Much of it was conducted at the top of Mr. Sylvester's healthy lungs, and it showed that all that has been said about Mr. Sylvester's being abusive, profane, combative and inaccurate was absolutely true in spades. Mr. Sylvester personally insulted and questioned the professional qualifications of the editors, described Safer as a "moocher" and implied he was drunk at the time, slandered two other correspondents, and . . . noted Safer was Canadian and therefore presumably disloyal.'

"Sylvester was asked to write an article for the issue of *Dateline* in which Safer's report appeared. He was asked a series of questions about the government and truth, which he chose not to answer."

Columnist Ralph de Toledano described another facet of Sylvester's paternalistic censorship: " . . . He has moved into the realm of foreign policy and dramatic criticism by forbidding a New York radio station to broadcast a dramatic program — 'Defeat by Default'

— which is critical of our military preparedness. Admitting that the program in question was 'well done,' Mr. Sylvester nevertheless frankly asserts that 'my personal reaction is that it is a very dangerous dramatization to present at this time.' "

De Toledano personally disagreed with the thesis of 'Defeat by Default.' It was his belief that America's defenses were better than the Administration would admit, but he was disturbed at Sylvester's brazen censorship: "It pains me just a little to harp on Mr. Sylvester's increasingly successful attempts to mold America's mass communications media to his own political bias. He is a pleasant and affable man, but like all doctrinaires he is beset by the conviction that unless his own ideology prevails, the nation will go to perdition in a hand-basket. Had he been held in line at the start, things might have moved differently, but his successes in muzzling Chief of Naval Operations Arleigh Burke, in humbling General Lyman Lemnitzer, now the Chairman of the Joint Chiefs of Staff, and in putting the fear of the Lord into military leaders who innocently believe that Communism is our enemy seems to have gone to his head."

STUART SYMINGTON was born on June 26, 1901 in Amherst, Massachusetts, son of Emily Harrison and William Symington. He married Evelyn Wadsworth. He is an alumnus of Yale University (B.A., 1923).

From 1923 until 1926, Symington worked as an iron molder for the Symington Company in Rochester, New York. In 1927, he became executive vice president of the company. From 1930 until 1935, he was president of the Colonial Radio Company in Rochester. From 1935 until 1937, he was president

of the Rustless Iron and Steel Company of Baltimore. From 1938 until 1945, he was president and chairman of the board of the Emerson Electric Manufacturing Company of St. Louis.

In 1945 and 1946, Symington spent two months as chairman of the U.S. Government's Surplus Property Board and four months as the Surplus Property Administrator. From February, 1946 until September, 1947, he was Assistant Secretary of War for Air. From September, 1947 until April, 1950, he was Secretary of the Air Force – the first to hold this position. From April, 1950 until May, 1951, he was chairman of the National Security Resources Board. From May, 1951 until January, 1952, he was Administrator of the Reconstruction Finance Corporation – a position he resigned to make his first campaign for political office. And, in November, 1952, as a Democrat he was elected to the U.S. Senate from Missouri. He was re-elected in 1958 and 1964.

As a freshman Senator in 1953, Symington received assignments to two very important committees: the Government Operations Committee and the Armed Services Committee. When he went on the Government Operations Committee, the late Senator Joseph R. McCarthy was chairman of the GOC's permanent investigations subcommittee. In 1953 and 1954, Symington, along with his Democrat colleagues and fellow committeemen John McClellan of Arkansas and Henry Jackson of Washington and Republican Charles Potter of Michigan, successfully disrupted McCarthy's efforts to uncover Communists and pro-Communists in the employ of the U.S. Government. Symington was especially culpable since he was a principal instigator of the charges against McCarthy which led to the famous

Army-McCarthy Hearings. In December, 1954, Symington joined all of his Democrat colleagues, twenty-two Republicans, and one Independent in a vote of condemnation against McCarthy.

On the surface, Symington's appointment to the Armed Services Committee could be understandable in light of his experience as Secretary of the Air Force and chairman of the National Security Resources Board. There is no doubt that Symington offered himself to the American public as an expert on military affairs. There were some critics in the background, however, who thought that Symington did somewhat less than a superlative job when he headed the Air Force. The space scientist Wernher von Braun called Symington's tenure the "lost years" in U.S. missile development. Said von Braun: "The United States had no ballistic missile program worth mentioning between 1945 and 1951. Those six years, during which the Russians obviously laid the groundwork for their large rocket program, are irretrievably lost."

Senator Lister Hill (D.-Ala.) complained that during Symington's Secretaryship "not one new aircraft or guided missile project was initiated by the Air Force." Hill was concerned about the Air Force's inadequacy at the outset of the Korean War, which occurred just two months after Symington resigned as Secretary. Hill claimed that because there had been no "aggressive approach to airpower research and development, we found ourselves in Korean combat with obsolete, piston-engine aircraft."

The Majority Leader in the Senate, Lyndon B. Johnson, said in July, 1950: "During this same period, from 1948 to the present, the Air Force – supposedly our first line of defense – has steadily decreased in size and effectiveness."

In his own defense, Symington attempted to shift the blame for the Air Force's weakness to President Truman and his Defense Secretary Louis Johnson. Four months after taking his Senate seat, Symington said: "If the nation had faced its national defense problem realistically five years ago [1948], there probably would have been no Korean War . . . . We learned a sad lesson from our former economy program." Symington, however, did not mention that he had been an economy buff while he was Secretary of the Air Force. In June, 1949, he said: "In our efforts to achieve military readiness we must not tax ourselves into defeat by economic collapse. It makes no difference whether the purpose of unbearable taxation is to finance military preparedness. The results would be the same: economic collapse." A month later, he said: "The Air Force believes that this country can have adequate military strength without committing economic suicide, and without surrendering to regimentation."

By the time that Symington was midway through his first Senatorial term, he talked of little else but national defense. But he had moved from a posture of economy to one of extravagance. And he justified his extravagance by accepting the Soviet Union's claims for superiority in air power, missile development, undersea power, and nuclear capability.

In the past few years, Symington has toned down somewhat in his speculative scaremongering and has talked some sense about the realities of air power in the Vietnam War. He has criticized the misuse of strategic air power and, for awhile, he was a firm advocate of using air power and other means to deliver crushing blows to North Vietnam's industrial centers and strategic port facilities. But when the Johnson Administration continued to show no interest in the tactics recommended by Symington, he backed down from his belligerent stance and moved leftward to join the "peace-by-negotiation" crowd. He has never become a complete peacenik. He still pays lip service to the gallantry of airmen who are fighting the wrong kind of air war.

On domestic matters, liberals have seldom had any reason to quarrel with Symington's voting record. In all his Senatorial years, he has been a very regular Democrat – the type admired by Americans for Democratic Action and the AFL–CIO's Committee on Political Education. As a border state Senator, the issue of segregation vis-à-vis the Supreme Court was a ticklish issue for Symington but he proved himself the master of evasion when he said: "I realize people in the South and many areas of the North, too, have a very difficult problem of adjustment, but I have confidence they are going to manage it, and manage it well in the true American tradition."

Symington has never been an aggressive legislator. He is and remains a cautious politician who has sought and received the support of business, labor, and farmers. He has gained a reputation as a fairly conservative Democrat yet he has been nothing less than a hack for the New Frontier and Great Society. He has called for a strong national defense against Communists yet has gone along with any and all disarmament agreements and proposals with the Soviet Union. Such is standard behavior for Symington. When there are two sides to an issue, he takes a stand on both but the weight of his commitment invariably shows heavier on the left.

ALBERT SZENT-GYÖRGYI was born on September 16, 1893 in Buda-

pest, Hungary, son of Josephine Lenhossek and Nickolas Szent-Györgyi. He married Martha Borbiro. He is an alumnus of the University of Budapest (M.D., 1917) and Cambridge University of England (Ph.D., 1927).

From 1931 until 1945, Szent-Györgyi was a professor of medical chemistry at the University of Szeged. From 1945 until 1947, he was a professor of biochemistry at the University of Budapest. In 1947, he came to the United States. He was naturalized in 1955. Since 1947, he has been research director at the Institute of Muscle Research at the Marine Biological Laboratories in Woods Hole, Massachusetts. In 1937 and again in 1955, he was awarded the Nobel prize in medical research.

Since at least 1962, Szent-Györgyi has been an active fellow traveler and leftwing pacifist. In 1962, he signed a call to a World Constitutional Convention along with readily recognizable Communists and pro-Communists. In 1963, he sponsored a visit to the United States by the Japanese Communist leader, Kaoru Yasui. In that same year, he was chairman of a "tribute to Linus Pauling" – an affair sponsored by Manachem Arnoni's *Minority of One* magazine, which from its beginnings in 1959 has been a propaganda vehicle for notorious leftwing pacifists and Communist fronters. Even North Vietnam's Communist dictator, Ho chi Minh, has used *Minority of One* as a propaganda outlet.

In 1964, Szent-Györgyi became a council member of the National Council for Civic Responsibility, a short-lived presidential campaign weapon, led by Arthur Larson, and aimed principally at anti-Communists. The genesis of the NCCR can be traced back to 1961 when the ultra-leftist labor leaders Walter and Victor Reuther dictated a memorandum to their friend Attorney General Robert F. Kennedy. The Reuthers called for the federal government, in cooperation with private agencies, to squelch conservatives and anti-Communists. And Larson's NCCR, with the likes of Szent-Györgyi and a host of veteran Communist fronters, was just one agency created for the Reuthers' purposes.

In 1965, Szent-Györgyi was a sponsor of the Medical Committee for Human Rights, a financial backstop for racial agitators who were plaguing the southern states. He has also been an active opponent of the House Committee on Un-American Activities. He has supported the leftwing, pacifist Women Strike for Peace and the National Committee for a Sane Nuclear Policy. In Massachusetts, he has been an active official of Political Action for Peace, which organization in 1965 solicited funds to defray the cost of renting Felix Greene's film, "China." (Greene is one of the better known propagandists for Mao Tse-tung's regime in this country.) Szent-Györgyi has spoken out on several occasions to urge the admission of Red China to the United Nations.

Szent-Györgyi, as befits a leftwing pacifist, has been active in opposition to the Vietnam War. And his sentiments on the war cannot help but comfort the enemy while they besmirch Szent-Györgyi's adopted country: "This senseless, hopeless Vietnam War tarnishes our good name . . . . The only principles we stand on are those laid down in our Declaration of Independence. These are often quoted by Ho chi Minh, so there can be no really basic difference between us, and hostilities could be stopped any minute by calling off our raids and inviting President Ho chi Minh to a conference." (*New York Times,* December 14, 1965.)

TELFORD TAYLOR was born on February 24, 1908 in Schenectady, New York, son of Marcia Jones and John Taylor. He married Mary Walker. He is an alumnus of Williams College (A.B., 1928; A.M., 1932) and Harvard University (LL.B., 1932).

In 1928 and 1929, Taylor was an instructor in history and political science at Williams college. In 1932 and 1933, he was a law clerk to the U.S. circuit judge in New York.

In 1933, Taylor began a career in government service which lasted until 1952. He was an assistant solicitor in the U.S. Department of the Interior (1933-1934); a senior attorney with the Agricultural Adjustment Administration (1934-1935); an associate counsel to the U.S. Senate Committee on Interstate Commerce (1935-1939); a special assistant to Attorney General of the United States (1939-1940); and, general counsel to the Federal Communications Commission (1940-1942).

Taylor became a military intelligence officer in 1942. From 1945 until 1949, he worked at the "war crimes" trials as a staff member for the chief of counsel and as United States chief of counsel. In 1951 and 1952, he was the administrator of the Small Defense Plants Administration. Taylor was a visiting lecturer at Yale Law School and Columbia Law School; then, in 1963, he became a professor of law at Columbia. He is the author of *Sword and Swastika; Grand Inquest; The March of Conquest;* and *The Breaking Wave.* He has also practiced law.

Taylor has been a national board member of Americans for Democratic Action, the center of the radical left in American politics. He has been chairman of the National Committee for an Effective Congress, a group which, since 1952, has campaigned for and financed ultra-leftist candidates for the House and Senate. His activities in NCEC brought about this comment in "On the Left" (*National Review,* February 1, 1956): "This paper has been honored by the so-called National Committee for an Effective Congress. An appeal for funds, signed by Telford Taylor, asks for financial aid to combat the nefarious designs of 'the new, well-heeled publication, *National Review.*' When he was chief prosecutor at Nuremberg, Taylor was charged publicly by [U.S.] Senator [William] Langer [R.-N.D.] with maintaining a staff 'composed of leftists and men who have since been exposed as Communists and members of Communist front organizations.' At the same time [U.S.] Representative George Dondero [R.-Mich.] charged that Taylor's staff was 'loaded with Communists and fellow travellers.' Justice Curtis Shake of the Indiana Supreme Court accused Taylor and his staff of hasty and ill-conceived action in threatening witnesses and engaging in unauthorized searches. Dr. Theophil Wurm, German Protestant Bishop, stated that Taylor's prosecuting staff employed 'criminal methods and abominable tortures to obtain testimony and confessions.' The same charge was repeated by Judge E. Van Roden of Pennsylvania. The *Daily Workers* of May 11, 1947, insisted that Taylor was an 'honest prosecutor.'"

Taylor's continuing activities with the National Committee for an Effective Congress caused Donald J. Lambro to write in *Human Events* (July 1, 1967): "Telford Taylor . . . was associated with the defense of leftwing union leader Harry Bridges in 1953 and authored the book, *Grand Inquest,* an attack on congressional investigations of Communism which was favorably reviewed in the *Daily Worker.* Taylor, in addition to defending Bridges, defended Junius Scales, North Carolina Communist Party chairman in 1956, on his appeal to the U.S. Supreme Court after conviction under the Smith Act. [Taylor's] defense of other leftist clients, including the Communist-controlled International Union of Mine, Mill and Smelter Workers in 1957, has won the applause of the *Daily People's World* and the *Daily Worker.*

"Taylor is known as ' . . . a perennial champion of leftists, whose professional talents have aided such individuals as Harry Bridges, various Smith Act defendants and union moguls with asserted Communist leanings,' according to Edward J. Mowery of the *Newark* (N.J.) *Star Ledger.*"

Mr. Mowery's comments came at a time when Taylor was being seriously mentioned as a possible head of the Central Intelligence Agency, sponsored by Walt Rostow who was then a special assistant for national security affairs to President Kennedy.

NORMAN THOMAS was born on November 20, 1884 in Marion, Ohio, son of Emma Mattoon and Welling Thomas. He married Frances Stewart. He is an alumnus of Princeton University (A.B., 1905) and Union Theological Seminary (B.D., 1911). He was ordained to the Presbyterian ministry in 1911 but resigned from the ministry twenty years later.

In 1913, Thomas joined the Socialist Party and became the party's leader in 1926. He was the Socialist Party's gubernatorial candidate in New York in 1924, the mayoralty candidate of New York City on two occasions, and the presidential candidate in every national election from 1928 through 1948. He has written more than a dozen books, all of which promote Socialism and/or pacifism.

Thomas has been affiliated with the American Fund for Public Service ("a major source for the financing of Communist Party enterprises"); the American Student Union ("Communist front"); the Consumer-Farmer Milk Cooperative ("Communist front"); the National Sharecroppers Fund ("Communist front"); Russian Reconstruction Farms ("Communist enterprise"); Workers Alliance ("Communist and subversive"); the National Committee to Abolish the House Un-American Activities Committee ("to lead and direct the Communist Party's 'Operation Abolition' campaign"); the United States Congress against War ("completely under the control of the Communist Party"); the American League against War and Fascism ("subversive and Communist"); the Consumers National Federation ("Communist front"); and, the North American Committee to Aid Spanish Democracy ("Communist").

Thomas has been an official of the leftwing pacifist Fellowship of Reconciliation; an officer of the socialist League for Industrial Democracy; a founder and officer of the American Civil Liberties Union, that motleyed collection of defenders of subversion, crime, and licentiousness; and officer of the National Committee for a Sane Nuclear Policy, (leftwing, pacifist); an officer of the 1966 National Voters' Pledge Campaign, which was led also by veteran Communist-fronter Reverend William Sloane Coffin and Sanford Gottlieb, the political director of the National Committee for a Sane Nuclear Policy. The Voter's Pledge Campaign was designed to support "peace" candidates, who would work for a cease-fire in Vietnam and encourage negotiations in which the Vietcong would be participants. He has been a sponsor of the 1965 Red-lined March on Washington for Peace in Vietnam; an officer of the 1967 Negotiation Now!, an ad hoc committee led by leftwing luminaries for appeasement in Vietnam, including Martin Luther King Jr., Joseph L. Rauh Jr., Victor Reuther, Arthur Schlesinger Jr., Reinhold Niehbuhr, and John Kenneth Galbraith; and, an officer of the leftwing American Committee on Africa. Thomas was also the head of the Institute for International Labor Research, financed by approximately one million dollars from the Central Intelligence Agency. One of the Institute's projects was the re-election of Juan Bosch, former Communist President of the Dominican Republic.

Thomas, along with Communist Party leader Gus Hall, was a featured speaker at the fortieth anniversary celebration of International Publishers (the Communist Party's main publishing firm) and at the eightieth birthday celebration of Alexander Trachtenberg, a Communist Party wheel horse.

On Thomas' eightieth birthday, Communist leaders Gus Hall and Henry Winston greeted Thomas in the pages of *The Worker:* "Progressive Americans in many walks of life are justly hailing you on your 80th Birthday as an outstanding American. We join in congratulating you on this occasion as a man dedicated to peace, the greatest challenge facing all humanity, as a partisan of civil rights, and as a lifelong fighter for civil liberties and adherent of socialism, our common goal." The Communists' tributes to Thomas were certainly deserved since there have been very few Communist projects and enterprises in the entire history of the Communist Party in America with which Thomas has not been publicly associated.

Thomas also received birthday greetings from Chief Justice Earl Warren and

Associate Justice Tom Clark. But the warmest greeting of all came from Vice President Hubert Humphrey who gushed: "America is a better land because of you."

LLEWELLYN THOMPSON was born on August 24, 1904 in Las Animas, Colorado. He married Jane Goelet. He is an alumnus of the University of Colorado (A.B., 1928).

Thompson entered the State Department in 1929. Over the next sixteen years, he held minor posts in Colombo, Geneva, Moscow, and London. From 1946 until 1949, he was in Washington, serving successively as chief of the division of Eastern European affairs and deputy director for European affairs, at the very time that Rumania, Bulgaria, Hungary, Poland, and Czecho-Slovakia were lost to the Communists who were aided and abetted in their seizures by the diplomatic duplicity and/or mendacious indifference of the State Department.

From the European desks, Thompson became deputy assistant secretary of state and, in 1950 and 1951, he was minister-counsellor in Rome.

From 1952 until 1955, Thompson was the U.S. High Commissioner to Austria and played a major role in negotiating and drafting the Austrian Peace Treaty with the Soviet Union. Between 1945 and 1955, twenty-one per cent of Austria's exports had been sent compulsorily and illegally to the Soviet Union and its satellites. The Soviet Union, at the same time, administered oilfields and more than three hundred industries in Eastern Austria, and shipped $108 million worth of goods annually to the Soviet Union and $25 million to their satellites from Austria. By the terms of Thompson's Austrian Treaty, Austria was forced to pay the Soviet Union —

over a ten-year period — $320 million worth of oil and manufactured goods in addition to property in Austria belonging to Germans, estimated as worth $1,500 million. The treaty also provided that the United States withdraw its troops from Austria where they had been a bridge between the NATO forces in Germany and those in Italy.

From Austria, Thompson went to the Soviet Union as U.S. Ambassador, serving from 1957 until 1962. He returned to Washington as Ambassador-at-Large and worked in the State Department as deputy under secretary of state for political affairs. In 1967, Thompson returned to the Soviet Union as U.S. Ambassador.

Thompson, during the past three Administrations, has proved to be one of the most persistent pleaders for accommodation with the Soviet Union. He pushes for peaceful cooperation between the U.S. and U.S.S.R. as if he were talking about two civilized neighbors instead of two nations that could not be more at war with one another. He is particularly anxious to promote more treaties concerning nuclear weapons and especially eager to dissuade the Soviet Union's leadership to abandon development of a costly anti-missile defense system. Why he wants to save them money, he has not explained. But then neither President Johnson nor Defense Secretary Robert McNamara offered an explanation when they urged the same thing.

ALEXANDER B. TROWBRIDGE was born on December 12, 1929 in Englewood, New Jersey, son of Julie Chamberlain and Alexander Trowbridge. He married Nancey Horst. He is an alumnus of Princeton University (B.A., 1951).

In 1950, Trowbridge was an assistant to U.S. Representative Franklin D.

Roosevelt Jr., the flaming liberal from New York. In 1951, Trowbridge was a trainee in the Central Intelligence Agency, but in that same year he joined the Marine Corps and saw service in the Korean War. According to a profile of Trowbridge in the *New York Times* (June 9, 1967), he thought of the U.S. Foreign Service after graduation from Princeton but "those were the days of low morale in the State Department because of the investigations of the late Senator Joseph R. McCarthy." Faced with this fictitious bogey, Trowbridge turned to George F. Kennan for advice. Kennan, the notable preacher of accommodation with the Communist bloc, was then at the Institute of Advanced Study in Princeton, New Jersey where his old friend J. Robert Oppenheimer, the security risk, was the director. Kennan urged Trowbridge to try the international oil business.

Trowbridge not only tried the oil business, he conquered it with a vengeance in a very short time. From 1955 to 1958, he was a marketing assistant for Caltex in Manila. In 1959, he joined Esso Standard Oil as an operations manager in Panama. In 1961, he was Esso's general manager in El Salvador and, in 1963, he became president and general manager of Esso Standard Oil in Puerto Rico. Then, according to the same *New York Times* profile, he received a phone call in February, 1965 from the White House. The call "was from John W. Macy Jr., President Johnson's chief talent scout as chairman of the Civil Service Commission. Mr. Macy had pulled Mr. Trowbridge's name from a vast file of 20,000 names of possible government appointees. [We can reasonably assume, if this saga is not apocryphal, that Trowbridge's membership in the Council of Foreign Relations put his name forward of most of the 20,000 names.] Mr. Macy wanted the young man as Assistant Secretary of Commerce for domestic and international business, and his first question was 'Are you interested in public service?' After a good deal of thought, Mr. Trowbridge decided he was, and he has not looked back since."

Trowbridge became Assistant Secretary of Commerce and, in 1967, was appointed Secretary of Commerce. And, as spokesman for the Commerce Department, Trowbridge has demonstrated that he truly belongs in Lyndon's Great Society. He has worked feverishly to sell the American people the insidious "bridges-of-understanding-through-East-West-trade" policy. While the United States wages war against the Communist bloc in Vietnam, Trowbridge boasts that more than 400 "non-strategic" items have been removed from the Commerce Department's Commodity Control List — items which are sent to our Communist enemies of the Vietnam War and items which are used most strategically by these enemies against American forces.

Trowbridge virtually ignores the hot war in Vietnam and reiterates the Lyndon Johnson platitude that "our objective is not to continue the Cold War, but to end it." While American soldiers are finding cold graves in the hot war of Vietnam, Trowbridge talks of "the soil of peaceful engagement" between the United States and our Communist enemies in "two-way trade in peaceful goods."

REXFORD GUY TUGWELL was born on July 10, 1891 in Sinclaireville, New York, son of Dessie Rexford and Charles Tugwell. He was married to, and divorced from, Florence Arnold. He then married Grace Falke. He is an alumnus of the Wharton School of Finance and Commerce at the University of Pennsylvania (B.S., 1915; A.M., 1916; Ph.D., 1922).

From 1915 until 1917, Tugwell was an economics instructor at the University of Pennsylvania. In 1917 and 1918, he was an assistant professor of economics at the University of Washington. From 1920 until 1937, he was on the economics faculty at Columbia University, serving successively as an instructor, assistant professor, associate professor, and professor.

In 1933, Tugwell took leave from his teaching duties at Columbia and went to work for the U.S. Department of Agriculture, under Secretary Henry A. Wallace. Tugwell served as Assistant Secretary and Undersecretary of Agriculture. Few New Deal braintrusters came into the Roosevelt Administration with a more flaming red background than Tugwell. He had campaigned in 1929 for the Socialist Party's mayoralty candidate for New York City, Norman Thomas. (This was at a time when the Communists were openly in support of Thomas.) Tugwell had been a member of the first American Trade Union Delegation to the Soviet Union – a Communist enterprise. When Tugwell returned from this junket, he set down his impressions in *Soviet Russia in the Second Decade*. His co-authors were Communist Robert W. Dunn and fellow-traveler Stuart Chase. The book was sold through Communist Party bookstores.

The disastrous federal farm policy promoted by Henry Wallace owed much to the inspiration of Tugwell with his obsession for government planning and regulation of the entire national economy.

In 1938, Tugwell became the chairman and head of the planning department of the New York City Planning Commission in the mayoralty of Fiorello LaGuardia, who successfully tried to be all things to all leftists.

In 1941, Tugwell became Chancellor of the University of Puerto Rico and, in that same year, Franklin Roosevelt appointed him as Governor of Puerto Rico, a post he held until 1946. Meanwhile, Tugwell became a member of the State Department's Caribbean Commission (1942-1947).

In 1946, Tugwell joined the faculty of the University of Chicago. From 1946 until 1957, he was a professor of political science, becoming professor emeritus in 1957. Since leaving Chicago's campus, Tugwell has done some teaching and/or research at the Fabian Socialist stronghold, the London School of Economics (1949-1950), Howard University in Washington, D.C., the University of Southern Illinois, and Columbia University.

Tugwell is the author of more than a dozen books and co-author of several others. In the full context of his output, which spans more than forty years, the only possible conclusion is that he is, and has been fully committed to, Socialism on a national and international scale. He has been affiliated with the socialist League for Industrial Democracy; the Committee for a Democratic Far Eastern Policy ("Communist"); Film Audiences for Democracy ("Communist front"); Films for Democracy ("Communist front"); *New Masses* ("Communist periodical"); and, the National Council of the Arts, Sciences and Professions ("a Communist front used to appeal to special occupational groups").

In 1945, Tugwell became a member of Robert M. Hutchins' Committee to Frame a World Constitution. After two and a half years, Tugwell and his fellow committeemen completed their world constitution which called for the complete abolition of nations in a world divided into nine societies and with a world government that would be absolutely totalitarian – about as retrogressive as a government could be. The "constitution" owed a great deal to the tenets of Marx, Hitler, and other maniacs who had planned to regiment every detail of every individual's life under a centralized political-economic-social order.

In 1964, Hutchins – who was then President of the Center for the Study of Democratic Institutions – once again beckoned to Tugwell. This time Hutchins had no such grandiose scheme in mind as a "world" constitution. He commissioned Tugwell to write a new constitution for the United States. And, for the past several years, Tugwell has been meeting with political scientists, sociologists, and other eggheads, seeking their suggestions and advice on a new constitution "that might enable the United States to function better as a nation in an age of revolutionary change." In the spring of 1968, Tugwell was working on his thirty-second draft. Thus far, his work is the answer to the wildest dream of the wildest Socialist and must even be comforting to Hutchins. The Constitution of the United States, as amended since 1789, according to Tugwell, is completely obsolete. Tugwell's constitution will solve all problems by focussing its attention on Planning – a planned economy and society, governed by planners, along lines laid down by the most elite of planners, made in the mold of Tugwell, Hutchins, and their internationally socialist minded colleagues at the Center for the Study of Democratic Institutions.

JOSEPH TYDINGS was born on May 4, 1928 in Asheville, North Carolina. He was adopted by Eleanor Davies and Millard Tydings. He married Virginia Campbell. He is an alumnus of the University of Maryland (B.A., 1951; LL.B., 1953). In 1952, he was admitted to the Maryland bar and began the private practice of law in Baltimore.

From 1955 until 1961, Tydings was a member of Maryland's House of Delegates. In 1960, he took a prominent role in the Kennedy presidential campaign and was particularly active in Maryland, Delaware, and Florida. In 1961, President Kennedy appointed him U.S. Attorney for Maryland. He served two years in this office.

In 1964, Tydings was elected to the U.S. Senate where he became a very close political crony of the late Robert F. Kennedy. He has been a completely reliable vote for organized labor and for the "great society's" welfare statism. He has been relatively quiet on foreign affairs although he has expressed his opinion that Red China should be given U.S. diplomatic recognition and membership in the United Nations. He gave his complete support to the consular treaty negotiated with the Soviet Union.

On the question of the Vietnam War, Tydings has given his support to the Johnsonian "no-win" policy coupled with the search for a negotiated "peace." But his most enthusiastic support in foreign affairs is reserved for any and all measures directed toward universal disarmament.

Tydings fancies himself to be a constitutional expert and in this role he pays lip service to states' rights. He maintains that the centralization of power in the federal government is mainly a result of the states abdicating their responsibilities. However, his first speech in the Senate and the brunt of his legislative energy as a Senator emphasized his antipathy for states' rights and constitutional processes. It all came about as a result of the Supreme Court's 1964 "one-man-one-vote" decision. The Republican leader, Senator Everett Dirksen, drafted an amendment — to offset the "one-man-one vote" ruling — which would have allowed each state to decide for itself whether representation in one of its legislative houses should be based on factors other than population. For Tydings it was anathema that the states should exercise their constitutional prerogative to amend the Constitution of the United States through constitutional processes. Tydings was one of the leaders in the successful fight in the Senate against the Dirksen Amendment.

Proponents of the Dirksen Amendment, however, did not give up the fight. In order to give their Amendment a further hearing, they proposed that a constitutional convention be called by Congress on application of the legislatures of two thirds of the states. Again it was an exercise of the states' constitutional prerogative, using nothing more than constitutional processes. But Tydings could not tolerate such an exercise of states' rights and gloomily warned that a constitutional convention would be "dominated by narrow commercial and agricultural interests and by rottenborough politicians who want to turn back the clock." Thus, during the most dramatic expression of states' rights activities in recent years, Tydings demonstrated that he is against such rights and contemptuous of constitutional processes.

In *Harper's* magazine (March, 1966) Tydings wrote: "There are grave dangers in the steady, almost inexorable growth of federal power. Necessary and justifiable as each single accretion of power may be, they add up to a centralization of power in Washington that has serious implications. This centralization . . . threatens our Jeffersonian principles of democracy and civil liberties." Unfortunately, Tydings has not adopted his own observations as a standard since it is virtually impossible to find where he has cast a vote against centralization of federal governmental power. As a matter of fact, in 1968, by his own admission, he offered the strongest federal gun control bill ever introduced to the Congress. He proposed the registration of every firearm in the United States and that a license be required for every purchase or possession of any firearm or ammunition in the United States. What made his proposals unusual is the fact that less than a year earlier he stated that such provisions were best left under the control of the individual states.

STEWART UDALL was born on January 31, 1920 in St. Johns, Arizona, son of Louise Lee and Levi Udall. He married Ermalee Webb. He is an alumnus of the University of Arizona (LL.B., 1948).

From 1948 until 1954, Udall practiced law in Tucson. From 1955 until 1961, he served in the House of Representatives, consistently voting for big government and against private enterprise, private ownership, and private property. Equally consistent were his votes against national security.

Since 1961, Udall has been Secretary of the Interior. Much of his time has been devoted to his duties as a lackey to Lady Bird Johnson as she wages her keep-America-beautiful campaign.

During Udall's tenure, he has acquired the reputation of a great conservationist but, in reality, the phoniness of this title was dramatized with his proposal to build two dams which would flood the Grand Canyon. He has been busy acquiring lands for the federal domain and creating national parks to build up the local prestige of Great Society congressmen. His contempt for private property was best expressed when he said, in 1966: "We have continued . . . to nurture ourselves on outmoded mythologies of . . . free enterprise, private property rights . . . . We have continued to hold to the twin idols of free enterprise and rugged individualism . . . . "

During Udall's tenure, with more funds and personnel available than ever before for the Bureau of Indian Affairs, the plight of American Indians on their government reservations has grown steadily worse. Udall has used his cabinet position to curry favor for the left. In 1966, he allowed Negro agitators to have a camp-in at Lafayette Park, directly across the street from the White House. In 1967, while the nation was still reeling from the epidemic of revolutionary riots in the cities, Udall said that "social change is often turbulent and we may look back on this and see it as a creative period in our history."

In 1966, Udall presented the Interior Department's Conservation Service Award to folksinger Woody Guthrie. Before two thousand government employees, whom Udall had assembled for the award ceremony, he praised Guthrie for summarizing in song "the struggles and deeply held conviction of those who love our land and fight to protect it." Then Udall announced that a Bonneville Power Administration substation in the Northwest was being named the Woody Guthrie Substation. In August, 1963, the Communist magazine *Mainstream's* entire issue had been devoted to Guthrie. It was a fitting tribute by the Communists since Guthrie had been one of them for over thirty years. He did his bit for the Communist Party, writing for *The Daily Worker, New Masses,* and other Communist Party journals, and he spread the Communist line through the more than one thousand folksongs he wrote. These songs form the basic repertoire for Communist and fellow-traveling folksingers today.

Then, in 1967, Udall dedicated the Terre Haute, Indiana home of Eugene V. Debs as a National Historic landmark. Debs was not only one of the most radical labor agitators in this country's history but on five occasions he was the Socialist Party candidate for the United States presidency.

LOUIS UNTERMEYER was born on October 1, 1885 in New York City, son of Julia Michael and Emmanuel Untermeyer. He has been married to Jean Starr, Virginia Moore, Esther Antin, and Bryna Ivens.

After a high school education, Untermeyer worked in his family's jewelry manufacturing business. At the age of thirty-eight, he retired from the business world and began his multi-faceted career as a poet, essayist, journalist, anthologist, editor, lecturer, radio commentator, and television panelist. At various times, he held editorial positions with the *American Mercury* and *The Seven Arts*. He lectured at numerous colleges and universities, including Amherst College, Knox College, Iowa State College, the University of Michigan, and the University of Kansas. He has written or edited at least ninety books including two autobiographies.

Untermeyer was a founder of *The Masses,* along with two pioneer American Communists, John Reed and Max Eastman. Untermeyer has also been affiliated with the American Society for Cultural Relations with Russia ("Communist front"); the John Reed Clubs ("Communist front"); the National

Council of American-Soviet Friendship ("subversive and Communist" – "specializing in pro-Soviet propaganda"); the *Liberator* ("Communist magazine"); the United American Artists ("Communist front"); the Veterans of the Abraham Lincoln Brigade ("subversive and Communist"); the World Peace Congress ("Communist front"); the Civil Rights Congress ("subversive and Communist"); the American Labor Party ("Communist front"); the Joint Anti-Fascist Refugee Committee ("subversive and Communist"); the League of American Writers ("subversive and Communist"); the World Federation of Democratic Youth ("Communist front"); *Masses and Mainstream* ("Communist publication"); the Mid-Century Conference for Peace ("aimed at assembling as many gullible persons as possible under Communist direction and turning them into a vast sounding board for Communist propaganda" – "a Communist front"); the National Committee to Defeat the Mundt Bill ("a Communist lobby"); and, the Voice of Freedom Committee ("subversive"). He has also been affiliated with the leftwing, pacifist National Committee for a Sane Nuclear Policy. He has petitioned to abolish the House Committee on Un-American Activities and has protested against the arrest, conviction, and imprisonment of Communists. He has participated in Communist-led May Day parades.

During World War II, Untermeyer was publications editor for Elmer Davis' Red-lined Office of War Information and editor of *Armed Services Editions*. He has been a U.S. delegate to the International Cultural Conferences in India (1961) and Japan (1963). During the Kennedy Administration, he was a consultant in poetry to the Library of Congress.

HAROLD C. UREY was born on April 29, 1893 in Walkerton, Indiana, son of Cora Reinoehl and Samuel Urey. He married Frieda Daum. He is an alumnus of the University of Montana (B.S., 1917) and the University of California (Ph.D., 1923).

From 1917 until 1919, Urey worked as a chemist with Barrett Chemical Company of Philadelphia. From 1919 until 1921, he was a chemistry instructor at the University of Montana. From 1924 until 1929, he was an associate in chemistry at The Johns Hopkins University. From 1929 until 1934, he was an associate professor in chemistry at Columbia University. From 1934 until 1945, he was a professor of chemistry at Columbia. From 1939 to 1942, he was the executive officer of Columbia's chemistry department. From 1942 until 1945, he was research director at Columbia's S.A.M. Laboratories.

In 1945, Urey began a seven-year term as distinguished service professor of chemistry at the University of Chicago's Institute of Nuclear Studies. From 1952 until 1958, he was the Martin A. Ryerson distinguished service professor at Chicago. Since 1958, he has been a professor of chemistry-at-large at the University of California. As a visiting lecturer, he has worked at Yale University, the University of Nebraska, the University of California, and – in England – at Oxford University and Cambridge University.

In his field, Urey has distinguished himself as the discoverer of the hydrogen atom of atomic weight two. And, in the development of the atomic bomb, Urey made his contribution through research on the production of heavy water and U235. He was awarded the Nobel prize in chemistry for 1934.

Urey has been affiliated with the

American Committee for Democracy and Intellectual Freedom ("Communist front" – "subversive and un-American"); the American Committee for Protection of Foreign Born [Americans] "subversive and Communist" – "one of the oldest auxiliaries of the Communist Party in the United States" – under the "complete domination" of the Communist Party); the American Committee to Save Refugees ("Communist enterprise"); the Committee of One Thousand ("Communist created and controlled front organization"); the Coordinating Committee to Lift the [Spanish] Embargo ("Communist front"); Friends of the Abraham Lincoln Brigade ("its officers and staff members were in the main [Communist] Party members and functionaries"); the Greater New York Emergency Conference on Inalienable Rights ("Communist front"); the League of American Writers ("subversive and Communist"); the National Council of American-Soviet Friendship ("subversive and Communist" – "specializing in pro-Soviet propaganda"); the National Emergency Conference ("Communist front"); the National Emergency Conference for Democratic Rights ("Communist front"); Veterans of the Abraham Lincoln Brigade ("subversive and Communist"); and, the National Committee to Secure Justice in the Rosenberg Case ("Communist front").

In the matter of the convicted atom bomb spies, the Rosenbergs, Urey gave the National Committee to Secure Justice in the Rosenberg Case its most dazzling propaganda contributions. "Without having been present at the trial of the Rosenbergs and with no legal training at all by which to test his opinions, Urey, nevertheless, did not hesitate to declare flatly that 'I found the testimony of the Rosenbergs more believable than that of the Greenglasses.' Urey's statement, first contained in a letter to Judge [Irving] Kaufman and published in the *New York Times* 'Letter Columns' on January 5, 1953, earned him banner headlines in the *Daily Worker.*" (House Committee on Un-American Activities, *Trial by Treason,* August 25, 1956, pp. 31-32.)

Urey has also demonstrated his sympathy for Communists by his appearance at a Paris gathering in 1947 of the World Federation of Scientific Workers, which was nothing but an international group of Communists and extreme pro-Communists.

Urey, as a hard-core fellow traveler, has naturally worked to abolish the House Committee on Un-American Activities. He has been an outstanding critic of any and all security measures designed to guard against subversion and espionage directed against the United States nuclear weapons program. Urey, as did so many scientists connected with the development of the A-bomb, adopted the position that post-World War II development of atomic weapons should be halted and that scientific discoveries should be shared with the Soviet Union.

EARL WARREN was born on March 19, 1891 in Los Angeles, son of Chrystal Hernlund and Methias Warren. He married Nina Meyers. He is an alumnus of the University of California (LL.B., 1912; J.D., 1914). He was admitted to the California bar in 1914.

From 1914 until 1917, Warren worked as a law clerk for a San Francisco law firm. In 1919, he was a clerk for the judiciary committee of the California Legislature. In 1919 and 1920, he was deputy city attorney for Oakland. From 1920 until 1923, he was a deputy district attorney for Alameda County.

From 1923 until 1925, he was chief deputy district attorney and, from 1925 until 1939, district attorney for Alameda County. From 1939 until 1943, he was Attorney General of California. From 1943 until 1953, he was Governor of California.

During Warren's fourteen years as Attorney General and Governor of California, the State became one of the most concentrated areas of activities for the Communist Party. Yet, as Warren was concluding his gubernatorial years and he sought to be a favorite-son presidential nominee in 1952, he said in his campaign literature: "We must be relentless in rooting out the agents of international communism, who are actively working within our Nation to bring about its destruction. In dealing with communism in all its aspects we must be direct, forthright – and when principle is involved – firm. Vaccilation or indecision will not improve our relations with Russia and her satellites."

In that same campaign literature, speaking on individual freedom, Warren said: "We must insist upon one law for all men and equal opportunity in life for all men. The heart of our Constitution is its Bill of Rights which guarantees to every individual in our country, regardless of race, creed or color and regardless of position in life, the precious rights of freedom of assembly, freedom of speech and freedom of worship. Anything that divides us or limits the opportunities for full American citizenship is injurious to the welfare of all." Yet, in 1942, as Attorney General, Warren shared responsibility with President Franklin Roosevelt for moving 110,000 Japanese residents and Japanese-American citizens from their homes, farms, and businesses in California to inland stockades. Warren's excuse was that he was trying to avert sabotage. The excuse fell completely apart when not a single saboteur was ever discovered among his victims. (Much of Warren's conduct as California's Governor must remain for future historians to evaluate. When he resigned the governorship in December 1953, he stipulated that his gubernatorial records be sealed for ten years or until his death. When the ten years had elapsed in December 1963, Warren requested that "these records be continued under seal during my lifetime or unless notified otherwise at a future date." As of 1968, that future date had not yet arrived.)

In his campaign literature, Warren supported free enterprise against socialism and a planned economy. Yet, in his gubernatorial years, he invariably supported welfare state legislation on a state and national level.

In 1928 Warren was an alternate delegate and, in 1932, a delegate to the Republican National Convention. From 1934 until 1936, he was chairman of the Republican State Central Committee of California. In 1936 and 1944, he led California delegations to the Republican National Convention. In 1944, he was keynote speaker and temporary chairman of the Republican National Convention. In 1948, he was the Republican Party's vice presidential nominee. (Harry Truman said of Warren that he was a Democrat who didn't know it.)

In 1952, Warren was a leader of the political chicanery which robbed Ohio's Senator Robert A. Taft of the Republican Party's presidential nomination. As a reward for the California delegation's votes which Warren threw his way, President Dwight Eisenhower appointed Warren as Chief Justice of the United States, which office he assumed on October 5, 1953. As credentials for the nation's highest office, Warren had absolutely no judicial experience. His private practice of law had been virtually barren. Neither Warren nor even his most idolatrous biographers have offered any pretensions to his legal scholarship.

Not long after he became Chief Justice, the Supreme Court was called the "Warren Court" by both friends and critics. In fifteen years, the "Warren Court" revolutionized traditional American judicial processes as it reversed longstanding decisions of the federal courts. By 1961, the veteran U.S. Senator Harry F. Byrd (D.-Va.) was moved to say: "Judicial usurpation of power has reached a peak with the Warren Court. Its decisions have invaded homes, handicapped police protection, disregarded State sovereignty, interfered with executive authority and usurped the powers of Congress. There is no doubt that the Warren Court is undermining our system and contributing to centralization of power; and thereby it is sapping our national strength. This makes us more vulnerable to destructive forces at home and abroad."

Warren, as the unmistakable leader of the Court, has written or concurred in decisions consistently on the side of centralized government versus state and local government; unions versus individuals; criminals versus society; Communists versus national security. Warren and his leftist colleagues have deliberately ignored the legislative intent of Congress and have written and re-written laws in direct violation of the Constitution. For legal evidence, they have substituted highly controversial theories of sociology, economics, and political science. They have re-written almost the entire Bill of Rights and much of the rest of the Constitution of the United States.

The Warren Court, yielding to the demands of the National Association for the Advancement of Colored People, the American Civil Liberties Union and other pressure groups, has advanced the cause of egalitarianism for Negroes in the name of so-called civil rights in areas of education, housing, and the franchise.

In its abuse of the Bill of Rights, the Warren Court has outlawed prayers and Bible reading in public schools; allowed the press media extreme latitude in protection against libel suits; provided immunities from punishment for murderers, rapists, pornographers, and other criminals; restricted severely police powers of surveillance, arrest, and interrogation; and, virtually eliminated the power of the several States to protect themselves from subversion.

In a complete usurpation of authority, the Warren Court assumed the power to reapportion seats in the House of Representatives and the several State legislatures and laid down the egalitarian "one-man, one-vote" rule for electing legislators.

The Warren Court has undermined the investigative power and authority of the House Committee on Un-American Activities and virtually mutilated the nation's most important internal security legislation, the Smith Act and the McCarran-Walter Act. On June 17, 1957 ("Red Monday"), the Warren Court made three such obviously pro-Communist decisions that Dorothy Healey, a Communist Party spokesman, hailed them by saying: "This is the greatest victory the Communist Party ever had." The Communists' *Daily Worker* called the decisions "liberty rulings" and "a milestone for Democracy" which "mark the definitive ending of the McCarthyian era in American life."

Along with his corruption of the judicial process, away from the court's chambers Warren has involved himself in extra-judicial affairs to the extent that his judicial impartiality and independence must be suspect. He and his wife have made at least six trips abroad at the taxpayers' expense under a State Department program of Education and Cultural Exchange — a situation which certainly makes Warren beholden to the Executive branch. Ironically, on at least three of these trips, the Warrens have visited the Communist tyrant Josip Broz Tito in Communist Yugoslavia. And the Warrens' expense-paid journeys have taken them to other Communist bloc nations including Poland and Czecho-Slovakia. The friendliness of hosts and visitors on these trips certainly casts a shadow over any decision made by Warren in relation to Communism and Communists.

Shortly after the news of President Kennedy's assassination reached him, Warren stated: "A great and good President has suffered martyrdom as a result of the hatred and bitterness that has been injected into the life of our nation by bigots, but his memory will always be an inspiration to Americans of good will everywhere." During the ceremonies attendant to the Kennedy funeral, Warren, in his eulogy to the late President, blamed the assassination on "forces of hatred and malevolence, such as today are eating their way into the bloodstream of American life." The press in this country and abroad interpreted Warren's remarks as directed against "rightwingers."

Four days after the assassination, the midweek edition of the Communists' *Worker* editorialized: "Justice and the internal security of the nation call for the most complete investigation and revelation of all factors which brought forth this heinous assassination. We believe that President Johnson on the one hand and Congress on the other should act at

once to appoint respective extraordinary investigating commissions with full power to conduct a searching inquiry into all the circumstances around the assassination of the President and murder of the suspect. Such an investigating commission, headed by the chief justice of the Supreme Court, should be composed of citizens and experts who enjoy the confidence of the nation."

Two days after the Communists' editorial appeared, President Lyndon Johnson appointed Warren to head the President's Commission on the Assassination of President Kennedy. Notwithstanding the fact that he had already prejudged the case; notwithstanding the fact that he would have to disqualify himself if the case against the alleged assassin ever reached the Supreme Court; notwithstanding the fact that he would have to neglect his Supreme Court duties while heading the Commission, Warren complied with Johnson's request — and the suggestion of the *Worker* — and accepted leadership of the Commission.

The report of the Warren Commission remains as controversial as any report ever offered by any governmental group. Much of the evidence gathered remains totally secretive. And, Warren's major contribution to the work of the Commission was his solicitude for Marina Oswald, widow of the alleged assassin and in her own right a provable liar and evasive witness before the Commission.

Warren, contrary to his predecessors in the office of Chief Justice, is a compulsive publicity seeker as he roams the world extolling the work of the United Nations, the pacifist cause of "world peace through world law," disarmament, so-called civil rights, and other measures and matters that have a direct bearing upon decisions which he must encounter on the Supreme Court.

His code of ethics is strange indeed, but no stranger than his behavior in the circumstances of his on-again, off-again resignation from the Supreme Court. On June 13, 1968, he submitted his resignation to President Johnson who announced the fact ten days later. On July 5, 1968, Warren said that he would not leave the Court unless the Senate confirmed Associate Justice Abe Fortas to be his successor. This sort of pressure, exerted by Warren upon the Senate, has no precedence in American history, and is simply one more example of Warren's contempt for the division of powers which is so characteristic of the Constitution of the United States.

ARTHUR WASKOW was born on October 12, 1933 in Baltimore, son of Hannah Osnowitz and Henry Waskow. He married Irene Elkin. He is an alumnus of Johns Hopkins University (B.A., 1954) and the University of Wisconsin (M.A., 1956; Ph.D., 1963).

From 1959 until 1961, Waskow was a legislative assistant to Representative Robert W. Kastenmeier (D.-Wisc.), one of the most leftist members of the Congress. From 1961 until 1963, he was a senior staff member of the Peace Research Institute (Washington, D.C.), one of the most prestigious organizations in the entire leftwing peace movement. Since 1963, he has been at the Institute for Policy Studies, where he is now a senior fellow. The IPS is nothing less than a leftwing propaganda agency for disarmament.

Waskow is the author of *The Limits of Defense* (1962) and *The Worried Man's Guide to World Peace* (1963), and a co-author with Stanley L. Newman of *American in Hiding*. He has also written for *Ramparts* magazine, the far-out leftist publication which clings to a line somewhere amid anarchism, out-and-out-pro-Communism, and ostentatious anti-Americanism. He once wrote a study for the U.S. Arms Control and Disarmament Agency in which he claimed that the Soviet occupation of Eastern and Central Europe had been beneficial for world peace. In 1965, he wrote a pamphlet ("Keeping the World Disarmed") for the Fund for the Republic's Center for the Study of Democratic Institutions. In it Waskow appealed for an international police force for a future demilitarized world. But, of all his writings, it is most probable that Waskow's most important contribution to leftwing pacifism was his "The Theory and Practice of Deterrence," in *The Liberal Papers*, edited by James Roosevelt and published in 1962.

In his *Liberal Papers* article, Waskow alleged that he had found "a number of officers and administrators, mainly in the Air Force, [who] are convinced that thermonuclear war is possible, conceivable, acceptable [!], and that it will be 'won' or 'lost' in the classical sense." For some esoteric reason, the Air Force is an especial center of concentration for the peacenik. (For example, see Peter Bryant's *Red Alert* and Eugene Burdick and Harvey Wheeler's *Fail-Safe,* in both of which Air Force personnel not only find thermonuclear war "acceptable" but inaugurate such warfare.) Of course, Waskow does not identify the "officers and administrators" by their rank, their experience, their credentials for making such profound judgments, their numbers, or state whether he found contrary opinions or how extensive his survey was among Air Force personnel and others in the several armed services. But, in the absence of any and all contrasting opinions, Waskow represents his alleged informants as the only group holding an opinion worthy of consideration. And he sets his informants up for easy demolition: "These men agree that it would be preferable to prevent such a war from taking place, but they think the only effective prevention is the establishment of a force capable of winning such a war and accepting the surrender of the enemy." Waskow obviously hopes that his readers will understand that it is evil to build such a massive preventive force that no enemy of the United States would dare to risk war and certain defeat. On the other hand, Waskow has the ideal solution. He would have international laws promulgated against natural armaments. An international police force would enforce such laws. Waskow's logic: "An international agreement effectively policed can conceivably deter any would-be aggressor." (He returned to that theme in more detail in his 1965 pamphlet, "Keeping the World Disarmed," but in neither case does Waskow harbor the thought that an international police force — controlled by the wrong people — could be perverted into an aggressive force.)

Until Waskow's international utopia could be realized, he offered plans for Congress on a national level. The Congress would create a National Peace Agency "to mobilize the techniques of social and natural science in the search for disarmament . . . scholars of all sorts would be encouraged to deal with the myriad question of reducing tensions in political, economic, military, and other fields."

Only a naive observer of the Washington scene would deny that Waskow, from his staff position with the Institute for Policy Studies, has a ready and easy access to the government's policy makers. It is equally certain that his scaremongering fanaticism reaches receptive ears among the disarmament advocates in the State and Defense Departments. It has become routine enchantment for cowering diplomats and civilian strategists to contemplate a mythical military-industrial complex, testing nuclear weapons in preparation for all-out nuclear warfare.

Waskow, however, does not oppose only future warfare. He has been a strong critic of U.S. involvement in Vietnam. To Waskow, the United States has made a "neo-imperial" strategic intervention (Waskow, "The New Student Movement," *Our Generation,* May, 1966). In Vietnam, "We have scarcely contributed to the peace of the world." (Speech at the Middle South Model United Nations at the University of North Carolina, February 12, 1965.) Unmentioned by Waskow: any contributions to world peace made in Vietnam by Ho chi Minh and his supporters in the Soviet Union, Red China, and in the rest of the world Communist apparatus.

At the Woodrow Wilson School of Politics at Princeton University on April 4, 1968, Waskow said: "Vietnam has proved that a real social revolution, as in Vietnam, can push one of the great world empires in world history to the edge of crisis." The aggression of Ho chi Minh, which Waskow calls a "social" revolution, is being opposed . by the "imperialist" United States but the owners of "the first permanent war machine in United States history and the most overwhelming in human history, are discovering that this war machine is useless — cannot win political victories." (Quoted in Joseph G. Herzberg's special dispatch to the *New York Times,* April 7, 1968.) It is "imperialist" ambition, not the danger from Communist aggression, says Waskow, that is responsible for the permanence of America's military establishment. And, of course, he does not even hint at the identity of any responsible military man who has ever claimed that our fighting force was designed to win political victories.

Away from the Institute for Policy Studies, Waskow has pushed his plea for disarmament through his activities in the leftwing, pacifist National Committee for a Sane Nuclear Policy. And, in 1966, he engaged in direct political activity as a member of the executive board, national councilman, and member of the convention steering committee of the National Conference for New Politics. It was Waskow who drafted almost the entire text of the formal call to a convention issued by the NCNP. It soon became evident that NCNP was a classical united front, third party movement largely controlled by the Communist Party.

THOMAS J. WATSON JR. was born on January 8, 1914 in Dayton, Ohio, son of Jeannette Kittridge and Thomas Watson. He married Olive Cawley. He is an alumnus of Brown University (B.A., 1937).

In 1937, Watson became a salesman for International Business Machines Corporation, which had been established by his father in the 1920's. From 1940 until 1946, he was in the U.S. Army Air Corps. After his distinguished military service, he returned to IBM and since 1946 he has been an executive in the corporation. He was president from 1952 until 1961 and, since 1961, has been IBM's chairman of the board.

There can be no denial of Watson's business acumen. He and his corporation enjoy the respect of industrial and business communities throughout the world. But Watson has not been a cobbler sticking to his last. While at the task of promoting his business interests, he has entered upon the fringes of the federal government in various capacities and into the ranks of internationalists. And, unwittingly or not, he has – in his writings and utterances – parroted the clichés of leftwing policy makers who are determined to use the resources of the United States for the purpose of creating a socialist one-world, dominated by Communist powers.

In the course of his business activities, Watson has traveled throughout the world. For reasons best known to himself, he has assumed that he is competent to speak authoritatively on matters far beyond the purview of his background and experience. For example, in 1959, he described as "uncommitted nations" Ghana, Guinea, North Korea, and North Vietnam. Of them, he said: "They have all undergone – or are undergoing – radical changes ... political, economic and social. These changes are inspired by a nationalistic fervor; an almost fanatic desire to thrust off the yoke of colonialism; to free themselves from imperialism; to establish self-rule and to achieve in their own right the dignity of being free .... I believe that one of the major keys to a peaceful and prosperous world is to be found in these under-developed and largely uncommitted areas of the world." Apparently it never was explained to Watson that each of these countries was thoroughly committed to the advance of international Communism or that each of them was a direct result of Communist diplomatic and political agitation or that each was ruled by Communist viceroys under the tolerance of Moscow and Peiping.

After a short visit to the Soviet Union in 1959, Watson expressed his reactions: "The enthusiasm of the average Russian for his system and what it has produced is amazing. They are proud and they believe in what they are doing. I'm sure when they go abroad as technicians assigned to an under-developed area, their pride and enthusiasm make them very effectve salesmen for Communism." Of course, Watson was not the first nor the last American businessman to receive the totally phony impression that he encountered "the average Russian" at work. He was not the first nor the last to be ignorant of the fact that he was allowed to see and hear only what his well-disciplined Communist guides allowed him to see and hear. He was not the first nor the last to ignore the fact that only trustworthy (by rigid Communist standards) technicians were allowed to leave the Soviet Union and that while in foreign lands they were under the constant and close scrutiny of Soviet security police. He was not the first nor the last to be oblivious to the fact that if any Soviet citizen did not display "pride and enthusiasm" for Communism while at home or abroad, his day of accounting would not be less than ruthless.

As have so many Americans, in and out of government, Watson displayed a flair for uncritical acceptance of Soviet claims for educational advancement, scientific achievements, military and space programs, industrial production, and foreign "aid" expenditures. Perhaps the extent of his naiveté was best demonstrated when he said: "Communism has raised the standard of living in Russia materially. Our democratic system has done much better under any comparison but attempts to prove the Soviet system an economic failure are wishful thinking." Watson and all of IBM's computers would be hard pressed trying to prove — even to the Kremlin's leaders — that the Soviet system has been an economic success.

United States foreign "aid" programs have received the enthusiastic support of Watson. He believes that such programs are necessary if the United States is going to beat the Soviet Union in a contest for the "all-important, uncommitted nations" so that the latter can be won over to western orientation. To Watson, foreign aid is "one of the very important ways of winning allies." What single ally the United States has ever won through foreign aid, Watson has never mentioned. But then his education in the realities of foreign "aid" programs has been sadly neglected. As a premise for his foreign "aid" propaganda, he has stated that "the Marshall Plan money was spent abroad to prevent the entire European Continent from becoming Communist satellites." If Watson had even a rudimentary knowledge of the Marshall Plan, he would know that Marshall Plan money was offered to, and rejected by, the Soviet Union and its satellites.

There can be no question that Watson has been welcomed into the higher echelons of the Liberal Establishment. He is a trustee of the Rockefeller Foundation which has contributed untold millions of dollars to leftwing causes and institutions throughout the world. He has been a member of the Council on Foreign Relations which has dominated the policy-making apparatus of the U.S. Department of State for the past three decades. He has been a member of the Business Advisory Council which is the CFR's patronage link to the federal government. He has been a member of the Committee for Economic Development, the CFR's major propaganda arm in the important work of socializing the American economy. He was a member of the Citizens Committee for International Development which propagandized for foreign "aid" programs during the Kennedy Administration. He has been on the board of directors of the Atlantic Council of the United States, an organization which stresses the need for closer cooperation, especially economic, between the United States and the socialist nations of western Europe. He has been on the public policy committee of the Advertising Council, a propaganda outfit which uses money contributed by American businesses to tout pet projects of the federal government. The boosts for the federal boondoggles are offered as a "public service" on radio, television, in newspapers and magazines, and even in commercial advertisements. In recent years, Watson has served the Kennedy and Johnson Administrations as a member of the Peace Corps Advisory Council and the President's Advisory Committee on Labor-Management Policy.

In 1967 and 1968, Watson's firm became a target of a campaign waged by Young Americans for Freedom. The action of YAF stemmed from the fact that IBM had been selling its sophisticated data processing systems to Communist Czecho-Slovakia, Communist Poland, Communist Hungary, Communist Bulgaria, and had announced its intention of selling its equipment to Communist East Germany. Since every one of these Communist countries was supporting the war effort of Communist North Vietnam, YAF argued that the continuance of trade with the enemy – the Communist bloc – was obviously in conflict with the best interests of the United States.

IBM officials insisted that the federal government had advised American businessmen to trade with the eastern European Communist countries. YAF, on the other hand, replied that because the federal government advises a policy does not mean that businessmen have to follow such advice.

IBM officials further argued that they were not trading strategic materials (strategic by governmental definition) to the Communists. YAF's answer was that the government's definition of strategic was much more liberal than it should be. But beyond that and accepting IBM's premise that the materials being traded were non-strategic, YAF countered by arguing that "our principal objection to trade in non-strategic items is that by trading with a Communist country, by definition you are giving them a commodity or items of equipment which they want and need to strengthen their economy."

Watson and other IBM officials, however, refused to recognize that the famous IBM machines were not only a boon to the economy of the Communist nations but that the same machines can be and are used as an integral part of military establishments in any country fortunate enough to have them.

Watson's and IBM's willingness to follow the advice of the State Department by sending machines to the Communist bloc were not unprecedented. In 1959, when the Soviet dictator Khrushchev was invited to visit the United States by Dwight Eisenhower, one of the Communist butcher's stops was at the IBM plant in San Jose, California. In a quarterly report to IBM's stockholders, Watson wrote of how "delighted" he was that Eisenhower had extended the invitation to Khrushchev and "in an attempt to be of assistance to the President and the State Department, I wrote a letter to the Chief of Protocol stating that IBM has a number of outstandingly modern plants and, like most American companies, we do our utmost to build up the role of the individual in IBM production. I suggested that it might be helpful to U.S. – Soviet relations if Chairman Khurshchev and his party could tour one of these plants."

579

The day came when Khrushchev arrived at IBM's facilities in San Jose. Watson escorted him around the plant and before the tour began gave Khrushchev some words of wisdom: "I told Chairman Khrushchev and his party that we believe employee welfare and good working conditions contribute to the dignity of the individual. We believe this dignity is the key to our industrial productivity, and that the American worker employed in the American way is unbeatable."

Khrushchev, while returning to Moscow, provided a sequel to Watson's homily: "When I was preparing for the trip to the United States . . . some people in America said: Khrushchev will come to our country, he will see our wealth, our strength, and he will change his views. Perhaps they hoped that I would change my views and abandon communist ideas. But, of course, only foolish people would think that."

ROBERT WEAVER was born on December 29, 1907 in Washington, D.C., son of Florence Freeman and Mortimer Weaver. He married Ella Haith. He is an alumnus of Harvard University (A.B., 1929; M.A., 1931; Ph.D., 1934). He is the author of *Negro Labor: A National Problem* (1946); *The Negro Ghetto* (1948); and *The Urban Complex* (1964).

In 1931 and 1932, Weaver was a professor of economics at the Agricultural and Technical College of North Carolina. From 1934 until 1938, he was an advisor on Negro Affairs to Secretary of the Interior Harold L. Ickes. From 1938 until 1940, he was a special assistant to Administrator Nathan Straus of the U.S. Housing Authority. In 1940, he was administrative assistant to Sidney Hillman (the pro-Communist labor leader) of the National Defense Advisory

Commission. In 1941 and 1942, he was chief of the Negro employment and training branch of the labor division in the Office of Production Management, and, in 1943, he held the same duties in the War Production Board. In 1944, he was director of Negro Manpower Service in the War Manpower Commission.

During his years in the New Deal, Weaver was the leader of the so-called "black cabinet" – Negro brain-trusters in the federal government. The function of the black cabinet was to attain for Negroes jobs in various federal boondoggles and occupancy of federal housing projects. Weaver's group performed its function quite efficiently. According to Richard Bardolph in his *The Negro Vanguard,* the high point of the black cabinet's influence came shortly before the 1940 presidential election. At a time when President Roosevelt was arriving in New York City's Pennsylvania Station, the President's press secretary Stephen Early pushed a Negro policeman to the floor. The black cabinet was asked to write a speech for the President so that Negroes would not be alienated by the incident. Weaver blocked this move and summoned the black cabinet to a meeting and the group made recommendations which Roosevelt immediately accepted. And within forty-eight hours, in response to the black cabinet, Benjamin O. Davis became the first Negro general in the U.S. Army; William H. Hastie became the first Negro civilian aide to the Secretary of War; and, Campbell C. Johnson became the first Negro civilian aide to the director of Selective Service.

In addition to his regular jobs in the New Deal, Weaver ran a federal survey of Negro white collar and skilled workers – a boondoggle that employed 1,800 people and cost more than $500,000.

For the Tennessee Valley Authority, he ran a survey of the TVA program and the participation of minority groups in it. As a consultant to the President's Advisory Committee on Education and as a member of the advisory committee of the National Youth Administration, he conducted other studies related to Negroes.

After leaving government service, Weaver was, for a short time, executive director of the Mayor's Committee on Race Relations in Chicago. In 1946, Weaver went to work for the United Nations Relief and Rehabilitation Administration. For UNRRA, he went to the Ukraine in the Soviet Union where he eventually became acting deputy chief of mission. He returned from this experience with high praise for the lack of discrimination and prejudice he witnessed under Communism. (Later, he admitted that his judgment was faulty: "I am afraid you see in Russia about as much understanding as you take there, and I did not take too much.")

From 1947 until 1949, Weaver was in Chicago. He was an official of the American Council on Race Relations, a board member of the Metropolitan Housing Council of Chicago, and an executive committee member of the National Committee on Housing. During this same period, he lectured at Northwestern University, the Teachers College of Columbia University, New York University, and the New School for Social Research.

From 1949 until 1955, Weaver was director of the opportunity fellowships program of the John Hay Whitney Foundation. He was also a member of the national selection committee for Fulbright scholarships, a member of the fellowship committee on the Julius Rosenwald Fund, and chairman of the faculty fellowship committee of the United Negro College Fund.

In 1955, Weaver became the deputy commissioner of the New York State Division of Housing. In December, 1955, Governor Averell Harriman appointed Weaver to be the Rent Administrator for the State of New York, with cabinet rank. He held this post until January, 1959. He then moved on to New York City where Mayor Robert Wagner appointed him vice chairman of the City's Housing and Redevelopment Board. While in this position, Weaver was also chairman of the board of directors of the National Association for the Advancement of Colored People.

On December 31, 1960, President-elect John F. Kennedy announced that Weaver would be apointed as Administrator of the U.S. Housing and Home Finance Agency. (Weaver was just one of many Americans for Democratic Action who would become part of the New Frontier.)

Weaver's nomination was the first in the Kennedy Administration to encounter delay and opposition in the Senate. Senator A. Willis Robertson, chairman of the Banking and Currency Committee which held hearings on the nomination, requested from President Kennedy a letter attesting that Weaver had undergone investigation by the Federal Bureau of Investigation and that the President was satisfied as to Weaver's loyalty. The President complied with Robertson's request.

In the background, Weaver had had some affiliations with Communist fronts and Communist projects. In 1937, he had been a discussion leader at the second National Negro Congress. The Congress was subversive and Communist. (There was also evidence that, in 1938, Weaver was scheduled to speak at an eastern regional conference of the NNC and, in 1940, was scheduled to appear at the third National Negro Congress.) In 1939, Weaver signed a letter circulated by the Negro People's Committee to Aid Spanish Democracy, a Communist front. In 1941, he was a member of the Washington Book Shop, a Communist front, although Weaver's resignation from the front was announced at a membership meeting of the Washington Book Shop on May 20, 1941. In 1941, Weaver made a small financial contribution to *Social Work Today,* a Communist magazine. In 1944, Weaver sponsored a testimonial dinner in honor of Ferdinand C. Smith, an alien Communist. In 1944, Weaver was a member of the executive board of Sidney Hillman's National Citizens Political Action Committee, which the Special House Committee on Un-American Activities described as the "Communist Party's supreme bid for power throughout its twenty-five years of existence in this country." In 1945, Weaver endorsed the program of the Council on African Affairs, a Communist front designed to provoke racial friction.

In his defense, Weaver admitted that he had been a dupe in his endorsement for the Council on African Affairs. His participation in the National Negro Congress he excused on grounds that the NNC had received greetings from President Franklin Roosevelt and other important persons. Furthermore, Weaver insisted that he had never been an active member of any subversive organization.

In the Senate hearings, Weaver received the complete support of the New York Senators Kenneth Keating and Jacob Javits, both Republicans, Senator Joseph S. Clark, Democrat of Pennsylvania, and Representative William Fitts Ryan, a Democrat from Manhattan. After some opposition on the floor of

the Senate, Weaver's nomination was confirmed on February 9, 1961.

One of President Kennedy's plans involved the establishment of a new Department of Urban Affairs and Housing. And, in January, 1962, Mr. Kennedy announced that if Congress did create the new department, Weaver would be his nomination for Secretary. It was not until November, 1965 that Congress acted upon Mr. Kennedy's proposal and created the Department of Housing and Urban Development. In January, 1966, President Lyndon Johnson said that after looking over three hundred potential candidates, he had decided to appoint Weaver as Secretary of HUD so as "to pursue the goal of bringing the full measure of the Great Society to our urban areas." Thus, Weaver became the first Negro in a presidential cabinet. Unlike 1961, there was little or no opposition to Weaver's nomination in the Senate.

Weaver has never been a flamboyant Negro leader. At the same time, he has never made a secret of the fact that he has used his public and private positions to promote Negro causes. And, at times, he has even been an apologist for Negro militants. In the Kennedy and Johnson Administrations, he made it clear that he wanted to use federal power to create multi-racial neighborhoods in cities and suburbs. He has proclaimed: "We must stop trying to weld all cultures in the United States. There is richness in our differences." But this sentiment does not square with his insistence that integration of blacks and whites be contrived by federal action – executive, legislative, judicial.

On May 14, 1968, Weaver announced that he would resign from the cabinet after the November presidential election. On the following day, it was announced that, effective January, 1969, he would become president of the new Bernard M. Baruch College of New York City's University. Said Weaver as his appointment was made: "I look forward to Baruch's program encouraging a marriage between Federal assistance and higher education in terms of the pressing needs of a preponderantly urban nation."

HARVEY WHEELER was born in 1918. He spent his childhood in Greensburg, Indiana. He attended Wabash College and Indiana University as an undergraduate. He received his Ph.D. from Harvard University.

Wheeler taught political science at Johns Hopkins University and Washington and Lee University. While at Washington and Lee, he was a consultant to the Center for the Study of Democratic Institutions for the Center's Study of the Political Process. Since 1959, he has been a full-time member of the Center's staff.

In 1962, Wheeler achieved great notoriety when he collaborated with the late Eugene Burdick in writing *Fail-Safe*, a book which achieved sales in the millions in hard-cover and paperback format. It was a Book-of-the-Month Club selection and later became a highly profitable motion picture. *Fail-Safe* had as its basic theme the inevitability of accidental nuclear warfare and the danger of such warfare being critical as of 1962. The book was not presented as science fiction but rather as the truth.

The most perceptive criticism of *Fail-Safe* has been presented by Sidney Hook in a *New Leader* book review (December 10, 1962) and in his own book *The Fail-Safe Fallacy*, published in 1963. Wheeler and Burdick presented a situation wherein the United States retaliatory bombing system became totally disorganized, causing six United States bombers to make a nuclear attack which destroyed Moscow. In atonement, the President of the United States ordered American bombers to demolish New York City. The full context of *Fail-Safe* was a scaremongering plea for disarmament and appeasement with the Soviet Union, along with an intellectually dishonest representation of the safeguards prepared by the American military to prevent accidental nuclear warfare. A few of Dr. Hook's observations are pertinent: (1) "It [*Fail-Safe*] is an emotionally surcharged political tract designed to prove that the greatest danger to the survival of free institutions in the world today is our defense system." (2) "To the extent that this [the inevitability of accidental nuclear warfare] is believed, it is certain to encourage the appeasement of Nikita Khrushchev, portrayed by the authors as a man of noble character and profound thought." (3) "The authors present Khrushchev as a man of tragic dimensions, more sinned against than sinning, reluctant to demand a cruel and gratuitous price for an accident which he agrees is no one's fault, a humanist and a reflective critic of Bolshevik Leninism. . . . He leaves the stage a philosopher pledged to reasonable compromise." (4) "*Fail-Safe* is also morally objectionable because of the colors in which it portrays the civilian experts on how to survive war if it is forced on us . . . by describing them as money-hungry monsters, their entire intellectual activity in behalf of a free society is called into question."

Since he achieved so much success as co-author of *Fail-Safe*, Wheeler has emerged as one of the most important academicians of the left. His writings have appeared in *Nation* magazine, the *Bulletin for Atomic Scientists*, and *Sat-*

urday Review, and he is the author of occasional papers published by the Center for the Study of Democratic Institutions.

In 1965, Wheeler became a sponsor and faculty member of the New Left School in Los Angeles. (Others connected with the NLS included Southern California's Communist Party Chairman Dorothy Healey; veteran Communist fronter Reverend Stephen Fritchman; "civil rights" agitators Jimmy Garrett of the Student Nonviolent Coordinating Committee and Don Smith of the Congress of Racial Equality; and, two of Wheeler's colleagues from the staff of the Center for the Study of Democratic Institutions, Richard Lichtman and Irving Lauchs.) From the beginning, the New Left School was obviously Marxist, but Wheeler explained that, as a "middle-aged liberal," his interest in the Marxist organization was "academic" rather than "activist." He said that he would teach a course in the history of radicalism and admitted his realization that the organizers of the NLS hoped it would become a headquarters for a variety of radical and/or Marxist protests, demonstrations, and propaganda activities.

In 1966, at a New Left conference in Los Angeles, Wheeler led a group which declared in a manifesto: "We call upon the unrepresented, the exploited, the alienated and the manipulated to join in the creation of a new politics dedicated to participatory democracy, to the elimination of imperialism, domestic and foreign, to the building of humanitarian communities, to insure security of mind and body to the enoblement of the conditions of life."

Elsewhere in his writings, Wheeler has made it clear that by "participatory democracy," he means planned socialism ("Many people equate planning with socialism. I believe this is a sound impulse.") And he has called for fundamental alterations of the Constitution of the United States to make national planning for a Socialist America a more feasible function of the federal government. (The distinguished political analyst Alice Widener has remarked on the striking similarities between Wheeler's blueprint for "participatory democracy" and Communist leader William Z. Foster's *Toward a Soviet America.*)

True to Marxian precepts, Wheeler's advocacy of socialism is not confined to national boundaries. The whole world, according to him, is beset by the problem of rich nations versus poor nations — a problem that can be solved only with the realization of "world ownership" of communication facilities, capital, and natural resources.

WILLIAM A. WIELAND was born on November 17, 1907 in New York City, son of Katherine Dooley and William Wieland. (When William was eight years of age, his widowed mother married Manuel Ralph Montenegro.) He married Lee Kukowska.

Wieland attended high school (1922-1923) in Cedarhurst, New York. In 1924 and 1925, he attended Classon Point Military Academy in Oakdale, New York. In 1925 and 1926, he attended Ruston Academy in Havana. (His stepfather and mother had moved to Cuba a few years earlier.) In 1926 and 1927, he studied at Villanova College in Pennsylvania. In September, 1927, he enlisted in the U.S. Army but in December, 1928 he purchased his discharge.

From 1928 until 1937, Wieland lived in Havana and, successively, he worked for the Morro Castle Supply Company, the General Electric Company, and the

Cuban Electric company. In 1932, he joined the *Havana Post,* working first as a reporter, and then becoming an editor in 1933. While employed by the *Post,* Wieland also worked for the Hearst Agencies, International News Service and Universal News Service. In 1935, the owner of the *Post* fired Wieland, accusing him of filching items from the Associated Press files. Shortly thereafter, Wieland began working for the Havas News Agency (French). In 1936, he rejoined the *Havana Post* as an editor and, in that same year, he left the employ of Havas. In June, 1937, he left the *Havana Post* and went to Washington, D.C. to work for the Associated Press. He remained with AP until 1941, and worked as a correspondent in Washington and New York.

In June, 1941, Wieland was called by Michael J. McDermott and asked to work for the State Department. (McDermott, at that time, was in charge of the State Department's Press and Public Relations Bureau. Wieland would later testify under oath that he first met McDermott in 1937 and that in 1940 he had discussed with McDermott the possibility of State Department employment.) Wieland accepted a position as a press attaché. He took a six-month leave of absence from AP, extended the leave at least twice, but actually remained with the State Department until 1968. Wieland began his work in the Foreign Service Auxiliary at an annual salary of $7,000 — an increase of $3,880 from his AP salary.

Wieland was sworn into service on June 2, 1941 but he did not fill out his State Department employment application until June 4 of that year. Twenty years later the Senate Internal Security Subcommittee found that Wieland had falsified his application in several ways.

Although he was supposed to list every occupation he had had, Wieland mentioned only his employment with the *Havana Post* and the Associated Press. He failed to state the reasons for leaving his places of employment and especially did not mention that he had been fired from the *Havana Post* because he had pirated the Associated Press files. And, although technically not instructed to do so, Wieland failed to mention any aliases he had used. (In 1947, when he filled out another form which did require an enumeration of aliases, he again failed to mention any. But, in sworn testimony, Wieland did admit that he had used the name William Arthur Montenegro in Havana. In 1960, Nathaniel Weyl, writing in his *Red Star Over Cuba,* stated as an unequivocal fact that "as a young man in Cuba, Wieland was associated with the terrorist ABC [revolutionary] organization. At that time he operated under the name of Guillermo Arturo Montenegro." As a Communist, Weyl — in 1932 and 1933 — had had direct dealings with the ABC leaders. Weyl was not a run-of-the-mill Communist. He belonged to the same Communist Party cell as Alger Hiss and, in the Party, Weyl's specific duties were involved with Latin American activities and with the top leaders of Cuba's Communist Party.)

Amid the circumstances of Wieland's initial employment with the State Department was his long-time friendship with Sumner Welles whose prominence and influence in the Roosevelt Administration's diplomatic corps was accentuated by his notorious and scandalous conduct as a homosexual. Wieland first met Welles in Havana in 1934. Although Wieland testified that he knew Welles mainly through their professional contacts and that their social relationship was quite limited, Wieland was known in

Havana as Welles' fair-haired boy. Whatever the extent of their relationship, the
fact remains that Wieland did admit that
Welles suggested in 1940 that it would
be a good idea for Wieland to enter State
Department service. From a financial
standpoint, if nothing else, it was a good
idea for Wieland whose income was more
than doubled by the move.

From 1941 until 1946, Wieland was
stationed at the U.S. Embassy in Rio de
Janeiro, where he served under Ambassadors Jefferson Caffrey, Adolf Berle, William Pawley, and Herschel Johnson. In
1945, Wieland took written and oral
tests to become a careerist in the Foreign
Service. (Wieland had been recommended for such a career by Herschel
Johnson whose ambassadorial career was
marred by his reputation as a homosexual. In 1961, Wieland was interrogated as
to whether he ever had to deal with the
problem of homosexuality in any way,
and he replied in the negative even
though two of his earliest State Department associates — Welles and Johnson —
were notorious as homosexuals.)

In October, 1946, Wieland received
his first appointment as a careerist in the
Foreign Service. His salary was $4,400 a
year, a considerable reduction from the
$7,000 a year he had been paid since
1941. But the initial monetary sacrifice
would reap dividends for Wieland within
a few years as promotions and salary
increases came rapidly his way in the
Latin American division of the State
Department. (At that time, the division
had become a special bailiwick for Communist agents. In 1945 and 1946,
Maurice Halperin was the divisional head
and he was successor to Lawrence Duggan. Halperin later fled the country to
work directly for his Soviet bosses.
Duggan, while federal investigators were
unraveling his espionage career, went to

his death out a window. He jumped or
was pushed.

In 1946, Wieland was appointed as
third secretary and vice consul at the
U.S. Embassy in Rio de Janeiro. Within a
month, he was transferred in the same
positions to Bogota, Columbia. From
1947 until 1949, he was second secretary and vice-consul at Bogota and, in
1949, became consul. It was in Bogota
that Wieland was a witness to Fidel
Castro's Communist activities in the uprising of 1948. Castro played such a
prominent part in the uprising that he
became unmistakably identified as a
Communist in reports which circulated
throughout the State Department, especially in its Latin American division.
(After Castro came to power, Wieland
suffered extraordinary lapses of memory
when interrogated as to the numerous
reports of Castro's activities which he
had seen in the circumstances surrounding the Bogotazo.)

In 1949, Wieland moved on to the
U.S. Embassy in San Salvador as consul.
From 1951 until 1953, he was consul in
Rio de Janeiro and, in 1954 and 1955,
he was consul in Quito, Ecuador. From
1955 until 1957, he was counselor to the
U.S. Embassy in Quito. In 1957, he was
assigned to Washington, D.C. as Special
Assistant for Public Affairs in the State
Department's Office of Inter-American
Affairs. Within three months, he became
Director of the Office of Middle Ameri-
can (Caribbean-Mexican) Affairs — a
position he held until 1960.

In 1957, shortly after Wieland took
over the Caribbean desk, Fidel Castro
and his Communist colleagues began to
apply pressure on the State Department
to follow a "hands-off" policy toward
Castro's revolutionary ambitions and,
above all else, to stop sending arms to
the legitimate Cuban regime of Fulgen-

cio Batista – a regime, by the way, for which Sumner Welles, Wieland's friend and sponsor, had a pathological hatred. On November 21, 1957, Wieland contributed to a position paper excoriating the alleged terrorism of the Batista government. On December 19, 1957, Wieland prepared "policy recommendations for restoration of normalcy in Cuba," the most important of which was that arms be withheld from Batista. In March, 1958, the State Department followed the Wieland-Castro recommendations and, in direct violation of existing agreements, U.S. arms-shipments to Batista were halted. Nine months later, Castro took over Cuba. Within a week of the Communist coup, the United States extended diplomatic recognition to the Castro regime – a move recommended by Wieland, who described Castro to his State Department colleagues as the leader of a group "oriented primarily toward moderation and the establishment of a prosperous, democratic Cuba with an honest government."

Wieland's strenuous and successful efforts to impose Castro's Communist tyranny upon Cuba did not go unnoticed. A former U.S. Ambassador to Cuba, Earl E.T. Smith, in testimony before the Senate Internal Security Subcommittee in 1960, portrayed Wieland as a Castro idolator. Smith's testimony was supplemented and corroborated by the testimony of former Ambassadors Arthur Gardner, William D. Pawley, and Robert C. Hill. But long before these individuals testified as to their personal experiences and observations of Wieland as a Castro booster and apologist, FBI agents and State Department security officials had been investigating Wieland's ideological sympathies. There had even been some efforts to fire Wieland. But during the Eisenhower Administration,

Undersecretary of State C. Douglas Dillon reasoned that if Wieland were fired, the Republican Party might suffer politically from a resulting scandal. Dillon felt it would be wise to send Wieland to an overseas post but State Department officials decided against this, and instead, moved Wieland away from the Caribbean desk and sent him to the Foreign Service School to study German, in preparation for a proposed assignment to Zurich, Switzerland.

In September, 1961, Wieland completed his studies of German and was assigned as Consul to Bremen – not Zurich. But before he had a chance to take up his new assignment, he was given a temporary position in the State Department's Office of Management. This occurred in October, 1961 and by that time Wieland had been interrogated at length on two occasions by the Senate Internal Security Subcommittee.

At a news conference on January 24, 1962, reporter Sarah McLendon attempted to ask President John F. Kennedy about Wieland. She characterized Wieland as a security risk who was helping to reorganize the Office of Security in the State Department. Mr. Kennedy raged at Mrs. McLendon and said that he and Secretary of State Rusk had full confidence in Wieland's character and abilities. A few weeks after the Kennedy-McLendon confrontation, Wieland was provided shelter and obscurity in the office of William J. Crockett, the State Department's Deputy Undersecretary of State for Administration. (Crockett, at that time, was allied with Abba Schwartz, the State Department's Administrator for Security and Consular Affairs, in an effort to get rid of Miss Frances Knight, the vigorous anti-Communist head of the Passport Office. Crockett was simultaneously wielding an administrative hatchet against Otto Otepka. Otepka, as a security officer in the State Department, had dug deeply into Wieland's record and had testified truthfully before the Senate Internal Security Subcommittee about the lack of security in the State Department. Crockett's protection of Wieland would later be hailed by leftwing columnist Carl Rowan: "When a lot of people ran from Wieland as though he were contaminated, Crockett gave him a job in his office. He then saw that Wieland got full benefit of every feasible piece of personnel and administrative machinery in an effort to clear his name.")

President Kennedy's highly emotional defense of Wieland caused the Senate Internal Security Subcommittee to recall him for further testimony. And, on October 16, 1962, the SISS released a report on Wieland which — to say the least — was highly critical of Wieland's activities and confirmed the worst criticisms which had been leveled by more than a hundred witnesses heard by the SISS in its several hearings on Wieland. (Among other items, the SISS reported that there was substantial evidence that Wieland's State Department files had been tampered with after President Kennedy had defended him.)

In February, 1964, Wieland was named as an administrative specialist in the State Department. Less than a month later, a three-man panel (retired Air Force Brigadier General Milton Summerfelt; former president of the Export-Import Bank Samuel Waugh; former Ambassador William J. Sebald) was hand-picked by the State Department to investigate Wieland. Within nine days, the panel concluded that Wieland should be cleared of any and all charges that he might be a security risk. Then Wieland's protector, William J. Crockett, submit-

ted the panel's report to the State Department's own Personnel Review Board and the Special Investigations Board of the Office of Security (Otepka was gone by this time) and, predictably, Wieland received a complete cost of whitewash. However, nothing was issued for public consumption until July, 1965, when the State Department deliberately released news of Wieland's "clearance" by Crockett's stooges on the same day that the SISS issued its own report, "The Wieland Case Updated." The State Department release claimed that its clearance of Wieland was concurred in by the FBI — an absolute lie which was put to rest immediately by FBI Director J. Edgar Hoover. On the other hand, the SISS report reaffirmed the damaging conclusions of the SISS's 1962 report on Wieland. But, on the day after the State Department and the SISS releases were issued, Wieland was assigned as counsel for consular affairs to Canberra, Australia. On October 10, 1965, he became consul general in Melbourne, Australia with a salary in excess of $24,000. In February, 1968, it was reported that Wieland had finally retired from the Foreign Service and was living in Hollywood, Maryland.

JEROME B. WIESNER was born on May 30, 1915 in Detroit, Michigan, son of Ida Friedman and Joseph Wiesner. He married Laya Wainger. He is an alumnus of the University of Michigan (B.S., 1937; M.S., 1940; Ph.D., 1950).

From 1937 until 1940, while in pursuit of his master's degree at Michigan, Wiesner was associate director of the University's broadcasting service and taught an undergraduate course in broadcasting techniques.

From 1940 until 1942, Wiesner was chief engineer of the Library of Congress. In these years, he spent most of his time traveling throughout the South as part of a team recording songs and folklore of the region. From 1942 until 1945, he was an electrical engineer in the Massachusetts Institute of Technology radiation laboratory. He held the same position, in 1945 and 1946, at the University of California's Los Alamos laboratory.

In 1946, Wiesner became a member of the faculty at MIT. In 1950, he became a professor of electrical engineering and, from 1949 until 1964, he served as associate director and director, successively, at the Institute's research laboratory of electronics. In 1964, Wiesner became dean of science and, in 1966, was named provost of MIT.

In 1958, Wiesner attended the Second Pugwash Conference at Lac Beauport, Canada. The Pugwash Conferences had been initiated by Communists and prominent fellow travelers for the purposes of selling out United States security and advancing the world conquest designs of international Communism.

In 1960, President-elect John F. Kennedy sent Wiesner and his MIT colleague Walt W. Rostow to the Sixth Pugwash Conference, being held in Moscow. (At that time, Rostow was on the staff of MIT's Center for International Study which was nothing less than a Central Intelligence Agency center. In Moscow, Rostow held a secret conference with the Soviet Union's First Deputy Minister Vasily V. Kuznetsox. Kuznetsov proposed that the United States curtail its first-strike weapons, including the B-70 Bomber. Such a move by the Americans, according to Kuznetsov, "would ease world tensions." Rostow became Kennedy's adviser for National Security Affairs and, within four months of the Rostow-Kuznetsov conference, Kennedy ordered the scrapping of all United States first-strike weapons.)

In Moscow, Wiesner proved to be the ideal partner for Rostow by telling the Soviet leaders what they wanted to hear. (Of course, neither Rostow nor Wiesner had any right to speak on behalf of the United States Government, but it was obvious that they were going to be influential members of the incoming Administration.)

Despite a total lack of experience in military matters or diplomacy, Wiesner was not a bit bashful in offering his advice to the Soviet leaders as to how they might get the United States to disarm. (The closest that Wiesner had come to the military was his membership on the U.S. Army's science advisory committee from 1956 to 1960, but this was only a part-time affiliation since Wiesner was busily directing MIT's electronics research laboratory in this period.) Wiesner, in a speech to the Pugwashers, said that he believed "in the importance of eliminating all military power from the arsenals of independent nations as rapidly as feasible." But he also believed that it would be "extremely difficult to achieve this goal in one mighty agreement and that it may be necessary to reach it through a series of steps in which the total available military force is successively reduced."

First steps toward Wiesner's disarmament utopia would naturally be taken by the United States. He advocated a system of mutual deterrence which would mean a parity of strategic power between the United States and the Soviet Union. Since the United States was obviously more powerful than the Soviet Union, Wiesner advocated that the United States initiate the scrapping of manned bombers and the abolition of further nuclear weapons tests and devel-

589

opment. And, in the diplomatic realm, the United States should reach an agreement with the Soviet Union to prohibit development of anti-missile systems.

The Soviet leaders probably thought that Wiesner was too good to be true as he advised them to build up their nuclear defensive strength to protect the Soviet Union from an American nuclear first-strike attack (the very type of attack which had been forsworn in United States policy). Wiesner further advised the Soviet leaders to protect their missile sites against American attacks – otherwise they would not be in a position to retaliate against the United States. For the United States, Wiesner advised that Americans not deploy an anti-missile system, lest the mutuality of deterrence would be imbalanced in favor of the United States. (During the Kennedy Administration, Wiesner implemented his 1960 advice by persuading President Kennedy to stop deployment of the Nike-Zeus missile and to dismantle most of the DEW [Distant Early Warning] Line stations which were built to alert the United States and Canada to Soviet attacks.)

General Thomas A. Lane has described Wiesner and his breed as "academicians and pacifists playing at peace." A *Saturday Review* (December 10, 1960) story on Wiesner said that he "looks upon arms control as almost a crusade" and although "any arms agreement with the Soviets may carry calculated risks, science must develop such an overwhelming case in support of the soundness of the calculated risk philosophy, that the fearful politician will have nothing left to hide behind."

Unfortunately, Wiesner did more than play with peace – he trifled with it as his "calculated risk philosophy" became the hallmark of the Kennedy Administra-

tion. Wiesner, the electrical engineer, who believed that Soviet Union leaders seem "to be quite reasonable," would successfully promote his disarmament mania as the keystone of U.S. diplomacy and military strategy.

In 1961, while he retained his ties with MIT, Wiesner became a special assistant to President Kennedy on science and technology and chairman of the President's science advisory committee. In a friendly article in the *New York Times* (September 3, 1961), Wiesner's position in the Kennedy Administration was described as "the top planner, arbitrator and counselor of scientific policy within the Government, and thus, throughout the scientific community at large . . . . Wiesner oversees the operations of all scientifically oriented agencies, such as the Defense Department, Atomic Energy Commission and National Science Foundation . . . .

"[He] operates behind a wall of White House secrecy, somewhat to the dismay of Congress which would like to be privy to his scientific policy advice . . . .

"Before joining the Administration, Wiesner made no secret of his belief that the United States at times had been almost as much to blame as the Soviet Union for blocking agreement on arms-control measures . . . . "

The *Times* certainly did not exaggerate Wiesner's influence upon the Kennedy Administration. In September, 1963 the U.S., by a vote of 80 to 19, approved the "limited" Moscow Nuclear Test Ban Treaty – a treaty which, even the State Department admits, has been violated by the Soviet Union. Wiesner's work for disarmament, however, was not completed.

In June, 1964, Wiesner took part in a disarmament conference, sponsored by the American Academy of Arts and

Sciences and the Soviet Academy of Sciences. The American conferees were supported by a $325,000 grant from the Ford Foundation. The conference was merely an offshoot of the Pugwash Conferences and most of the participants were veteran Pugwashers. (Wiesner, who attended the Pugwash Conferences in 1958 and 1960, presented a paper to be read at the 1961 conference and was scheduled to attend the 1964 conference.) The June, 1964 conference was held in Dedham, Massachusetts and at Harvard University where the American and Soviet participants discussed further measures of arms control. Although none of the Americans were officially designated representatives of the government, their participation was approved by the White House, State Department, and the Arms Control and Disarmament Agency. If there had been any doubt on that score, it was resolved in October, 1964, when Wiesner was commissioned by President Lyndon Johnson to be chairman of a committee on Arms Control and Disarmament for the 1965 White House Conference on International Cooperation.

The most widely publicized report to come out of that conference was the one from Wiesner's committee — a report which became popularly known as the Wiesner-Gilpatric Report (Roswell Gilpatric had been a Deputy Secretary of Defense in the Kennedy Administration). Wiesner's penchant for appeasement was evident throughout the amazing recommendations made in the Report.

The United States, said the Report, should "at a minimum" continue "to seek coordinated methods, with or without formal agreements, to destroy weapons deemed obsolete or superfluous ... Most generally, we consider such deeper cuts in strategic inventories — on the order of a one-third cut — to be worth serious consideration." The Wiesner team favored the decimation of the United States strategic weapons inventory as a unilateral measure if necessary but if an agreement was made with the Soviet Union, then the Wiesner team would not insist upon inspection provisions.

The Wiesner-Gilpatric Report recommended that the United States "take the lead in seeking a non-aggression pact between NATO and the Warsaw Treaty Organizations" — which, of course, would stamp the United States seal of approval on the Soviet captivity of Eastern Europe. And, to resolve all doubts that appeasement was the order of the day, the Report also recommended that all American troops be withdrawn from Central Europe — a longtime desire of the Soviet leaders.

Red China was not neglected. The Wiesner-Gilpatric Report advised President Johnson to negotiate directly with the Chinese Communists on disarmament and to "support suitable initiatives" to gain United Nations membership for Red China.

Wiesner's old preoccupation with an anti-missile system also came to the fore. The Report strongly urged that the United States not deploy its defensive missile system for at least three years even if the Soviet Union refused to go along with such a moratorium. And if the moratorium was successively negotiated with the Soviet Union, the United States should not insist upon an inspection system. (Wiesner evidently held to his belief that the Soviet Union's leaders seemed "to be quite reasonable.") Even the *Washington Star*, which has moved steadily leftward in recent years, commented: "What baffles us ... is the Wiesner group's bland faith in the thought that an agreement with the Kremlin — explicit or tacit — is a guarantee of anything."

Other proposals made by the Wiesner-Gilpatric team were equally outrageous and brazen — so much so that Lyndon Johnson, the self-anointed prince of peace, showed little enthusiasm over Wiesner's handiwork. But Wiesner has proven to be indefatigable in his quest for appeasement through disarmament.

In 1966, Wiesner spoke on behalf of the Institute for Policy Studies which was conducting brainwashing sessions for congressional assistants by exposing them to the disarmament fanaticism of Seymour Melman, Marcus Raskin, and Arthur Waskow. If Wiesner couldn't work through the White House, perhaps Congress would buy his bill of goods. Then, on January 22, 1967, Sunday newspapers throughout the nation carried an extensive article written for the Associated Press by Wiesner. It was a massive effort by Wiesner to have the general public jump on the surrender bandwagon. The same sort of ploy was made on July 10, 1967, when Wiesner held a press conference at New York City's Overseas Press Club. He spoke on behalf of a ban-the-bomb group, the Educational Committee to Halt the Spread of Nuclear Weapons, and he announced that he was presenting an "open letter" to President Johnson. In the "letter" Wiesner urged Johnson to begin immediate negotiations with the Chinese Communists to achieve nuclear arms control and to avoid "another costly and dangerous arms cycle in missile defense." Wiesner could have saved his breath and ink on the latter point. Johnson's Defense Secretary Robert S. McNamara, against the unanimous recommendations of the Joint Chiefs of

Staff, had refused to construct a missile defense system. This is just what the Wiesner-Gilpatric Report of 1965 had advised. (Of course, the Soviet Union began to construct its missile defense system at the very time that the Wiesner-Gilpatric Report was presented to Johnson's White House Conference in 1965.)

Although Wiesner is no longer on the Washington, D.C. scene, he has not kept out of touch. In October, 1967, Wiesner — at his home in Watertown, Massachusetts — was host to a party of individuals who seem never to be very far from the seat of power. The star attraction at the party was Soviet Ambassador Anatoliy Dobrynin whose conversation captivated such well-known guests as Adam Yarmolinsky, formerly of the Defense Department; Richard N. Goodwin, formerly a speech writer for Presidents Kennedy and Johnson and author of the Alliance for Progress Act; Leona Baumgartner, former Assistant Secretary of State in the foreign aid program; former U.S. Senator Maurine Neuberger; Robert Manning, editor of *Atlantic Monthly* magazine and a former Asssistant Secretary of State for Public Affairs; Paul Doty of the Harvard University faculty and a veteran of at least six Pugwash Conferences; and, President Howard Johnson of MIT. Wiesner was renewing his friendship with Ambassador Dobrynin — a friendship which began when Wiesner was one of the three American negotiators (the others were Ambassador Averell Harriman and Carl Kaysen, director of the Institute for Advanced Studies) who concluded the 1963 Moscow Nuclear Test Ban Treaty.

ROY WILKINS was born on August 30, 1901 in St. Louis, Missouri, son of Mayfield Edmonson and William Wilkins. He married Aminda Badeau. He is an an important factor in bringing the plight of the Negro people, along with other underprivileged groups, more sharply to the attention of those parties which have been in power. You have asked me my attitude toward the coming Communist convention and of the work of the Communist Party, though I myself can't sincerely embrace Communism as my conviction. Nevertheless, there is no doubt in my mind that the program and demands of the Communists have been emboldened by the basic and basically right demands put forth."

Wilkins may not have embraced Communism as his conviction but he certainly contributed to its strength from his high-ranking position on the NAACP's secretariat. In 1937, he spoke for the International Labor Defense, the American section of the International Red Aid which had its headquarters in Moscow. The International Labor Defense, as the legal arm of the Communist Party, was nothing less than part of an international network of organizations for the defense of Communist lawbreakers. Also, in 1937, he sponsored a joint meeting of the subversive and Communist American League against War and Fascism and the Communist-controlled American Friends of the Chinese People. And, in 1937, he attended the congress of the American League for Peace and Democracy, a subversive and Communist organization formed to succeed the American League against War and Fascism in an effort to create public sentiment on behalf of a foreign policy adapted to the interests of the Soviet Union.

In 1938, Wilkins was on the executive board of the Medical Bureau and North American Committee to Aid Spanish Democracy. The Communist Party had thrown itself wholeheartedly into the campaign for support of the Spanish

alumnus of the University of Minnesota (A.B., 1923).

From 1923 until 1931, Wilkins was managing editor of the *Kansas City* (Mo.) *Call,* a Negro weekly. He had gained some experience in journalism during his college days as night editor of the university newspaper and as editor of the *St. Paul Appeal,* a Negro weekly.

In 1931, Wilkins began his career on the staff of the National Association for the Advancement of Colored People (he had been secretary of a local NAACP chapter while at the University of Minnesota). For eighteen years, he was assistant executive secretary of the NAACP. For fifteen of those years, he also served as editor of the NAACP's official publication *The Crisis.* In 1949 and 1950, he was acting executive secretary of the NAACP and, in 1950, he was also the administrator of internal affairs for the organization. Since 1955, he has been the NAACP's executive secretary.

In recent years, Wilkins has taken great pains to create an image of himself as a responsible moderate in the area of civil rights. He eschews black power militancy, never directly encourages violence, and carefully cultivates the "ins" (he has been a very close confidant of Presidents John F. Kennedy and Lyndon B. Johnson).

There was a time, however, when Wilkins was not too worried about his image. In 1936, at a time when Franklin and Eleanor Roosevelt could not have been more patronizing toward Negroes, Wilkins was proving to be most grateful to the Communists, as he said: "The greatest significance undoubtedly attends the 1936 convention of the Communist Party. It must be patent to anyone who has kept track of the news that the political left-wing – and especially the Communist program – has been

Loyalist cause, recruiting men and organizing multifarious so-called relief organizations such as the Medical Bureau. Also, in 1938, he sponsored the Conference on Pan-American Democracy, a Communist front which defeated Luiz Carlos Prestes, a Brazilian Communist leader and former member of the executive committee of the Communist International.

In 1939, Wilkins was a speaker at the New York State convention of the Workers Alliance, a subversive and Communist organization.

In 1942, Wilkins was a member of the International Juridical Association, an organization which actively defended Communists and consistently followed the Communist Party line.

In 1944, Wilkins was a supporter of the International Workers Order, one of the strongest Communist organizations.

In 1949, Wilkins spoke before the Physician's Forum which was organized primarily by the Communist Party. Also, in 1949, the *Daily Worker* quoted Wilkins as telling a press conference that he had voted for Benjamin J. Davis, a national leader of the Communist Party, in the previous New York City election.

After 1949, Wilkins became somewhat more discreet in his public associations. He did make one slip, however, in 1965 when *Freedomways,* a Communist-supported Negro quarterly, memorialized W.E.B. DuBois, the famous Negro Communist. Wilkins submitted his tribute to DuBois, which was published along with tributes from such Communists as Paul Robeson, Herbert Aptheker, and James E. Jackson.

Wilkins' dubious associations and affiliations have not made him *persona non grata* in government circles. In 1941, he was a consultant to the War Board on the training and placement of Negroes in the armed forces. In 1945, he was a consultant to the U.S. delegation at the United Nations' organizing conference in San Francisco. In 1967, he was appointed by President Lyndon Johnson to be a member of the National Advisory Commission on Civil Disorders. In 1968, he was chairman of the U.S. delegation at the International Conference on Human Rights in Tehran, Iran.

Perhaps the highlight of Wilkins' career came in March, 1967 when he received the annual Freedom House Award. Secretary of State Dean Rusk, who attended the function, read a message from Lyndon Johnson who called Wilkins "one of the true leaders, not only of our time, but of all time . . . a unique American whose contributions transcend the boundaries of both time and territory."

Wilkins is undoubtedly one of the suavest spokesmen for Negroes in the civil rights area. He does preach nonviolence as a tactic, but at the same time, lards his speeches with references to police brutality and lynching and three-hundred-years-of-deprivation — just enough to keep militants from rejecting him. As for riots, Wilkins is extremely careful never to blame Negroes for instigating them and he characterizes riots as a "grass roots revolt" against conditions imposed upon Negroes. He never hints that anarchists, Communists, and black revolutionaries are conspiring to cause riots. And whatever solutions he offers to Negroes' problems inevitably entails large expenditures of money by the federal government.

Aside from civil rights, Wilkins has associated himself with the leftwing-pacifist Women's International League for Peace and Freedom. In 1964, he urged the U.S. Government to withdraw support from the anti-Communist regime of Moise Tshombe in the Congo's Katanga Province.

Wilkins has held high office in the American Civil Liberties Union. In 1964, he was a member of the National Council for Civic Responsibility, an election year's drive by the Democratic Party against anti-Communists. The NCCR was inspired by Walter Reuther and led by the original "modern" Republican Arthur Larson. In 1966, Wilkins became a member of the Institute for American Democracy, a revival of Larson's NCCR and an elite representative group of leftists who specialized in anti-anti-Communist activities and utterances.

In 1964, Wilkins attained an excellent forum for his soft-sell agitation when he began to write a weekly column for the *Des Moines Register and Tribune Syndicate*. His ·writings, however, did not dwell upon civil rights as he frequently expounded on the political virtues of liberals and on the vices of conservatives and anti-Communists. But to his credit, his column has never reached the depths he managed in 1963, when he commented on the assassination of President Kennedy: "Quite properly, the perceptive among us point the finger at the vocal vermin, the poison pen 'patriots,' the suave salesmen of superiority, the analyzing anesthetists and the hawkers of hate. These people, not the miserable Oswald, slew John Fitzgerald Kennedy."

G. MENNEN WILLIAMS was born on February 23, 1911 in Detroit, son of Elma Mennen and Henry Williams. He married Nancy Quirk. He is an alumnus of Princeton University (A.B., 1933) and the University of Michigan (J.D., 1936).

From 1936 until 1938, Williams was an attorney for the Social Security Board in Washington, D.C. In 1938 and 1939, he was an assistant to Michigan's Attorney General. From 1939 until 1941, he was in the U.S. Department of Justice, serving, successively, as an executive assistant to the Attorney General, executive assistant to the Department's general counsel, and member of the Department's criminal division. In 1946 and 1947, he was deputy director of the Office of Price Administration in Michigan. In 1947 and 1948 he was a liquor control commissioner in Michigan.

While at Princeton, Williams was president of the Young Republicans Club. He became a Democrat during his years at the University of Michigan. In 1948, as a Democrat, he was elected Governor of Michigan. He was re-elected to that office five consecutive times. In 1960, when he did not seek a seventh gubernatorial term, he was appointed by President John Kennedy to be Assistant Secretary of State for African Affairs, a newly created post.

As Governor of Michigan from 1949 until 1961, Williams was merely a stooge for Walter Reuther. He was completely beholden to the United Auto Workers and the rest of organized labor for his office. His extravagant administration and his bias for labor endeared him to the Americans for Democratic Action. (Williams' further liberal credentials include his membership in the radical United World Federalists, his support of the leftwing-pacifist National Committee for a Sane Nuclear Policy, and his utter commitment ot the United Nations. He has also been a longtime advocate of Red China's admission to United Nations membership.)

As Assistant Secretary for African Affairs, Williams was a diplomatic disaster for the United States and a boon to the Communists. Within a few weeks of his appointment, he declared that U.S. policy was "Africa for the Africans" —

the very slogan used by black African revolutionaries, who were being supported by Communists from the Soviet Union and Red China.

Once Williams began to travel throughout Africa, he demonstrated a strong penchant for fawning over Communist leaders: Algeria's Ben Bella, Kenya's Jomo Kenyatta, Ghana's Kwame Nkrumah, and Guinea's Sékou Touré. (In 1962, Williams made very strong recommendations for U.S. aid to Touré, who, in 1961, had been given the Lenin "Peace" Prize, an award reserved for those who have made substantive contributions to the cause of international Communism.) In defiance of overwhelming evidence, Williams declared unequivocally, in 1962, that, "No African leader is going to become a Communist."

Whereas he had nothing but kind words and apologies for Communist and pro-Communist leaders in Africa, Williams was bitterly critical of the Spanish and Portuguese in Africa, Rhodesia, South Africa, and the Tsombe regime in the Congo's Katanga Province — all of which were demonstrably anti-Communist.

During his several extended trips throughout Africa, Williams also played the role of a buffoon for the amusement of his hosts but to the embarrassment of the United States.

In 1966, Williams resigned his State Department job to campaign for the U.S. Senate seat held by Republican Robert Griffin. Williams was defeated and went into semi-retirement. Inexplicably, in 1968, President Lyndon Johnson appointed Williams to be U.S. Ambassador to the Philippines.

WILLIAM A. WILLIAMS was born on June 12, 1921 in Atlantic, Iowa, son of Mildred Appleman and William Williams. He is an alumnus of the United States Naval Academy (B.S., 1944), the University of Leeds in England, and the University of Wisconsin (M.A., 1948; Ph.D., 1950).

Prior to 1957, Williams taught history at Washington and Jefferson College, Bard College, Ohio State University, and the University of Oregon. Since 1957, he has been on the faculty of the University of Wisconsin where he is a professor of history. He has been an activist in the "civil rights" movement and in Socialist politics. He has been the recipient of grants from the Ford Foundation, the Fund for Social Analysis ("Communist propaganda organization"), the Louis B. Rabinowitz Foundation, and the University of Wisconsin Graduate Research Committee.

Williams is the author of *American-Russian Relations, 1784-1947; The Shaping of American Diplomacy, 1763-1955; The Tragedy of American Diplomacy; The Contours of American History; The United States, Cuba and Castro;* and *The Great Evasion.* He has been a contributor to *The Nation* and *Commentary* magazines, as well as *Monthly Review* ("pro-Communist" and "pro-Soviet") and *New World Review* ("subversive").

The "pro-Communist" and "pro-Soviet" periodical *Monthly Review* recommended as a gift book Williams' *The United States, Cuba and Castro,* which is understandable since the book is nothing short of pro-Castro propaganda.

Alger Hiss, writing in the *National Guardian* of March 12, 1962, heaped praises on Williams' *The Contours of American History,* which was published by the firm of Marzani and Munsell, which publishes pro-Communist literature.

In a review of Williams' *The Great Evasion,* sociology professor Don Martindale of the University of Minnesota said that it "is not a study in social science nor an essay in social and cultural history, but a missionary pamphlet by a self-appointed apologist of the secular theology of Marxism. It rests upon faith in the sainthood of Marx as the infallible prophet of contemporary history."

Williams has been affiliated with the National Committee of the American Forum for Socialist Education (under Communist "inspiration and domination"); the Emergency Civil Liberties Committee ("Communist front" — "subversive"); and, the National Committee to Secure Justice for Morton Sobell ("Communist campaign"). He has petitioned to abolish the House Committee on Un-American Activities.

In 1965, Williams was a member of the Inter-University Committee for a Public Hearing on Vietnam, sponsors of the anti-Vietnam "teach-in" movement, which the Communist propaganda apparatus exploited for purely Communist purposes. And he helped to organize and participated in a two-day "teach-in" at the University of Wisconsin.

DAGMAR WILSON was born on January 25, 1916 in New York City, daughter of Marion Ballin and César Saerchinger. She married Christopher Wilson. She is an alumna of University College (London), where she received, in 1936, a diploma in fine arts.

From 1936 until 1939, she was an art teacher in London. In 1940 and 1941, she was an assistant art teacher in the Lincoln School of Teacher's College in New York City. From 1943 until 1946, she was a graphic artist for the co-ordinator for inter-American affairs in the State Department. Since 1946, she has been a free-lance artist and illustrator in Washington, D.C.

In 1961, Mrs. Wilson founded the Women Strike for Peace movement. The alleged circumstances surrounding the birth of WSP have been described in a flattering sketch of Mrs. Wilson (Alvin Shuster's "Close-up of a 'Peace Striker,' " *New York Times* magazine, May 7, 1962), which is used by WSP as promotional literature: "Her crusade is in many ways informal and it started almost casually. The idea came to Mrs. Wilson one day last September while she was sitting with her husband Christopher (an aide at the British Embassy) and some friends in the backyard of her house in Georgetown. They were talking about the jailing in London that day of Bertrand Russell for his part in anti-nuclear-bomb demonstrations.

"I realized this was a man who had worked all his life for peace. He was speaking out for humanity. I called up a few friends and the next thing I knew we had this women's movement. They called their friends. And they in turn called others. And they all wrote letters to friends in other cities."

On November 1, 1961 — less than two months after her back yard inspiration — Mrs. Wilson and her WSP conducted demonstrations in sixty cities across the nation. An estimated 50,000 women marched for disarmament and against the resumption of nuclear testing by the United States. Mrs. Wilson sent letters to Mrs. Nikita Khrushchev and Mrs. John F. Kennedy, both of whom sent sympathetic responses, assuring Mrs. Wilson that their husbands, Dictator Khrushchev and President Kennedy, were working strenuously for peace.

In January, 1962, Mrs. Wilson conducted a demonstration before the White House and President Kennedy gave WSP a tremendous propaganda boost by describing the feminine agitators as "extremely earnest" and "concerned as we all are of the possibility of nuclear war." (On January 15, Mrs. Wilson's group had become officially Women's International Strike for Peace.)

In February, 1962, seventy members of Mrs. Wilson's WISP were invited to the Soviet Union's mission at the United Nations where they spoke to Soviet Ambassador Valerian. A. Zorin.

In April, 1962, Mrs. Wilson led a WISP delegation to Geneva. She was accompanied by Mrs. Cyrus Eaton, wife of the notorious pro-Communist industrialist, and Mrs. Martin Luther King, wife of the racist agitator. The American delegates were joined in Geneva by women from other countries. In Geneva, while the perennial disarmament conference was going on, the WISP group met with the diplomatic missions of the United States and the Soviet Union. And, from Geneva, Mrs. Wilson and her cohorts sent a cable to President Kennedy asking that he give them an American military base near the Soviet Union so that the base could be disarmed and converted into a "cultural exchange center."

Mrs. Wilson and her WISP delegates returned to the United States, very disappointed at not getting the military base. And Mrs. Wilson was critical of the United States as the roadblock to peace: "I believe the Russians want to disarm. They really have everything to gain by disarming. They do not have private money tied up in the armament industry so they won't have the vested interests profiting from the arms race. If they could, they obviously would like to provide more for the material needs of their people."

As for the military base that WISP had sought from President Kennedy, Mrs. Wilson said: "That would really impress them [the Russians]. They are very sensitive about the bases surrounding them. They are aware of our building of military might more and more each day. They think we are getting substantially stronger than they. The base idea is the most obvious. I sensed in Geneva the Russians are intensely fearful and terrified of war."

While U.S.-U.S.S.R. negotiations for a test-ban treaty were underway, Mrs. Wilson considered the United States government to be most unreasonable in its demand that there be inspection sites within the Soviet Union: "There are enough stations. I don't know what kind they are — all over the world able to tell what they're testing. And the Russians don't want us on their territory until we're really disarmed . . . . I think they are diffident to show us their marbles. And I think it is unfair for us to say we want to go in and look at them."

In April, 1962, a WISP group held a vigil outside the White House to protest U.S. atmospheric nuclear testing; in July, another group demonstrated at the Nevada nuclear testing site; and, also in July, Mrs. Wilson led a twelve-member delegation of WISP to Moscow for a two-week visit as guests of the Soviet Women's Committee. In Moscow, the American women appealed to Mrs. Nikita Khrushchev to join them in their anti-nuclear testing protests.

From its very beginnings, WISP was riddled with Communists and Communist-fronters. "At the first big show in California, in front of the Oakland City Hall, on November 1, 1961, 90 women participated. Of these, 32 were recognized as active Communist Party members or members of various pro-Communist organizations. At a rally in

San Francisco's Golden Gate Park in the spring of 1962 there were more than 50 hard-core Communists, pro-Communists and fellow travelers among the 1,200 persons present." (Irene Corbally Kuhn, "Lysistratas of the Bomb," *National Review,* January 5, 1963.)

In his excellent study of leftwing, pacifist groups, Mr. James Drummey (" 'Peace' — A Communist Hoax," *American Opinion,* January, 1965) described how the Communist Party, USA welcomed the advent of WISP: "A unique feature of WISP is its contention that it is not an organization, but rather a movement. Ruth Gage-Colby, international coordinator of WISP, explained this in a speech she delivered to the Moscow World 'Peace' Congress in 1962: "Women's Strike for Peace has not organized. They have no elections, no officers, no dues. They are a network of rapid communication, using telephones, telegrams and group visits to government officials on chartered buses, trains and planes.' The Communists were quick to see the value in setting up fronts as *movements.* They could thus seek to block and impede congressional investigations which would find it more difficult to investigate a Communist front with no formal organization, no officers, no members, and no records. Communist Arnold Johnson claimed that this distinction 'confounded the House Un-American Activities Committee during those dramatic hearings when the peacewomen won the support of the press and the public.' "

The dramatic hearings, as Johnson called them, took place December 11-13, 1962, before the House Committee on Un-American Activities ("Communist Activities in the Peace Movement"). HCUA's announced purpose for the hearings was "to determine the extent of Communist infiltration in peace organizations . . . with special reference to the Women Strike of Peace . . . . " Twelve women, who were among the leaders of the New York branch of WISP, were called to testify. Ten of the twelve women pleaded their constitutional privilege under the Fifth Amendment when asked if they were currently members of the Communist Party. Of the other two women, one flatly refused to say whether she was a Communist; the twelfth woman said that she hadn't been a Communist during the previous five years, but she would not say whether she had agreed at the time she formally left the party to continue supporting its policies and objectives.

Mrs. Wilson's testimony before the HCUA was an exemplary bit of double-talk and evasion. She denied being any kind of leader in WISP. She admitted her role as founder but said that every woman in the movement was a leader, working on her own initiative for the cause of peace. And, although Mrs. Wilson was the only witness at the hearings with no apparent Communist affiliations, she was not the least bit concerned that Communists had moved into the leadership of WISP. For her part, she would do nothing to prevent such a Communist takeover. By her logic, there were no leaders but everyone was a leader. It was all rather vague but there could be no doubt that the leader-less WISP could amass tens of thousands of women in simultaneous demonstrations in scores of cities, shouting the same slogans and brandishing identical picket signs.

The HCUA hearings did not stall the growth of WISP and, by the end of 1963, as they celebrated their second anniversary, the non-leaders of WISP were claiming a membership of 500,000 — all leaders.

In 1963, Mrs. Wilson – along with Russ Nixon, the general manager of the Communist weekly *National Guardian*, and Donna Allen, an active member of WISP – interceded with the State Department to gain entry into the United States for Kaoru Yasui, a prominent Japanese Communist and a recipient of the Lenin "Peace" Prize. The intercession was successful and Yasui visited the United States on a ten-day speaking tour which began in Honolulu in November, 1963, when the notorious red labor leader Harry Bridges held a "stop-work-meeting" to hear Yasui, the head of the pro-Communist Japan Council, speak against A and H-Bombs.

In 1964, the House Committee on Un-American Activities, which – at that time – was charged with the responsibility of surveillance over the McCarran-Walter Immigration Act of 1952, investigated the visit of Communist Yasui as part of a study to determine whether U.S. government agencies were improperly granting special waivers to foreigners who should not be allowed to enter the United States. From March 12 to September 9, 1964, the HCUA held nine executive sessions in its study of the waiver practices. On December 7, 1964, Nixon, Mrs. Allen, and Mrs. Wilson appeared under subpoena at HCUA's tenth executive session. It was explained that they had been summoned because of their role in arranging Yasui's visit and because testimony heard in previous executive sessions indicated that they might have information as to possible abuses of the immigration laws by U.S. government agencies.

Nixon protested that HCUA was in executive session and refused to be sworn to testify unless the hearing were made public. Mrs. Wilson was sworn, but refused to answer questions and also protested the executive nature of the hearing. Donna Allen took an affirmation, rather than an oath. She refused to give her name and address or to answer any questions of the HCUA in protest to the executive session. On December 10, 1964, the HCUA voted unanimously to report the conduct of the three witnesses to the Speaker of the House. On December 11, the Speaker certified to the U.S. Attorney for the District of Columbia that Allen, Nixon, and Wilson were in contempt of the Congress. On December 30, the three witnesses were indicted by a federal grand jury on charges of contempt. On February 26, 1965, defense motions to dismiss the indictments were denied and the three were tried and found guilty of the charges on April 8. On June 4 each of the defendants was sentenced to pay a fine of $100 and to serve jail terms of four to twelve months, the execution of the sentences being suspended. The three defendants then successfully appealed their convictions to the U.S. Court of Appeals. (A national committee, Defenders of 3 against HCUA, had been organized and it was publicized in the Communist press to raise funds for Allen, Nixon, and Wilson.)

By 1965, Mrs. Wilson and WISP were devoting less of their energy to hysterical outbursts against nuclear testing and were concentrating on the Vietnam War. Through "teach-ins" and marches and newspaper advertisements, they followed the Communist line by portraying the United States as a barbaric aggressor against innocent Vietnamese women and children caught up in a "civil war." Said WISP in one of its widely-printed newspaper ads: "One neglected pathway to peace is the United Nations. We ask that the United States honor its commitment to world law by a formal submission of the Vietnam dispute to the U.N. We ask for a United Nations *cease fire and free election* in South Vietnam. The Vietnamese may elect leaders we don't like. They may choose a form of government we despise – but that's their affair, as our elections are our own affair."

In July, 1965, a delegation of WISP went to Jakarta, Indonesia, where it met with a delegation of Vietcong and North Vietnamese women. The American and Communist women signed a declaration deploring U.S. "military aggression" and calling for "American women to work with dedication to stop the war in Vietnam." Indonesia's Communist President Achmed S. Sukarno told the WISP delegates how happy he was that they had chosen Indonesia as their meeting place with the Communist women for their talks on "world peace." The Communist press in this country and elsewhere was delirious in its praise of the WISP junket.

In August, 1967, Mrs. Wilson, accompanied by two other members of WISP, journeyed to Hanoi to meet with the North Vietnamese Women's Union. The trip was made in defiance of a State Department ban against travel to the enemy's territory but Mrs. Wilson is immune from any punishment by federal officials. Upon her return from North Vietnam, she pulled out all the stops with her bleeding-heart drivel: "I felt so passionately angry I wanted to take up a gun and shoot back [at American bombers]. I never thought I'd want to do that in my life." – "It's so fiendish. Here you are tilling the fields or walking to school and you think, 'Where are we supposed to go? What are we supposed to do?' Taking a gun in your hand is the only kind of relief you can have – or running for shelter which is what we did. All one's normal feelings of national loyalty go out the window. You have no idea of who the enemy is – the enemy is war and violence. It's a fallacy that bombing will weaken them [the North Vietnamese]. It just strengthens the resistance. Everything we were feeling was not as intense as what they were feeling."

Ho chi Minh could not have improved upon Mrs. Wilson's observations that he would not be bullied into peace negotiations. To Mrs. Wilson, her visit to the enemy's land "is more like visiting a family. They are totally united. Everyone suffers together and they understand each other's sufferings. There's a need to take in the children whose parents have been killed – they become everybody's children." She found a "totally unified" Vietnam: "I don't think there's anyone left in Vietnam, north or south, who isn't with the resistance movement [sic] against America. It's only the few who profit from the American presence who are loyal."

Mrs. Wilson did not visit Saigon or any other place in South Vietnam. She made no mention of South Vietnamese casualties or the atrocities committed by the Vietcong. Her only target for criticism was the United States – but, as she admitted, when she was in the heart of the enemy's country, her national loyalty to the United States went out the window.

WILLARD WIRTZ was born on March 14, 1912 in De Kalb, Illinois, son of Alpha White and William Wirtz. He married Mary Quisenberry. As an undergraduate, he attended Northern Illinois State Teachers College and the University of California (Berkeley). He is an alumnus of Beloit College of Wisconsin (A.B., 1933) and Harvard University (LL.B.,1937).

In 1933 and 1934, Wirtz was a high school teacher. From 1937 until 1939, he was an instructor at the University of Iowa. From 1939 until 1942, he was an assistant professor of law at Northwestern University.

In 1942 and 1943, Wirtz was assistant general counsel to the Board of Economic Warfare. From 1943 until 1945, he was general counsel to the War Labor Board. In 1946, he was chairman of the National Wage Stabilization Board. From 1946 until 1954, he was a professor of law at Northwestern University. From 1955 until 1961, he practiced law as a partner of the late Adlai Stevenson.

In 1961 and 1962, Wirtz was Under Secretary of Labor. Since 1962, he has been Secretary of Labor

From his cabinet position, Wirtz has waged a campaign of harassment against employers in industry and agriculture. He has urged legislation providing double pay for overtime in order to force employers to hire more workers. He has recommended a full year's paid sabbatical leave for workers in every industry. He has assumed that it is his responsibility as Secretary of Labor to fight against "right-to-work" laws and bring about compulsory unionism. He has used high-power pressure upon corporations to make them surrender unconditionally to union demands or face the loss of their government contracts. He has proposed federal legislation for a thirty-five hour work week. In the face of overwhelming contradictory evidence, he has propagandized that automation kills jobs permanently and thus he recommends feather-bedding to offset such job losses.

Wirtz has caused severe economic hardship to fruit and vegetable growers by his arbitrary restrictions upon the use of experienced foreign migrant fruit and vegetable pickers. He has compelled some farmers to pay higher than legal minimum wages.

In the Kennedy and Johnson Administrations, Wirtz lobbied vigorously for every federal boondoggle concerned with panaceas for unemployment. In an extraordinary gesture of contempt for common sense, he ruled that federal convicts, while serving prison sentences, could establish their eligibility for unemployment benefits and also qualify for the Social Security program's payments. On another occasion, he proposed a two-year program of free public education for everybody sixty years of age and over.

Despite severe criticism on the part of congressmen and business and industrial leaders, Wirtz' position in the Kennedy and Johnson Administrations has been impregnable since he is the virtual stooge of organized labor's top leaders, George Meany and Walter Reuther, whose campaign support is vital to the Democrat Party. Wirtz has also proved useful to both Administrations by serving as a stalking horse to make the most asinine socialistic proposals, designed to cultivate votes among Negroes, women, or some other segment of the population.

In Wirtz' family background, there is an element which would be of some concern to a security-minded Administration. In the 1940's, Wirtz' brother Robert was a notorious organizer for the Communist Party. (And, in the 1960's Robert's son, Stephen, has been active in radical student agitation in California.) As was indicated in a *National Review Bulletin* (August 30, 1966) commentary: "A Cabinet member's brother, privy to numerous casual intimations, is in just such a position to gut security as the well-placed Penkovsky was in the Soviet Union. Even if Robert Wirtz has broken with the Party, it would be easy and expected for the Communists to try to pressure or blackmail him through past associations. The possibility of Communist blackmail has long been considered, properly, so massive a risk to security in sensitive cases as to justify the denial of a security clearance. Secretary Wirtz must hold a top clearance to sit in the President's cabinet. The pertinent questions, therefore, are: Does the government know of the adverse information on Robert Wirtz? If so, why, by what procedure and by whom were normal security requirements waived to grant a clearance to Secretary Wirtz?

"It may very well be that investigators are conclusively satisfied that Willard is beyond any possible reach of his brother Robert, but it would be reassuring to know that the activities and associations of the brother of this cabinet member have been checked out. . . ."

WILLIAM WORTHY was born in 1923 in Boston, Massachusetts. He graduated from Bates College in Maine with a bachelor's degree in sociology. He was a Nieman fellow at Harvard University (1956-1957) and a Ford Foundation fellow in African studies (1959-1960).

For at least the past thirteen years, Worthy has been in journalism. In 1955, he went to Moscow as a correspondent for the *Baltimore Afro-American* and the Columbia Broadcasting System. In 1956, he visited Communist Hungary. In that same year, he attempted to visit South Africa after being refused a visa to enter that country. Also, in 1956, he went to Red China in defiance of a United States ban on such travel. In 1957, the State Department refused to renew his passport.

In 1961, Worthy went to Communist Cuba. He became a strong apologist for the Castro regime and became an activist in the Castro-subsidized Fair Play for Cuba Committee. In 1962, Worthy was indicted and convicted in a Federal court for having returned from Cuba without a U.S. passport, in violation of the McCarran-Walter Immigration and Nationality Act of 1952. Worthy's conviction became a celebrated cause for protest by Communists and fellow travelers. The leftwing Workers Defense League rallied to Worthy's side and insisted that it would carry his appeal to the U.S. Supreme Court if necessary. The necessity did not arise since Worthy's conviction was overthrown by the U.S. Court of Appeals on grounds that the law prohibiting a citizen from leaving or entering the U.S. with a valid passport was unconstitutional. The U.S. Department of Justice decided not to seek a review of the case before the Supreme Court.

In 1965, Worthy — without a passport — traveled to Indonesia, North Vietnam, Cambodia, and Malaysia. On at least one occasion in 1965, he wrote an article on Malaysia for the Communist weekly *National Guardian.* (In the past, Worthy had written for the Socialists' *New America*).

Worthy is a racist agitator, an outspoken proponent for black militancy. Writing in the *Boston Sunday Globe* (April 21, 1968), Worthy issued a thinly disguised call for black revolutionaries to plan and strike in a war of professional sabotage against "white racist" America. He cautioned Negroes that they were not ready for success and he warned them that they faced tremendous odds. As part of his scaremongering, he offered this fantasy: "Together with its gung ho allies in the CIA and in the military, the radical right is going to erupt politically — and perhaps militarily with an attempted putsch — when the white

United States is defeated by Vietnamese nationalism. When the rightists grab onto a domestic scapegoat, Negroes and Negro 'rioters' will be the most obvious target . . . .

"The CIA is a key element among the forces arrayed against the revolutionary movement. Ever since its establishment in 1947, it has bribed and assassinated inconvenient men of color in various countries, in order to salvage and enlarge the U.S. empire. The same CIA will not hesitate to use the same means to smash revolutionary threats in Roxbury [Massachusetts] and elsewhere in the colonial heartland. Imperialism is a racist racket."

Worthy had previously stated that race problems would not be solved in this country except through "a drastic, Castro-type revolution." And when the black supremacists had successfully revolted, he suggested mass jailings in "humanely operated rehabilitation centers" for the enemies of the revolutionary regime. He also insisted that evidence of subversive activities gathered by the Federal Bureau of Investigation should be burned and that FBI Director J. Edgar Hoover should be jailed.

Worthy's revolutionary sentiments have reached large reading audiences in *Esquire* magazine (1964 and 1967) and he has lectured at universities and colleges across the nation. He has stated that he is not nor has he ever been a Communist.

QUINCY WRIGHT was born on December 28, 1890 in Medford, Massachusetts, son of Elizabeth Sewall and Philip Wright. He married Louise Leonard. He is an alumnus of Lombard College of Illinois (A.B., 1912) and the University of Illinois (A.M., 1913; Ph.D., 1915).

In 1915 and 1916, Wright was a research fellow at the University of Pennsylvania. From 1916 until 1919, he was an instructor in international law at Harvard University. From 1919 until 1923, he was on the political science faculty at the University of Minnesota as an assistant professor, associate professor, and professor. From 1923 until 1956, he was on the faculty at the University of Chicago, successively, as a professor of political science and professor of international law, becoming professor emeritus in 1956. In 1956 and 1957, he was a visiting research scholar at the Carnegie Endowment for International Peace. In 1957 and 1958, he was a visiting professor of international law at the School for International Studies in New Delhi (he returned to the same position in 1962). From 1958 until 1961, he was a professor of international law at the University of Virginia, becoming professor emeritus in 1961. In 1962 and 1963, he was a visiting professor of international relations at Columbia University.

In 1943 and 1944, Wright was a consultant to the Foreign Economic Administration in the Department of State. In 1945, he was a technical adviser at the Nuremberg Trials. In 1949, he was a consultant to UNESCO. In 1949, and 1950, he was a consultant to the U.S. High Commissioner in Germany.

Among Wright's most recent books are *The Role of International Law in the Elimination of War; The Strengthening of International Law;* and *International Law and the United Nations.* He was also a contributor to James Roosevelt's *The Liberal Papers* which was no less than a manifesto on foreign policy prepared by extreme leftwingers including H. Stuart Hughes, Vera Micheles Dean, Arthur

Waskow, David Riesman, and Walter Millis.

Wright has been one of this country's most ardent apologists for the United Nations. He has been affiliated with the Institute of Pacific Relations ("a vehicle used by the Communists to orientate American far eastern policies toward Communist objectives"); the National Committee for a Sane Nuclear Policy (leftwing, pacifist); the National Voters' Pledge Campaign of 1966, which was led by Socialist Norman Thomas, veteran Communist-fronter Reverend William Sloane Coffin, and Sanford Gottlieb, the political director of the National Committee for a Sane Nuclear Policy. The Voters' Pledge Campaign was designed to support "peace" candidates, who would work for a cease-fire in Vietnam and encourage negotiations in which the Vietcong would be participants. He was also affiliated with the Inter-University Committee for a Public Hearing on Viet Nam, sponsors of the anti-Vietnam "teach-in" movement, which the Communist propaganda apparatus exploited for purely Communist purposes. He is a non-resident member of the Council on Foreign Relations, the informal supra-State Department of the United States. He is a past-president of the leftwing American Association of University Professors.

HENRY WRISTON was born on July 4, 1889 in Laramie, Wyoming, son of Jennie Atcheson and Henry Wriston. He was married to the late Ruth Bigelow. He is married to Marguerite Woodworth. He is an alumnus of Wesleyan University (A.B., 1911; A.M., 1912) and Harvard University (Ph.D., 1922).

From 1914 until 1925, Wriston was at Wesleyan University, serving successively as an instructor, associate profes-sor and professor of history. From 1925 until 1937, he was president of Laurence College in Wisconsin. From 1937 until 1955, he was president of Brown University.

While at Brown, Wriston moved into the high echelons of the ultra-liberal internationalists. He served as a trustee of two of the most prestigious leftwing-pacifist groups: the World Peace Foundation (1943-1954). From 1953 until 1964, he was president of the Council on Foreign Relations. His tenure coincided with the unmistakable development that the CFR became easily recognizable as the informal supra-State Department of the United States through the saturation of foreign policy-making positions by CFR members. And, from 1943 until 1967, Wriston was on the editorial advisory board of the CFR's quarterly magazine *Foreign Affairs.* The quarterly, through its editor Hamilton Fish Armstrong and its editorial advisory board, has offered a most hospitable forum to the ultra-liberal internationalists, American and foreign, as they drive toward their one-world goal, at the expense of American sovereignty and security and for the advantage of Communist and Socialist regimes everywhere.

In 1955, Wriston became the executive director of the American Assembly, an affiliate of Columbia University. The Assembly was instituted in 1950 by Dwight Eisenhower, then Columbia's president. The Assembly's offices are at Columbia's Graduate School of Business but the Assembly's semi-annual conferences are held at Arden House, a gift of Averell Harriman and located at Harriman, New York, fifty miles north of New York City. Prior to each Assembly conference, authorities are hired to write background papers. Then, at Arden House, about sixty men and women meet for several days "to discuss the Assembly topic and consider alternatives for national policy."

Wriston, after three years as executive director (1955-1958) of the Assembly, became president in 1958 and chairman of the board of trustees in 1962. He retired in 1967.

There was no conflict of interest between Wriston's high and coterminous positions in the CFR and the American Assembly. The Assembly's meetings were controlled from beginning to end by CFR personnel. To the meetings came businessmen, scientists, government officials, leaders from organized labor, military officers, press representatives, educators, publishers, religious leaders, jurists, and officials of major foundations. They were confronted with a topic of national and international import on which few of them could claim any real expertise. Under such circumstances, the Assembly's sessions became brainwashing rituals conducted by ultra-liberals who were foisted upon the conferees by Wriston. And when the sessions were concluded, the conferees had gone through the motions of endorsing what Wriston and his propagandists had decided beforehand.

As time went on, an extensive list of ultra-liberal, ultra-leftist causes received the rubber-stamped approval of an impressive roster of American leaders — policy makers, opinion molders, legislators, and administrators from the public and private sectors.

Under Wriston's direction, American Assembly meetings were held not only at Arden House but at university campuses throughout the United States and some were held at various locations in Canada. These were not merely ivory-tower conclaves. The recommendations which emanated from the Assembly's meetings were easily identifiable as the working policies — foreign and domestic — of the federal government. In general, on the domestic scene, there was an increased demand for the centralization of power in the federal government to complete the socialization of the United States. In foreign policy, every facet of United States relations with the rest of the world was subject to the recommendations of the Assembly: diplomatic relations with Canada, Japan, Latin America, eastern Europe, western Europe, The Philippines, Red China, the Soviet Union, and Africa; arms control; disarmament; "cultural" exchange; trade relations with the Communist bloc; the uses of atomic power; population control; and outer space. The hallmarks of a United States foreign policy as recommended by Wriston's CFR-American Assembly alliance include appeasement with the Communist powers through treaties dealing with progressive steps toward disarmament, through increased trade and cultural relations with the Communist bloc along the lines of Lyndon Johnson's "bridges-to-the East" program, through more reliance upon the United Nations as the arbiter of peace for the entire world, and through the continuance of American financial aid to Socialist and Communist regimes on every continent.

Not content with the enormous influence he could exert through his CFR-American Assembly positions, Wriston served simultaneously on the Public Policy Committee of the Advertising Council which, in its own literature, says that "its sole function is to conduct national advertising campaigns in the country's interest." Many of the campaigns are inoffensive and non-controversial. But others are complementary to Wriston's efforts to promote a socialized America in a collectivist one-world as they extol the virtues of the United Nations, the Peace Corps, and the federal government's increasing interference in the economic and social life of the nation. The ideological flavor of the Public Policy Committee on which Wriston served may be judged by the leftwing posture of his colleagues who included Joseph Beirne, Sarah Blanding, Ralph Bunche, Roscoe Drummond, Elmo Roper, and Paul Hoffman.

In 1960, President Dwight Eisenhower appointed Wriston to be chairman of a National Goals Commission which was instructed to "identify the great issues of our generation and describe our objectives in these areas." As might be expected, Wriston's Goals Commission was simply a gathering of the Council on Foreign Relations clan, offering another rationalized plea for an American welfare state and for a U.S. foreign policy wherein the heaviest reliance would be upon a strengthened United Nations organization.

ADAM YARMOLINSKY was born on November 17, 1922 in New York City, son of Babette Deutsch and Avrahm Yarmolinsky. He married Harriet Rypins. He is an alumnus of Harvard University (A.B., 1943) and Yale University (LL.B., 1948).

In 1948 and 1949, Yarmolinsky was law clerk to Chief Judge C.E. Clark of the U.S. Court of Appeals. Then briefly, he was an associate in a law firm. In 1950 and 1951, he was law clerk to Associate Justice Stanley Reed of the U.S. Supreme Court. From 1951 until 1955, he was an associate in a law firm.

From 1955 until 1957, Yarmolinsky was director, then secretary, of the Washington office of the Fund for the Republic. While with the Fund, Yarmo-

linsky wrote a report (*Case Studies in Personnel Security*) which cost the Fund $192,170. Frank Kluckhohn in his *Lyndon's Legacy* described Yarmolinsky's methodology: "These were cases involving government employees charged with Communist activities or otherwise being security or loyalty risks. The cases Yarmolinsky selected had been handled mainly by a small group of lawyers who often represent Communists. He interviewed these lawyers and the accused government employees to form the basis of his study on federal security.

"Yarmolinsky then proceeded to write his report. His selection of the 50 cases he described in his study, his method of collecting and evaluating the information, and his subsequent editing of the government hearings produced a highly slanted and highly distorted attack on federal security procedures.

"It was perhaps not entirely Yarmolinsky's fault that he did not get the entire government viewpoint on these 50 cases, because under the Eisenhower Administration personnel files were treated as confidential and classified to protect personnel and he was thus not permitted access to any of them.

"However, a comparison between the complete published hearings of the accused loyalty and security risks, and Yarmolinsky's version of the hearings in his Fund study, shows that he edited the hearings extensively, deleting words, phrases, sentences and paragraphs in such a way as to give the impression that the accused security risks had not been given fair hearings. In one instance, for example, a question was asked and Yarmolinsky deleted the entire answer, to create not only a false impression, but one which was exactly contrary to the facts."

Yarmolinsky did his work so well in attacking the federal loyalty and security programs, that the left wing adopted his study as the definitive hatchet to wield against such programs.

In 1957, Yarmolinsky became public affairs director for Doubleday, the publishing house. In 1959, he left Doubleday and returned to law practice, serving as a legal consultant to several tax-exempt foundations.

During the Kennedy presidential campaign, Yarmolinsky worked for Kennedy's brother-in-law Sargent Shriver. The two men set to work recruiting and screening individuals for jobs in the Kennedy Administration. They selected more than seventy lawyers, mostly from the left wing, and placed them in high-level government jobs.

Yarmolinsky knew a leftwinger when he encountered one. His parents had been mixed up in Communist and Communist front activities since the 1920's, and Yarmolinsky in his teenage years — as he admitted publicly — had a few associations with Communist Party activities.

Defense Secretary Robert McNamara had Yarmolinsky as his special assistant and deputy from 1961 until 1964. In this job, Yarmolinsky controlled appointments and patronage, in connection with the hiring and firing of personnel in the Defense Department. And McNamara had a firm ally in Yarmolinsky as the Defense Secretary set out to reduce the influence of military men in military matters and place the military men under tight-knit control of civilians. Part of the McNamara-Yarmolinsky program was to muzzle military leaders so that their public remarks would be rigidly censored if they wished to speak out against the enemy — the Communists.

McNamara and Yarmolinsky, with the full approval of President Kennedy, conducted further civilian interference of the military by transforming U.S. military bases into instruments of political and social pressure under the announced purpose of ending racial discrimination in the armed forces. A Washington attorney, Gerhard Gesell, chairman of a presidential Committee on Equal Opportunity in the Armed Forces submitted a report, written by a Negro official of the National Association for the Advancement of Colored People. All seven members of Gesell's committee either belonged to the NAACP or Americans for Democratic Action. The Defense Department, following the Gesell report's recommendations, was to enforce the will of the NAACP-ADA.

McNamara, in 1963, began issuing directives, written by Yarmolinsky, to implement the Gesell report. Military base commanders were ordered to declare "off limits" to all servicemen any business establishments in the local communities that allegedly practiced racial discrimination. Another directive designed a "monitor" system to receive Negroes' complaints at military bases. The complaints would be relayed (outside the usual military chain of command) to the Pentagon where a civilian "political adviser" would review the complaints. Yarmolinsky was determined to apply the entire power of the Defense Department to coerce the southern States into rapid and total integration — not just military bases, but also the entire communities surrounding the bases. Yarmolinsky was so obsessed with integration that, in 1961, he asked the service academies, especially Annapolis, to forget about competitive entrance examinations. He wanted "special" examinations so that Negro applicants would receive preferential treatment.

In 1964, Yarmolinsky began working with Sargent Shriver to outline Lyndon Johnson's so-called war on poverty. Shriver was to be director of the Office of Economic Opportunity, war headquarters – and, Yarmolinsky was to be his deputy. Southern congressmen refused to support the enabling legislation unless they were guaranteed that Yarmolinsky would not be in the program. Yarmolinsky did not become Shriver's deputy but remained in his Pentagon job, spending half his time, however, at the White House selecting "talent" for Shriver's poverty war. In 1965, McNamara named Yarmolinsky his deputy assistant for international affairs – an appointment that did not require confirmation by the Senate. Yarmolinsky resigned from government service in 1966 to take his present position at Harvard University as a law professor.

STEPHEN YOUNG was born on May 4, 1889 near Norwalk, Ohio, son of Belle Wagner and Stephen Young. He married Ruby Dawley. He is an alumnus of Western Reserve University (LL.B., 1911). He was admitted to the Ohio bar in 1911 and began his law practice in Norwalk.

From 1913 until 1917, Young was a member of Ohio's House of Representatives. In 1917 and 1918, he was an assistant prosecutor and, in 1919 and 1920, chief assistant prosecutor for Cuyahoga County.

In 1922 and 1930, respectively, Young was an unsuccessful candidate for attorney general and governor of Ohio.

In 1931 and 1932, he was a member of Ohio's Commission On Unemployment Insurance.

From 1933 until 1937, Young – as a Democrat – served two terms in the U.S. House of Representatives. In 1936, he was unsuccessful in his bid for the gubernatorial nomination. From 1937 until 1939, he was a special counsel to Ohio's Attorney General.

From 1941 until 1943, Young served another term in the U.S. House of Representatives. In 1943, he entered military service and after World War II resumed his private law practice in Cleveland, Ohio and Washington, D.C. From 1949 until 1951, he served a term in the U.S. House of Representatives but, in 1950, was an unsuccessful candidate for re-election. In 1956, he was an unsuccessful candidate for the attorney generalship of Ohio. Since 1959, he has been in the U.S. Senate.

Throughout his four terms in the House and two terms in the Senate, Young has been nothing more than a rubber-stamp liberal vote for the Democrat side. In 1959, Young emerged from obscurity when he agreed to speak at a New York dinner sponsored by the Emergency Civil Liberties Committee. Prior to Young's engagement, the House Committee on Un-American Activities and the Senate Internal Security Subcommittee had investigated the ECLC.

The HCUA reported: "The Emergency Civil Liberties Committee is an organization with headquarters in New York, whose avowed purpose is to abolish the House Committee on Un-American Activities and discredit the FBI .... The committee finds that the Emergency Civil Liberties Committee, established in 1951, although representing itself as a non-Communist group, actually operates as a front for the Communist Party. It has repeatedly assisted, by means of funds and legal aid, Communists involved in Smith Act violations and similar legal proceedings. One of its chief activities has been and still is the dissemination of voluminous Communist propaganda material."

The SISS reported: "To defend the cases of Communist lawbreakers, fronts have been devised making special appeals in behalf of civil liberties and reaching out far beyond the confines of the Communist Party itself. Among these organizations are the . . . Emergency Civil Liberties Committee. When the Communist Party itself is under fire these fronts offer a bulwark of protection."

American Legionnaires of Ohio asked their fellow Legionnaire Young to cancel his scheduled appearance before the ECLC. Young's reply consisted of a defense of the ECLC and a tirade against the legionnaires: "You self-appointed censors" — "self-proclaimed super-duper 100% American Firsters" — "you professional veterans" — "you self-proclaimed breast-beating patriots" — "you self-appointed vigilantes" — "you loud-mouthed publicity-seeking professional veterans." In turn, the Ohio legionnaires passed a resolution of censure against their comrade Young.

The 1959 episode with the ECLC was not Young's only or last obeisance to the left. (In 1964, Young sent his greetings to an ECLC "Bill of Rights" dinner.) When Ohio State University's president banned a campus speech scheduled to be made by the Communist leader Herbert Aptheker, Young protested on behalf of Aptheker, using the customary bleeding-heart appeals for "freedom of speech" and "academic freedom." When some Americans — government officials and private citizens — tried to block the

election of Communist Cheddi Jagan as head of British Guiana's government, Young was bitterly critical of them.

Anti-Communist congressional investigations are, in Young's opinion, nothing more than "witch hunts." His softness toward Communism has carried over into the area of foreign affairs. In 1966, he advocated that the United States extend diplomatic recognition to Outer Mongolia, which has been under the absolute control of the Soviet Union since 1924. But Young, in disregard of the Soviet Union's total commitment to the North Vietnamese war effort against the United States and its allies in Vietnam, said in 1966: "Today the Soviet Union is veering toward capitalism . . . is no longer the menace it once was to the peace of the world."

For the anti-Communist Franco regime in Spain, Young has urged a complete severance of all relations by the United States — an action he has not suggested be taken against Communist regimes.

In one of his patented outbursts, Young pinpointed his version of the anti-Americans: " . . . In my opinion, Facist-minded directors of the NAM [National Association of Manufacturers] and the United States Chamber of Commerce — and I can personally name several [which he never did] — are in reality enemies of our free enterprise system and the American way of life."

In the past few years, Young has had much to say about the Vietnam War. And in that matter, he is completely on the side of the doves. He views the conflict as a civil war. He has repeatedly called for a halt to the bombing of North Vietnam and for conclusive peace negotiations. He despises the Saigon regime and can see no United States interest served by the defeat of the Communists in Vietnam. In his zeal to be a peacenik, he has gone so far as to describe Secretary of State Dean Rusk as a warhawk. (This ranks in silliness with his assertion that there have been no acts of appeasement in the Truman, Kennedy, or Johnson Administrations. Only Eisenhower, he asserts, was guilty of appeasement when he negotiated the truce in Korea.)

Young couples his demands for "peace" in Vietnam with a vigorous campaign for disarmament in which he is completely willing to trust the word of Communist regimes. In his opinion, wars result from an armaments race, not from Communist perfidy.

WHITNEY YOUNG JR. was born on July 31, 1921 in Lincoln Ridge, Kentucky, son of Laura Ray and Whitney Young. He married Margaret Buchner. He is an alumnus of Kentucky State College (B.S., 1941) and the University of Minnesota (M.A., 1947). During World War II, while in the U.S. Army, he studied electrical engineering for two years at Massachusetts Institute of Technology. In 1961, he was a visiting scholar, under a Rockefeller Foundation grant, at Harvard University. He is the author of *To Be Equal* (1964).

From 1947 until 1950, Young was director of industrial relations and vocational guidance of the St. Paul (Minnesota) Urban League. In 1948 and 1949, he supervised field work students of the Atlanta University School of Social Work and the University of Minnesota School of Social Work. In 1949, he was a lecturer at the College of St. Catherine in St. Paul. From 1950 until 1953, he was executive secretary of the Omaha (Nebraska) Urban League. From 1950 until 1954, he was an instructor at the School of Social Work of the University of Nebraska. In 1951 and 1952, he lectured at Creighton University in Omaha. From 1954 until 1961, he was dean of Atlanta University's School of Social Work.

Since 1961, Young has been the executive director of the National Urban League, which presently is the parent organization of more than eighty local leagues in as many cities throughout the United States.

During his years with the NUL, Young has enjoyed remarkably favorable press notices. Among Negro leaders, he enjoys the distinction of being hailed — almost unexceptionally — as the epitome of moderation. He is described accurately as having easy access to the White House, to business leaders, and to heads of large foundations. In most instances, he is portrayed as aloof from politics and at odds with black militants. By his public actions and utterances, however, Young reveals himself as an ultra-liberal politician, a socialist ideologue, an affiliate of ultra-leftwingers, and a suave but militant racist agitator.

In 1963, Young began to agitate for a federal government-financed "Domestic Marshall Plan," involving the expenditure of 145 billion dollars over a ten-year period on Negroes. His cry was that the Negro needs "more-than-equal" treatment because of a "discrimination gap." In the hackneyed liberal fashion, he bemoaned "more than three centuries of abuse, humiliation, segregation and bias" as the Negroes' lot in the white society of America. (At various times, Young has described the American society as "sick," "racist," "more immoral than most," and one that "lives by the gun and the bullet." He offers, as model societies, the welfare states of Britain and Sweden.)

In 1964, Young and the National Urban League went all-out to defeat Barry Goldwater by calling upon all

Negroes to vote against the Republican presidential nominee in order to avoid a calamitous future. In his personal plea for Goldwater's defeat, Young said that "voters will make a mistake from which the nation may never recover if out of fear and misunderstanding of the race problem they permit the election of those who would encourage extremists and racists, those who ignore the problems of poverty, ill-health, and inadequate education, and those who see big business as an evil but who are indifferent to big social problems." After branding Goldwater as the leader of racists, extremists, and enemies of the poor, Young stumped for his friend Lyndon Johnson whom Young hoped would avoid the middle-of-the-road by having a strong liberal Democrat Party platform and a liberal vice president.

Young's support of leftwing Democrats has brought to him prestigious positions in the high councils of government. He has been a member of the presidential Commission on Technology, Automation and Economic Progress; the special presidential Task Force on Urban Affairs; the presidential Commission on Law Enforcement and Administration of Justice; the presidential Commission on Youth; the national advisory council of the U.S. Office of Economic Opportunity; the advisory council on vocational education of the U.S. Office of Education; the advisory committee on Equal Opportunity in the Armed Forces; the advisory committee on juvenile delinquency of the Department of Justice; the advisory committee for the Department of Health, Education and Welfare; the national planning committee of the 1960 White House Conference on Children and Youth; and, consultant to the U.S. Public Health Service.

Young's name is also well-known in liberal circles as a national committeeman for the Adlai E. Stevenson Memorial Fund, a trustee of the John Fitzgerald Kennedy Library Corporation, a trustee of the Eleanor Roosevelt Memorial Foundation, and a member of the national advisory council of the AFL-CIO's Community Services Activities. He has also served as president of the National Conference on Social Welfare. In this latter position he practically invited social workers to incite poor people as he offered his dictate: "The social worker must plant the spark and the seed of change and indignation in the mind of every citizen in want."

Among his other affiliations is Young's membership in Franklin Littell's Institute for American Democracy, an elite representative group of Leftists who have specialized in anti-anti-Communist activities and utterances. Young has also served as an executive committee member of the leftwing Citizens Crusade against Poverty which was founded by Walter Reuther, using a million-dollar "donation" from the United Automobile Workers. In this venture, Young aligned himself with the racist agitators Martin L. King Jr. and James Farmer, the Socialist Party leader Michael Harrington, the pacifist baby doctor Benjamin Spock, the leftwing farm organizer James Patton, and the defamation expert Dore Schary of the Anti-Defamation League. Ordinarily, Young does not associate himself with leftwing organizations but he has been a sponsor of the leftwing-pacifist Women's International League for Peace and Freedom and he did join some leftwing Negro agitators in petitioning the Johnson Administration to withdraw any support it might have given to the anti-Communist Premier Moise Tshombe of the Congo.

When Young first became the executive director of the National Urban League, he presented himself to the American public as having the primary objective of obtaining jobs for Negroes through persuasive but peaceful methods. Superficially, Young was acting independently of racist agitators. Once he had established this public posture of reasonableness, he began to become just another black power advocate. He and the National Urban League took part in the 1963 March on Washington, the 1965 Selma to Montgomery March, and James Meredith's "walk" through Mississippi.

Young joined black and white leftists in their demands for civilian review boards and human relations courses for police. And, as time went on, he discarded caution and adopted the typical racist agitator's jargon — "the real problem is racism, the bigotry of white people" — "[Martin L. King's assassination] was spawned by a society which has relentlessly demonstrated to Negroes that they don't belong" — "[don't call them riots, but rather] spontaneous expressions of pent-up anger and frustration by an oppressed people."

When Lyndon Johnson's National Advisory Commission on Civil Disorders placed the entire blame for the nation's riots on a white racist society, Young offered his complete endorsement of the findings. He insisted that there were no conspiracies behind the racial turmoil that beset the nation — the single cause was white racism.

In 1968, at the Congress of Racial Equality's annual convention, Young supported the revolutionary slogan of "black power." He has portrayed the United States as a nation with twenty-five million Negroes as second-class citizens. He insists that the U.S. government should provide homes and jobs and a guaranteed annual income for Negroes. He supports the Office of Economic Opportunity and its offshoots in the so-called War on Poverty but only if the federal government continues to increase its spending on these boondoggles. Where he once went through the motion of spurning activists who carried picket signs, engaged in sit-ins, marches and other demonstrations, Young — after he had developed his public image as a moderate — told his fellow Negroes how to get Opportunity: "We must march to Parent-Teacher Association meetings, to libraries, to voting booths. We must march to party caucuses, to adult education classes, to vocational and apprenticeship training courses. We must march to decision-making meetings on town zoning, urban renewal, health, welfare, and education."

How far Young has advanced away from moderation can be understood by his complete tolerance of Sterling Tucker's leadership of the Washington Urban League, the most important local of the National Urban League. Said Tucker in 1967: "I view rioting as a tool of communication that more and more people will accept. Man needs to be heard, needs people to respond to him." In 1968, Tucker demonstrated that he was not merely talking in abstract terms about rioting as he joined the Black United Front where the most forceful personality was the revolutionary militant Stokely Carmichael.

HOWARD ZINN was born on August 24, 1922 in New York City, son of Jennie Rabinowitz and Edward Zinn. He married Roslyn Schechter. He is an alumnus of New York University (B.A., 1951) and Columbia University (M.A., 1952; Ph.D., 1958).

Zinn was a history instructor at Upsala College, from 1953 until 1956, and a history lecturer at Brooklyn College in 1955 and 1956. At Spelman College in Atlanta, from 1956 until 1963. Zinn was chairman of the history department and a social science professor. While at Spelman, he held a fellowship at Harvard University's Center for Far Eastern Studies and was director of the Non-Western Studies Program at the Atlanta University Center. Since 1964, he has been an associate professor of government at Boston University. Zinn's books include *La Guardia in Congress; SNCC: The New Abolitionists; The Southern Mystique;* and *Vietnam: The Logic of Withdrawal.*

Zinn has been an active "civil rights" agitator and his contributions to the black powerites have been the subject of very favorable comments in the Communist press.

Zinn's leftwing pronouncements cover a wide range of topics. He has described Red China's role in the Korean War as "primarily a defense one, undertaken reluctantly." He has spoken out publicly against alleged "persecutions" under the Internal Security Act. He has been an advisor to the explosive Student Non-Violent Coordinating Committee, and is a friendly associate of the demagogic Stokely Carmichael. He has urged Negroes to take up arms "to scare the federal government into action." He has called for the impeachment and removal of Lyndon Johnson as "a dramatic denunciation of brutality in foreign relations (I am speaking of Vietnam, of course) and an affirmation of the democratic process in national politics (I mean the natural right of recall). In its historic significance it would be comparable to the action of the 20th Party Congress in the Soviet Union, which excoriated Stalin because he killed too many people in the course of building his Great Society."

In 1967, Zinn was an initial sponsor of the National Student Strike for Peace, which was led by Communist Bettina Aptheker. (In 1966, Zinn had sponsored a testimonial dinner to Bettina's father, Communist Herbert Aptheker.) Also, in 1967, Zinn sponsored the Call for Vietnam Week, which had as its purpose "to undermine and sabotage U.S. resistance to Communist military aggression in Vietnam."

INDEX OF ORGANIZATIONS